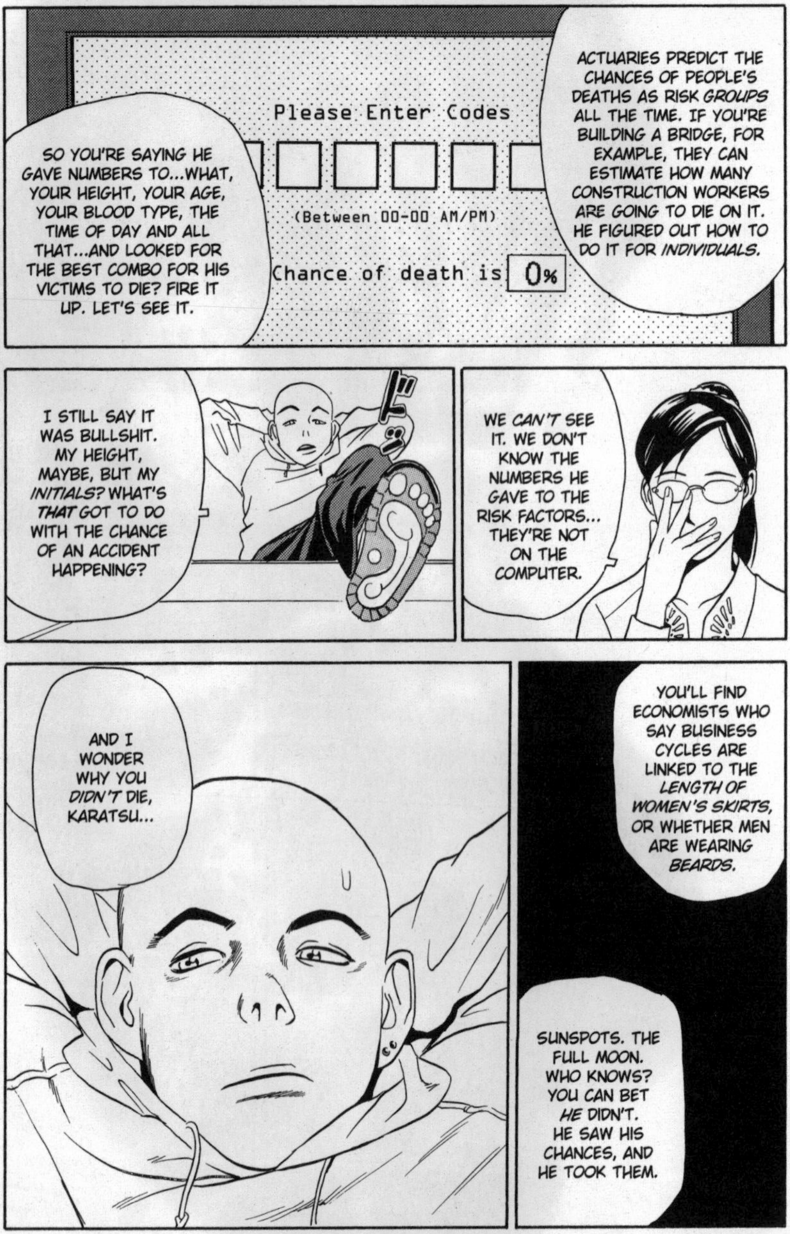
ACTUARIES PREDICT THE CHANCES OF PEOPLE'S DEATHS AS RISK *GROUPS* ALL THE TIME. IF YOU'RE BUILDING A BRIDGE, FOR EXAMPLE, THEY CAN ESTIMATE HOW MANY CONSTRUCTION WORKERS ARE GOING TO DIE ON IT. HE FIGURED OUT HOW TO DO IT FOR *INDIVIDUALS.*
Please Enter Codes
(Between 00-00 AM/PM)
Chance of death is 0%
SO YOU'RE SAYING HE GAVE NUMBERS TO...WHAT, YOUR HEIGHT, YOUR AGE, YOUR BLOOD TYPE, THE TIME OF DAY AND ALL THAT...AND LOOKED FOR THE BEST COMBO FOR HIS VICTIMS TO DIE? FIRE IT UP. LET'S SEE IT.
WE *CAN'T* SEE IT. WE DON'T KNOW THE NUMBERS HE GAVE TO THE RISK FACTORS... THEY'RE NOT ON THE COMPUTER.
I STILL SAY IT WAS BULLSHIT. MY HEIGHT, MAYBE, BUT MY *INITIALS?* WHAT'S *THAT* GOT TO DO WITH THE CHANCE OF AN ACCIDENT HAPPENING?
YOU'LL FIND ECONOMISTS WHO SAY BUSINESS CYCLES ARE LINKED TO THE *LENGTH OF WOMEN'S SKIRTS,* OR WHETHER MEN ARE WEARING *BEARDS.*
SUNSPOTS. THE FULL MOON. WHO KNOWS? YOU CAN BET *HE* DIDN'T. HE SAW HIS CHANCES, AND HE TOOK THEM.
AND I WONDER WHY YOU *DIDN'T* DIE, KARATSU...

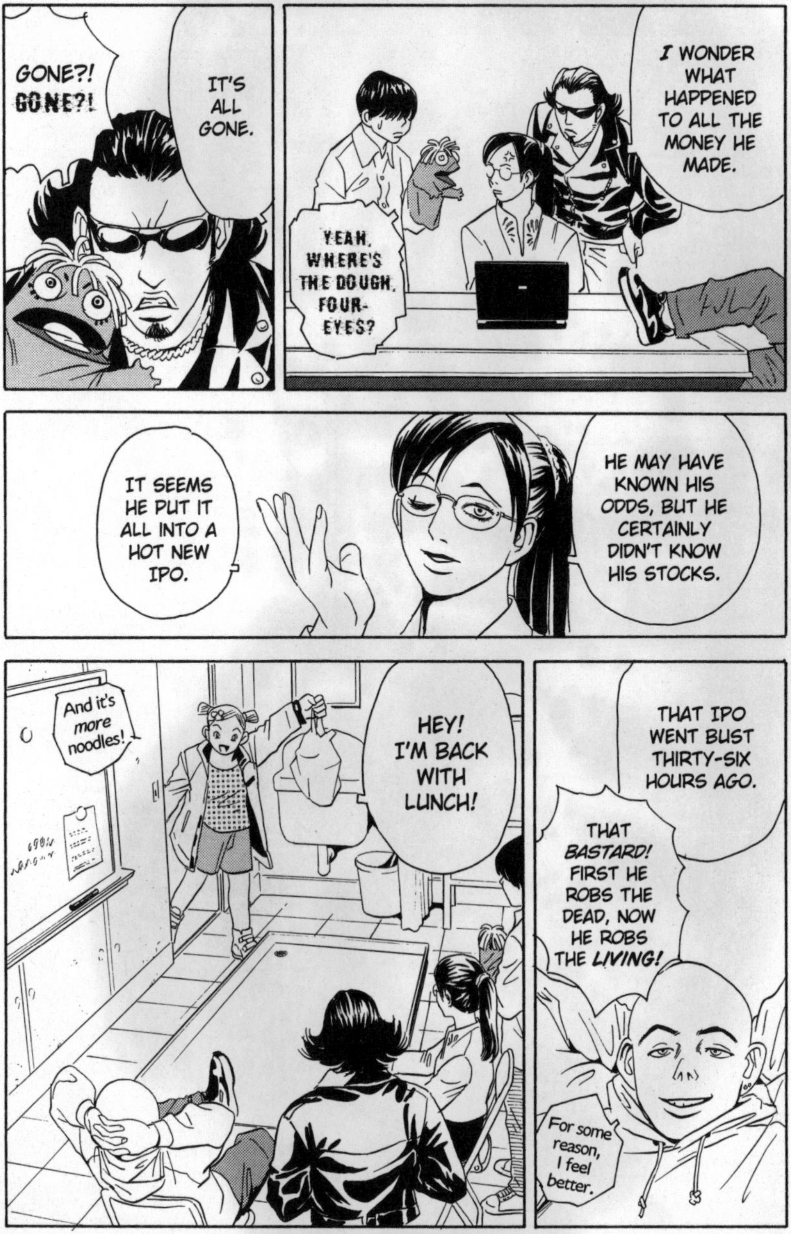
I WONDER WHAT HAPPENED TO ALL THE MONEY HE MADE.
YEAH, WHERE'S THE DOUGH, FOUR-EYES?
IT'S ALL GONE.
GONE?! GONE?!
HE MAY HAVE KNOWN HIS ODDS, BUT HE CERTAINLY DIDN'T KNOW HIS STOCKS.
IT SEEMS HE PUT IT ALL INTO A HOT NEW IPO.
THAT IPO WENT BUST THIRTY-SIX HOURS AGO.
THAT *BASTARD!* FIRST HE ROBS THE DEAD, NOW HE ROBS THE ***LIVING!***
For some reason, I feel better.
HEY! I'M BACK WITH LUNCH!
And it's *more* noodles!

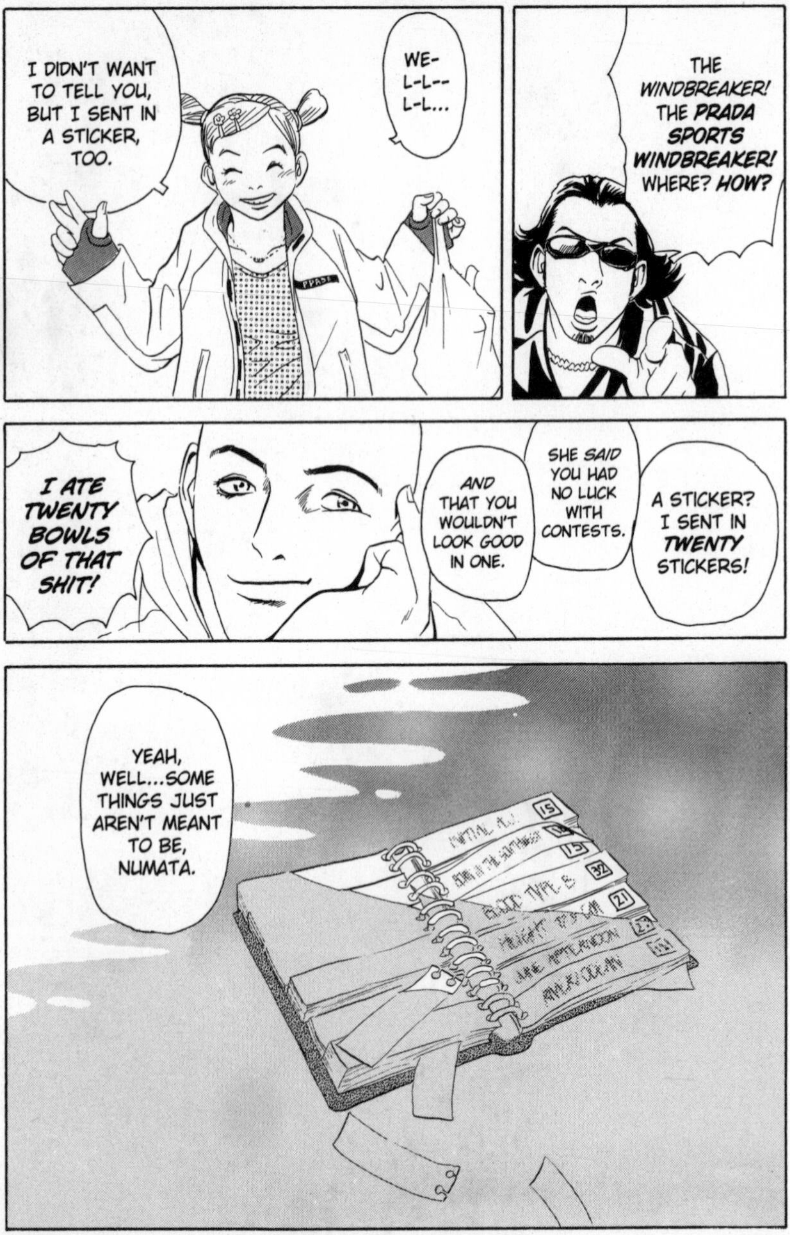
THE *WINDBREAKER!* THE ***PRADA SPORTS WINDBREAKER!*** WHERE? ***HOW?***
WE-L-L--L-L...
I DIDN'T WANT TO TELL YOU, BUT I SENT IN A STICKER, TOO.
A STICKER? I SENT IN ***TWENTY*** STICKERS!
SHE *SAID* YOU HAD NO LUCK WITH CONTESTS.
AND THAT YOU WOULDN'T LOOK GOOD IN ONE.
I ATE TWENTY BOWLS OF THAT SHIT!
YEAH, WELL...SOME THINGS JUST AREN'T MEANT TO BE, NUMATA.

4th delivery: september rain—the end
continued in *the kurosagi corpse delivery service* vol. 2

DISJECTA MEMBRA

SOUND FX GLOSSARY AND NOTES ON KUROSAGI VOL. 1 BY TOSHIFUMI YOSHIDA
introduction and additional comments by the editor

TO INCREASE YOUR ENJOYMENT of the distinctive Japanese visual style of this manga, we've included a guide to the sound effects (or "FX") used in this manga adaptation of the anime film. It is suggested the reader not constantly consult this glossary as they read through, but regard it as supplemental information, in the manner of footnotes. If you want to imagine it being read aloud by Osaka, after the manner of her lecture to Sakaki on hemorrhoids in episode five, please go right ahead. In either Yuki Matsuoka or Kira Vincent-Davis's voice—I like them both.

Japanese, like English, did not independently invent its own writing system, but instead borrowed and modified the system used by the then-dominant cultural power in their part of the world. We still call the letters we use to write English today the "Roman" alphabet, for the simple reason that about 1600 years ago the earliest English speakers, living on the frontier of the Roman Empire, began to use the same letters the Romans used to write their Latin language, to write out English.

Around that very same time, on the other side of the planet, Japan, like England, was another example of an island civilization lying across the sea from a great empire, in this case, that of China. Likewise, the Japanese borrowed from the Chinese writing system, which then as now consists of thousands of complex symbols—today in China officially referred to in the Roman alphabet as *hanzi*, but which the Japanese pronounce as *kanji*. For example, all the Japanese characters you see on the front cover of *The Kurosagi Corpse Delivery Service*—the seven which make up the original title and the four each which make up the creators' names—are examples of kanji. Of course, all of them were hanzi first; although the Japanese did later invent some original kanji of their own, just as new hanzi have been created over the centuries as Chinese evolved.

(Note that whereas both *kanji* and *hanzi* are methods of writing foreign words in Roman letters, "kanji" gives English speakers a fairly good idea of how the Japanese word is really pronounced—*khan-gee*—whereas "hanzi" does not—in Mandarin Chinese it sounds something like *n-tsuh*). The reason is fairly simple: whereas the most commonly used method of writing Japanese in Roman letters, called the Hepburn system, was developed by a native English speaker, the most commonly used method of writing Chinese in Roman letters, called the Pinyin system, was developed by native Mandarin speakers. In fact Pinyin was developed to help teach Mandarin pronunciation to speakers of other Chinese dialects; unlike Hepburn, it was not intended as a learning tool for English speakers *per se*, and hence has no particular obligation to "make sense" to English speakers or, indeed, users of

other languages spelled with the Roman alphabet).

Whereas the various dialects of Chinese are written entirely in hanzi, it is impractical to render the Japanese language entirely in them. To compare once more, English is a notoriously difficult language in which to spell properly, and this is in part because it uses an alphabet designed for another language, Latin, whose sounds are different. The challenges the Japanese faced in using the Chinese writing system for their own language were even greater, for whereas spoken English and Latin are at least from a common language family, spoken Japanese is unrelated to any of the various dialects of spoken Chinese. The complicated writing system Japanese evolved represents an adjustment to these differences.

When the Japanese borrowed hanzi to become kanji, what they were getting was a way to write out (remember, they already had ways to *say*) their vocabulary. Nouns, verbs, many adjectives, the names of places and people—that's what kanji are used for, the fundamental data of the written language. The practical use and processing of that "data"—its grammar and pronunciation—is another matter entirely. Because spoken Japanese neither sounds nor functions like Chinese, the first work-around tried was a system called *manyogana*, where individual kanji were picked to represent certain syllables in Japanese (a similar method is still used in Chinese today to spell out foreign names).

The commentary in *Katsuya Terada's The Monkey King* (also available from Dark Horse, and also translated by To-shifumi Yoshida) notes the importance that not only Chinese, but Indian culture had on Japan at this time in history—particularly, Buddhism. It is believed the Northeast Indian *Siddham* script studied by Kukai (died 835 AD), founder of the Shingon sect of Japanese Buddhism, inspired him to create the solution for writing Japanese still used today. Kukai is credited with the idea of taking the manyogana and making the shorthand versions of them now known simply as *kana*. The improvement in efficiency was dramatic—a kanji, used previously to represent a sound, that might have taken a dozen strokes to draw, was now reduced to three or four.

Unlike the original kanji it was based on, the new kana had *only* a sound meaning. And unlike the thousands of kanji, there are only 46 kana, which can be used to spell out any word in the Japanese language, including the many ordinarily written with kanji (Japanese keyboards work on this principle). The same set of 46 kana is written two different ways depending on their intended use; cursive style, *hiragana*, and block style, *katakana*. Naturally, sound FX in manga are almost always written out using kana.

Kana works somewhat differently than the Roman alphabet. For example, while there are separate kana for each of the five vowels (the Japanese order is not A-E-I-O-U as in English, but A-I-U-E-O), there are, except for "n," no separate kana for consonants (the middle "n" in the word ninja illustrates this exception). Instead, kana work by grouping together consonants with vowels: for example, there are five kana for sounds starting

with "k," depending on which vowel follows it—in Japanese vowel order, they go KA, KI, KU, KE, KO. The next set of kana begins with "s" sounds, so SA, SHI, SU, SE, SO, and so on. You will observe this kind of consonant-vowel pattern in the FX listings for *Kurosagi* Vol. 1 below.

Katakana are almost always used for manga sound FX, but on occasion (often when the sound is one made by a person) hiragana are used instead. In *Kurosagi* Vol. 1 you can see one of several examples on page 21, panel 3, when Karatsu smacks the back of his head with a "PACHIN" sound, which in hiragana style is written ぱちん. Note its more cursive appearance compared to the other FX. If it had been written in katakana style, it would look like パチン.

To see how to use this glossary, take an example from page 3: "3.1 FX: BAKO BAKO BAKO—sound of a distant helicopter." 3.1 means the FX is the one on page 3, in panel 1 (in this case, of course, the only panel on the page). BAKO BAKO BAKO are the sounds these kana—バコ/バコ/バコ—literally stand for. After the dash comes an explanation of what the sound represents (in some cases, such as this one, it will be less obvious than others). Note that in cases where there are two or more different sounds in a single panel, an extra number is used to differentiate them from right to left (for example, 7.3.1 and 7.3.2); or, in cases where right and left are less clear (for example, 18.7.1 and 18.7.2) in clockwise order.

The use of kana in these FX also illustrates another aspect of written Japanese—its flexible reading order. For example,

the way you're reading the pages and panels of this book in general: going from right-to-left, and from top to bottom—is the order in which Japanese is also written in most forms of print: books, magazines, and newspapers. However, if you look closely those kana examples given above, you'll notice something interesting. They read "Western" style—left-to-right! In fact, many of the FX in *Kurosagi* (and manga in general) read left-to-right. On page 141 you can even find them going in both directions—141.1 is going right-to-left, but 141.5 is going left-to-right. This kind of flexibility is also to be found on Japanese web pages, which themselves usually read left-to-right. In other words, Japanese doesn't simply read "the other way" from English; the Japanese themselves are used to reading it in several different directions.

As might be expected, some FX "sound" short, and others "sound" long. Manga represent this in different ways. One of many examples of "short sounds" in *Kurosagi* Vol. 1 is to be found in 7.3, with its BUCHI and DOSA. Note the small ツ mark at the end of each. This is ordinarily the katakana for the sound "tsu," but its half-size use at the end of FX like this means the sound is the kind which stops or cuts off suddenly; that's why these sounds are written as BUCHI and DOSA and not BUCHITSU and DOSATSU—you don't "pronounce" the TSU in such cases.

Note the small "tsu" has another occasional use *inside*, rather than at the end, of a particular FX, as seen in 7.6's NCCHI ZUN CHAKA NCCHI ZUZUCHAKA— here it's at work between the "N" ン and

the "CHI" チ to indicate a doubling of the consonant sound that follows it.

There are three different ways you may see "long sounds"—where a vowel sound is extended—written out as FX. One is with an ellipsis, as in 19.3's VUUUUN. Another is with an extended line, as in 70.1's MIIIIN MIN MIN. Still another is by simply repeating a vowel several times, as in 141.1's KIIII. As a visual element in manga, FX are an art rather than a science, and are used in a less rigorous fashion than kana are in standard written Japanese.

The explanation of what the sound represents may sometimes be surprising; but every culture "hears" sounds differently. Note that manga FX do not even necessarily represent literal sounds; for example 153.1 FX: SHIN—in manga this is the figurative "sound" of silence. 14.1 FX: BIKU, representing a shudder, is another one of this type. Such "mimetic" words, which represent an imagined sound, or even a state of mind, are called *gitaigo* in Japanese. Like the onomatopoeic *giseigo* (the words used to represent literal sounds—i.e., most FX in this glossary are classed as giseigo), they are also used in colloquial speech and writing. A Japanese, for example, might say that something bounced by saying PURIN, or talk about eating by saying MUGU MUGU. It's something like describing chatter in English by saying "yadda yadda yadda" instead.

One important last note: all these spelled-out kana vowels should be pronounced as they are in Japanese: "A" as *ah*, "I" as *eee*, "U" as *ooh*, "E" as *eh*, and "O" as *oh*.

2.1 Note that all four chapter titles in this volume are the names of songs by Hiromi Ota, a J-pop singer who had a popular debut in the 1970s.

3.1 **FX: BAKO BAKO BAKO—** sound of a distant helicopter

6.1 **FX: BUN BUN BUBUN**—sound of buzzing flies

7.1 **FX/balloon: PIKUN**—twitch

7.2 **FX: BIKU BIKUN BIKUN—** sound of body convulsing

7.3.1 **FX/white: BUCHI**—sound of rope snapping

7.3.2 **FX/balloon: DOSA**—sound of body thudding on ground

7.5 **FX: ZU ZURU**—sound of body dragging itself on the ground

7.6 **FX: NCCHI ZUN CHAKA NCCHI ZUZUCHAKA**—sound of music being overheard on someone's headphones

10.1 **FX: TSUU TSUKU TSUU CHA ZUNCHAKA ZUTCHA TSUU TSUKU ZUN**—sound of music being overheard on someone's headphones

10.2 Aokigahara Forest is a real place, and it really is famous for suicides. Japan, incidentally, has about twice the suicide rate of the U.S. Translator Toshifumi Yoshida notes that the location first gained notoriety when novelist Seicho Matsumoto wrote his book *Tower of the Sea*, where a character commits suicide in Aokigahara. When the novel was made into a TV movie in 1973, Aokigahara became synonymous with suicide.

10.3 FX: BAKO BAKO BAKO— sound of a helicopter

10.4 These boxes also exist, and are located at various points along the forest paths. Yoshida notes their messages tend to be blunt; rather than reassuring people life isn't so hopeless, the flyers ask potential suicides to consider: "You may think you will leave a beautiful corpse, but your body will be ravaged by wildlife before rotting and eventually leaving only your bones." The translator points interested readers to http://www.tanteifile.com/baka/ 2002/ 09/22_01_shinrei2_04/ which documents a group of reporters going into Aokigahara. They claim that their compasses became useless, and to have eventually stumbled across someone's personal effects, including a copy of a notorious "Perfect Suicide" how-to manual with blood on the pages. Note the "Suicide Preven- tion Message Box" is just like the one seen here (except in this version, its sign has been translated into English).

11.3 FX: PURAN—sound of an arm falling out of the stretcher

13.6.1 FX: NU—hand reaching for shoulder

14.1 FX: BIKU—scared shudder

14.5 FX: PA PA—sound of a camera flash

17.1 FX: PAKU PAKU—sound of the puppet's mouth flapping. Note the game *Pac-Man* was named for this FX. I asked Japanese Licensing Manager (and translator of DH's *Reiko the Zombie Shop*) Michael

Gombos why, if that was the case, Pac-Man doesn't go "paku paku"— I always heard the sound he makes as "waku waku." Mr. Gombos replied that *is* "paku paku"—a case that only demonstrates the point made above about different cultures hearing things differently.

17.4 FX: PAN PAN—brushing dirt off pants

18.7.1 FX: BUUUN—buzzing fly

18.7.2 FX/balloon: PITA—sound of fly landing on eye

19.1 FX: BUUUN BUBUUUN— buzzing flies

19.2 FX: BUBUN—sound of flies

19.3 FX: BUUUUN—buzzing flies

19.5 FX: BA—sound of Karatsu turning around quickly

20.1.1 FX: BUBUN—sound of flies

20.1.2 FX: BUUUUN—buzzing flies

20.1.3 FX: BUUUUN—more buzzing flies

20.2 FX: BUUUUN—buzzing flies

21.3 FX: PACHIN—slapping own head

21.4 FX: KOKI—cracking neck

21.5 FX: GA—footstep

21.6 FX: ZA—kneeling into leaves

22.5 FX: PITA—sound of hand placed on body

22.6 Until fairly recent decades, an ancient tradition was to be found in Japan (and particularly in north- eastern Honshu, where Kuro Karatsu is from) where young blind girls would be chosen to undergo a harsh religious initiation involving starvation, exposure to cold, and

the memorization of *sutras*, Buddhist prayers (see 11.4). At the end they were considered *Itako*, spiritualists who could now contact the dead. It is said that elderly itako still practice their calling, but in contemporary popular culture the concept has been expanded—for example, Anna in Hiroyuki Takei's manga *Shaman King* is an itako, even though she is sighted. Of course, Karatsu is neither blind nor female, but see the translator's comments for 44.1 below.

26.3   **FX: SHUBO**—lighter being lit

26.4   **FX/balloon: FUUU**—exhaling smoke

27.4   **FX: GUSHI**—putting out cigarette

27.6   **FX: GOGOGOGO**—sound of the furnace burning

28.2   **FX: GORORORO**—sound of the table being rolled out of the furnace

32.1   **FX: BAN**—placing hand on body

34.2   **FX/balloon: HIRA**—sound of lottery ticket sliding out of notebook

35.4   **FX/balloon: KATA KATATA**—typing sound

36.1-4 If you want to grow up to be an editor and get good car insurance rates (see 167.3 below) it is especially important to practice good spelling online, as that is where people do most of their writing these days. I personally think teachers should practice this with students if they've got computers in class. Never mind the porn filters, we need bad grammar filters to protect our children.

37.1.1   **FX/black: GAYA GAYA**—crowd noise

37.1.2   **FX/white: WAI WAI**—more crowd noise

38.1   **FX: PII PAA PII POPOPOP PII PO**—cell ringing

38.5   **FX: PUWAAAAN**—sound of train

39.1   **FX: GATAN GOTON GATAN GOTOTON**—sound of train on the tracks

40.4   **FX: ZEI ZEI**—panting

40.5   **FX: DOSA**—putting body down

41.1   **FX: SHUGOGOGO**—sound of a propane stove

41.2   "Numacchi," as you might guess, is a cute way of saying "Numata."

42.2   **FX: MOZO**—body bag moving

42.3   **FX/balloon: JI**—zipper starting to open

42.4   **FX: JIIIII**—zipper unzipping

43.1   **FX/Balloons: ZU ZURI**—dragging sound

44.1   The translator theorizes that the mysterious spirit that accompanies Karatsu may be a traditional itako who was an ancestor of his. Judging by the events of this volume, Karatsu himself is not necessarily aware of her (if it indeed is a "her") presence, and no one else can see her either. The identity of this spirit is one of the as-yet unresolved mysteries of the story.

44.4   **FX: GABA**—getting up suddenly

45.1   **FX/balloon: KII**—sound of cab braking.

45.2   **FX: GACHA**—car door opening

45.3   **FX/balloon: BURORORO**—cab driving away

46.4 FX: GURI—putting his dowsing ring on

46.6 FX: CHARIIIN—the dowsing pendulum making a ringing sound

47.2 FX/balloon: KASA—rustling leaves

47.3 FX/balloons: KARI GARIRI—sound of nails scratching then digging into outside wall

48.1 FX: BAN—hand slamming into window

48.2 FX: BAN BAN BAN BAN—palm hammering on window

49.1 FX: BAN BAN BAN BAN BAN—more hammering

49.2 FX: BASHAAAN—sound of breaking glass

49.3 FX: BA—hand grabbing ledge

49.4 FX: ZURI—body lifting up

49.5 FX: ZUZUZU—body slowly climbing in

50.1 FX: DOSA—sound of body landing in room

50.2 FX: ZUZU—body dragging itself on floor

50.3 FX: DO—back bumping into wall

51.1 FX: DAAAAAN—sound of a shotgun firing

51.3 Sasaki's remark is so bizarre by American standards it might almost seem a mistake—but that's what she said. Very few Japanese own actual firearms (if they do, it would be a shotgun or rifle for hunting, as portrayed here—private ownership of handguns is, practically speaking, forbidden) and even if they did, they would be unlikely to think of them as home-defense weapons. Very roughly, Japan has one one-hundredth the gun death rate of the U.S.; should certain crimes portrayed in this manga seem shocking, it is worth bearing in mind that Japan in real life is a considerably less violent and more law-abiding society than our own.

51.5 FX: KIII—door creaking

54.1 FX: PA PA—lights coming on

56.1 FX: SU—Karatsu stepping forward

58.1.1 FX/white: BIKUN BIKUN—body starting to twitch

58.1.2 FX/black: GUGU—body starting to rise

58.2 FX: ZU ZU—body starting to stand

59.2 FX: BAKOON—blam

59.3 FX: GIRO—glare

59.4.1 FX/white: BETA BETA—sound of bare feet walking

59.4.2 FX/black: GASHA—reloading sound

60-61.1 FX: BA—sound of Yuki's corpse grabbing her father

62.2 FX: HA—coming out of trance

62.4.1 FX/small: PORO—parts falling off of face

62.4.2 FX: GEBOBOBO—vomiting blood

62.5 FX: BACHA BETA—body falling onto Yamakawa's face

62.6.1 FX/white: BECHA—loud bloody splash

62.6.2 FX/black: DO—an organ hitting floor

63.1 **FX: DOCHA**—body falling in a wet thud

63.2 **FX/balloons: GEHO GEHO**—coughing

64.4 **FX/balloon: GOHO GEHO**—coughing up smoke

65.1 **FX: PAKU PAKU**—puppet's mouth moving

65.2 **FX: PURU PURU**—small trembling

65.6 **FX: ZU**—picking up ticket

66.3 **FX: GATA GOTO GATAN**—sound of a older car's suspension

66.4.1 FX/white: PASUN PUSUN PAN—sound of an old car's engine

66.4.2 FX/black: GATA GOTO KISHI—more old suspension noise

67.1 **FX: GATA GATAN GOTO GAKON**—old car sounds

67.2 **FX: GOTO GOTON GATAN**—more old car sounds

66.3 **FX: GOTO GATA**—still some more

68.1 **FX: GAKO GAKO**—old car noises

68.2 **FX/balloon: KIKII**—sound of brakes

68.3 **FX: PINPOOON**—doorbell sound

69. 1 *Tono Monogatari*, or "Tales of Tono" (the first "o" in "Tono" is pronounced long, and you will thus sometimes see it spelled in English as *Touno* or *Tohno*) is a classic collection of Japanese folklore, first published in 1910 or 1912 (reports vary). Kunio Yanagita, touring Japan as a government agricultural and trade inspector, became interested in the traditional stories he would hear while visiting various localities.

Aozasa Village is associated with the modern city of Tono in Iwate Prefecture, and, like the Aokigahara Forest featured in "Less Than Happy," is a real place. You can see images of the Dendera Field where this chapter opens at: http://www.sukima.com/12_touhoku00_04/02dendera.htm Note that the original version of the quote on this page goes into much greater detail; for example, Yanagita remarked that Aozasa Village's Dendera Field was also used by the neighboring locales Kamisato, Ashiraga, and Ishida.

69.2 **FX: PATAMU**—sound of a book closing.

69.3 The mountain story to which he refers is that of *Uba Sute Yama*, literally "Elder Cast Off Mountain." There is a similar story in Japanese folklore called *The Ballad of Narayama*, which would seem to refer to a different mountain.

70.1 **FX: MIIIIIN MIN MIN MIIIIIN MIN MIN**—sound of cicadas.

70.4 **FX: DOSUN**—thud

74.2 **FX: KUN KUKUN**—sound of the pendulum tugging

74.3 He literally did say "Bingo!" in the original Japanese. Do they play it there, or just use the expression? When was the last time you saw someone play bingo in a manga?

75.3 Such an altar would ordinarily contain ritual objects used in daily Buddhist worship, including a symbolic offering of food—hence Makino's theory about the rat. An excellent image of how a home altar such as this might be arranged

ordinarily in the *Jodo Shinshu* sect (there are many) of Buddhism can be seen at: http://shinmission_sg.tripod.com/id36.html

76.1   **FX: GAKON**—altar door forced open

77.6   **FX: PITA**—sound of fingertips touching corpse

79.4   **FX: GACHA**—sound of door opening

81.4   Originally Karatsu compared it to a Japanese TV show called *Otakara Kanteidan*, "Treasure Appraisers," but its premise is very similar to PBS's *Antiques Roadshow*, so the editor just plugged that in.

83.6   **FX: GUI**—putting on ring

83.7   **FX: CHARIIIN**—the pendulum chain ringing as he drops the weighted end

85.1   **FX: HYUUUU**—sound of wind

85.5   **FX: PECHI PECHI**—tapping the sign

86.5   **FX/balloon: GIKU**—gulp sound effect

86.6   **FX/balloon: KUI KUI**—sounds of fingers pointing down

87.1   **FX: GATA GATA GATA**—sound of the car rattling

87.2   **FX: GOGOGOGOGOGO**—sound of the car on the highway

88.4   **FX: GARARAN**—sound of trash being moved around

89.3   **FX: KUN**—arm suddenly swinging over to point

89.4   **FX/small: GASA DOSA**—sound of rustling bushes followed by a thud

90.1   **FX: DODO**—running sound

90.2   **FX: BURORORO**—truck starting to drive off

90.3   **FX/balloon: ZA**—stepping onto the road

91.1   **FX: BAN**—sound of fist hitting windshield

91.2   **FX: PARA PARA**—sound of glass shards falling

92.1   **FX: GWOOO**—speeding down highway

93.1   **FX: KOAAAA**—sound of a crow

93.2   **FX/balloon: KOAAA**—more cawing

94.2-3   8000 yen a month *is* dirt cheap, even for such basic accommodations, but oddly enough a sixty-year-old apartment building might be more easily thought "ancient" in Tokyo than in many younger American cities. By contrast, in the editor's neighborhood in Portland (the oh-so-trendy NW 23rd) there are a dozen or more apartment buildings dating from the 1920s and 1930s—including the Irving, where Gus Van Sant shot *Drugstore Cowboy*, as the plaque outside will be glad to tell you. Makino's mention that the place is sixty years old implies the apartment was built during the Second World War (this story first appeared in the Japanese magazine *Psycho Ace*—a spinoff of *Shonen Ace* named, naturally, for its hit manga *MPD Psycho*—in late 2000) and was therefore one of the relatively few to survive that era. However, in Tokyo, even a thirty-year-old building might be thought ripe for redevelopment. Japan's construction sector is much larger

than America's relative to the country's size, with political clout that often leads both to things getting built for which there is no need (shorelines filled with those caltrop-like breakwaters you see in anime, highways to nowhere) and to things getting torn down without good reason (i.e., "old" buildings). It's only the editor's opinion, but this may be one of the reasons why Tokyo, surely one of the greatest cities of the world, is generally lacking in great or even attractive architecture. Why bother, when it's just going to get bulldozed in another generation? Mamoru Oshii touched on this theme in his films *Patlabor 1* and *Jin-Roh*.

95.3 The sign says "Quiet in the hallway!"

96.4 **FX: PITA**—fingertips touching body

98.3 **FX: KIII**—creaking door

98.6 **FX: GACHARI**—sound of altar door being locked

100.1 **FX: NUKU**—standing up

101.1 **FX: MYAA MYAA**—sound of gulls

101.2 Note the bag marked "Kadokawa"— the original publishers of *The Kurosagi Corpse Delivery Service*.

103.3 **FX/balloon: ZA**—sound of sandals in gravel

104.2 **FX: ATA FUTA**—panicked sound

105.4 **FX: KUN KUN**—sound of pendulum tugging

105.7 **FX: ZA**—footstep

113.4 **FX: SHAKIN**—sound of scissors closing

116.1 **FX/balloons: GAKI GAKI BAKI**—pry bar hitting car trunk

117.2 **FX: BAKAN**—trunk breaking open

120.2 **FX: MUGYU**—sound of the others squeezing in close

120.4 Saburo is a character from Machiko Hasegawa's manga of everyday life, *Sazae-San*, which ran from 1946 to 1974, and has been a regular anime show since 1969. It's one of the few manga of which it can probably be said that *every* Japanese person has heard of it— everyone, that is, except Makino.

121.1 **FX: GIKU**—gulp

121.2 **FX: BATAN**—quickly closed trunk

124.2 **FX: SUU**—sound of gauze pressed on body

124.4 **FX: GACHA**—door opening

125.5 **FX/balloon: KACHA**—camera shutter

127.1 **FX/small: KOKI**—neck crack

129.1 **FX: GACHA**—opening door

129.3 **FX: BATAM**—closing door

130.4 **FX: GATA**—starting to get up out of chair

132.3 **FX: PAN PAN**—hitting sheet of paper

132.4 **FX: PORI PORI**—scratching head

135.5 **FX/balloon: PAPAAN**—honking horn

138.3 **FX: BAKAN**—striking locker door

139.1 **FX/balloon: KACHA**—door opening

139.2 **FX: GO**—foot bumping severed head

140.1 FX: GAPA—sound of a freezer being opened

140.3 FX/balloons: GAKI GAN GAKIN—sound of something hitting doorknob

140.4 FX/balloon: KACHARI—sound of door unlatching

141.1 FX: KIIII—door creaking open

141.5 FX: JIIII—sound of opening zipper

146.1.1 FX/white: BIKU BIKU—body starting to convulse

146.1.2 FX/black: GABA—eyes popping open

146.3 FX: GATA GATA KATA GATA—headless body starting to shake

147.1 FX: GASHI—headless body grabbing Tsutsui

147.2 FX: GYUUU—arms squeezing Tsutsui

147.3 FX: BATAN—headless body falling and hitting ground

147.4 FX: HETA—Tsutsui slumping down to the ground

147.5 FX/balloons: PAKU PAKU—sound of flapping mouths

148.1.1 FX/balloon: PAKU PAKURI—sound of flapping mouths

148.1.2 FX/balloon: PAKU PAKU—sound of flapping mouths

148.2.1 FX/balloon: PAKU—sound of flapping mouths

148.2.2 FX/balloon: PAKU PAKU—sound of flapping mouths

148.3.1 FX/white: KPFU—sound of a refrigerator door popping open

148.3.2 FX/Black: WASA WASA WASA—arms inside plastic backs reaching out

149.1.1 FX/black: YORO—stagger

149.1.2 FX/white: PATA—sound of a footstep on bare tile

150-151.1 FX: BA—corpse suddenly lashing out.

152.3 FX: DO—body crumpling into Tsutsui's lap

152.4 FX: KAKUN—hand suddenly stopping movement

152.5 FX: PITA—flapping mouth suddenly going silent

153.1 FX: SHIN—sound of silence

154.1 FX: KASHU—sound of beer can opening

154.3 FX: ZAZAAAAN—crashing waves

155.3 FX: ZAAAN ZAZAAAN—sound of distant waves

158.2 FX: ZU ZUU—noodle-slurping noises

159.6.1 FX: SUKU—Karatsu standing up

159.6.2 FX/balloons: KOKI KOKI—cracking back

160.2 FX: CHAPOON—splash of a pebble hitting water

160.3 FX: YURAI—sound of a body floating in water

161.1 FX: DOCHA—wet thud

161.2 FX: ZA—sound of Karatsu kneeling in gravel

162.2 FX: SU—taking hands off body

165.1 FX/balloon: KACHA—hanging up phone

167.1 FX/balloons: HAA HAA HAA— panting

167.3 FX/balloons: PAKU PAKU— sound of flapping mouth. Somewhat suspiciously, perhaps, neither Yata nor the puppet are seen to be breathing hard in this panel. Recently, when the editor was getting a new car insurance policy, he got to the point in the interview with the agent where they ask for your profession. When he said, "editor," the agent noted cheerfully that this seemed to drop my premium considerably. It's a good thing I didn't mention the "manga" part.

168.1 FX: PARA PARA— flipping through book

168.1 The editor is himself a Virgo male with blood type O, so he will certainly take this under advisement.

169.2 FX: GURUN— sound of world spinning

169.3 FX: DO GA DOGA— sound of Yata falling down steps

170.1 119, rather than 911, is the emergency number for fire and ambulance in Japan, as well as Taiwan and South Korea (although unlike the U.S., Japan has a separate number for emergency calls to the police— namely, 110).

170.2 FX/balloon: PIPEPE PEEPU PIPAPAPA— cell ringing

170.3 FX/balloon: PIPA— answering phone

171.3 FX: PATA— sound of a book closing

172.5 FX: KACHA— opening car door

173.3 FX: GORORON GORORO— sky rumbling

173.5 FX: SU— raising arm

173.6 FX/balloon: JIII— zipper closing

173.7 FX: PARA— flipping though book

174.1 FX: KARI KARI KARI KYUD-WOOOON— air crackling then a loud lightning strike

174.2 FX: DOGOGOGOGOGO— loud rumbling sound

175.3 FX/balloon: PIPAAPI PIPA-PAPIPA PIIPIPA– cell ringing

175.4 FX: PII PA PII PA PI PIPOPA— cell continuing to ring

175.5 FX/balloon: PIPA— answering cell

176.5 FX/balloon: TSUU TSUU TSUU— disconnect tone

176.6 FX: BA BA— looking around quickly

176.7 FX/balloons: POTSU POTSU POTSU— raindrops

177.1 FX: ZAAAAA— pouring rain

178.1 FX: MOGU MOGU— eating sounds

179.3 FX/balloons: PIPI PIPI— an e-mail notice beep from cell

179.4 FX/balloon: PI— button press sound

180.2 FX/balloon: KACHI— putting cable into cell

180.3 FX: PA PA— file opening on computer

181.3 FX/balloon: KACHI— mouse click

183.1 FX: PEE PAPI PIPAPAPIPU PIPA— cell ringing

184.4 FX: TON—putting book down

184.5 FX: PARA PARA—flipping though pages

185.1.1 FX: PATAN—flipping page

185.1.2 FX: PATAN—page sections being flipped over

185.4 FX/balloon: KATA KATATA—clicking way on keyboard

187.1 FX: DOSA—dropping body bag

187.4 FX/balloon: PIPAPA PIPAPU-PAPA PIPAPI—cell ringing

189.3 FX: JIWA—water level rising

189.4 FX: GOGOGOGOGO—distant rumbling of rushing water

189.5 FX: GOGOGOGOGO—getting louder

190-191.1 FX: DWOOOOO—rushing wall of water

192.1 FX: GOBAAAAA—water rushing by

192.2 FX: GOGOGO—rushing water sound

192.4 FX: GOGOGOGOGO—rushing water

193.3 FX/balloon: PIKU—hand twitching

193.5 FX: GOGOGOGO—rushing water

194.1 FX: ZAZAAAN—rushing river water being kicked up

194.2 FX: BASHA BASHA BASHA—sound of splashing

194.3 FX: ZABABABA—sound of Karatsu pulling his body out of the water

195.2.1 FX: KWOOOO—sound of a plane flying overhead

195.2.2 FX/balloon: KIRA—glint of light in the air

195.3 FX: HIIIIII—sound of something falling

195.4 FX: HEEEEEEE—getting louder

196.1 FX: PAKIII—sound of a bolt falling through glasses at terminal velocity into eye socket

197.2 FX: ZABO—book falling into water

STAFF D

Embalming
[エンバーミング]：死体修復

STAFF E

Channeling
[チャネリング]：宇宙人と交信

STAFF E'

Puppet
[マペット]：宇宙人が憑依

→

お届け物は死体です。

黒鷺死体宅配便
the KUROSAGI corpse delivery service

story
EIJI OTSUKA

art
HOUSUI YAMAZAKI

original cover design
BUNPEI YORIFUJI

translation
TOSHIFUMI YOSHIDA

editor and english adaptation
CARL GUSTAV HORN

lettering and touch-up
IHL

contents

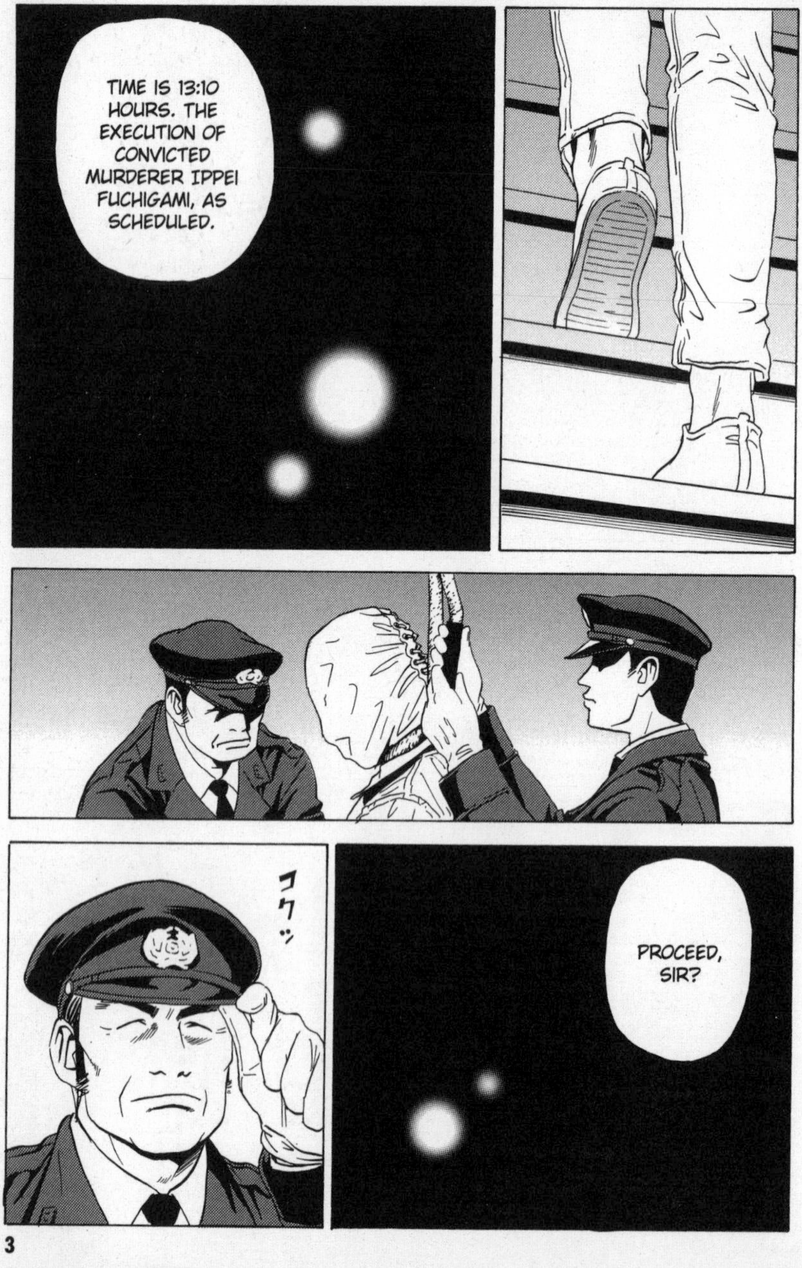
TIME IS 13:10 HOURS. THE EXECUTION OF CONVICTED MURDERER IPPEI FUCHIGAMI, AS SCHEDULED.
PROCEED, SIR?
コクッ

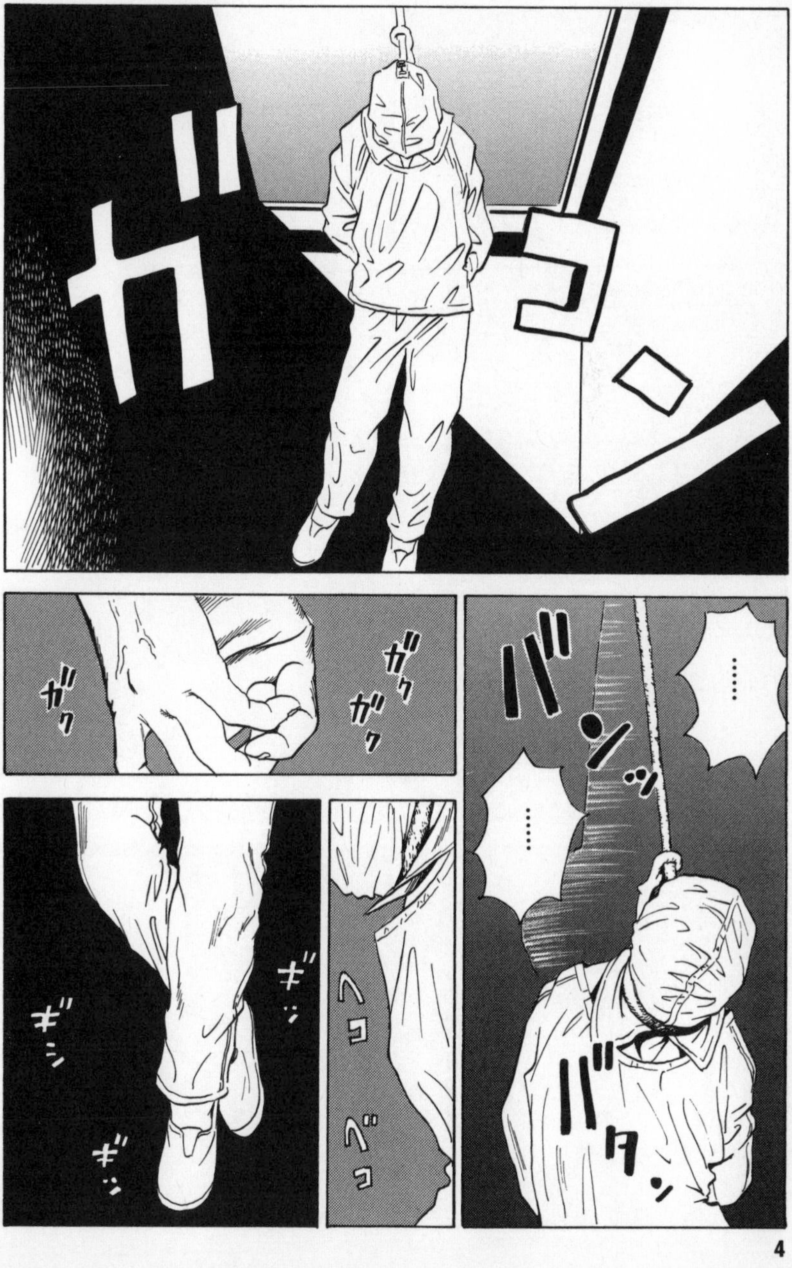

ガコン
……
バンッ
……
バタン
ガク
ガク
ガク
ベコ
ベコ
ギッ
ギシ
ギッ

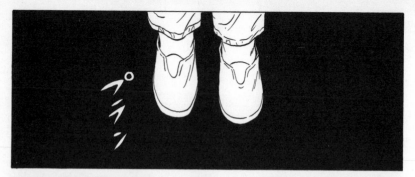

TIME IS 13:24 HOURS. THE DEATH OF IPPEI FUCHIGAMI IS CONFIRMED.

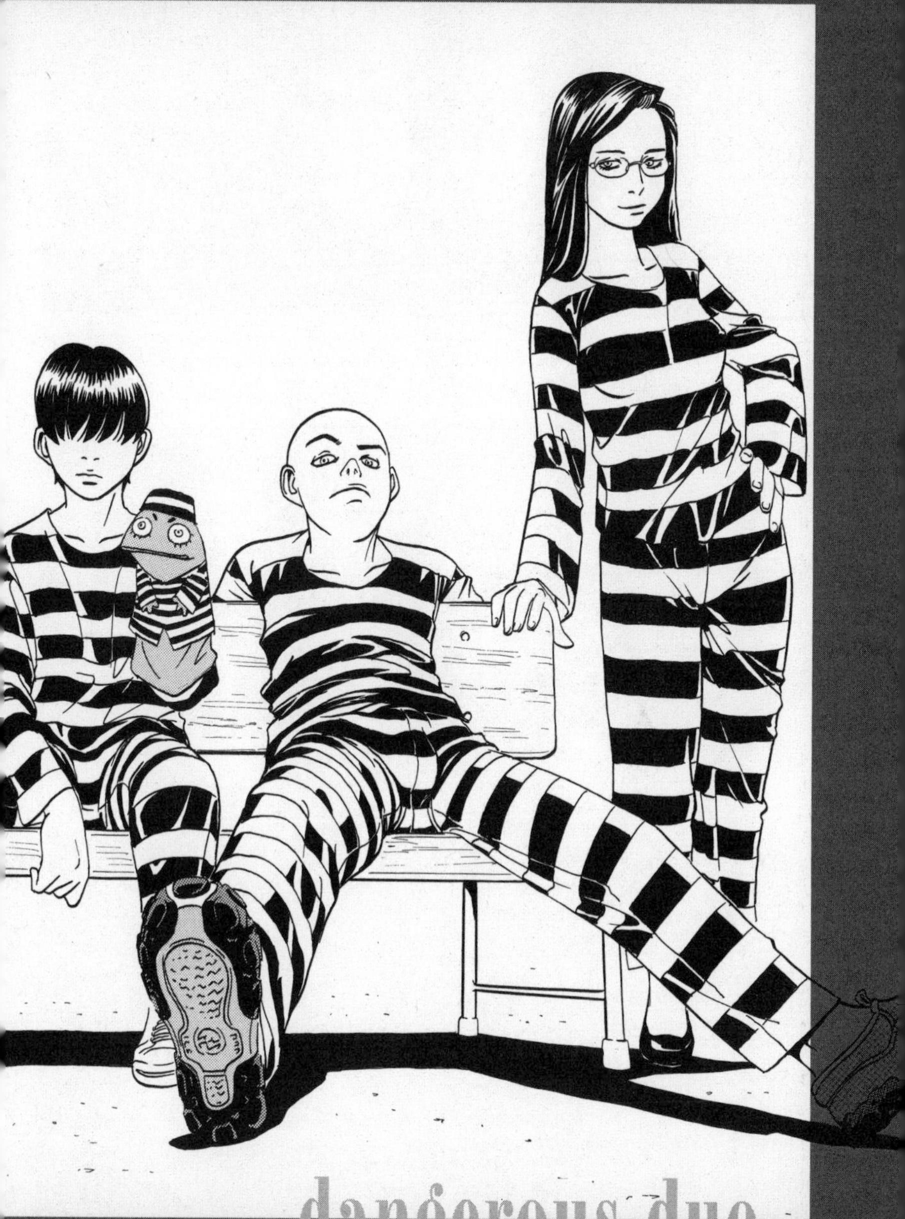

dangerous duo

1st delivery 危険なふたり

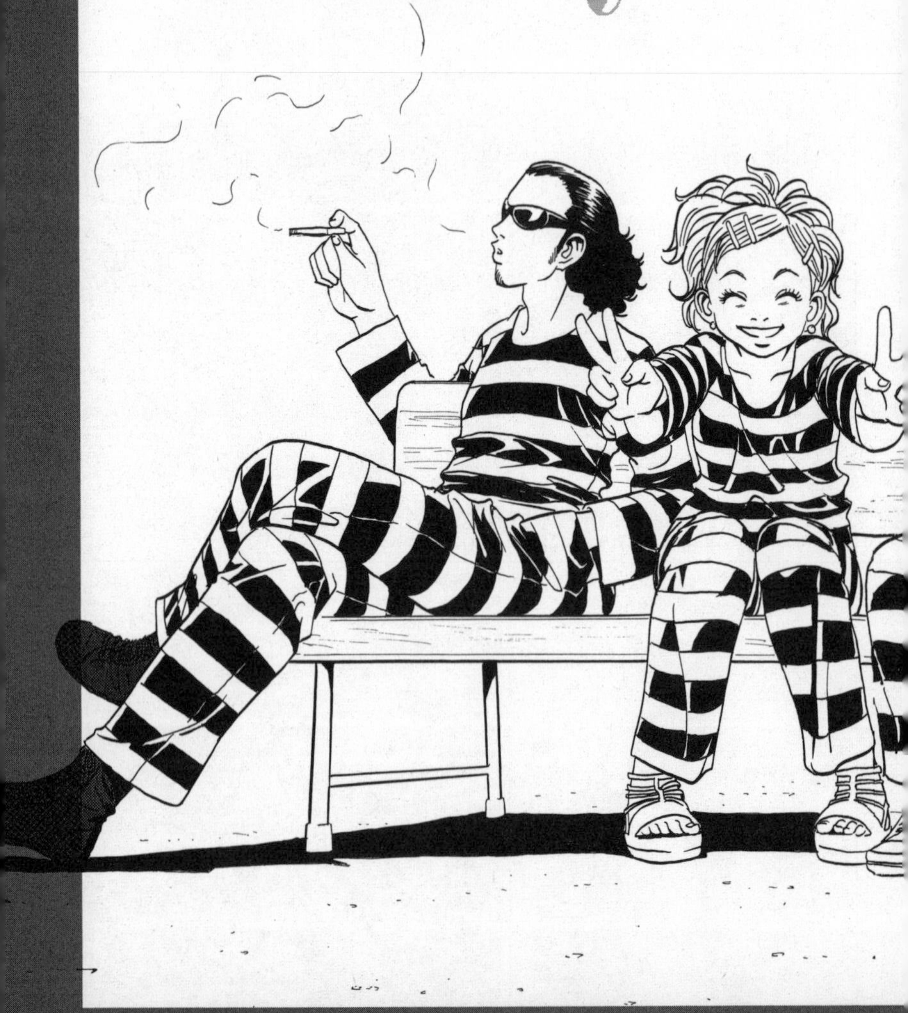

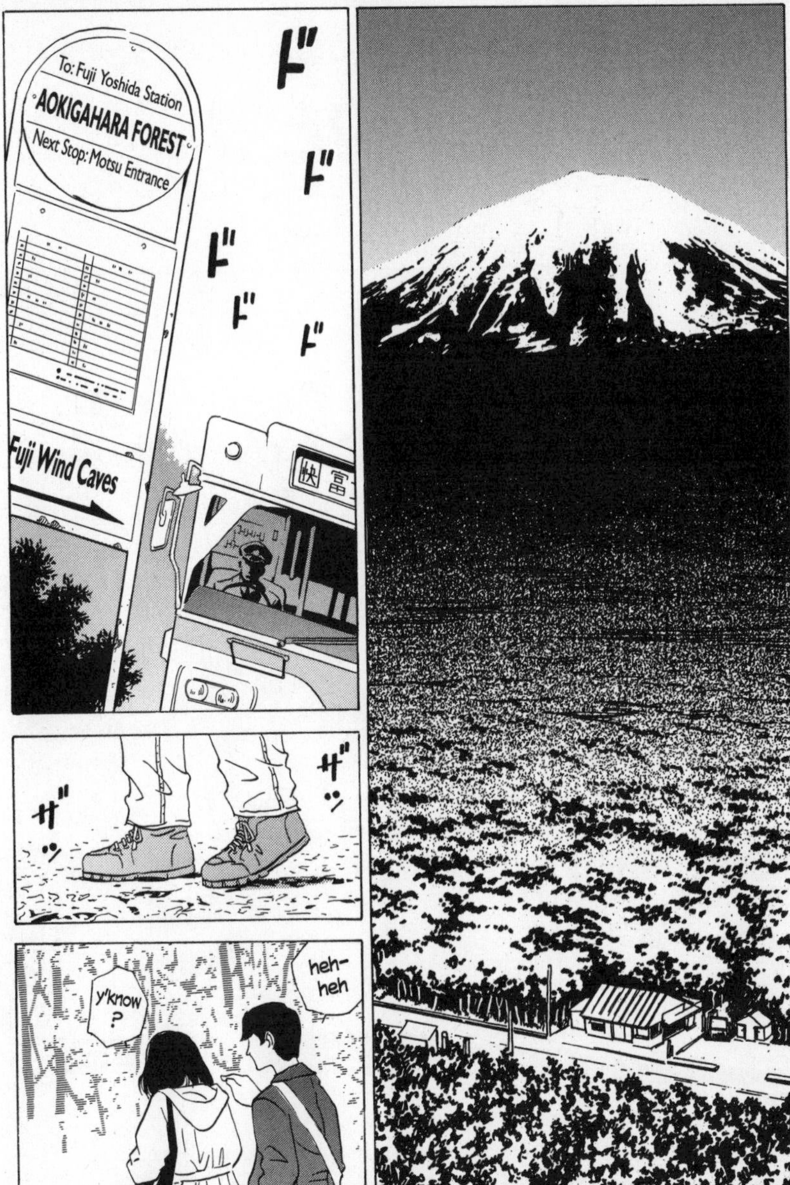
To: Fuji Yoshida Station
AOKIGAHARA FOREST
Next Stop: Motsu Entrance
Fuji Wind Caves
ド
ド
ド
ド
ド
ザッ
ザッ
heh-heh
y'know?

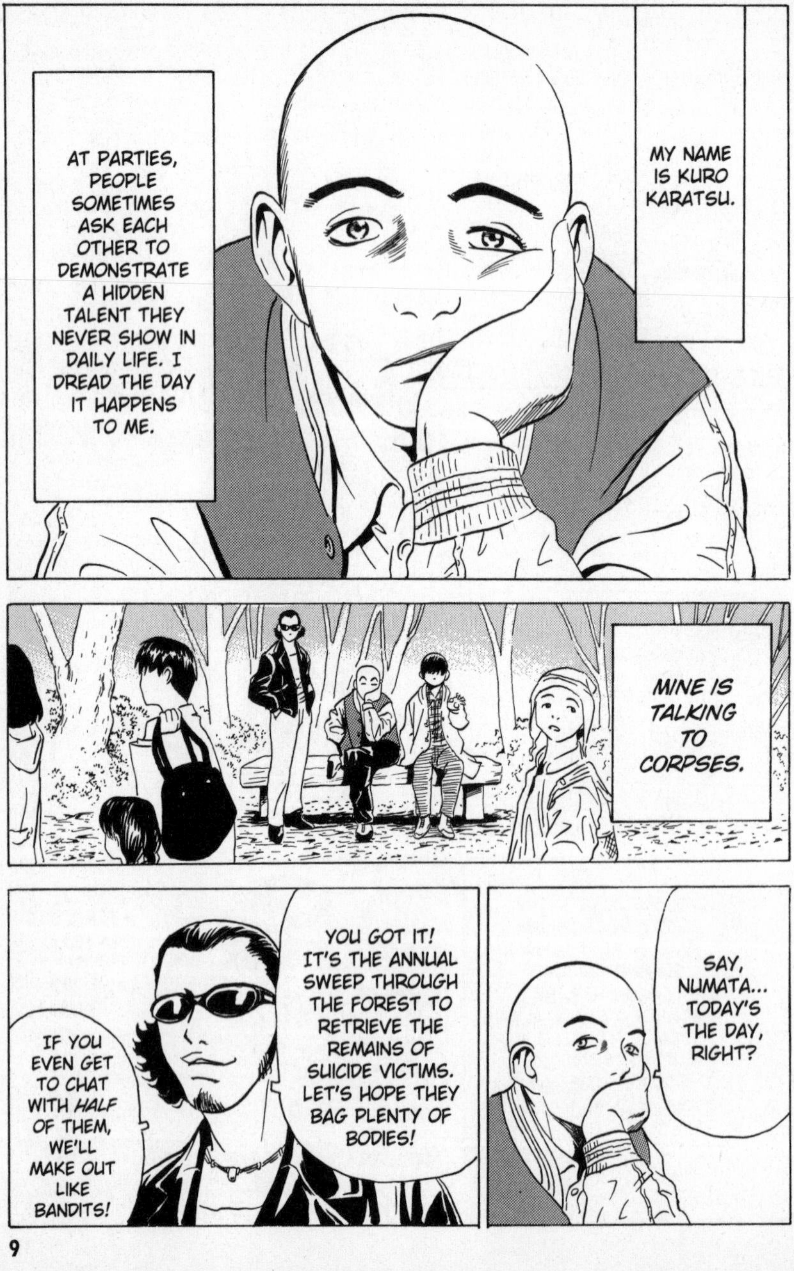
MY NAME IS KURO KARATSU.
AT PARTIES, PEOPLE SOMETIMES ASK EACH OTHER TO DEMONSTRATE A HIDDEN TALENT THEY NEVER SHOW IN DAILY LIFE. I DREAD THE DAY IT HAPPENS TO ME.
MINE IS TALKING TO CORPSES.
SAY, NUMATA... TODAY'S THE DAY, RIGHT?
YOU GOT IT! IT'S THE ANNUAL SWEEP THROUGH THE FOREST TO RETRIEVE THE REMAINS OF SUICIDE VICTIMS. LET'S HOPE THEY BAG PLENTY OF BODIES!
IF YOU EVEN GET TO CHAT WITH *HALF* OF THEM, WE'LL MAKE OUT LIKE BANDITS!

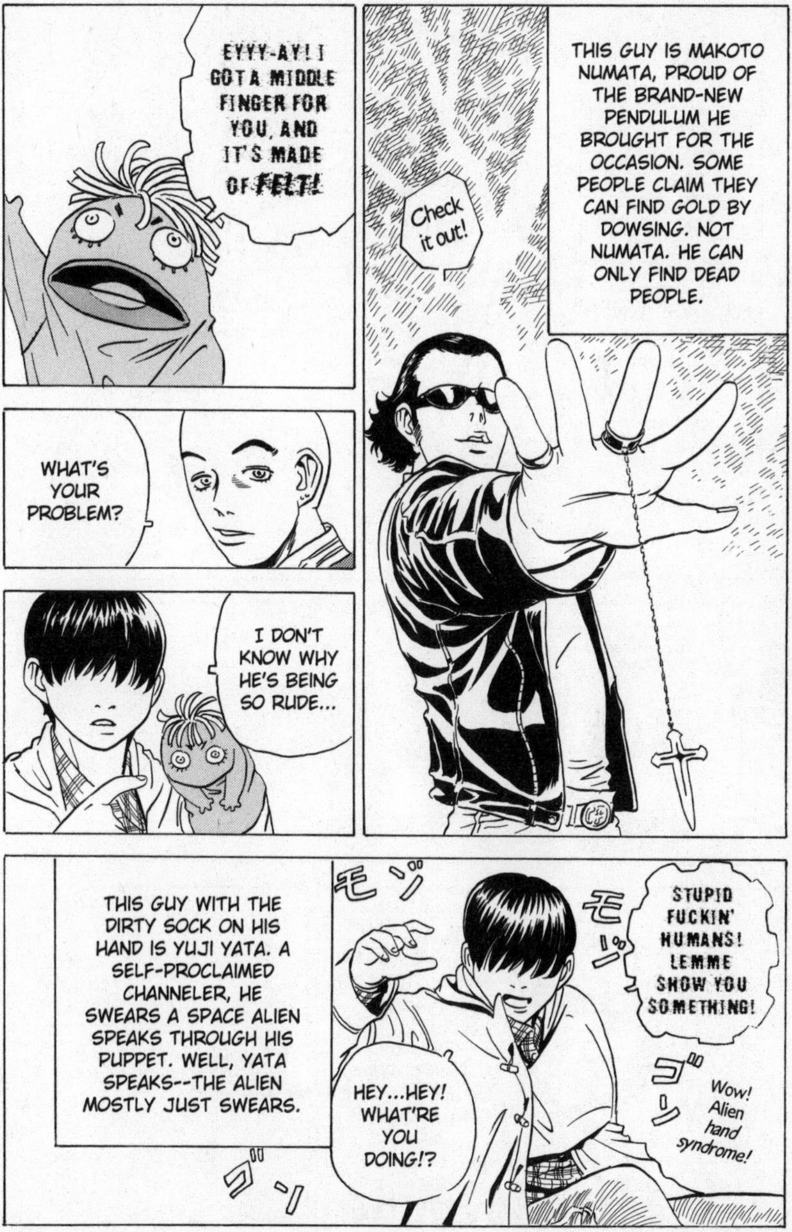
THIS GUY IS MAKOTO NUMATA, PROUD OF THE BRAND-NEW PENDULUM HE BROUGHT FOR THE OCCASION. SOME PEOPLE CLAIM THEY CAN FIND GOLD BY DOWSING. NOT NUMATA. HE CAN ONLY FIND DEAD PEOPLE.
Check it out!
EYYY-AY! I GOT A MIDDLE FINGER FOR YOU, AND IT'S MADE OF FELT!
WHAT'S YOUR PROBLEM?
I DON'T KNOW WHY HE'S BEING SO RUDE...
STUPID FUCKIN' HUMANS! LEMME SHOW YOU SOMETHING!
モゾ
モゾ
ゴン
Wow! Alien hand syndrome!
HEY...HEY! WHAT'RE YOU DOING!?
THIS GUY WITH THE DIRTY SOCK ON HIS HAND IS YUJI YATA. A SELF-PROCLAIMED CHANNELER, HE SWEARS A SPACE ALIEN SPEAKS THROUGH HIS PUPPET. WELL, YATA SPEAKS--THE ALIEN MOSTLY JUST SWEARS.
ゴン

CAN YOUR SPECIES *READ* YET? IT WAS POSTED ON YOUR UNIVERSITY BULLETIN BOARD!
NOTICE OF CANCELLATION
31ST ANNUAL SUICIDE VICTIM SEARCH
The Fuji Yoshida Police and Fire Departments regret to announce the cancellation of this year's search of Aokigahara Forest, previously announced for October 20th. In a recent survey of visitors to Fuji Hakone Izu National Park, 63% stated that they were prompted to come to Aokigahara by media coverage promoting the forest as the "Suicide Spot," the "Hanging Hangout," or the "Seek-End Getaway." In an attempt to improve our image and encourage healthier use of our precious natural resources, we have decided to cancel the annual search. We regret any inconvenience caused to the public.
Fuji Yoshida Public Safety Bureau
パサッ
INCONVENIENCE"? "*INCONVENIENCE*"?! WE'RE GONNA BE OUT THREE MILLION YEN, *EASY!!!*
AWWW, *MAN!*

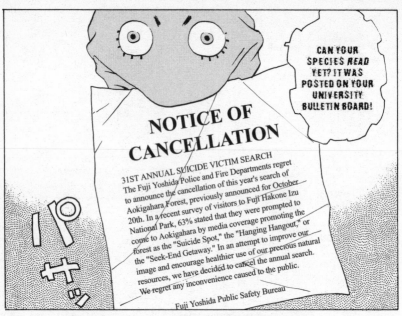

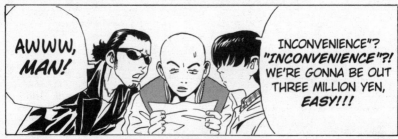

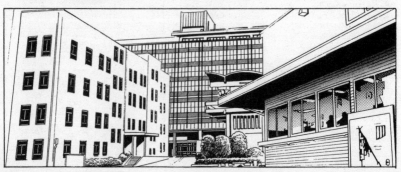

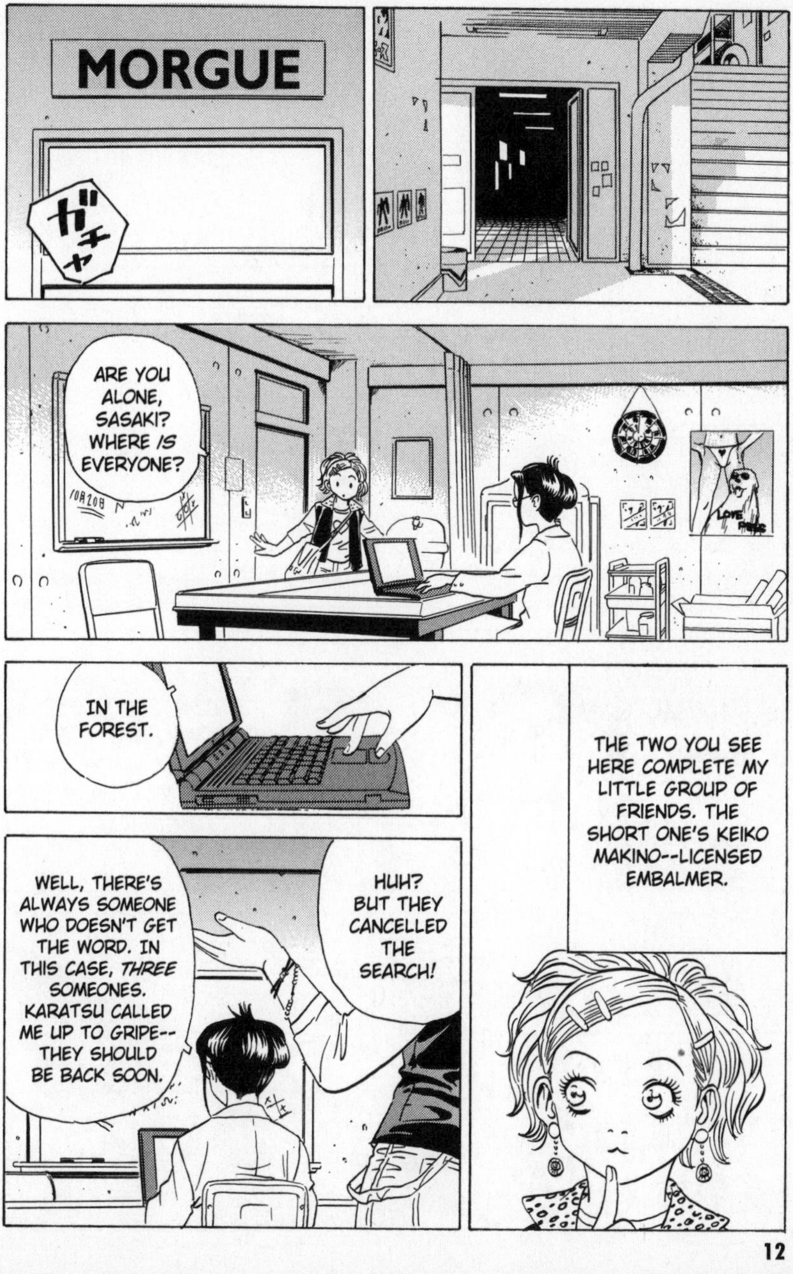
MORGUE
ガチャ
ARE YOU ALONE, SASAKI? WHERE *IS* EVERYONE?
THE TWO YOU SEE HERE COMPLETE MY LITTLE GROUP OF FRIENDS. THE SHORT ONE'S KEIKO MAKINO--LICENSED EMBALMER.
IN THE FOREST.
HUH? BUT THEY CANCELLED THE SEARCH!
WELL, THERE'S ALWAYS SOMEONE WHO DOESN'T GET THE WORD. IN THIS CASE, *THREE* SOMEONES. KARATSU CALLED ME UP TO GRIPE-- THEY SHOULD BE BACK SOON.

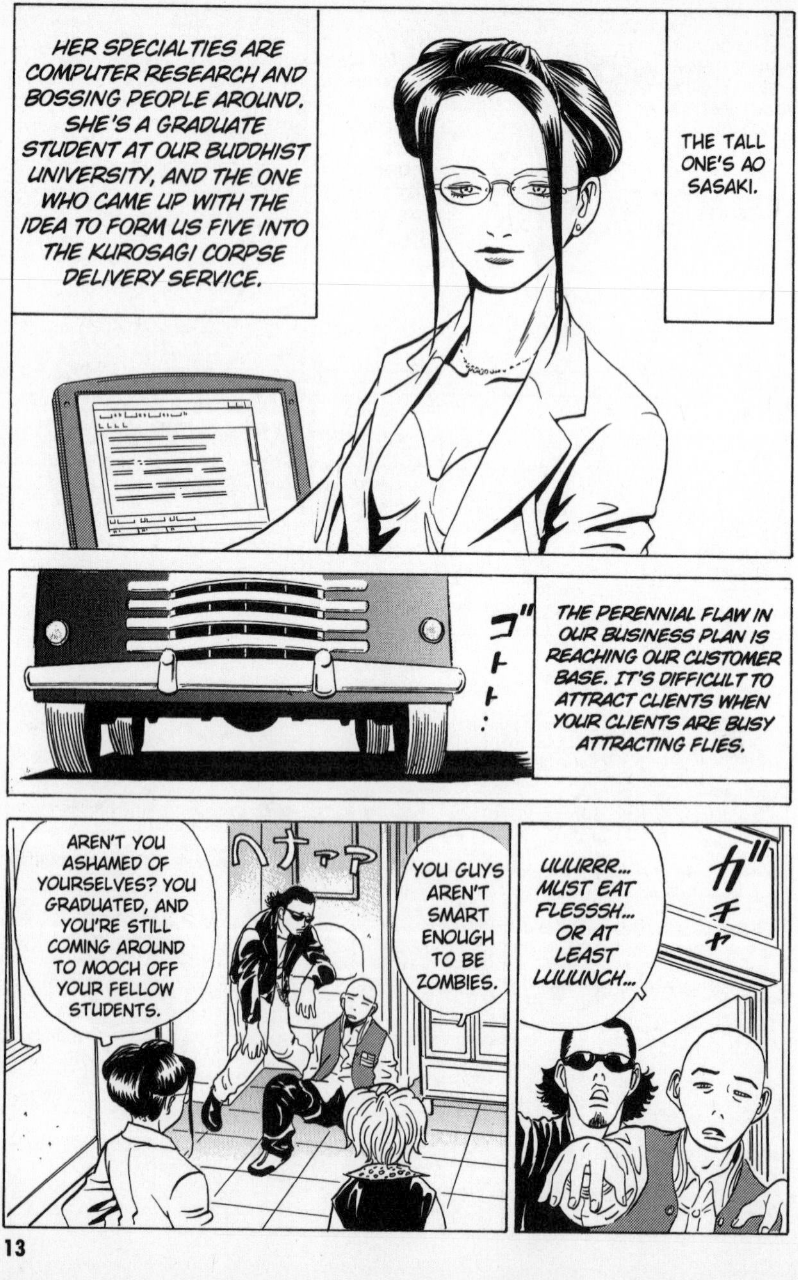

THE TALL ONE'S AO SASAKI.
HER SPECIALTIES ARE COMPUTER RESEARCH AND BOSSING PEOPLE AROUND. SHE'S A GRADUATE STUDENT AT OUR BUDDHIST UNIVERSITY, AND THE ONE WHO CAME UP WITH THE IDEA TO FORM US FIVE INTO THE KUROSAGI CORPSE DELIVERY SERVICE.
THE PERENNIAL FLAW IN OUR BUSINESS PLAN IS REACHING OUR CUSTOMER BASE. IT'S DIFFICULT TO ATTRACT CLIENTS WHEN YOUR CLIENTS ARE BUSY ATTRACTING FLIES.
ゴトト…
ガチャ
UUURRR... MUST EAT FLESSSH... OR AT LEAST LUUUNCH...
YOU GUYS AREN'T SMART ENOUGH TO BE ZOMBIES.
ヘナァア
AREN'T YOU ASHAMED OF YOURSELVES? YOU GRADUATED, AND YOU'RE STILL COMING AROUND TO MOOCH OFF YOUR FELLOW STUDENTS.

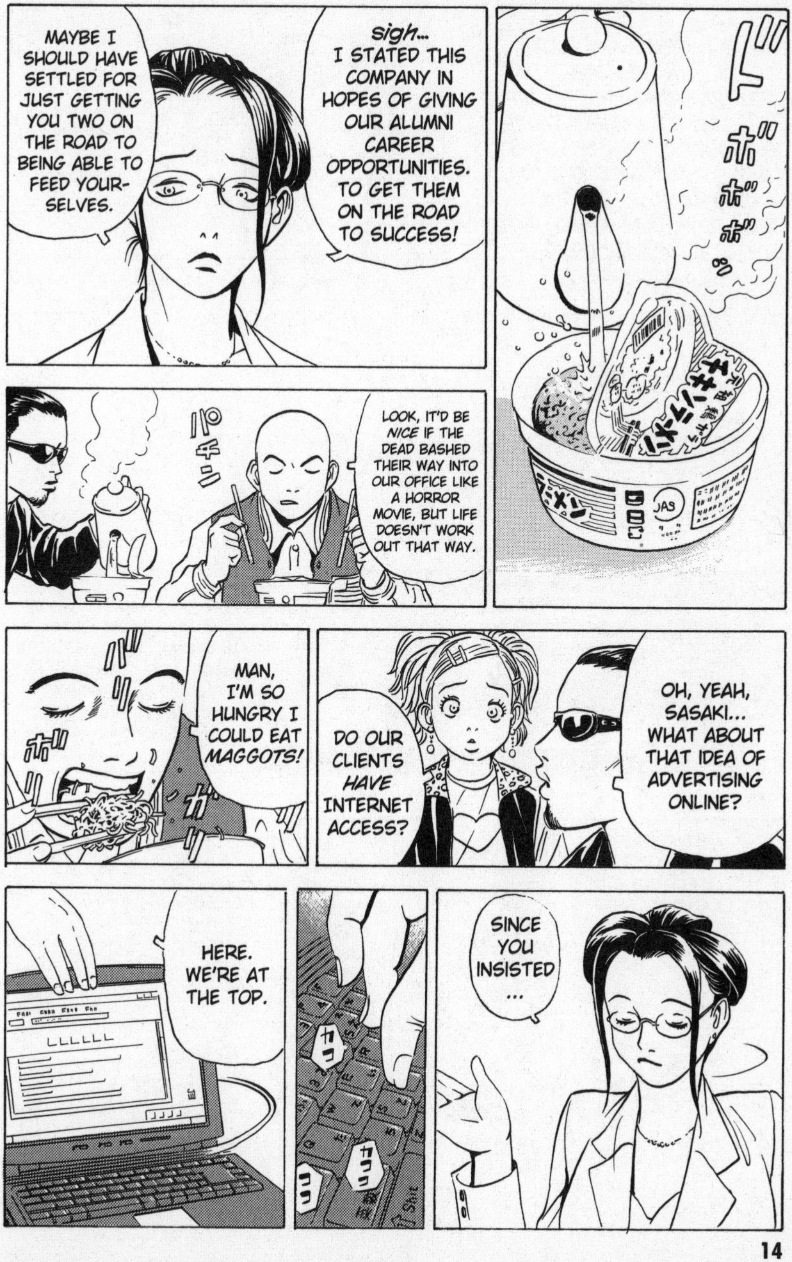
sigh... I STATED THIS COMPANY IN HOPES OF GIVING OUR ALUMNI CAREER OPPORTUNITIES. TO GET THEM ON THE ROAD TO SUCCESS!
MAYBE I SHOULD HAVE SETTLED FOR JUST GETTING YOU TWO ON THE ROAD TO BEING ABLE TO FEED YOUR-SELVES.
LOOK, IT'D BE *NICE* IF THE DEAD BASHED THEIR WAY INTO OUR OFFICE LIKE A HORROR MOVIE, BUT LIFE DOESN'T WORK OUT THAT WAY.
OH, YEAH, SASAKI... WHAT ABOUT THAT IDEA OF ADVERTISING ONLINE?
DO OUR CLIENTS *HAVE* INTERNET ACCESS?
MAN, I'M SO HUNGRY I COULD EAT *MAGGOTS!*
SINCE YOU INSISTED ...
HERE. WE'RE AT THE TOP.

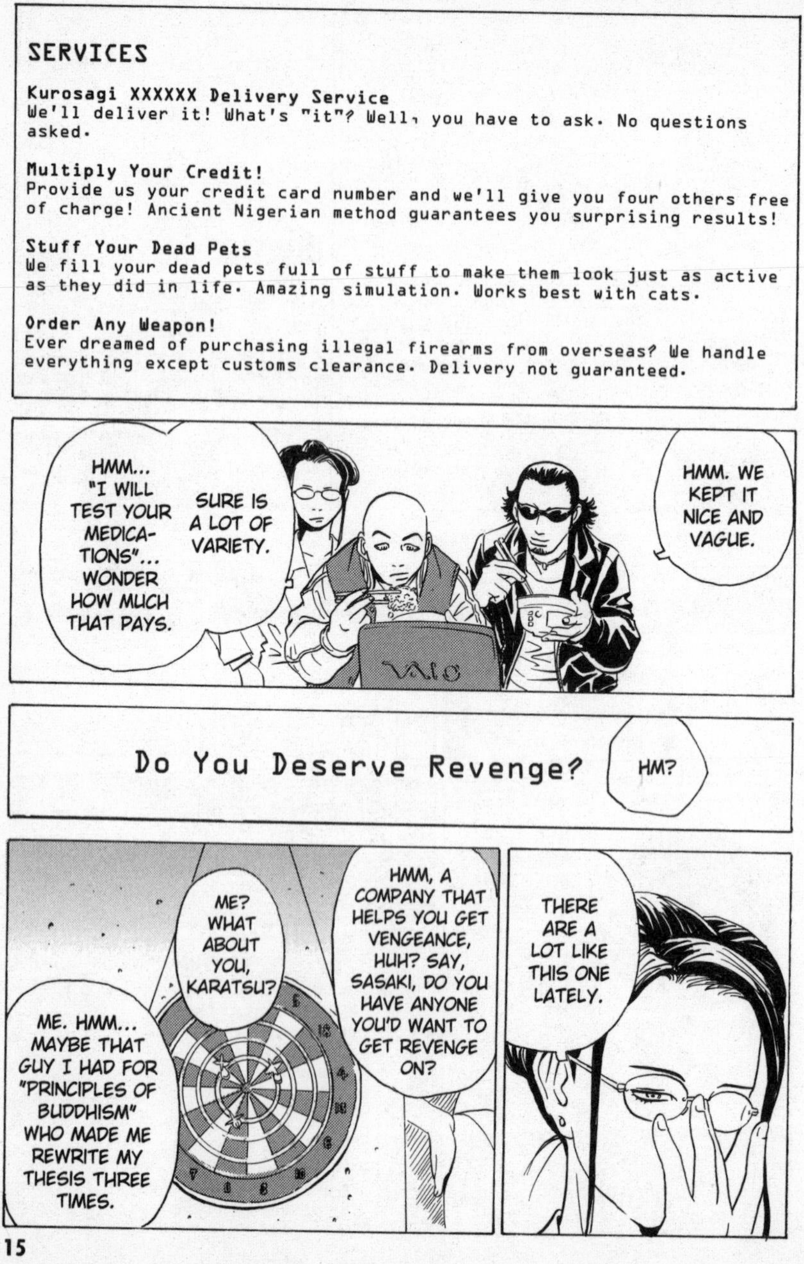
SERVICES
Kurosagi XXXXXX Delivery Service
We'll deliver it! What's "it"? Well, you have to ask. No questions asked.
Multiply Your Credit!
Provide us your credit card number and we'll give you four others free of charge! Ancient Nigerian method guarantees you surprising results!
Stuff Your Dead Pets
We fill your dead pets full of stuff to make them look just as active as they did in life. Amazing simulation. Works best with cats.
Order Any Weapon!
Ever dreamed of purchasing illegal firearms from overseas? We handle everything except customs clearance. Delivery not guaranteed.
HMM. WE KEPT IT NICE AND VAGUE.
SURE IS A LOT OF VARIETY.
HMM... "I WILL TEST YOUR MEDICA-TIONS"... WONDER HOW MUCH THAT PAYS.
VAIO
HM?
Do You Deserve Revenge?
THERE ARE A LOT LIKE THIS ONE LATELY.
HMM, A COMPANY THAT HELPS YOU GET VENGEANCE, HUH? SAY, SASAKI, DO YOU HAVE ANYONE YOU'D WANT TO GET REVENGE ON?
ME? WHAT ABOUT YOU, KARATSU?
ME. HMM... MAYBE THAT GUY I HAD FOR "PRINCIPLES OF BUDDHISM" WHO MADE ME REWRITE MY THESIS THREE TIMES.

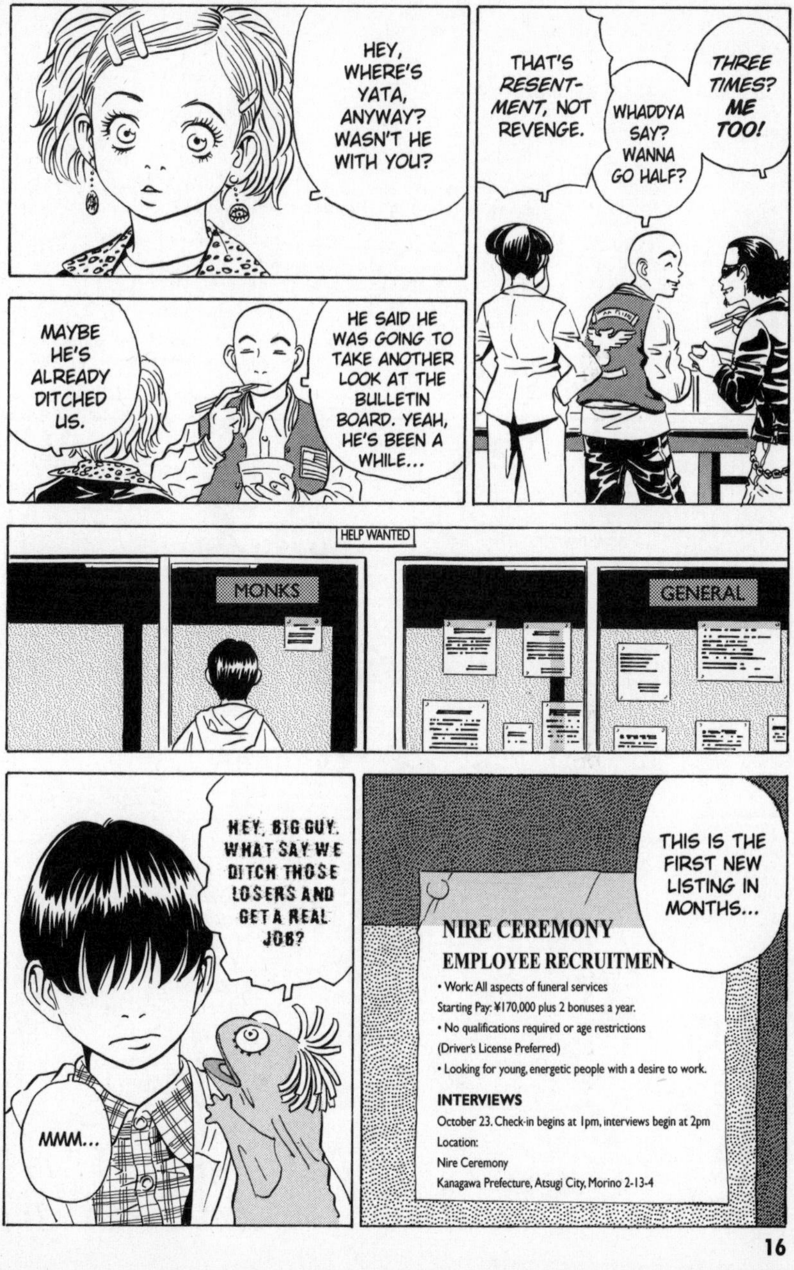

THREE TIMES? ME TOO!
WHADDYA SAY? WANNA GO HALF?
THAT'S RESENTMENT, NOT REVENGE.
HEY, WHERE'S YATA, ANYWAY? WASN'T HE WITH YOU?
HE SAID HE WAS GOING TO TAKE ANOTHER LOOK AT THE BULLETIN BOARD. YEAH, HE'S BEEN A WHILE...
MAYBE HE'S ALREADY DITCHED US.
HELP WANTED
GENERAL
MONKS
THIS IS THE FIRST NEW LISTING IN MONTHS...
NIRE CEREMONY
EMPLOYEE RECRUITMENT
• Work: All aspects of funeral services
Starting Pay: ¥170,000 plus 2 bonuses a year.
• No qualifications required or age restrictions
(Driver's License Preferred)
• Looking for young, energetic people with a desire to work.
INTERVIEWS
October 23. Check-in begins at 1pm, interviews begin at 2pm
Location:
Nire Ceremony
Kanagawa Prefecture, Atsugi City, Morino 2-13-4
HEY, BIG GUY. WHAT SAY WE DITCH THOSE LOSERS AND GET A REAL JOB?
MMM...

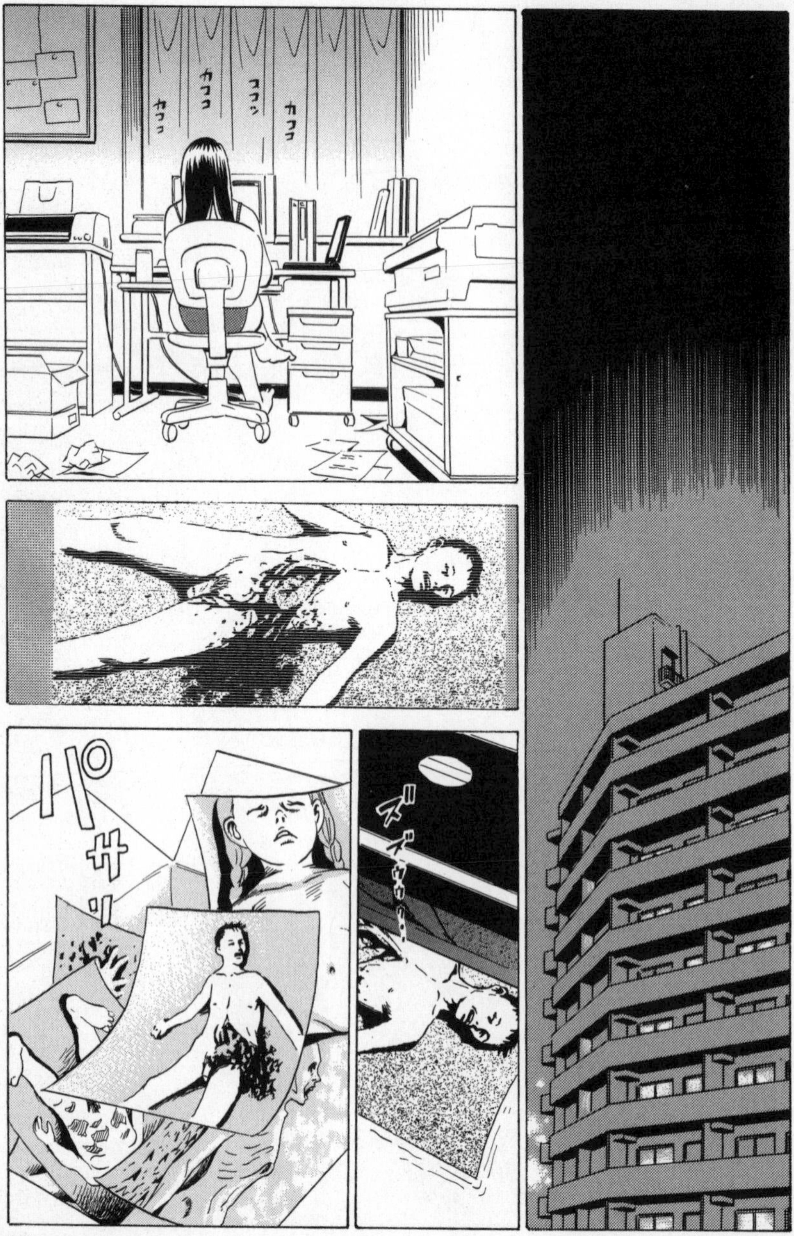
カココ
ココッ
カココ
カココ
ズズゥゥ…
パサッ

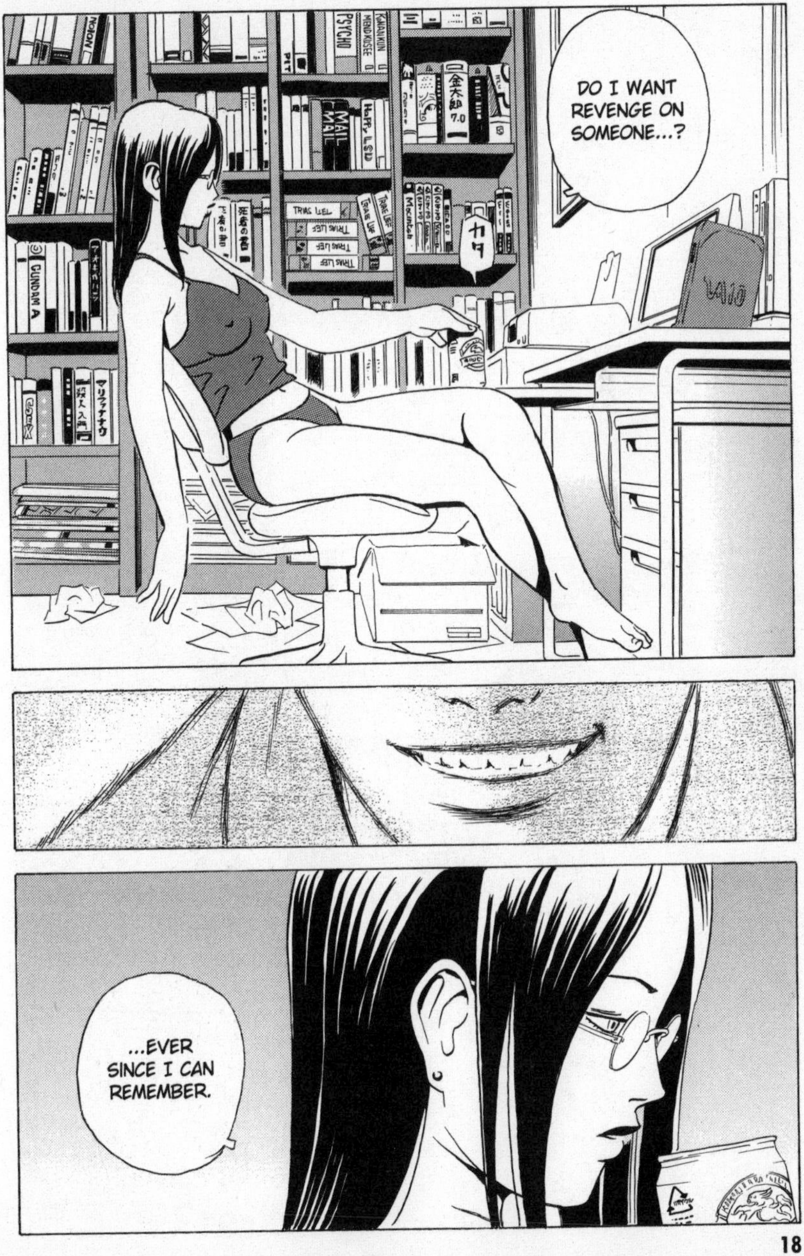
DO I WANT REVENGE ON SOMEONE...?
カタ
...EVER SINCE I CAN REMEMBER.

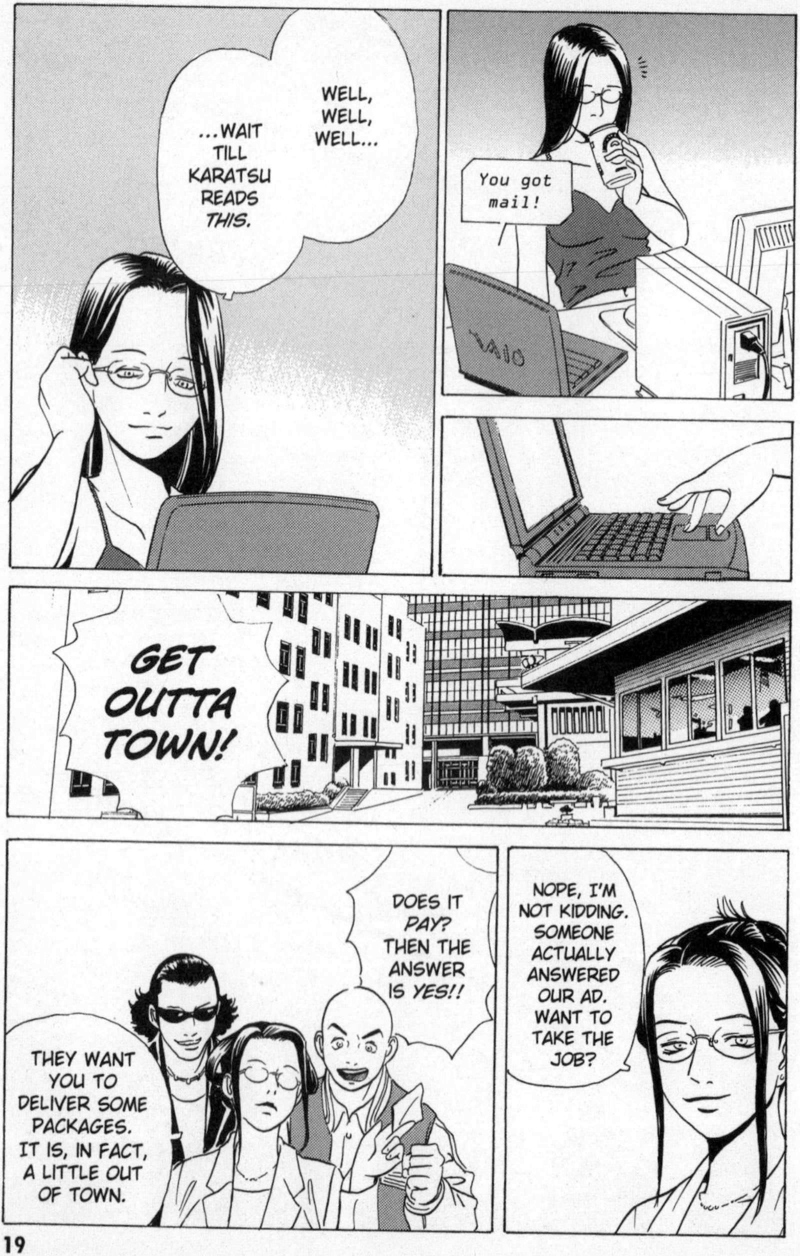
You got mail!
WELL, WELL, WELL...
...WAIT TILL KARATSU READS *THIS.*
GET OUTTA TOWN!
NOPE, I'M NOT KIDDING. SOMEONE ACTUALLY ANSWERED OUR AD. WANT TO TAKE THE JOB?
DOES IT *PAY?* THEN THE ANSWER IS *YES!!*
THEY WANT YOU TO DELIVER SOME PACKAGES. IT IS, IN FACT, A LITTLE OUT OF TOWN.

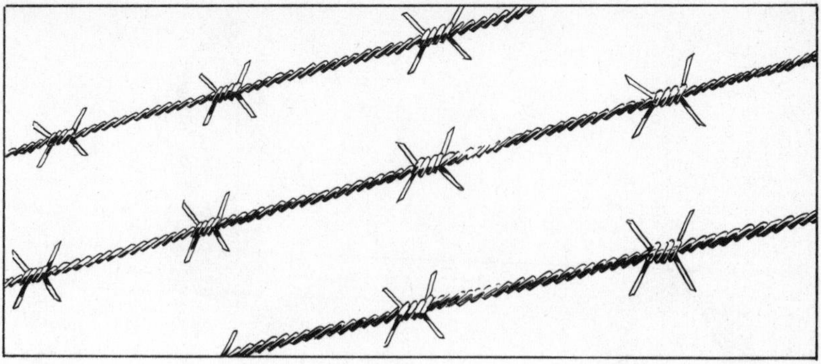
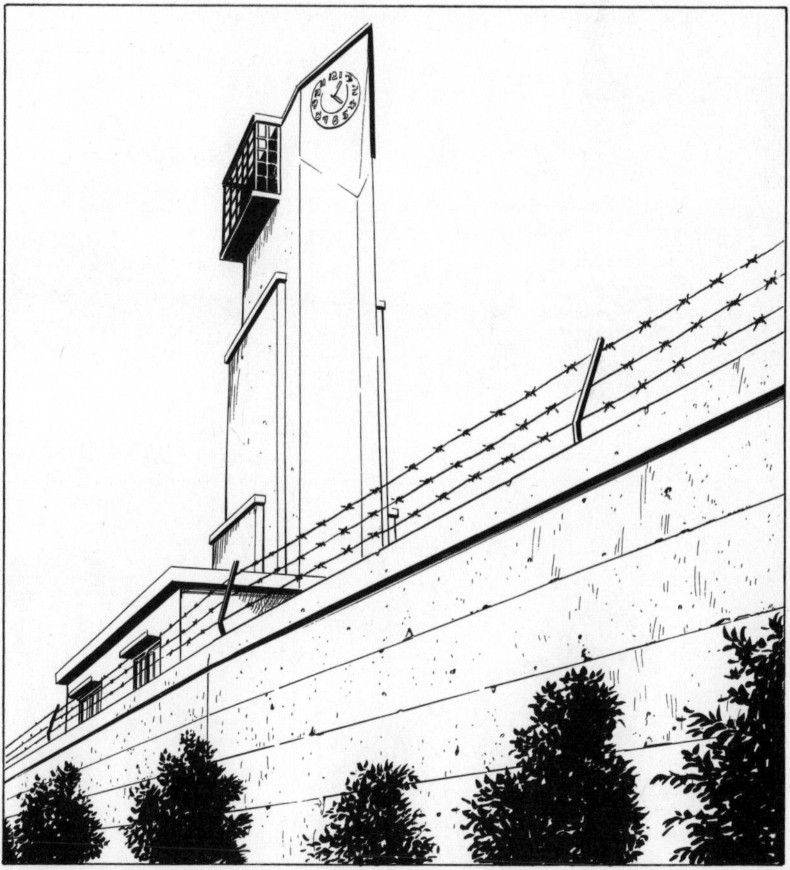

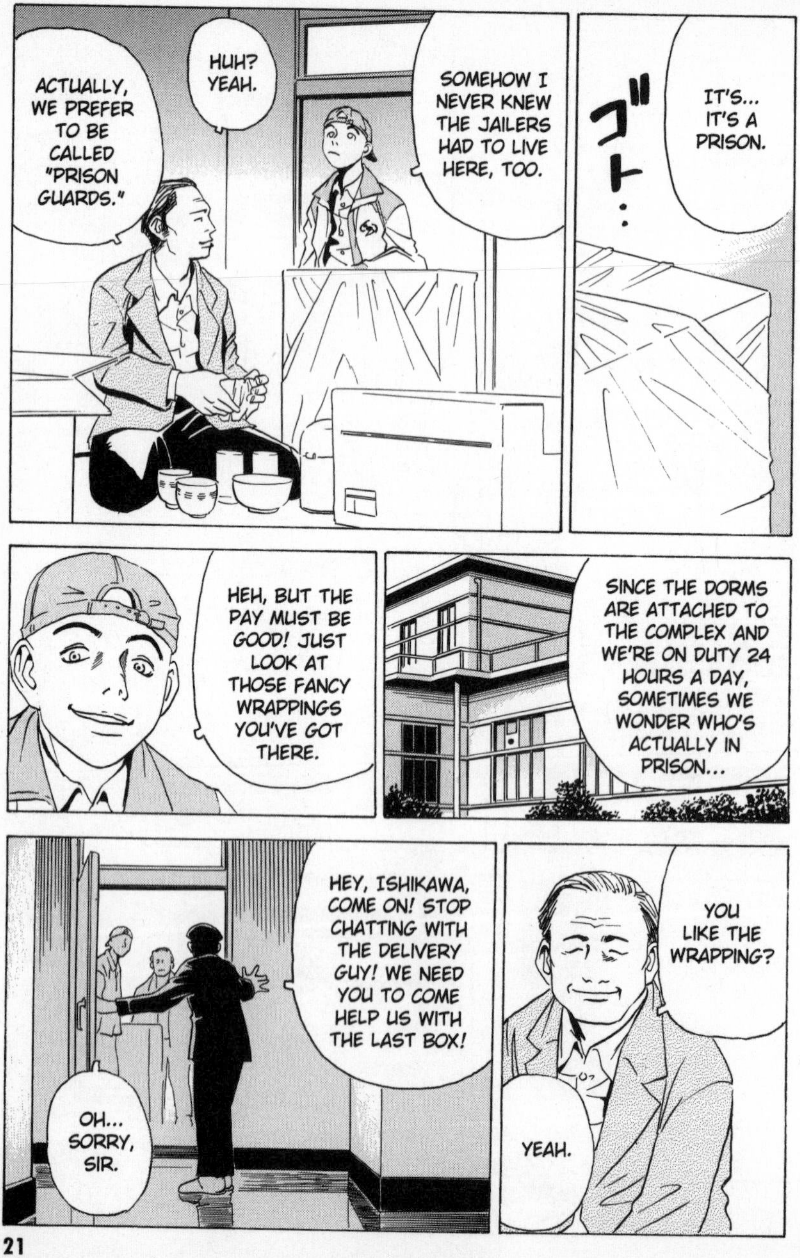
ゴト..
IT'S... IT'S A PRISON.
SOMEHOW I NEVER KNEW THE JAILERS HAD TO LIVE HERE, TOO.
HUH? YEAH.
ACTUALLY, WE PREFER TO BE CALLED "PRISON GUARDS."
SINCE THE DORMS ARE ATTACHED TO THE COMPLEX AND WE'RE ON DUTY 24 HOURS A DAY, SOMETIMES WE WONDER WHO'S ACTUALLY IN PRISON...
HEH, BUT THE PAY MUST BE GOOD! JUST LOOK AT THOSE FANCY WRAPPINGS YOU'VE GOT THERE.
YOU LIKE THE WRAPPING?
YEAH.
HEY, ISHIKAWA, COME ON! STOP CHATTING WITH THE DELIVERY GUY! WE NEED YOU TO COME HELP US WITH THE LAST BOX!
OH... SORRY, SIR.

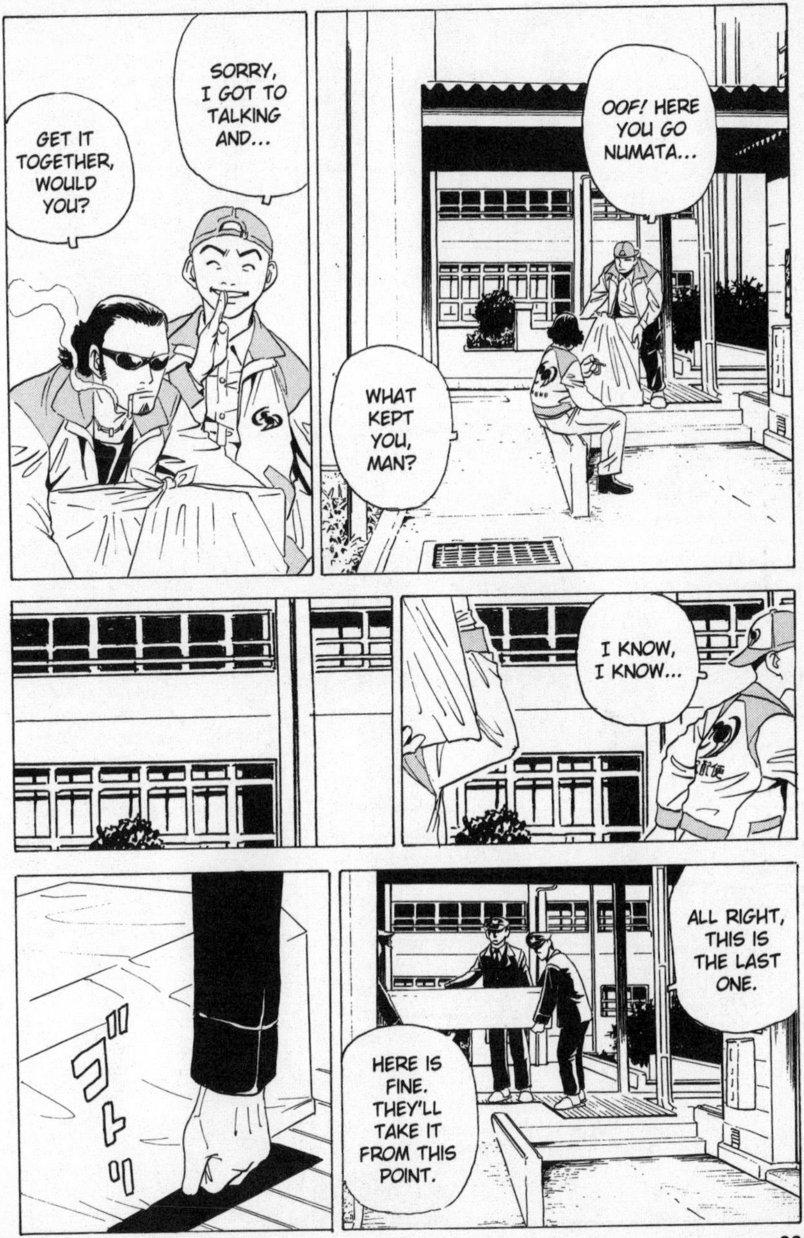

OOF! HERE YOU GO NUMATA...
WHAT KEPT YOU, MAN?
SORRY, I GOT TO TALKING AND...
GET IT TOGETHER, WOULD YOU?
I KNOW, I KNOW...
ALL RIGHT, THIS IS THE LAST ONE.
HERE IS FINE. THEY'LL TAKE IT FROM THIS POINT.
ゴトッ

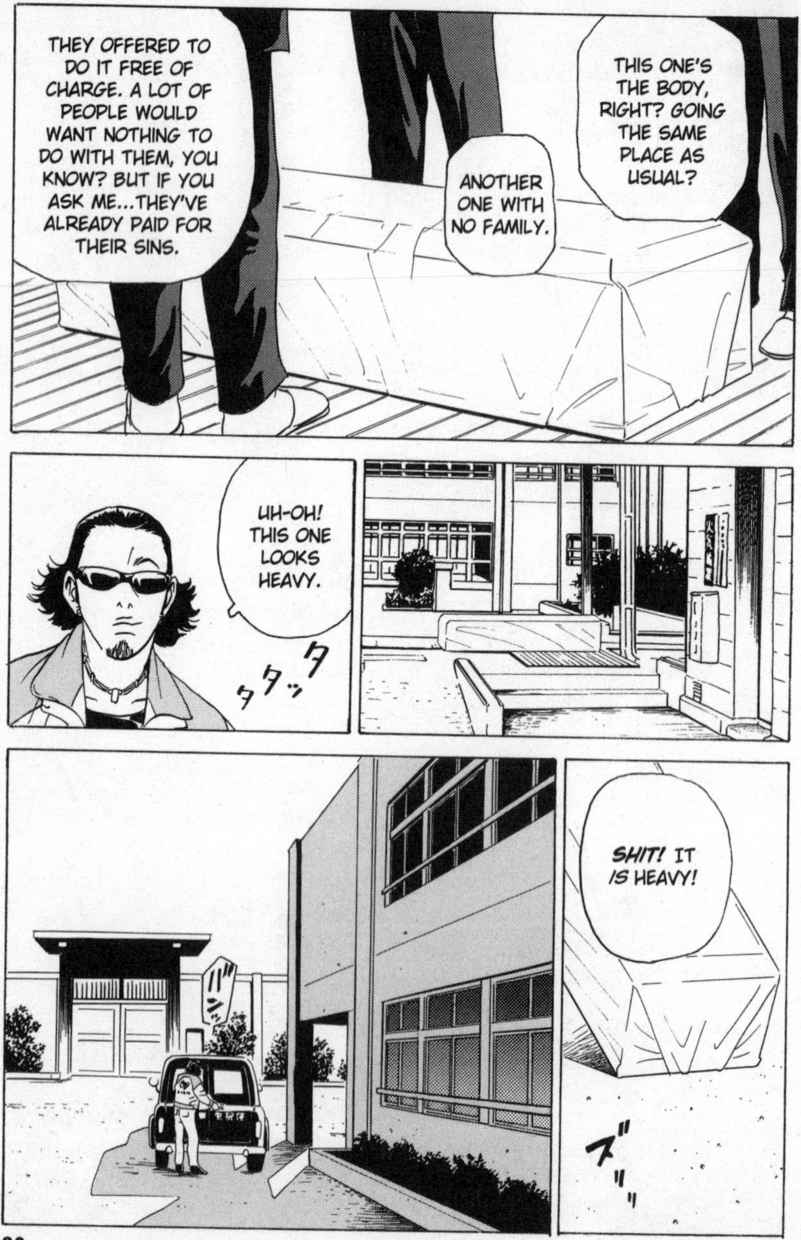
THIS ONE'S THE BODY, RIGHT? GOING THE SAME PLACE AS USUAL?
ANOTHER ONE WITH NO FAMILY.
THEY OFFERED TO DO IT FREE OF CHARGE. A LOT OF PEOPLE WOULD WANT NOTHING TO DO WITH THEM, YOU KNOW? BUT IF YOU ASK ME...THEY'VE ALREADY PAID FOR THEIR SINS.
UH-OH! THIS ONE LOOKS HEAVY.
SHIT! IT *IS* HEAVY!

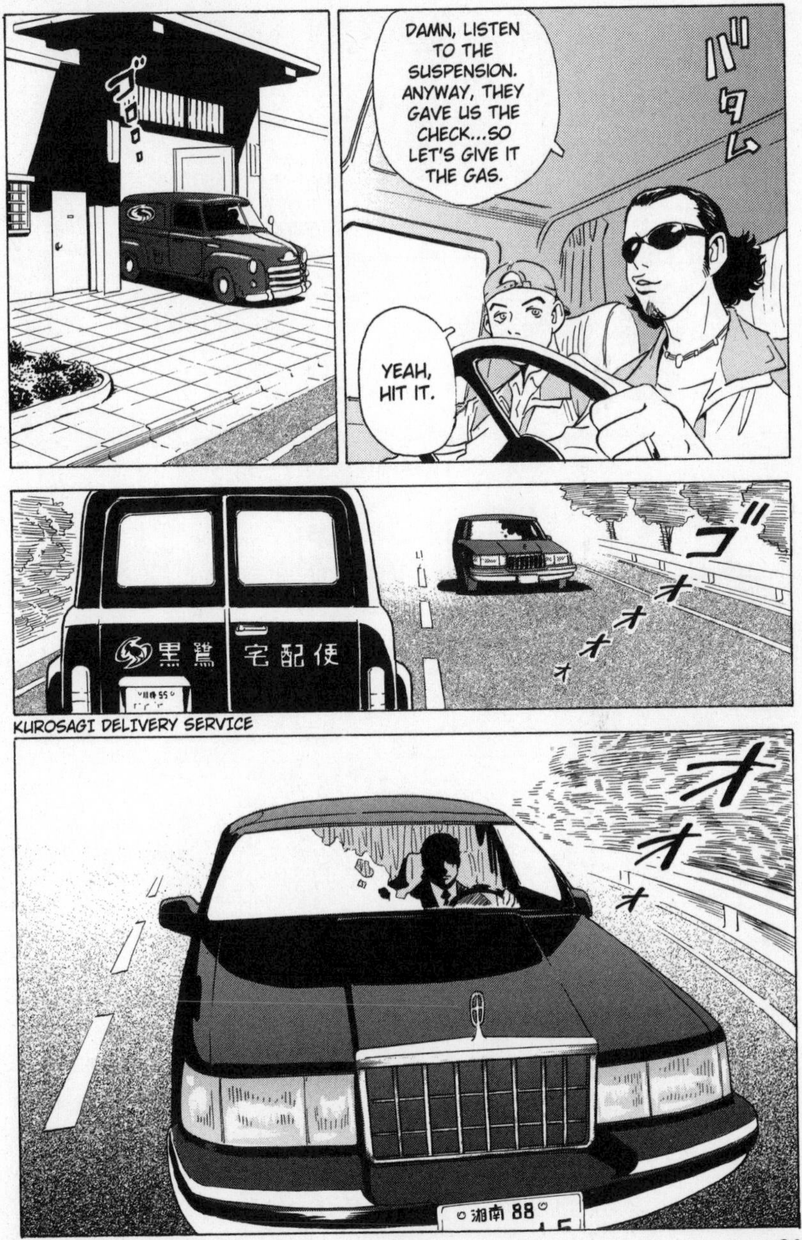
バタム
DAMN, LISTEN TO THE SUSPENSION. ANYWAY, THEY GAVE US THE CHECK...SO LET'S GIVE IT THE GAS.
YEAH, HIT IT.
ゴロロ
ゴオオオオ
黒鷺 宅配便
KUROSAGI DELIVERY SERVICE
オオオ
湘南 88

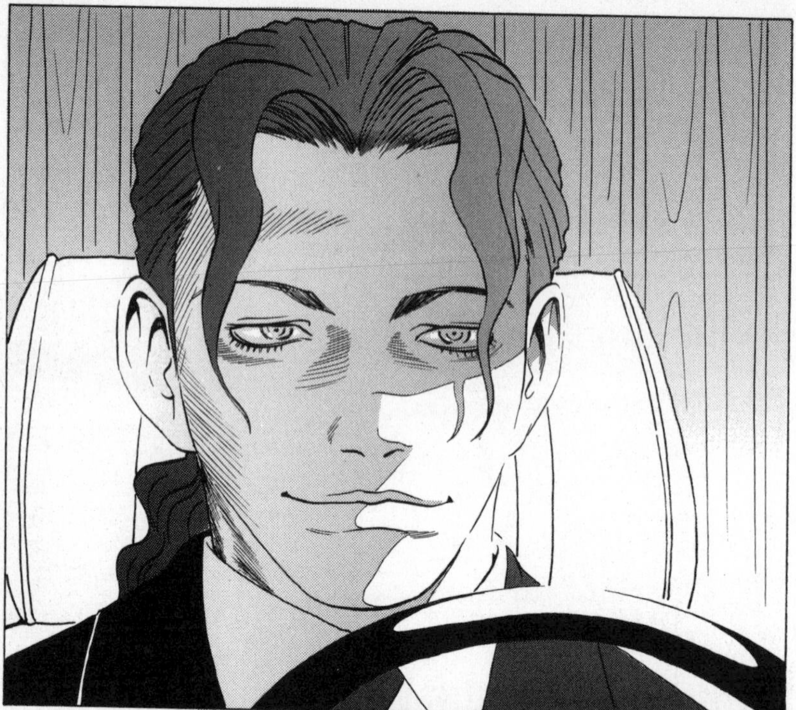

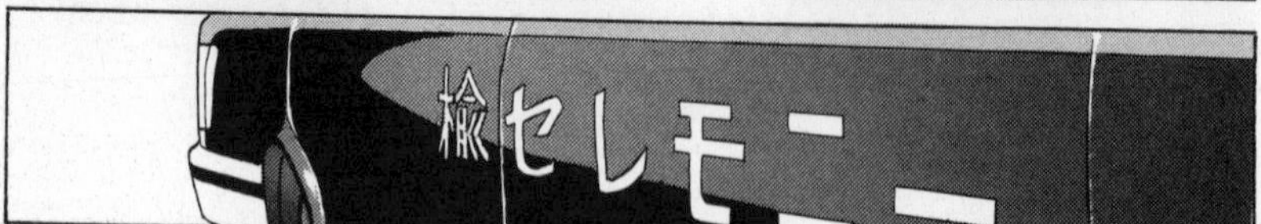
楡セレモニー

NIRE CEREMONY

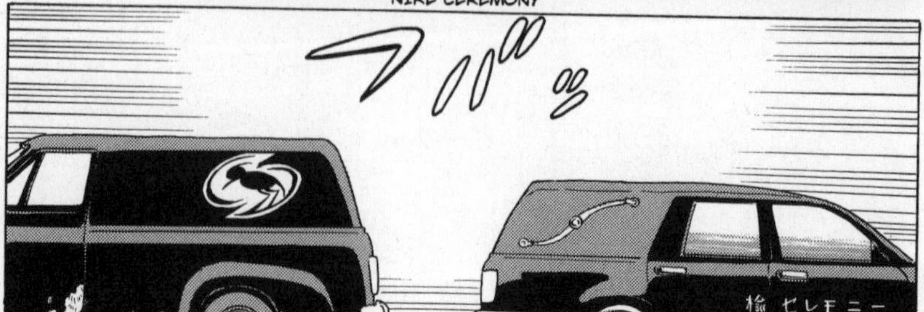
フバッ
楡 セレモニー

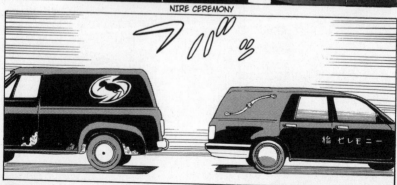

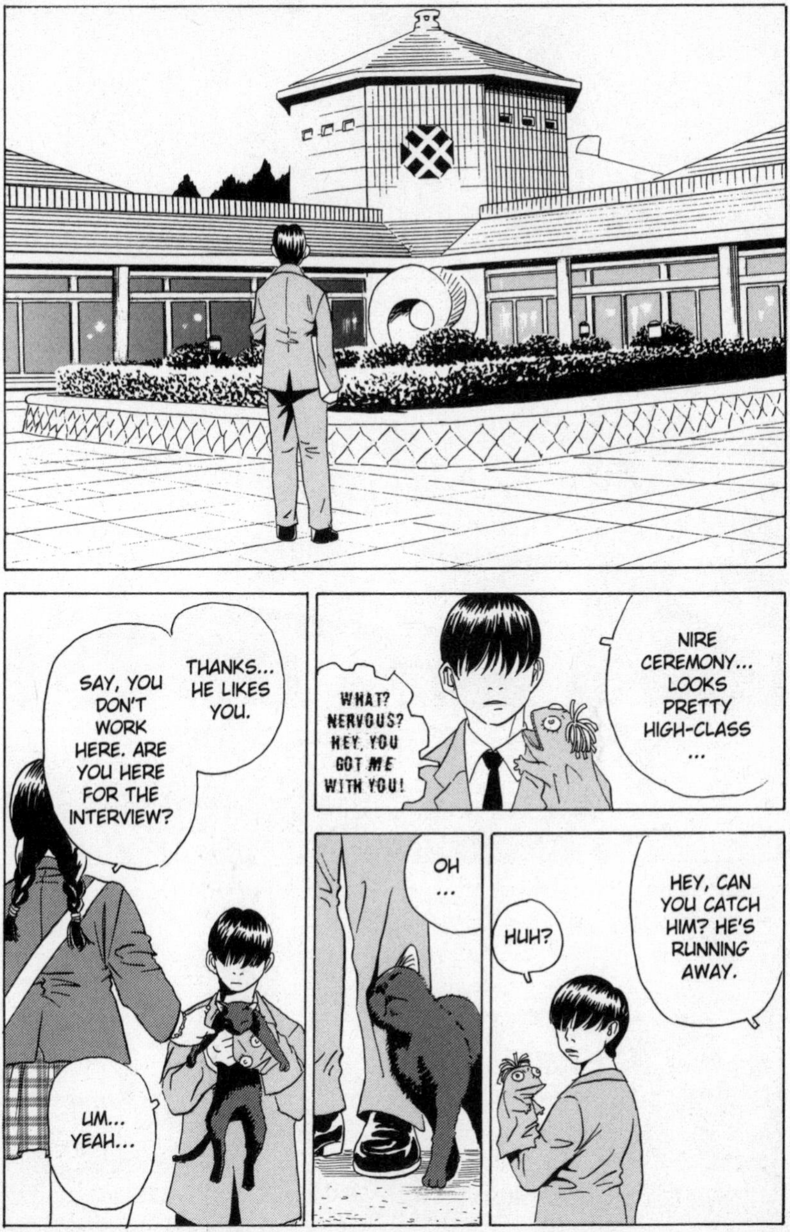
NIRE CEREMONY... LOOKS PRETTY HIGH-CLASS ...
WHAT? NERVOUS? HEY, YOU GOT ME WITH YOU!
HEY, CAN YOU CATCH HIM? HE'S RUNNING AWAY.
HUH?
OH ...
THANKS... HE LIKES YOU.
SAY, YOU DON'T WORK HERE. ARE YOU HERE FOR THE INTERVIEW?
UM... YEAH...

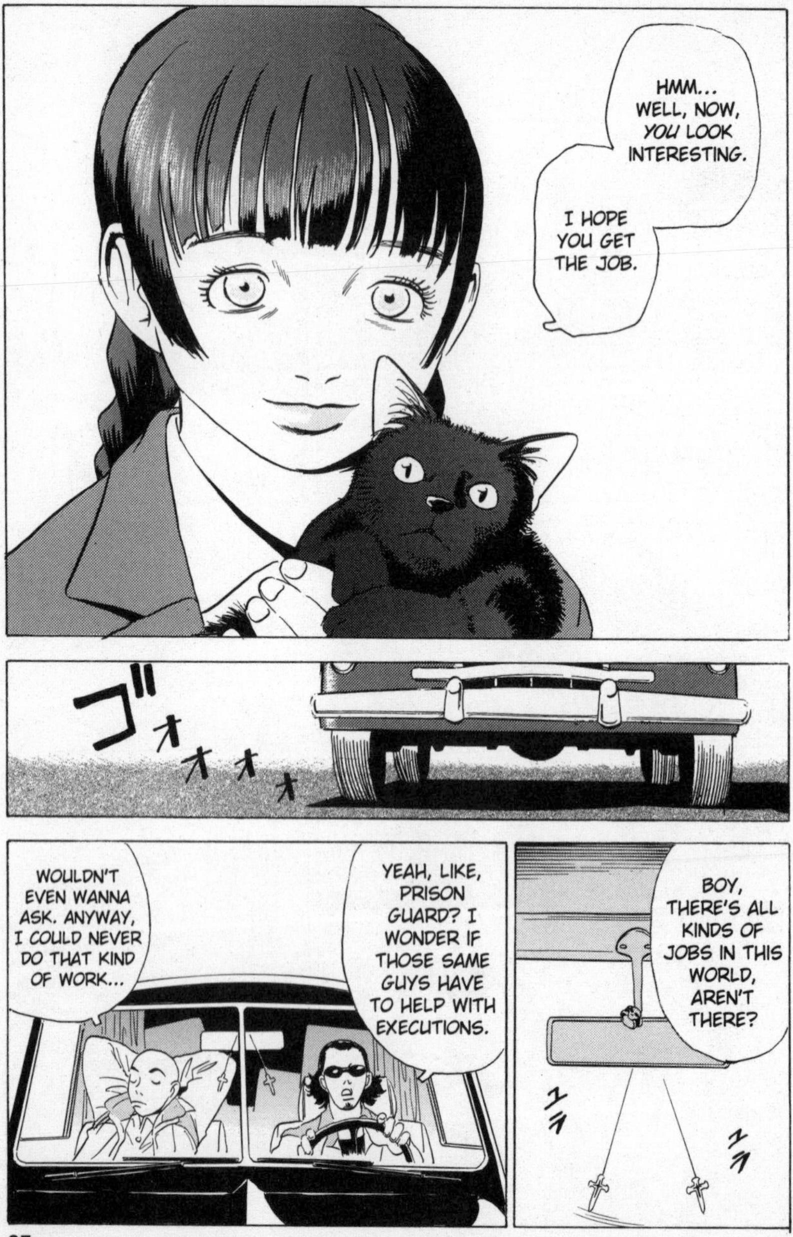
HMM... WELL, NOW, *YOU* LOOK INTERESTING.
I HOPE YOU GET THE JOB.
ゴォォォォ
BOY, THERE'S ALL KINDS OF JOBS IN THIS WORLD, AREN'T THERE?
ユラ
ユラ
YEAH, LIKE, PRISON GUARD? I WONDER IF THOSE SAME GUYS HAVE TO HELP WITH EXECUTIONS.
WOULDN'T EVEN WANNA ASK. ANYWAY, I COULD NEVER DO THAT KIND OF WORK...

...SAY, NUMATA.

YEAH?

IS THAT THING SWINGING?

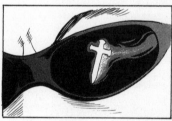

IT'S PROBABLY JUST THE CAR...

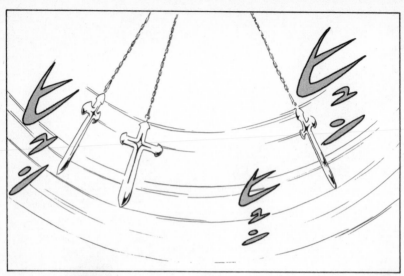

MR. NUMATA... NOW THAT STRIKES ME AS A CONTAINER OF SUSPICIOUS DIMENSIONS.

IN RETROSPECT, MR. KARATSU... THE WEIGHT OF THE BOX ALSO DEMANDS FURTHER INQUIRY.

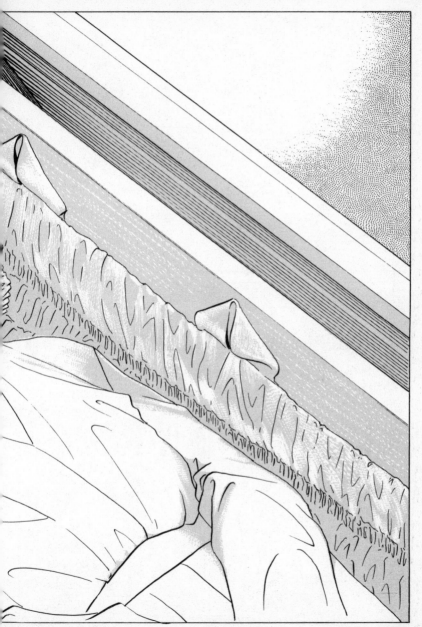

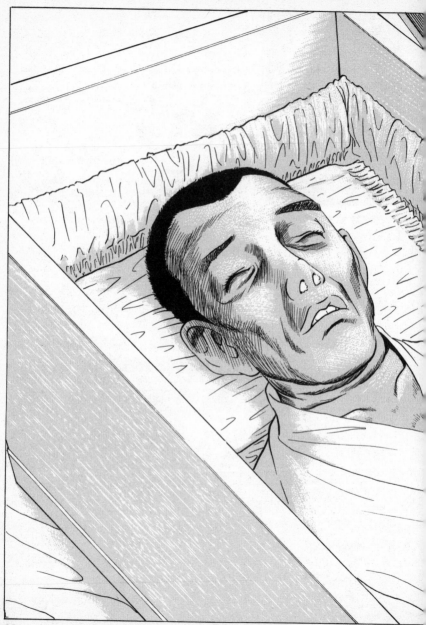

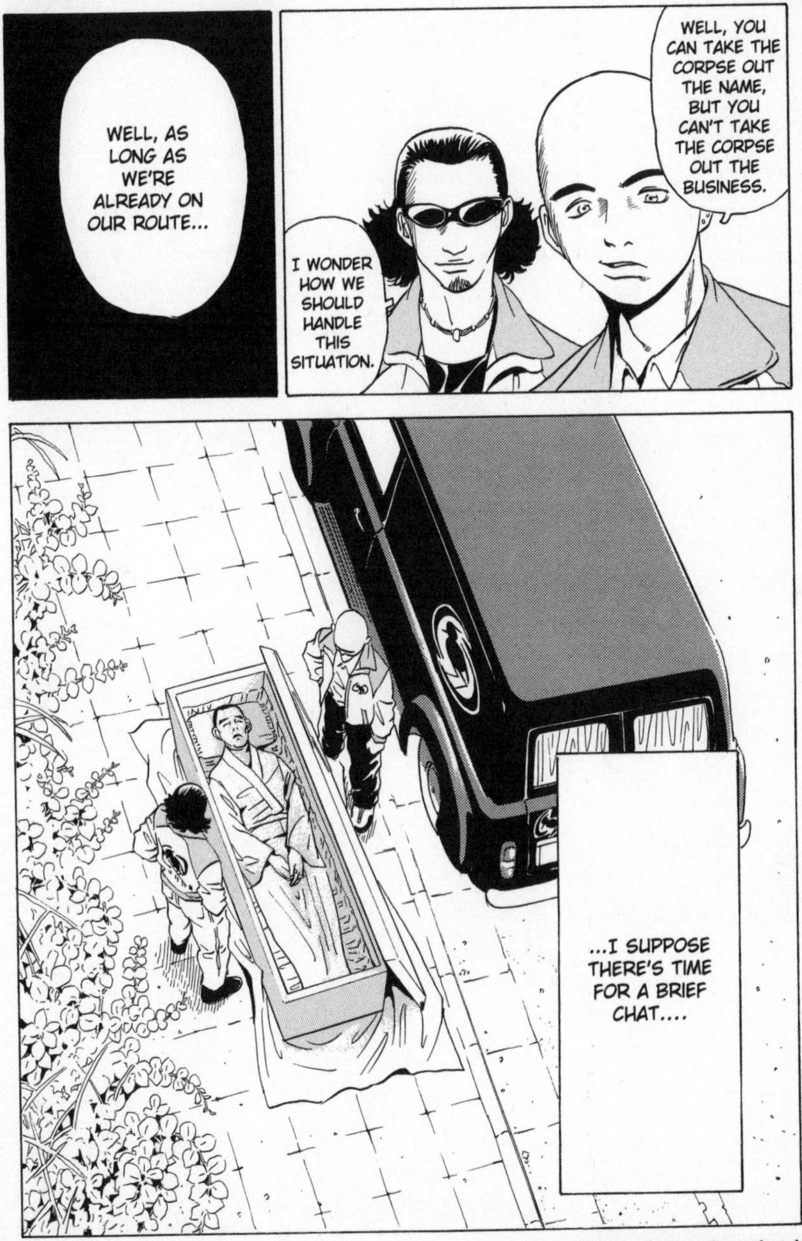
WELL, YOU CAN TAKE THE CORPSE OUT THE NAME, BUT YOU CAN'T TAKE THE CORPSE OUT THE BUSINESS.
I WONDER HOW WE SHOULD HANDLE THIS SITUATION.
WELL, AS LONG AS WE'RE ALREADY ON OUR ROUTE...
...I SUPPOSE THERE'S TIME FOR A BRIEF CHAT....

1st delivery: dangerous duo—the end

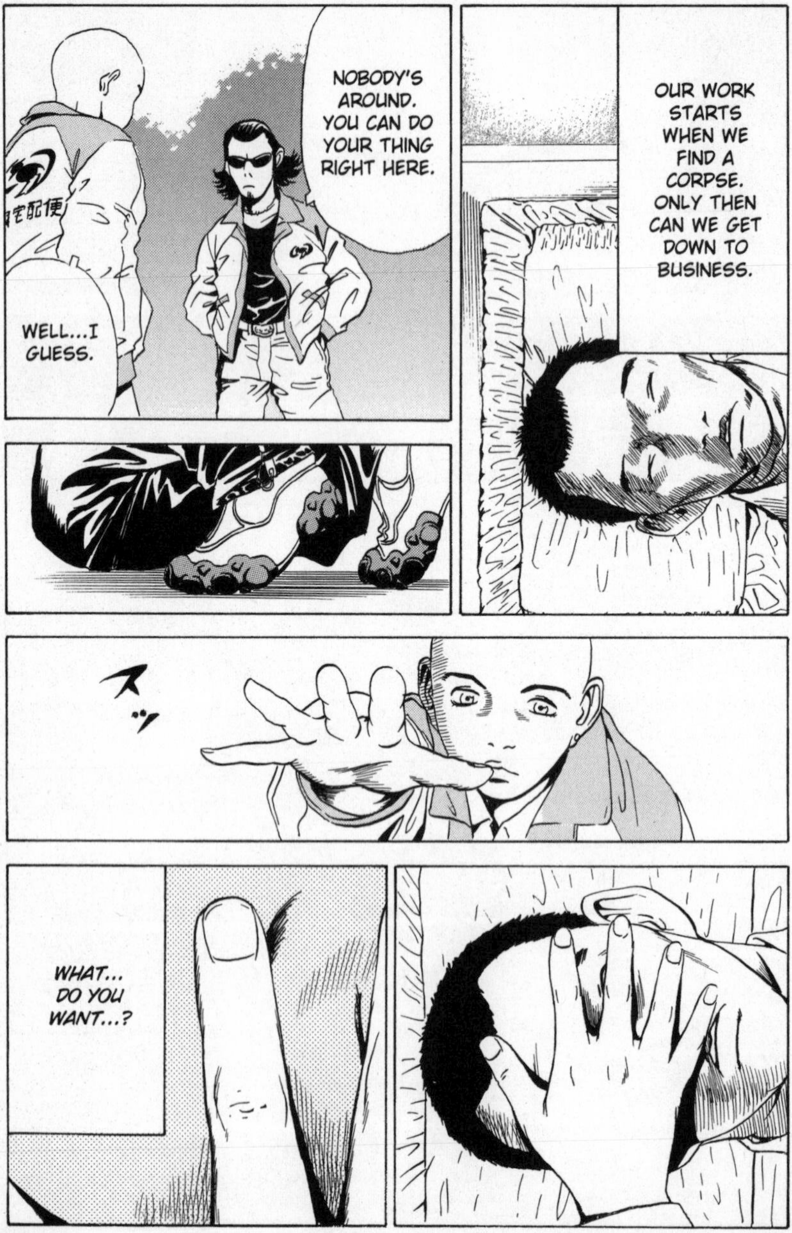
OUR WORK STARTS WHEN WE FIND A CORPSE. ONLY THEN CAN WE GET DOWN TO BUSINESS.
NOBODY'S AROUND. YOU CAN DO YOUR THING RIGHT HERE.
WELL...I GUESS.
スッ
WHAT... DO YOU WANT...?

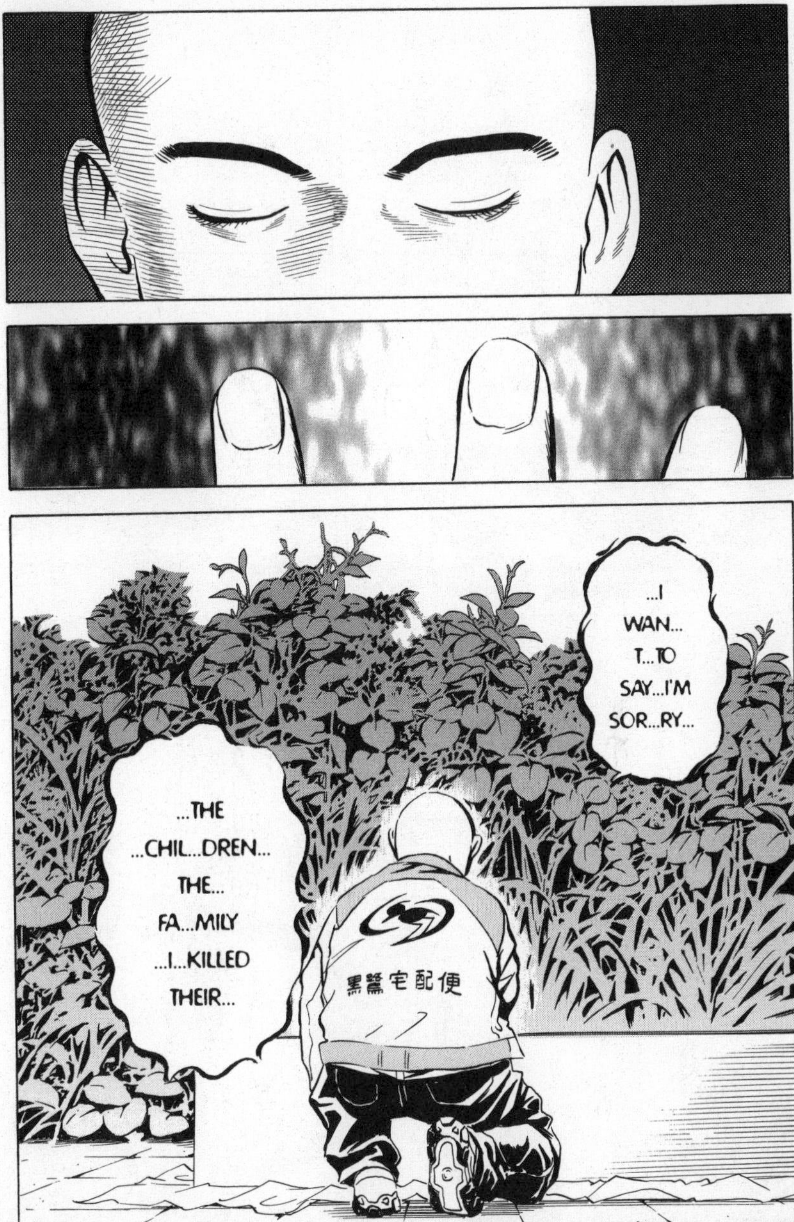
...I WAN... T...TO SAY...I'M SOR...RY...
...THE ...CHIL...DREN... THE... FA...MILY ...I...KILLED THEIR...
黒鷺宅配便

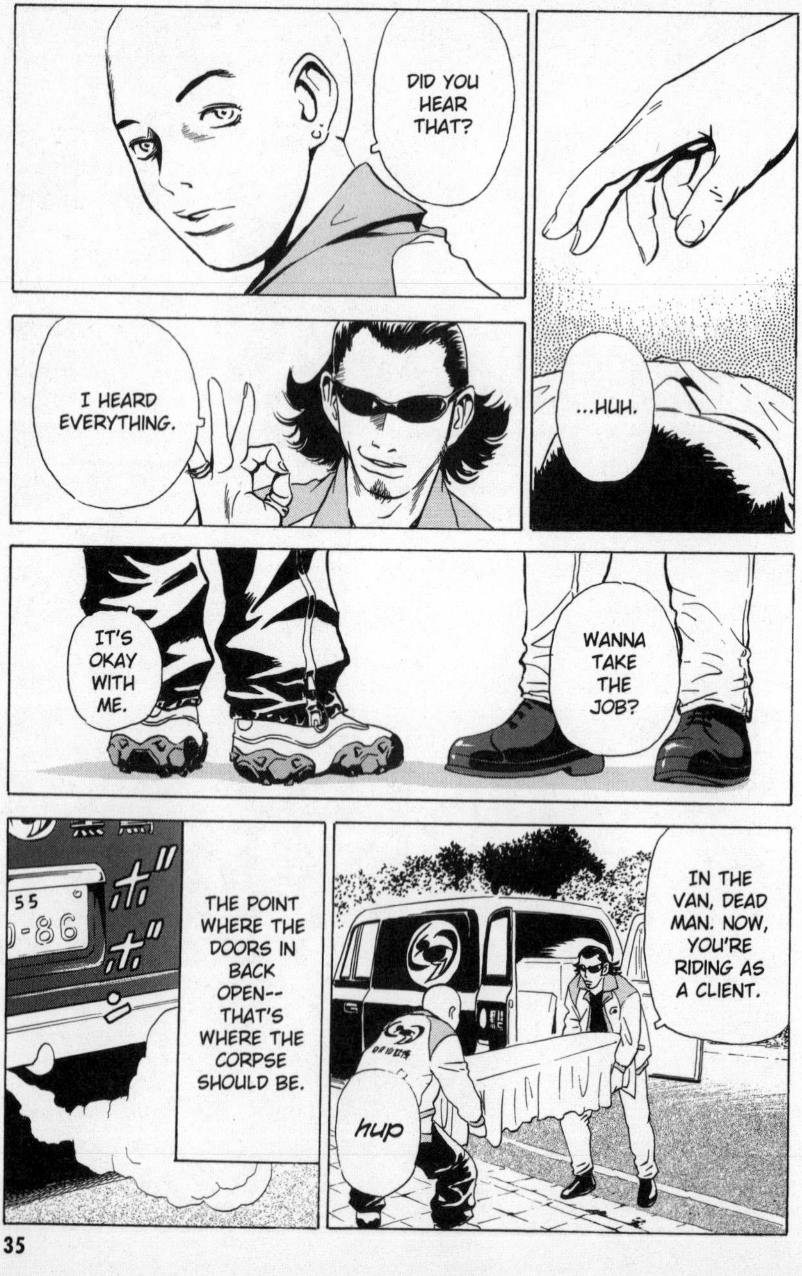
...HUH.
DID YOU HEAR THAT?
I HEARD EVERYTHING.
WANNA TAKE THE JOB?
IT'S OKAY WITH ME.
IN THE VAN, DEAD MAN. NOW, YOU'RE RIDING AS A CLIENT.
hup
THE POINT WHERE THE DOORS IN BACK OPEN--THAT'S WHERE THE CORPSE SHOULD BE.
ボ
ボ

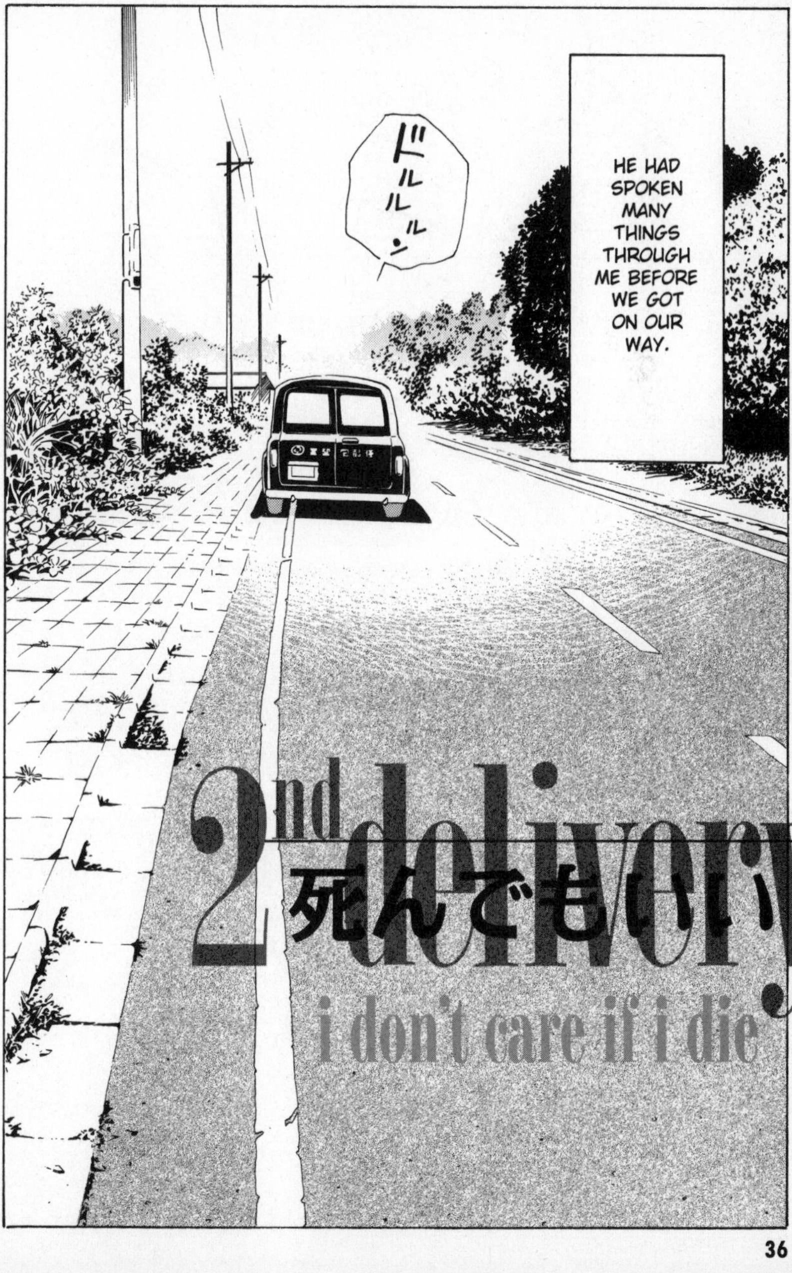
HE HAD SPOKEN MANY THINGS THROUGH ME BEFORE WE GOT ON OUR WAY.
ドルルルン
2nd delivery
死んでもいい
i don't care if i die

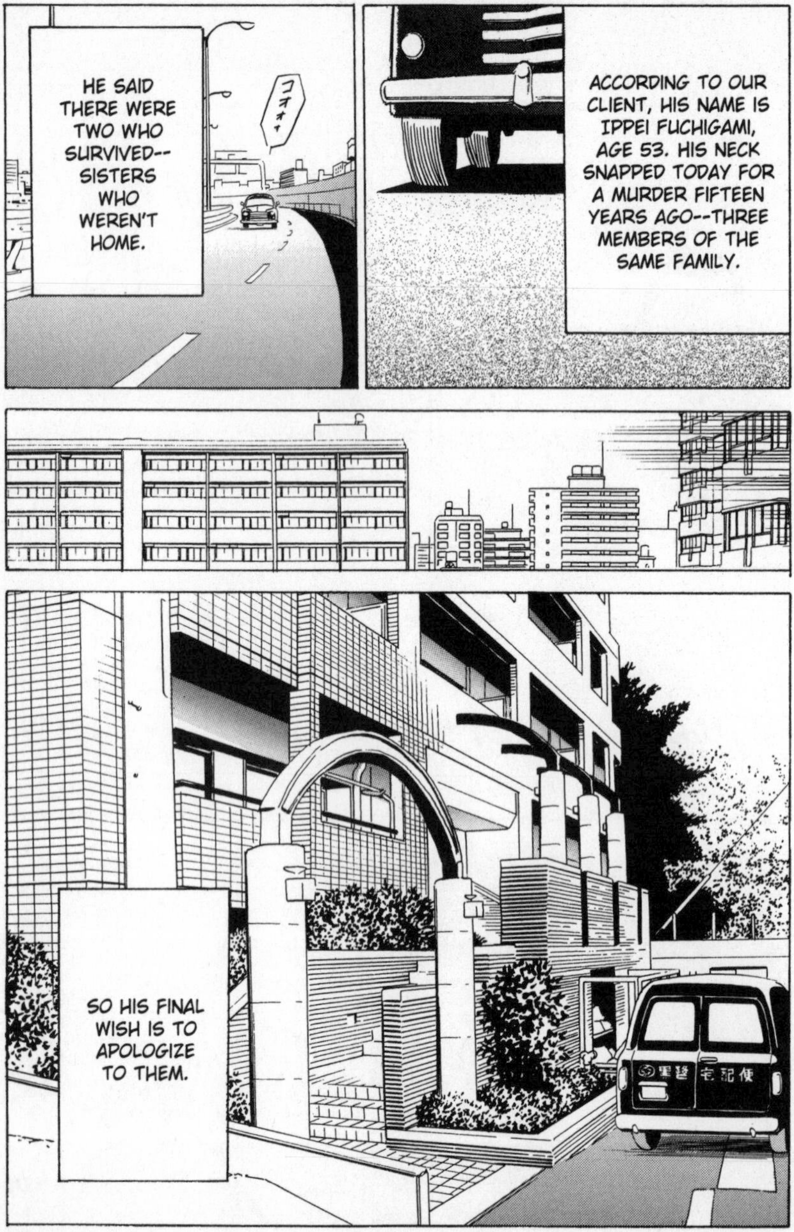
ACCORDING TO OUR CLIENT, HIS NAME IS IPPEI FUCHIGAMI, AGE 53. HIS NECK SNAPPED TODAY FOR A MURDER FIFTEEN YEARS AGO--THREE MEMBERS OF THE SAME FAMILY.
HE SAID THERE WERE TWO WHO SURVIVED--SISTERS WHO WEREN'T HOME.
コオォォ
SO HIS FINAL WISH IS TO APOLOGIZE TO THEM.

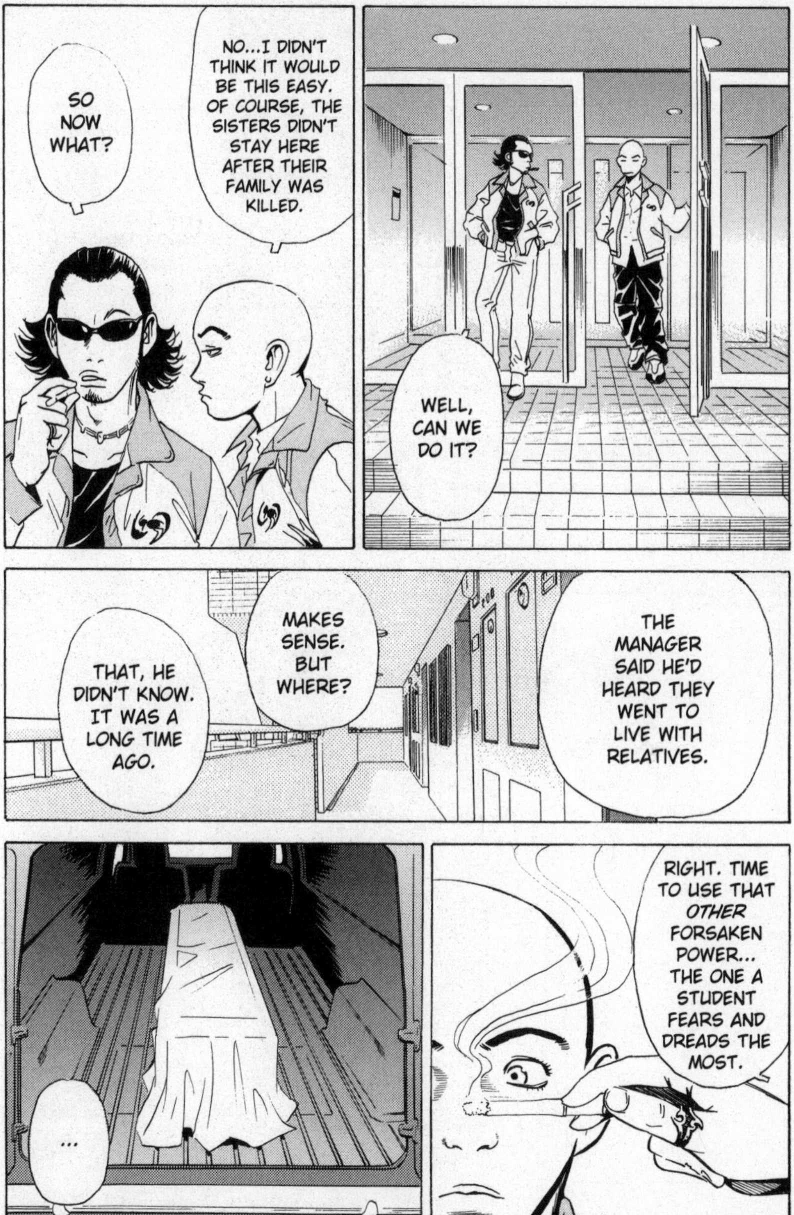
WELL, CAN WE DO IT?
NO...I DIDN'T THINK IT WOULD BE THIS EASY. OF COURSE, THE SISTERS DIDN'T STAY HERE AFTER THEIR FAMILY WAS KILLED.
SO NOW WHAT?
THE MANAGER SAID HE'D HEARD THEY WENT TO LIVE WITH RELATIVES.
MAKES SENSE. BUT WHERE?
THAT, HE DIDN'T KNOW. IT WAS A LONG TIME AGO.
RIGHT. TIME TO USE THAT *OTHER* FORSAKEN POWER... THE ONE A STUDENT FEARS AND DREADS THE MOST.
...

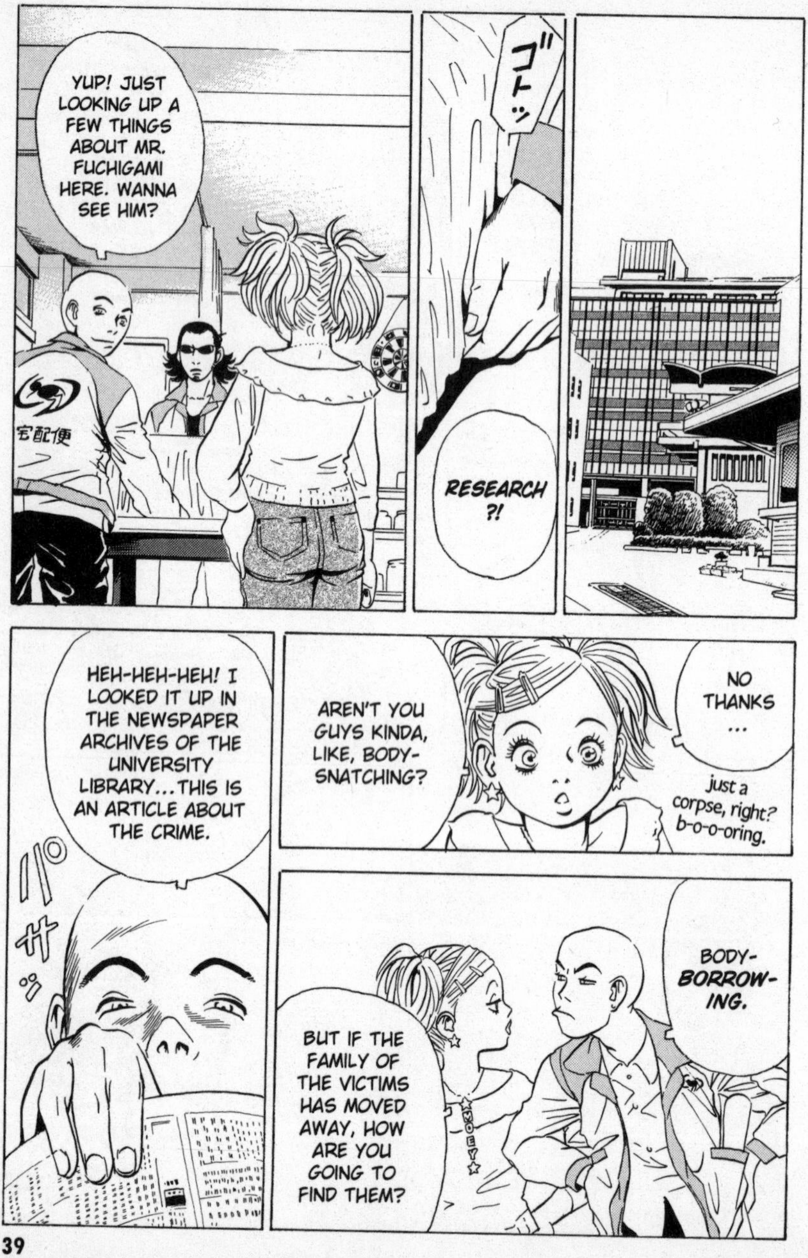
ゴトッ
RESEARCH ?!
YUP! JUST LOOKING UP A FEW THINGS ABOUT MR. FUCHIGAMI HERE. WANNA SEE HIM?
宅配便
NO THANKS ...
just a corpse, right? b-o-o-oring.
AREN'T YOU GUYS KINDA, LIKE, BODY-SNATCHING?
BODY-BORROWING.
BUT IF THE FAMILY OF THE VICTIMS HAS MOVED AWAY, HOW ARE YOU GOING TO FIND THEM?
HEH-HEH-HEH! I LOOKED IT UP IN THE NEWSPAPER ARCHIVES OF THE UNIVERSITY LIBRARY...THIS IS AN ARTICLE ABOUT THE CRIME.
パサッ

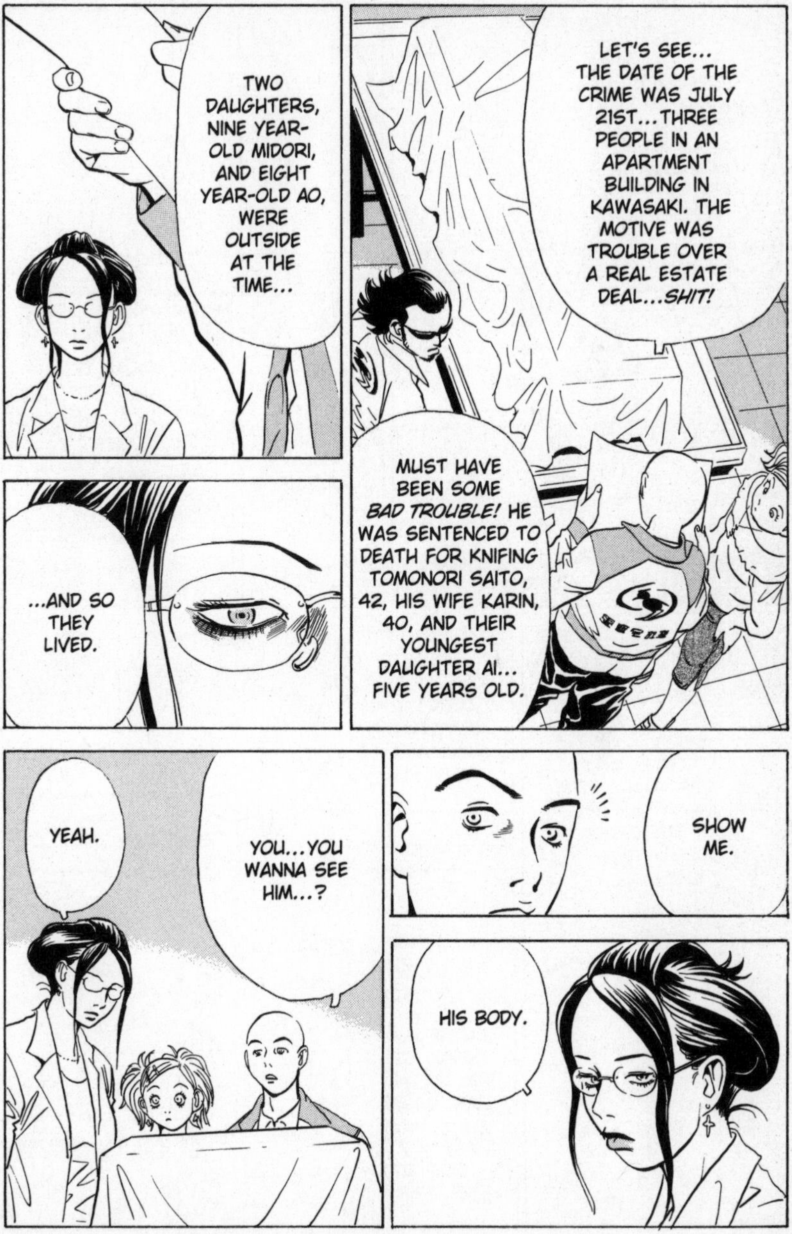
LET'S SEE... THE DATE OF THE CRIME WAS JULY 21ST... THREE PEOPLE IN AN APARTMENT BUILDING IN KAWASAKI. THE MOTIVE WAS TROUBLE OVER A REAL ESTATE DEAL... *SHIT!*
MUST HAVE BEEN SOME *BAD TROUBLE!* HE WAS SENTENCED TO DEATH FOR KNIFING TOMONORI SAITO, 42, HIS WIFE KARIN, 40, AND THEIR YOUNGEST DAUGHTER AI... FIVE YEARS OLD.
TWO DAUGHTERS, NINE YEAR-OLD MIDORI, AND EIGHT YEAR-OLD AO, WERE OUTSIDE AT THE TIME...
...AND SO THEY LIVED.
SHOW ME.
HIS BODY.
YOU... YOU WANNA SEE HIM...?
YEAH.

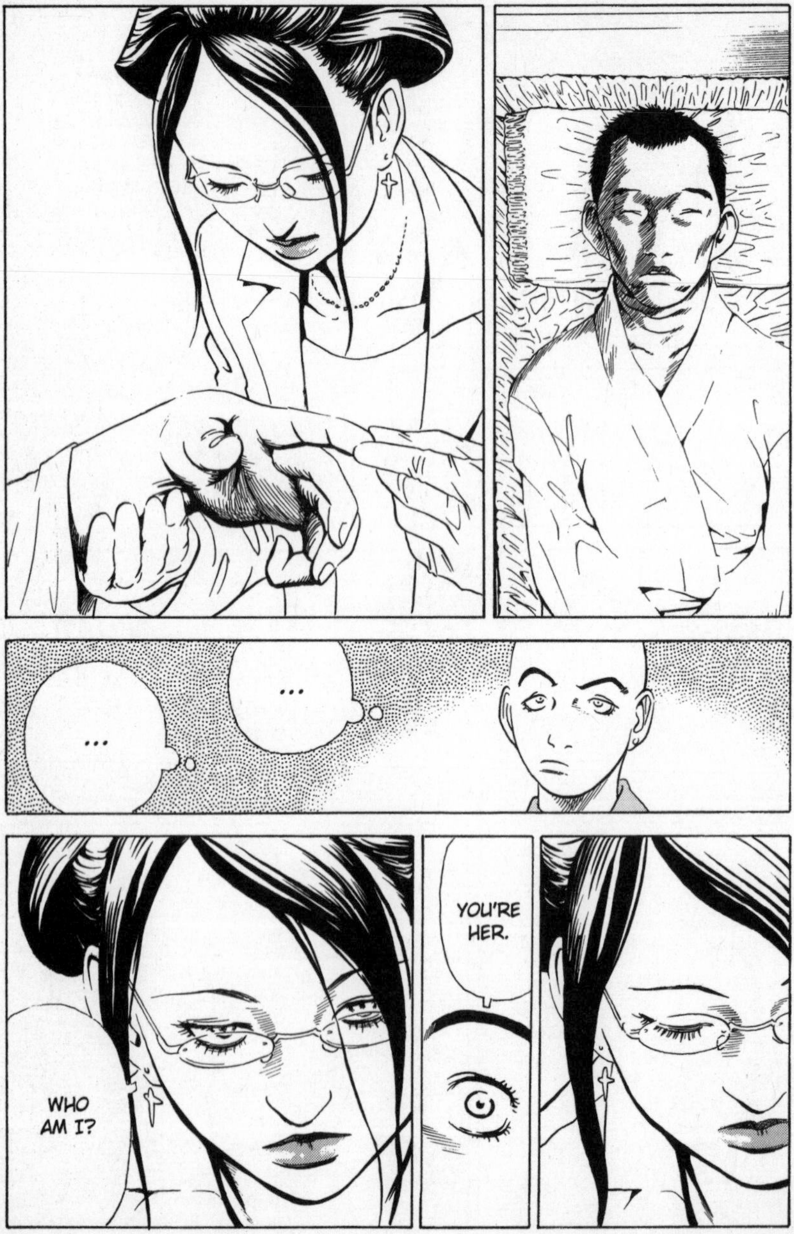
...
...
YOU'RE HER.
WHO AM I?

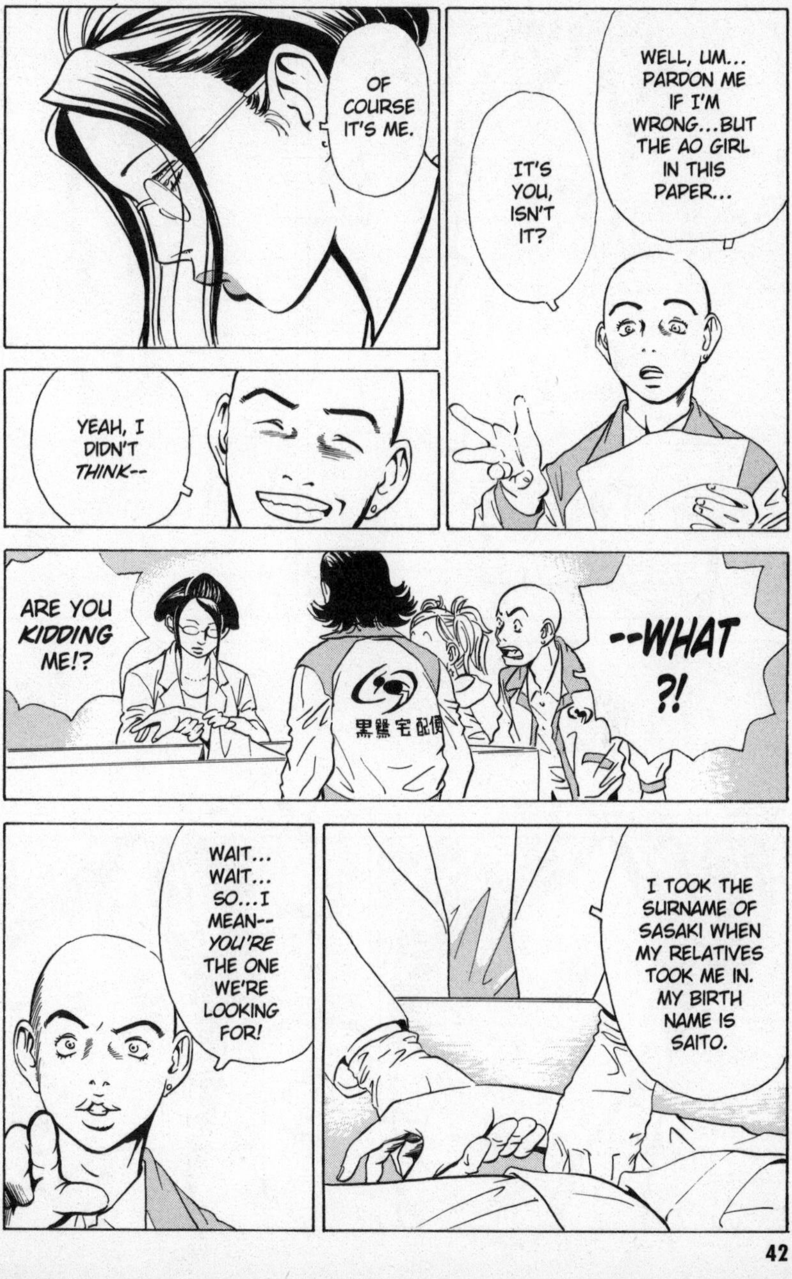
WELL, UM... PARDON ME IF I'M WRONG...BUT THE AO GIRL IN THIS PAPER...
IT'S YOU, ISN'T IT?
OF COURSE IT'S ME.
YEAH, I DIDN'T *THINK*--
--*WHAT* ?!
ARE YOU *KIDDING* ME!?
I TOOK THE SURNAME OF SASAKI WHEN MY RELATIVES TOOK ME IN. MY BIRTH NAME IS SAITO.
WAIT... WAIT... SO...I MEAN-- *YOU'RE* THE ONE WE'RE LOOKING FOR!

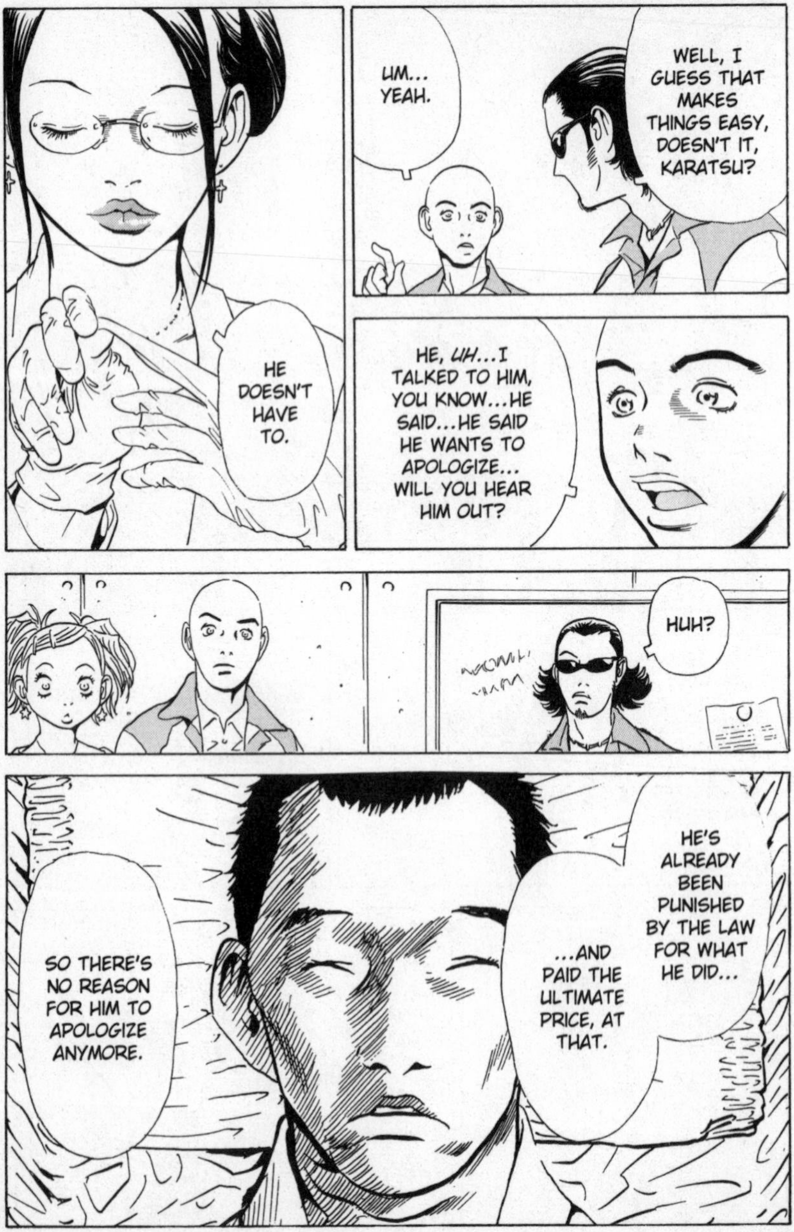

WELL, I GUESS THAT MAKES THINGS EASY, DOESN'T IT, KARATSU?
UM... YEAH.
HE, *UH*...I TALKED TO HIM, YOU KNOW...HE SAID...HE SAID HE WANTS TO APOLOGIZE... WILL YOU HEAR HIM OUT?
HE DOESN'T HAVE TO.
HUH?
HE'S ALREADY BEEN PUNISHED BY THE LAW FOR WHAT HE DID...
...AND PAID THE ULTIMATE PRICE, AT THAT.
SO THERE'S NO REASON FOR HIM TO APOLOGIZE ANYMORE.

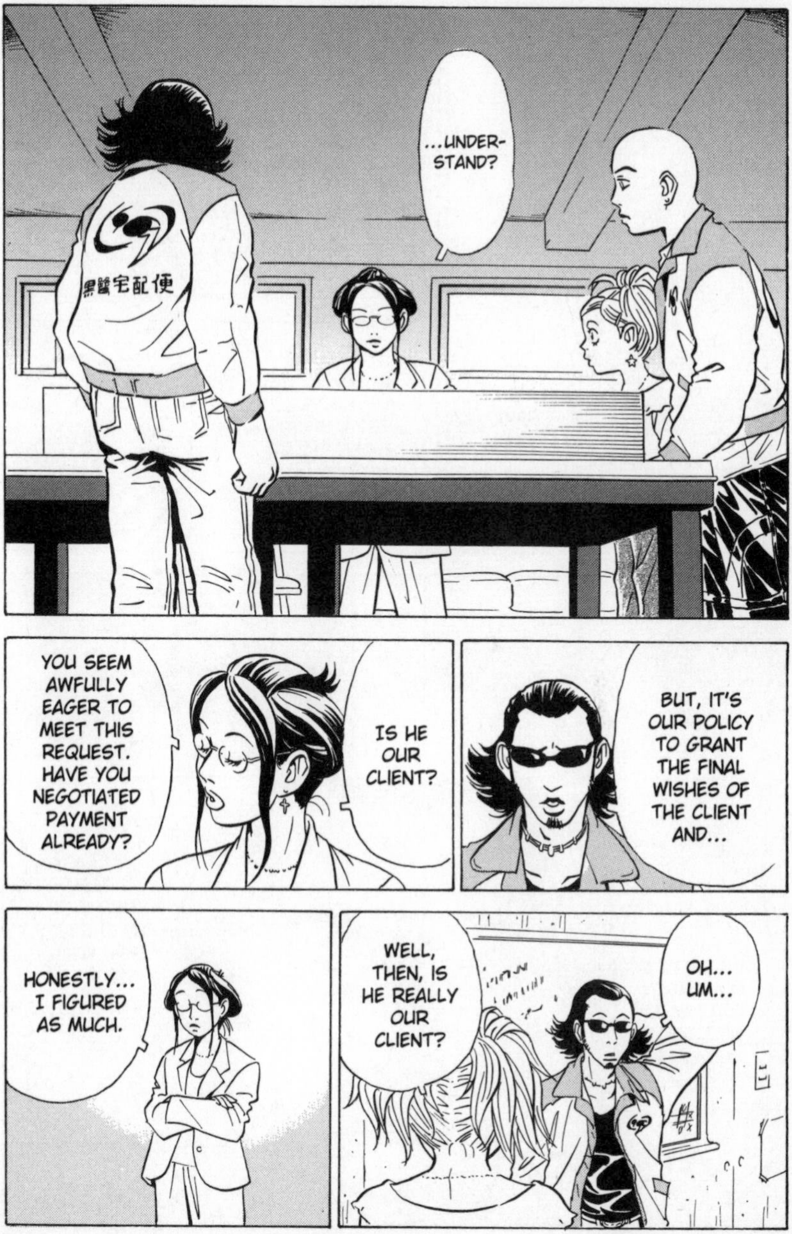
...UNDER-
STAND?
黒鷺宅配便
BUT, IT'S OUR POLICY TO GRANT THE FINAL WISHES OF THE CLIENT AND...
IS HE OUR CLIENT?
YOU SEEM AWFULLY EAGER TO MEET THIS REQUEST. HAVE YOU NEGOTIATED PAYMENT ALREADY?
OH... UM...
WELL, THEN, IS HE REALLY OUR CLIENT?
HONESTLY... I FIGURED AS MUCH.

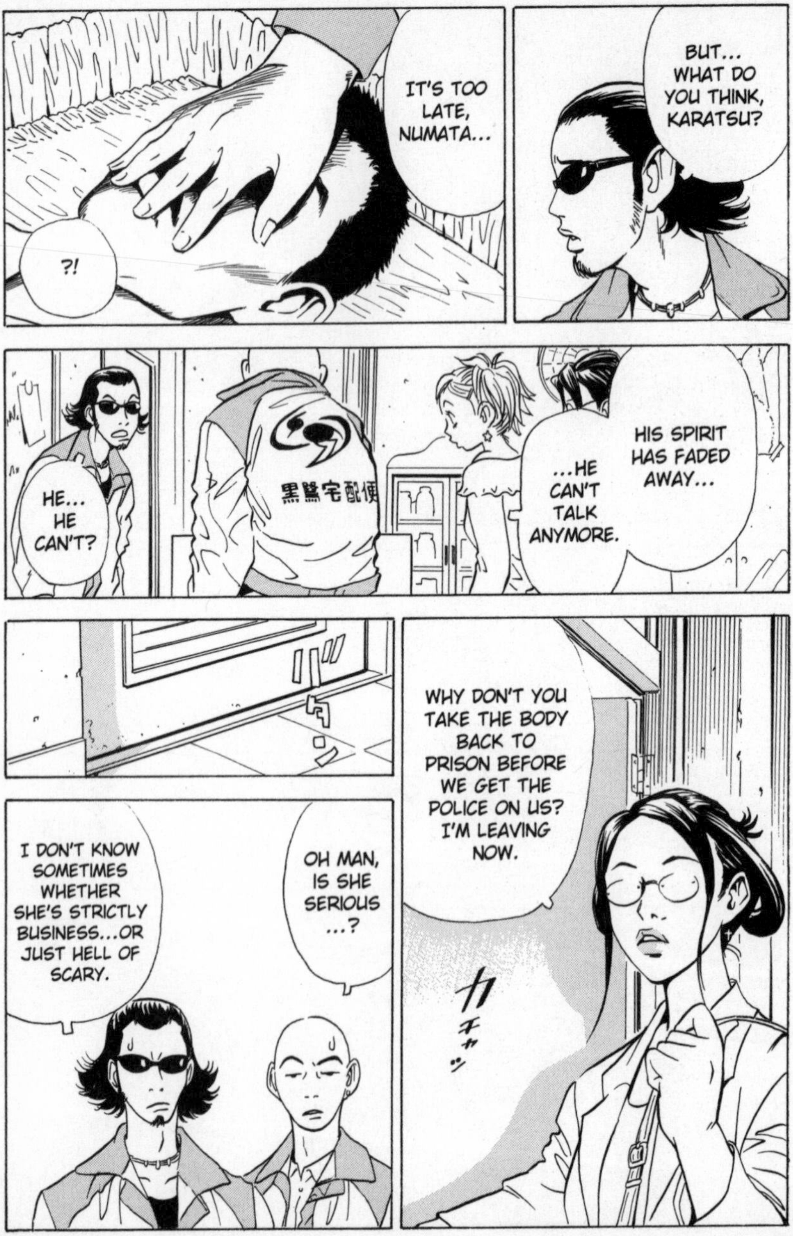
BUT... WHAT DO YOU THINK, KARATSU?
IT'S TOO LATE, NUMATA...
?!
HIS SPIRIT HAS FADED AWAY...
...HE CAN'T TALK ANYMORE.
黒鷺宅配便
HE... HE CAN'T?
WHY DON'T YOU TAKE THE BODY BACK TO PRISON BEFORE WE GET THE POLICE ON US? I'M LEAVING NOW.
OH MAN, IS SHE SERIOUS ...?
I DON'T KNOW SOMETIMES WHETHER SHE'S STRICTLY BUSINESS...OR JUST HELL OF SCARY.

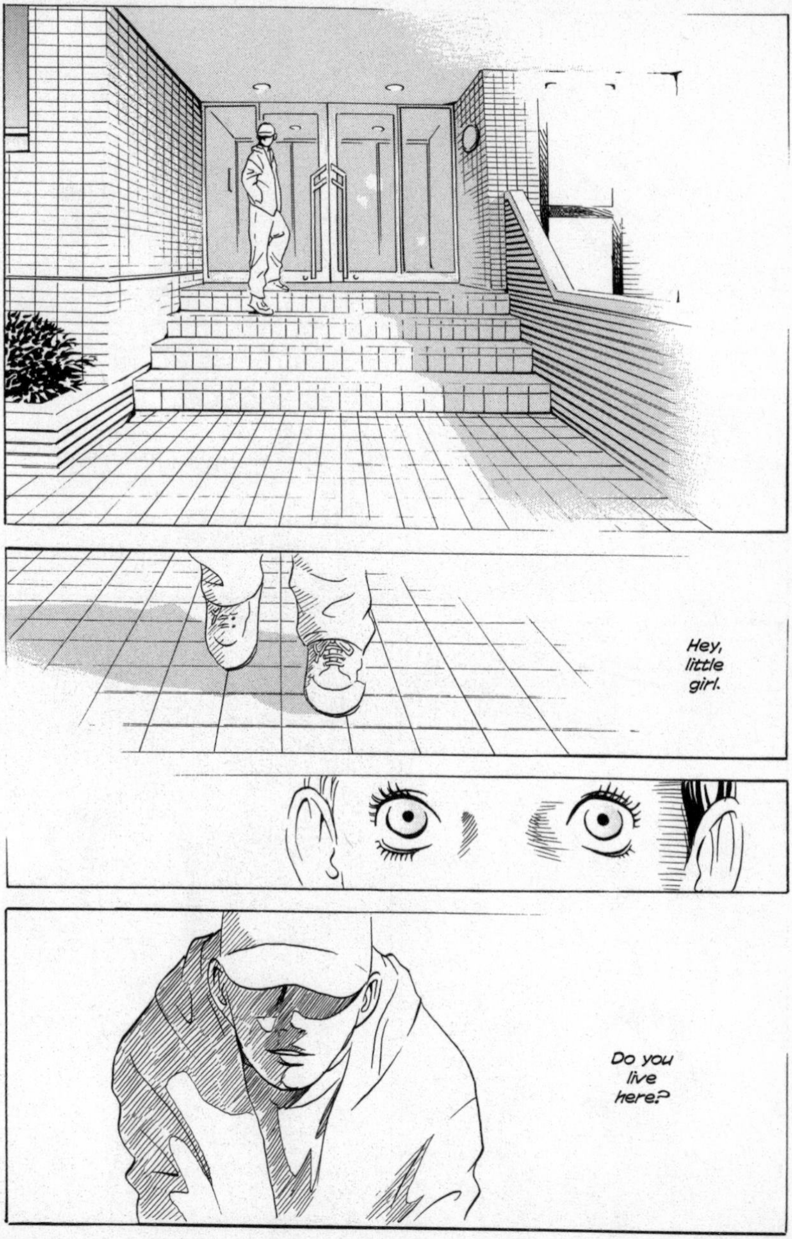
Hey, little girl.
Do you live here?

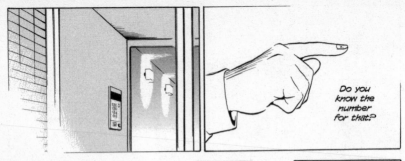

Do you know the number for that?
Do you know the combination for the door?
I guess you're too little to know.
Um... I know.
You do? Will you tell me?
Ummm... 0... 9... 3... 7!

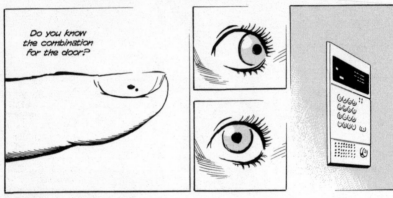

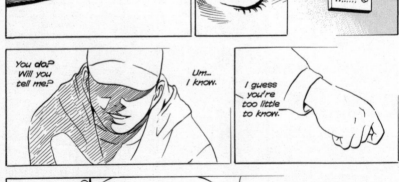

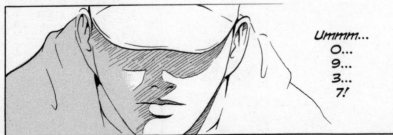

...Thank you, little girl.

Sis?

What is it...sis?

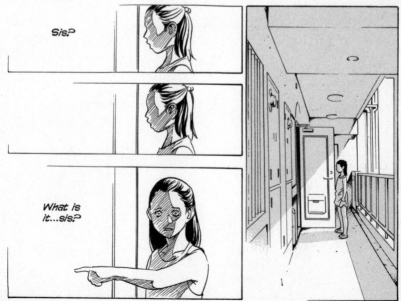

48

たたっ

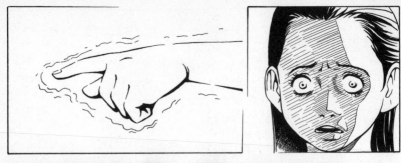

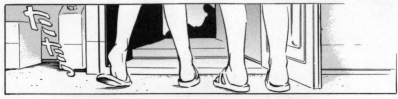

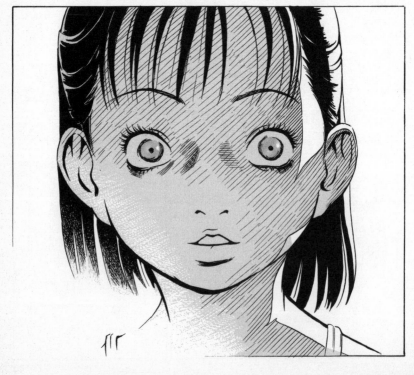

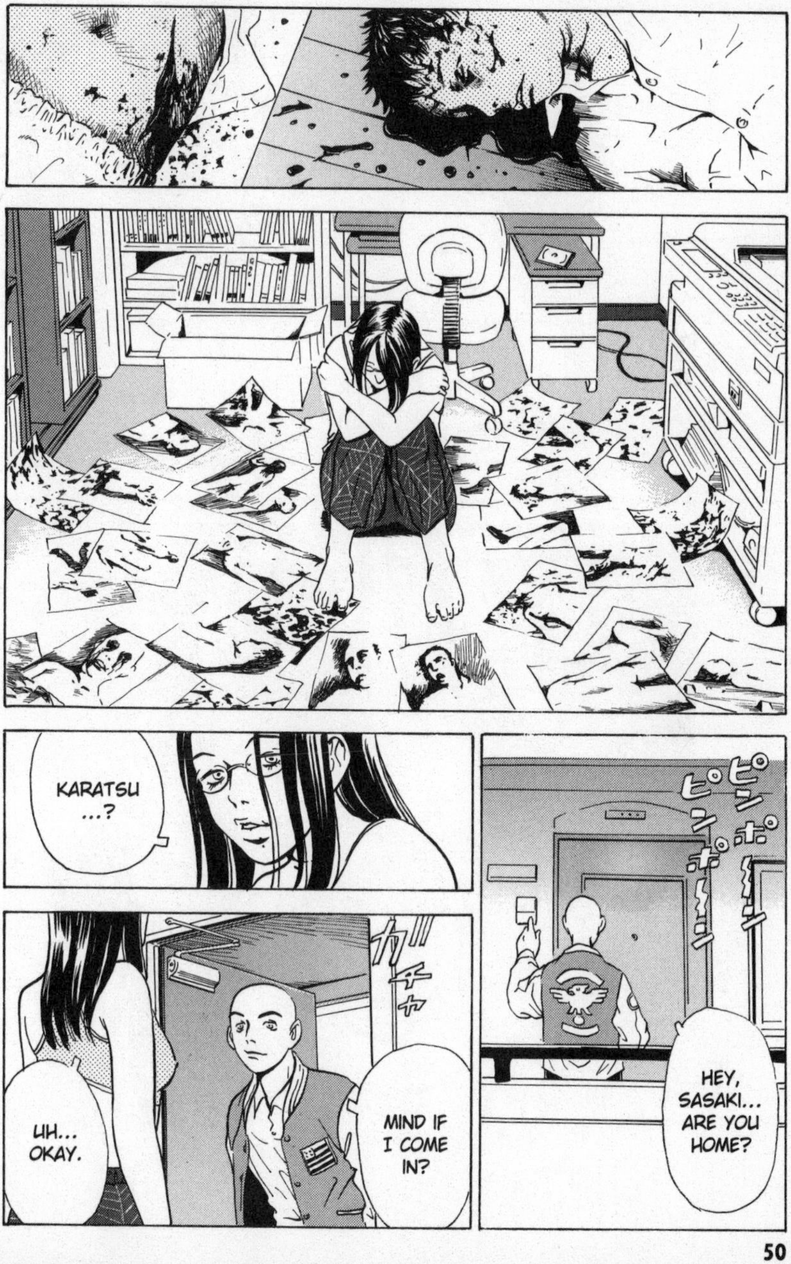
HEY, SASAKI... ARE YOU HOME?
KARATSU ...?
ガチャ
MIND IF I COME IN?
UH... OKAY.

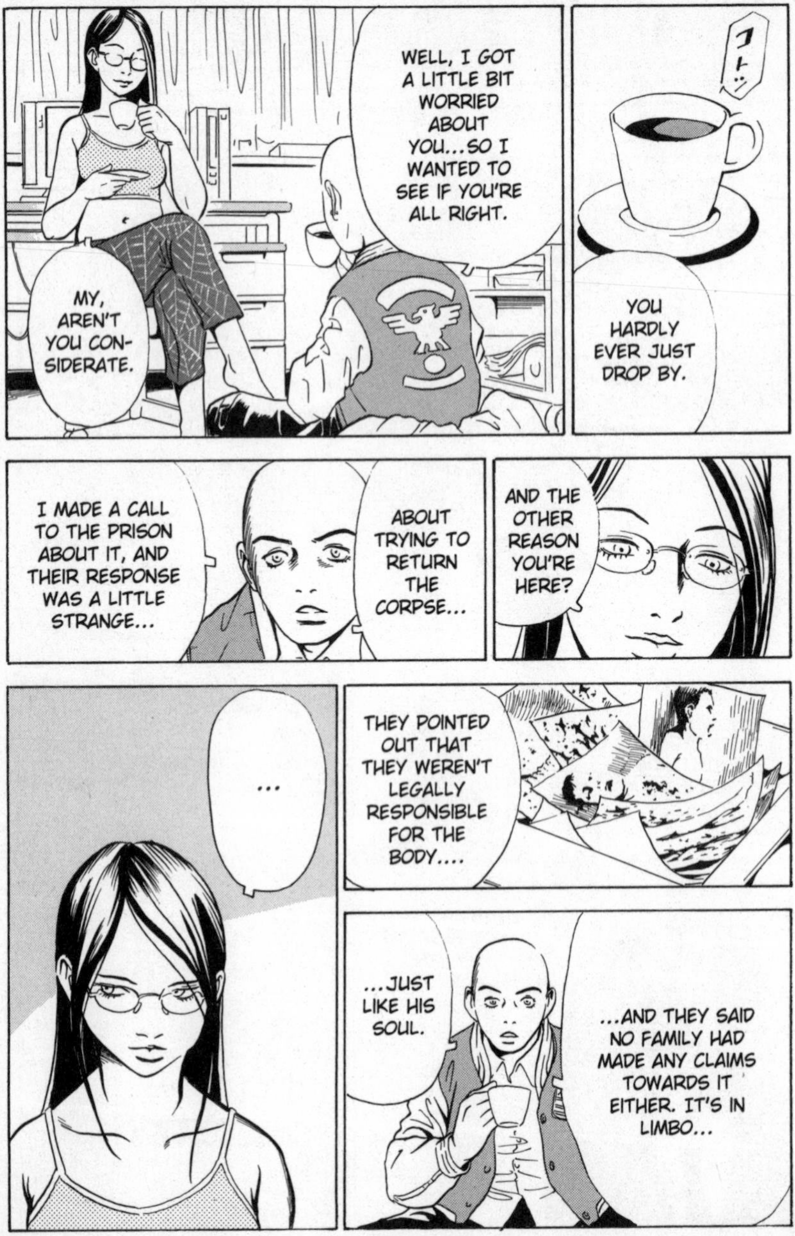

コトッ
YOU HARDLY EVER JUST DROP BY.
WELL, I GOT A LITTLE BIT WORRIED ABOUT YOU...SO I WANTED TO SEE IF YOU'RE ALL RIGHT.
MY, AREN'T YOU CON-SIDERATE.
AND THE OTHER REASON YOU'RE HERE?
ABOUT TRYING TO RETURN THE CORPSE...
I MADE A CALL TO THE PRISON ABOUT IT, AND THEIR RESPONSE WAS A LITTLE STRANGE...
THEY POINTED OUT THAT THEY WEREN'T LEGALLY RESPONSIBLE FOR THE BODY....
...AND THEY SAID NO FAMILY HAD MADE ANY CLAIMS TOWARDS IT EITHER. IT'S IN LIMBO...
...JUST LIKE HIS SOUL.
...

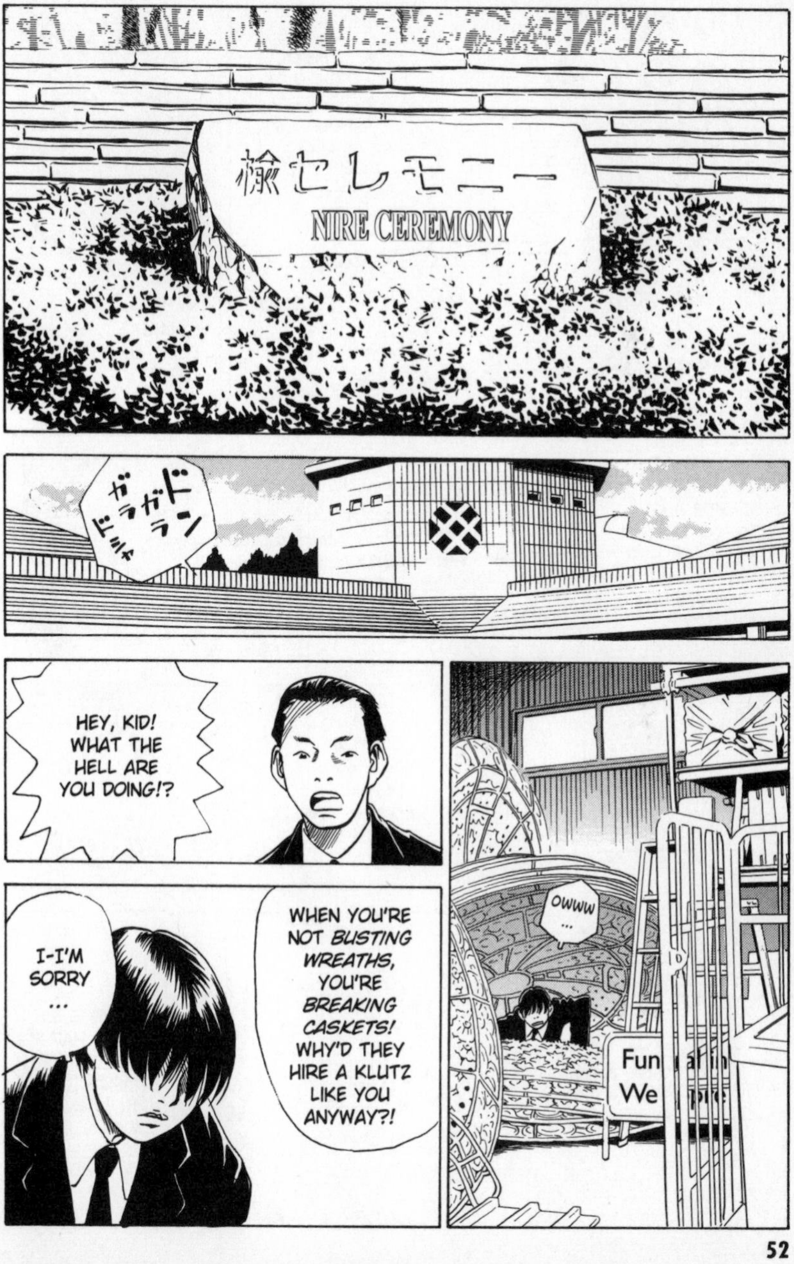
楡セレモニー
NIRE CEREMONY
ドン
ガラガラ
ドシャ
OWWW ...
HEY, KID! WHAT THE HELL ARE YOU DOING!?
WHEN YOU'RE NOT *BUSTING* *WREATHS*, YOU'RE *BREAKING* *CASKETS*! WHY'D THEY HIRE A KLUTZ LIKE YOU ANYWAY?!
I-I'M SORRY ...

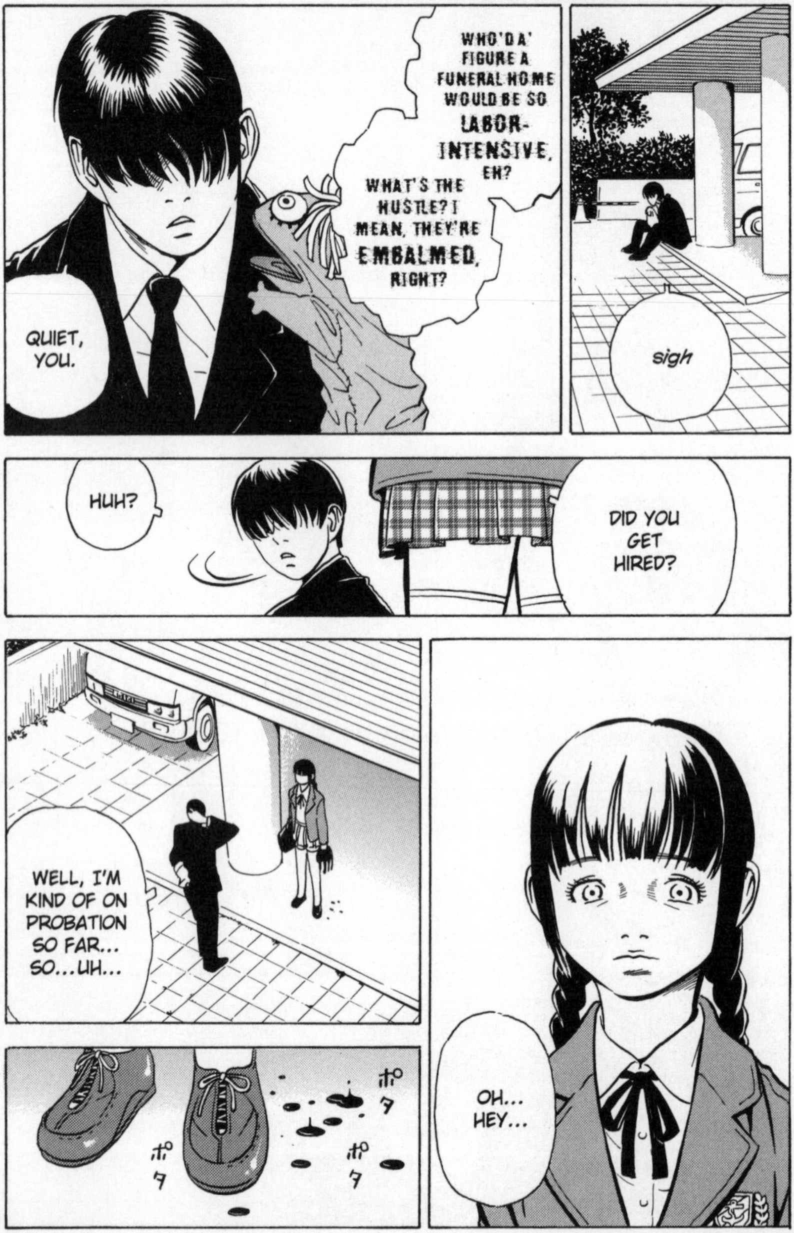
sigh
WHO'D A' FIGURE A FUNERAL HOME WOULD BE SO LABOR-INTENSIVE, EH?
WHAT'S THE HUSTLE? I MEAN, THEY'RE EMBALMED, RIGHT?
QUIET, YOU.
DID YOU GET HIRED?
HUH?
OH... HEY...
WELL, I'M KIND OF ON PROBATION SO FAR... SO...UH...
ポタ
ポタ
ポタ

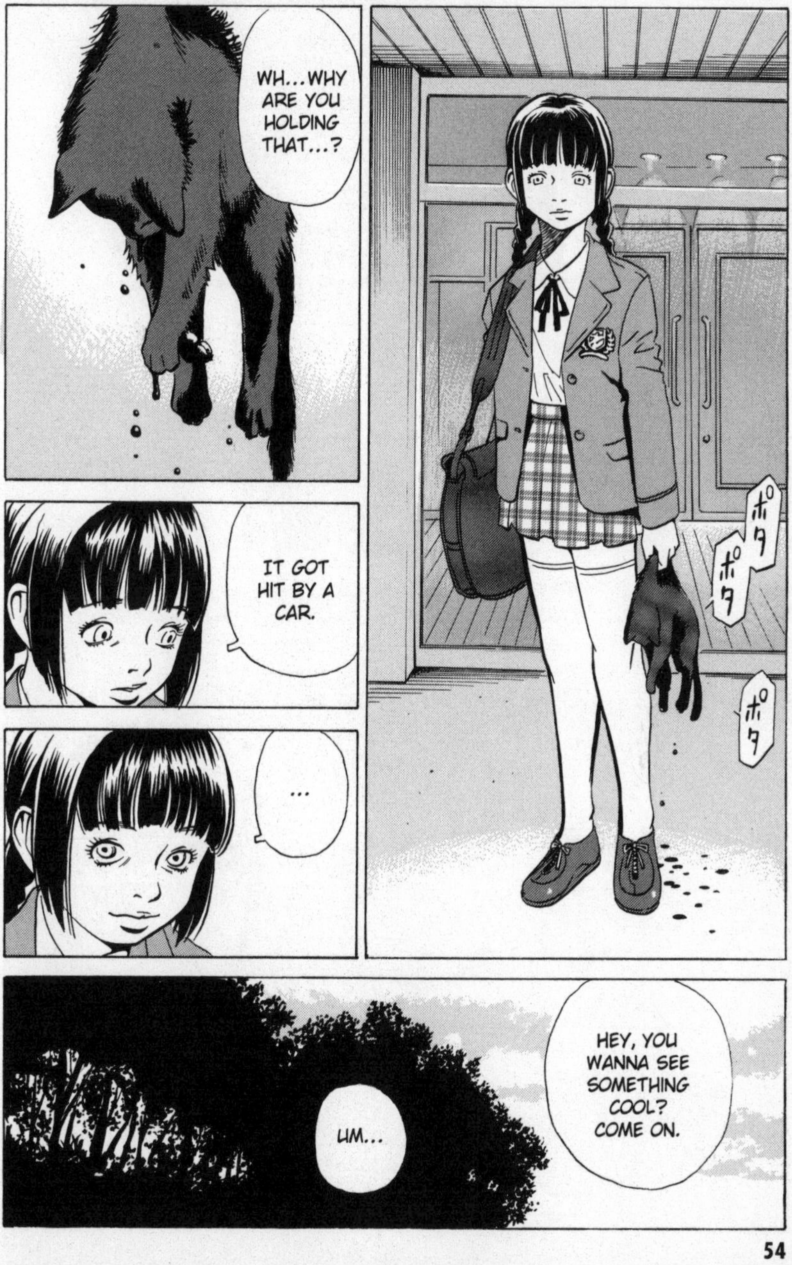
ポタ
ポタ
ポタ
WH...WHY ARE YOU HOLDING THAT...?
IT GOT HIT BY A CAR.
...
HEY, YOU WANNA SEE SOMETHING COOL? COME ON.
UM...

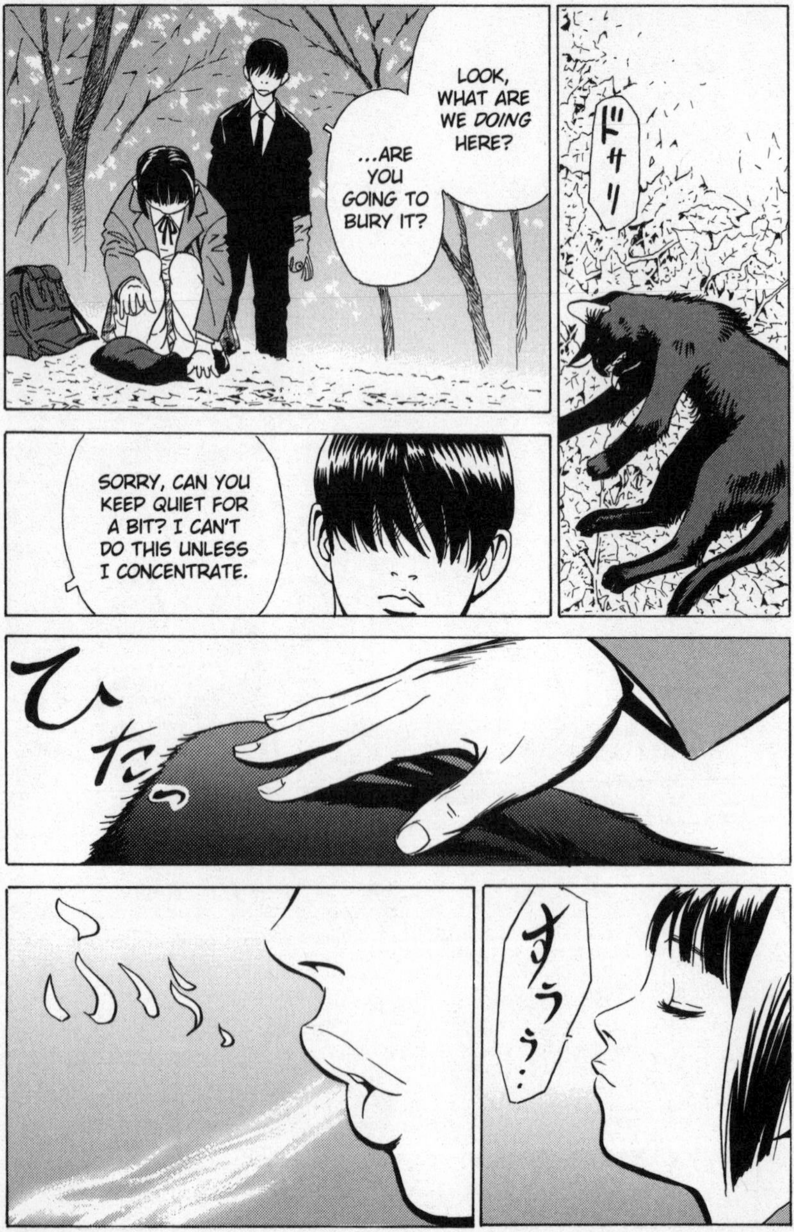
ドサリ
LOOK, WHAT ARE WE *DOING* HERE?
...ARE YOU GOING TO BURY IT?
SORRY, CAN YOU KEEP QUIET FOR A BIT? I CAN'T DO THIS UNLESS I CONCENTRATE.
ひたっ
すぅぅ..
ふぅぅ

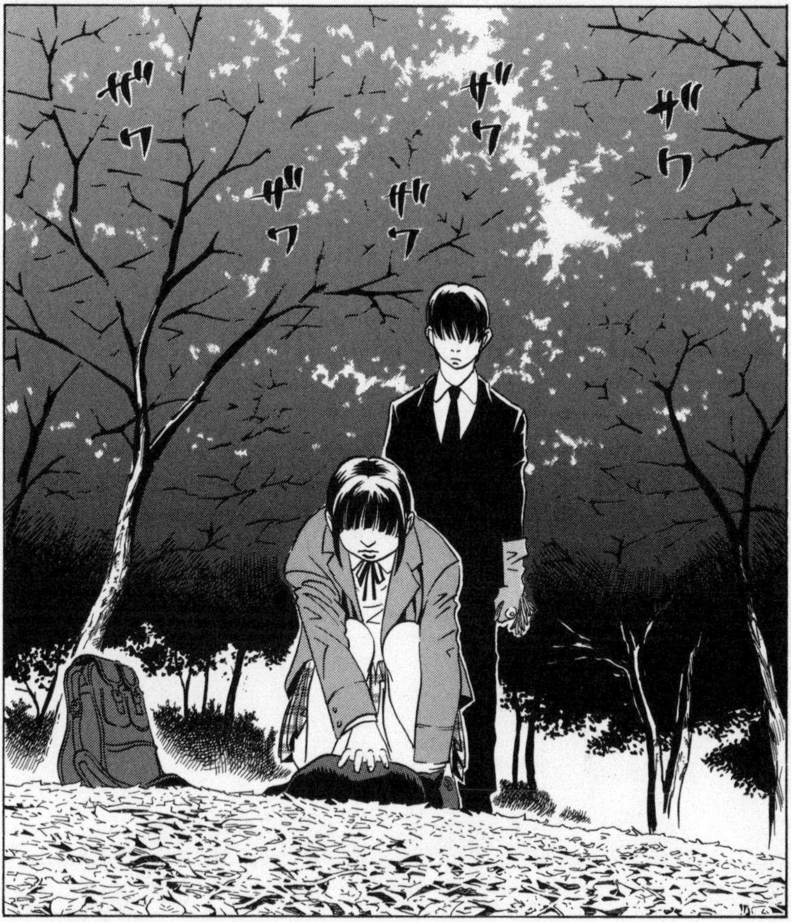
ザワ
ザワ
ザワ
ザワ
ザワ

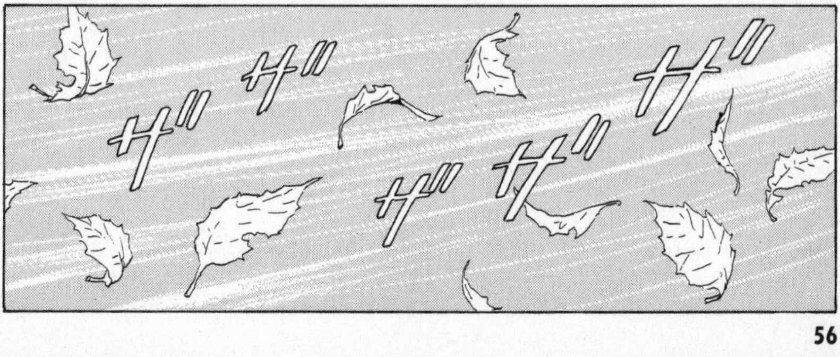
ザ
ザ
ザ
ザ
ザ

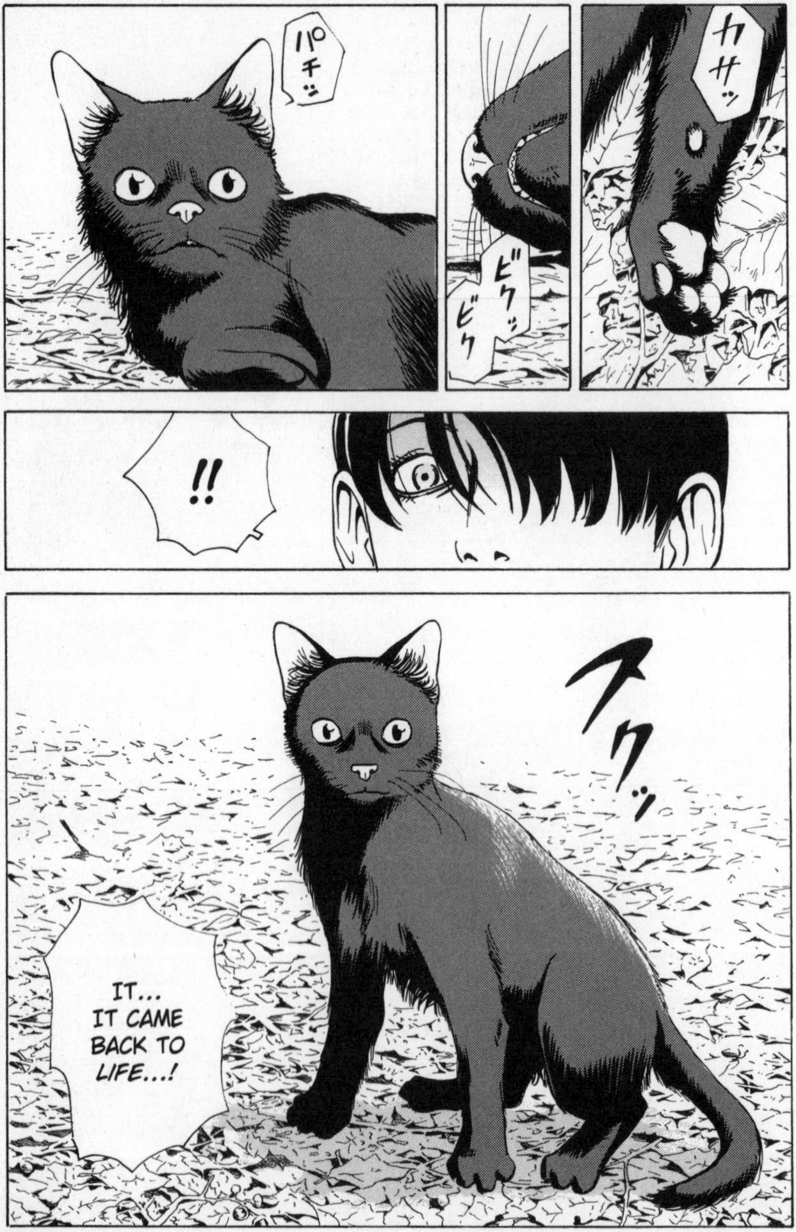
カサッ
ビクッ
ビク
パチッ
!!
スクッ
IT... IT CAME BACK TO LIFE...!

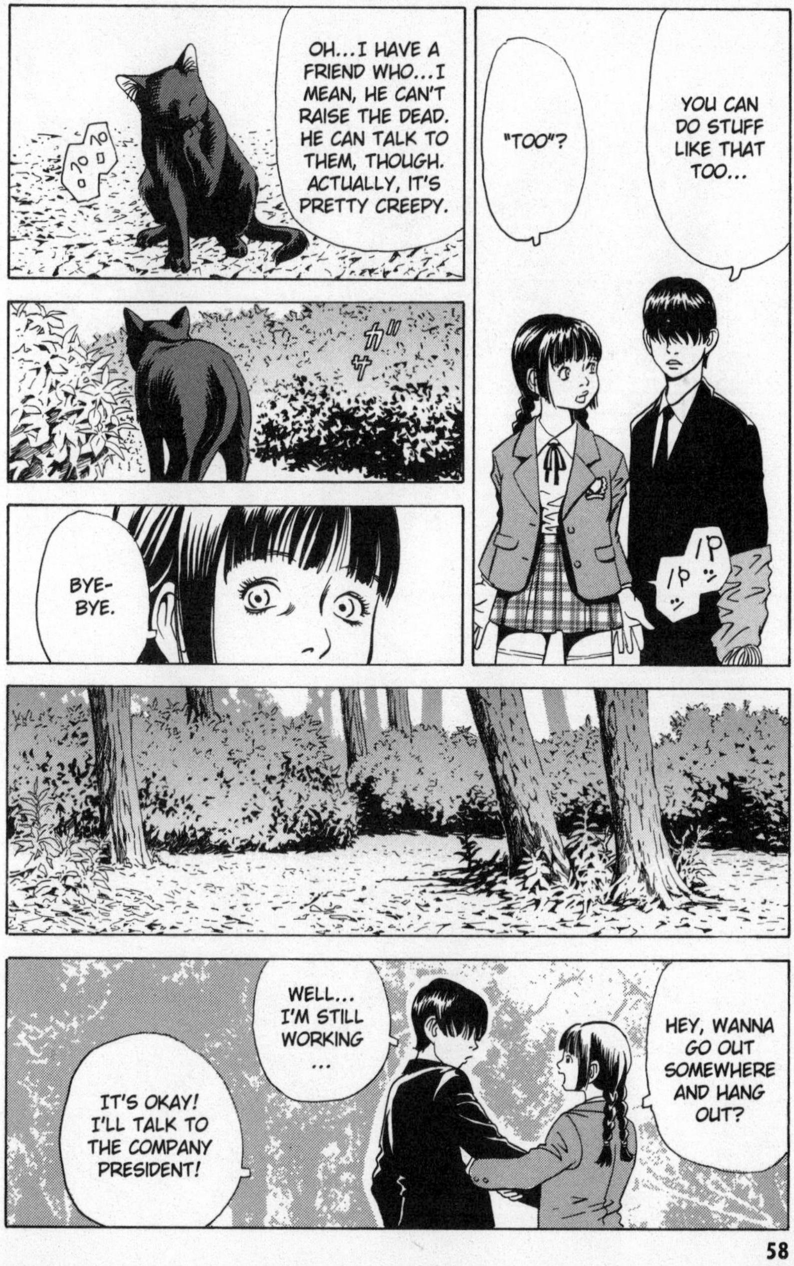
YOU CAN DO STUFF LIKE THAT TOO...
"TOO"?
パッ パッ
OH...I HAVE A FRIEND WHO...I MEAN, HE CAN'T RAISE THE DEAD. HE CAN TALK TO THEM, THOUGH. ACTUALLY, IT'S PRETTY CREEPY.
ガサ
BYE-BYE.
HEY, WANNA GO OUT SOMEWHERE AND HANG OUT?
WELL... I'M STILL WORKING ...
IT'S OKAY! I'LL TALK TO THE COMPANY PRESIDENT!

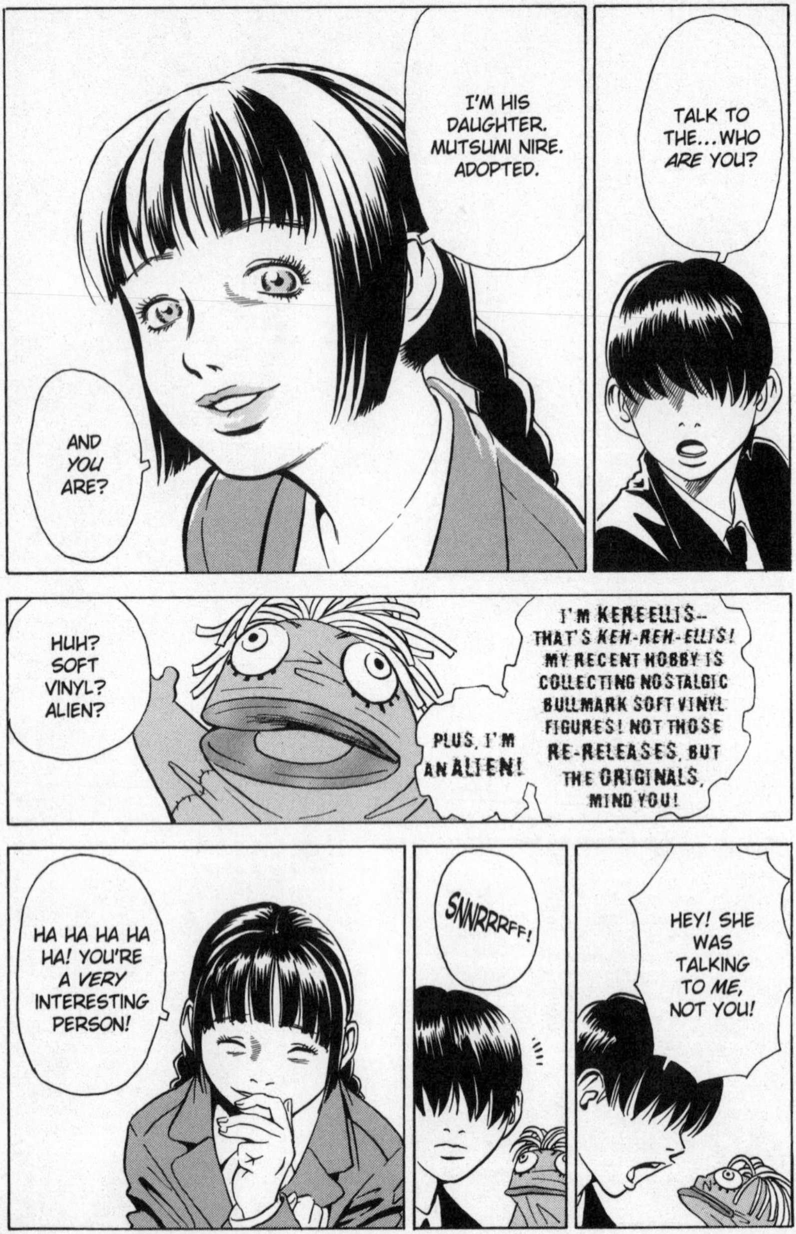
TALK TO THE...WHO *ARE* YOU?
I'M HIS DAUGHTER. MUTSUMI NIRE. ADOPTED.
AND *YOU* ARE?
I'M KERE ELLIS-- THAT'S *KEH-REH-ELLIS!* MY RECENT HOBBY IS COLLECTING NOSTALGIC BULLMARK SOFT VINYL FIGURES! NOT THOSE RE-RELEASES, BUT THE ORIGINALS, MIND YOU!
PLUS, I'M AN ALIEN!
HUH? SOFT VINYL? ALIEN?
HEY! SHE WAS TALKING TO *ME*, NOT YOU!
SNNRRRFF!
HA HA HA HA HA! YOU'RE A *VERY* INTERESTING PERSON!

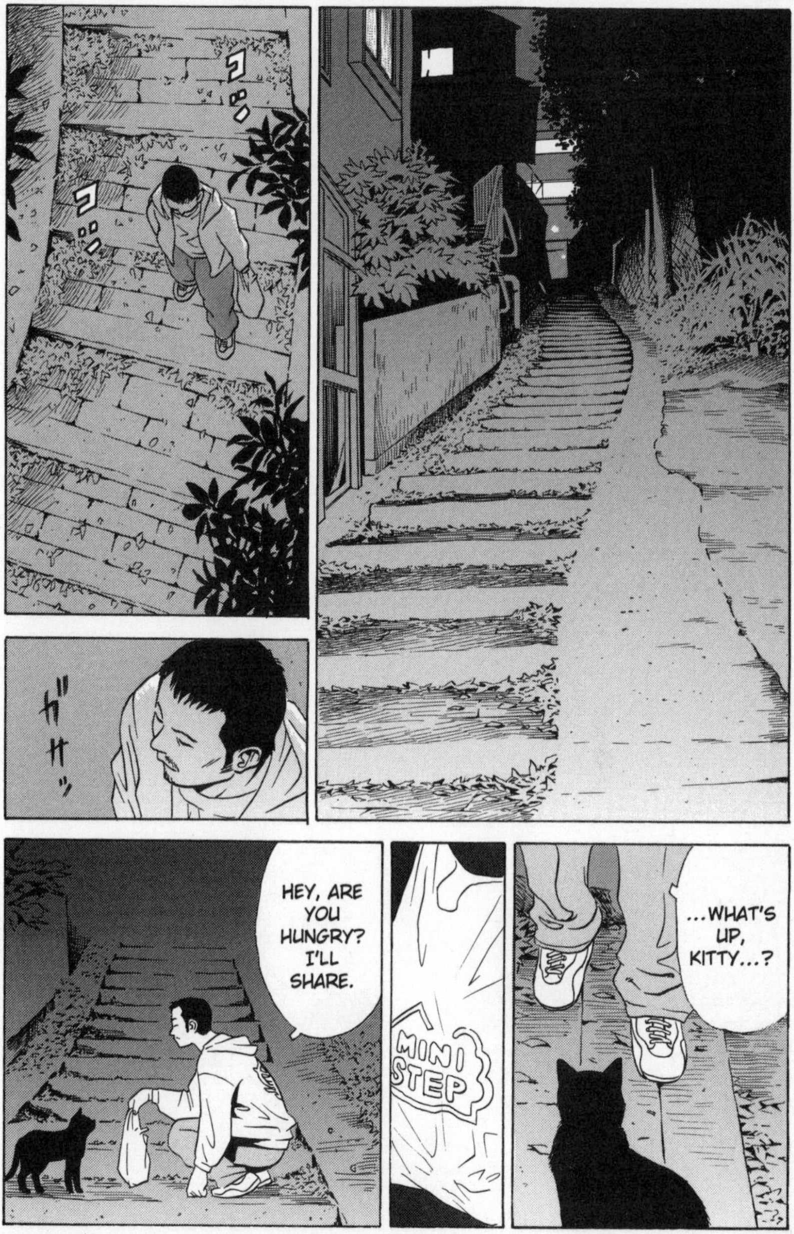
ガサッ
...WHAT'S UP, KITTY...?
MINI STEP
HEY, ARE YOU HUNGRY? I'LL SHARE.

GOTTA LITTLE FRANK HERE...
プラン
プルン
HEY? YOU WANT IT?
SHIT! WHY'D YOU BITE ME?!
WHY...
...EEYAAGH!!

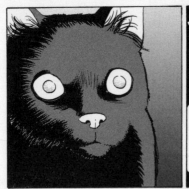

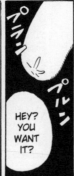

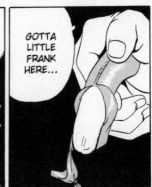

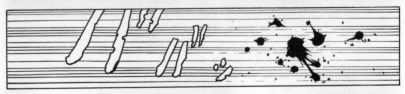

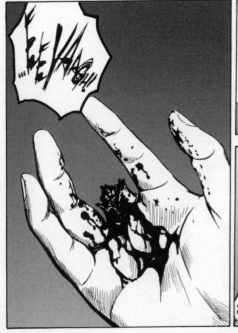

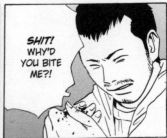

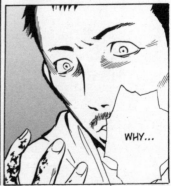

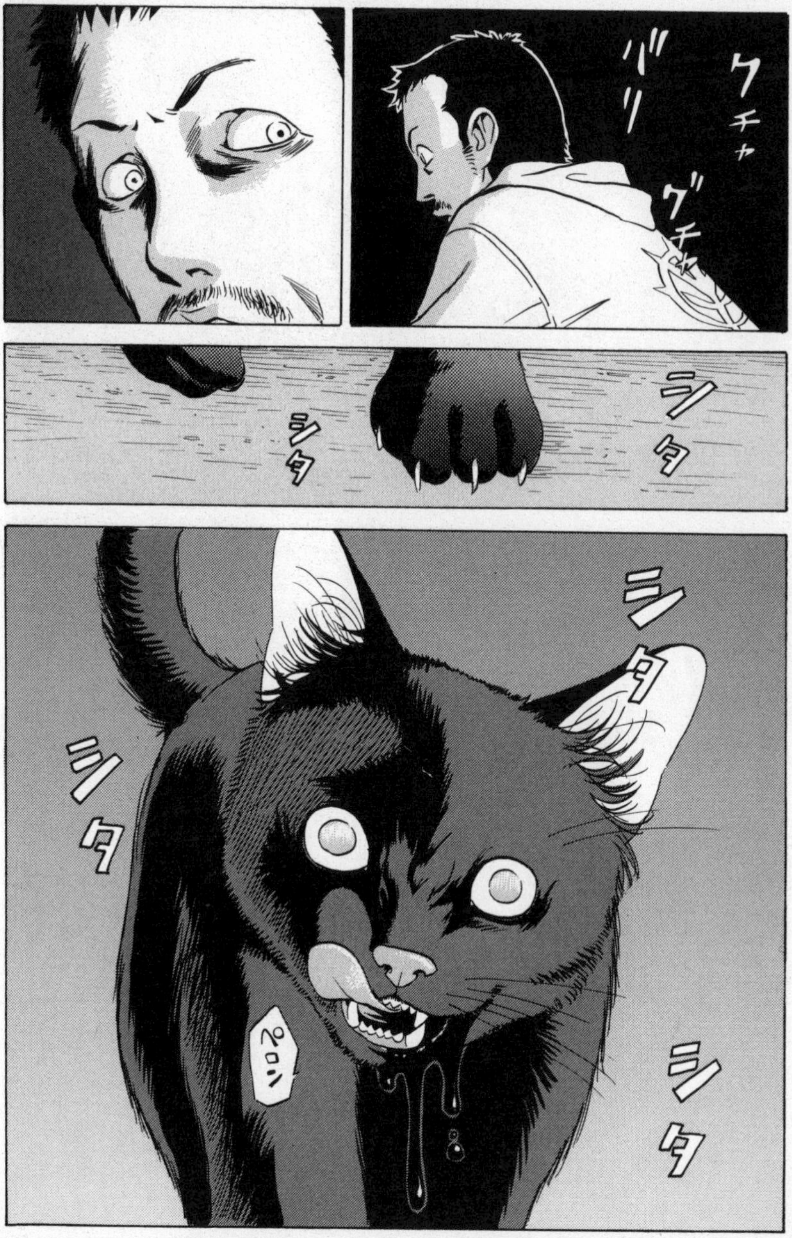
クチャ
グチャ
バリ
シタ
シタ
シタ
シタ
ペロン
シタ

2nd delivery: i don't care if i die—the end

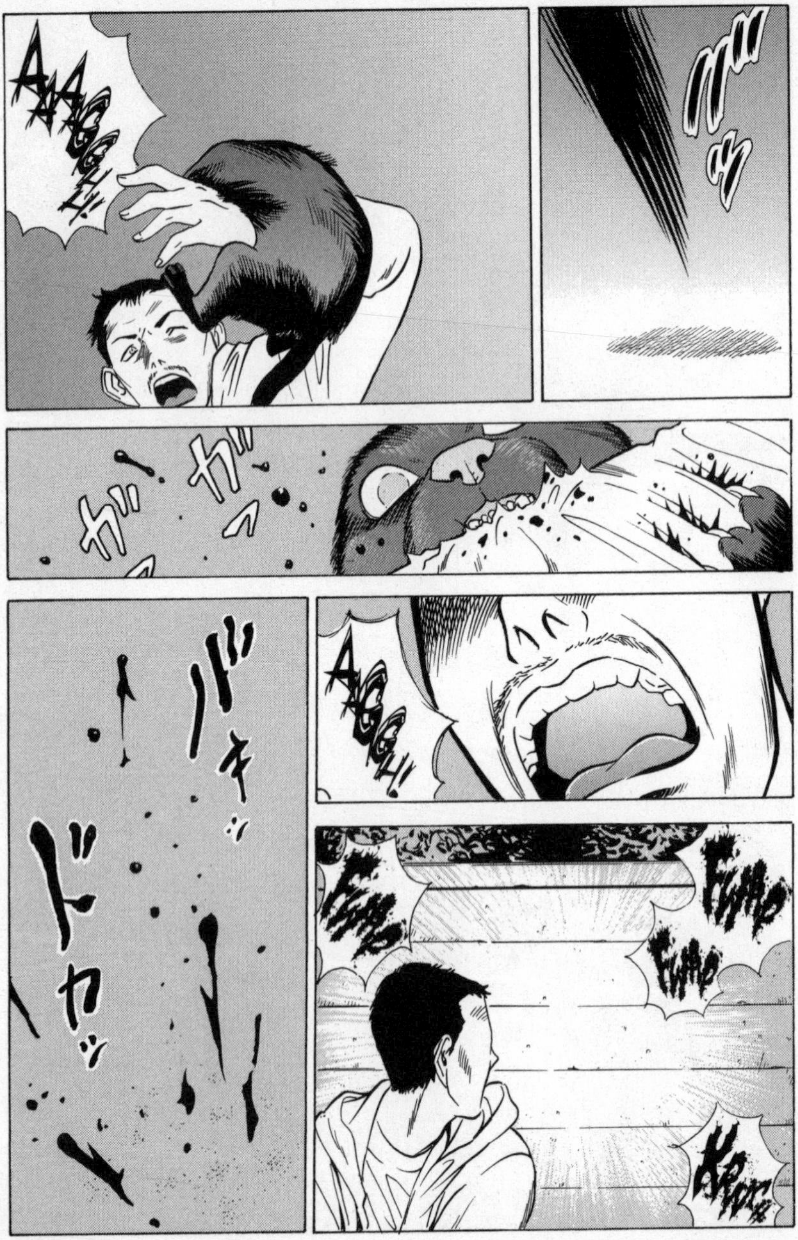
AAAGGH!!
ガッ
ガッ
AAAGGH!!
バキッ
ドカッ

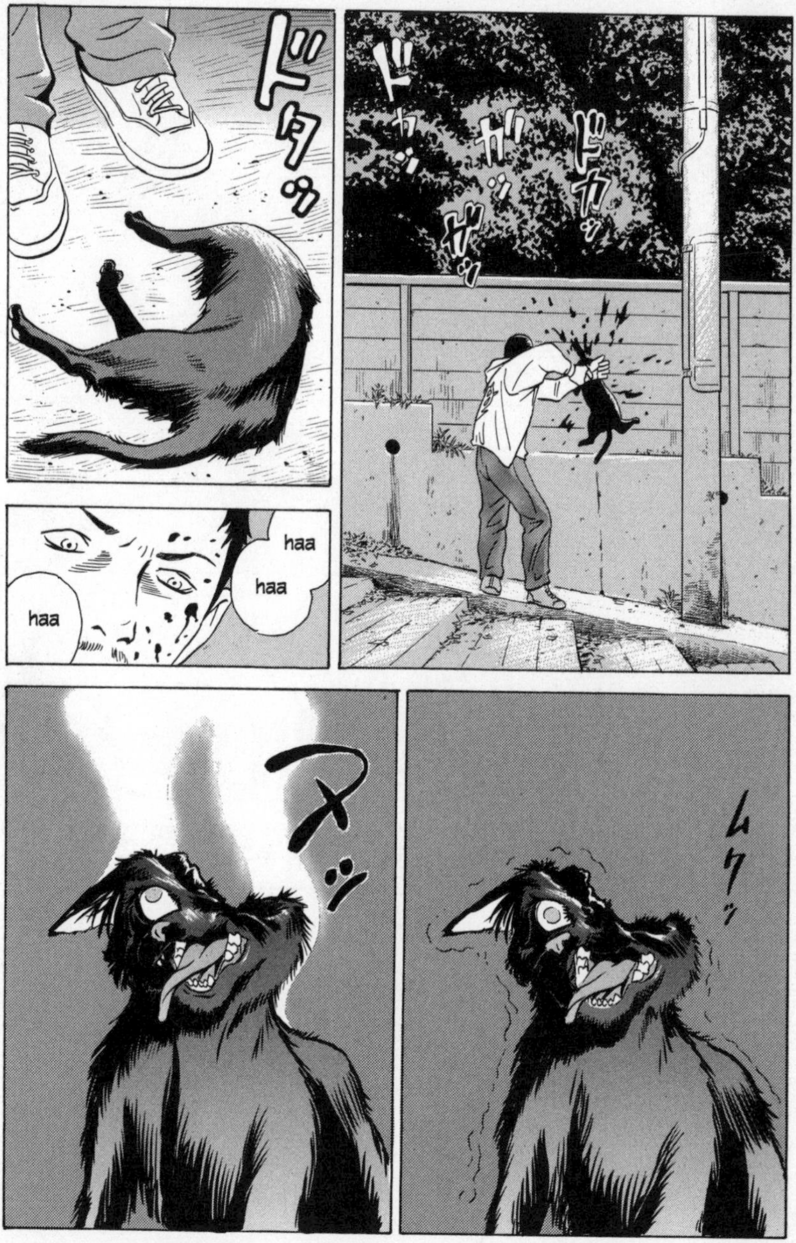
ドカッ
ガリッ
ドカッ
ザッ
ドタッ
haa
haa
haa
ムクッ
ヌッ

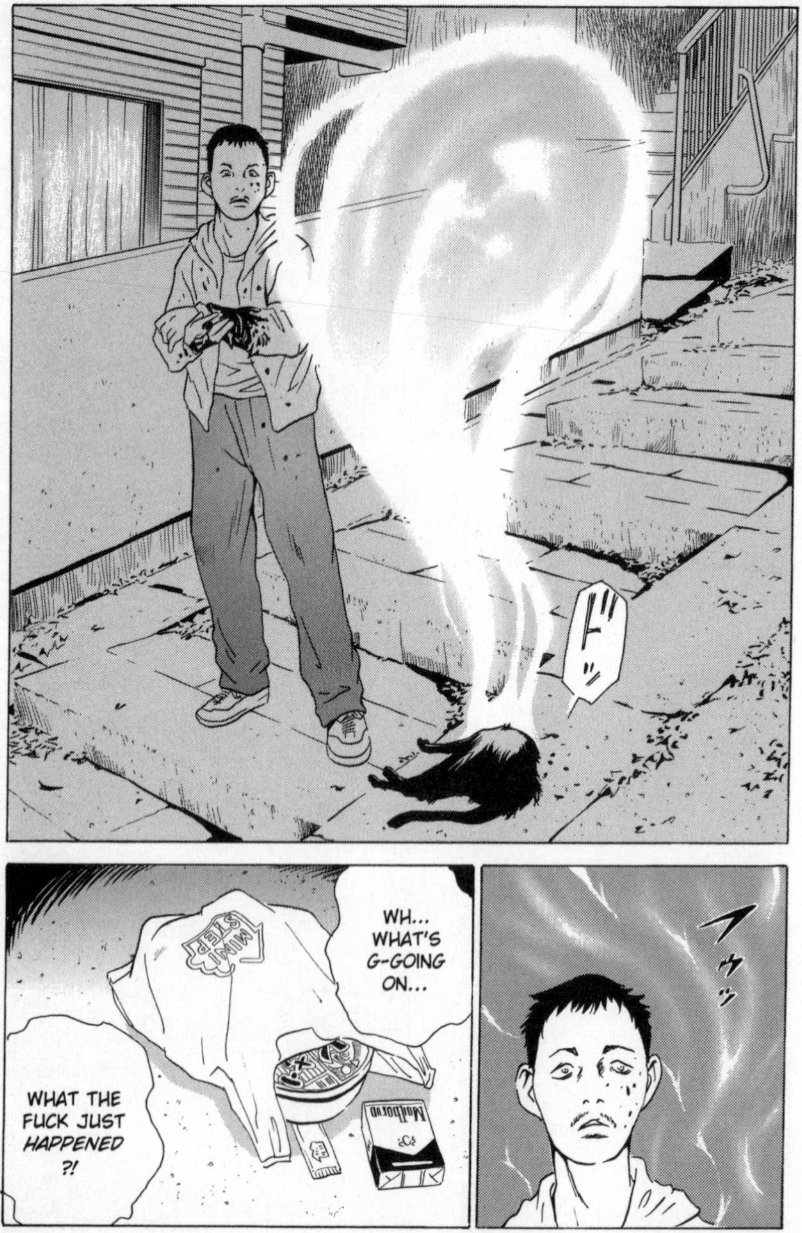
ドッ
WH... WHAT'S G-GOING ON...
WHAT THE FUCK JUST *HAPPENED* ?!

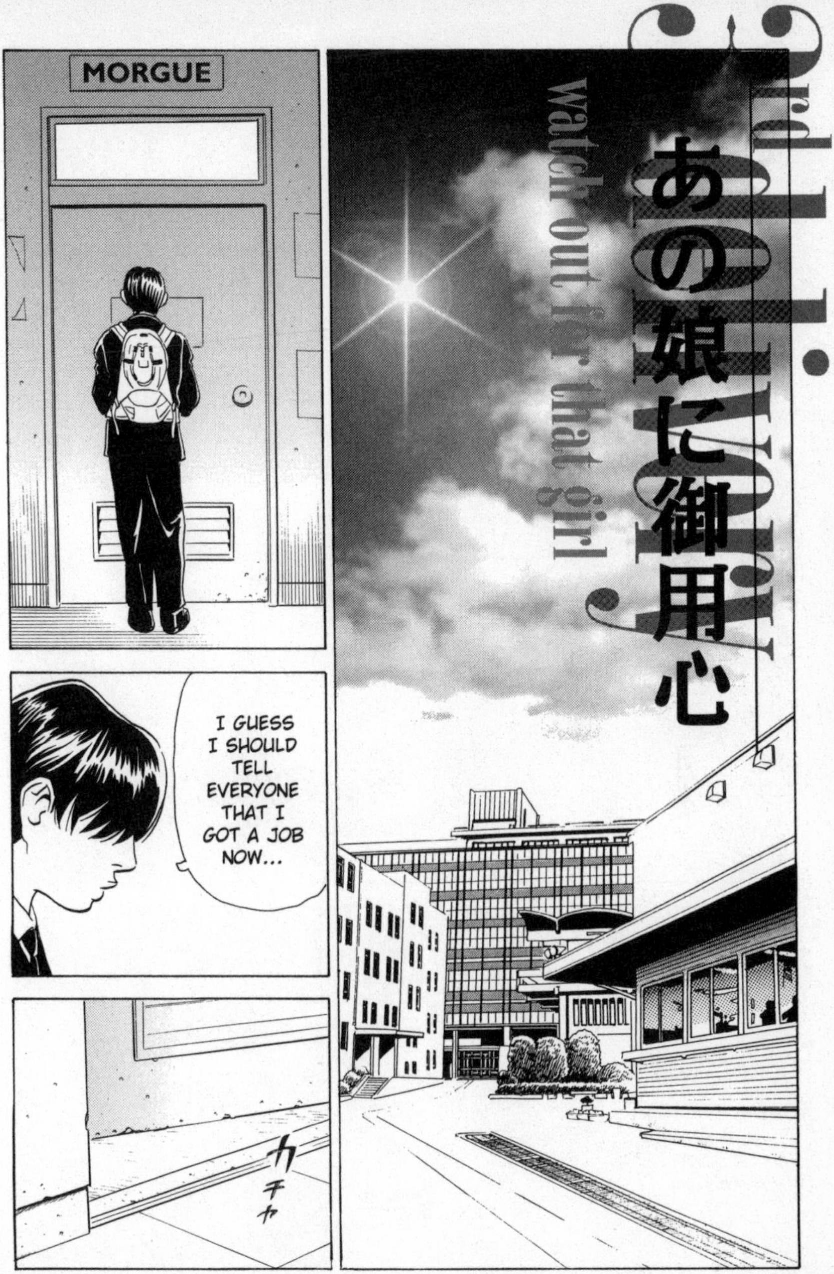
あの娘に御用心
watch out for that girl
MORGUE
I GUESS I SHOULD TELL EVERYONE THAT I GOT A JOB NOW...
カチャ

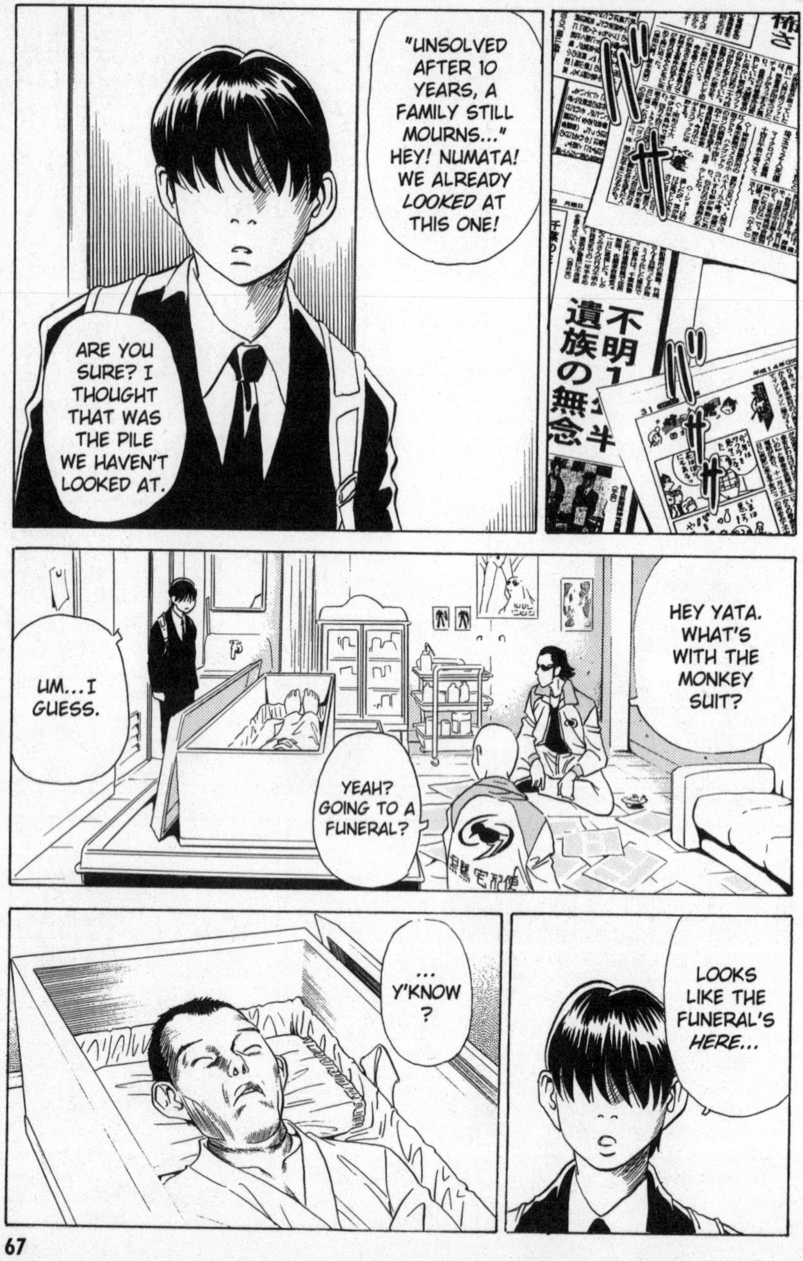
遺族の無念
"UNSOLVED AFTER 10 YEARS, A FAMILY STILL MOURNS..." HEY! NUMATA! WE ALREADY *LOOKED* AT THIS ONE!
ARE YOU SURE? I THOUGHT THAT WAS THE PILE WE HAVEN'T LOOKED AT.
HEY YATA. WHAT'S WITH THE MONKEY SUIT?
YEAH? GOING TO A FUNERAL?
UM...I GUESS.
LOOKS LIKE THE FUNERAL'S *HERE*...
... Y'KNOW ?

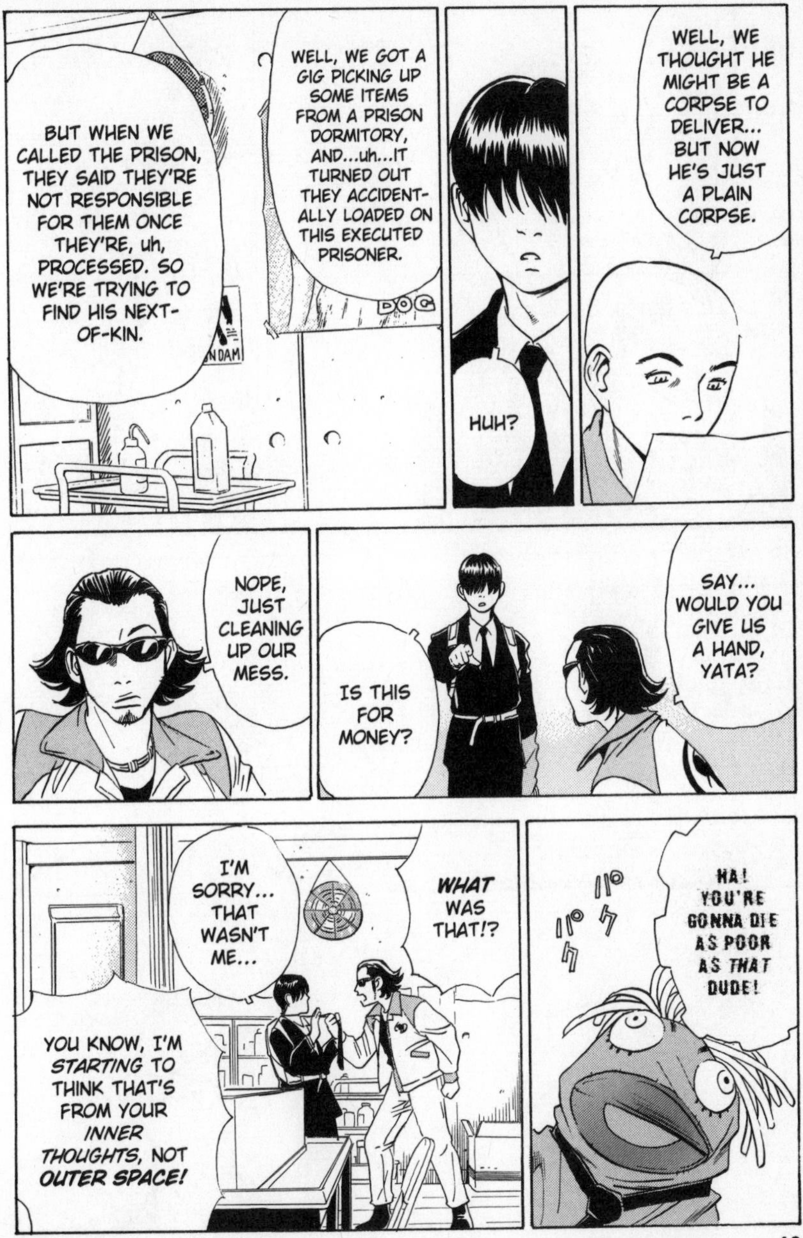
WELL, WE THOUGHT HE MIGHT BE A CORPSE TO DELIVER... BUT NOW HE'S JUST A PLAIN CORPSE.
HUH?
WELL, WE GOT A GIG PICKING UP SOME ITEMS FROM A PRISON DORMITORY, AND...uh...IT TURNED OUT THEY ACCIDENTALLY LOADED ON THIS EXECUTED PRISONER.
BUT WHEN WE CALLED THE PRISON, THEY SAID THEY'RE NOT RESPONSIBLE FOR THEM ONCE THEY'RE, uh, PROCESSED. SO WE'RE TRYING TO FIND HIS NEXT-OF-KIN.
SAY... WOULD YOU GIVE US A HAND, YATA?
IS THIS FOR MONEY?
NOPE, JUST CLEANING UP OUR MESS.
HA! YOU'RE GONNA DIE AS POOR AS *THAT* DUDE!
パク
パク
WHAT WAS THAT!?
I'M SORRY... THAT WASN'T ME...
YOU KNOW, I'M *STARTING* TO THINK THAT'S FROM YOUR *INNER THOUGHTS*, NOT *OUTER SPACE*!

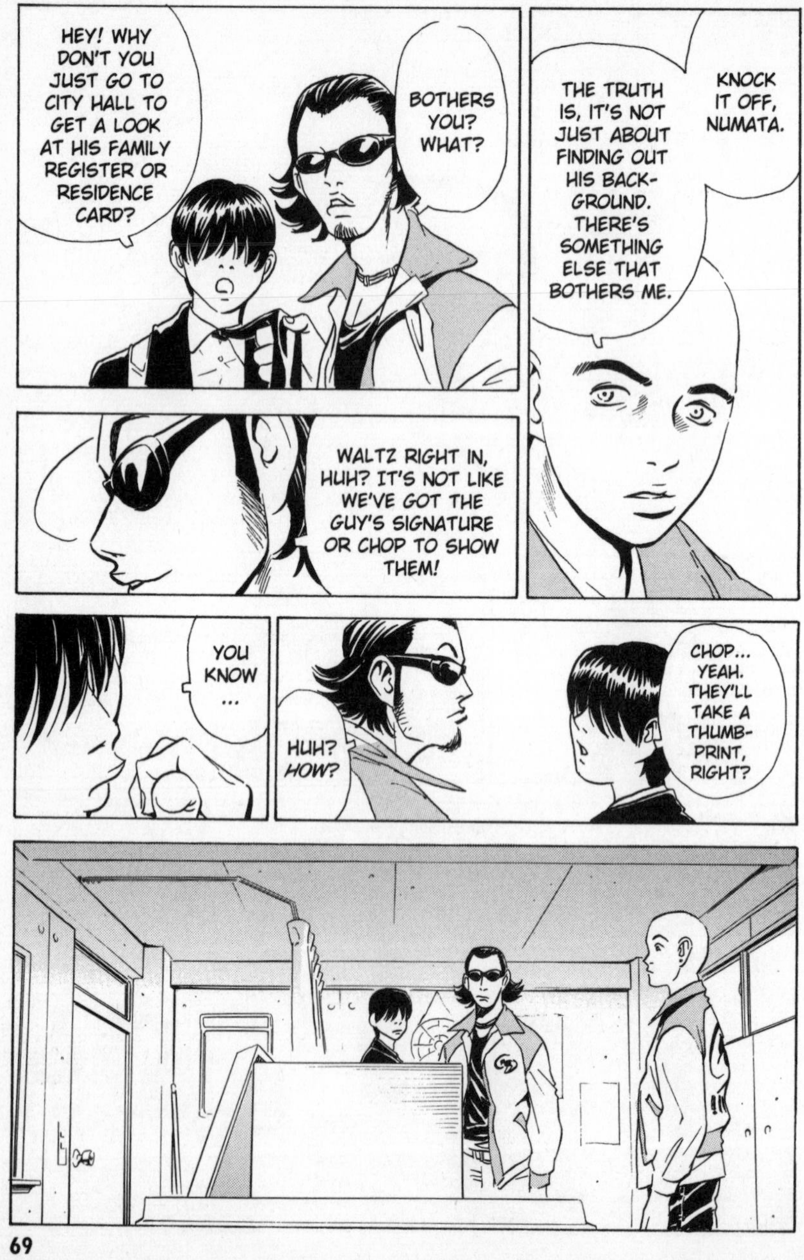
KNOCK IT OFF, NUMATA.
THE TRUTH IS, IT'S NOT JUST ABOUT FINDING OUT HIS BACK-GROUND. THERE'S SOMETHING ELSE THAT BOTHERS ME.
BOTHERS YOU? WHAT?
HEY! WHY DON'T YOU JUST GO TO CITY HALL TO GET A LOOK AT HIS FAMILY REGISTER OR RESIDENCE CARD?
WALTZ RIGHT IN, HUH? IT'S NOT LIKE WE'VE GOT THE GUY'S SIGNATURE OR CHOP TO SHOW THEM!
CHOP... YEAH. THEY'LL TAKE A THUMB-PRINT, RIGHT?
HUH? *HOW?*
YOU KNOW ...

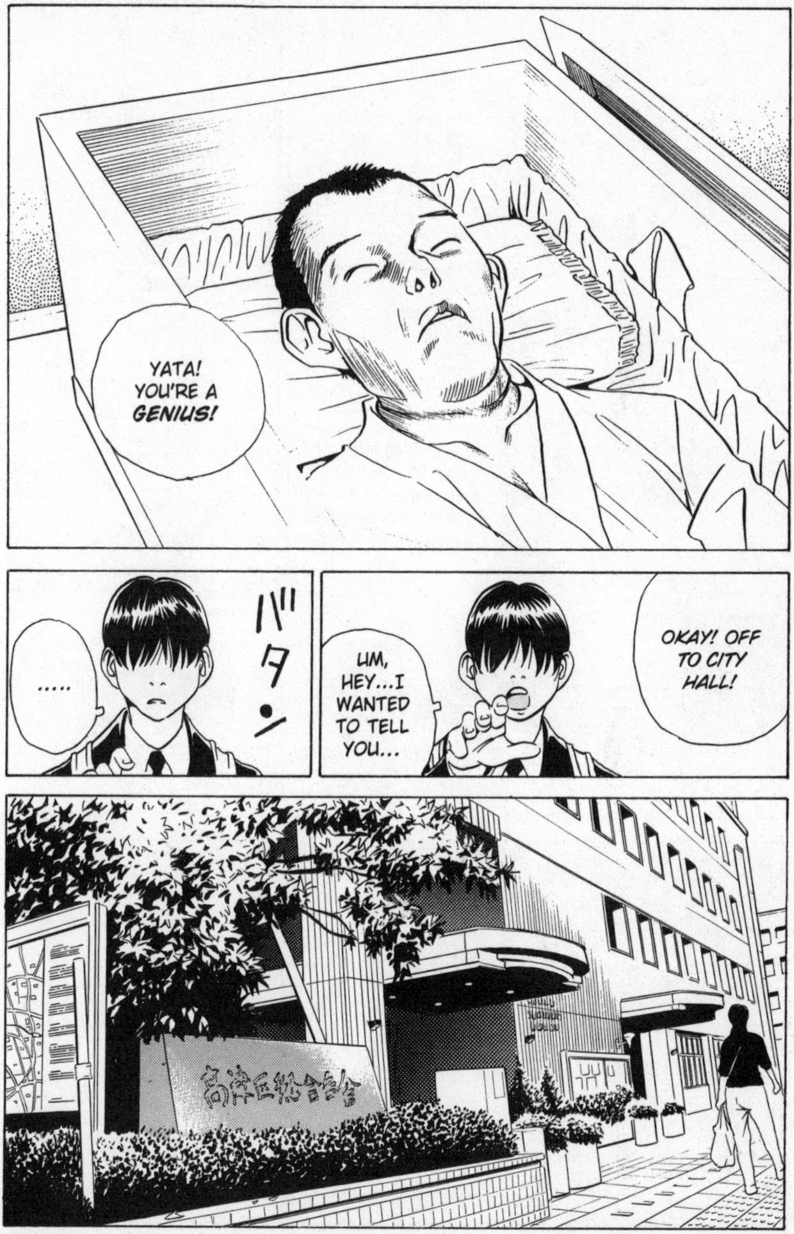
YATA! YOU'RE A GENIUS!
OKAY! OFF TO CITY HALL!
UM, HEY...I WANTED TO TELL YOU...
バタン
.....

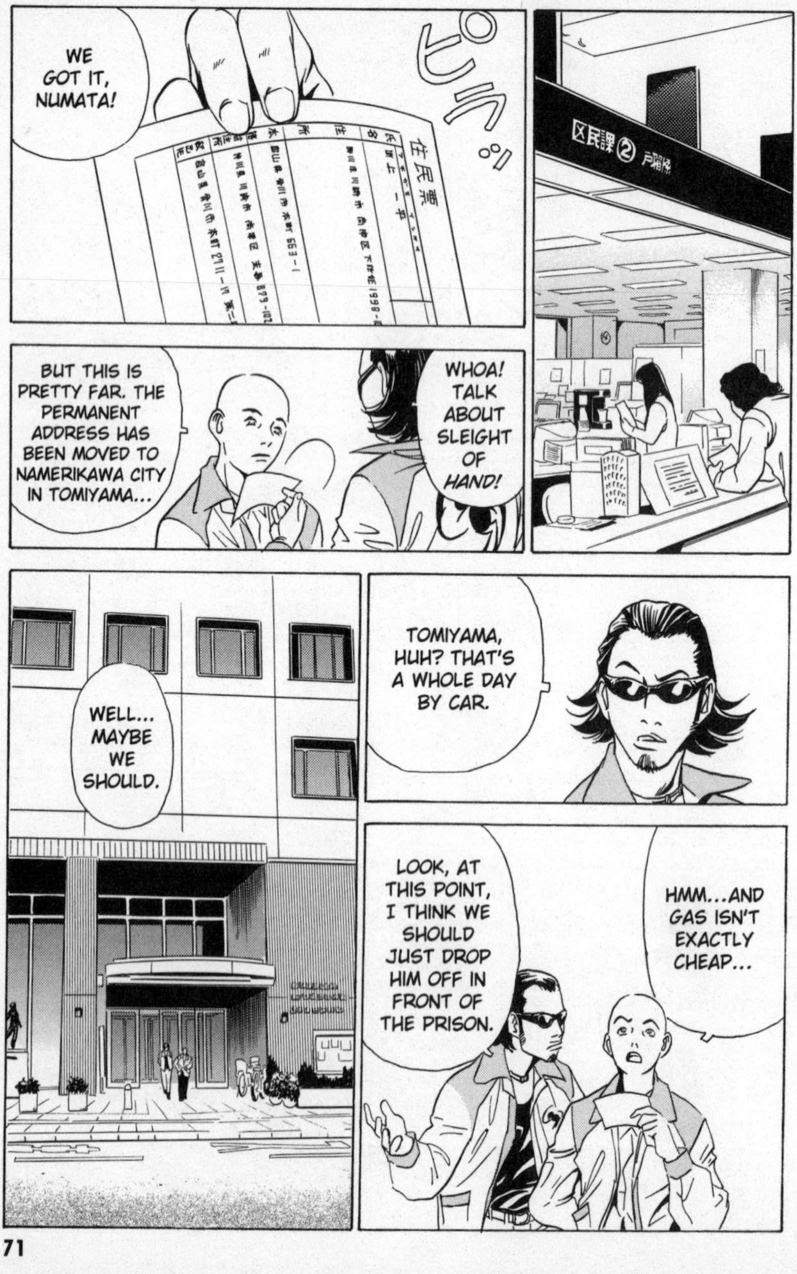

区民課 ② 戸籍係
ピラッ
WE GOT IT, NUMATA!
住民票
WHOA! TALK ABOUT SLEIGHT OF HAND!
BUT THIS IS PRETTY FAR. THE PERMANENT ADDRESS HAS BEEN MOVED TO NAMERIKAWA CITY IN TOMIYAMA...
TOMIYAMA, HUH? THAT'S A WHOLE DAY BY CAR.
HMM...AND GAS ISN'T EXACTLY CHEAP...
LOOK, AT THIS POINT, I THINK WE SHOULD JUST DROP HIM OFF IN FRONT OF THE PRISON.
WELL... MAYBE WE SHOULD.

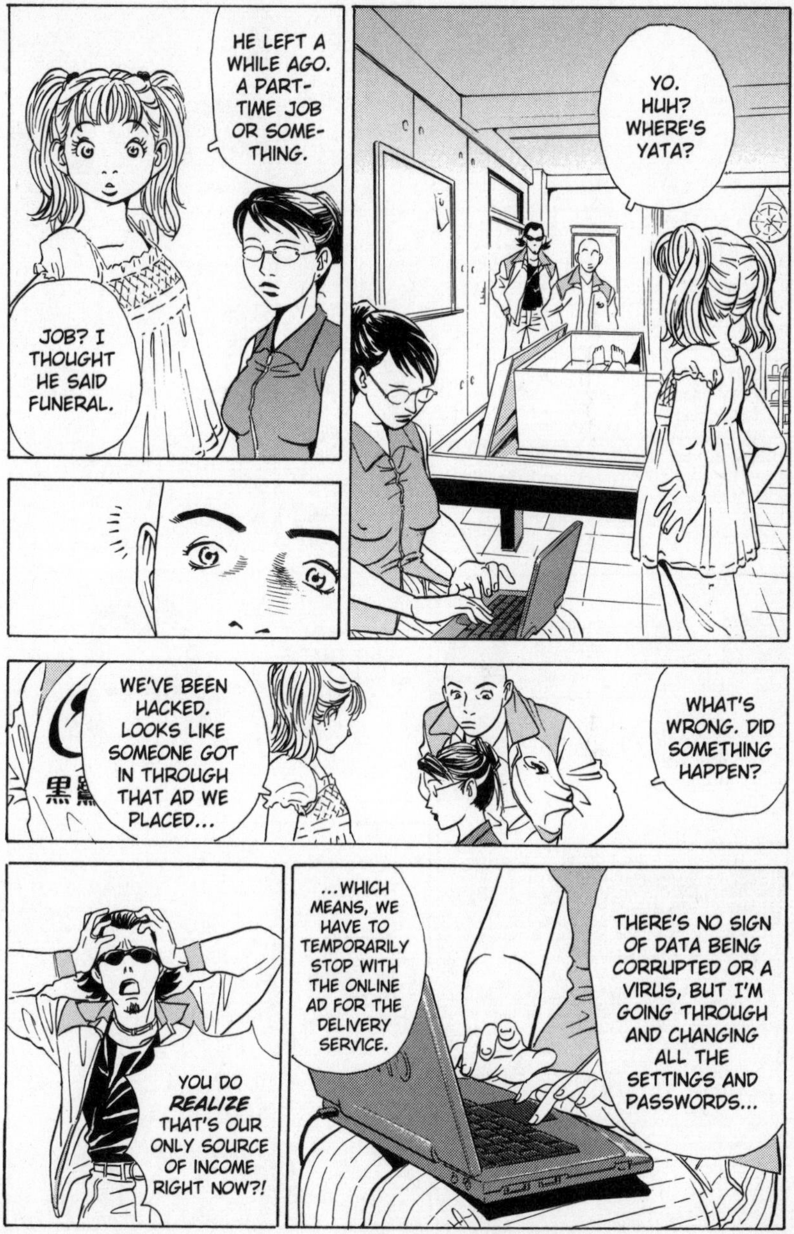
YO. HUH? WHERE'S YATA?
HE LEFT A WHILE AGO. A PART-TIME JOB OR SOME-THING.
JOB? I THOUGHT HE SAID FUNERAL.
WHAT'S WRONG. DID SOMETHING HAPPEN?
WE'VE BEEN HACKED. LOOKS LIKE SOMEONE GOT IN THROUGH THAT AD WE PLACED...
THERE'S NO SIGN OF DATA BEING CORRUPTED OR A VIRUS, BUT I'M GOING THROUGH AND CHANGING ALL THE SETTINGS AND PASSWORDS...
...WHICH MEANS, WE HAVE TO TEMPORARILY STOP WITH THE ONLINE AD FOR THE DELIVERY SERVICE.
YOU DO *REALIZE* THAT'S OUR ONLY SOURCE OF INCOME RIGHT NOW?!

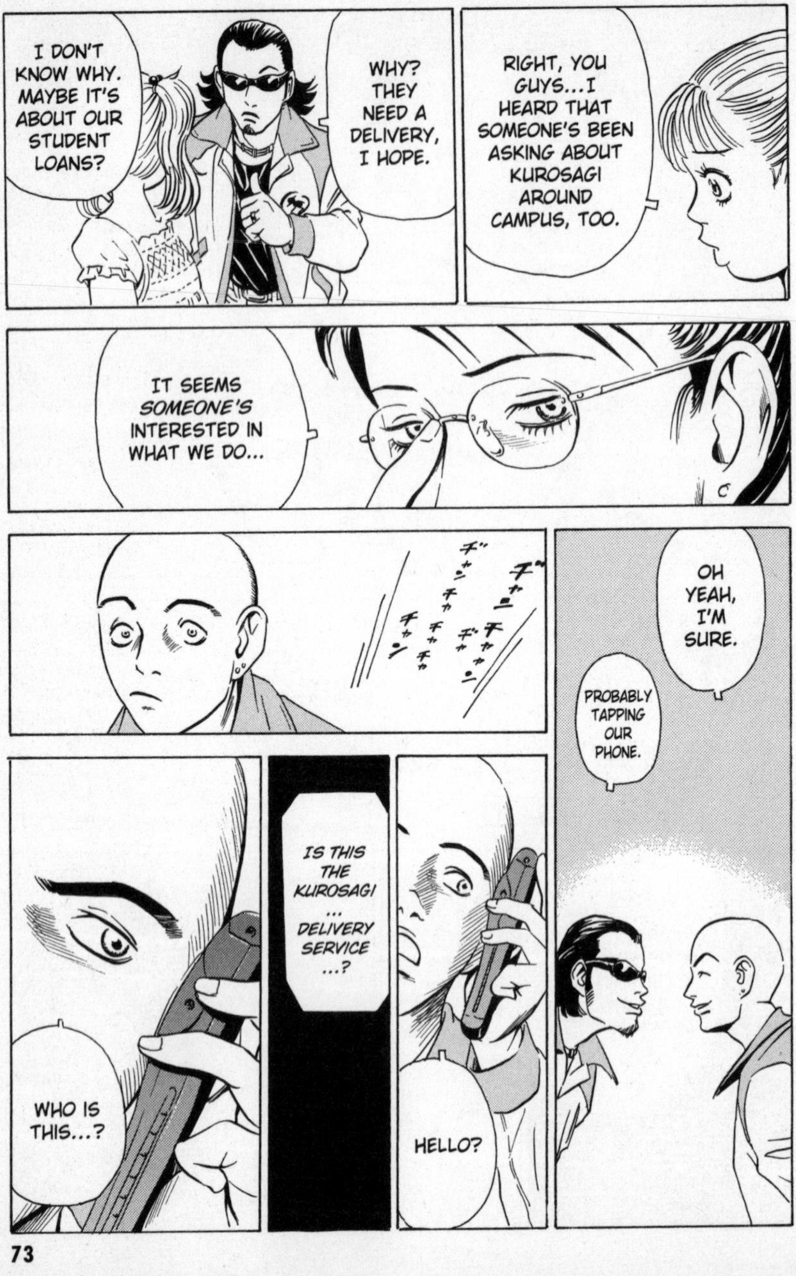
RIGHT, YOU GUYS...I HEARD THAT SOMEONE'S BEEN ASKING ABOUT KUROSAGI AROUND CAMPUS, TOO.
WHY? THEY NEED A DELIVERY, I HOPE.
I DON'T KNOW WHY. MAYBE IT'S ABOUT OUR STUDENT LOANS?
IT SEEMS *SOMEONE'S* INTERESTED IN WHAT WE DO...
OH YEAH, I'M SURE.
PROBABLY TAPPING OUR PHONE.
HELLO?
IS THIS THE KUROSAGI ... DELIVERY SERVICE ...?
WHO IS THIS...?

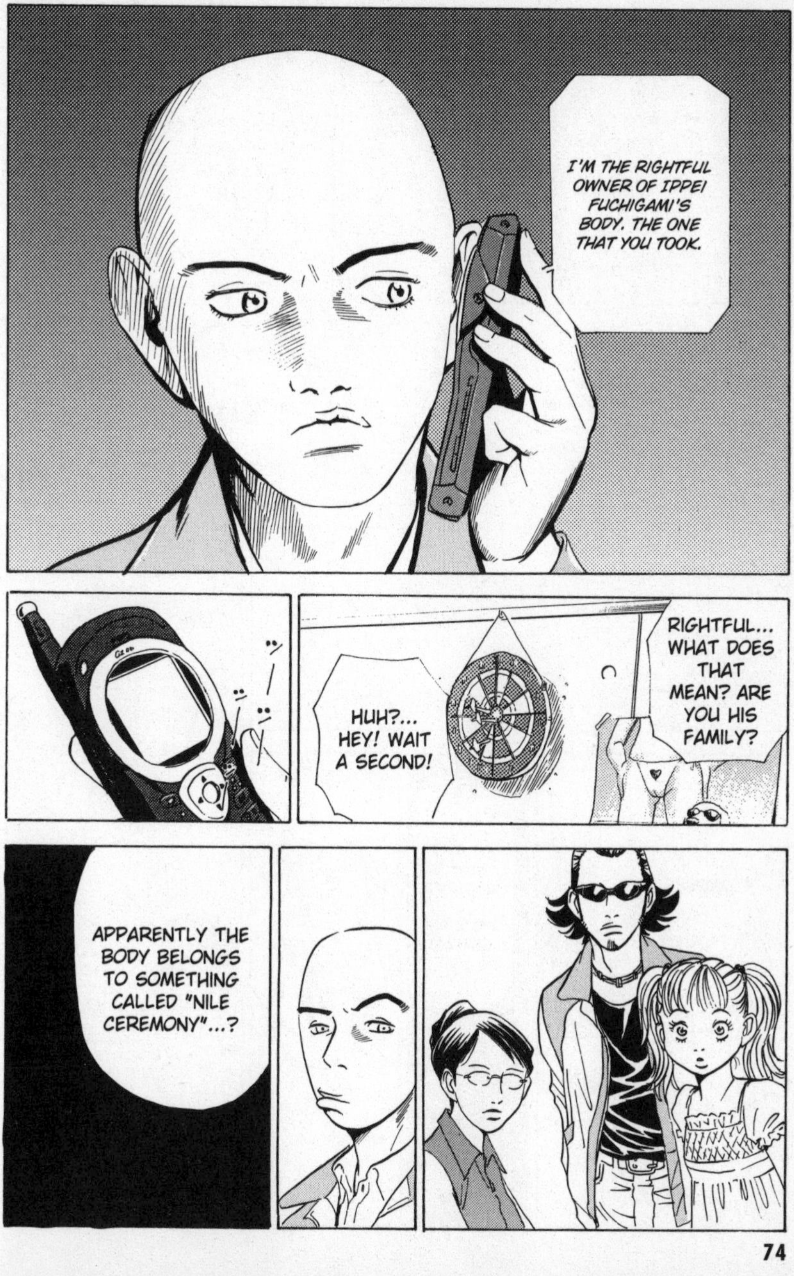
I'M THE RIGHTFUL OWNER OF IPPEI FUCHIGAMI'S BODY. THE ONE THAT YOU TOOK.
RIGHTFUL... WHAT DOES THAT MEAN? ARE YOU HIS FAMILY?
HUH?... HEY! WAIT A SECOND!
APPARENTLY THE BODY BELONGS TO SOMETHING CALLED "NILE CEREMONY"...?

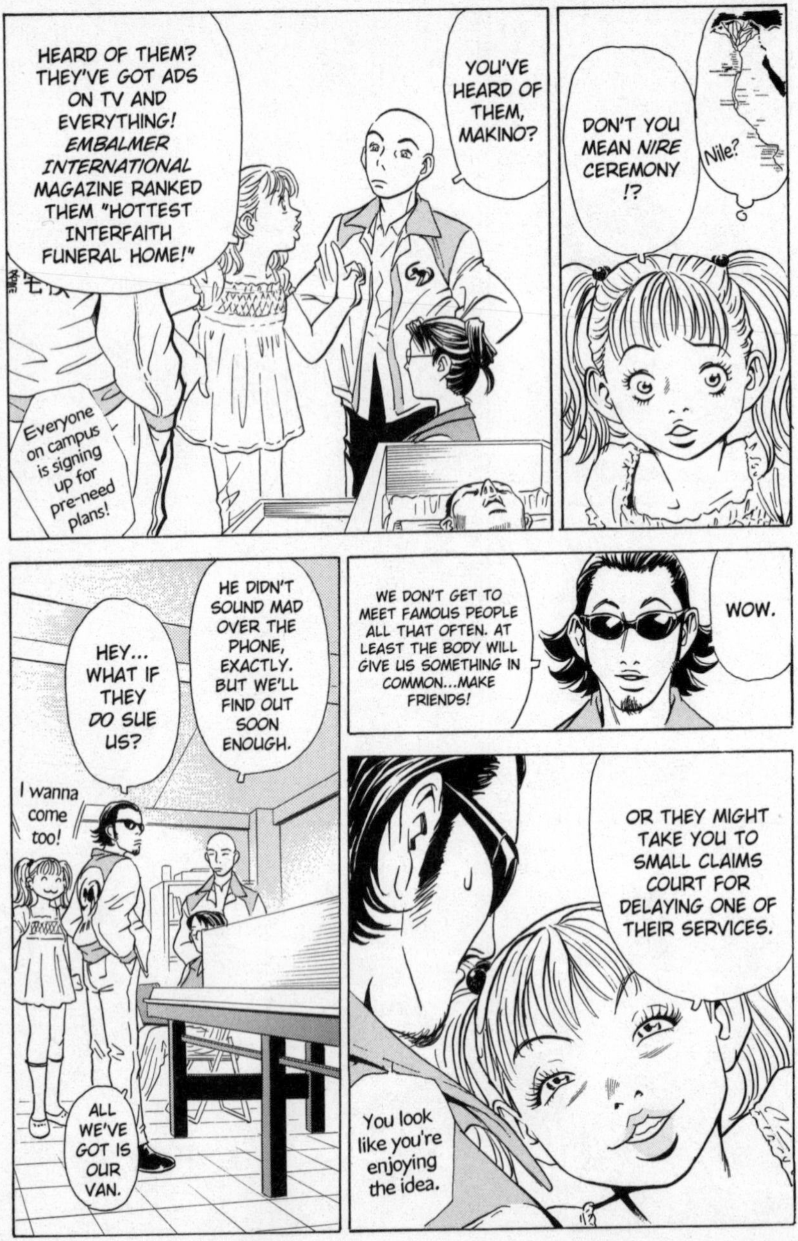
DON'T YOU MEAN *NIRE* CEREMONY !?
Nile?
YOU'VE HEARD OF THEM, MAKINO?
HEARD OF THEM? THEY'VE GOT ADS ON TV AND EVERYTHING! *EMBALMER INTERNATIONAL* MAGAZINE RANKED THEM "HOTTEST INTERFAITH FUNERAL HOME!"
Everyone on campus is signing up for pre-need plans!
WOW.
WE DON'T GET TO MEET FAMOUS PEOPLE ALL THAT OFTEN. AT LEAST THE BODY WILL GIVE US SOMETHING IN COMMON...MAKE FRIENDS!
OR THEY MIGHT TAKE YOU TO SMALL CLAIMS COURT FOR DELAYING ONE OF THEIR SERVICES.
You look like you're enjoying the idea.
HE DIDN'T SOUND MAD OVER THE PHONE, EXACTLY. BUT WE'LL FIND OUT SOON ENOUGH.
HEY... WHAT IF THEY *DO* SUE US?
I wanna come too!
ALL WE'VE GOT IS OUR VAN.

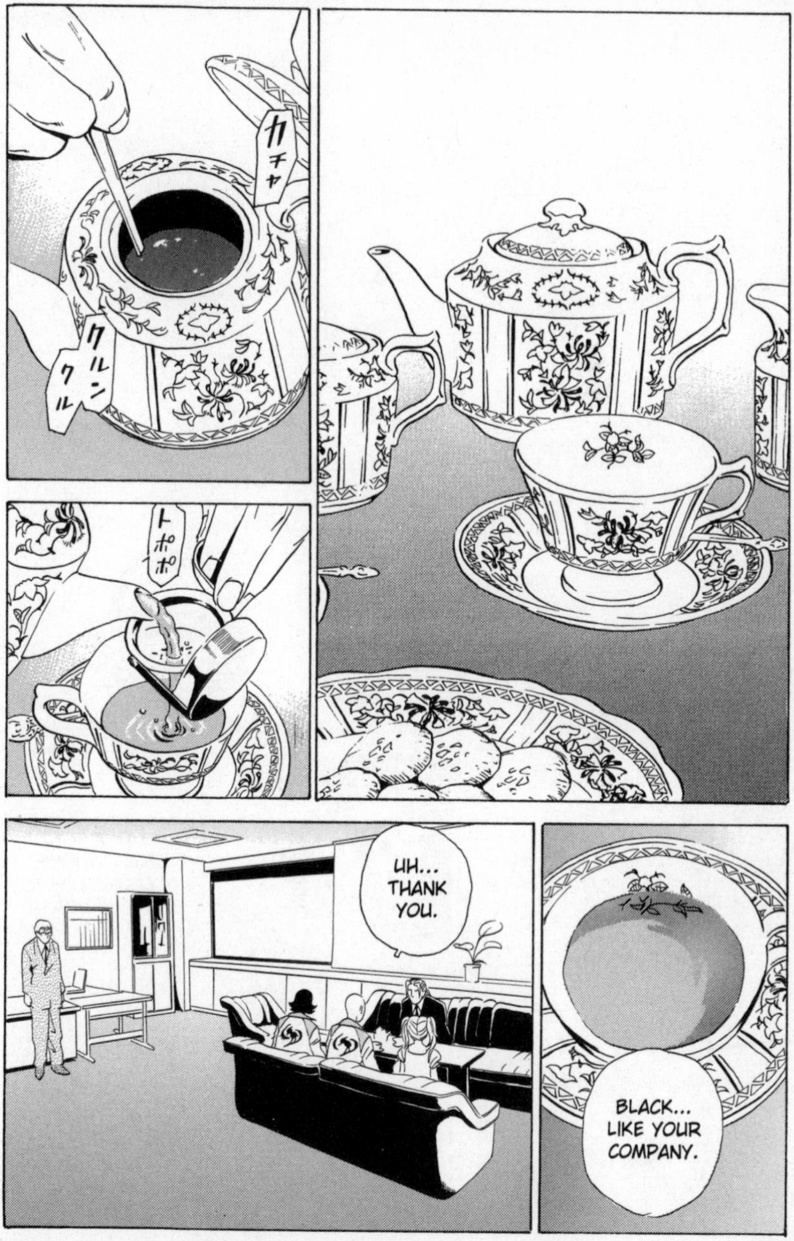
カチャ
クルンクル
トポポ
BLACK... LIKE YOUR COMPANY.
UH... THANK YOU.

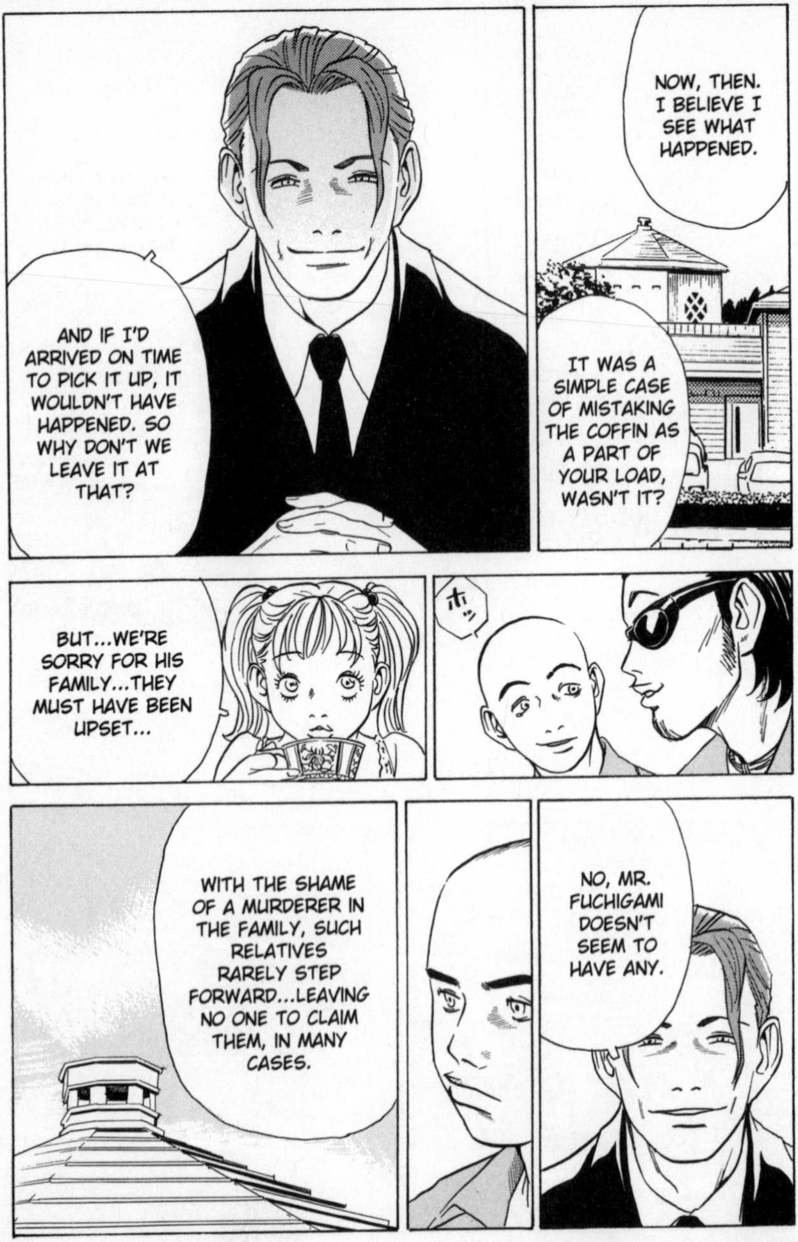
NOW, THEN. I BELIEVE I SEE WHAT HAPPENED.
IT WAS A SIMPLE CASE OF MISTAKING THE COFFIN AS A PART OF YOUR LOAD, WASN'T IT?
AND IF I'D ARRIVED ON TIME TO PICK IT UP, IT WOULDN'T HAVE HAPPENED. SO WHY DON'T WE LEAVE IT AT THAT?
ホッ
BUT...WE'RE SORRY FOR HIS FAMILY...THEY MUST HAVE BEEN UPSET...
NO, MR. FUCHIGAMI DOESN'T SEEM TO HAVE ANY.
WITH THE SHAME OF A MURDERER IN THE FAMILY, SUCH RELATIVES RARELY STEP FORWARD...LEAVING NO ONE TO CLAIM THEM, IN MANY CASES.

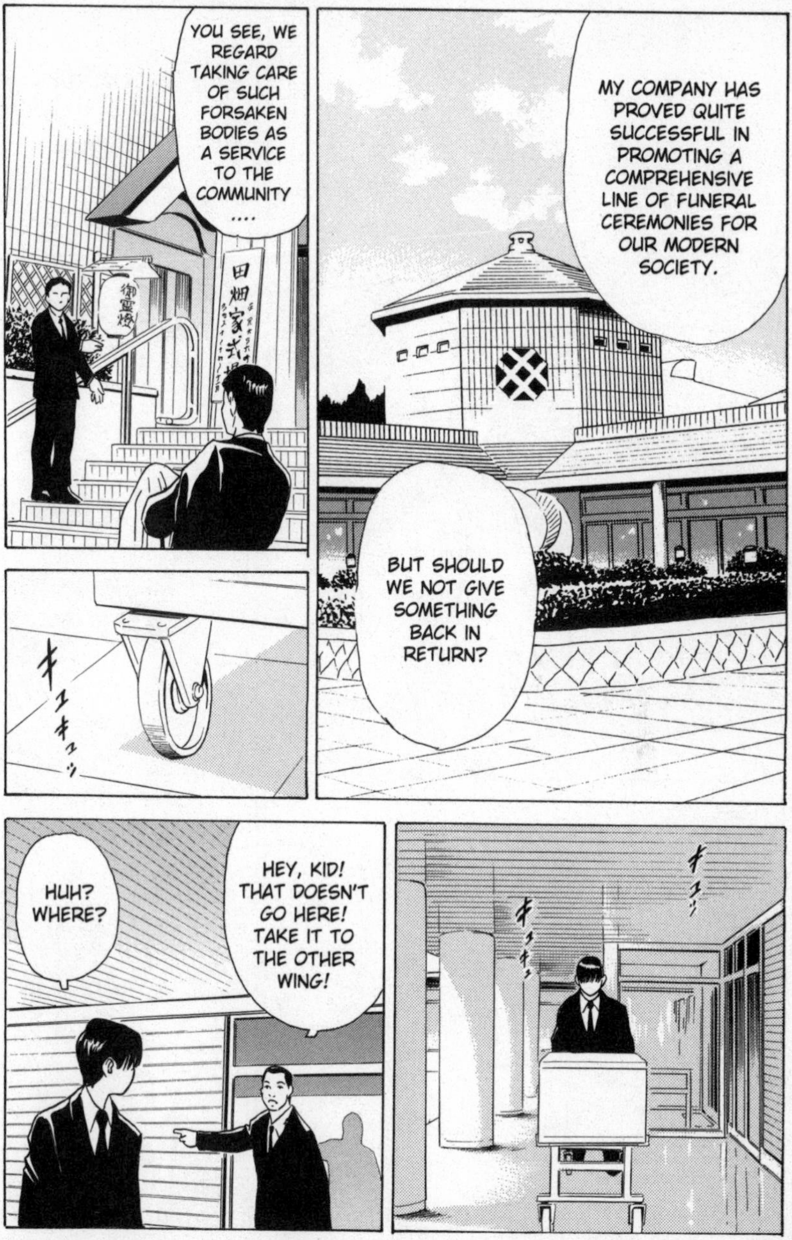
MY COMPANY HAS PROVED QUITE SUCCESSFUL IN PROMOTING A COMPREHENSIVE LINE OF FUNERAL CEREMONIES FOR OUR MODERN SOCIETY.
BUT SHOULD WE NOT GIVE SOMETHING BACK IN RETURN?
YOU SEE, WE REGARD TAKING CARE OF SUCH FORSAKEN BODIES AS A SERVICE TO THE COMMUNITY ....
田畑家式場
御霊燈
キュキュッ
キュッ
キュキュ
HEY, KID! THAT DOESN'T GO HERE! TAKE IT TO THE OTHER WING!
HUH? WHERE?

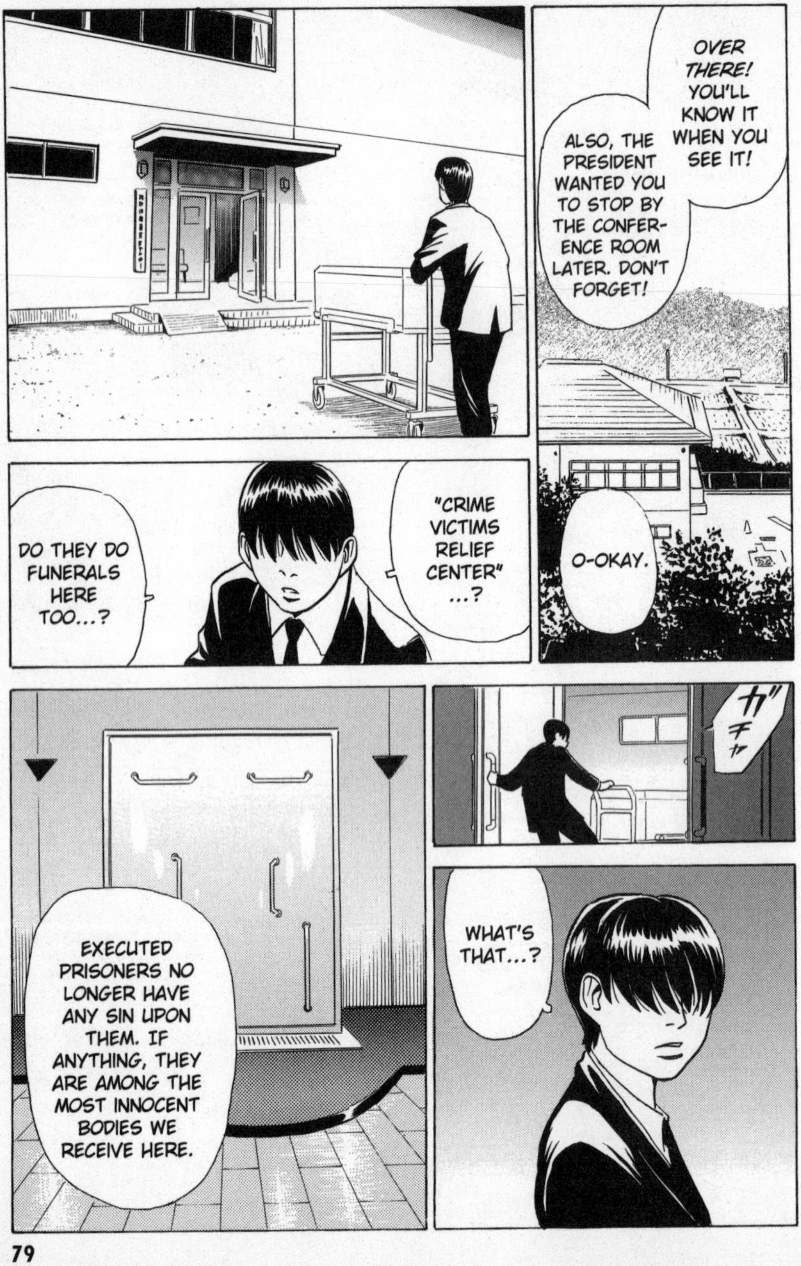
OVER THERE! YOU'LL KNOW IT WHEN YOU SEE IT!
ALSO, THE PRESIDENT WANTED YOU TO STOP BY THE CONFERENCE ROOM LATER. DON'T FORGET!
O-OKAY.
"CRIME VICTIMS RELIEF CENTER" ...?
DO THEY DO FUNERALS HERE TOO...?
ガチャ
WHAT'S THAT...?
EXECUTED PRISONERS NO LONGER HAVE ANY SIN UPON THEM. IF ANYTHING, THEY ARE AMONG THE MOST INNOCENT BODIES WE RECEIVE HERE.

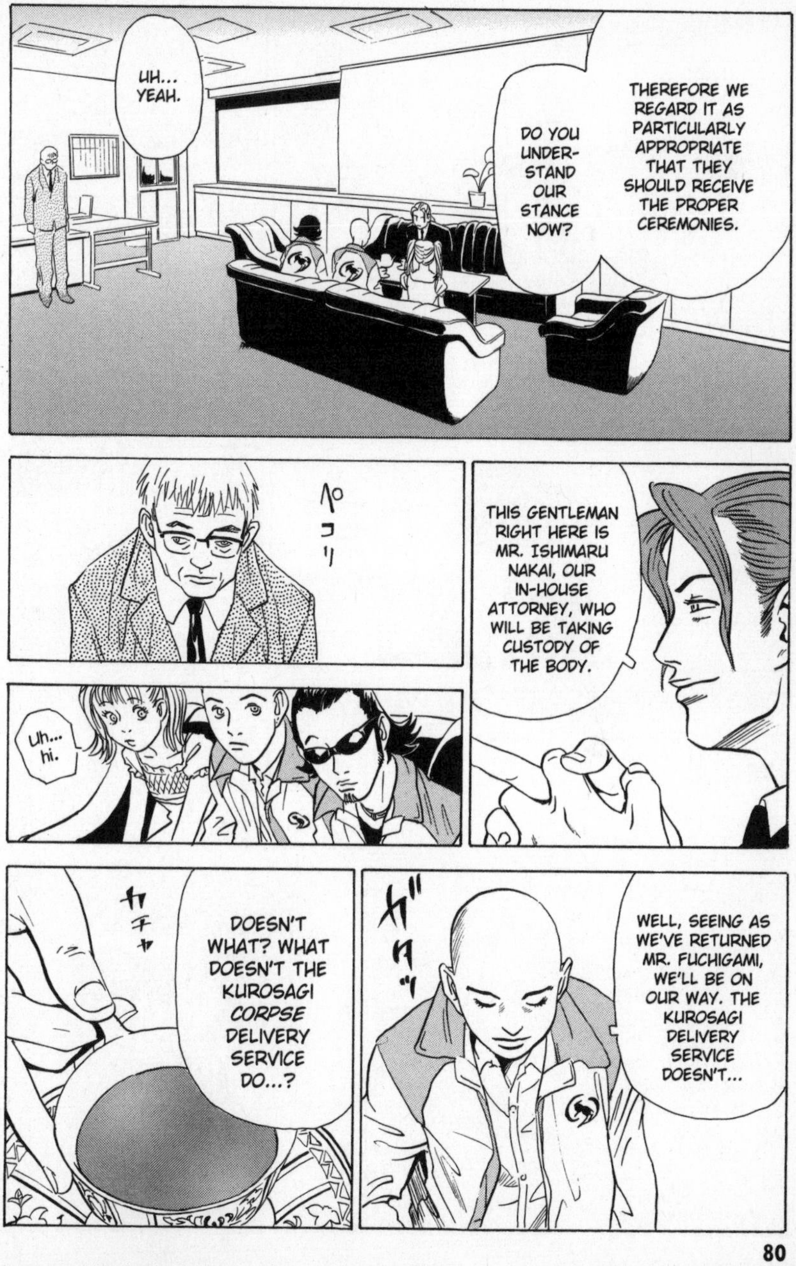
THEREFORE WE REGARD IT AS PARTICULARLY APPROPRIATE THAT THEY SHOULD RECEIVE THE PROPER CEREMONIES.
DO YOU UNDER-STAND OUR STANCE NOW?
UH... YEAH.
THIS GENTLEMAN RIGHT HERE IS MR. ISHIMARU NAKAI, OUR IN-HOUSE ATTORNEY, WHO WILL BE TAKING CUSTODY OF THE BODY.
ペコリ
Uh... hi.
WELL, SEEING AS WE'VE RETURNED MR. FUCHIGAMI, WE'LL BE ON OUR WAY. THE KUROSAGI DELIVERY SERVICE DOESN'T...
ガタッ
DOESN'T WHAT? WHAT DOESN'T THE KUROSAGI *CORPSE* DELIVERY SERVICE DO...?
カチャ

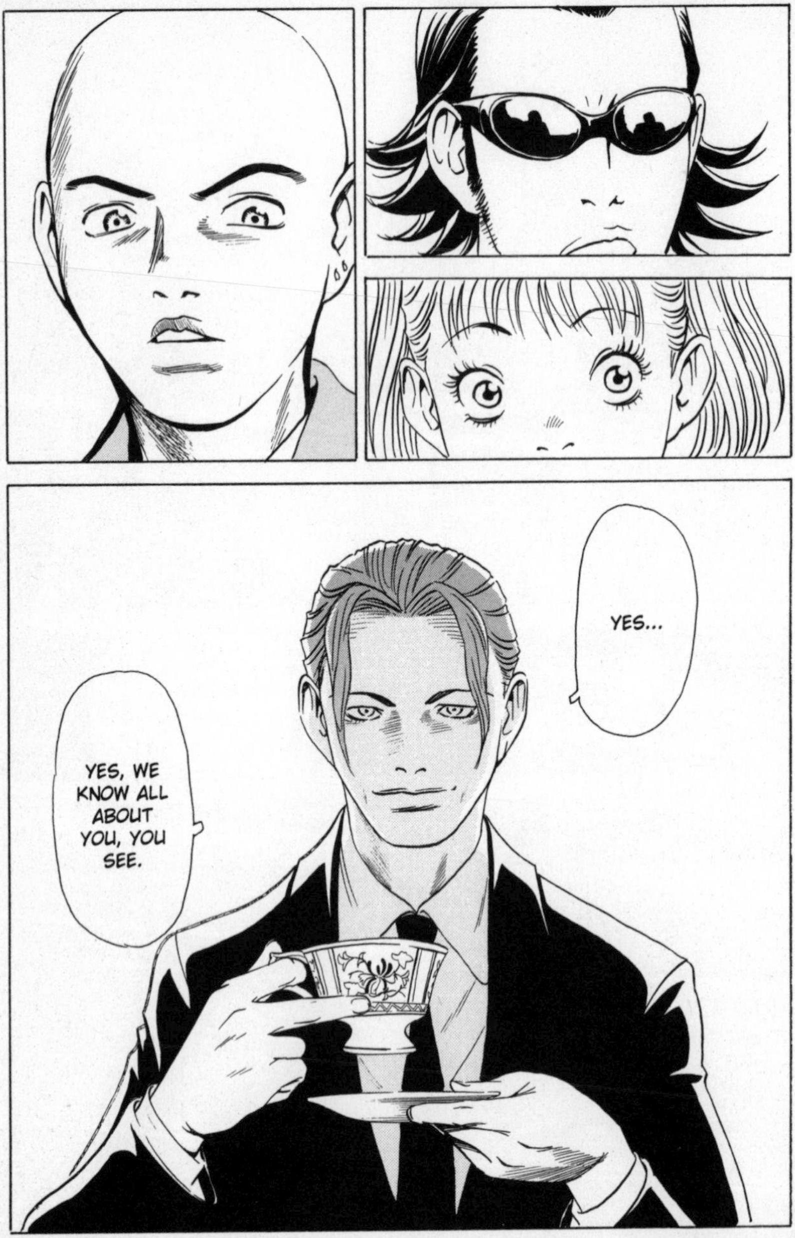
YES...
YES, WE KNOW ALL ABOUT YOU, YOU SEE.

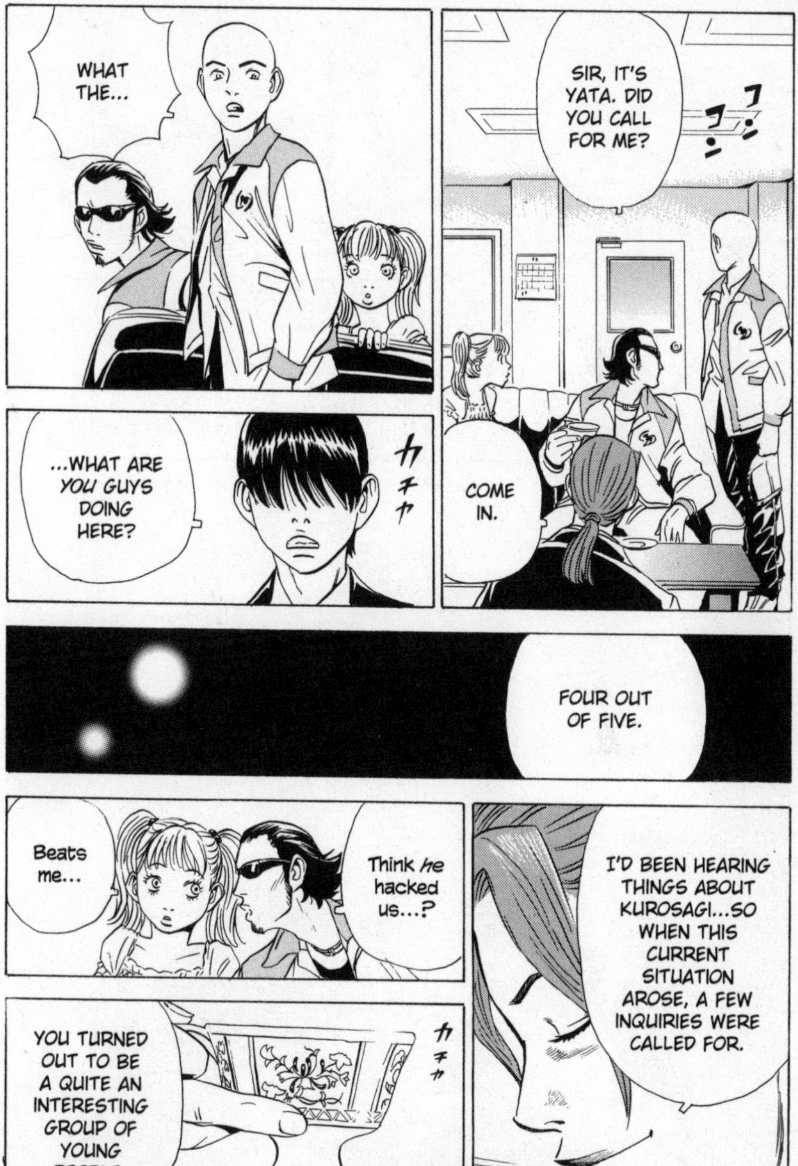

SIR, IT'S YATA. DID YOU CALL FOR ME?
コン コン
COME IN.
WHAT THE...
...WHAT ARE *YOU* GUYS DOING HERE?
カチャ
FOUR OUT OF FIVE.
I'D BEEN HEARING THINGS ABOUT KUROSAGI...SO WHEN THIS CURRENT SITUATION AROSE, A FEW INQUIRIES WERE CALLED FOR.
Think *he* hacked us...?
Beats me...
カチャ
YOU TURNED OUT TO BE A QUITE AN INTERESTING GROUP OF YOUNG PEOPLE.

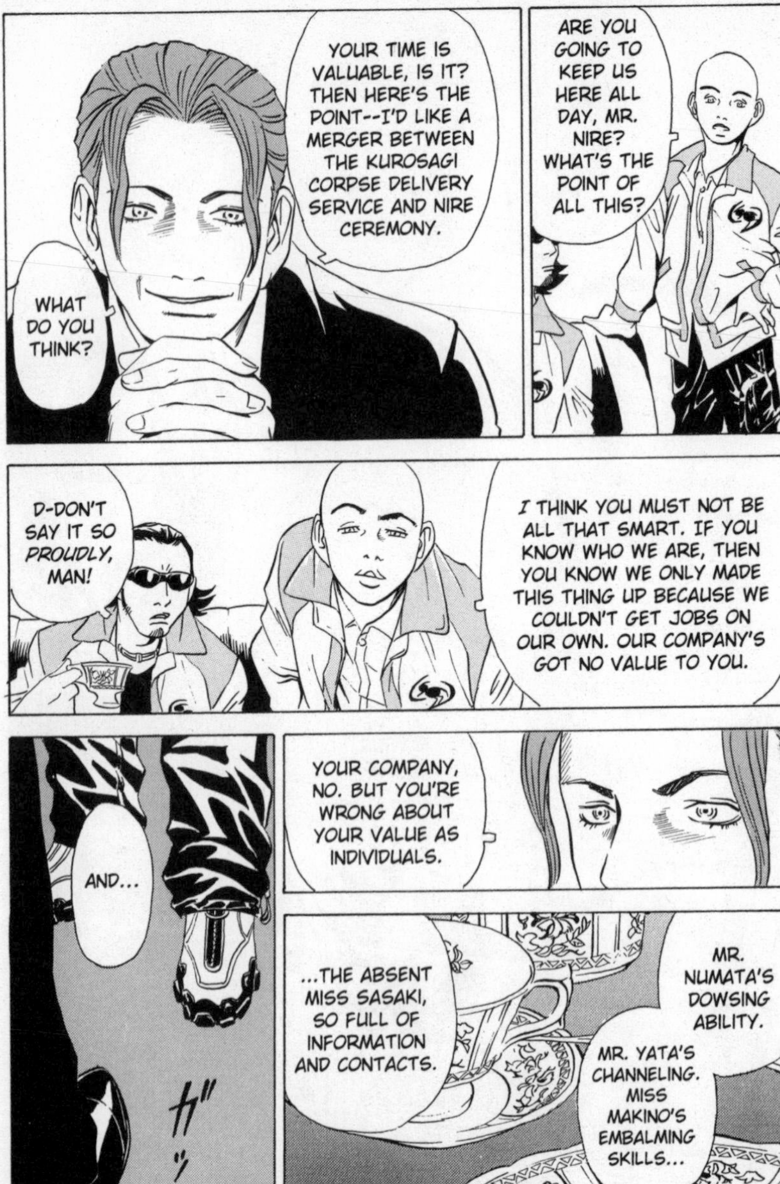
ARE YOU GOING TO KEEP US HERE ALL DAY, MR. NIRE? WHAT'S THE POINT OF ALL THIS?
YOUR TIME IS VALUABLE, IS IT? THEN HERE'S THE POINT--I'D LIKE A MERGER BETWEEN THE KUROSAGI CORPSE DELIVERY SERVICE AND NIRE CEREMONY.
WHAT DO YOU THINK?
I THINK YOU MUST NOT BE ALL THAT SMART. IF YOU KNOW WHO WE ARE, THEN YOU KNOW WE ONLY MADE THIS THING UP BECAUSE WE COULDN'T GET JOBS ON OUR OWN. OUR COMPANY'S GOT NO VALUE TO YOU.
D-DON'T SAY IT SO *PROUDLY*, MAN!
YOUR COMPANY, NO. BUT YOU'RE WRONG ABOUT YOUR VALUE AS INDIVIDUALS.
MR. NUMATA'S DOWSING ABILITY.
MR. YATA'S CHANNELING. MISS MAKINO'S EMBALMING SKILLS...
...THE ABSENT MISS SASAKI, SO FULL OF INFORMATION AND CONTACTS.
AND...
ガッ

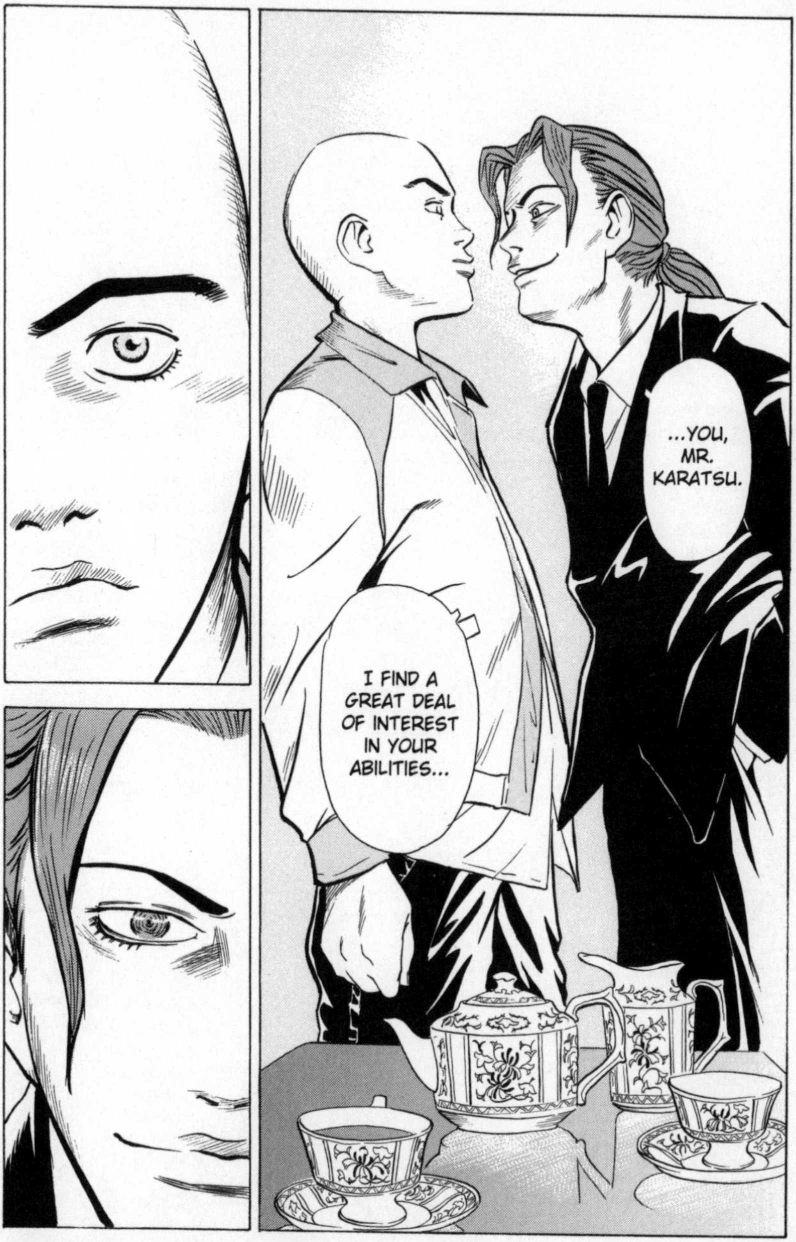
...YOU, MR. KARATSU.
I FIND A GREAT DEAL OF INTEREST IN YOUR ABILITIES...

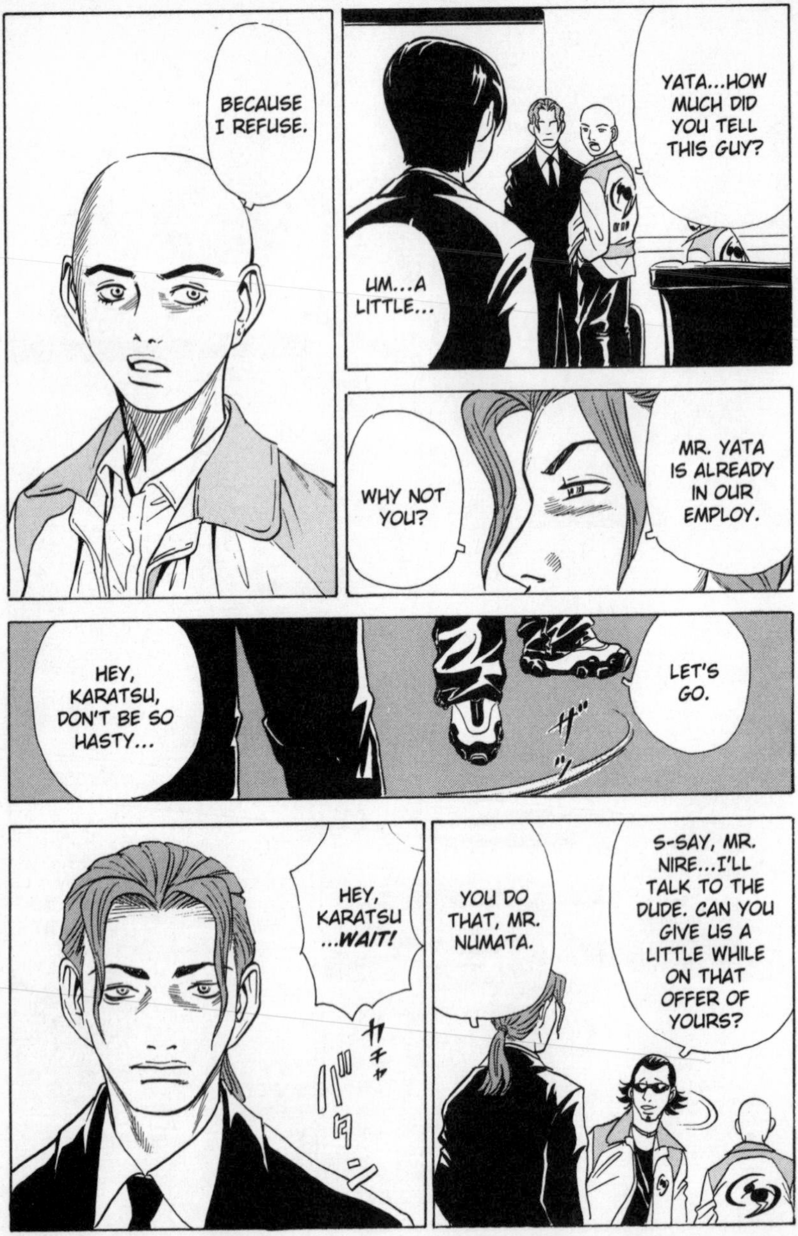
YATA...HOW MUCH DID YOU TELL THIS GUY?
UM...A LITTLE...
MR. YATA IS ALREADY IN OUR EMPLOY.
WHY NOT YOU?
BECAUSE I REFUSE.
LET'S GO.
HEY, KARATSU, DON'T BE SO HASTY...
S-SAY, MR. NIRE...I'LL TALK TO THE DUDE. CAN YOU GIVE US A LITTLE WHILE ON THAT OFFER OF YOURS?
YOU DO THAT, MR. NUMATA.
HEY, KARATSU ...*WAIT!*
カチャ
バタン

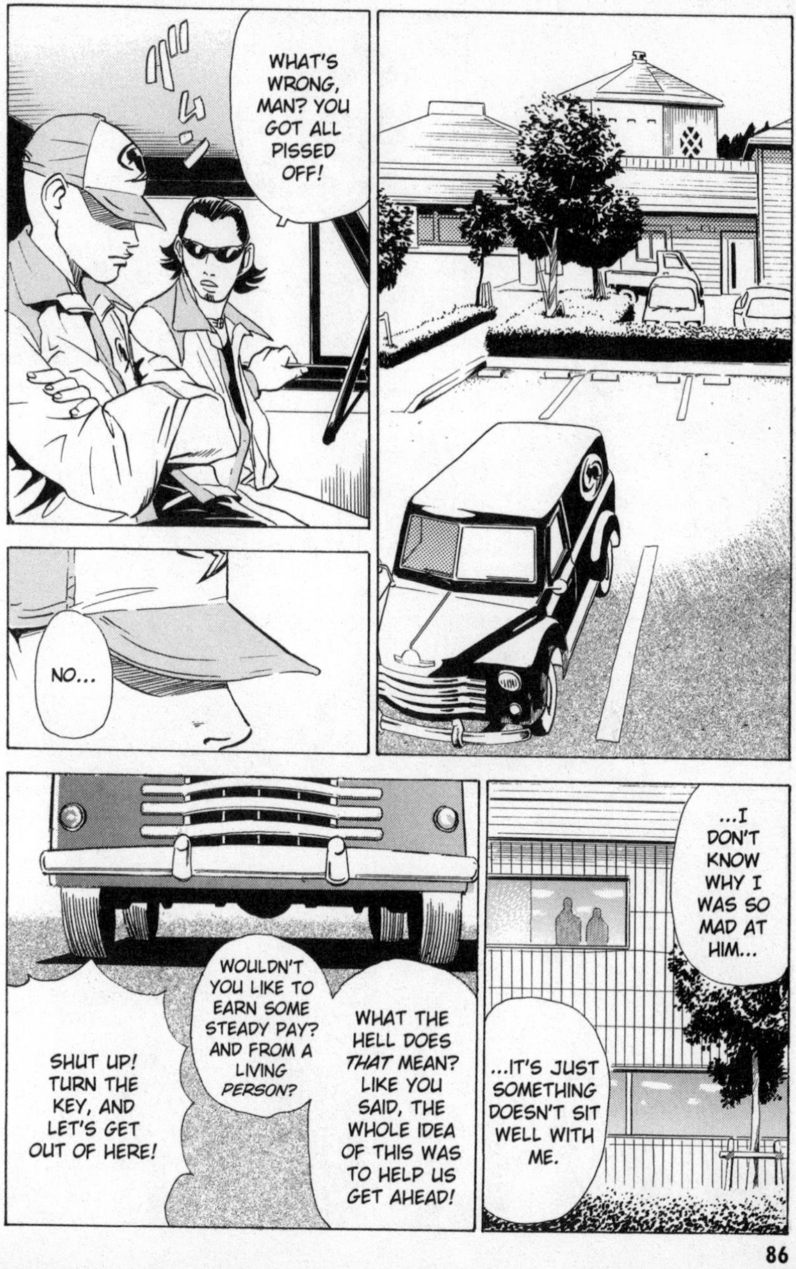
WHAT'S WRONG, MAN? YOU GOT ALL PISSED OFF!
NO...
...I DON'T KNOW WHY I WAS SO MAD AT HIM...
...IT'S JUST SOMETHING DOESN'T SIT WELL WITH ME.
WOULDN'T YOU LIKE TO EARN SOME STEADY PAY? AND FROM A LIVING *PERSON*?
WHAT THE HELL DOES *THAT* MEAN? LIKE YOU SAID, THE WHOLE IDEA OF THIS WAS TO HELP US GET AHEAD!
SHUT UP! TURN THE KEY, AND LET'S GET OUT OF HERE!

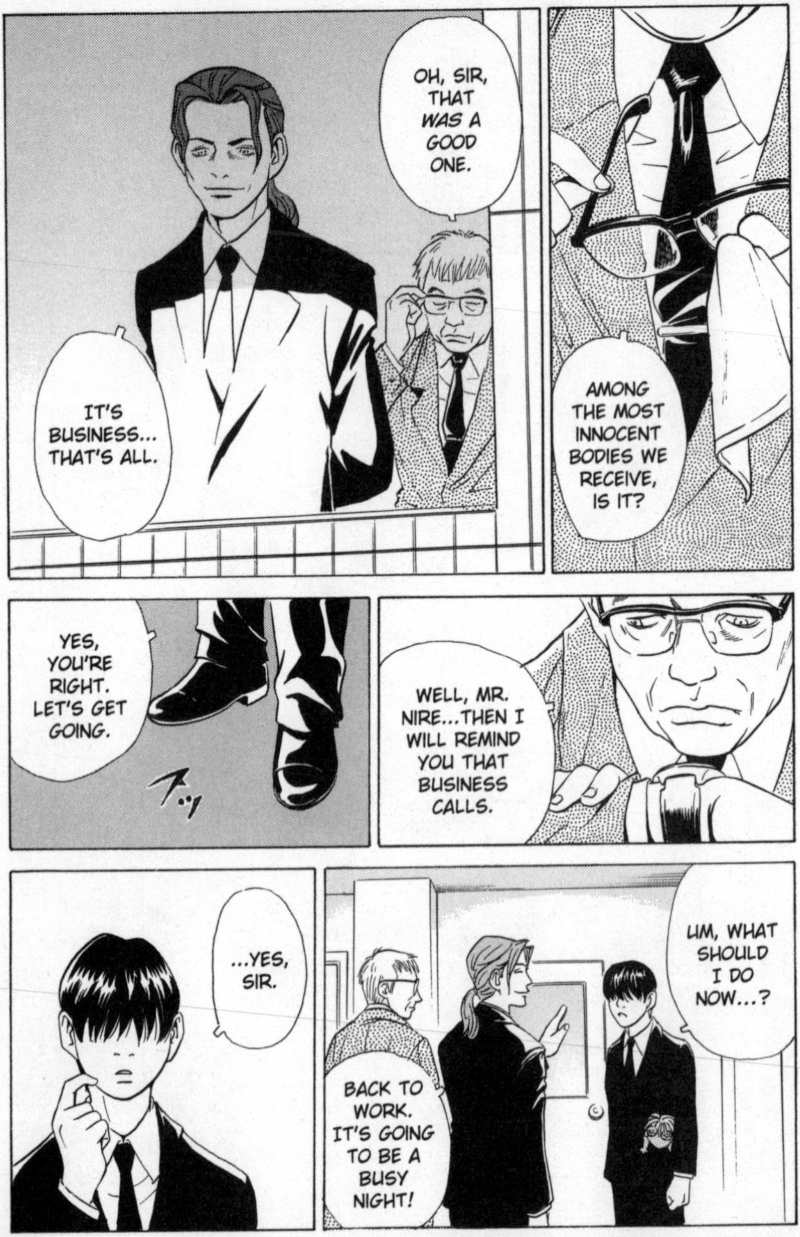
AMONG THE MOST INNOCENT BODIES WE RECEIVE, IS IT?
OH, SIR, THAT WAS A GOOD ONE.
IT'S BUSINESS... THAT'S ALL.
WELL, MR. NIRE...THEN I WILL REMIND YOU THAT BUSINESS CALLS.
YES, YOU'RE RIGHT. LET'S GET GOING.
スッ
UM, WHAT SHOULD I DO NOW...?
BACK TO WORK. IT'S GOING TO BE A BUSY NIGHT!
...YES, SIR.

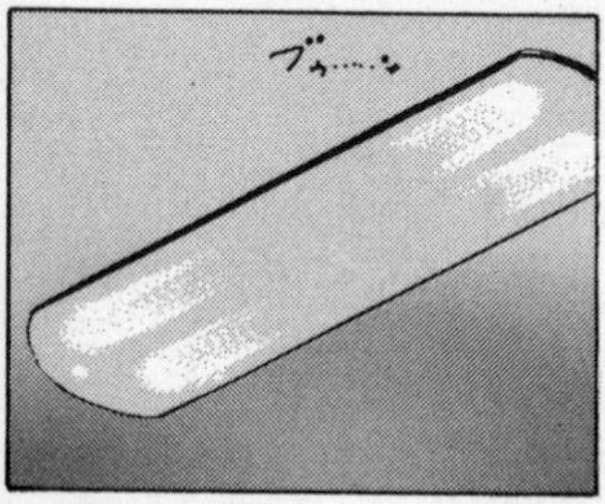
ブゥ…ン
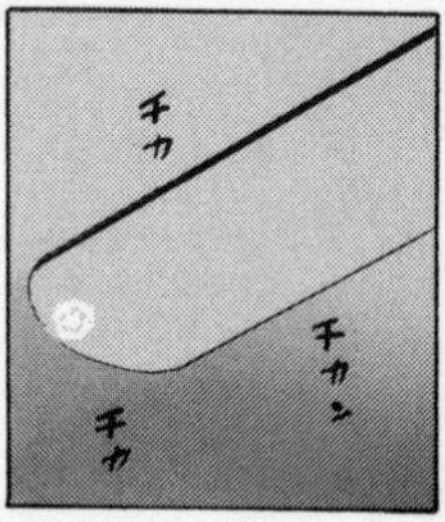
チカ
チカン
チカ
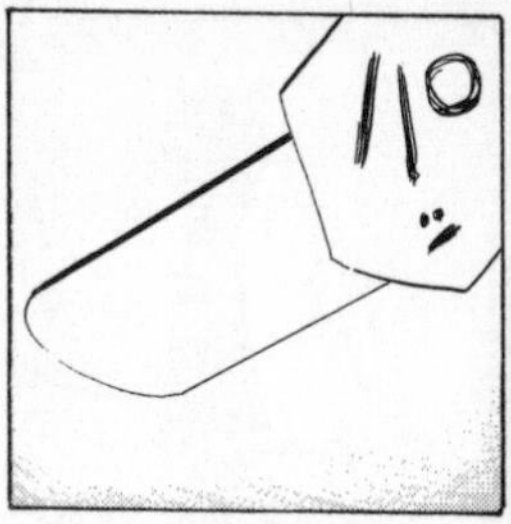
パッ
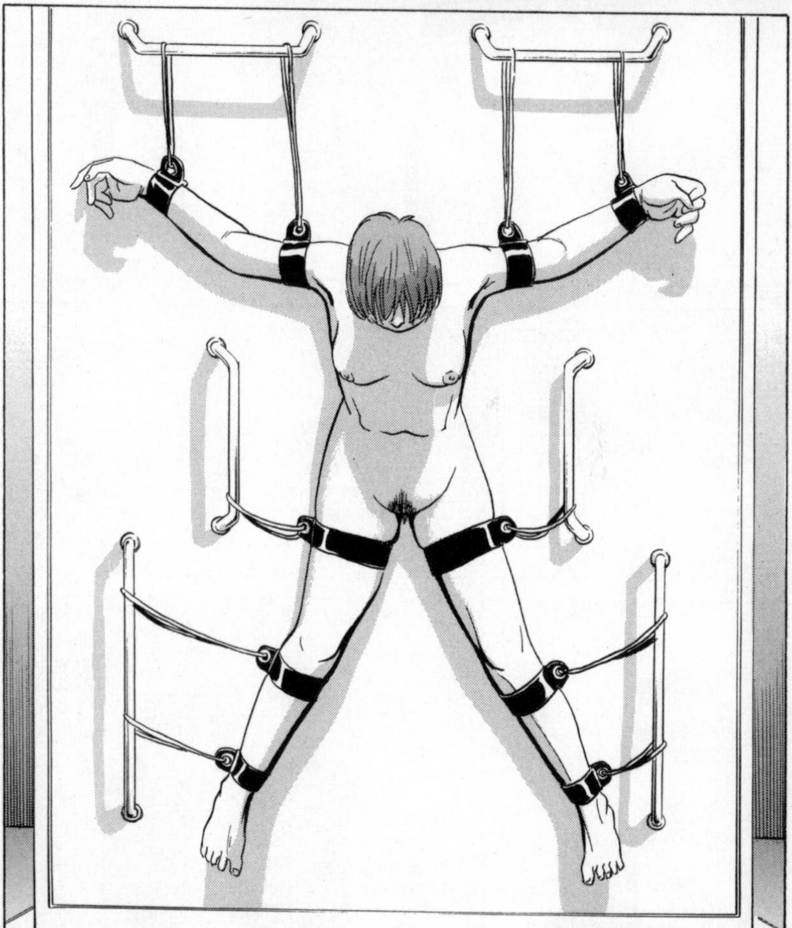

コッ

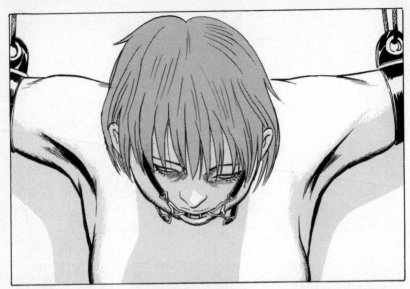

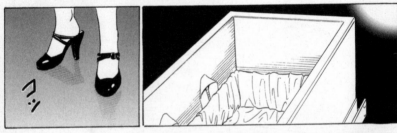

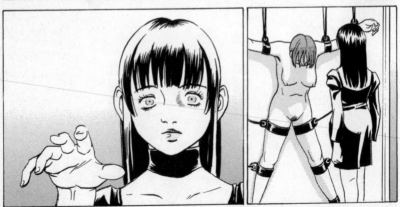

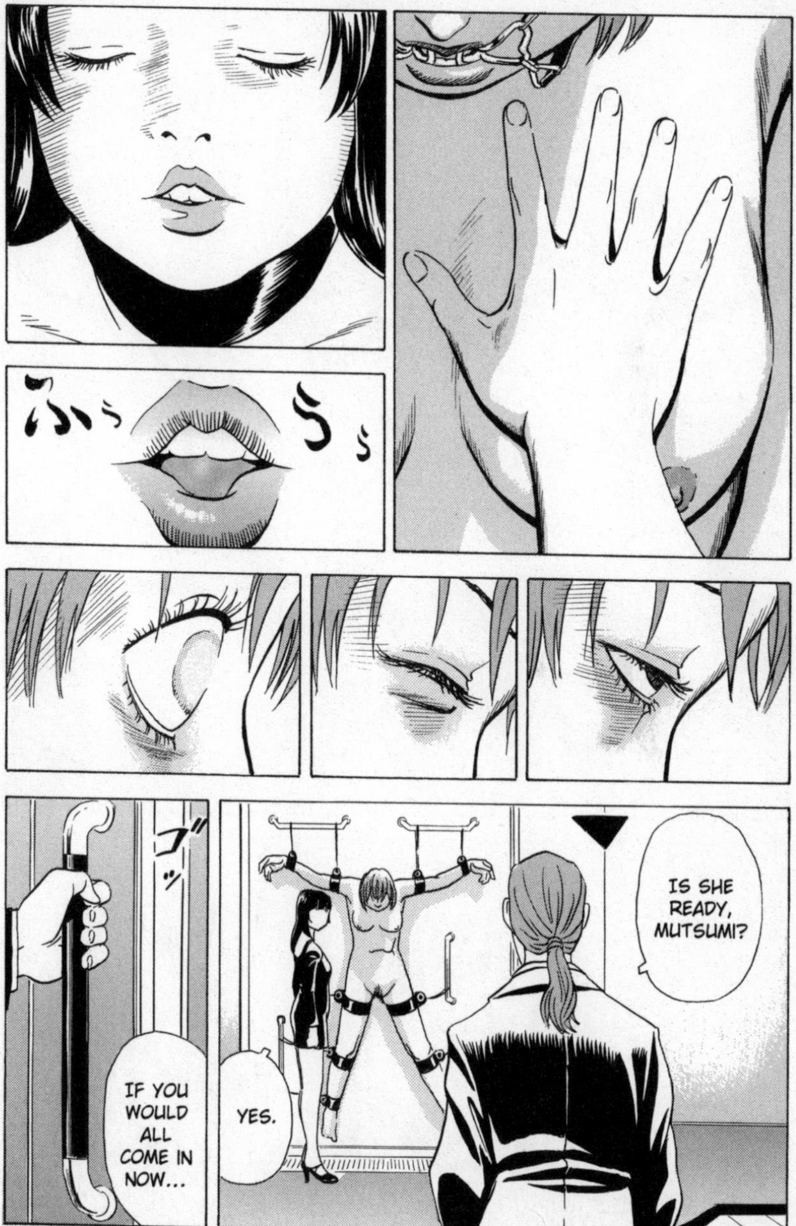
IS SHE READY, MUTSUMI?
YES.
ゴッ
IF YOU WOULD ALL COME IN NOW...

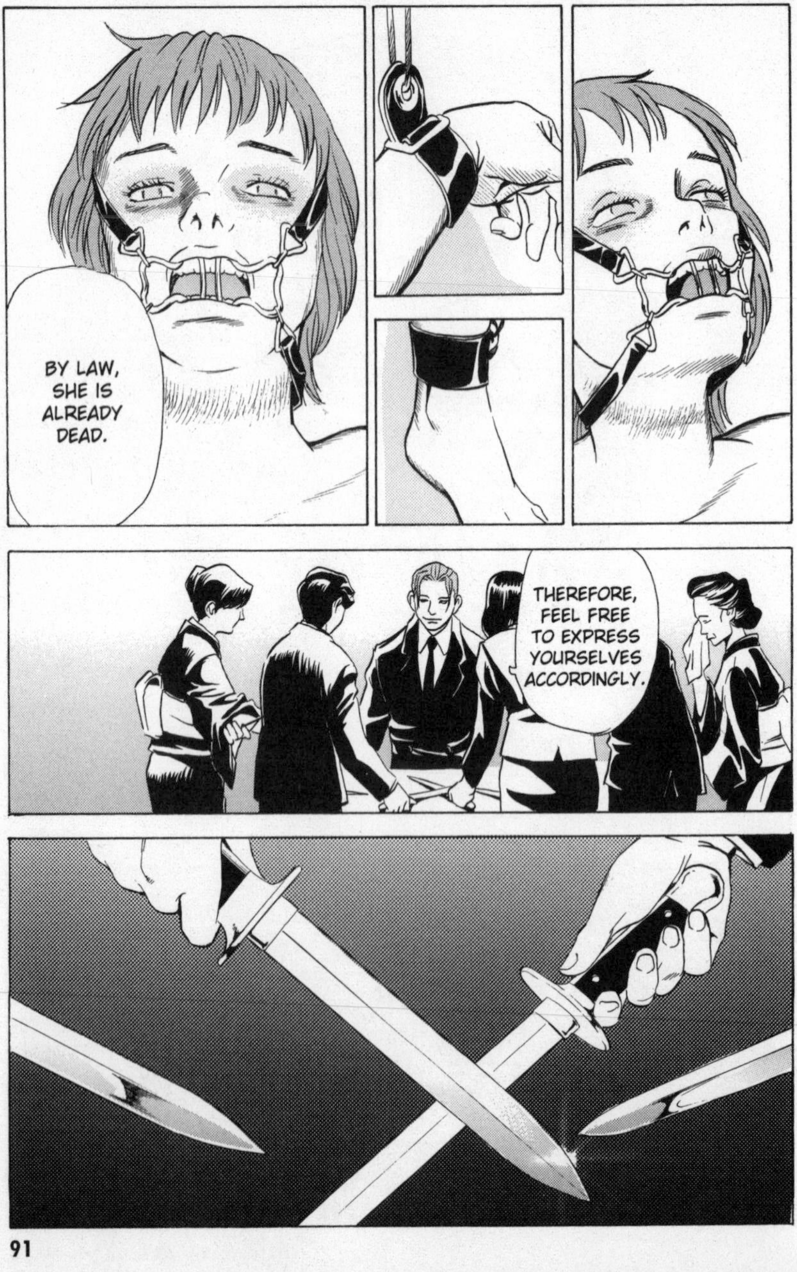
BY LAW, SHE IS ALREADY DEAD.
THEREFORE, FEEL FREE TO EXPRESS YOURSELVES ACCORDINGLY.

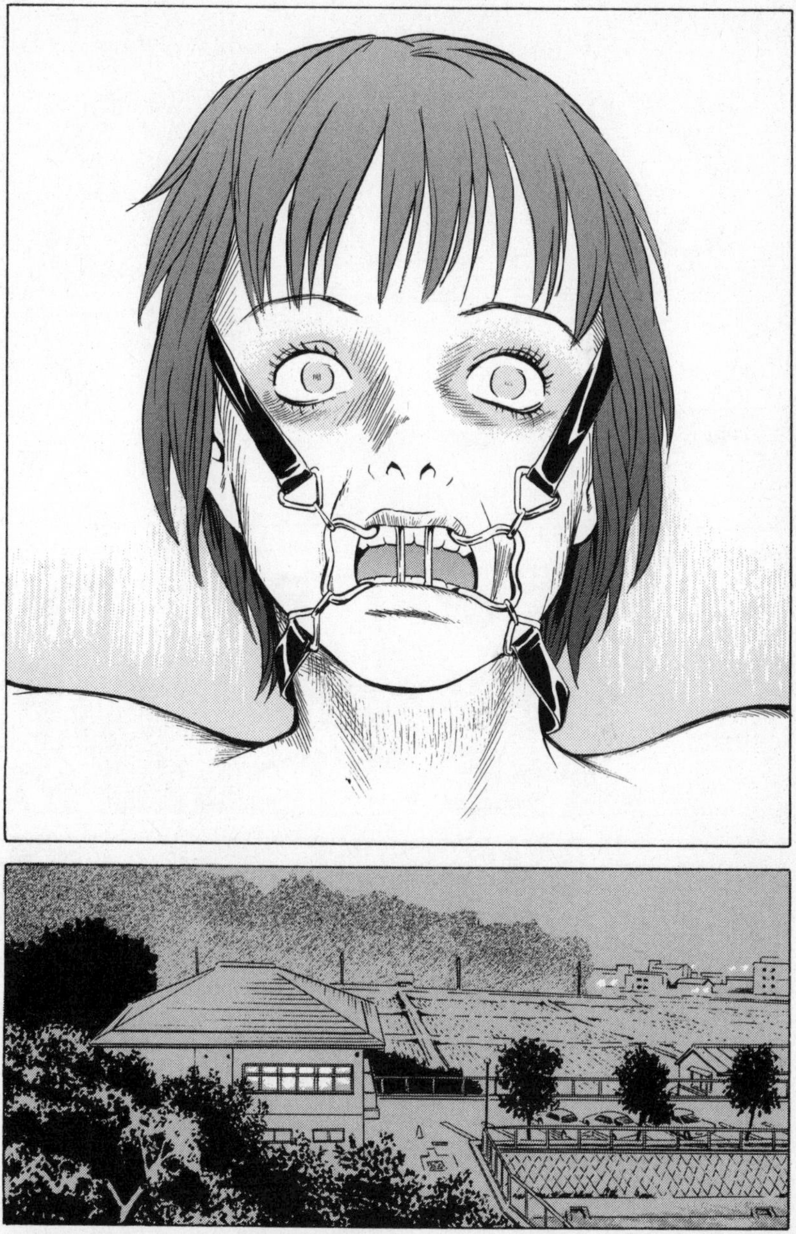

3rd delivery: watch out for that girl—the end

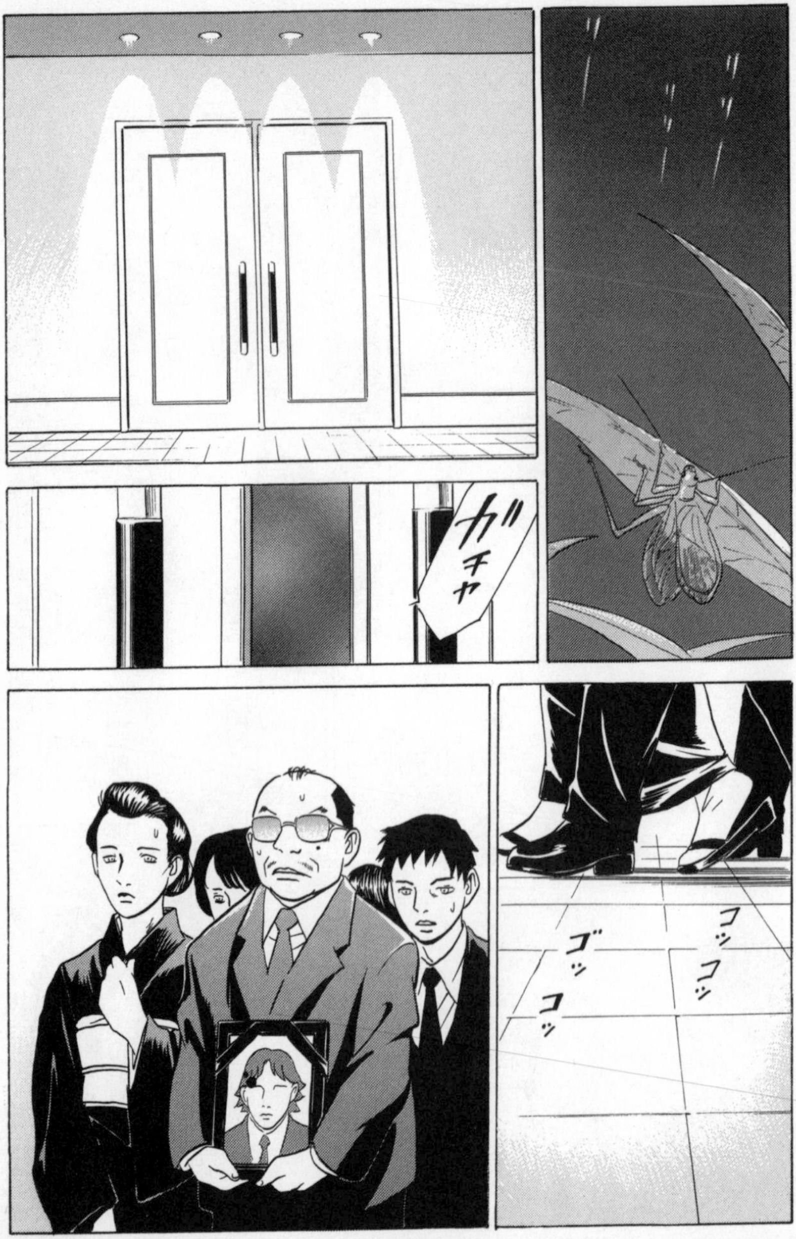
ガチャ
コッコッ
ゴッ
コッ

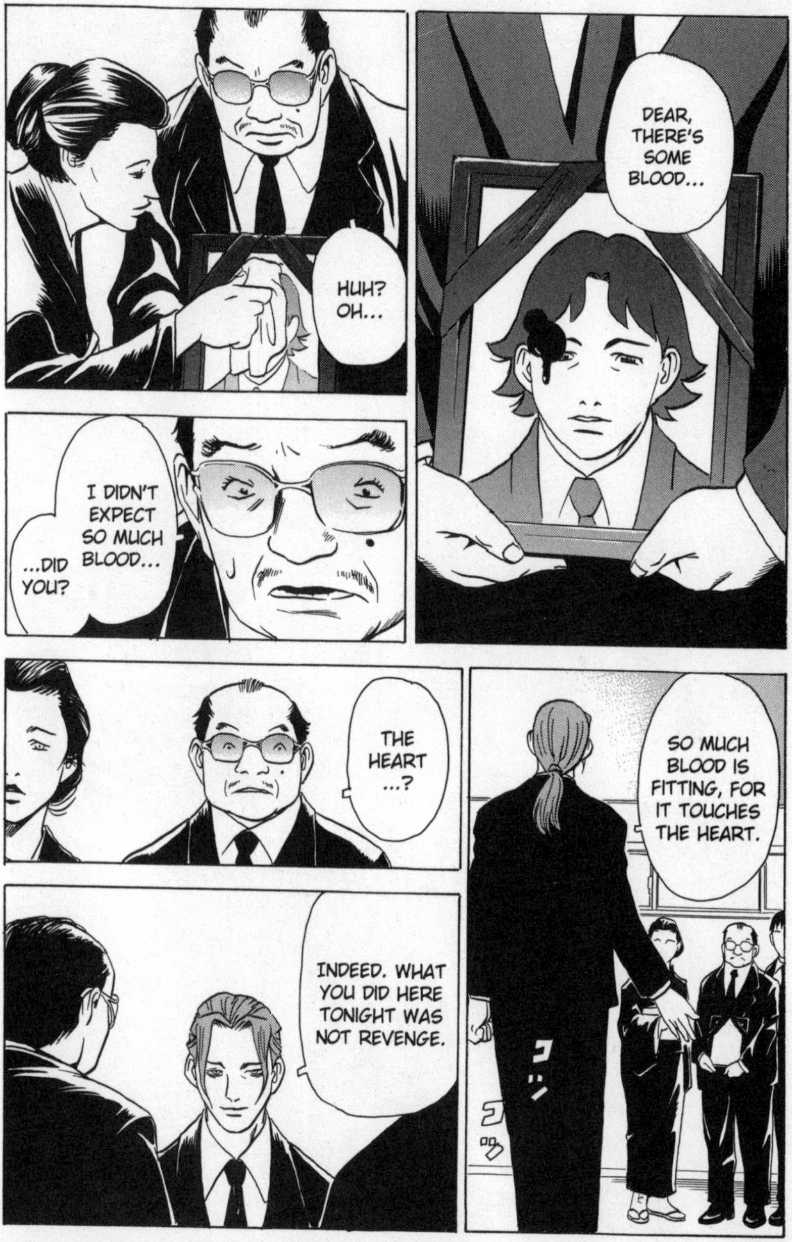
DEAR, THERE'S SOME BLOOD...
HUH? OH...
I DIDN'T EXPECT SO MUCH BLOOD...
...DID YOU?
SO MUCH BLOOD IS FITTING, FOR IT TOUCHES THE HEART.
THE HEART ...?
INDEED. WHAT YOU DID HERE TONIGHT WAS NOT REVENGE.

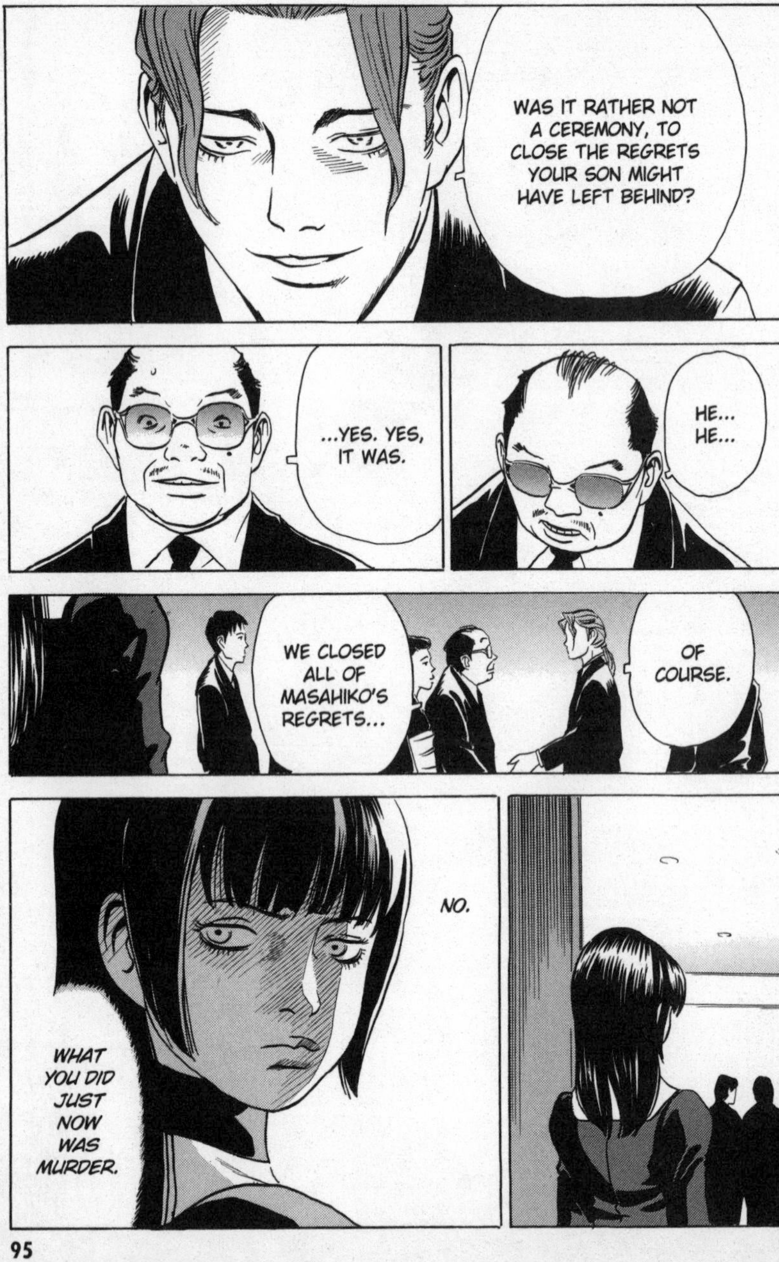
WAS IT RATHER NOT A CEREMONY, TO CLOSE THE REGRETS YOUR SON MIGHT HAVE LEFT BEHIND?
HE... HE...
...YES. YES, IT WAS.
OF COURSE.
WE CLOSED ALL OF MASAHIKO'S REGRETS...
NO.
WHAT YOU DID JUST NOW WAS MURDER.

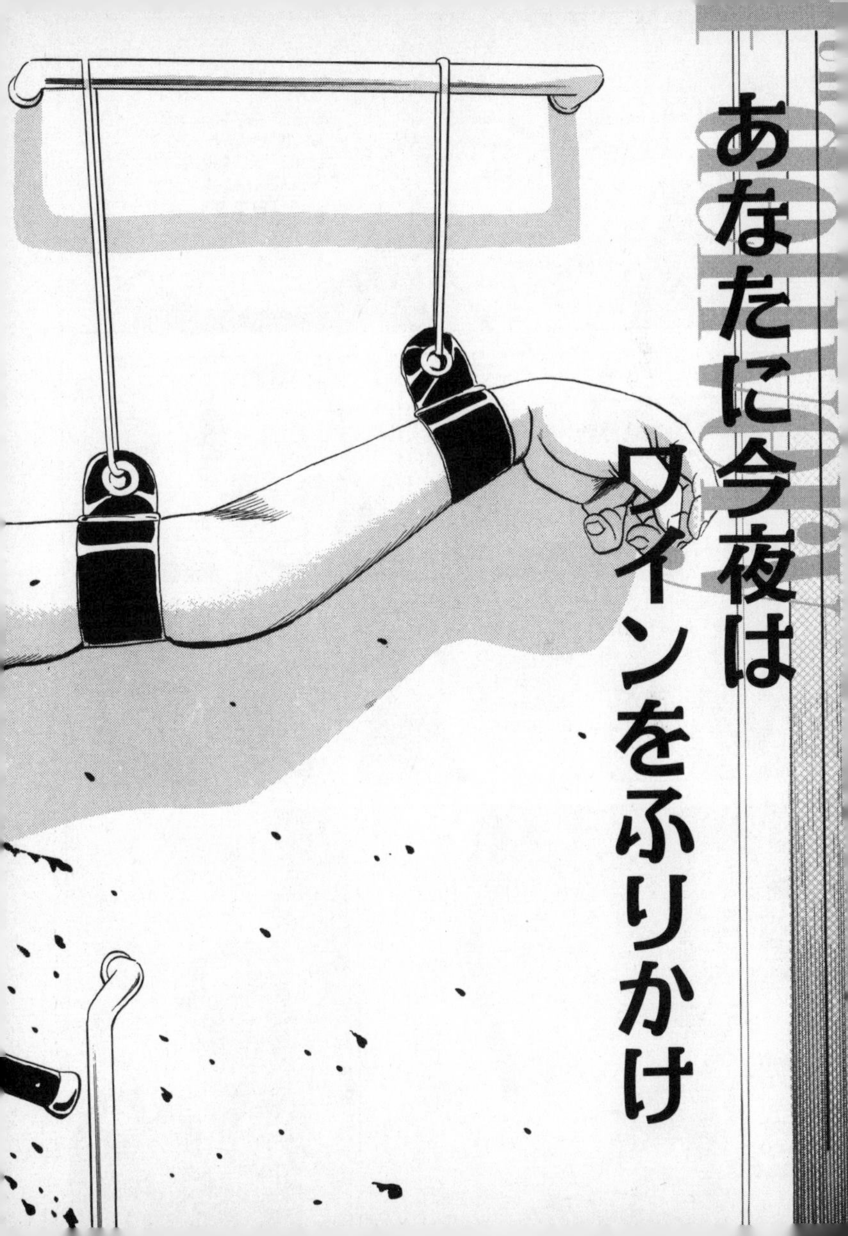
あなたに今夜は
ワインをふりかけ

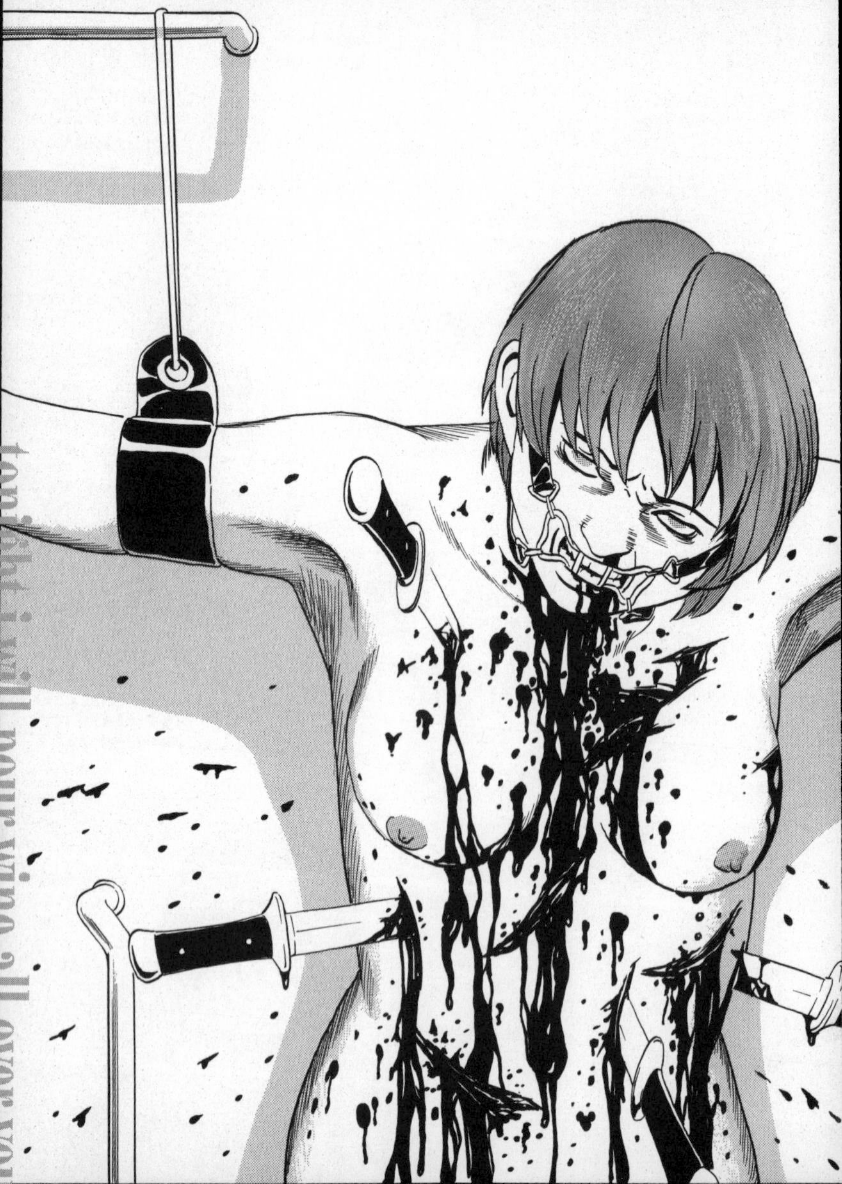
tonight i will pour wine all over you

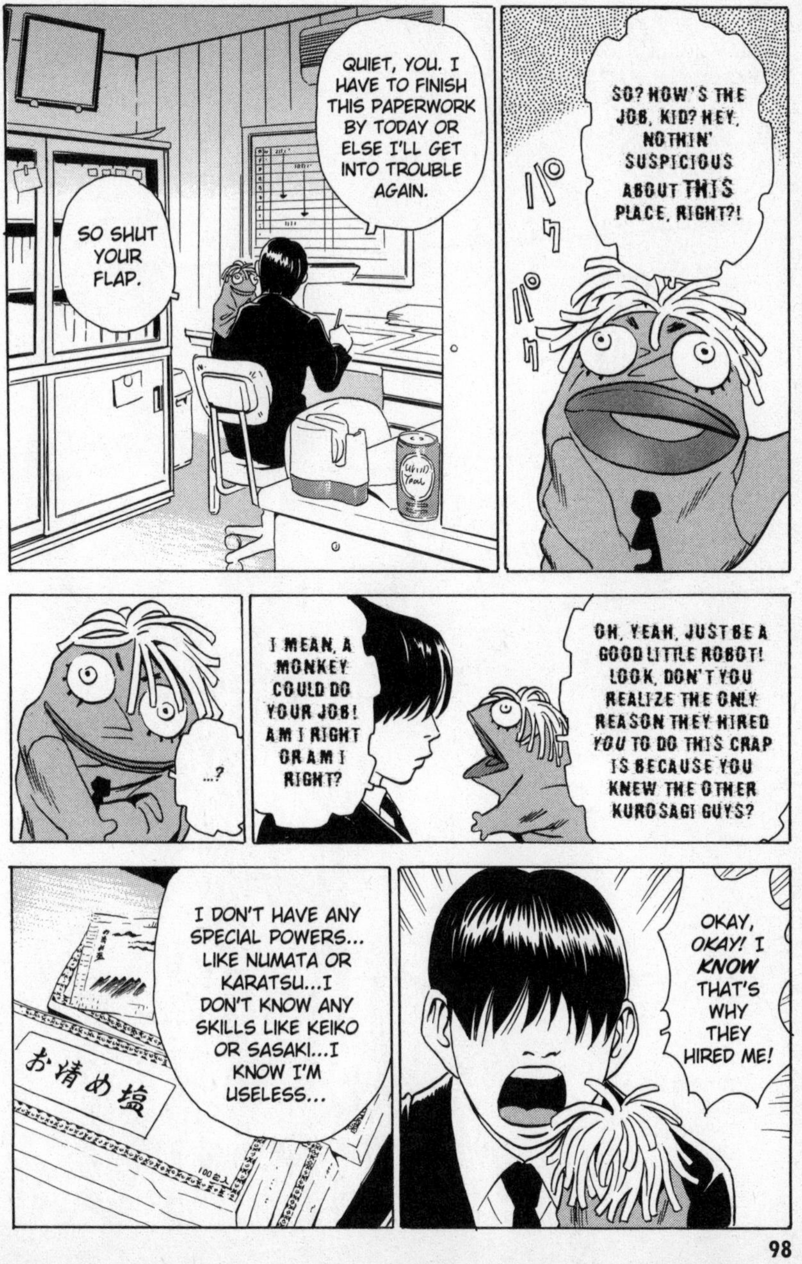
SO? HOW'S THE JOB, KID? HEY, NOTHIN' SUSPICIOUS ABOUT THIS PLACE, RIGHT?!
パクパク
QUIET, YOU. I HAVE TO FINISH THIS PAPERWORK BY TODAY OR ELSE I'LL GET INTO TROUBLE AGAIN.
SO SHUT YOUR FLAP.
OH, YEAH, JUST BE A GOOD LITTLE ROBOT! LOOK, DON'T YOU REALIZE THE ONLY REASON THEY HIRED *YOU* TO DO THIS CRAP IS BECAUSE YOU KNEW THE OTHER KUROSAGI GUYS?
I MEAN, A MONKEY COULD DO YOUR JOB! AM I RIGHT OR AM I RIGHT?
...?
OKAY, *OKAY!* I ***KNOW*** THAT'S WHY THEY HIRED ME!
I DON'T HAVE ANY SPECIAL POWERS... LIKE NUMATA OR KARATSU...I DON'T KNOW ANY SKILLS LIKE KEIKO OR SASAKI...I KNOW I'M USELESS...
お清め塩

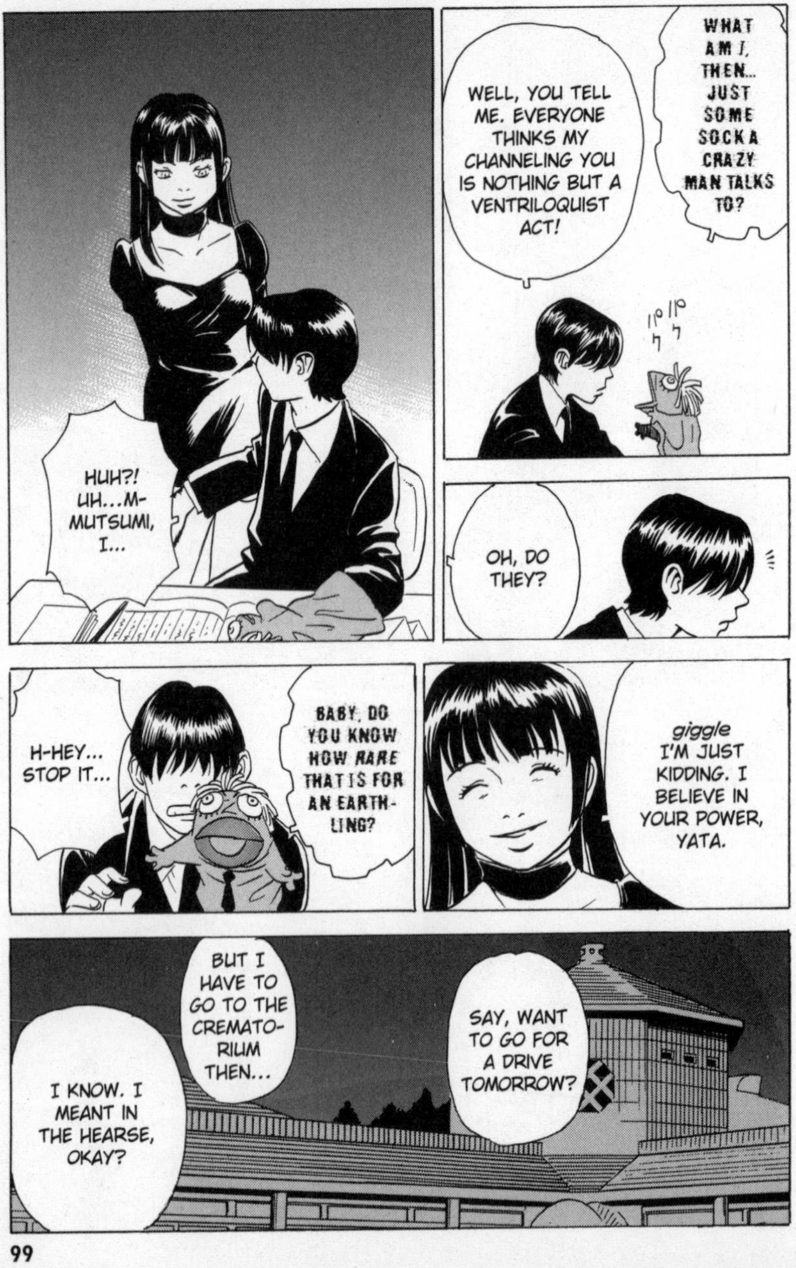
WHAT AM I, THEN... JUST SOME SOCK A CRAZY MAN TALKS TO?
WELL, YOU TELL ME. EVERYONE THINKS MY CHANNELING YOU IS NOTHING BUT A VENTRILOQUIST ACT!
OH, DO THEY?
HUH?! UH...M-MUTSUMI, I...
giggle I'M JUST KIDDING. I BELIEVE IN YOUR POWER, YATA.
BABY, DO YOU KNOW HOW RARE THAT IS FOR AN EARTH-LING?
H-HEY... STOP IT...
SAY, WANT TO GO FOR A DRIVE TOMORROW?
BUT I HAVE TO GO TO THE CREMATO-RIUM THEN...
I KNOW. I MEANT IN THE HEARSE, OKAY?

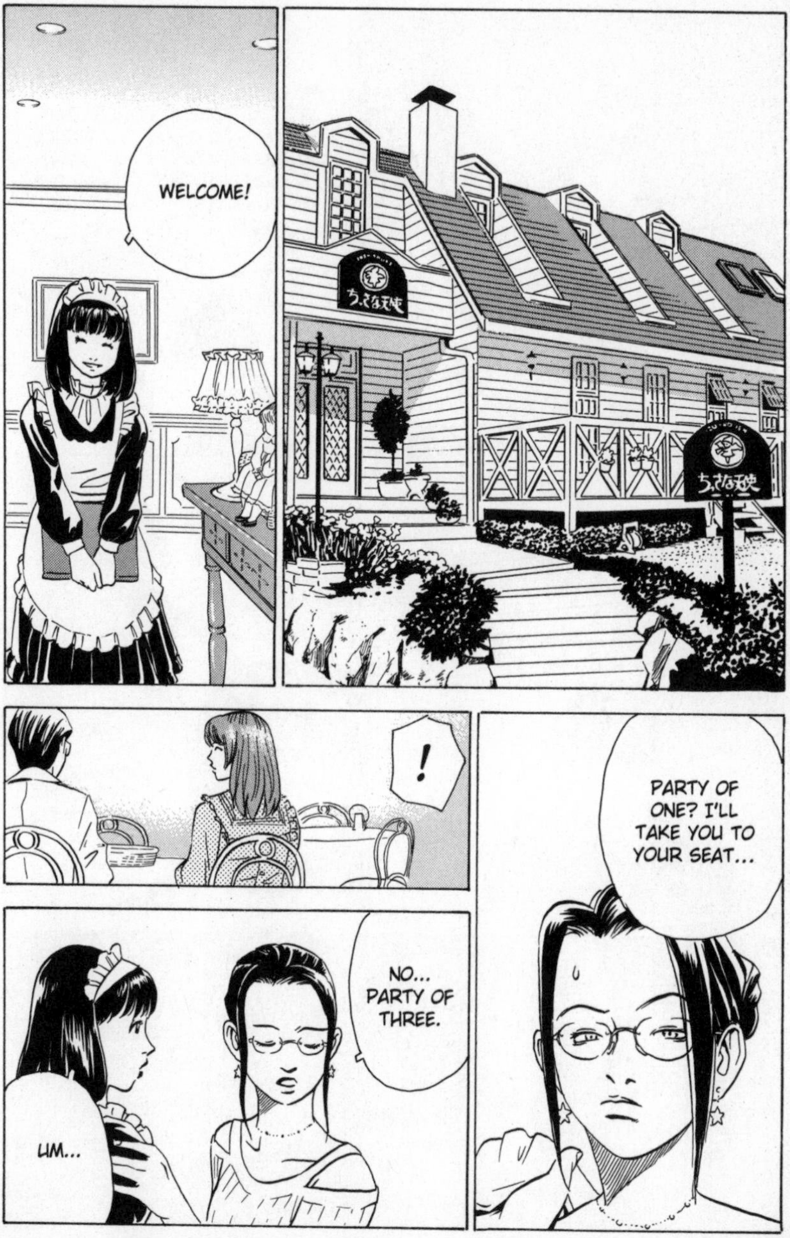
WELCOME!
PARTY OF ONE? I'LL TAKE YOU TO YOUR SEAT...
!
NO... PARTY OF THREE.
UM...

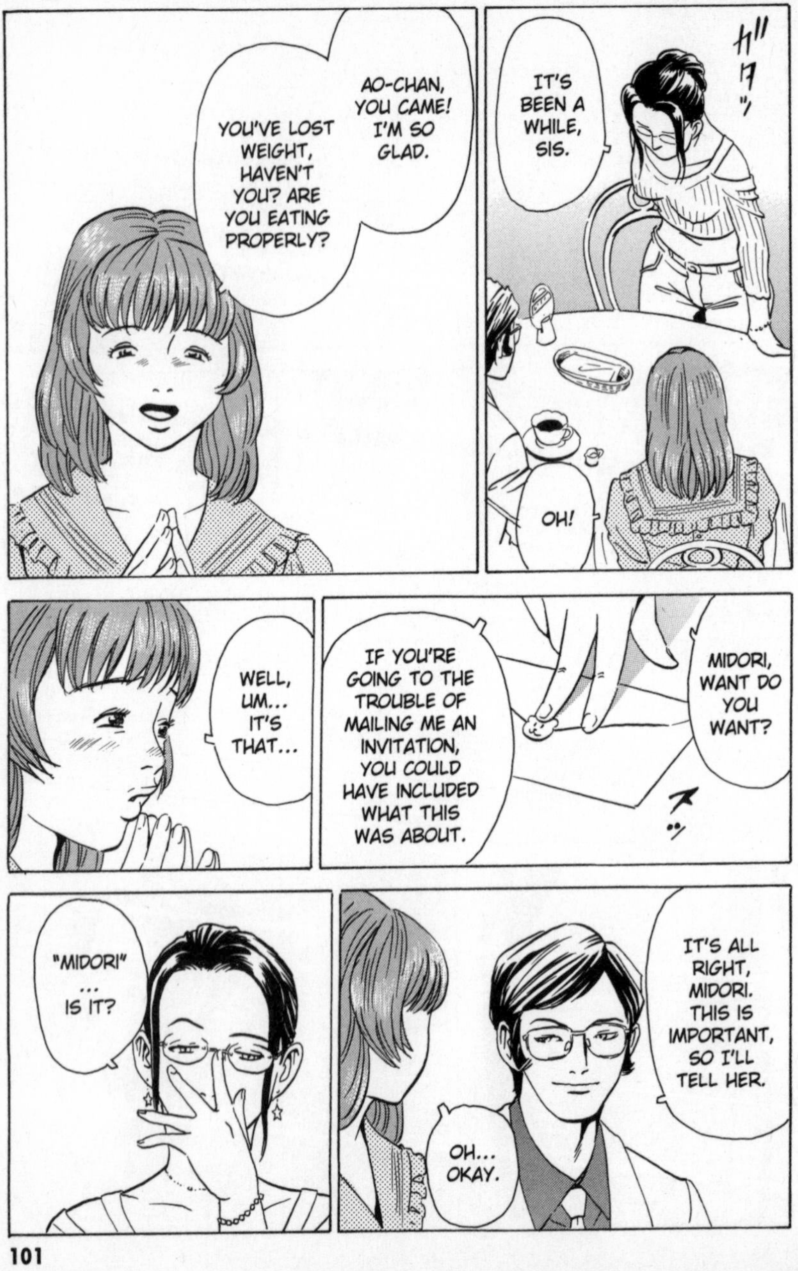
ガタッ
IT'S BEEN A WHILE, SIS.
OH!
AO-CHAN, YOU CAME! I'M SO GLAD.
YOU'VE LOST WEIGHT, HAVEN'T YOU? ARE YOU EATING PROPERLY?
MIDORI, WANT DO YOU WANT?
スッ
IF YOU'RE GOING TO THE TROUBLE OF MAILING ME AN INVITATION, YOU COULD HAVE INCLUDED WHAT THIS WAS ABOUT.
WELL, UM... IT'S THAT...
IT'S ALL RIGHT, MIDORI. THIS IS IMPORTANT, SO I'LL TELL HER.
OH... OKAY.
"MIDORI" ... IS IT?

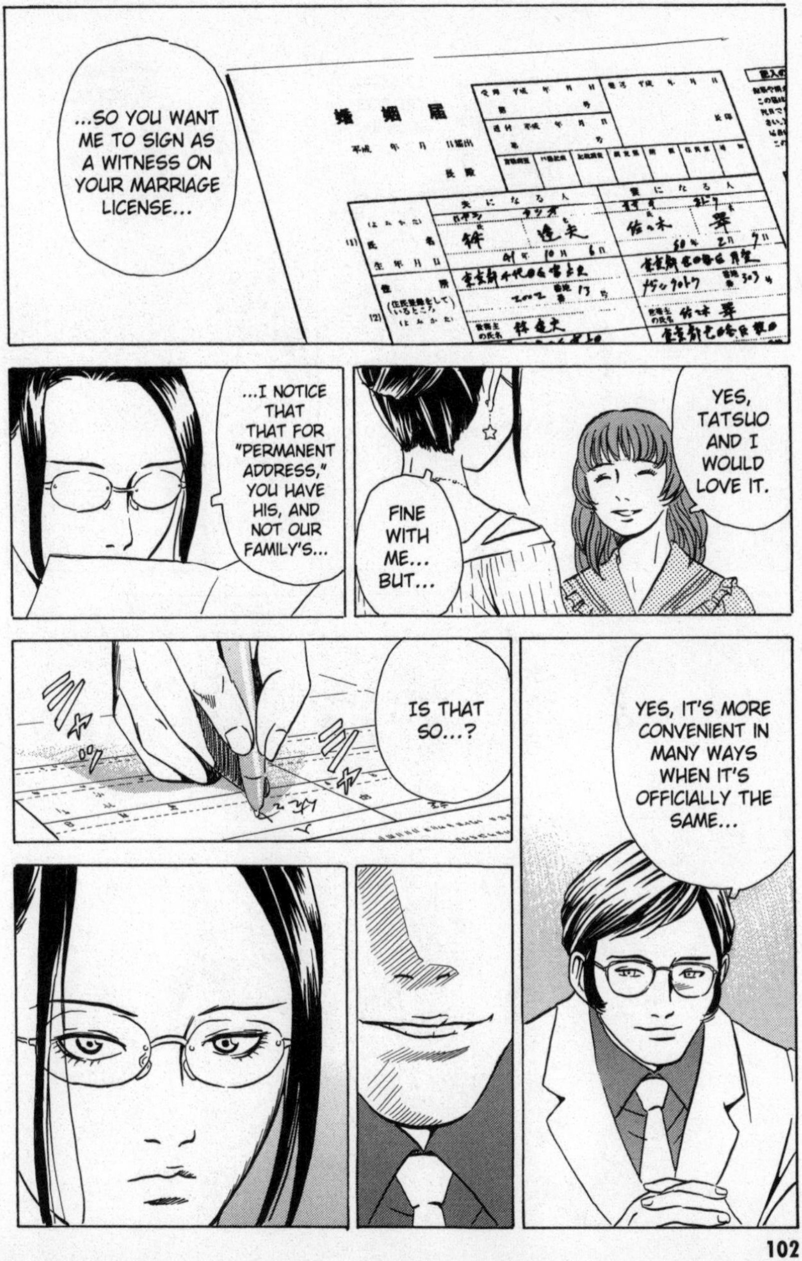
...SO YOU WANT ME TO SIGN AS A WITNESS ON YOUR MARRIAGE LICENSE...
YES, TATSUO AND I WOULD LOVE IT.
FINE WITH ME... BUT...
...I NOTICE THAT THAT FOR "PERMANENT ADDRESS," YOU HAVE HIS, AND NOT OUR FAMILY'S...
YES, IT'S MORE CONVENIENT IN MANY WAYS WHEN IT'S OFFICIALLY THE SAME...
IS THAT SO...?

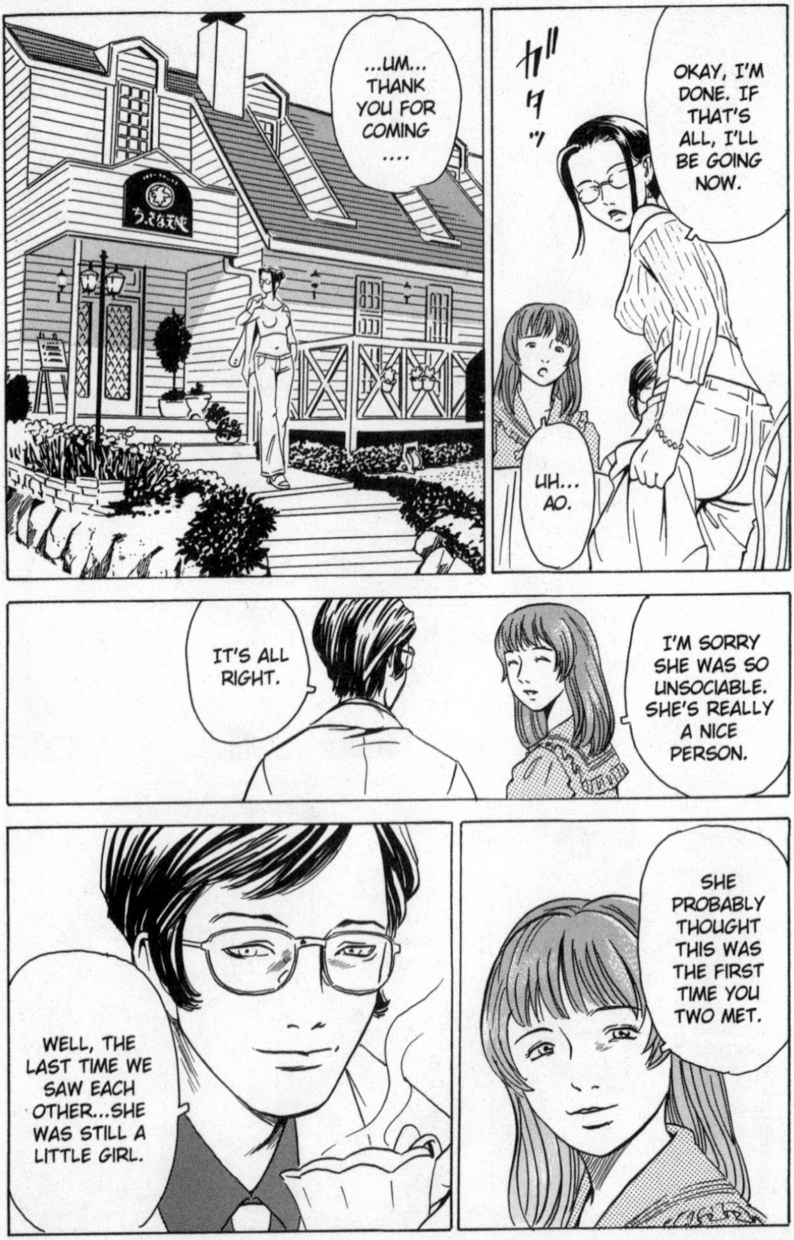
ガタッ
OKAY, I'M DONE. IF THAT'S ALL, I'LL BE GOING NOW.
UH... AO.
...UM... THANK YOU FOR COMING ....
I'M SORRY SHE WAS SO UNSOCIABLE. SHE'S REALLY A NICE PERSON.
IT'S ALL RIGHT.
SHE PROBABLY THOUGHT THIS WAS THE FIRST TIME YOU TWO MET.
WELL, THE LAST TIME WE SAW EACH OTHER...SHE WAS STILL A LITTLE GIRL.

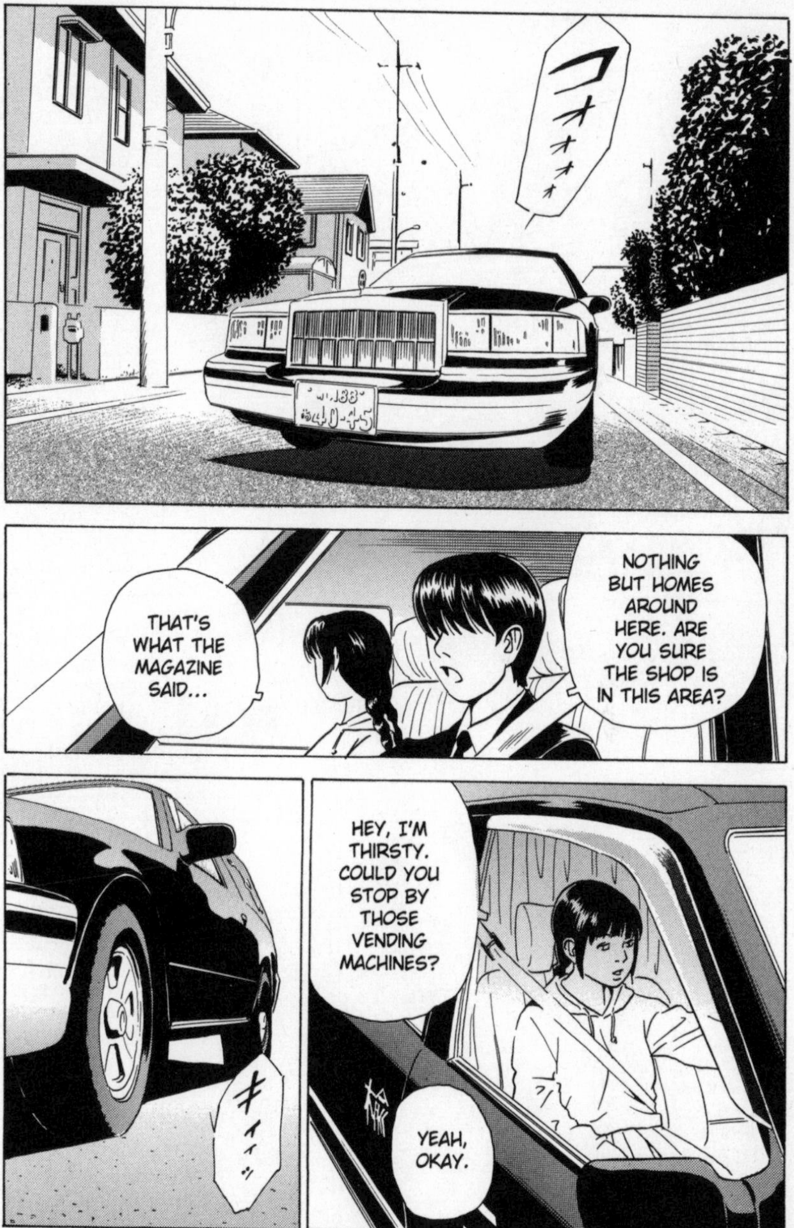
コオオオオ
NOTHING BUT HOMES AROUND HERE. ARE YOU SURE THE SHOP IS IN THIS AREA?
THAT'S WHAT THE MAGAZINE SAID...
HEY, I'M THIRSTY. COULD YOU STOP BY THOSE VENDING MACHINES?
YEAH, OKAY.
キイイッ

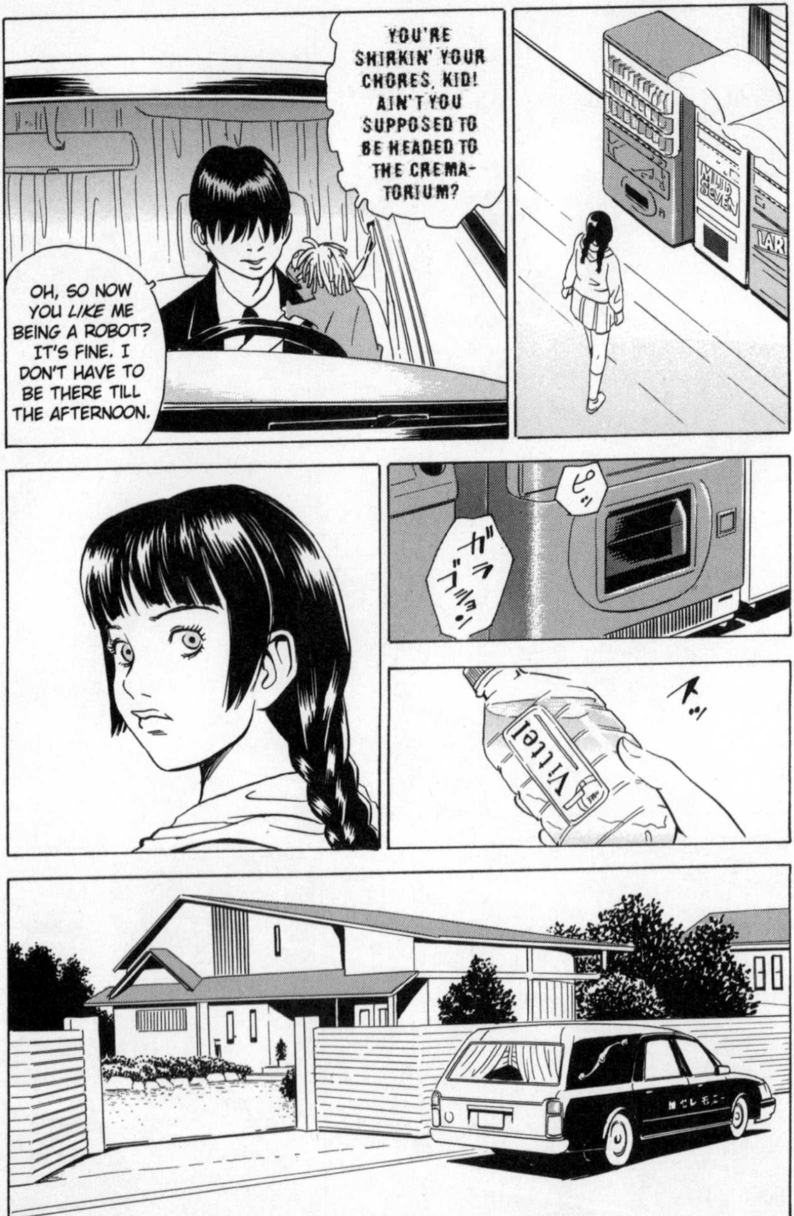
MILD SEVEN
YOU'RE SHIRKIN' YOUR CHORES, KID! AIN'T YOU SUPPOSED TO BE HEADED TO THE CREMA-TORIUM?
OH, SO NOW YOU *LIKE* ME BEING A ROBOT? IT'S FINE. I DON'T HAVE TO BE THERE TILL THE AFTERNOON.
ピッ
ガラゴション
スッ
Vittel

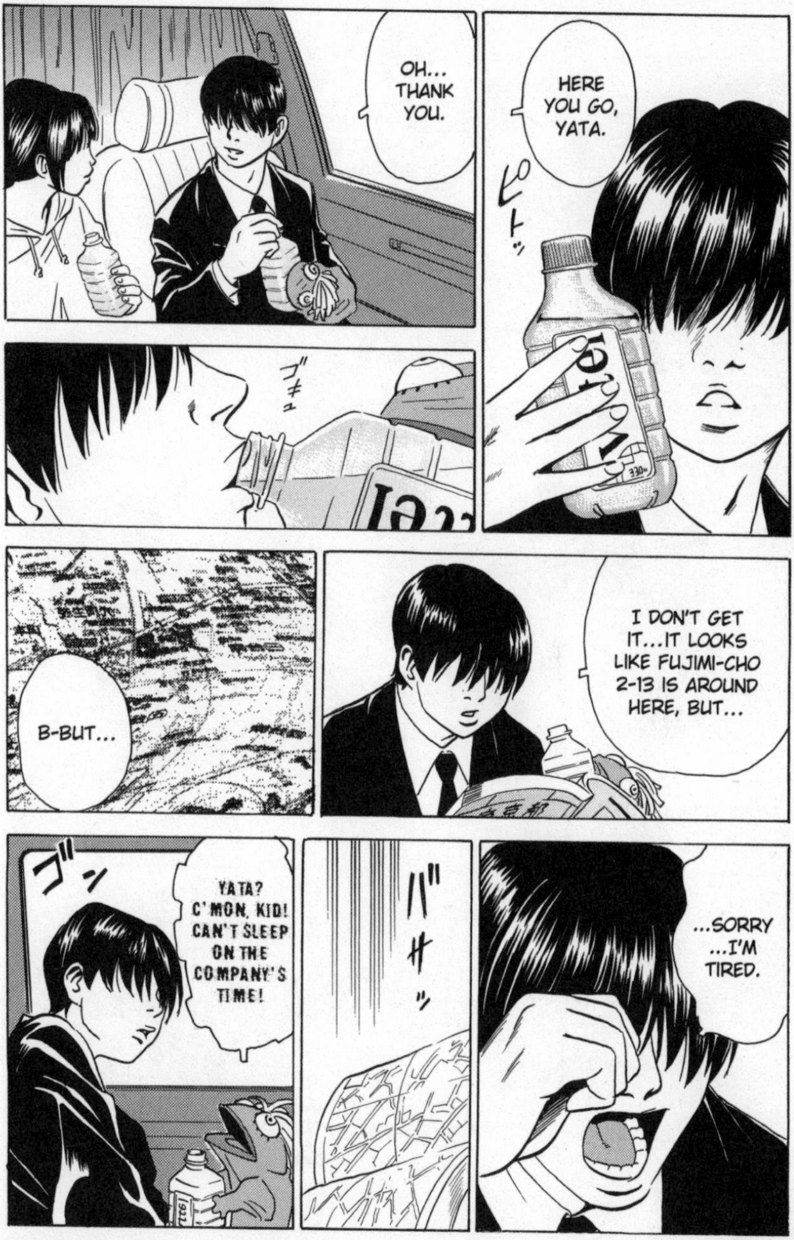
HERE YOU GO, YATA.
ピトッ
OH... THANK YOU.
ゴキュ
I DON'T GET IT...IT LOOKS LIKE FUJIMI-CHO 2-13 IS AROUND HERE, BUT...
B-BUT...
...SORRY ...I'M TIRED.
バサッ
ゴン
YATA? C'MON, KID! CAN'T SLEEP ON THE COMPANY'S TIME!

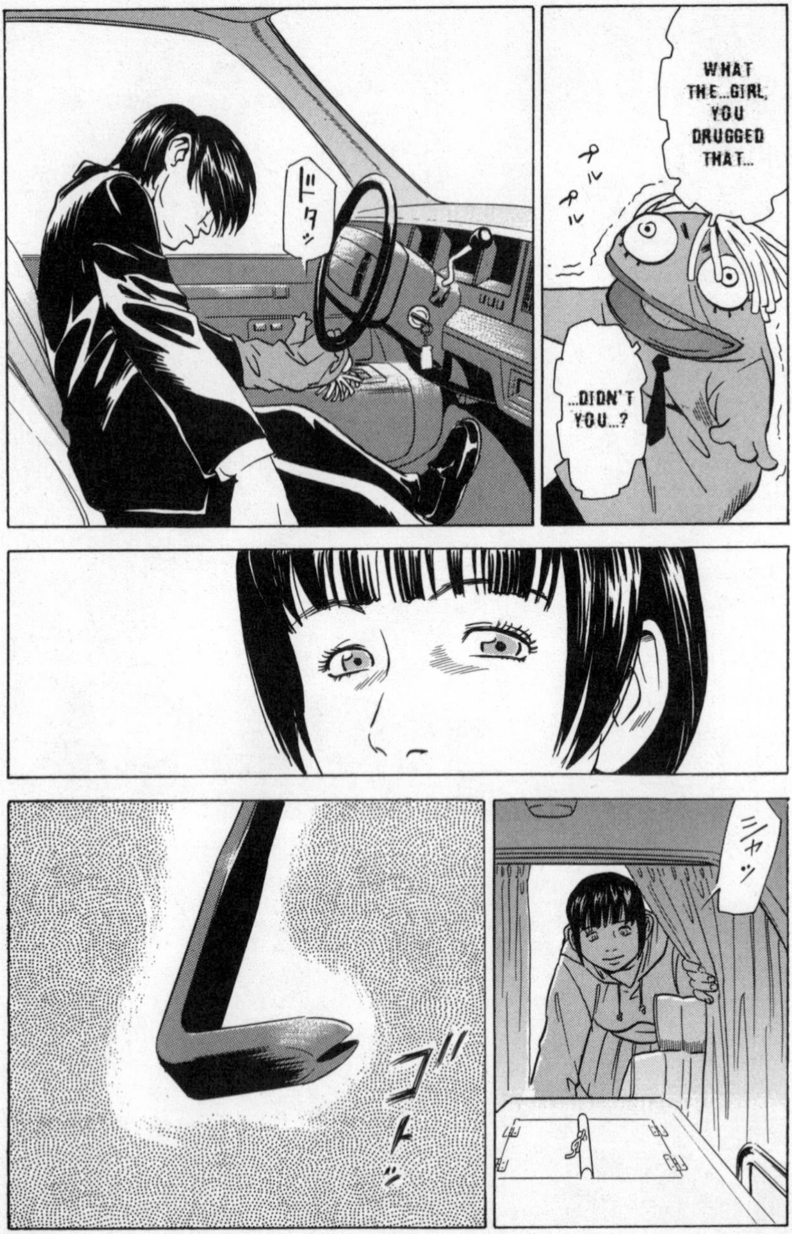
WHAT THE...GIRL, YOU DRUGGED THAT...
プルプル
...DIDN'T YOU...?
ドタッ
シャッ
ゴトッ

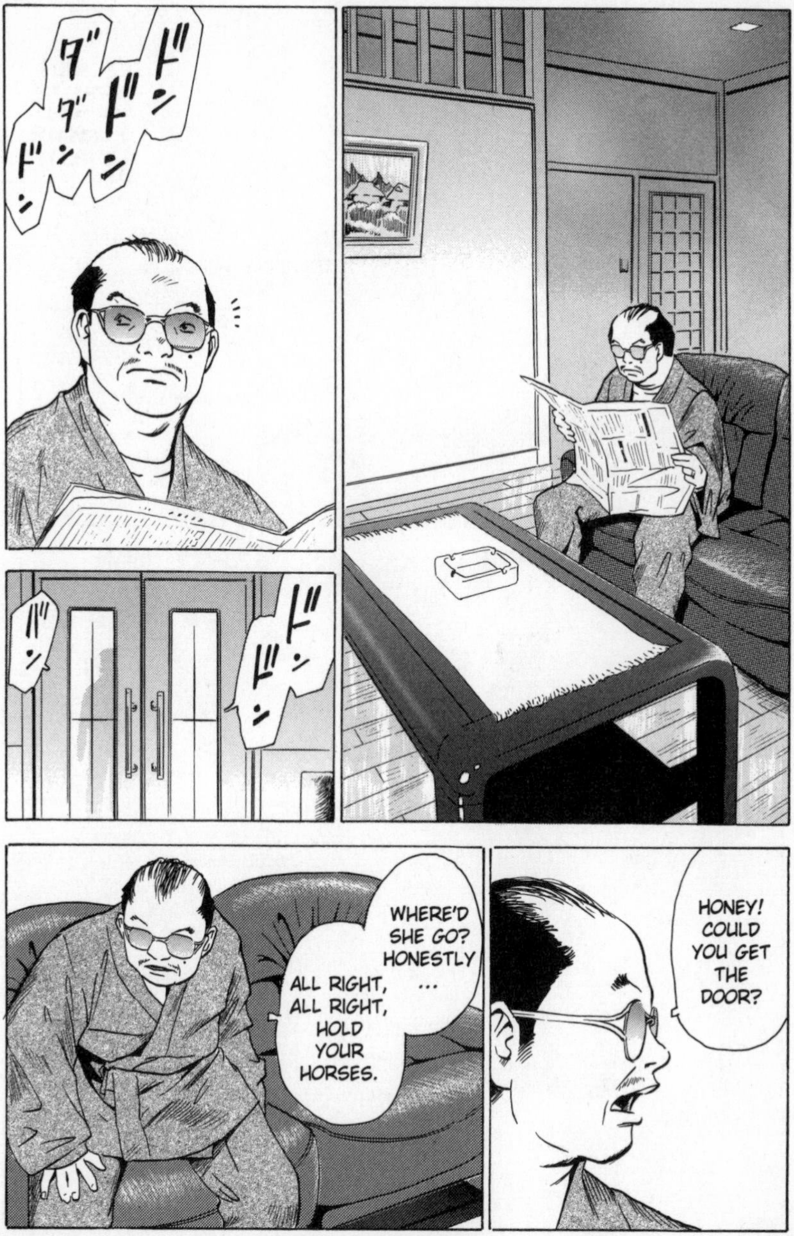
ドンドン
ダダン
ドン
ドンドン
バン
HONEY! COULD YOU GET THE DOOR?
WHERE'D SHE GO? HONESTLY ...
ALL RIGHT, ALL RIGHT, HOLD YOUR HORSES.

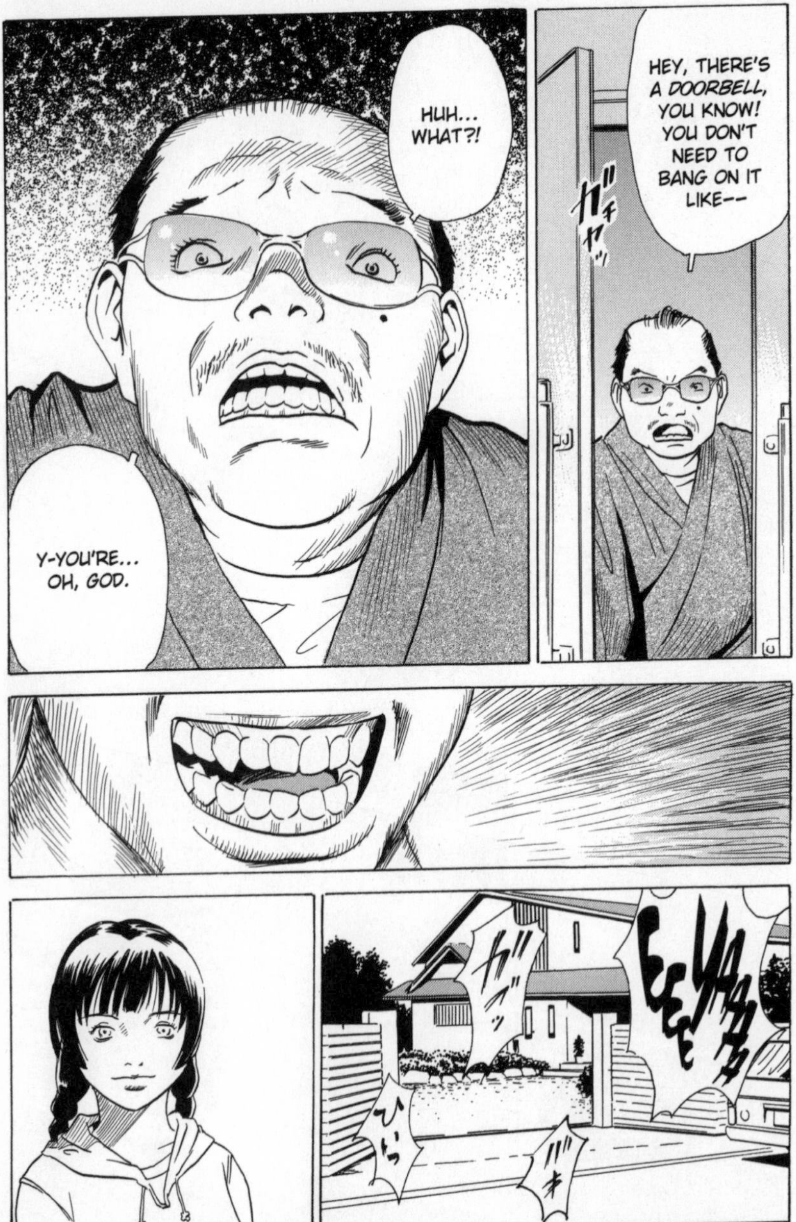
HEY, THERE'S A *DOORBELL*, YOU KNOW! YOU DON'T NEED TO BANG ON IT LIKE--
ガチャッ
HUH... WHAT?!
Y-YOU'RE... OH, GOD.

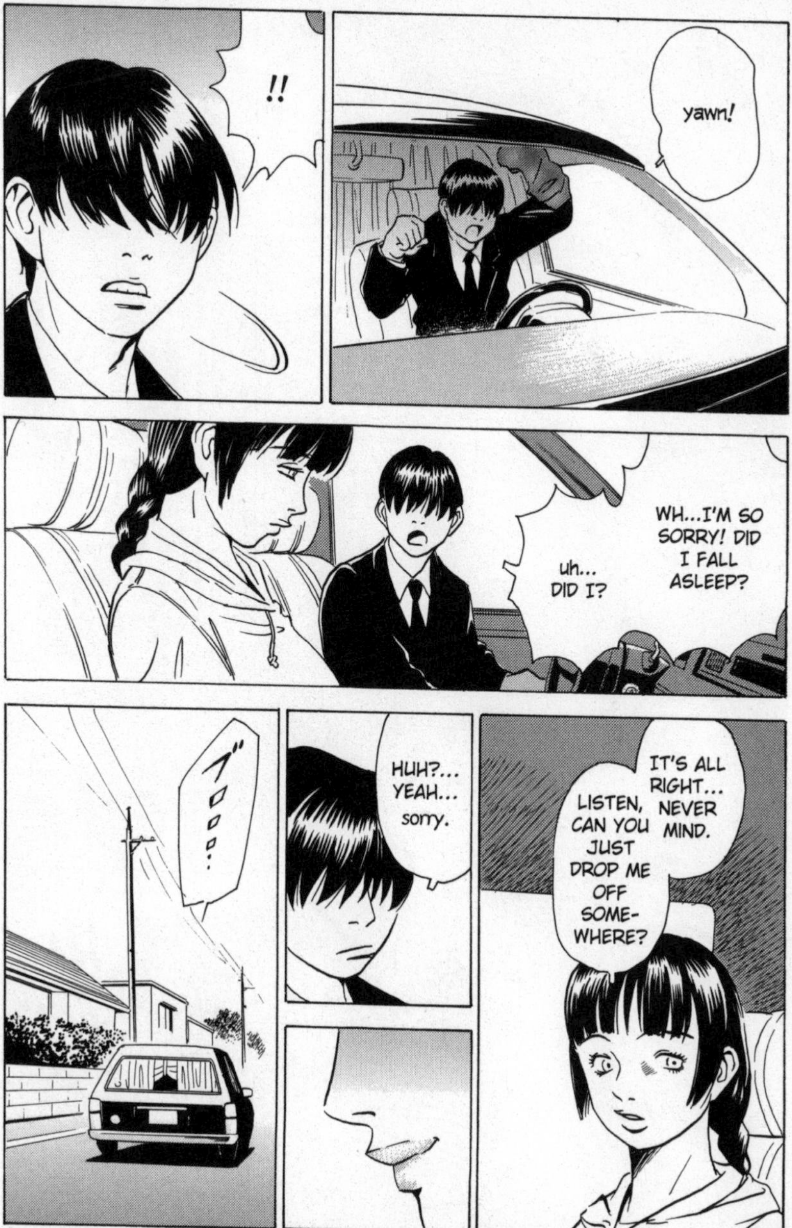
yawn!
!!
WH...I'M SO SORRY! DID I FALL ASLEEP?
uh... DID I?
IT'S ALL RIGHT... NEVER MIND.
LISTEN, CAN YOU JUST DROP ME OFF SOME-WHERE?
HUH?... YEAH... sorry.
ブロロロロ…

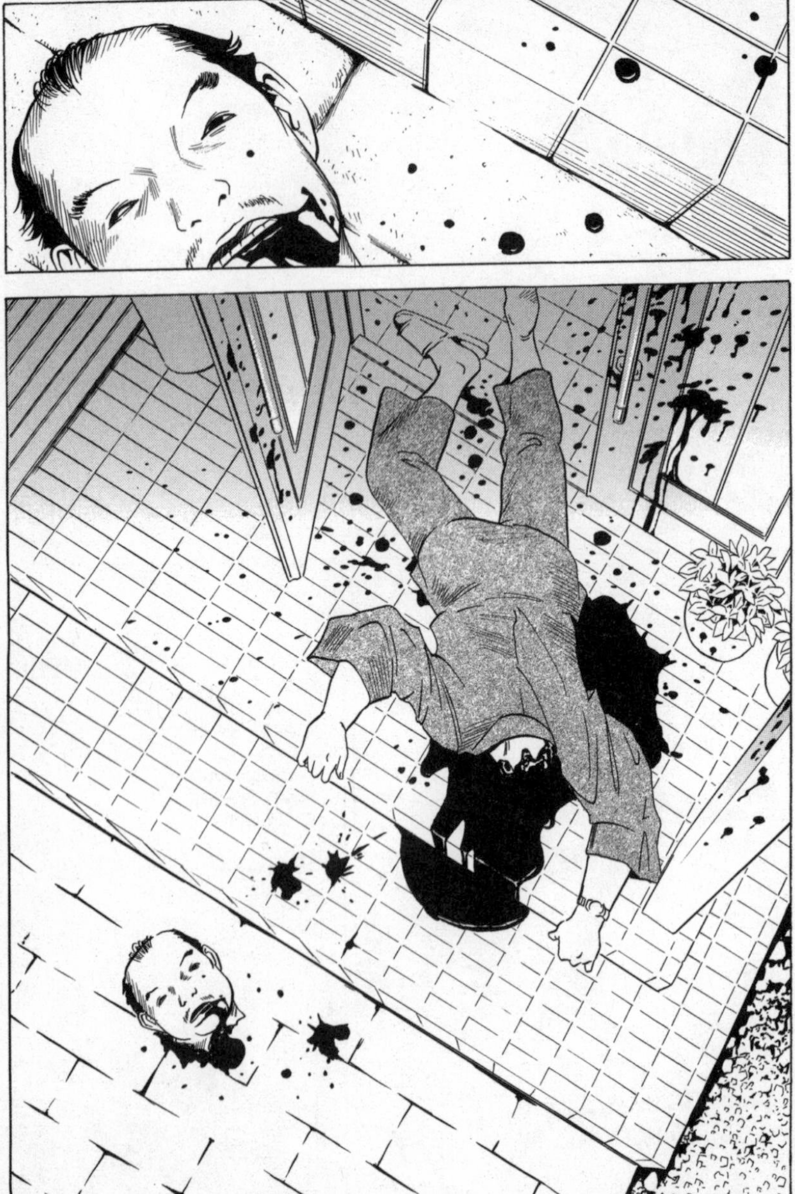

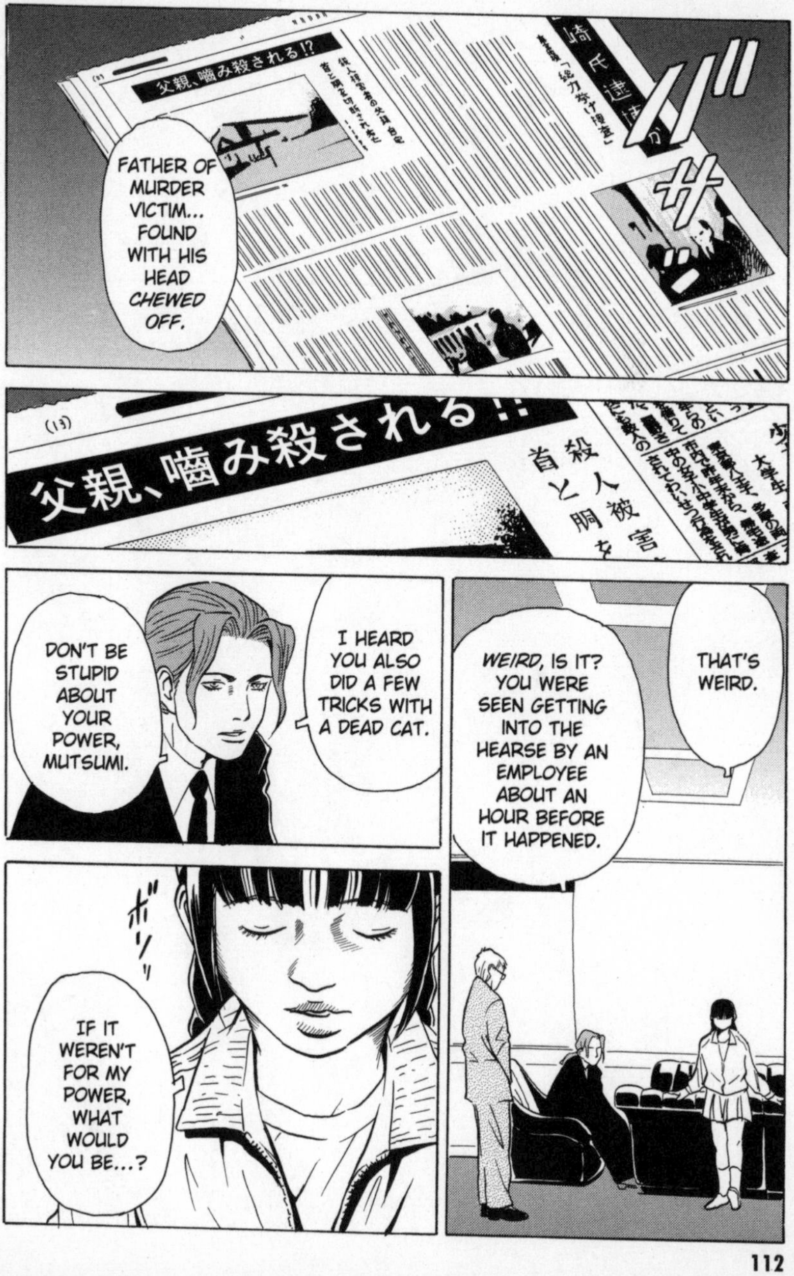
父親、噛み殺される!?
FATHER OF MURDER VICTIM... FOUND WITH HIS HEAD *CHEWED* OFF.
父親、噛み殺される!!
THAT'S WEIRD.
WEIRD, IS IT? YOU WERE SEEN GETTING INTO THE HEARSE BY AN EMPLOYEE ABOUT AN HOUR BEFORE IT HAPPENED.
I HEARD YOU ALSO DID A FEW TRICKS WITH A DEAD CAT.
DON'T BE STUPID ABOUT YOUR POWER, MUTSUMI.
ボソッ
IF IT WEREN'T FOR MY POWER, WHAT WOULD YOU BE...?

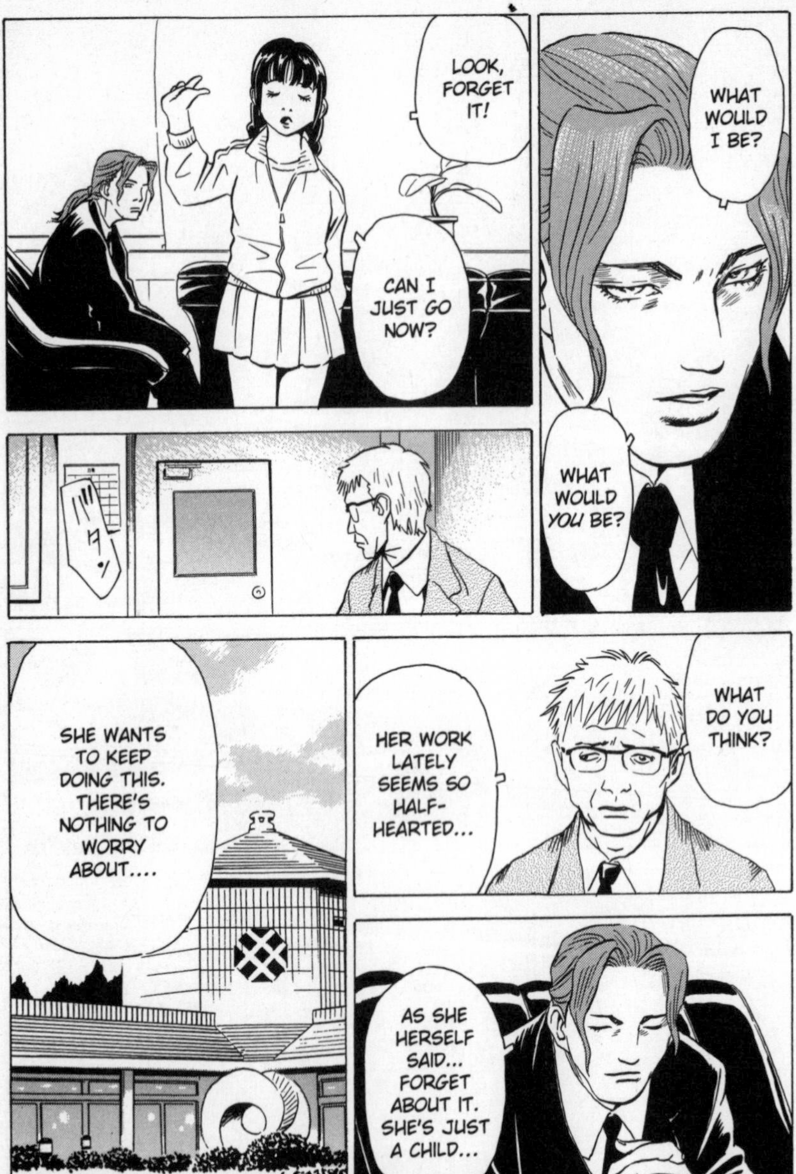
WHAT WOULD I BE?
WHAT WOULD YOU BE?
LOOK, FORGET IT!
CAN I JUST GO NOW?
バタン
WHAT DO YOU THINK?
HER WORK LATELY SEEMS SO HALF-HEARTED...
AS SHE HERSELF SAID... FORGET ABOUT IT. SHE'S JUST A CHILD...
SHE WANTS TO KEEP DOING THIS. THERE'S NOTHING TO WORRY ABOUT....

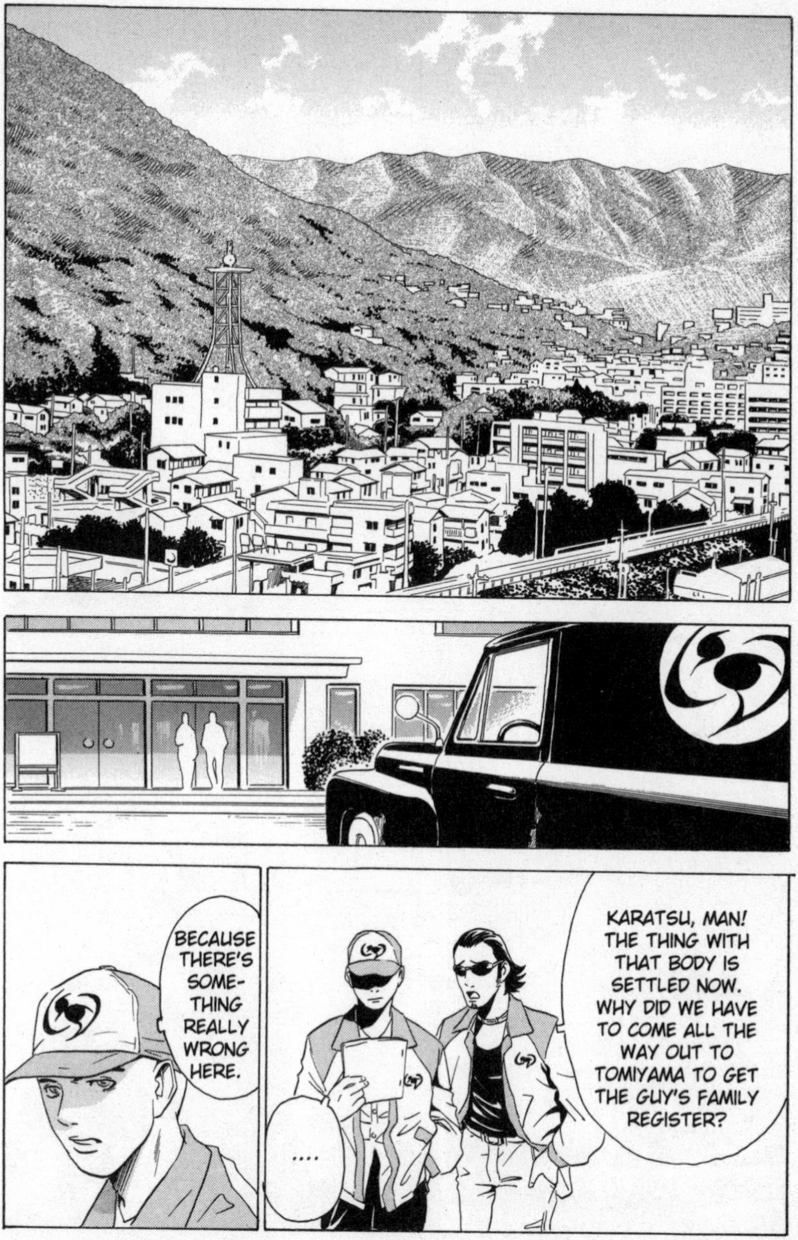
KARATSU, MAN! THE THING WITH THAT BODY IS SETTLED NOW. WHY DID WE HAVE TO COME ALL THE WAY OUT TO TOMIYAMA TO GET THE GUY'S FAMILY REGISTER?
....
BECAUSE THERE'S SOME-THING REALLY WRONG HERE.

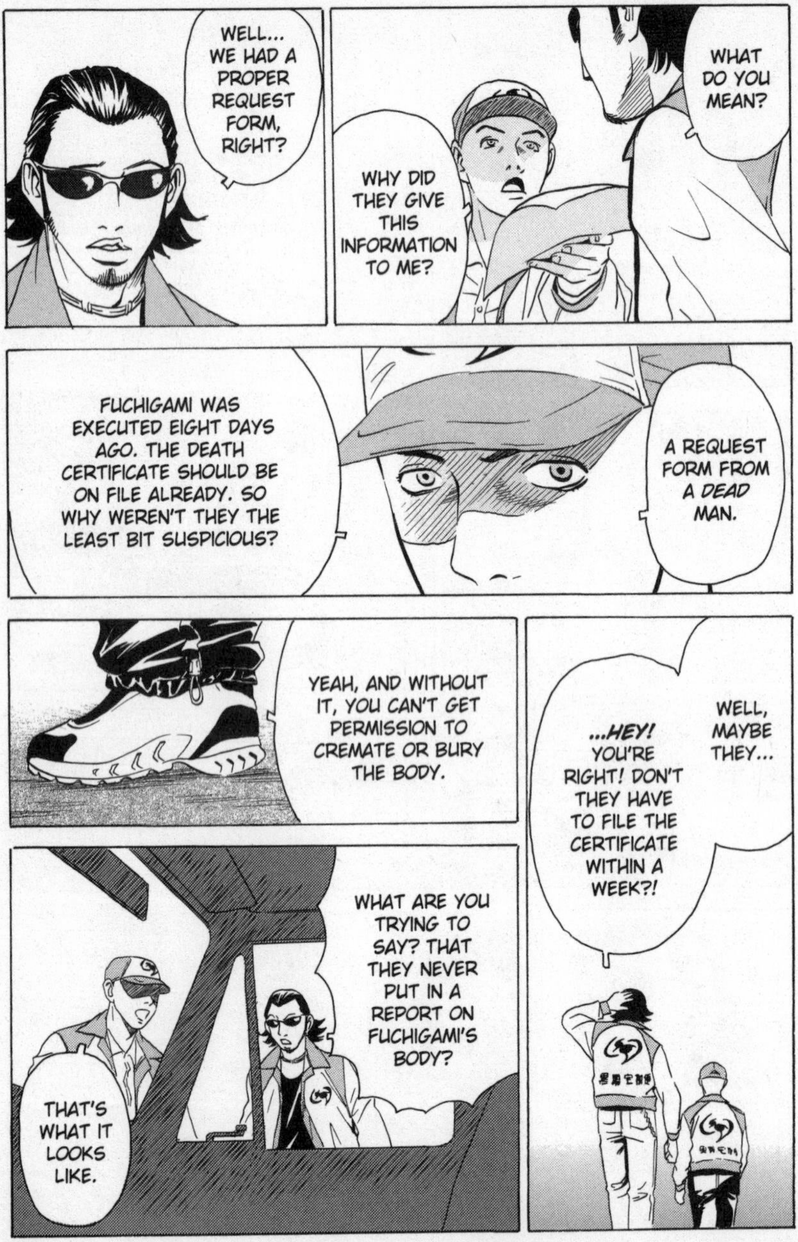
WHAT DO YOU MEAN?
WHY DID THEY GIVE THIS INFORMATION TO ME?
WELL... WE HAD A PROPER REQUEST FORM, RIGHT?
A REQUEST FORM FROM A *DEAD* MAN.
FUCHIGAMI WAS EXECUTED EIGHT DAYS AGO. THE DEATH CERTIFICATE SHOULD BE ON FILE ALREADY. SO WHY WEREN'T THEY THE LEAST BIT SUSPICIOUS?
WELL, MAYBE THEY...
...HEY! YOU'RE RIGHT! DON'T THEY HAVE TO FILE THE CERTIFICATE WITHIN A WEEK?!
YEAH, AND WITHOUT IT, YOU CAN'T GET PERMISSION TO CREMATE OR BURY THE BODY.
WHAT ARE YOU TRYING TO SAY? THAT THEY NEVER PUT IN A REPORT ON FUCHIGAMI'S BODY?
THAT'S WHAT IT LOOKS LIKE.

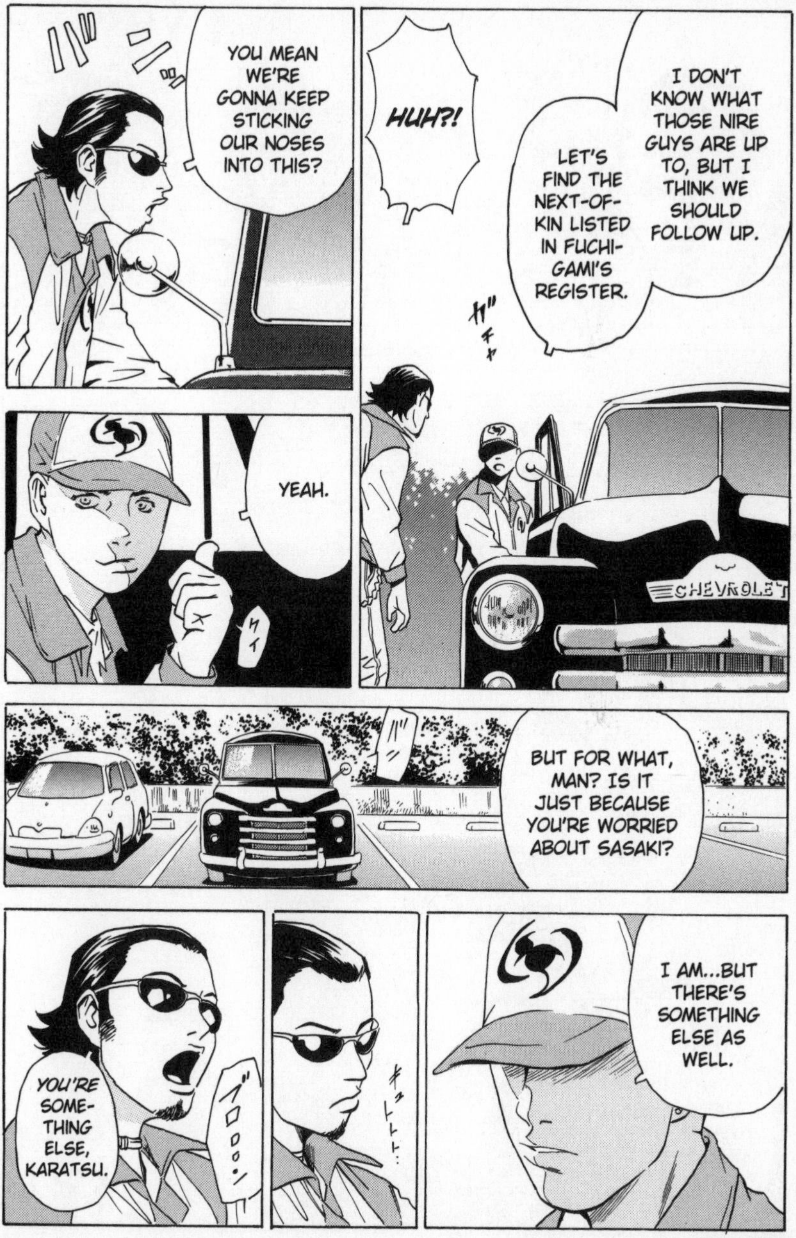
I DON'T KNOW WHAT THOSE NIRE GUYS ARE UP TO, BUT I THINK WE SHOULD FOLLOW UP.
LET'S FIND THE NEXT-OF-KIN LISTED IN FUCHIGAMI'S REGISTER.
HUH?!
YOU MEAN WE'RE GONNA KEEP STICKING OUR NOSES INTO THIS?
YEAH.
CHEVROLET
BUT FOR WHAT, MAN? IS IT JUST BECAUSE YOU'RE WORRIED ABOUT SASAKI?
I AM...BUT THERE'S SOMETHING ELSE AS WELL.
YOU'RE SOMETHING ELSE, KARATSU.

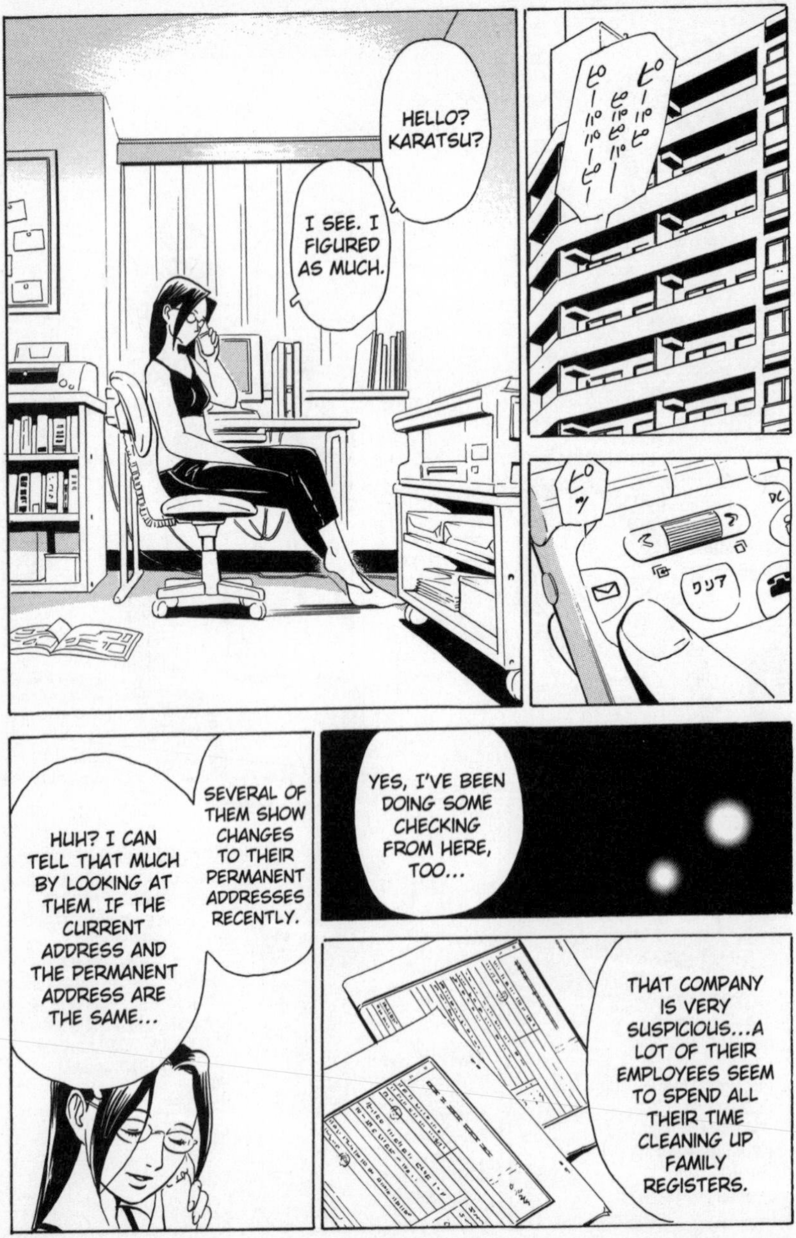
ピーパピ ピパピパー ピーパパーピー
ピッ
クリア
HELLO? KARATSU?
I SEE. I FIGURED AS MUCH.
YES, I'VE BEEN DOING SOME CHECKING FROM HERE, TOO...
THAT COMPANY IS VERY SUSPICIOUS...A LOT OF THEIR EMPLOYEES SEEM TO SPEND ALL THEIR TIME CLEANING UP FAMILY REGISTERS.
SEVERAL OF THEM SHOW CHANGES TO THEIR PERMANENT ADDRESSES RECENTLY.
HUH? I CAN TELL THAT MUCH BY LOOKING AT THEM. IF THE CURRENT ADDRESS AND THE PERMANENT ADDRESS ARE THE SAME...

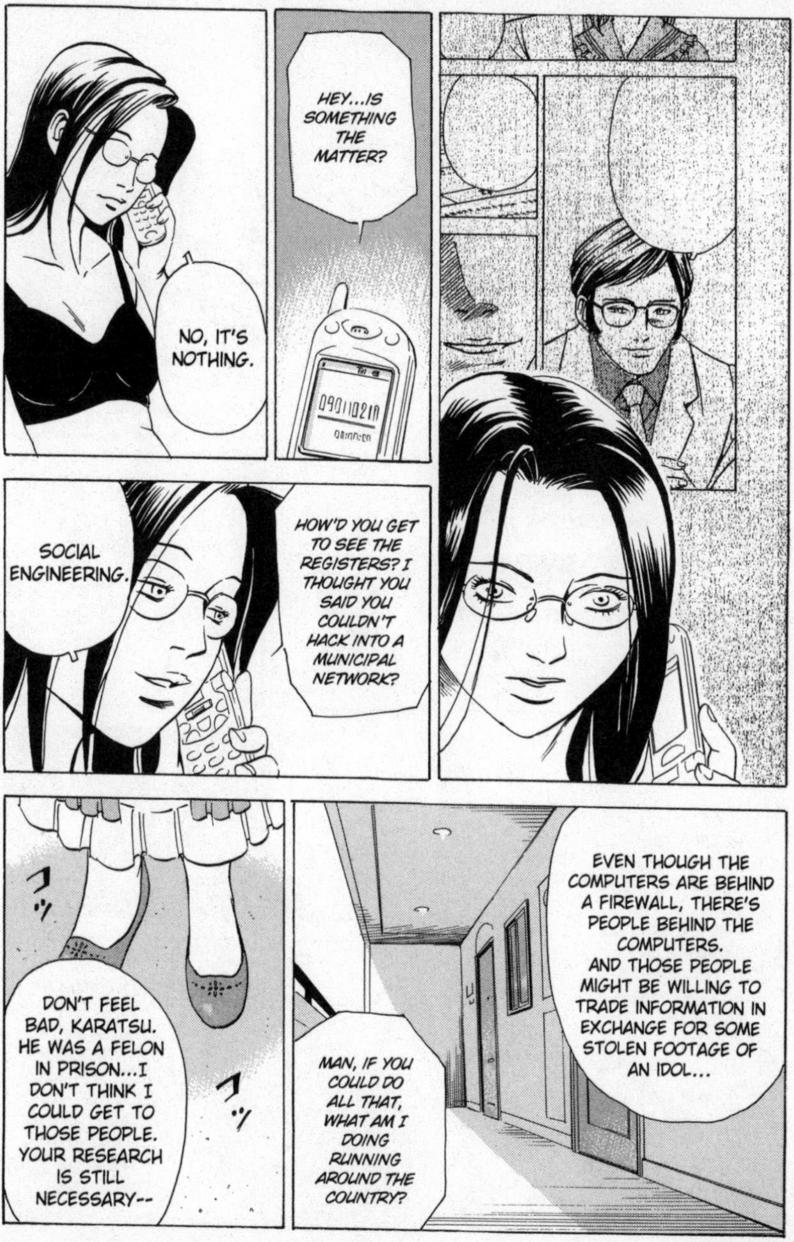
HEY...IS SOMETHING THE MATTER?
NO, IT'S NOTHING.
HOW'D YOU GET TO SEE THE REGISTERS? I THOUGHT YOU SAID YOU COULDN'T HACK INTO A MUNICIPAL NETWORK?
SOCIAL ENGINEERING.
EVEN THOUGH THE COMPUTERS ARE BEHIND A FIREWALL, THERE'S PEOPLE BEHIND THE COMPUTERS. AND THOSE PEOPLE MIGHT BE WILLING TO TRADE INFORMATION IN EXCHANGE FOR SOME STOLEN FOOTAGE OF AN IDOL...
MAN, IF YOU COULD DO ALL THAT, WHAT AM I DOING RUNNING AROUND THE COUNTRY?
コッ
コッ
DON'T FEEL BAD, KARATSU. HE WAS A FELON IN PRISON...I DON'T THINK I COULD GET TO THOSE PEOPLE. YOUR RESEARCH IS STILL NECESSARY--

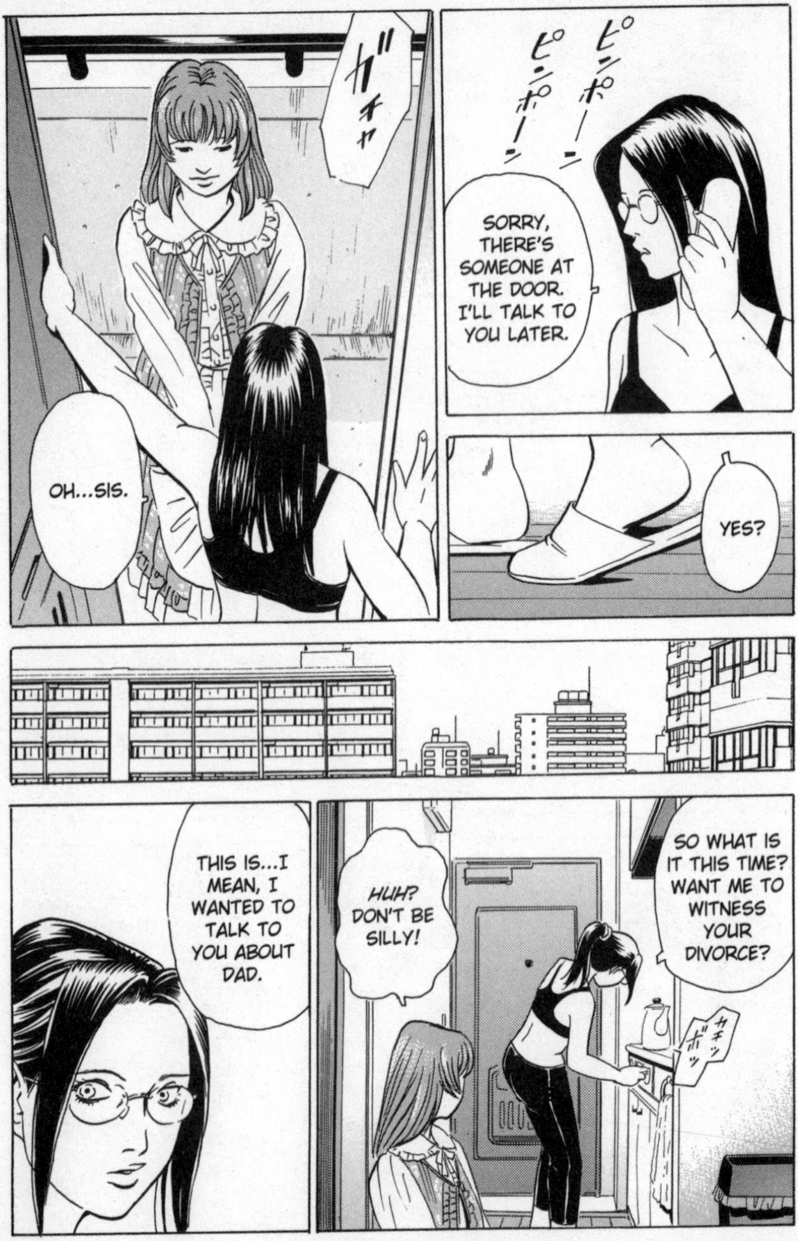
ピンポーン
ピンポーン
SORRY, THERE'S SOMEONE AT THE DOOR. I'LL TALK TO YOU LATER.
YES?
ガチャ
OH...SIS.
SO WHAT IS IT THIS TIME? WANT ME TO WITNESS YOUR DIVORCE?
カチッ
ボッ
HUH? DON'T BE SILLY!
THIS IS...I MEAN, I WANTED TO TALK TO YOU ABOUT DAD.

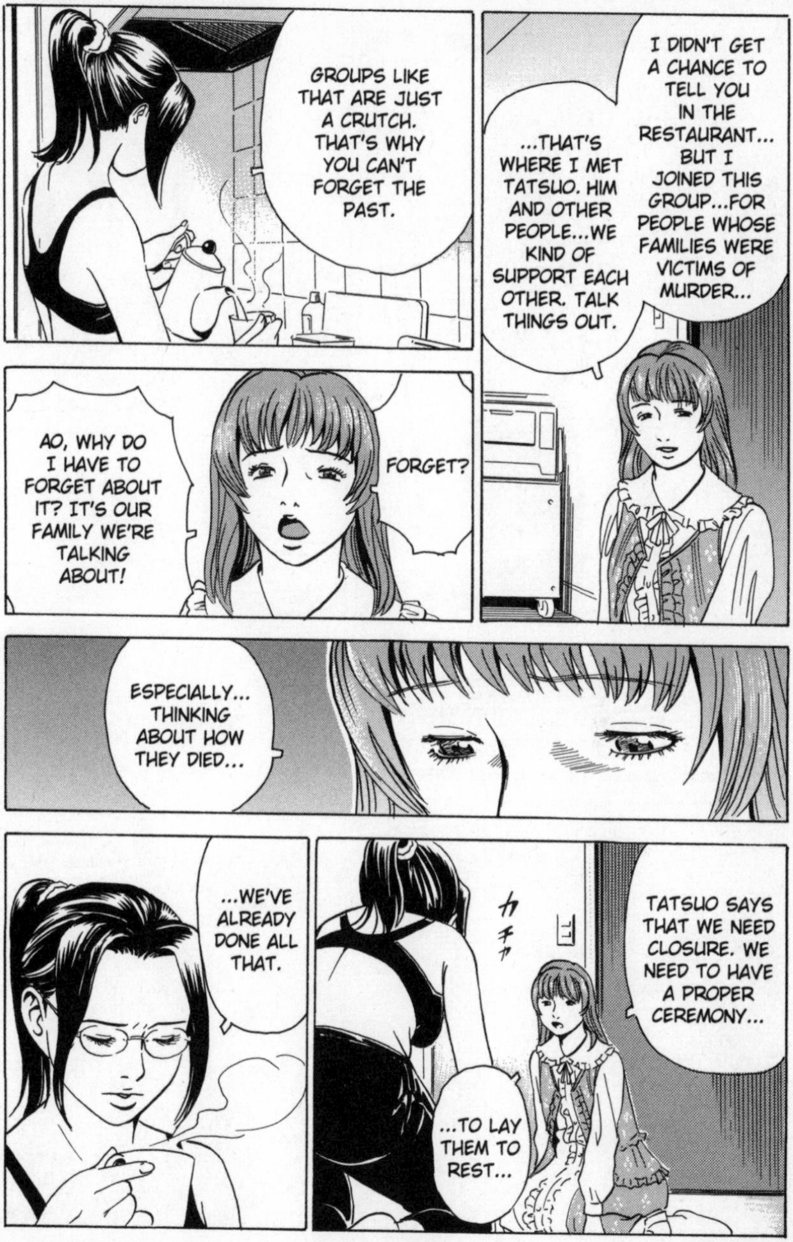

I DIDN'T GET A CHANCE TO TELL YOU IN THE RESTAURANT... BUT I JOINED THIS GROUP...FOR PEOPLE WHOSE FAMILIES WERE VICTIMS OF MURDER...
...THAT'S WHERE I MET TATSUO. HIM AND OTHER PEOPLE...WE KIND OF SUPPORT EACH OTHER. TALK THINGS OUT.
GROUPS LIKE THAT ARE JUST A CRUTCH. THAT'S WHY YOU CAN'T FORGET THE PAST.
FORGET?
AO, WHY DO I HAVE TO FORGET ABOUT IT? IT'S OUR FAMILY WE'RE TALKING ABOUT!
ESPECIALLY... THINKING ABOUT HOW THEY DIED...
TATSUO SAYS THAT WE NEED CLOSURE. WE NEED TO HAVE A PROPER CEREMONY...
カチャ
...TO LAY THEM TO REST...
...WE'VE ALREADY DONE ALL THAT.

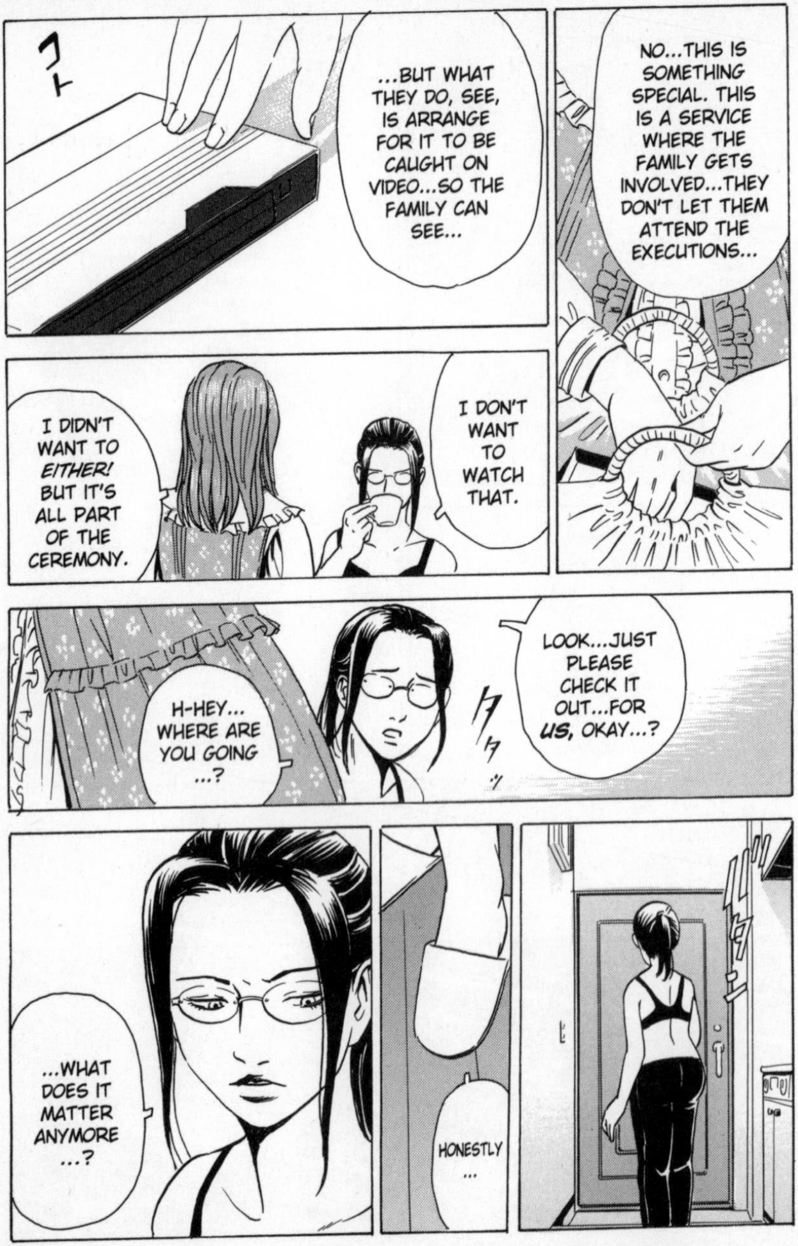
NO...THIS IS SOMETHING SPECIAL. THIS IS A SERVICE WHERE THE FAMILY GETS INVOLVED...THEY DON'T LET THEM ATTEND THE EXECUTIONS...
...BUT WHAT THEY DO, SEE, IS ARRANGE FOR IT TO BE CAUGHT ON VIDEO...SO THE FAMILY CAN SEE...
コト
I DON'T WANT TO WATCH THAT.
I DIDN'T WANT TO *EITHER!* BUT IT'S ALL PART OF THE CEREMONY.
LOOK...JUST PLEASE CHECK IT OUT...FOR **US**, OKAY...?
H-HEY... WHERE ARE YOU GOING ...?
HONESTLY ...
...WHAT DOES IT MATTER ANYMORE ...?

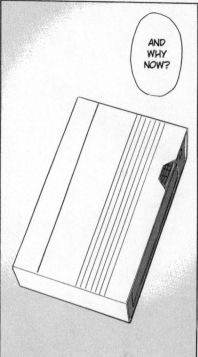

AND WHY NOW?

DID YOU GIVE IT TO HER?

DON'T WORRY ...

YES... BUT...

...I'M SURE YOUR SISTER WILL SOON SEE THINGS OUR WAY.

4th delivery: tonight i will pour wine all over you—the end

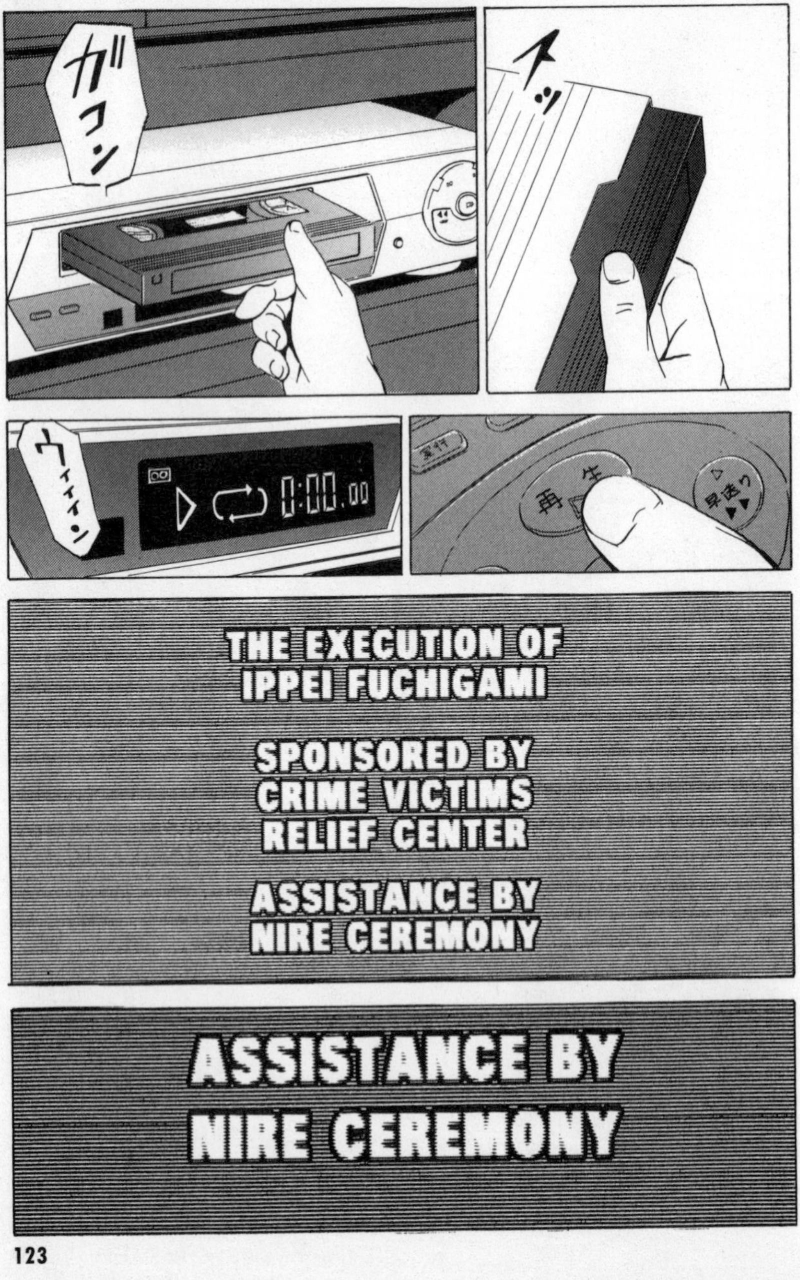
スッ
ガコン
再生
早送り
ウィイイン
THE EXECUTION OF
IPPEI FUCHIGAMI
SPONSORED BY
CRIME VICTIMS
RELIEF CENTER
ASSISTANCE BY
NIRE CEREMONY
ASSISTANCE BY
NIRE CEREMONY

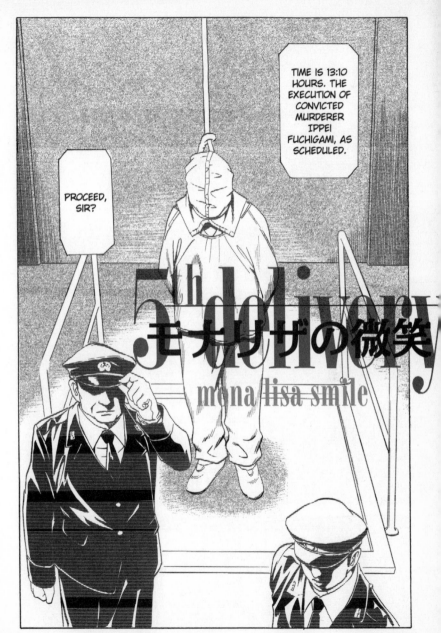

TIME IS 13:10 HOURS. THE EXECUTION OF CONVICTED MURDERER IPPEI FUCHIGAMI, AS SCHEDULED.

PROCEED, SIR?

5th delivery
モナ・リザの微笑
mona lisa smile

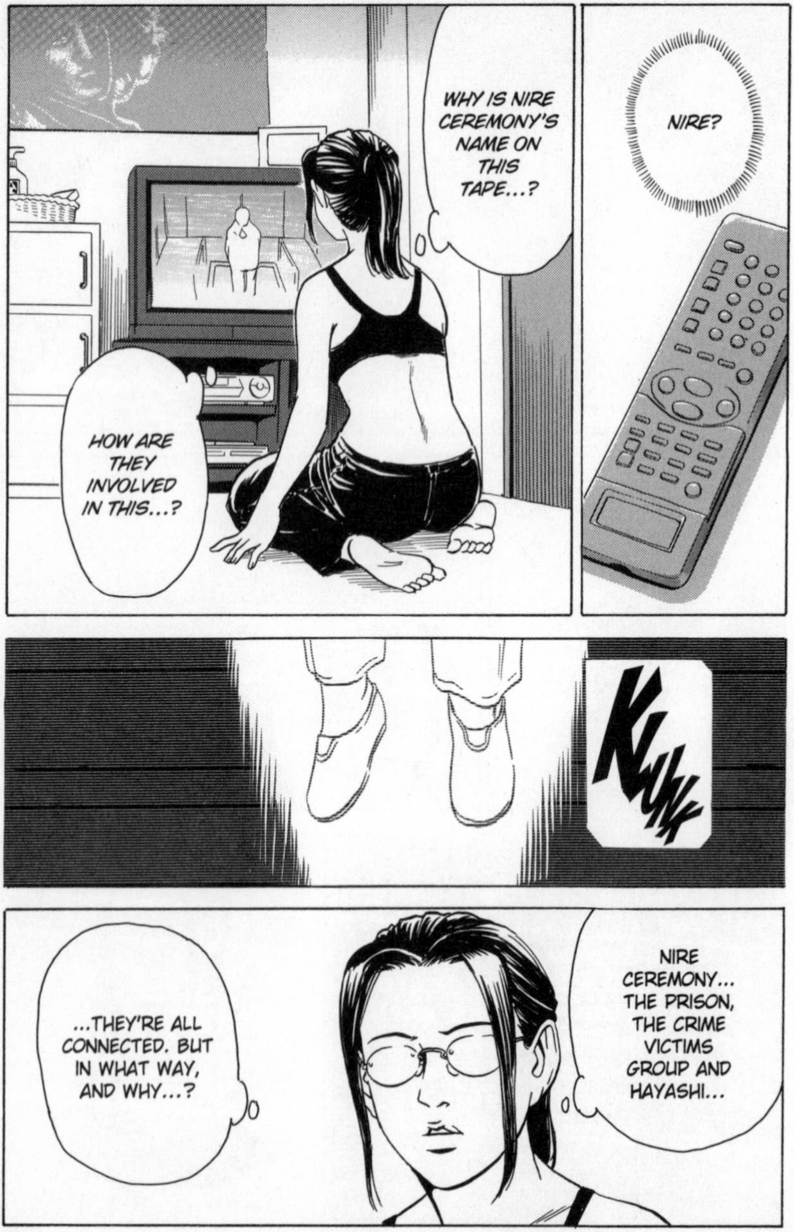
NIRE?
WHY IS NIRE CEREMONY'S NAME ON THIS TAPE...?
HOW ARE THEY INVOLVED IN THIS...?
KLUNK
NIRE CEREMONY... THE PRISON, THE CRIME VICTIMS GROUP AND HAYASHI...
...THEY'RE ALL CONNECTED. BUT IN WHAT WAY, AND WHY...?

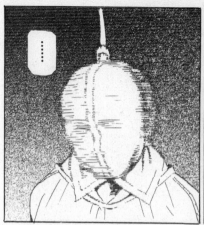

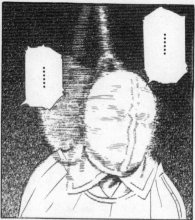

TIME IS 13:24 HOURS. THE DEATH OF IPPEI FUCHIGAMI IS CONFIRMED.

The following footage is of our ultimate service, in which you will be able to clear away the regrets of your loved ones with your own hands. It is called the Fugutaiten. Please observe closely.

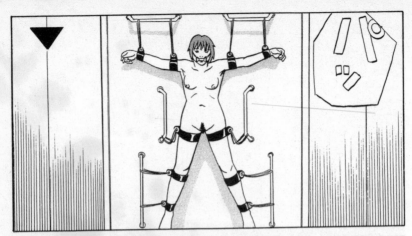

WHAT
ARE
THEY...

...WHAT
ARE
THEY
DOING...

127

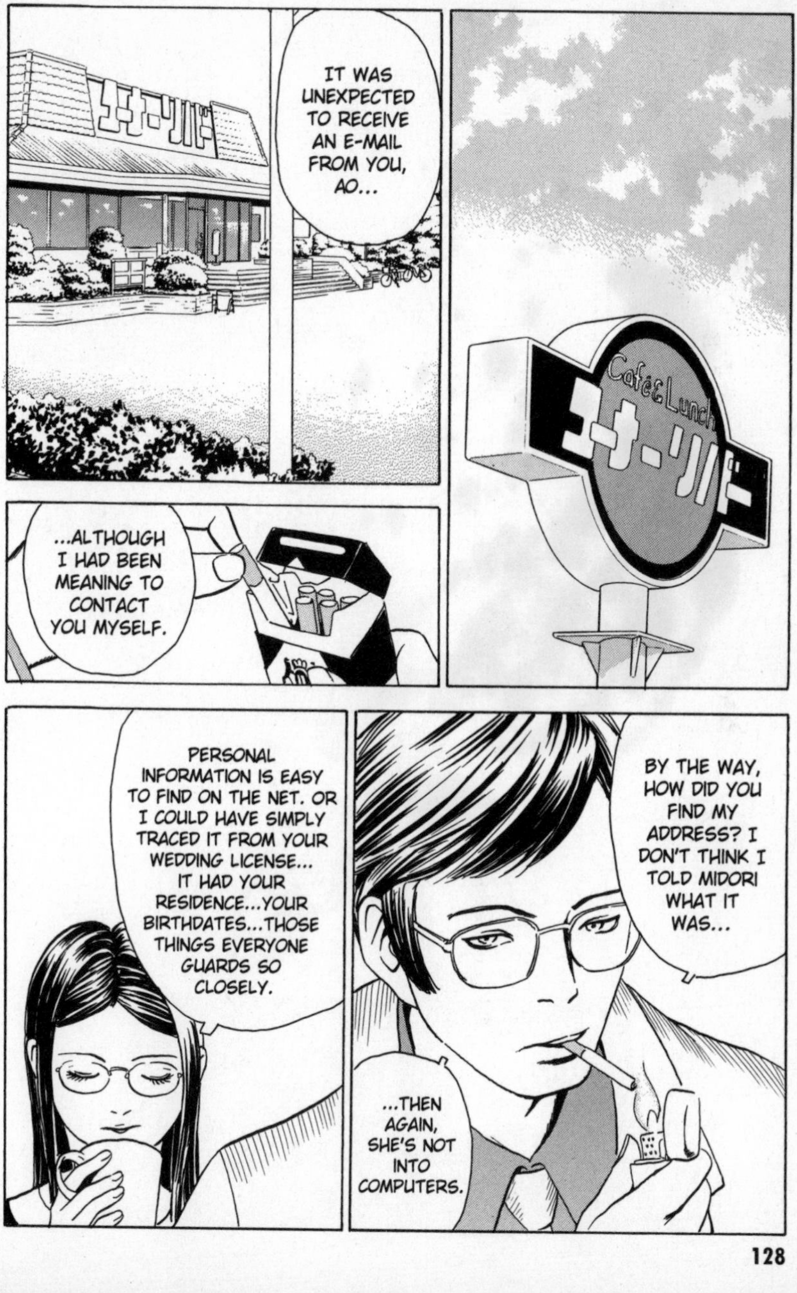
Café&Lunch
IT WAS UNEXPECTED TO RECEIVE AN E-MAIL FROM YOU, AO...
...ALTHOUGH I HAD BEEN MEANING TO CONTACT YOU MYSELF.
BY THE WAY, HOW DID YOU FIND MY ADDRESS? I DON'T THINK I TOLD MIDORI WHAT IT WAS...
...THEN AGAIN, SHE'S NOT INTO COMPUTERS.
PERSONAL INFORMATION IS EASY TO FIND ON THE NET. OR I COULD HAVE SIMPLY TRACED IT FROM YOUR WEDDING LICENSE... IT HAD YOUR RESIDENCE...YOUR BIRTHDATES...THOSE THINGS EVERYONE GUARDS SO CLOSELY.

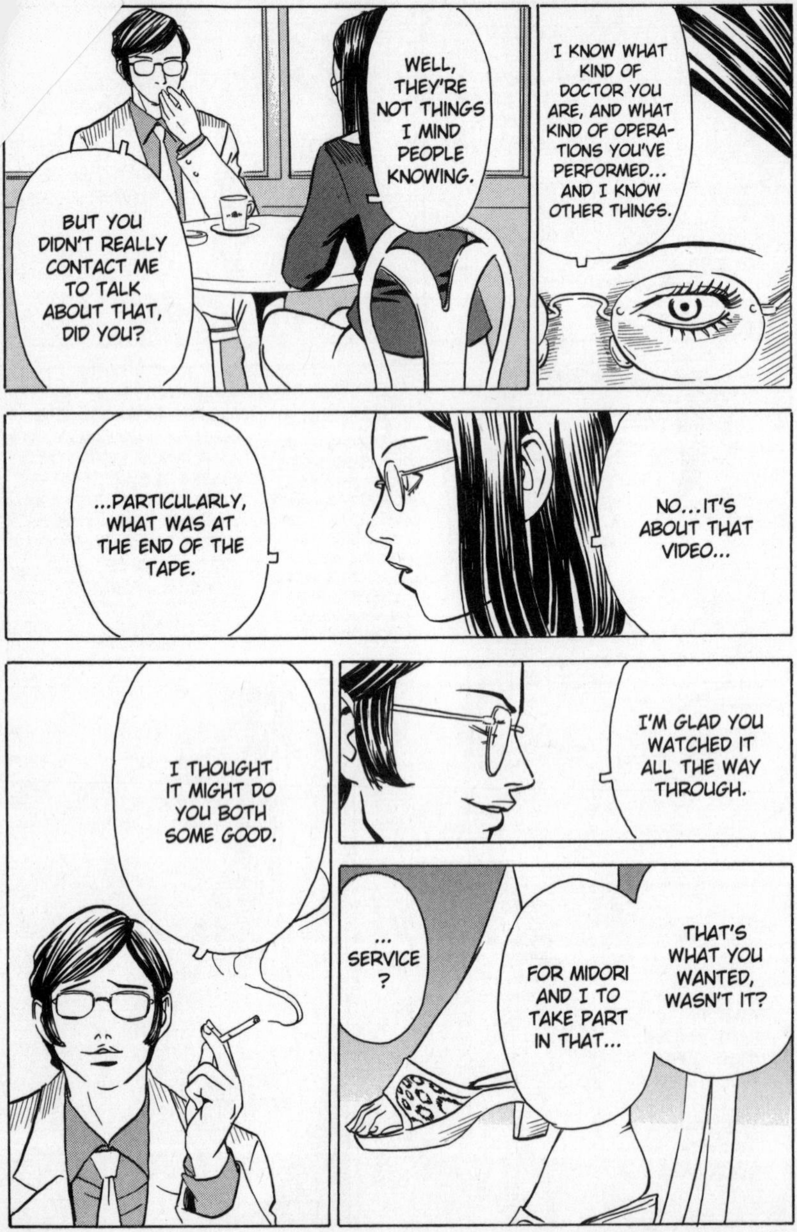
I KNOW WHAT KIND OF DOCTOR YOU ARE, AND WHAT KIND OF OPERATIONS YOU'VE PERFORMED... AND I KNOW OTHER THINGS.
WELL, THEY'RE NOT THINGS I MIND PEOPLE KNOWING.
BUT YOU DIDN'T REALLY CONTACT ME TO TALK ABOUT THAT, DID YOU?
NO...IT'S ABOUT THAT VIDEO...
...PARTICULARLY, WHAT WAS AT THE END OF THE TAPE.
I'M GLAD YOU WATCHED IT ALL THE WAY THROUGH.
THAT'S WHAT YOU WANTED, WASN'T IT?
FOR MIDORI AND I TO TAKE PART IN THAT...
...SERVICE?
I THOUGHT IT MIGHT DO YOU BOTH SOME GOOD.

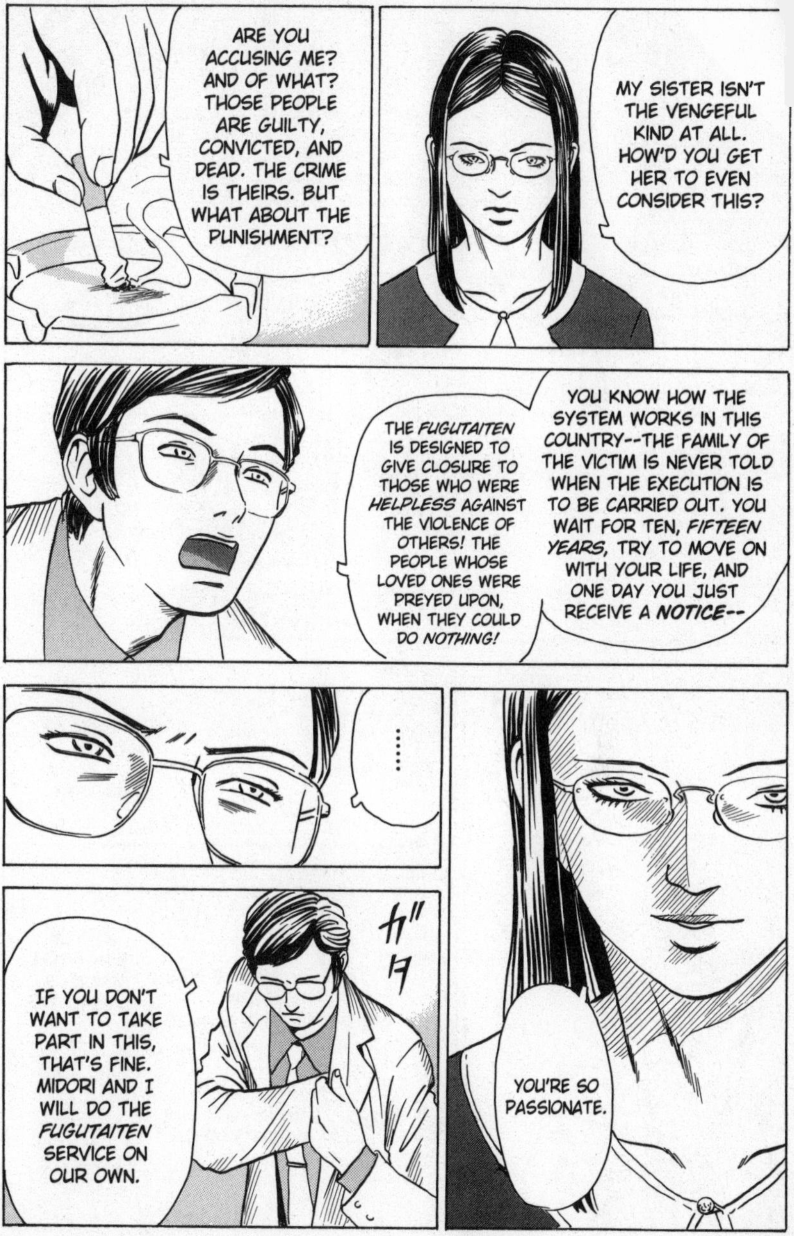
MY SISTER ISN'T THE VENGEFUL KIND AT ALL. HOW'D YOU GET HER TO EVEN CONSIDER THIS?
ARE YOU ACCUSING ME? AND OF WHAT? THOSE PEOPLE ARE GUILTY, CONVICTED, AND DEAD. THE CRIME IS THEIRS. BUT WHAT ABOUT THE PUNISHMENT?
YOU KNOW HOW THE SYSTEM WORKS IN THIS COUNTRY--THE FAMILY OF THE VICTIM IS NEVER TOLD WHEN THE EXECUTION IS TO BE CARRIED OUT. YOU WAIT FOR TEN, *FIFTEEN YEARS*, TRY TO MOVE ON WITH YOUR LIFE, AND ONE DAY YOU JUST RECEIVE A ***NOTICE***--
THE *FUGUTAITEN* IS DESIGNED TO GIVE CLOSURE TO THOSE WHO WERE *HELPLESS* AGAINST THE VIOLENCE OF OTHERS! THE PEOPLE WHOSE LOVED ONES WERE PREYED UPON, WHEN THEY COULD DO *NOTHING!*
YOU'RE SO PASSIONATE.
......
ガタ
IF YOU DON'T WANT TO TAKE PART IN THIS, THAT'S FINE. MIDORI AND I WILL DO THE *FUGUTAITEN* SERVICE ON OUR OWN.

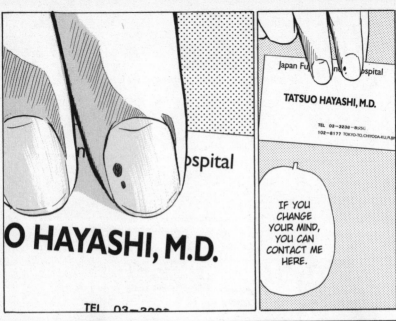

Japan Fu... ...n... ...ospital

TATSUO HAYASHI, M.D.

TEL 03-3238-8550
102-8177 TOKYO-TO, CHIYODA-KU, FUJI...

O HAYASHI, M.D.

TEL 03-3238...

IF YOU CHANGE YOUR MIND, YOU CAN CONTACT ME HERE.

...WHO ARE YOU?

クッ
クッ

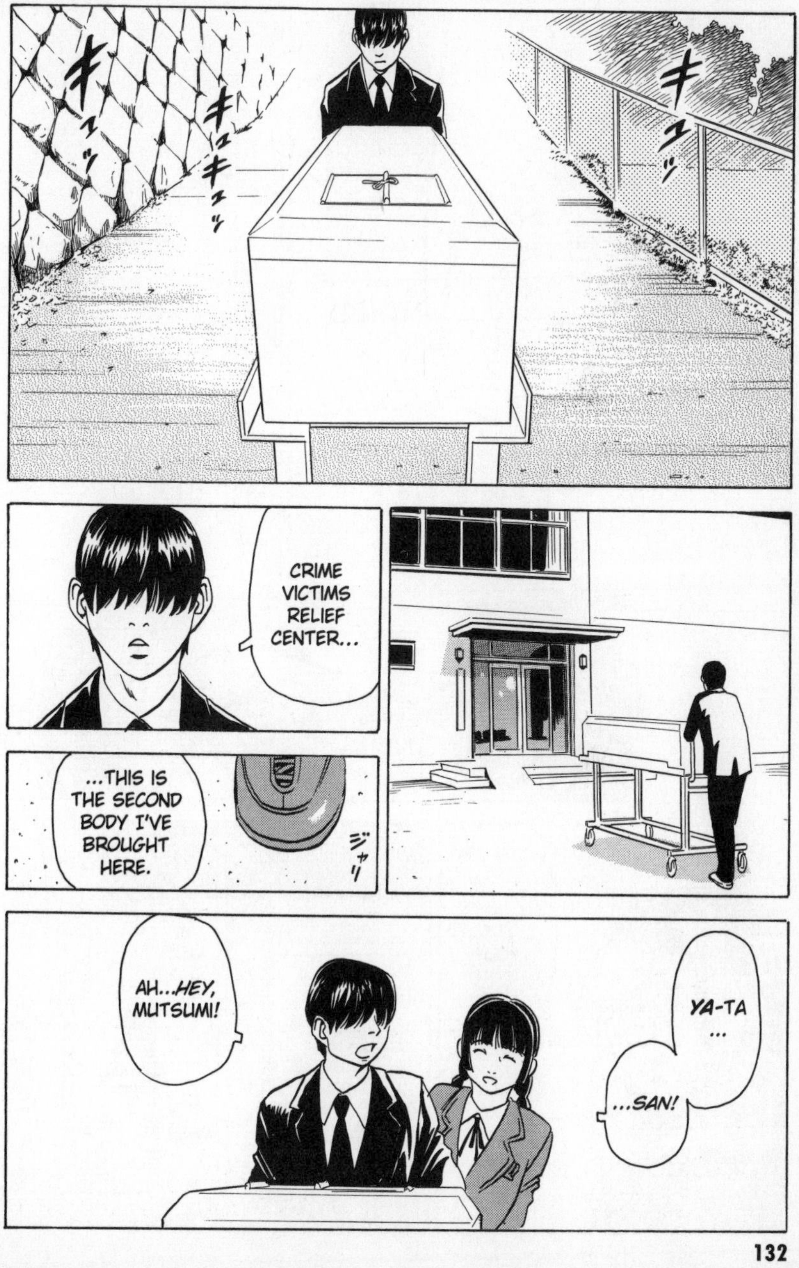
キュッ
キュキュッ
キュッ
CRIME VICTIMS RELIEF CENTER...
...THIS IS THE SECOND BODY I'VE BROUGHT HERE.
ジャリ
YA-TA ...
...SAN!
AH...HEY, MUTSUMI!

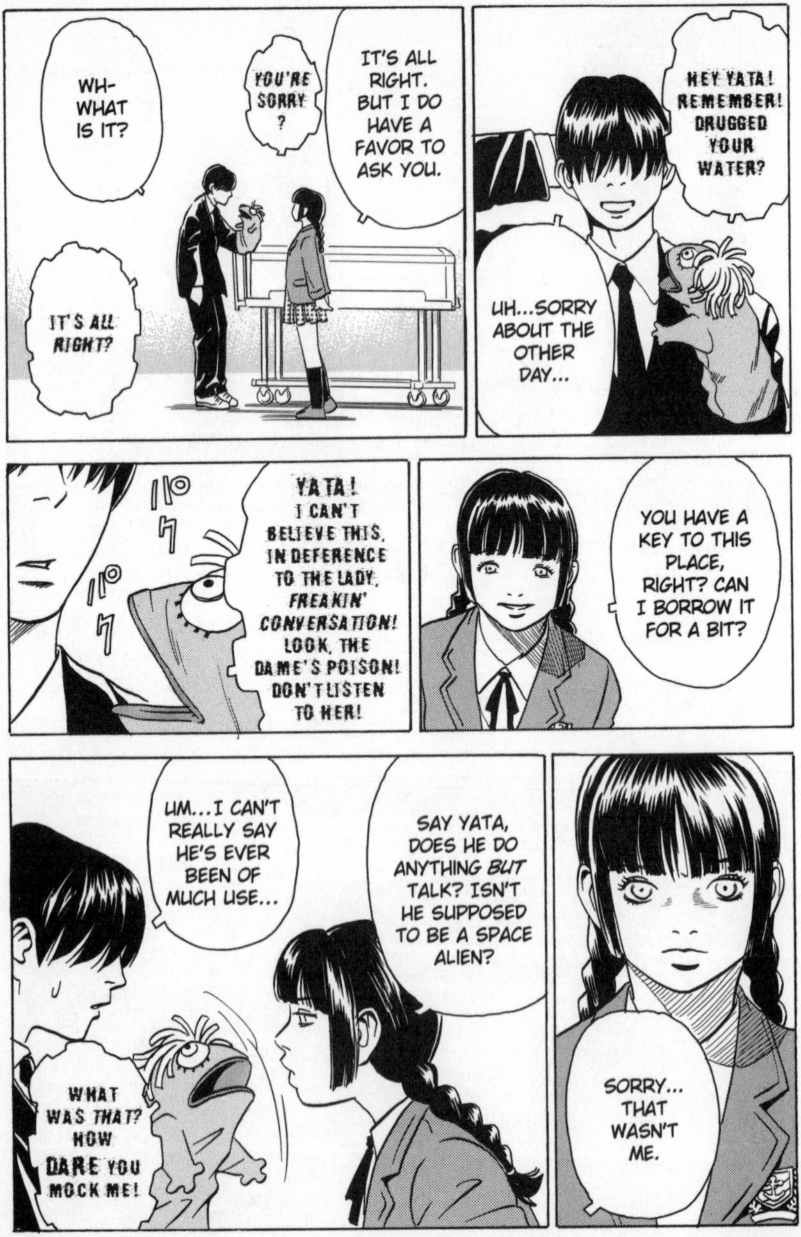
HEY YATA! REMEMBER! DRUGGED YOUR WATER?
UH...SORRY ABOUT THE OTHER DAY...
IT'S ALL RIGHT. BUT I DO HAVE A FAVOR TO ASK YOU.
YOU'RE SORRY?
WH-WHAT IS IT?
IT'S ALL RIGHT?
YOU HAVE A KEY TO THIS PLACE, RIGHT? CAN I BORROW IT FOR A BIT?
YATA! I CAN'T BELIEVE THIS. IN DEFERENCE TO THE LADY. *FREAKIN' CONVERSATION!* LOOK, THE DAME'S POISON! DON'T LISTEN TO HER!
パク
パク
SORRY... THAT WASN'T ME.
SAY YATA, DOES HE DO ANYTHING *BUT* TALK? ISN'T HE SUPPOSED TO BE A SPACE ALIEN?
UM...I CAN'T REALLY SAY HE'S EVER BEEN OF MUCH USE...
WHAT WAS *THAT*? HOW **DARE** YOU MOCK ME!

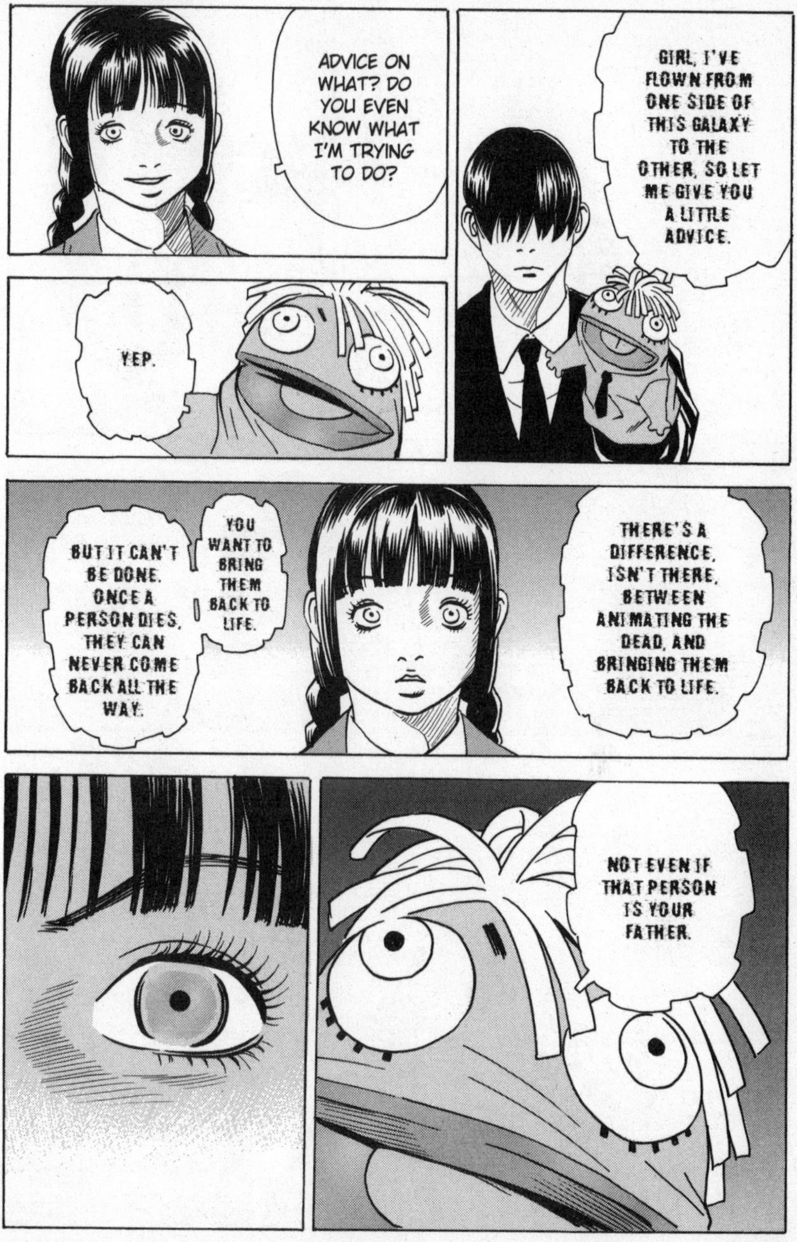
GIRL, I'VE FLOWN FROM ONE SIDE OF THIS GALAXY TO THE OTHER, SO LET ME GIVE YOU A LITTLE ADVICE.
ADVICE ON WHAT? DO YOU EVEN KNOW WHAT I'M TRYING TO DO?
YEP.
THERE'S A DIFFERENCE, ISN'T THERE, BETWEEN ANIMATING THE DEAD, AND BRINGING THEM BACK TO LIFE.
YOU WANT TO BRING THEM BACK TO LIFE.
BUT IT CAN'T BE DONE. ONCE A PERSON DIES, THEY CAN NEVER COME BACK ALL THE WAY.
NOT EVEN IF THAT PERSON IS YOUR FATHER.

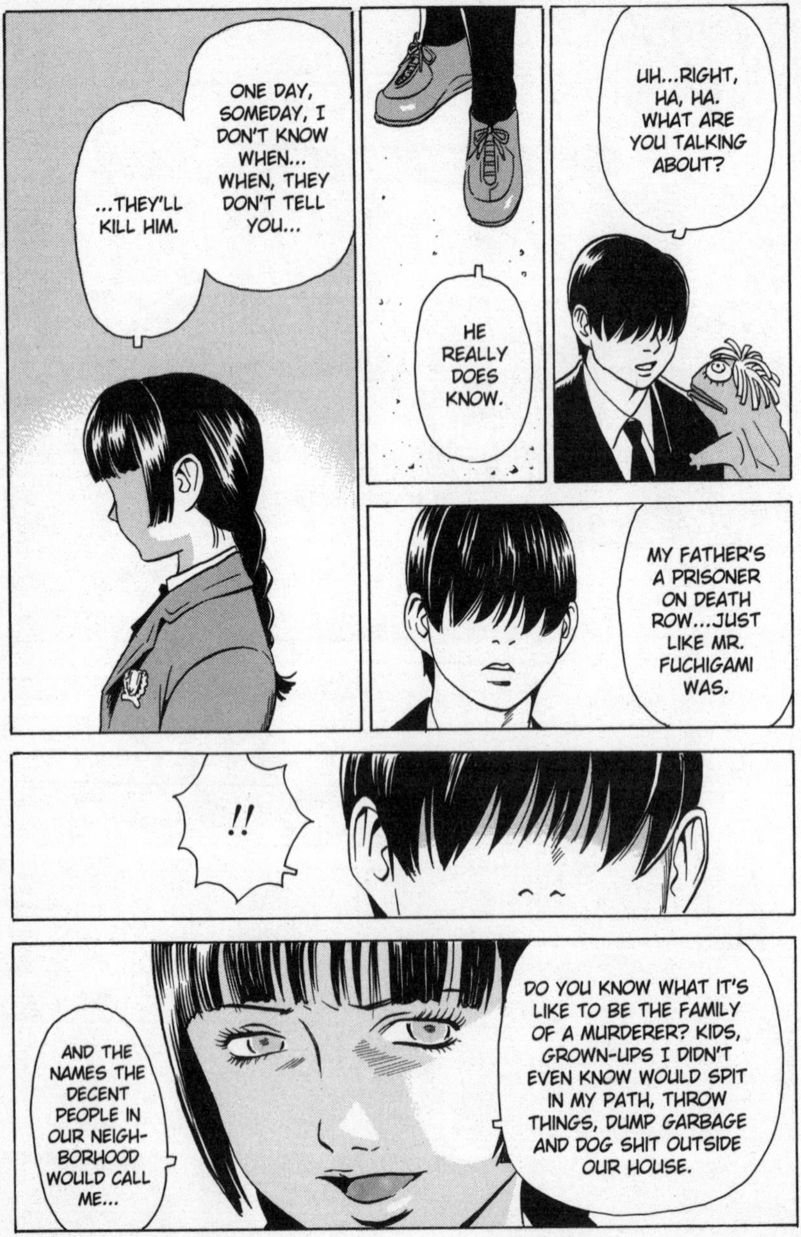
UH...RIGHT, HA, HA. WHAT ARE YOU TALKING ABOUT?
HE REALLY DOES KNOW.
MY FATHER'S A PRISONER ON DEATH ROW...JUST LIKE MR. FUCHIGAMI WAS.
ONE DAY, SOMEDAY, I DON'T KNOW WHEN... WHEN, THEY DON'T TELL YOU...
...THEY'LL KILL HIM.
!!
DO YOU KNOW WHAT IT'S LIKE TO BE THE FAMILY OF A MURDERER? KIDS, GROWN-UPS I DIDN'T EVEN KNOW WOULD SPIT IN MY PATH, THROW THINGS, DUMP GARBAGE AND DOG SHIT OUTSIDE OUR HOUSE.
AND THE NAMES THE DECENT PEOPLE IN OUR NEIGH-BORHOOD WOULD CALL ME...

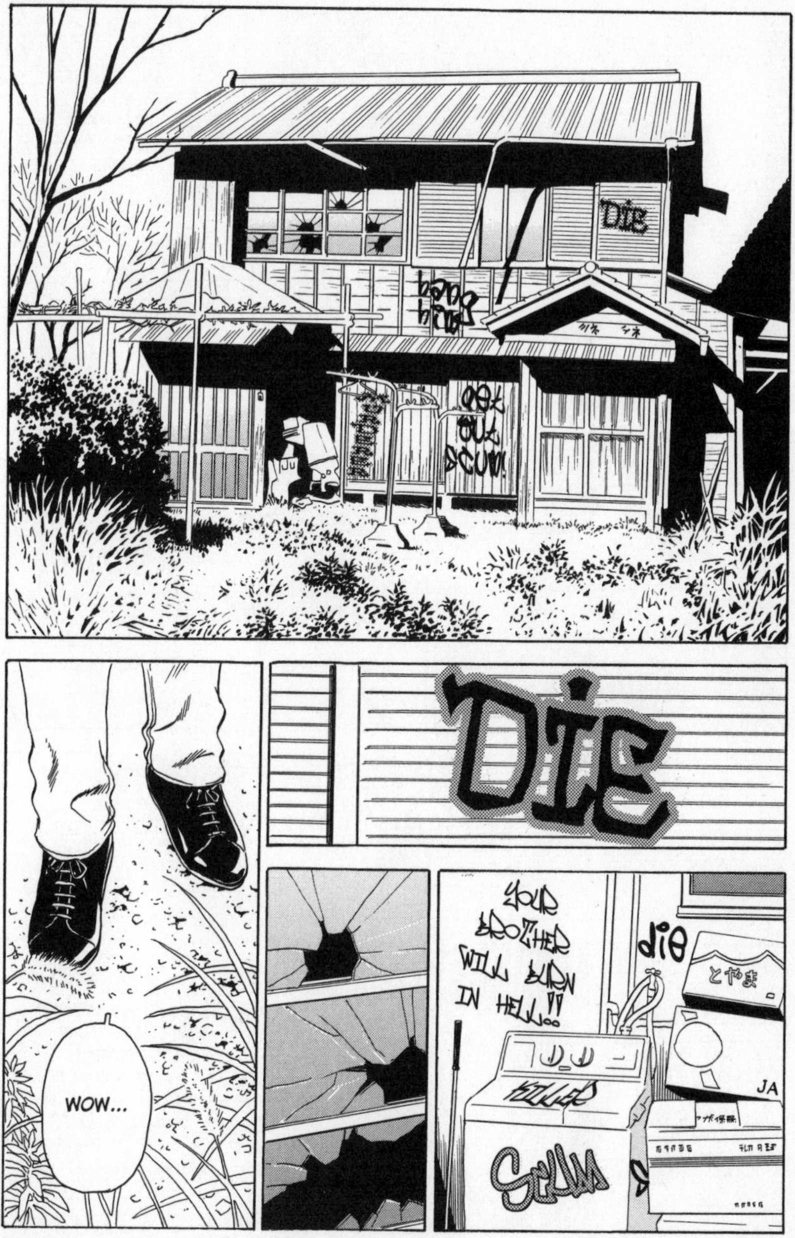
DIE
GET OUT SCUM!
DIE
YOUR BROTHER WILL BURN IN HELL!!..
die
とやま
JA
KILLER
SCUM
WOW...

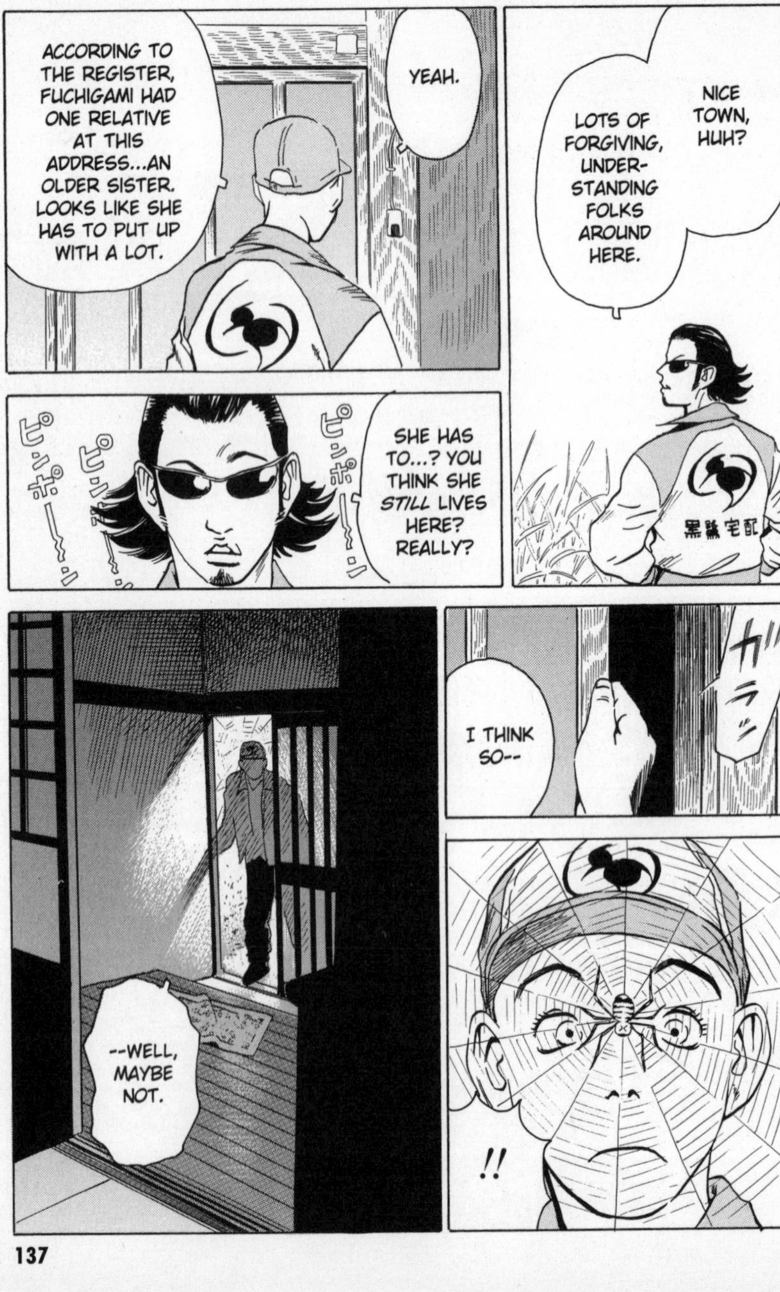
NICE TOWN, HUH?
LOTS OF FORGIVING, UNDER-STANDING FOLKS AROUND HERE.
黒鷺宅配
ACCORDING TO THE REGISTER, FUCHIGAMI HAD ONE RELATIVE AT THIS ADDRESS...AN OLDER SISTER. LOOKS LIKE SHE HAS TO PUT UP WITH A LOT.
YEAH.
ピンポーン~
SHE HAS TO...? YOU THINK SHE STILL LIVES HERE? REALLY?
ピンポーン~
ピンポーン~
ガラッ
I THINK SO--
!!
--WELL, MAYBE NOT.

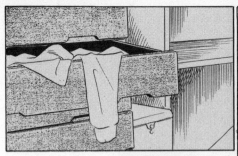

HEY KARATSU, THIS IS LOOKING LIKE A WASTED TRIP...

I MEAN SHE NEVER CLAIMED THE BODY, RIGHT? I'M THINKING SHE MUST HAVE CUT ALL TIES AND MOVED AWAY. MAYBE EVEN CHANGED HER NAME.

WHO COULD BLAME HER, RIGHT...?

THERE'S RICE STILL IN THE COOKER. IT DOESN'T LOOK LIKE SHE WENT FAR.

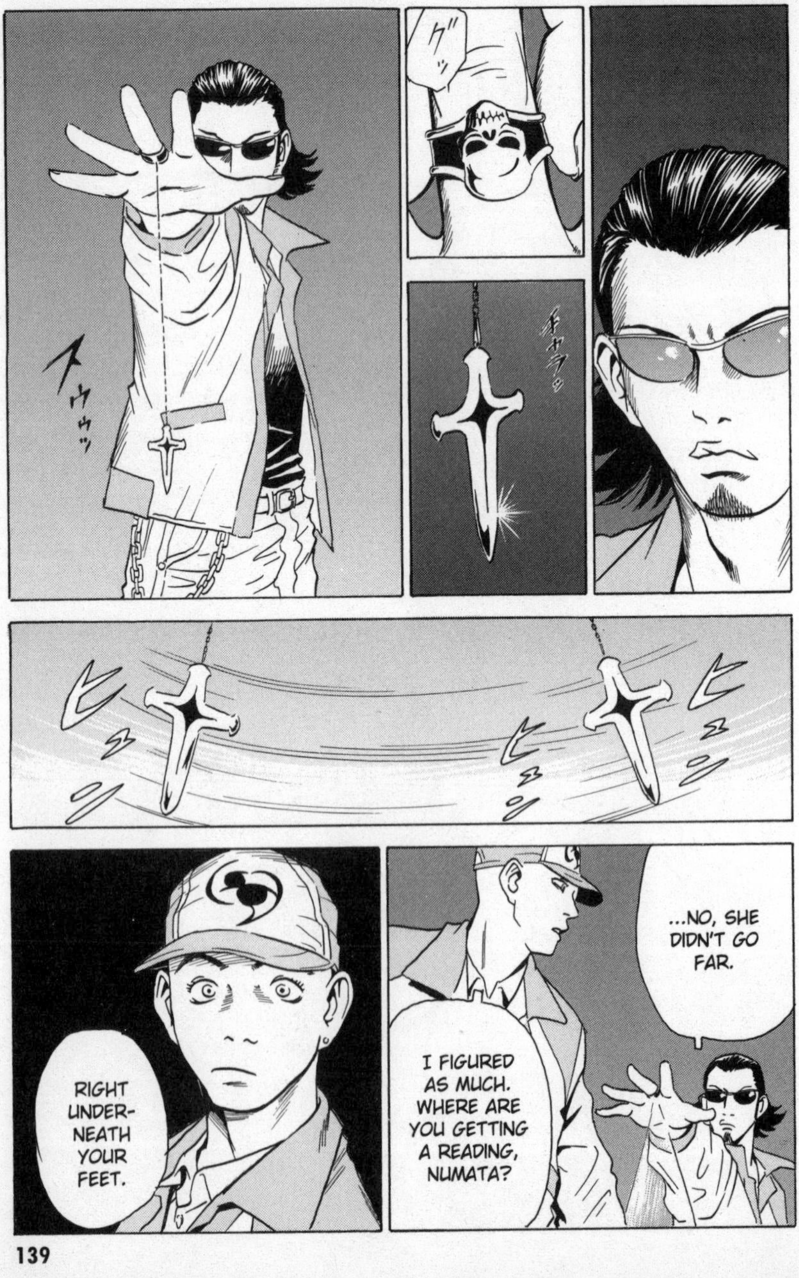
...NO, SHE DIDN'T GO FAR.
I FIGURED AS MUCH. WHERE ARE YOU GETTING A READING, NUMATA?
RIGHT UNDERNEATH YOUR FEET.

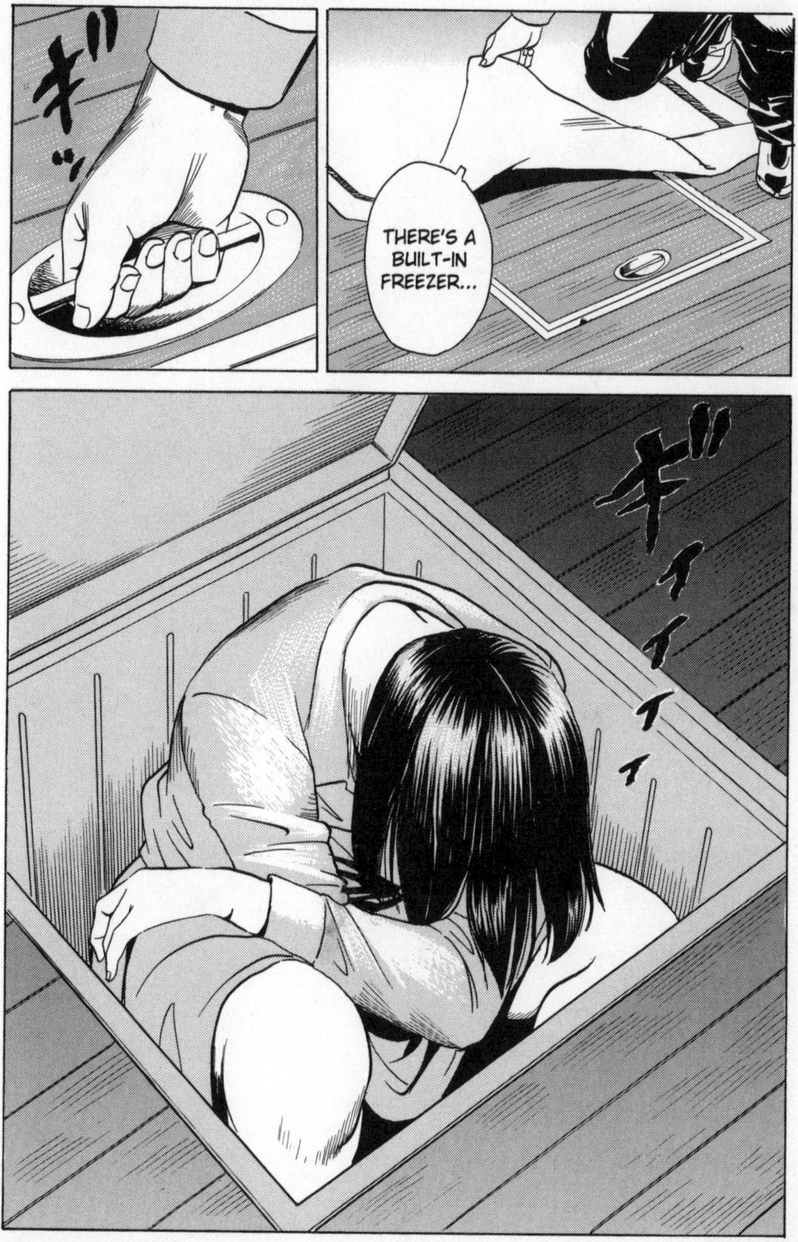
THERE'S A BUILT-IN FREEZER...

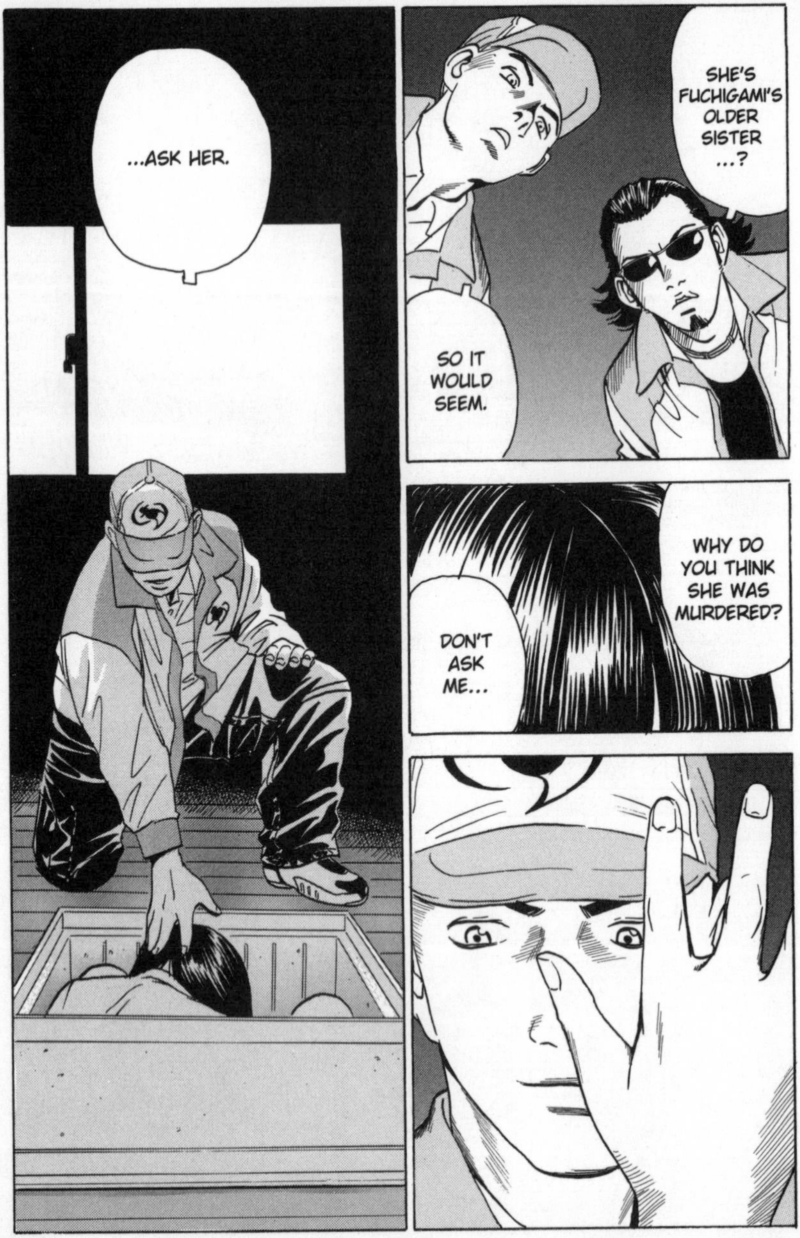
SHE'S FUCHIGAMI'S OLDER SISTER ...?
SO IT WOULD SEEM.
WHY DO YOU THINK SHE WAS MURDERED?
DON'T ASK ME...
...ASK HER.

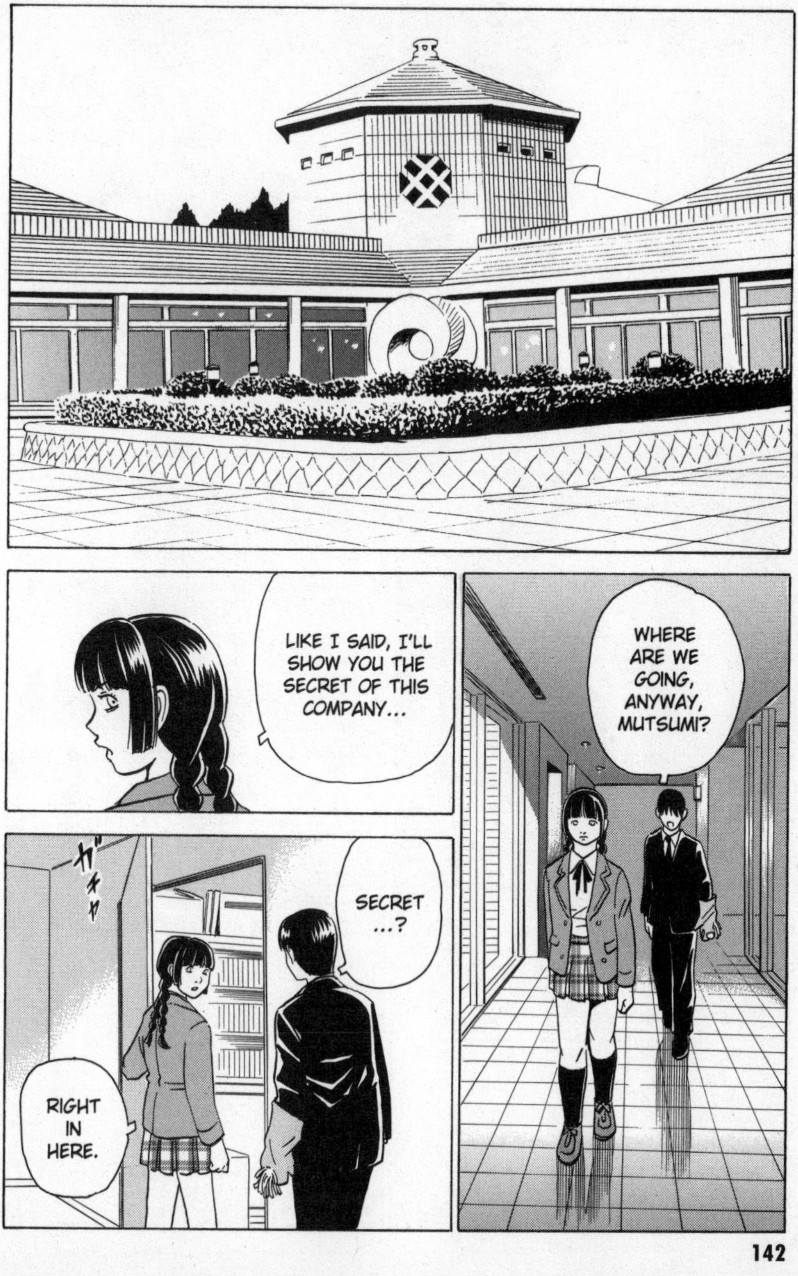
WHERE ARE WE GOING, ANYWAY, MUTSUMI?
LIKE I SAID, I'LL SHOW YOU THE SECRET OF THIS COMPANY...
ガチャ
SECRET ...?
RIGHT IN HERE.

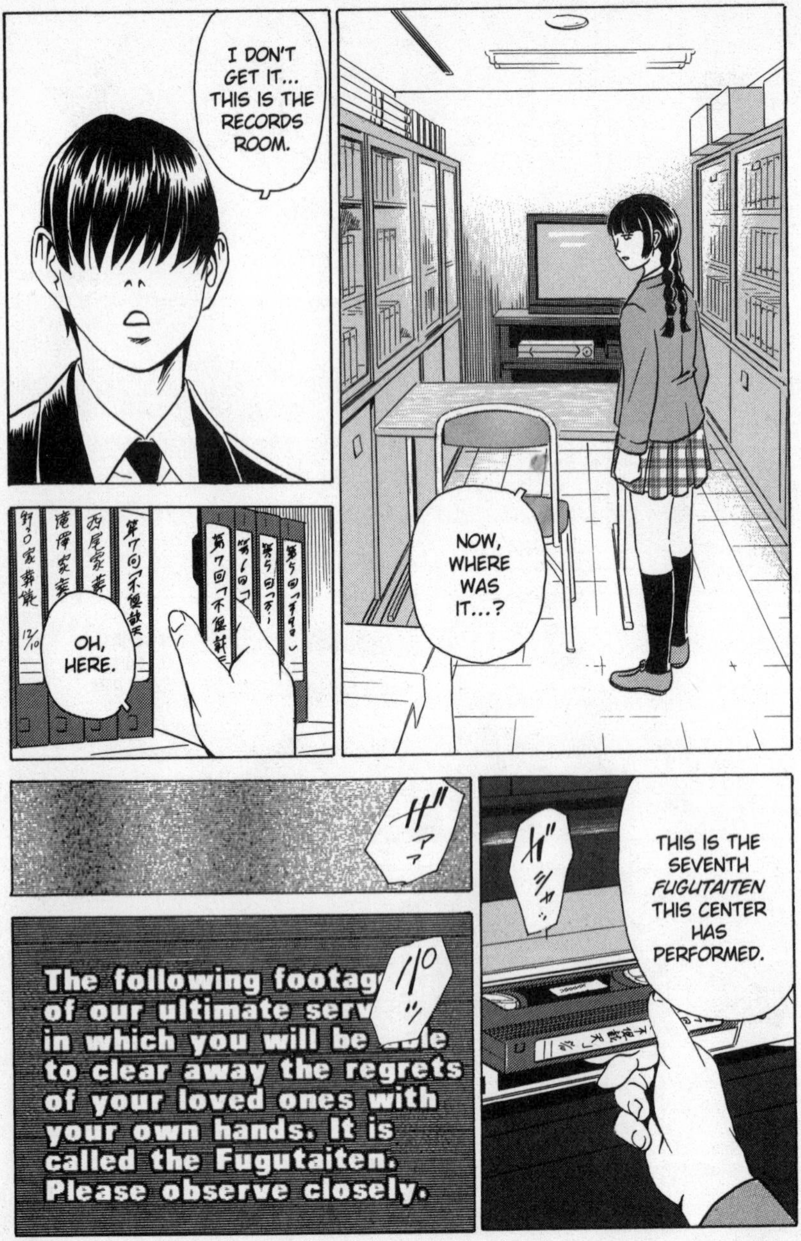
NOW, WHERE WAS IT...?
I DON'T GET IT... THIS IS THE RECORDS ROOM.
OH, HERE.
ガシャッ
THIS IS THE SEVENTH *FUGUTAITEN* THIS CENTER HAS PERFORMED.
ザァァ
パッ
The following footag
of our ultimate serv
in which you will be
to clear away the regrets
of your loved ones with
your own hands. It is
called the Fugutaiten.
Please observe closely.

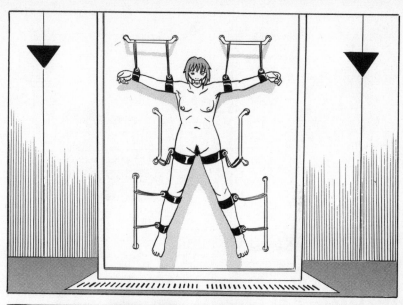

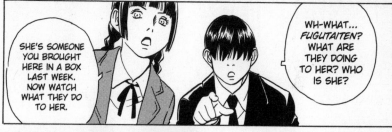

WH-WHAT... FUGUTAITEN? WHAT ARE THEY DOING TO HER? WHO IS SHE?
SHE'S SOMEONE YOU BROUGHT HERE IN A BOX LAST WEEK. NOW WATCH WHAT THEY DO TO HER.
BY LAW, SHE IS ALREADY DEAD.
THEREFORE, FEEL FREE TO EXPRESS YOURSELVES ACCORDINGLY.

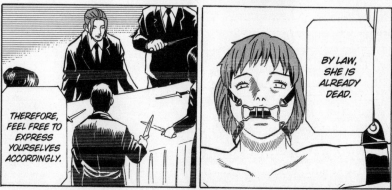

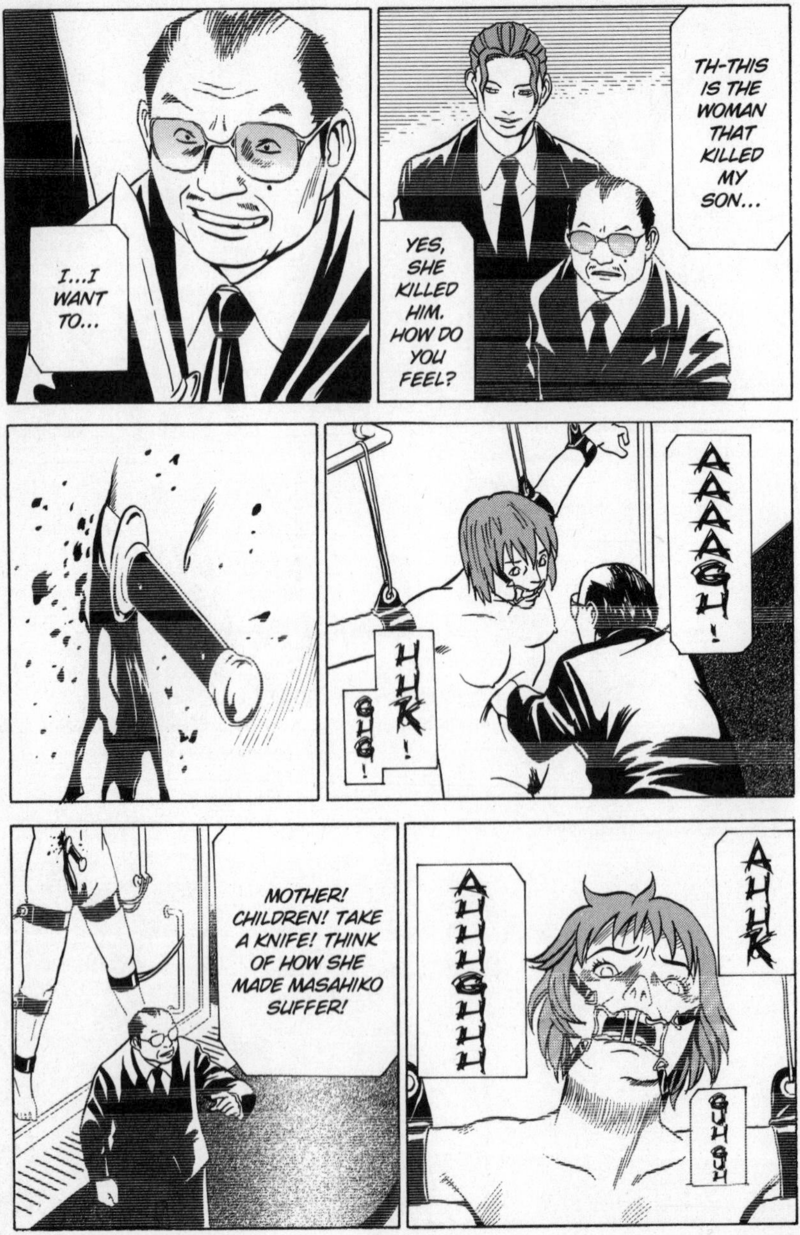
TH-THIS IS THE WOMAN THAT KILLED MY SON...
YES, SHE KILLED HIM. HOW DO YOU FEEL?
I...I WANT TO...
AAAAAGH!
HHK!
GHG!
AHHK
AHHHGHHH
GHGH
MOTHER! CHILDREN! TAKE A KNIFE! THINK OF HOW SHE MADE MASAHIKO SUFFER!

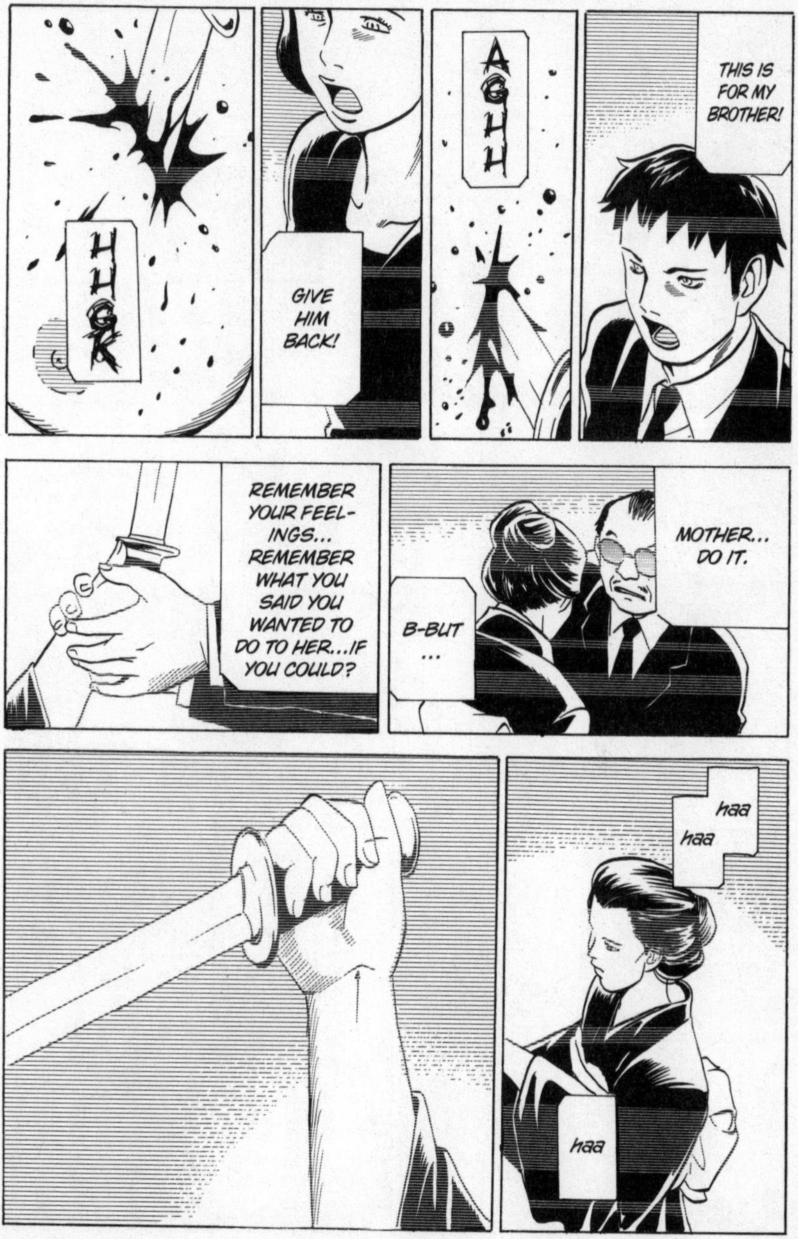

THIS IS FOR MY BROTHER!
AGHH
GIVE HIM BACK!
HHGK
MOTHER... DO IT.
B-BUT ...
REMEMBER YOUR FEEL-INGS... REMEMBER WHAT YOU SAID YOU WANTED TO DO TO HER...IF YOU COULD?
haa
haa
haa

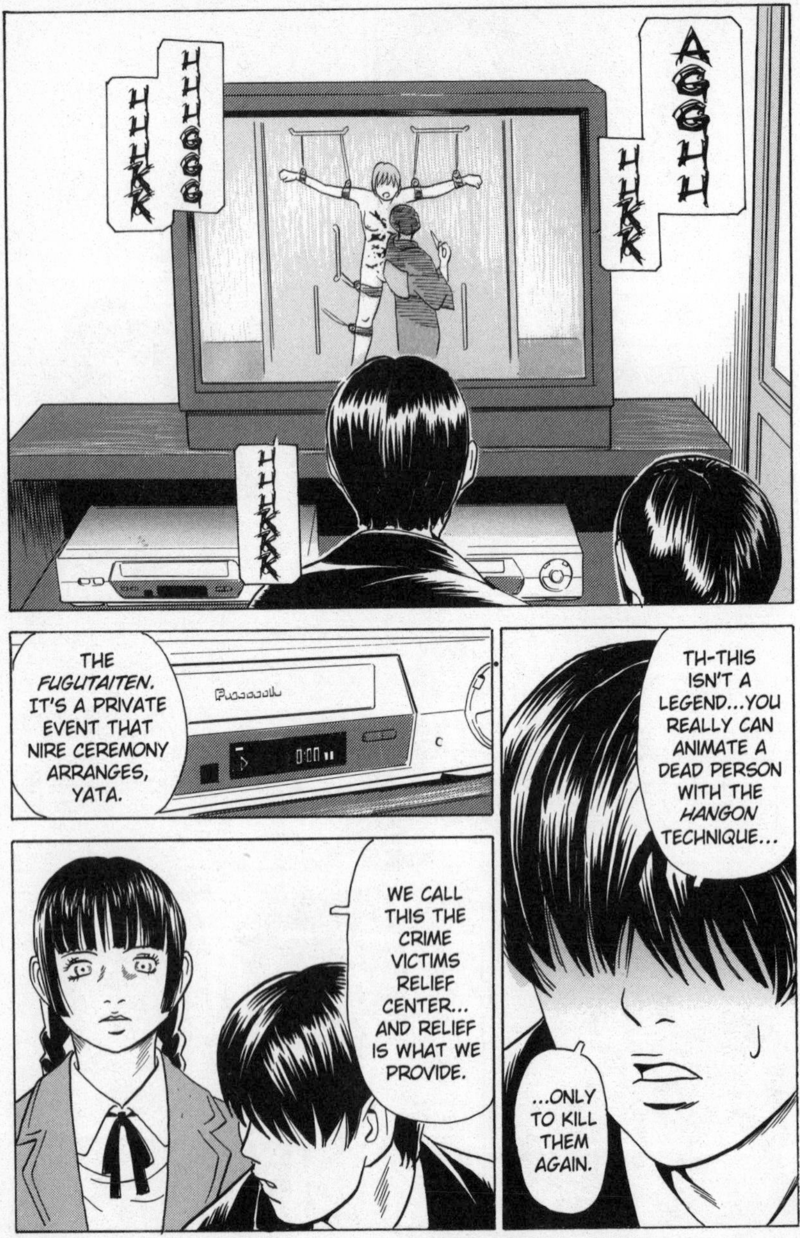
AGGHH
HHKK
HHHGGG
HHHKK
HHHKKK
TH-THIS ISN'T A LEGEND...YOU REALLY CAN ANIMATE A DEAD PERSON WITH THE *HANGON* TECHNIQUE...
...ONLY TO KILL THEM AGAIN.
THE *FUGUTAITEN*. IT'S A PRIVATE EVENT THAT NIRE CEREMONY ARRANGES, YATA.
WE CALL THIS THE CRIME VICTIMS RELIEF CENTER... AND RELIEF IS WHAT WE PROVIDE.

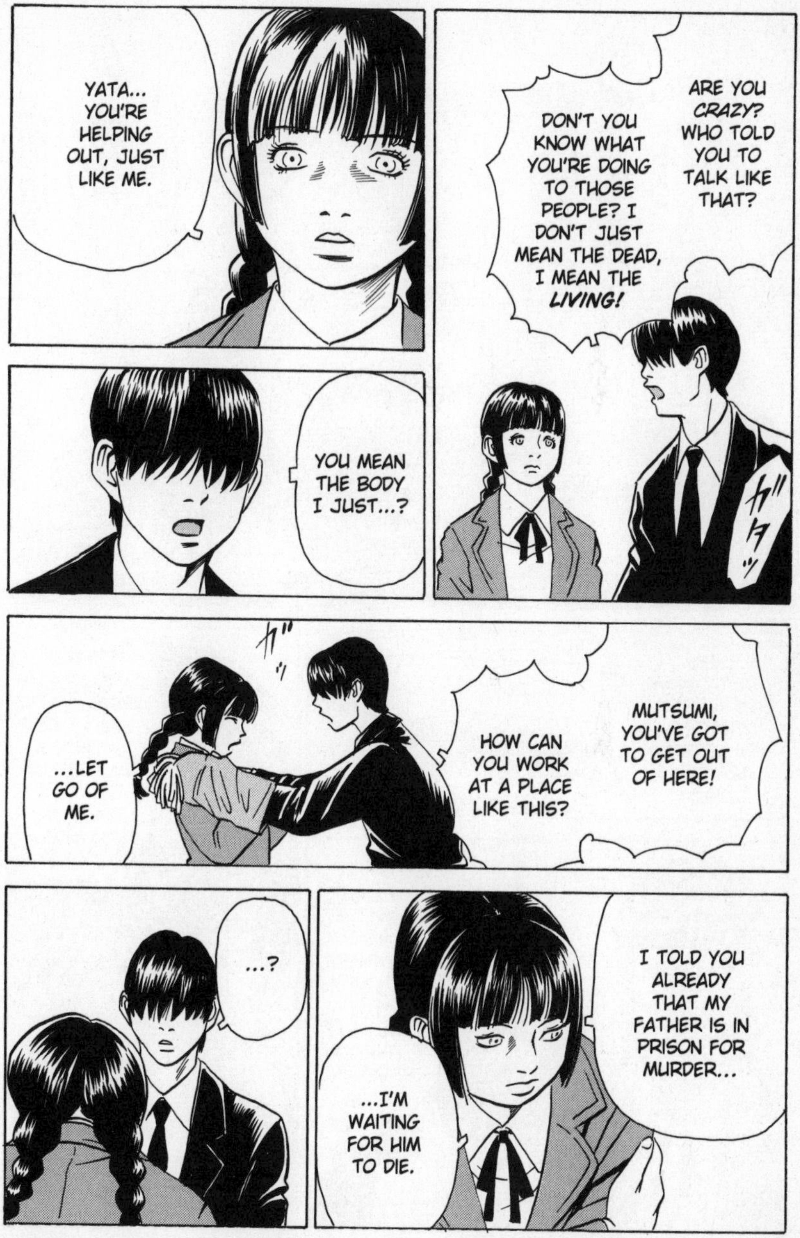
ARE YOU CRAZY? WHO TOLD YOU TO TALK LIKE THAT?
DON'T YOU KNOW WHAT YOU'RE DOING TO THOSE PEOPLE? I DON'T JUST MEAN THE DEAD, I MEAN THE LIVING!
ガタッ
YATA... YOU'RE HELPING OUT, JUST LIKE ME.
YOU MEAN THE BODY I JUST...?
ガッ
MUTSUMI, YOU'VE GOT TO GET OUT OF HERE!
HOW CAN YOU WORK AT A PLACE LIKE THIS?
...LET GO OF ME.
I TOLD YOU ALREADY THAT MY FATHER IS IN PRISON FOR MURDER...
...I'M WAITING FOR HIM TO DIE.
...?

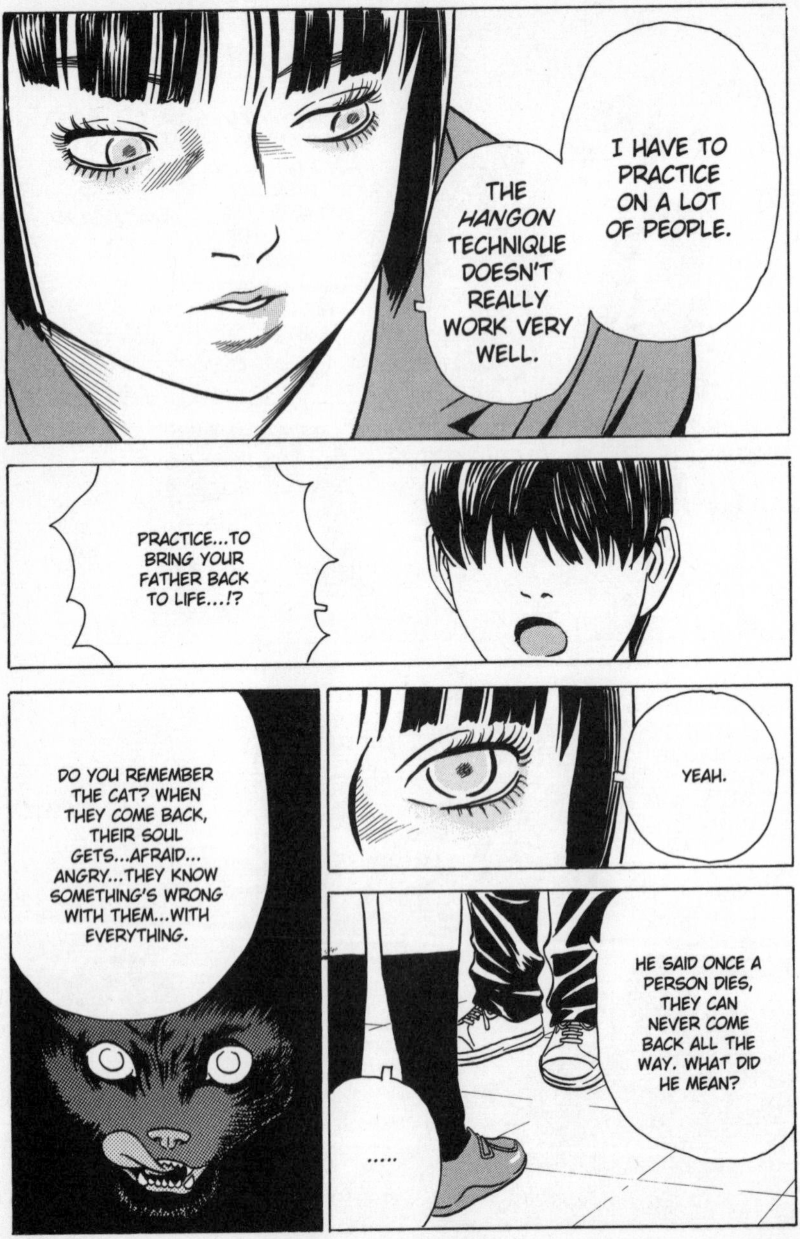

I HAVE TO PRACTICE ON A LOT OF PEOPLE.
THE *HANGON* TECHNIQUE DOESN'T REALLY WORK VERY WELL.
PRACTICE...TO BRING YOUR FATHER BACK TO LIFE...!?
YEAH.
HE SAID ONCE A PERSON DIES, THEY CAN NEVER COME BACK ALL THE WAY. WHAT DID HE MEAN?
.....
DO YOU REMEMBER THE CAT? WHEN THEY COME BACK, THEIR SOUL GETS...AFRAID... ANGRY...THEY KNOW SOMETHING'S WRONG WITH THEM...WITH EVERYTHING.

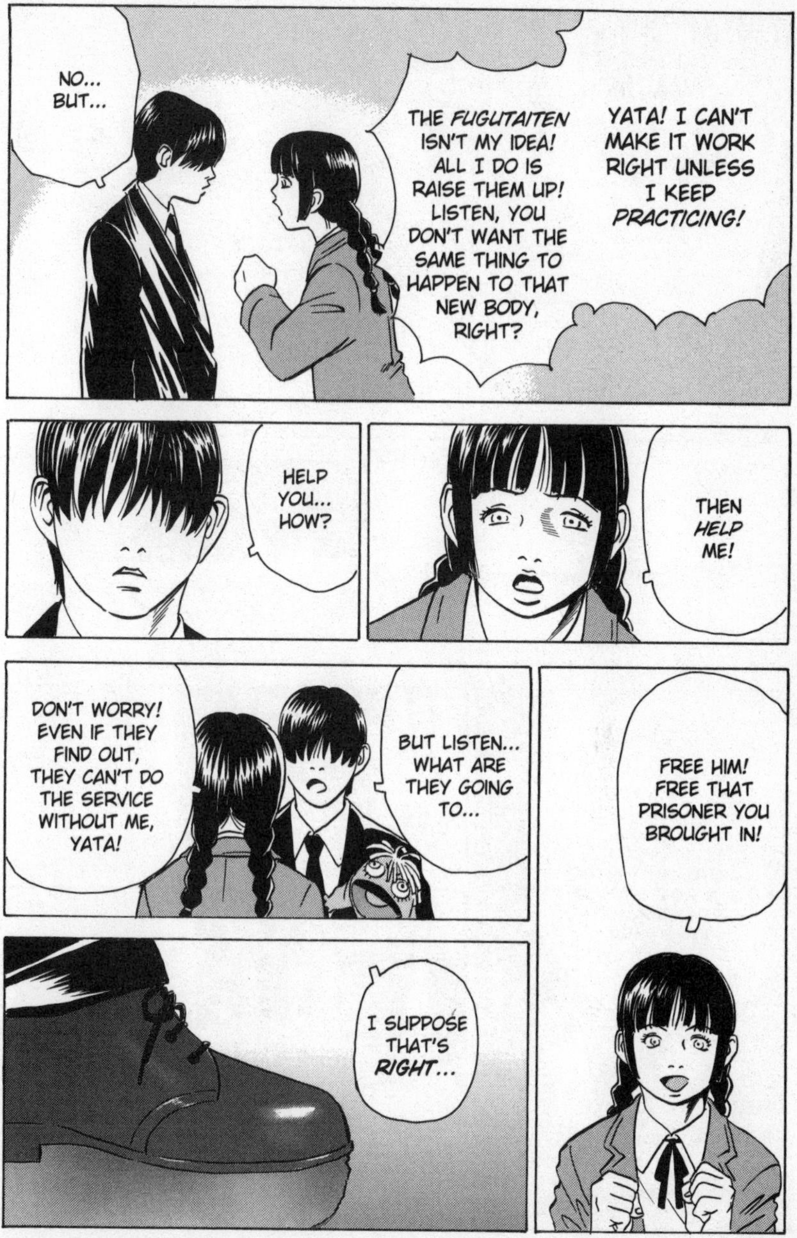
YATA! I CAN'T MAKE IT WORK RIGHT UNLESS I KEEP *PRACTICING!*
THE *FUGUTAITEN* ISN'T MY IDEA! ALL I DO IS RAISE THEM UP! LISTEN, YOU DON'T WANT THE SAME THING TO HAPPEN TO THAT NEW BODY, RIGHT?
NO... BUT...
THEN *HELP* ME!
HELP YOU... HOW?
FREE HIM! FREE THAT PRISONER YOU BROUGHT IN!
BUT LISTEN... WHAT ARE THEY GOING TO...
DON'T WORRY! EVEN IF THEY FIND OUT, THEY CAN'T DO THE SERVICE WITHOUT ME, YATA!
I SUPPOSE THAT'S *RIGHT*...

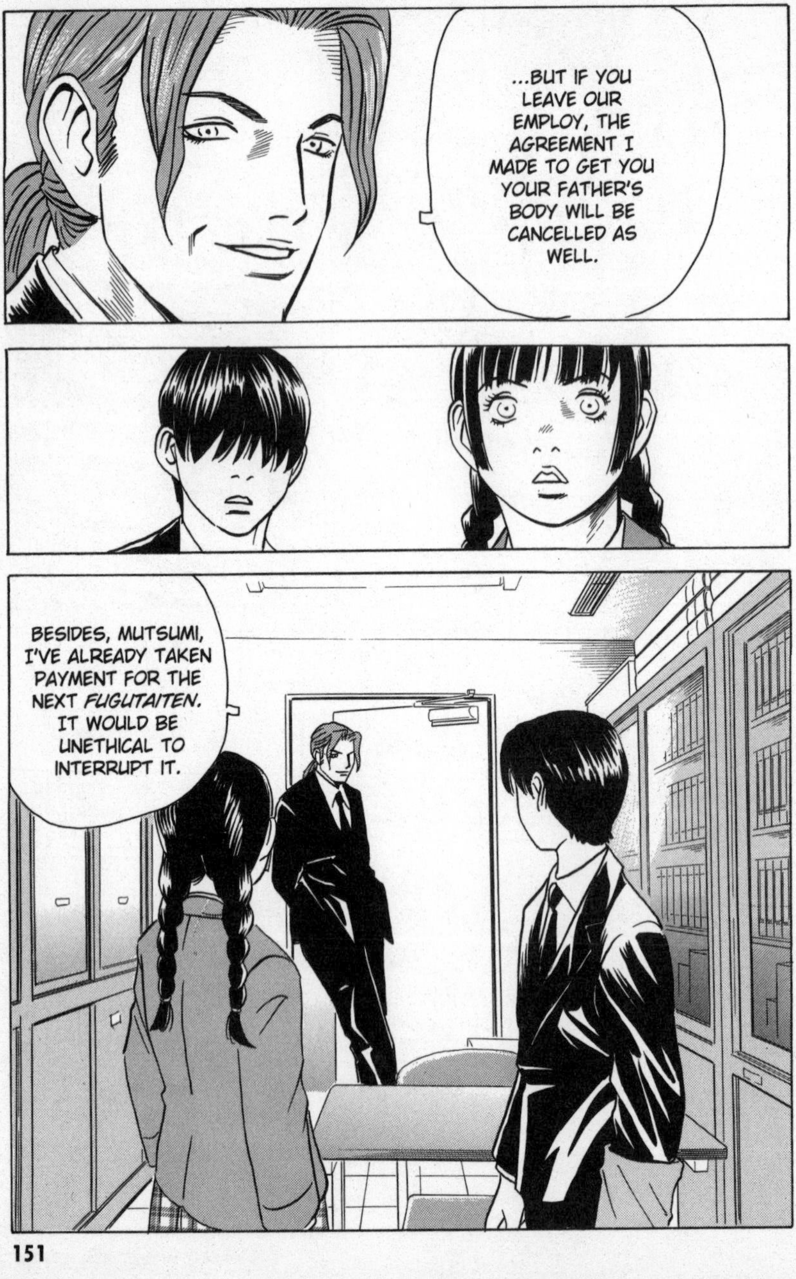
...BUT IF YOU LEAVE OUR EMPLOY, THE AGREEMENT I MADE TO GET YOU YOUR FATHER'S BODY WILL BE CANCELLED AS WELL.
BESIDES, MUTSUMI, I'VE ALREADY TAKEN PAYMENT FOR THE NEXT *FUGUTAITEN*. IT WOULD BE UNETHICAL TO INTERRUPT IT.

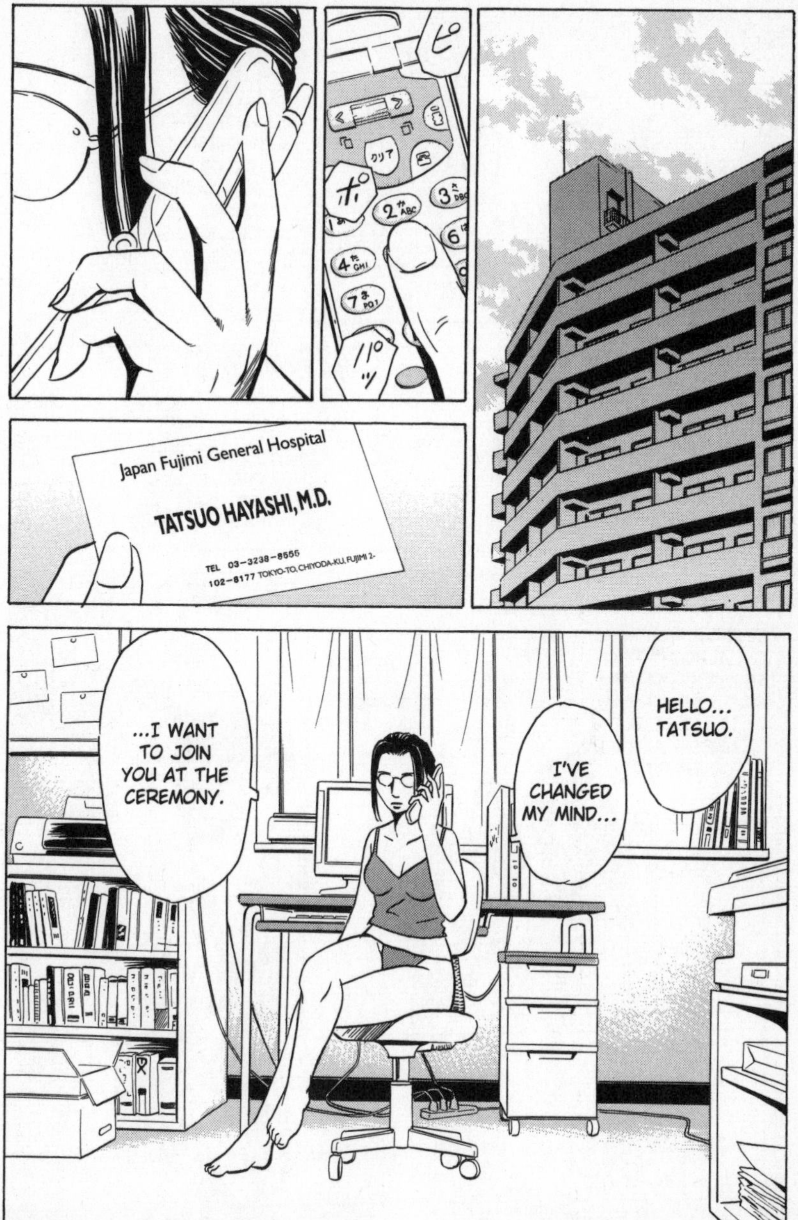
ピ
クリア
ポ
パッ
Japan Fujimi General Hospital
TATSUO HAYASHI, M.D.
TEL 03-3238-8555
102-8177 TOKYO-TO, CHIYODA-KU, FUJIMI 2-
HELLO... TATSUO.
I'VE CHANGED MY MIND...
...I WANT TO JOIN YOU AT THE CEREMONY.

5th delivery: mona lisa smile—the end

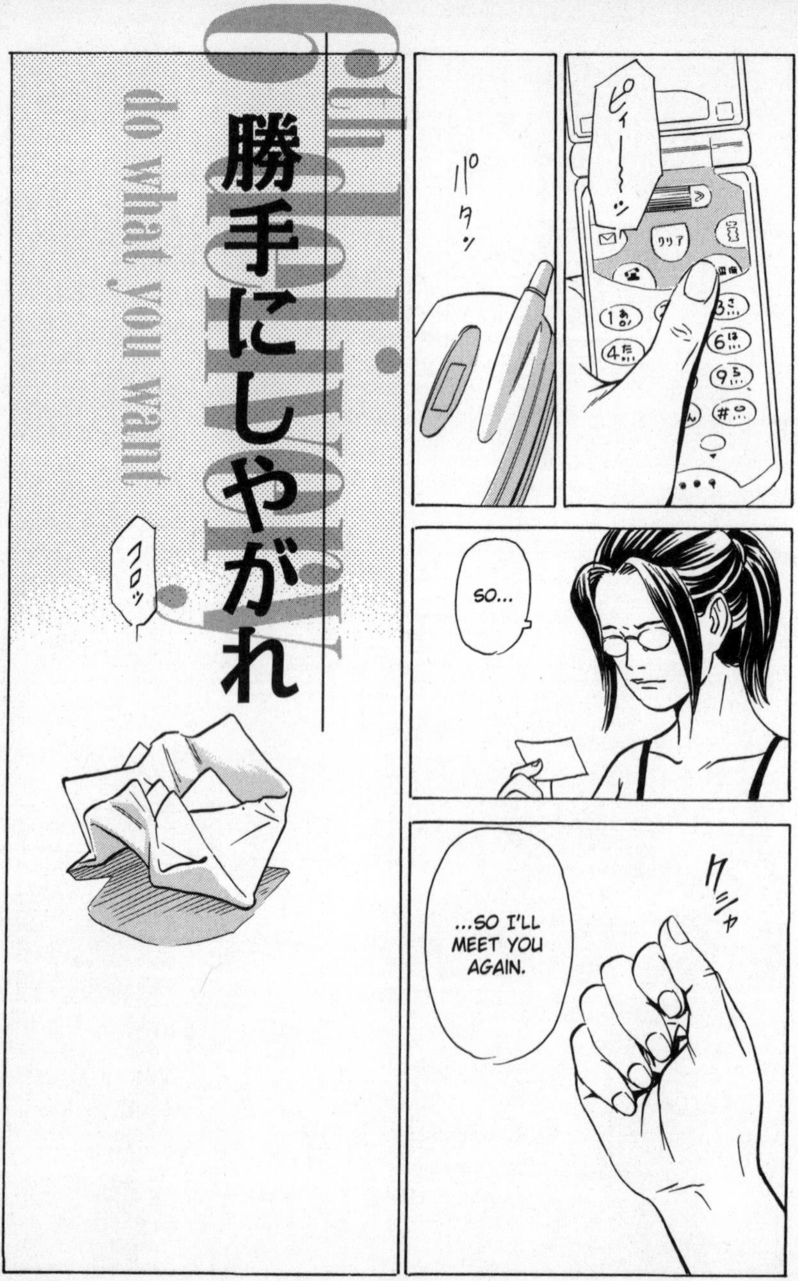
ピィ～～ッ
パタッ
SO...
...SO I'LL MEET YOU AGAIN.
クシャ
勝手にしやがれ
do what you want
コロッ

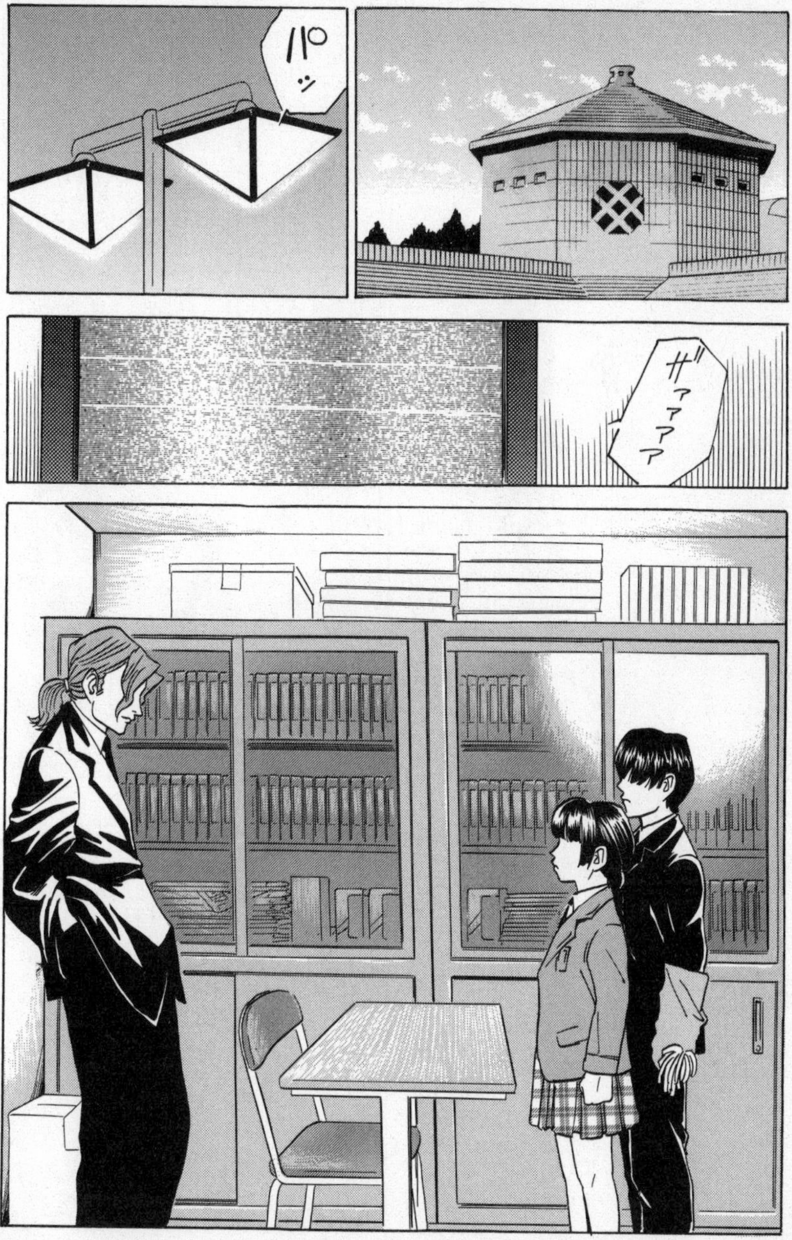
パッ
ザァアアア

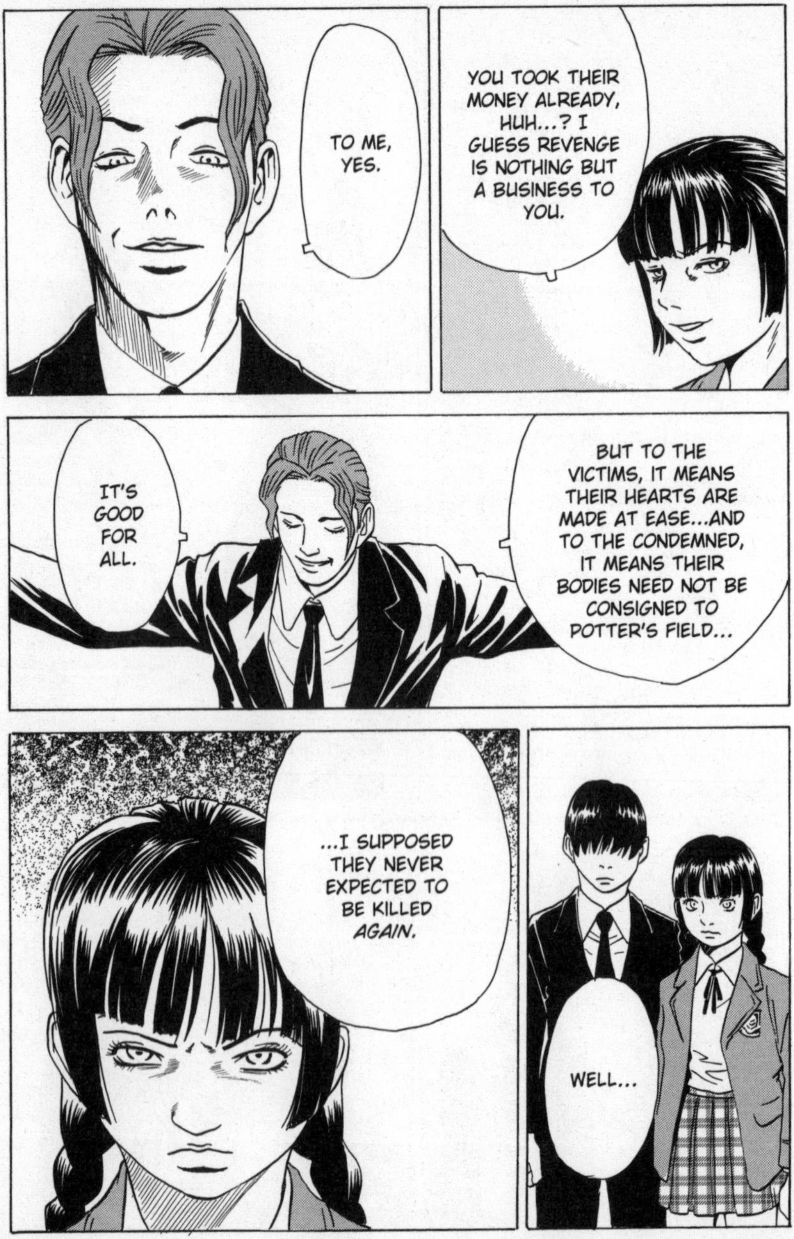
YOU TOOK THEIR MONEY ALREADY, HUH...? I GUESS REVENGE IS NOTHING BUT A BUSINESS TO YOU.
TO ME, YES.
BUT TO THE VICTIMS, IT MEANS THEIR HEARTS ARE MADE AT EASE...AND TO THE CONDEMNED, IT MEANS THEIR BODIES NEED NOT BE CONSIGNED TO POTTER'S FIELD...
IT'S GOOD FOR ALL.
WELL...
...I SUPPOSED THEY NEVER EXPECTED TO BE KILLED *AGAIN*.

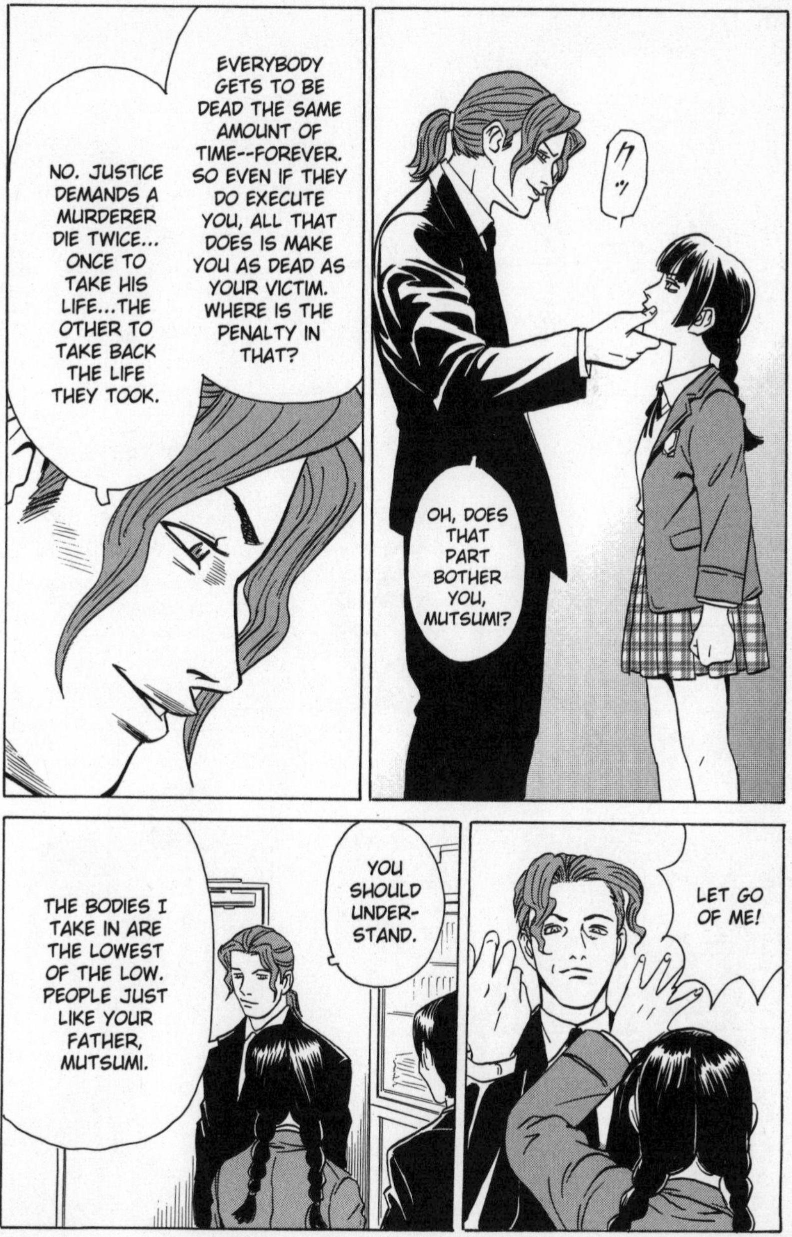

EVERYBODY GETS TO BE DEAD THE SAME AMOUNT OF TIME--FOREVER. SO EVEN IF THEY DO EXECUTE YOU, ALL THAT DOES IS MAKE YOU AS DEAD AS YOUR VICTIM. WHERE IS THE PENALTY IN THAT?
クッ
OH, DOES THAT PART BOTHER YOU, MUTSUMI?
NO. JUSTICE DEMANDS A MURDERER DIE TWICE... ONCE TO TAKE HIS LIFE...THE OTHER TO TAKE BACK THE LIFE THEY TOOK.
LET GO OF ME!
YOU SHOULD UNDER-STAND.
THE BODIES I TAKE IN ARE THE LOWEST OF THE LOW. PEOPLE JUST LIKE YOUR FATHER, MUTSUMI.

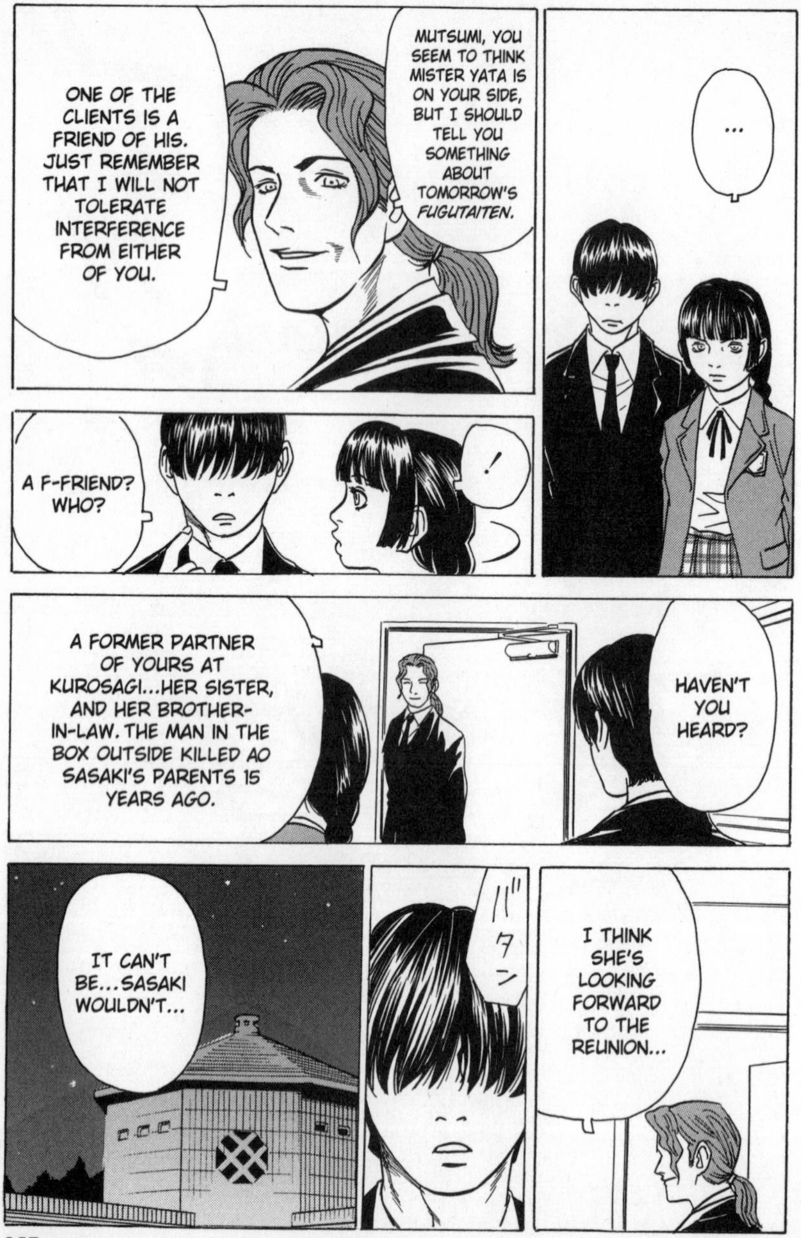
...
MUTSUMI, YOU SEEM TO THINK MISTER YATA IS ON YOUR SIDE, BUT I SHOULD TELL YOU SOMETHING ABOUT TOMORROW'S *FUGUTAITEN.*
ONE OF THE CLIENTS IS A FRIEND OF HIS. JUST REMEMBER THAT I WILL NOT TOLERATE INTERFERENCE FROM EITHER OF YOU.
!
A F-FRIEND? WHO?
HAVEN'T YOU HEARD?
A FORMER PARTNER OF YOURS AT KUROSAGI...HER SISTER, AND HER BROTHER-IN-LAW. THE MAN IN THE BOX OUTSIDE KILLED AO SASAKI'S PARENTS 15 YEARS AGO.
I THINK SHE'S LOOKING FORWARD TO THE REUNION...
バタン
IT CAN'T BE...SASAKI WOULDN'T...

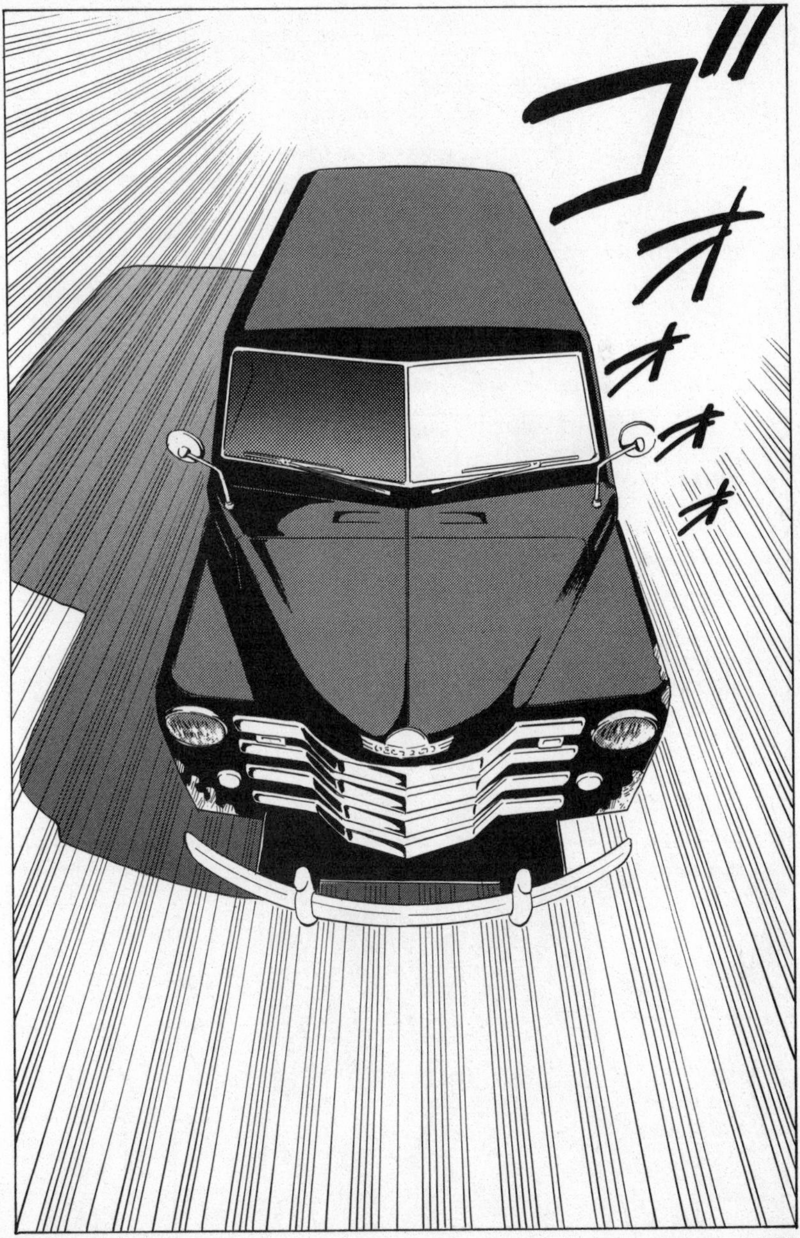
ゴオォォォ

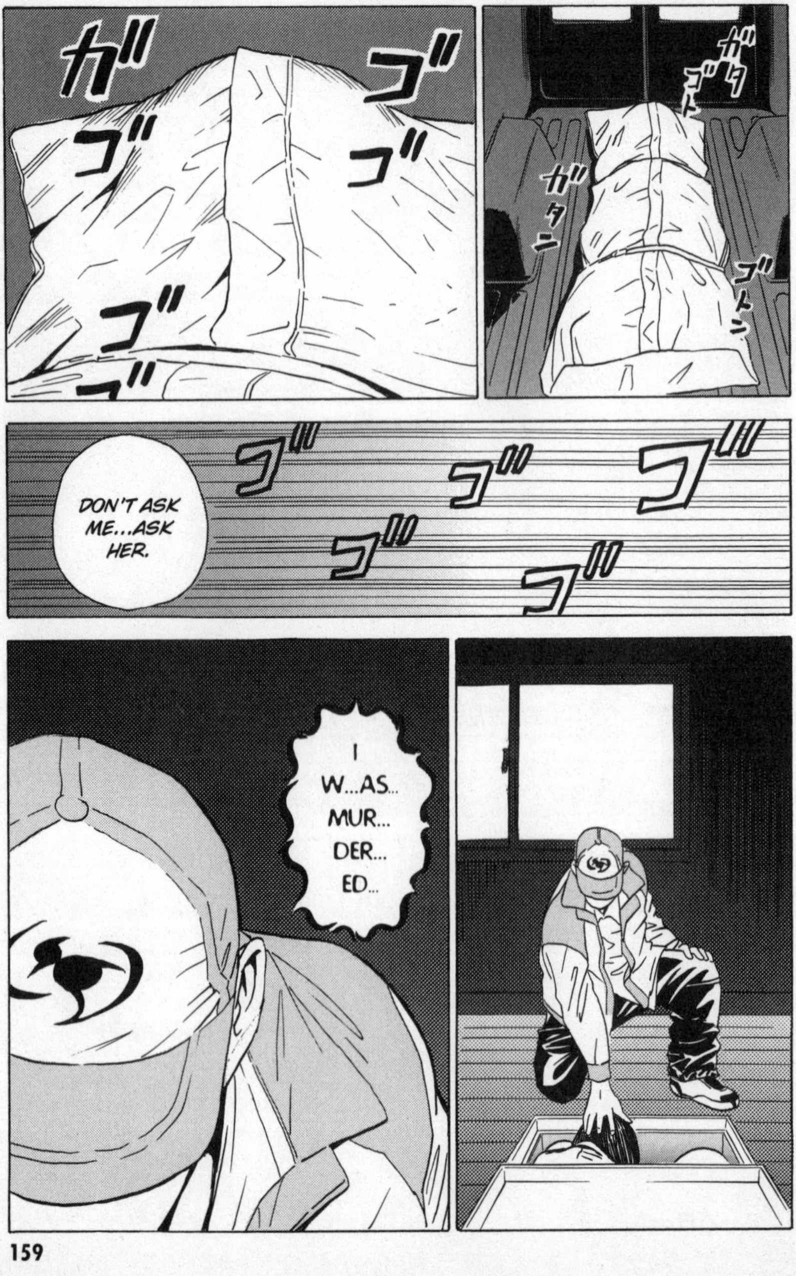
ガタゴト
ガタン
ゴトン
ガ
ゴ
ゴ
ゴ
ゴ
ゴ
ゴ
ゴ
ゴ
ゴ
DON'T ASK ME...ASK HER.
I W...AS... MUR... DER... ED...

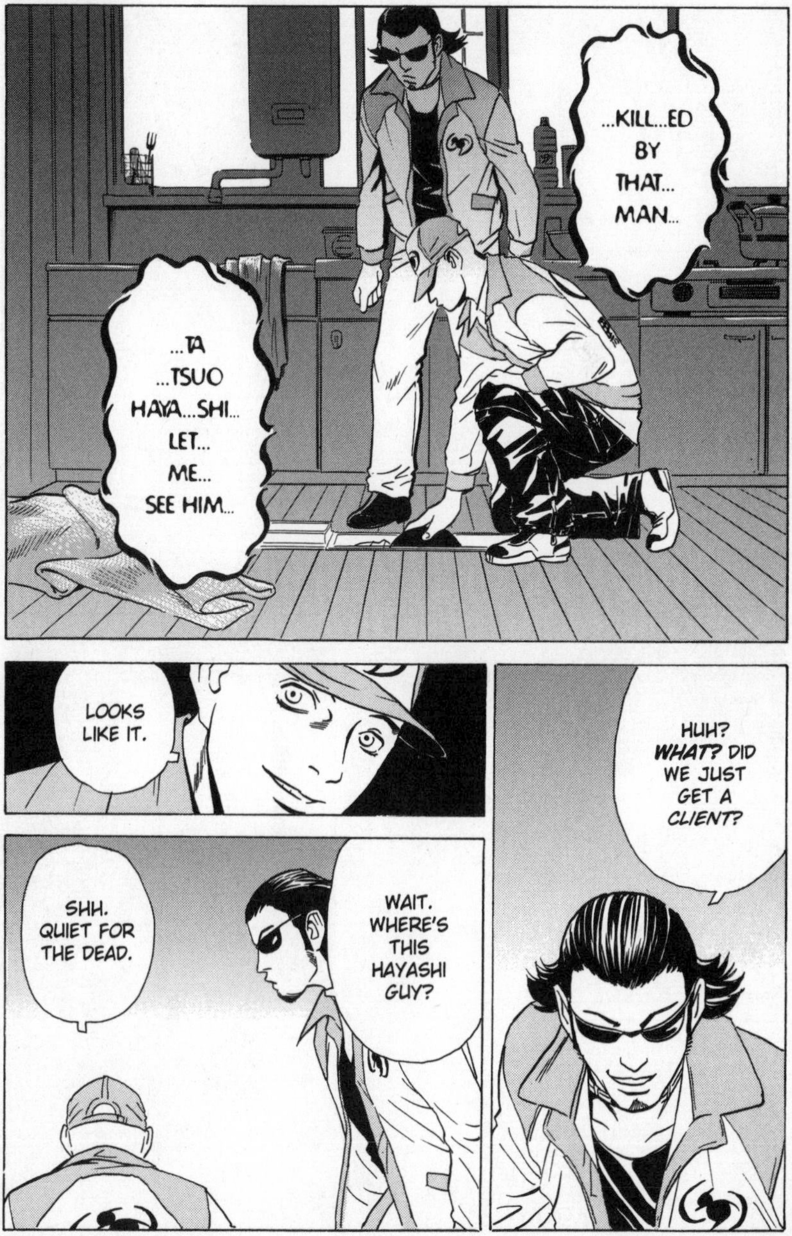
...KILL...ED BY THAT... MAN...
...TA ...TSUO HAYA...SHI... LET... ME... SEE HIM...
HUH? *WHAT?* DID WE JUST GET A *CLIENT?*
LOOKS LIKE IT.
WAIT. WHERE'S THIS HAYASHI GUY?
SHH. QUIET FOR THE DEAD.

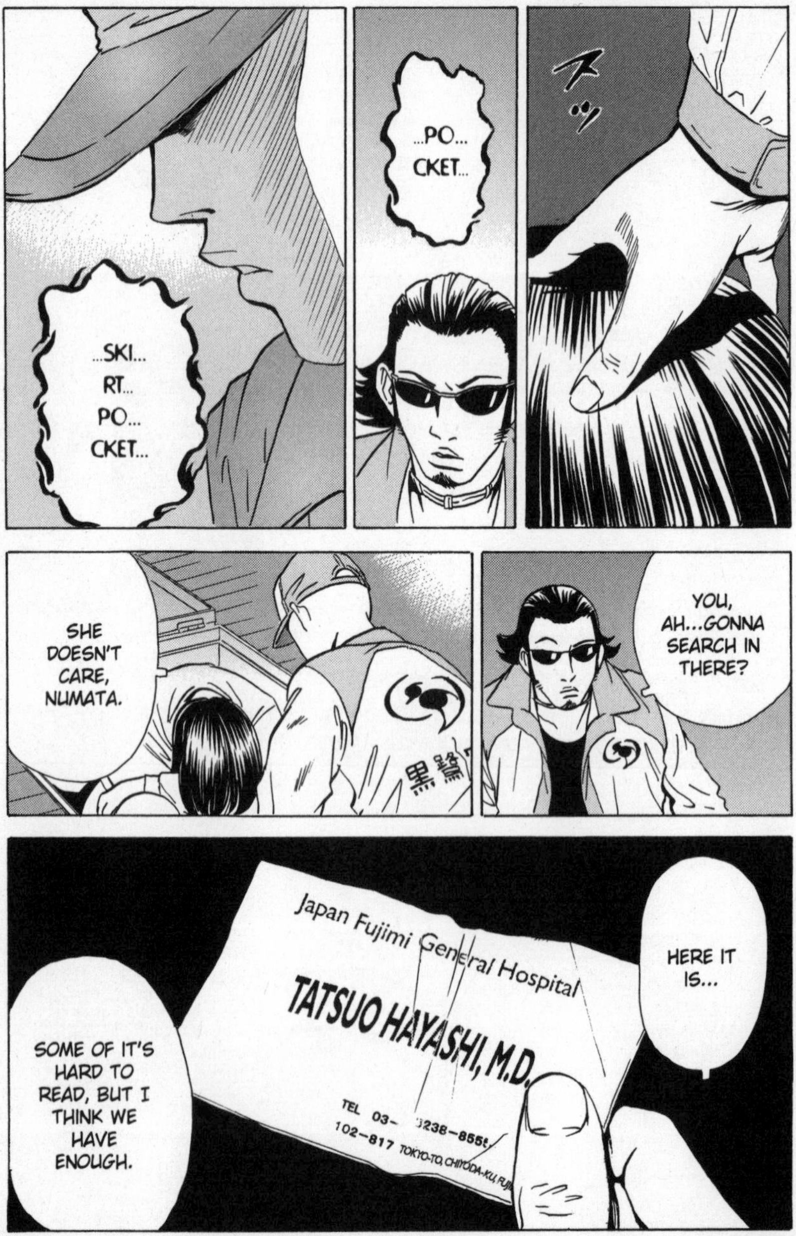
ズッ
...PO... CKET...
...SKI... RT... PO... CKET...
YOU, AH...GONNA SEARCH IN THERE?
SHE DOESN'T CARE, NUMATA.
HERE IT IS...
Japan Fujimi General Hospital
TATSUO HAYASHI, M.D.
SOME OF IT'S HARD TO READ, BUT I THINK WE HAVE ENOUGH.

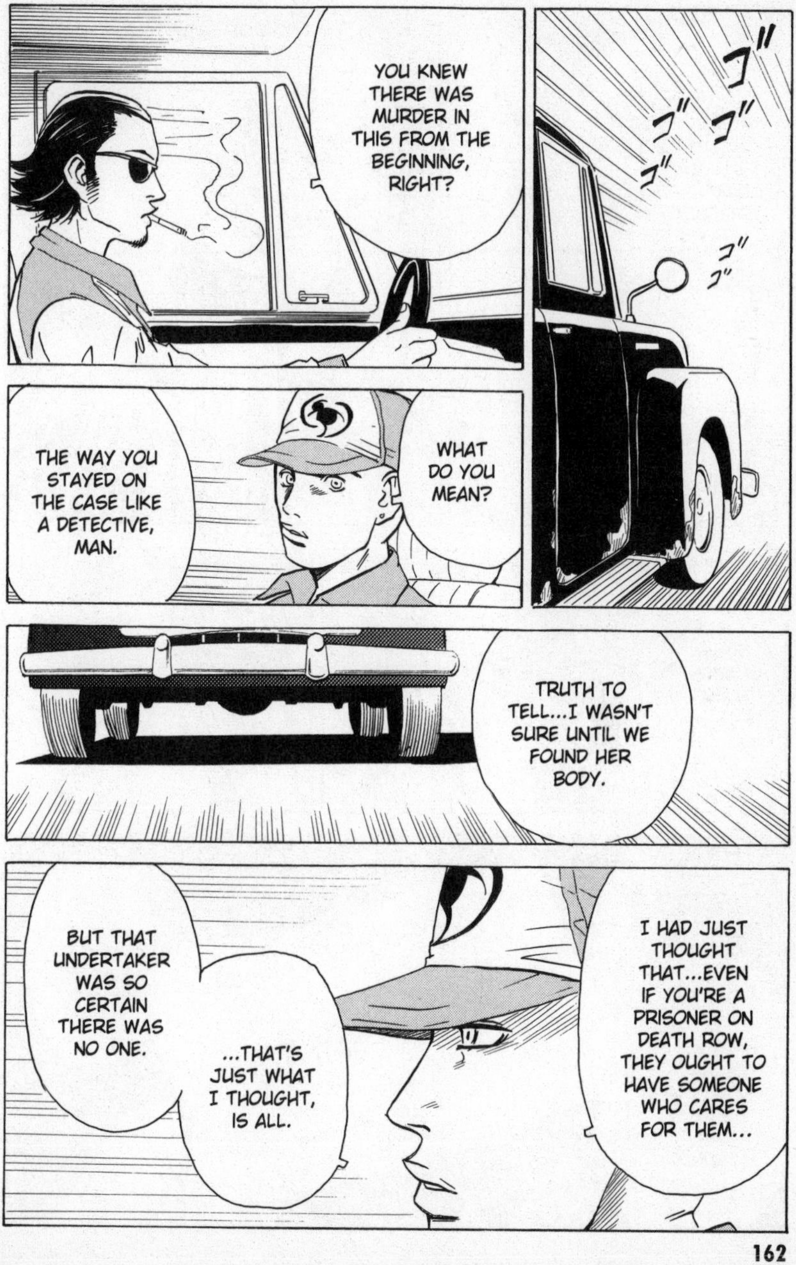
ゴ ゴ ゴ ゴ
ゴ ゴ
YOU KNEW THERE WAS MURDER IN THIS FROM THE BEGINNING, RIGHT?
WHAT DO YOU MEAN?
THE WAY YOU STAYED ON THE CASE LIKE A DETECTIVE, MAN.
TRUTH TO TELL...I WASN'T SURE UNTIL WE FOUND HER BODY.
BUT THAT UNDERTAKER WAS SO CERTAIN THERE WAS NO ONE.
I HAD JUST THOUGHT THAT...EVEN IF YOU'RE A PRISONER ON DEATH ROW, THEY OUGHT TO HAVE SOMEONE WHO CARES FOR THEM...
...THAT'S JUST WHAT I THOUGHT, IS ALL.

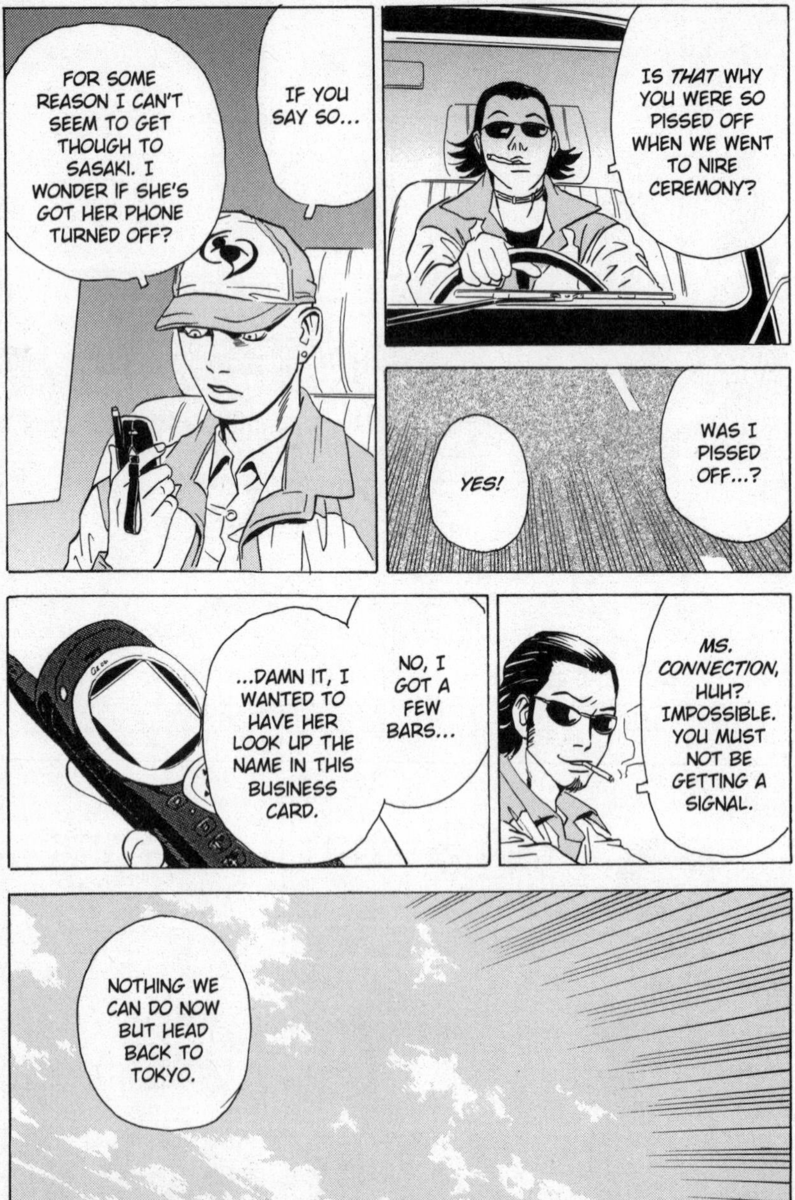

IS *THAT* WHY YOU WERE SO PISSED OFF WHEN WE WENT TO NIRE CEREMONY?
WAS I PISSED OFF...?
YES!
IF YOU SAY SO...
FOR SOME REASON I CAN'T SEEM TO GET THOUGH TO SASAKI. I WONDER IF SHE'S GOT HER PHONE TURNED OFF?
MS. CONNECTION, HUH? IMPOSSIBLE. YOU MUST NOT BE GETTING A SIGNAL.
NO, I GOT A FEW BARS...
...DAMN IT, I WANTED TO HAVE HER LOOK UP THE NAME IN THIS BUSINESS CARD.
NOTHING WE CAN DO NOW BUT HEAD BACK TO TOKYO.

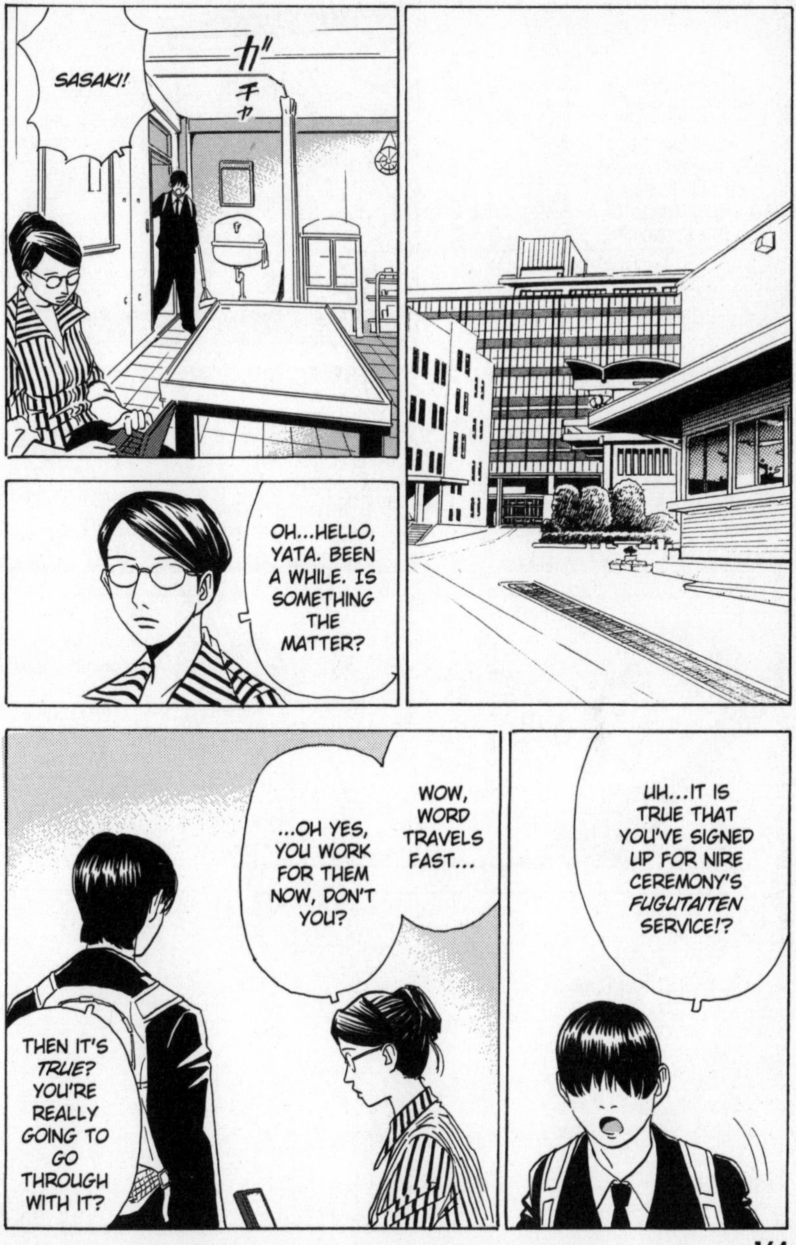
SASAKI!
ガチャ
OH...HELLO, YATA. BEEN A WHILE. IS SOMETHING THE MATTER?
UH...IT IS TRUE THAT YOU'VE SIGNED UP FOR NIRE CEREMONY'S *FUGUTAITEN* SERVICE!?
WOW, WORD TRAVELS FAST...
...OH YES, YOU WORK FOR THEM NOW, DON'T YOU?
THEN IT'S *TRUE*? YOU'RE REALLY GOING TO GO THROUGH WITH IT?

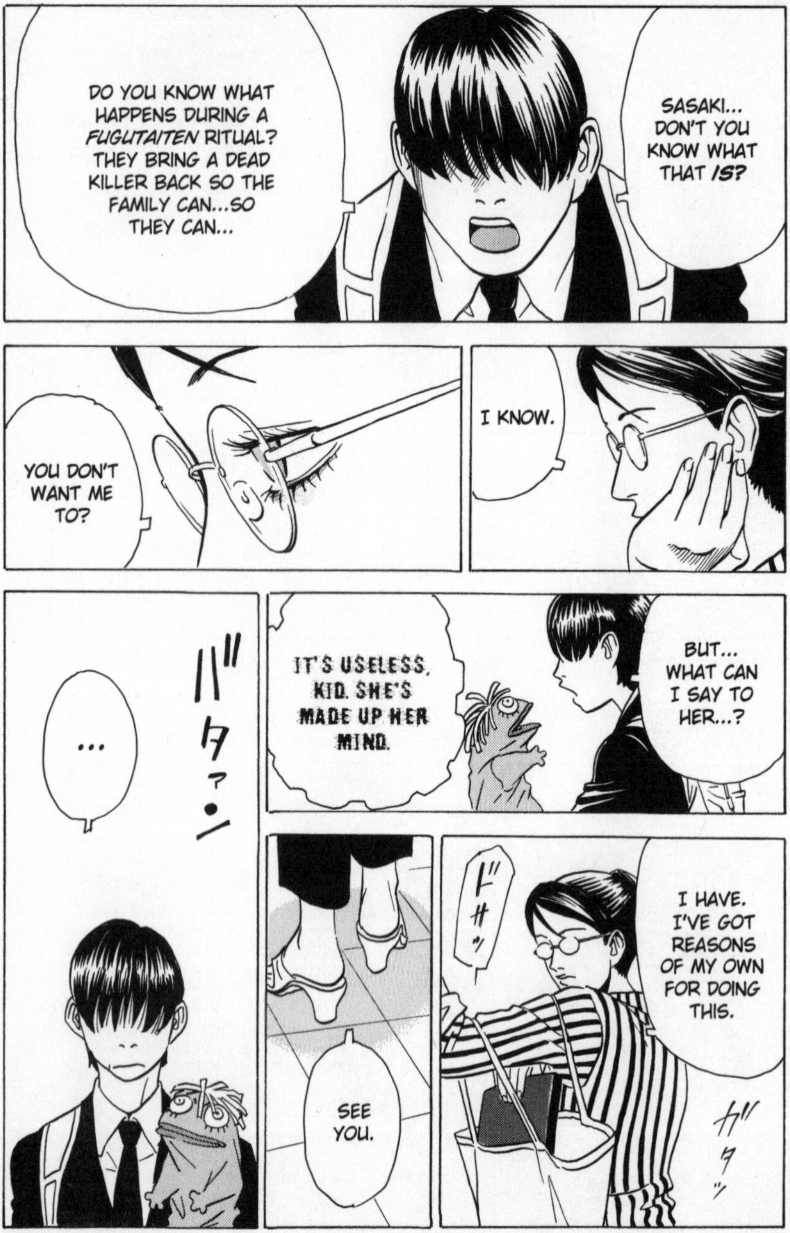
SASAKI... DON'T YOU KNOW WHAT THAT *IS?*
DO YOU KNOW WHAT HAPPENS DURING A *FUGUTAITEN* RITUAL? THEY BRING A DEAD KILLER BACK SO THE FAMILY CAN...SO THEY CAN...
I KNOW.
YOU DON'T WANT ME TO?
BUT... WHAT CAN I SAY TO HER...?
IT'S USELESS, KID. SHE'S MADE UP HER MIND.
I HAVE. I'VE GOT REASONS OF MY OWN FOR DOING THIS.
ガタッ
ドサッ
SEE YOU.
バタァン
...

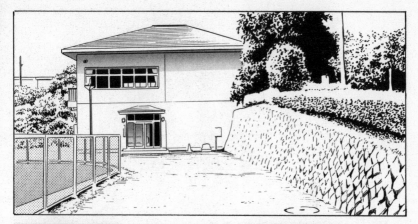

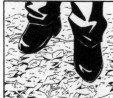

NO ADMITTANCE
ARE YOU SURE ABOUT THIS, MUTSUMI?
IT'LL BE FINE. I GOT THE KEY TO THIS BACK DOOR, SO WE WON'T BE SEEN GOING INTO THE CENTER.
...WHAT I'M TALKING ABOUT IS THAT YOU STILL WANT TO DO THIS, EVEN THOUGH THE PRESIDENT TOLD YOU NOT TO...

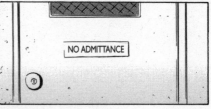

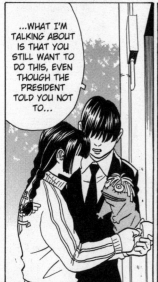

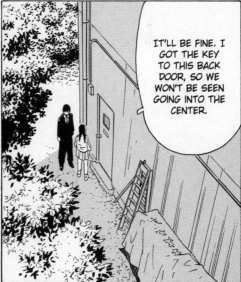

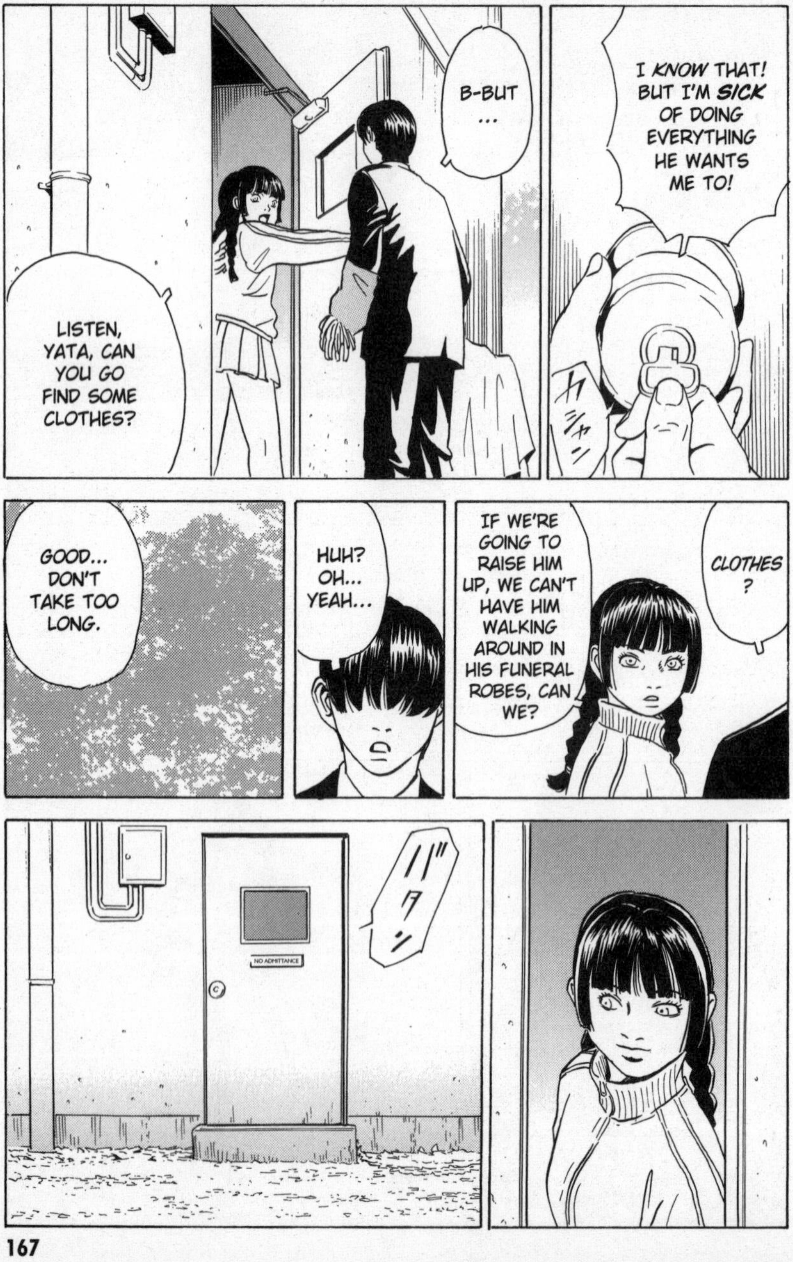
I KNOW THAT! BUT I'M SICK OF DOING EVERYTHING HE WANTS ME TO!
カシャン
B-BUT ...
LISTEN, YATA, CAN YOU GO FIND SOME CLOTHES?
CLOTHES ?
IF WE'RE GOING TO RAISE HIM UP, WE CAN'T HAVE HIM WALKING AROUND IN HIS FUNERAL ROBES, CAN WE?
HUH? OH... YEAH...
GOOD... DON'T TAKE TOO LONG.
バタン
NO ADMITTANCE

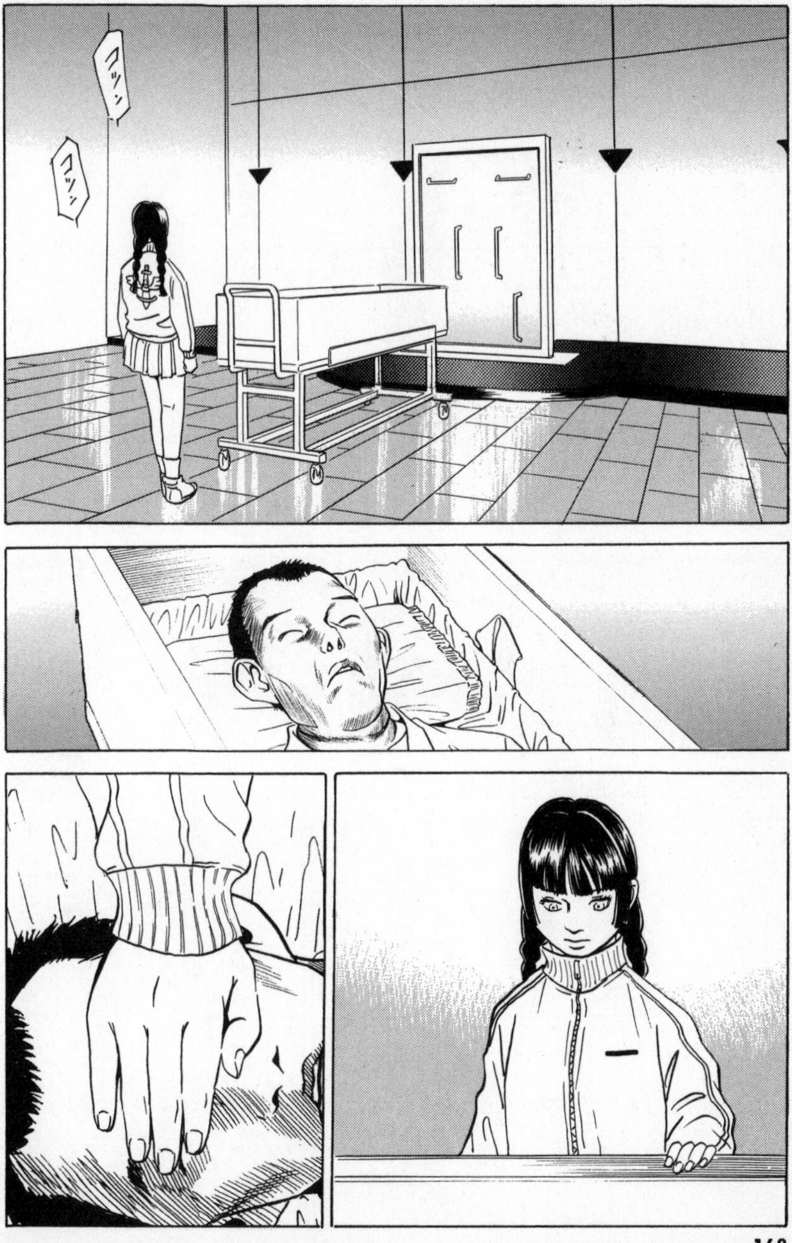
コツン
コツン

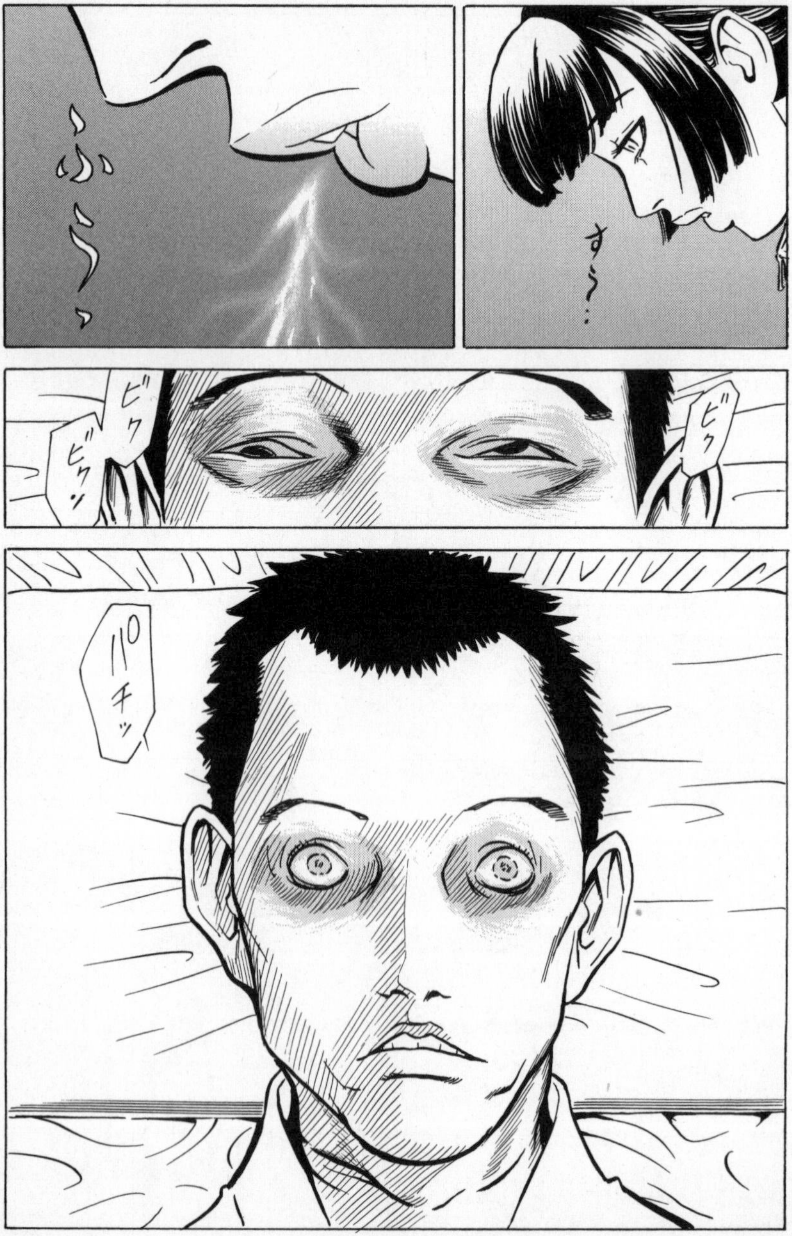

すぅ…
ふう
ビク
ビクビクッ
パチッ

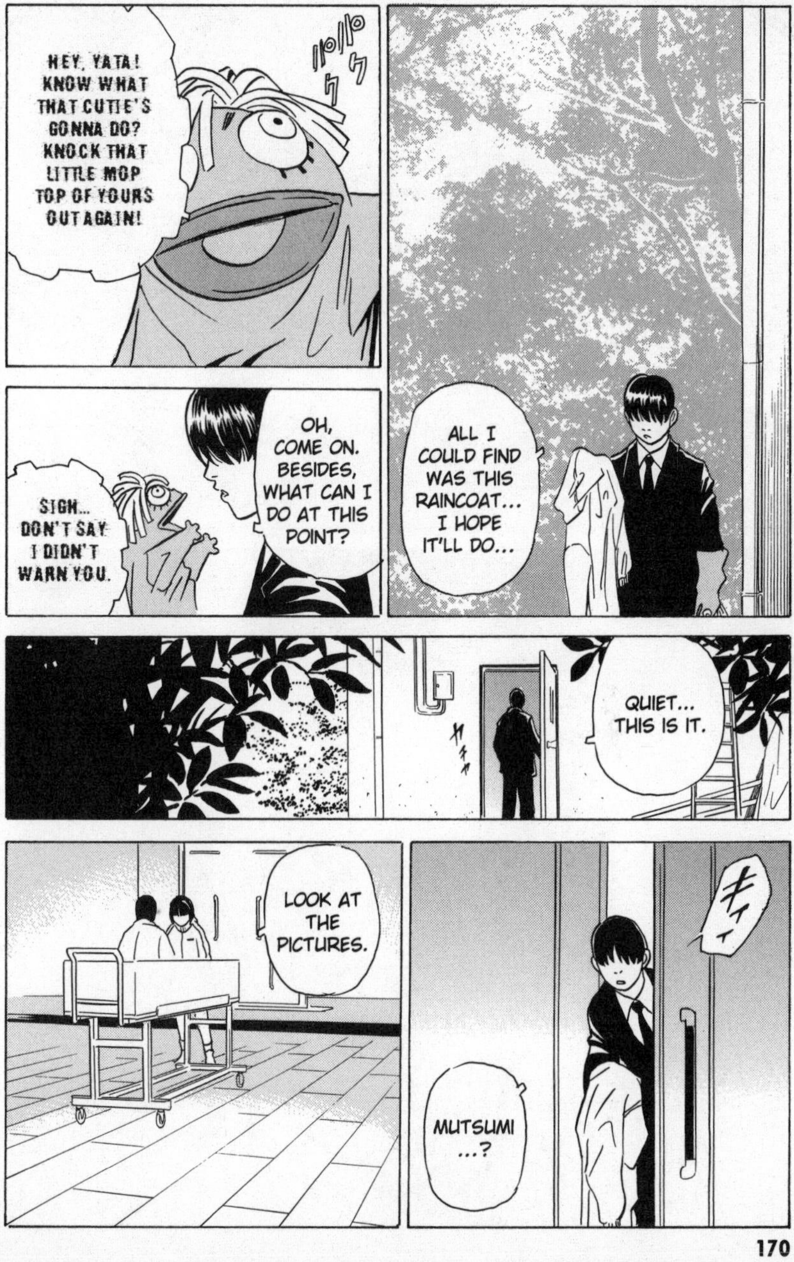
ALL I COULD FIND WAS THIS RAINCOAT... I HOPE IT'LL DO...
パクパク
HEY, YATA! KNOW WHAT THAT CUTIE'S GONNA DO? KNOCK THAT LITTLE MOP TOP OF YOURS OUT AGAIN!
OH, COME ON. BESIDES, WHAT CAN I DO AT THIS POINT?
SIGH... DON'T SAY I DIDN'T WARN YOU.
QUIET... THIS IS IT.
ガチャ
キィィ
MUTSUMI ...?
LOOK AT THE PICTURES.

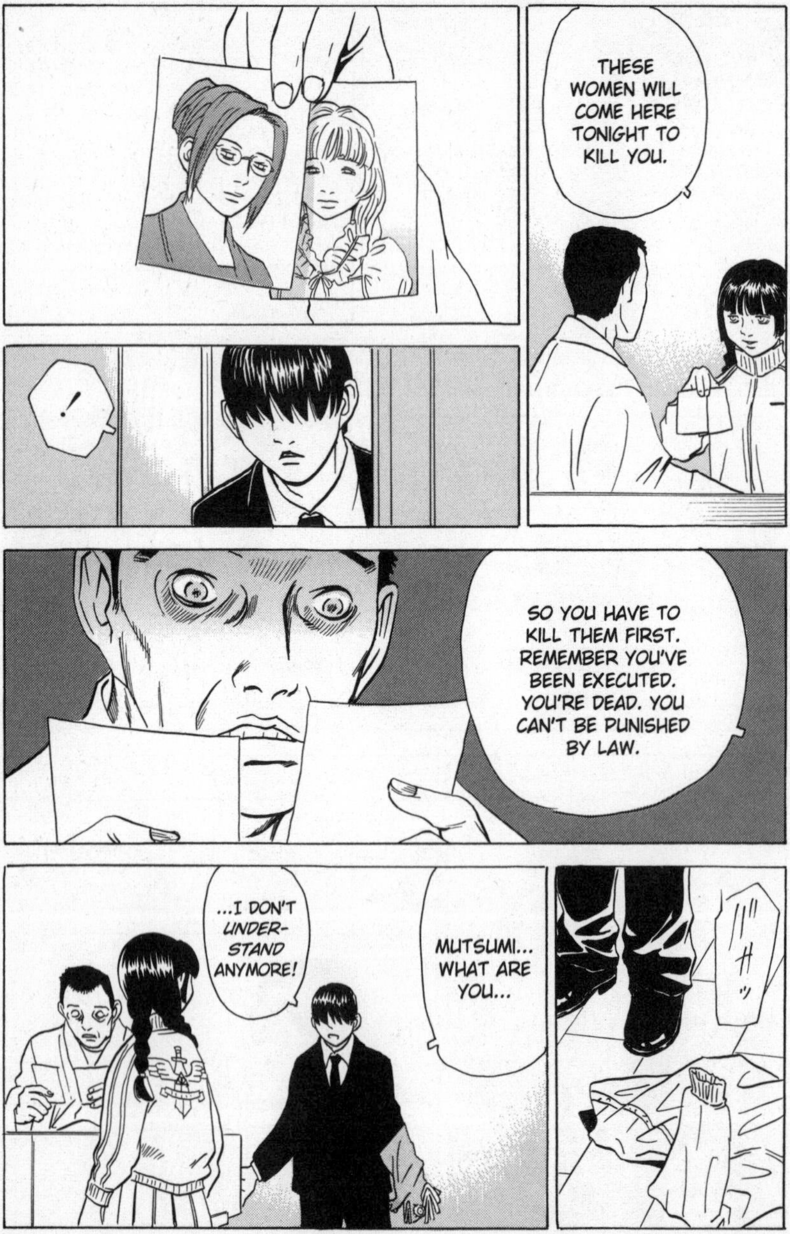
THESE WOMEN WILL COME HERE TONIGHT TO KILL YOU.
!
SO YOU HAVE TO KILL THEM FIRST. REMEMBER YOU'VE BEEN EXECUTED. YOU'RE DEAD. YOU CAN'T BE PUNISHED BY LAW.
ガッ
MUTSUMI... WHAT ARE YOU...
...I DON'T UNDER-STAND ANYMORE!

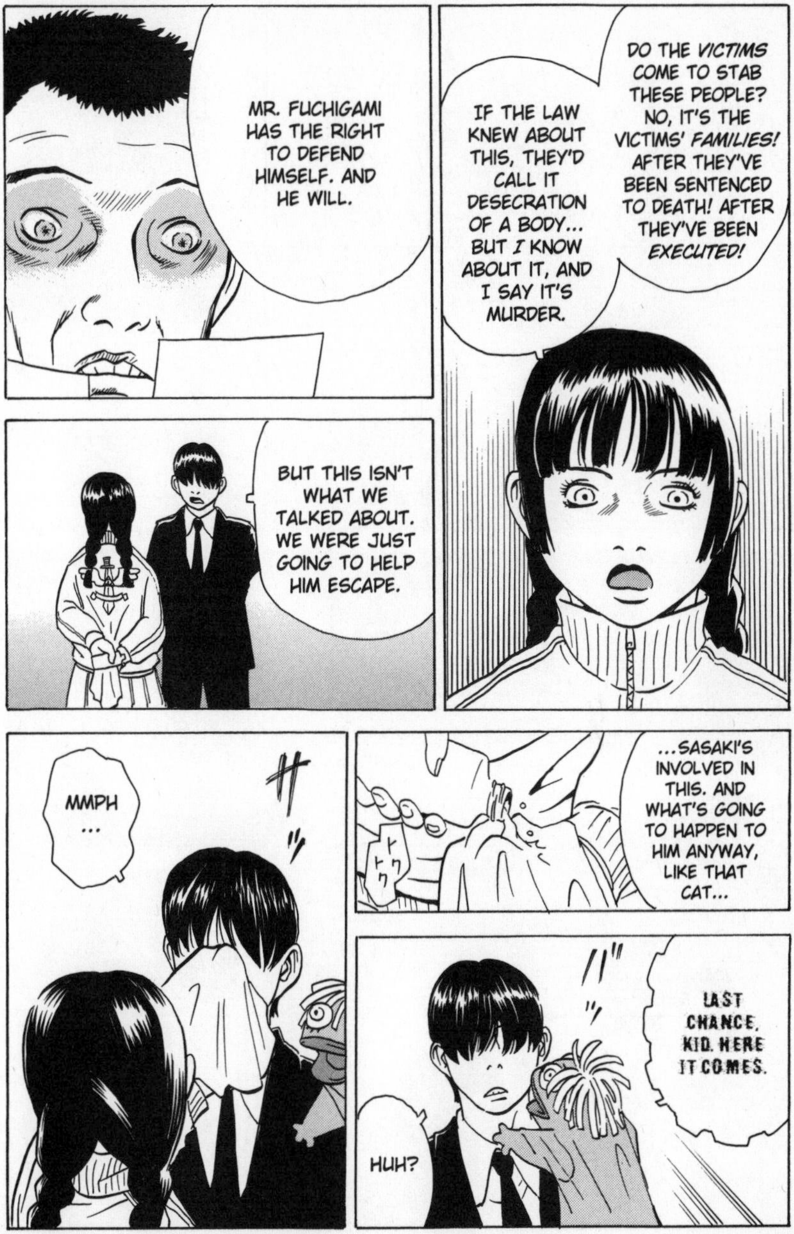
DO THE *VICTIMS* COME TO STAB THESE PEOPLE? NO, IT'S THE VICTIMS' *FAMILIES!* AFTER THEY'VE BEEN SENTENCED TO DEATH! AFTER THEY'VE BEEN *EXECUTED!*
IF THE LAW KNEW ABOUT THIS, THEY'D CALL IT DESECRATION OF A BODY... BUT *I* KNOW ABOUT IT, AND I SAY IT'S MURDER.
MR. FUCHIGAMI HAS THE RIGHT TO DEFEND HIMSELF. AND HE WILL.
BUT THIS ISN'T WHAT WE TALKED ABOUT. WE WERE JUST GOING TO HELP HIM ESCAPE.
...SASAKI'S INVOLVED IN THIS. AND WHAT'S GOING TO HAPPEN TO HIM ANYWAY, LIKE THAT CAT...
トクトク
LAST CHANCE, KID. HERE IT COMES.
HUH?
MMPH ...

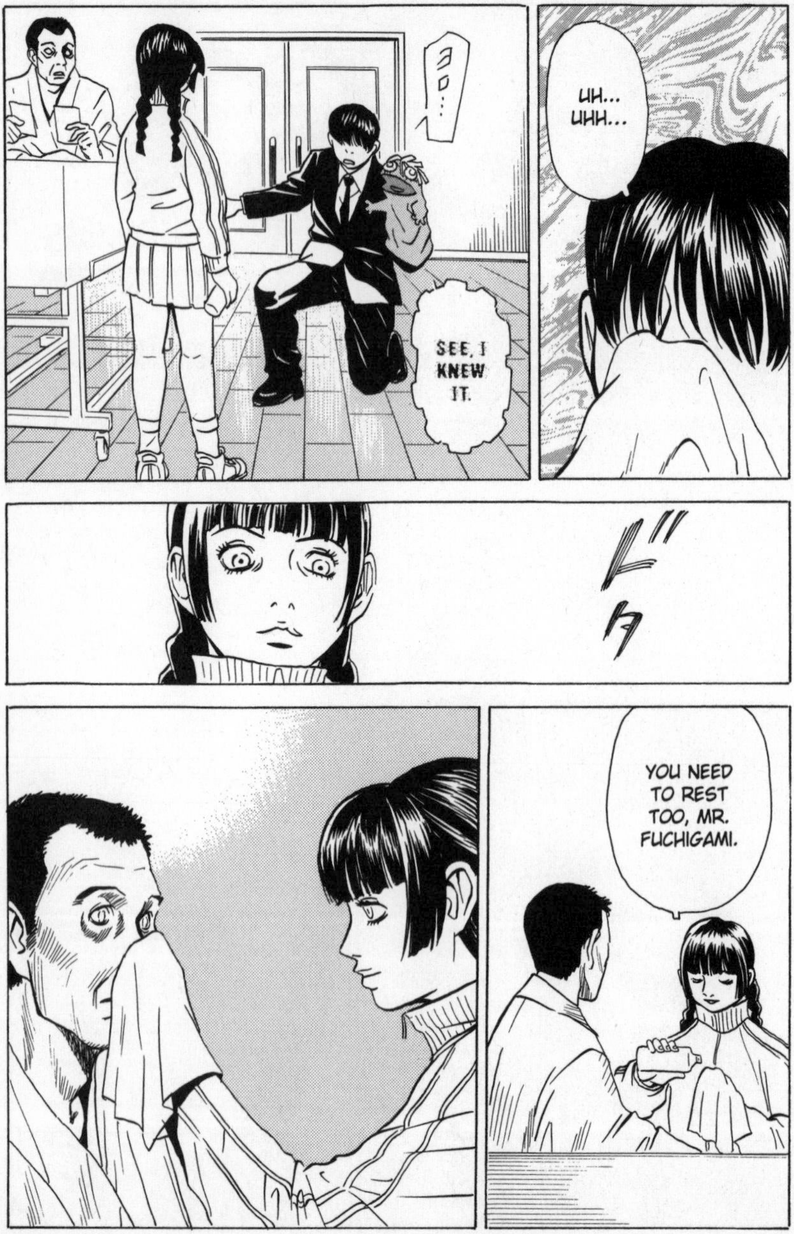
UH... UHH...
ヨロ…
SEE, I KNEW IT.
ビク
YOU NEED TO REST TOO, MR. FUCHIGAMI.

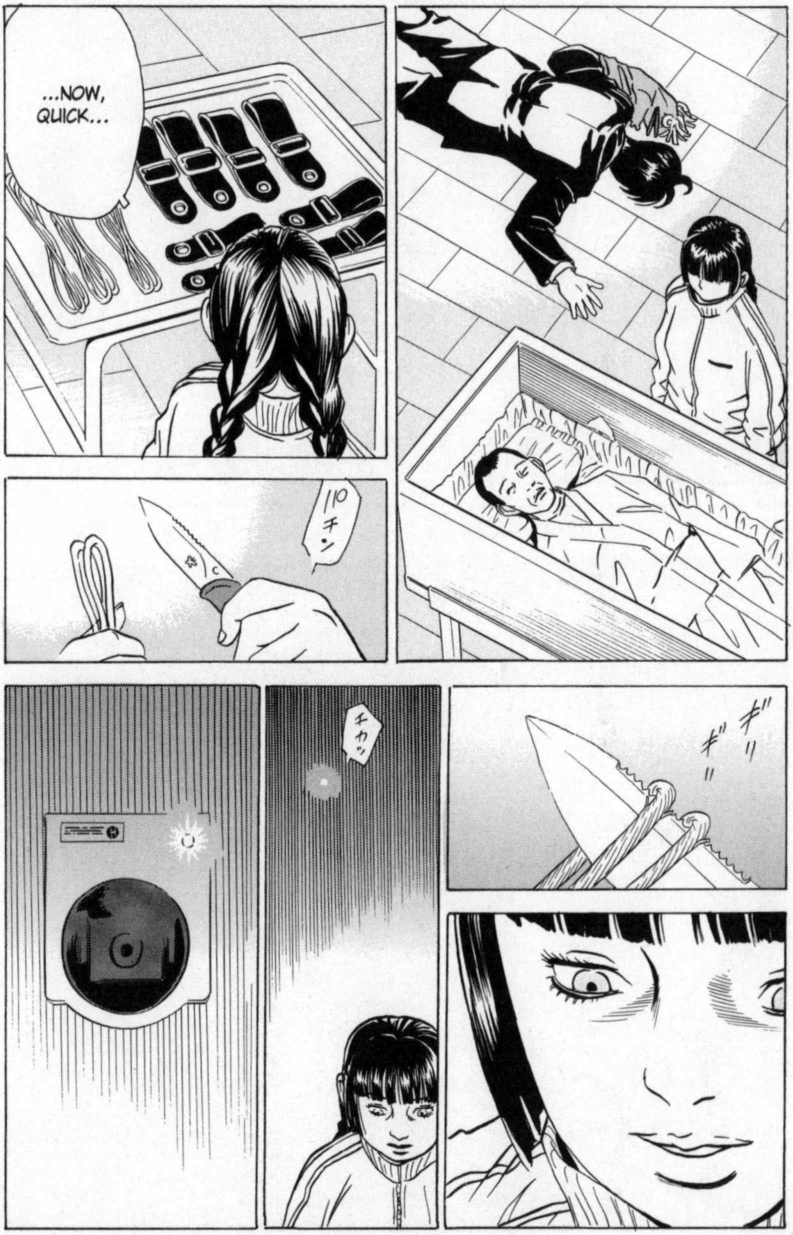
...NOW, QUICK...
パチン
ギリギリ
チカッ

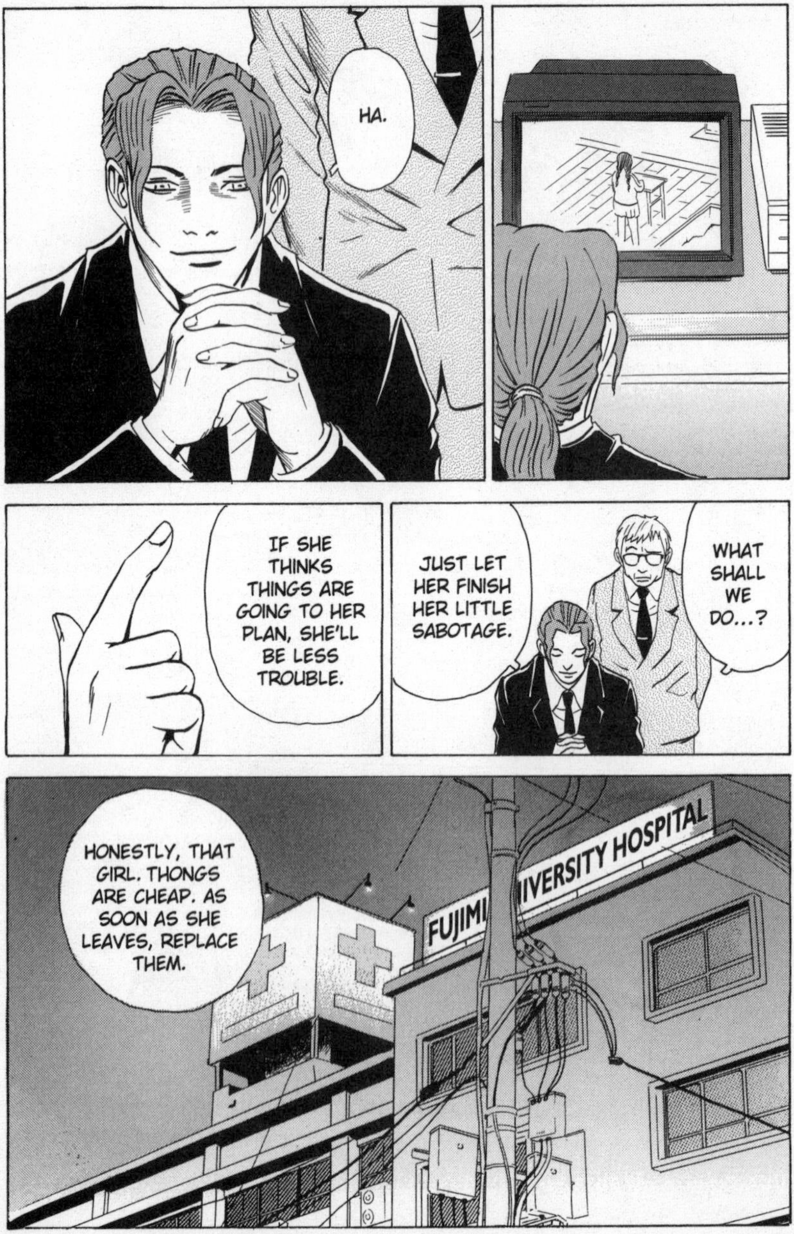
HA.
WHAT SHALL WE DO...?
JUST LET HER FINISH HER LITTLE SABOTAGE.
IF SHE THINKS THINGS ARE GOING TO HER PLAN, SHE'LL BE LESS TROUBLE.
FUJIMI
VERSITY HOSPITAL
HONESTLY, THAT GIRL. THONGS ARE CHEAP. AS SOON AS SHE LEAVES, REPLACE THEM.

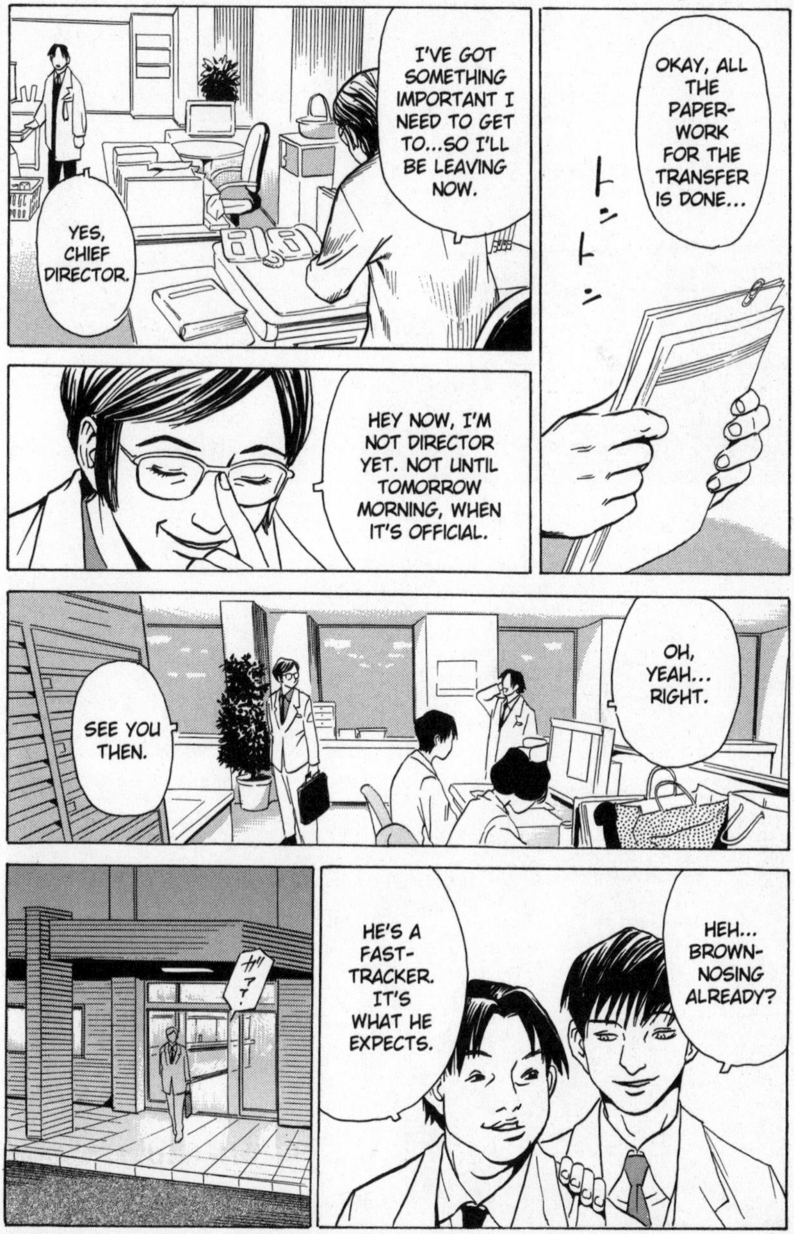
OKAY, ALL THE PAPER-WORK FOR THE TRANSFER IS DONE...
トン トン
I'VE GOT SOMETHING IMPORTANT I NEED TO GET TO...SO I'LL BE LEAVING NOW.
YES, CHIEF DIRECTOR.
HEY NOW, I'M NOT DIRECTOR YET. NOT UNTIL TOMORROW MORNING, WHEN IT'S OFFICIAL.
OH, YEAH... RIGHT.
SEE YOU THEN.
HEH... BROWN-NOSING ALREADY?
HE'S A FAST-TRACKER. IT'S WHAT HE EXPECTS.
ガァァ

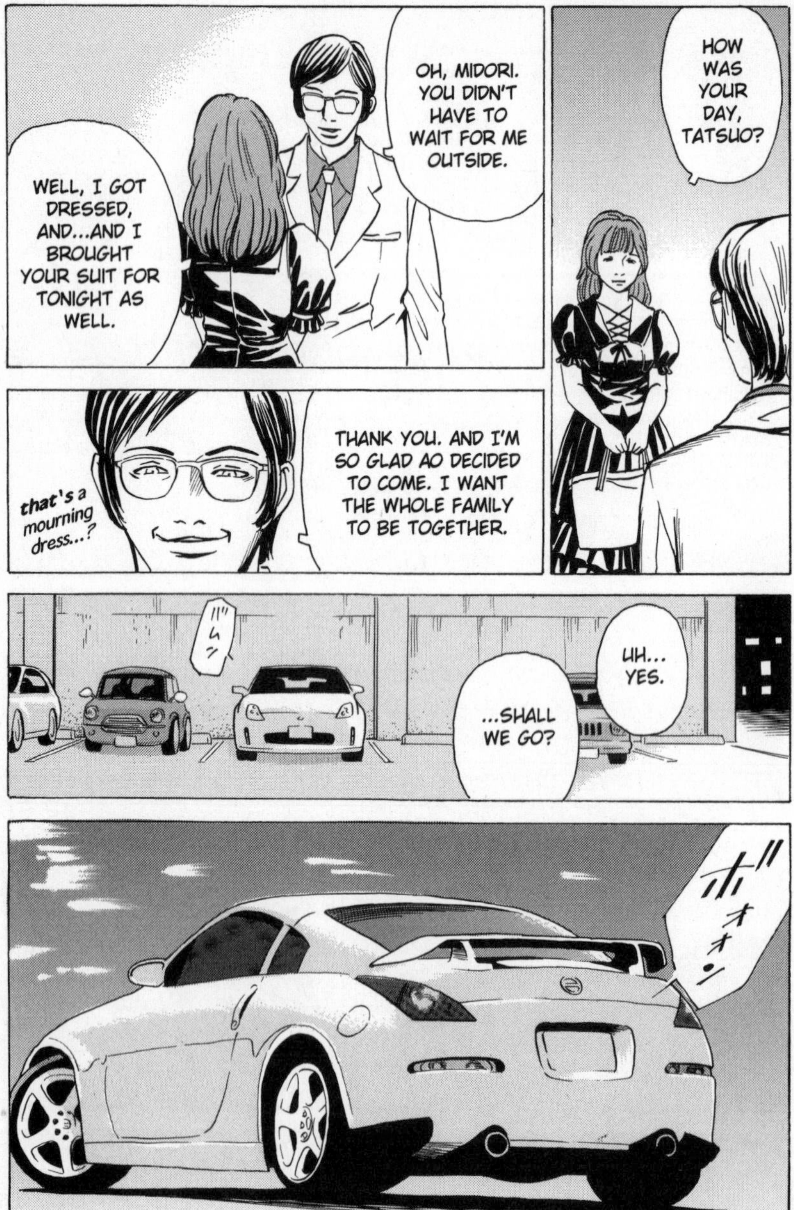
HOW WAS YOUR DAY, TATSUO?
OH, MIDORI. YOU DIDN'T HAVE TO WAIT FOR ME OUTSIDE.
WELL, I GOT DRESSED, AND...AND I BROUGHT YOUR SUIT FOR TONIGHT AS WELL.
THANK YOU. AND I'M SO GLAD AO DECIDED TO COME. I WANT THE WHOLE FAMILY TO BE TOGETHER.
that's a mourning dress...?
バムッ
UH... YES.
...SHALL WE GO?
ボオオン

MAN, THE MOMENT WE GET BACK INTO THE CITY, WE HIT THIS TRAFFIC JAM. THE BODY'S GOING TO ROT BEFORE WE GET THERE.

NAH, I GET THE FEELING MR. FUCHIGAMI'S GOT STAYING POWER. BETTER SEE IF I CAN GET A HOLD OF SASAKI AGAIN.

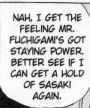

HELLO KARATSU... WHAT HAVE I BEEN DOING? OH...I HAD A FEW THINGS I NEEDED TO TAKE CARE OF...

SO, WHAT'S GOING ON...?

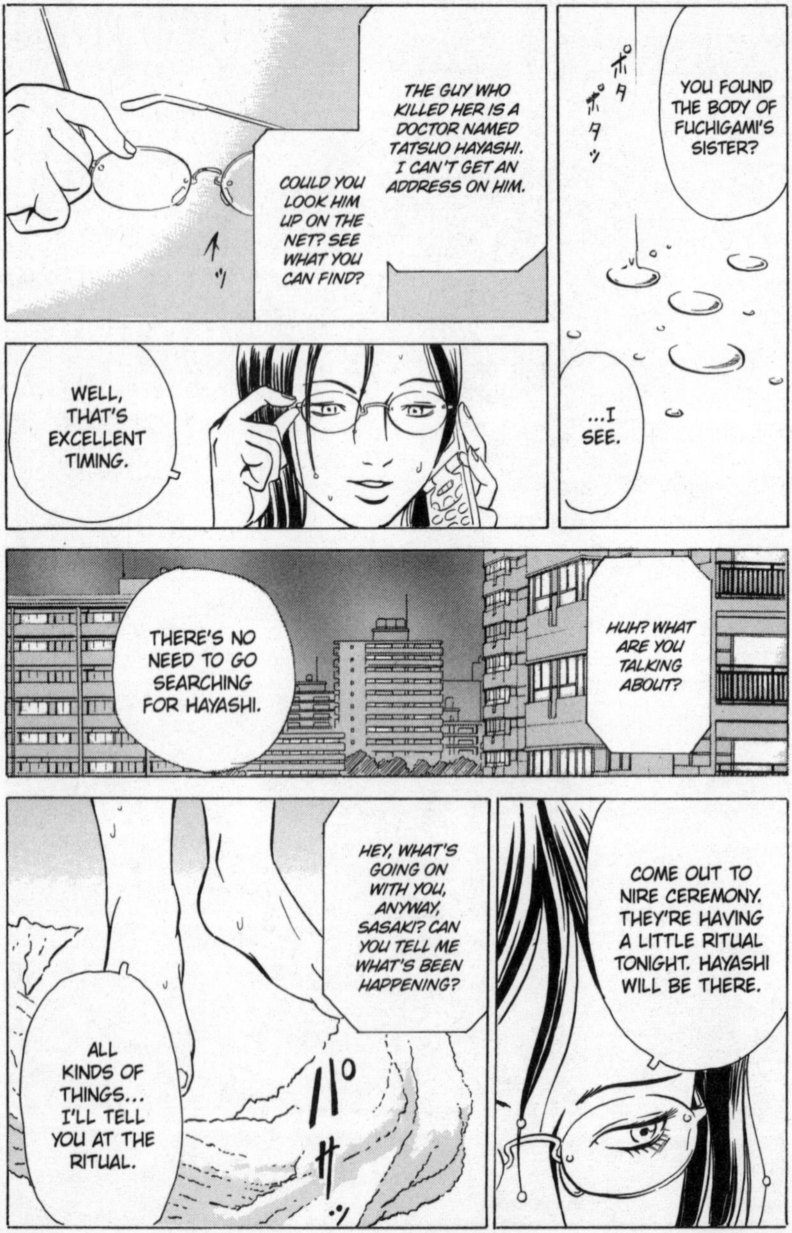
YOU FOUND THE BODY OF FUCHIGAMI'S SISTER?
...I SEE.
THE GUY WHO KILLED HER IS A DOCTOR NAMED TATSUO HAYASHI. I CAN'T GET AN ADDRESS ON HIM.
COULD YOU LOOK HIM UP ON THE NET? SEE WHAT YOU CAN FIND?
WELL, THAT'S EXCELLENT TIMING.
HUH? WHAT ARE YOU TALKING ABOUT?
THERE'S NO NEED TO GO SEARCHING FOR HAYASHI.
COME OUT TO NIRE CEREMONY. THEY'RE HAVING A LITTLE RITUAL TONIGHT. HAYASHI WILL BE THERE.
HEY, WHAT'S GOING ON WITH YOU, ANYWAY, SASAKI? CAN YOU TELL ME WHAT'S BEEN HAPPENING?
ALL KINDS OF THINGS... I'LL TELL YOU AT THE RITUAL.

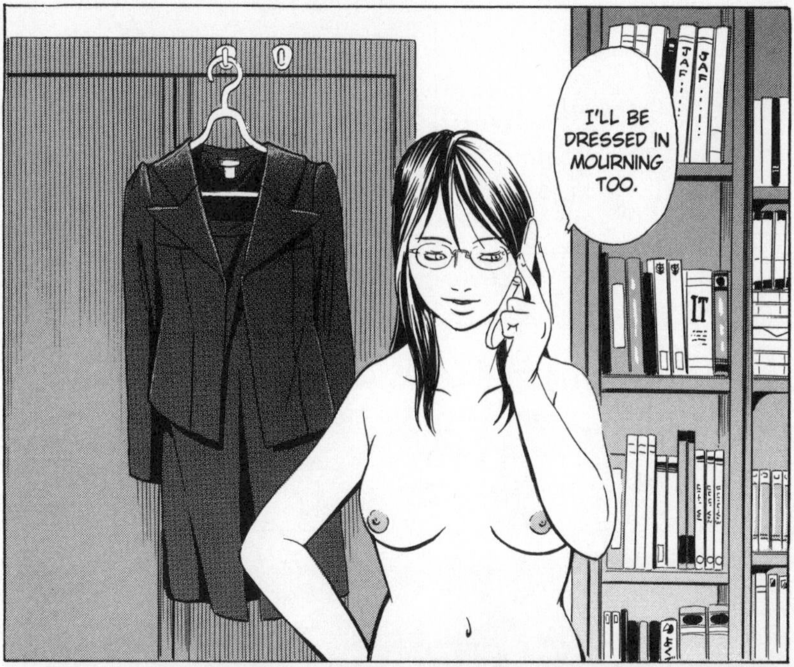
I'LL BE DRESSED IN MOURNING TOO.

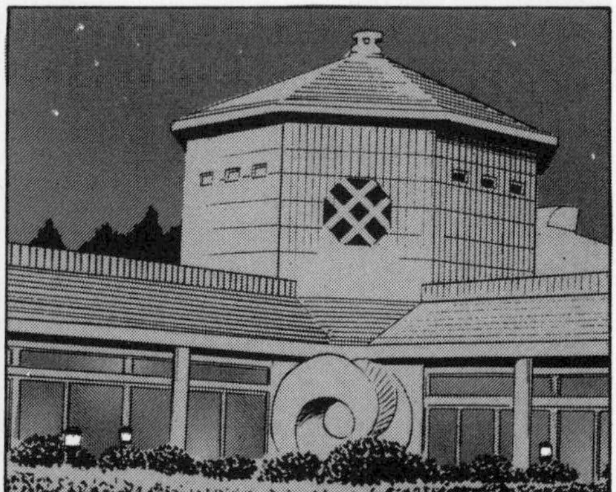

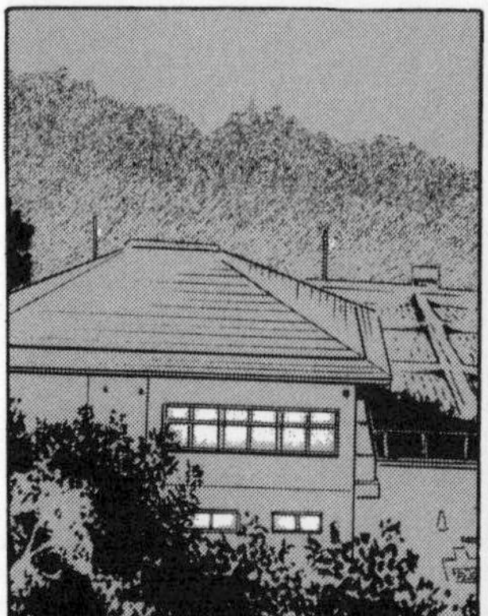

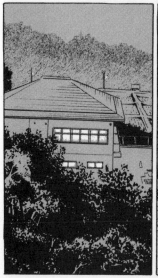

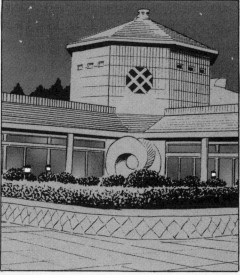

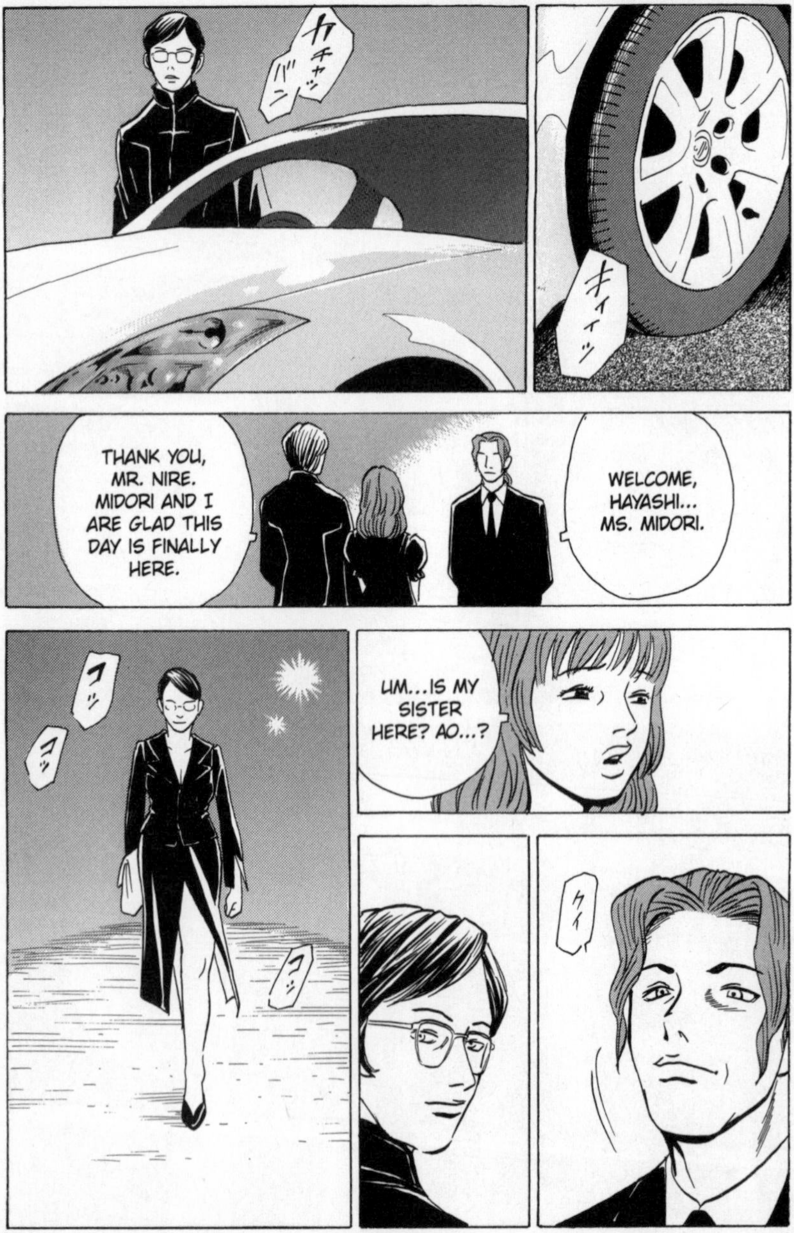
キイイッ
カチャッ
バン
WELCOME, HAYASHI... MS. MIDORI.
THANK YOU, MR. NIRE. MIDORI AND I ARE GLAD THIS DAY IS FINALLY HERE.
UM...IS MY SISTER HERE? AO...?
クイ
コツ
コツ
コツ

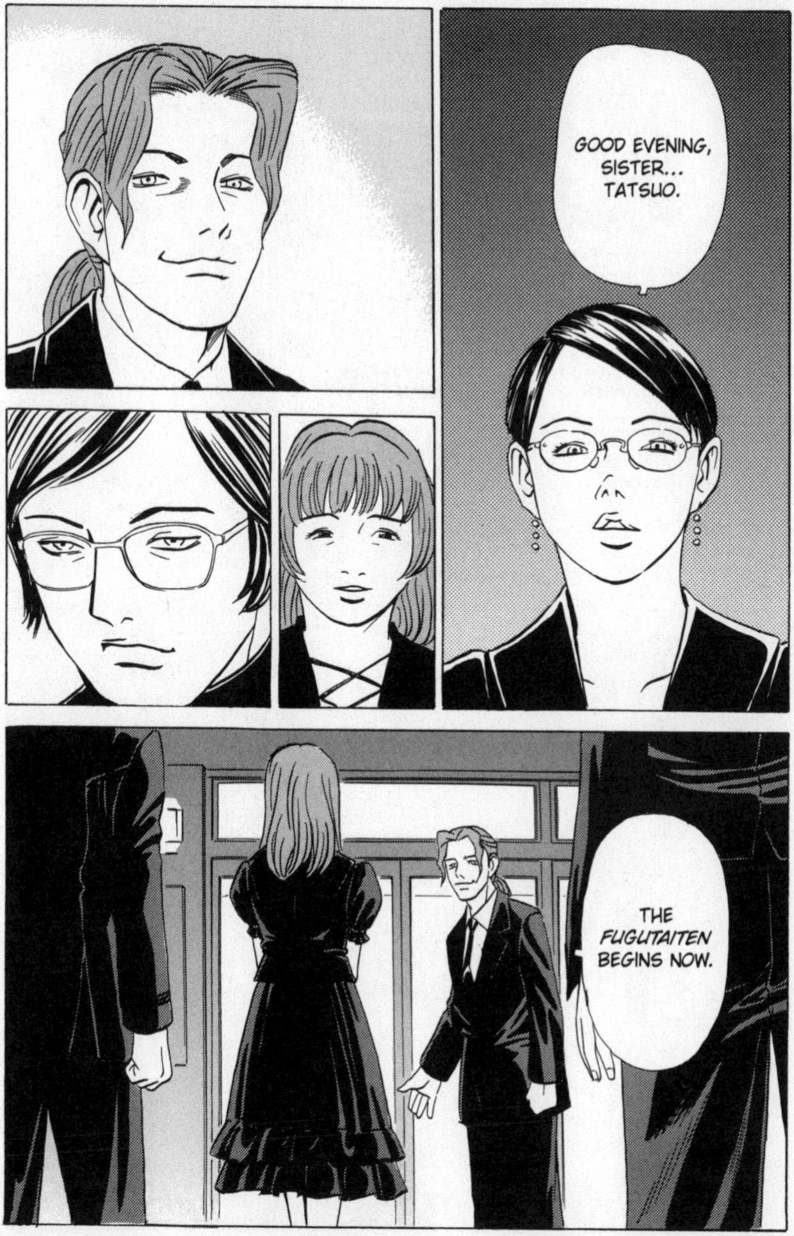
GOOD EVENING, SISTER... TATSUO.
THE FUGUTAITEN BEGINS NOW.

6th delivery: do what you want—the end

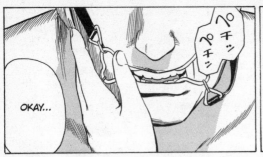

OKAY...

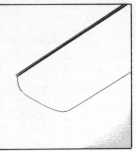

...TIME TO WAKE UP.

7th delivery

時の過ぎゆくままに

as time goes by

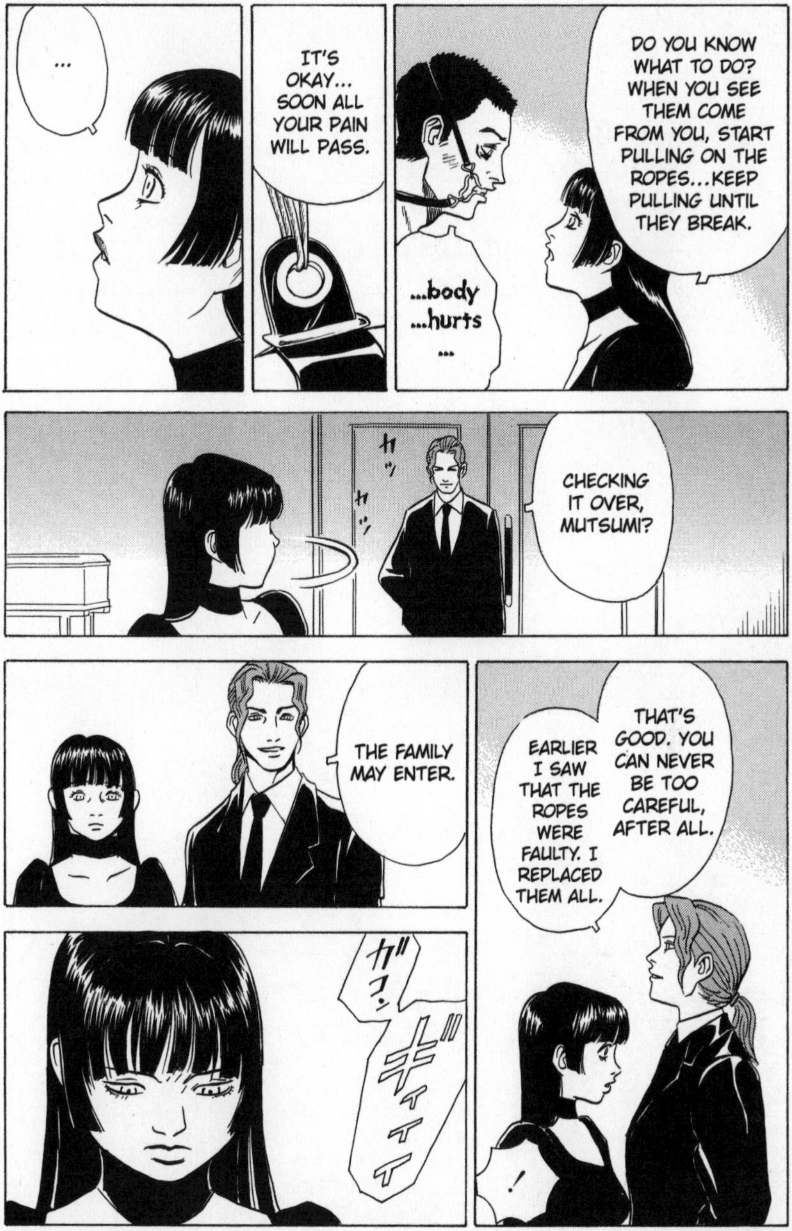
DO YOU KNOW WHAT TO DO? WHEN YOU SEE THEM COME FROM YOU, START PULLING ON THE ROPES...KEEP PULLING UNTIL THEY BREAK.
...body ...hurts ...
IT'S OKAY... SOON ALL YOUR PAIN WILL PASS.
...
カッ
カッ
CHECKING IT OVER, MUTSUMI?
THAT'S GOOD. YOU CAN NEVER BE TOO CAREFUL, AFTER ALL.
EARLIER I SAW THAT THE ROPES WERE FAULTY. I REPLACED THEM ALL.
!
THE FAMILY MAY ENTER.
ガコン
ギィィィ

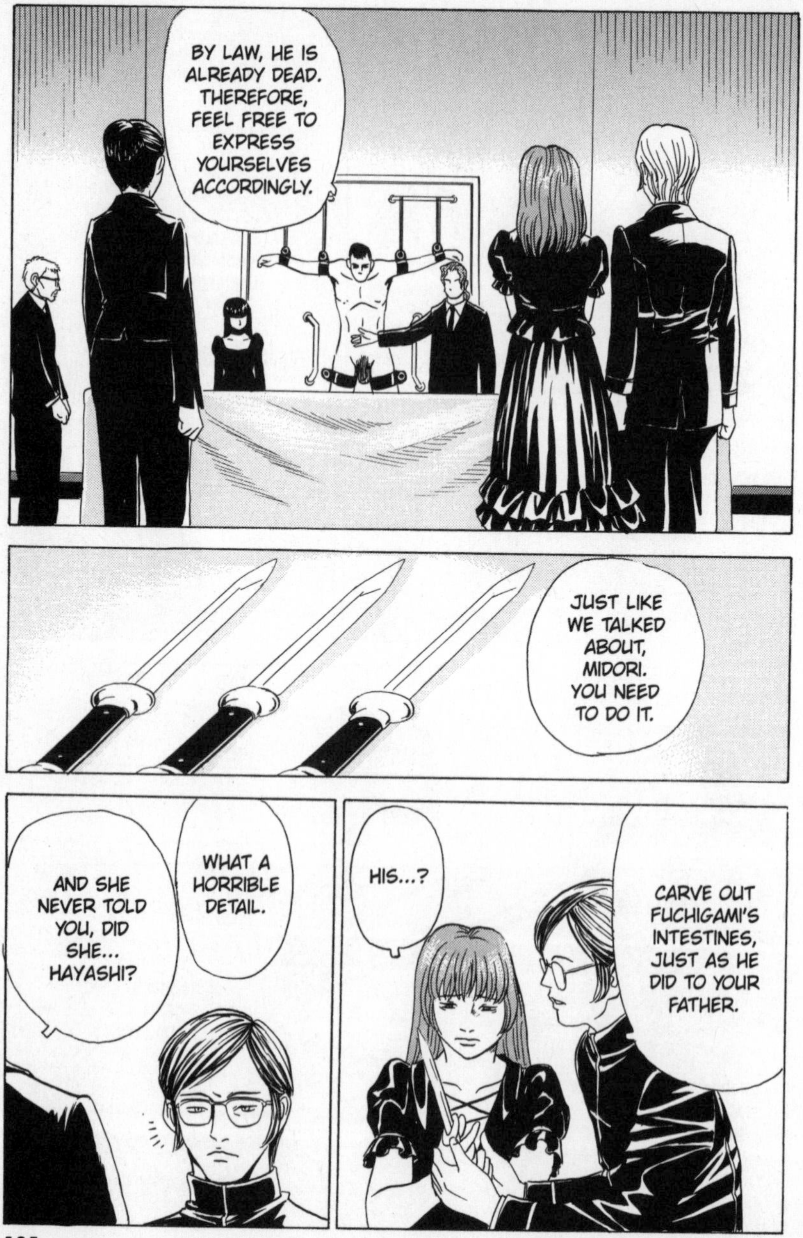
BY LAW, HE IS ALREADY DEAD. THEREFORE, FEEL FREE TO EXPRESS YOURSELVES ACCORDINGLY.
JUST LIKE WE TALKED ABOUT, MIDORI. YOU NEED TO DO IT.
CARVE OUT FUCHIGAMI'S INTESTINES, JUST AS HE DID TO YOUR FATHER.
HIS...?
WHAT A HORRIBLE DETAIL.
AND SHE NEVER TOLD YOU, DID SHE... HAYASHI?

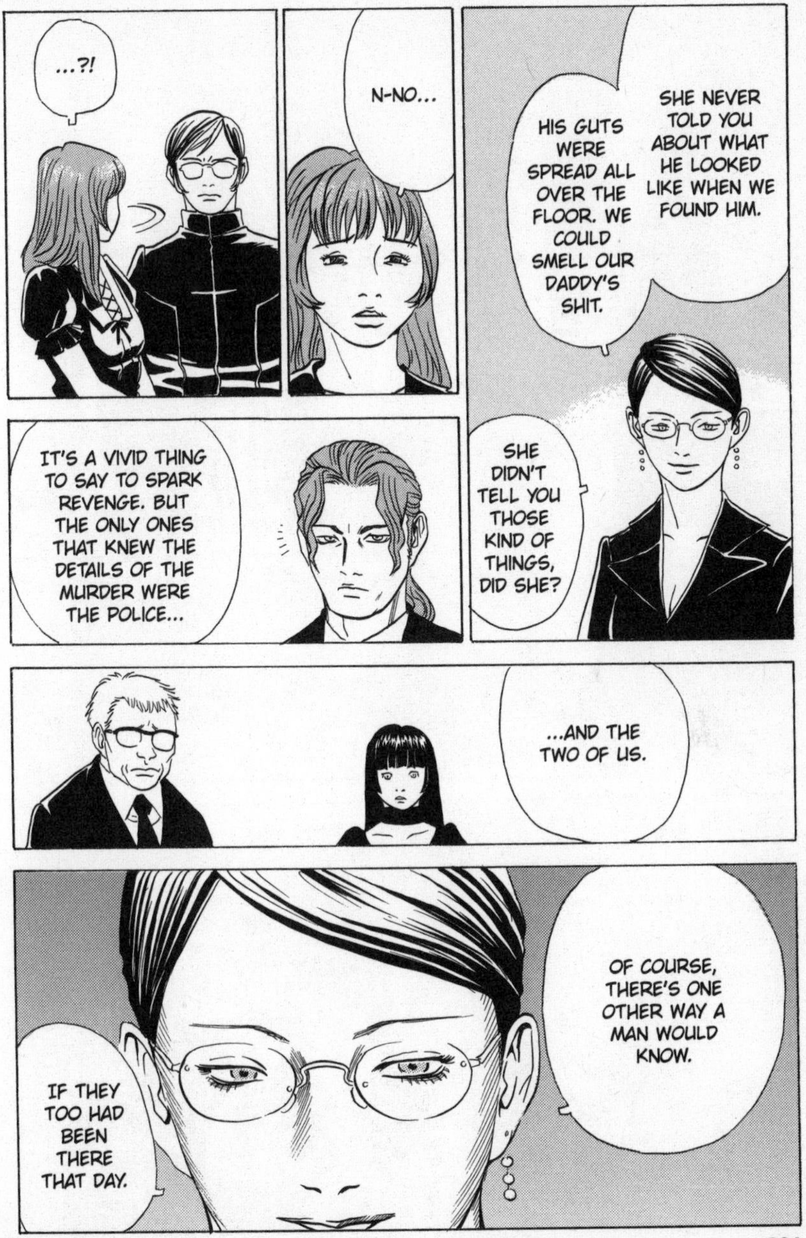
SHE NEVER TOLD YOU ABOUT WHAT HE LOOKED LIKE WHEN WE FOUND HIM.
HIS GUTS WERE SPREAD ALL OVER THE FLOOR. WE COULD SMELL OUR DADDY'S SHIT.
SHE DIDN'T TELL YOU THOSE KIND OF THINGS, DID SHE?
N-NO...
...?!
IT'S A VIVID THING TO SAY TO SPARK REVENGE. BUT THE ONLY ONES THAT KNEW THE DETAILS OF THE MURDER WERE THE POLICE...
...AND THE TWO OF US.
OF COURSE, THERE'S ONE OTHER WAY A MAN WOULD KNOW.
IF THEY TOO HAD BEEN THERE THAT DAY.

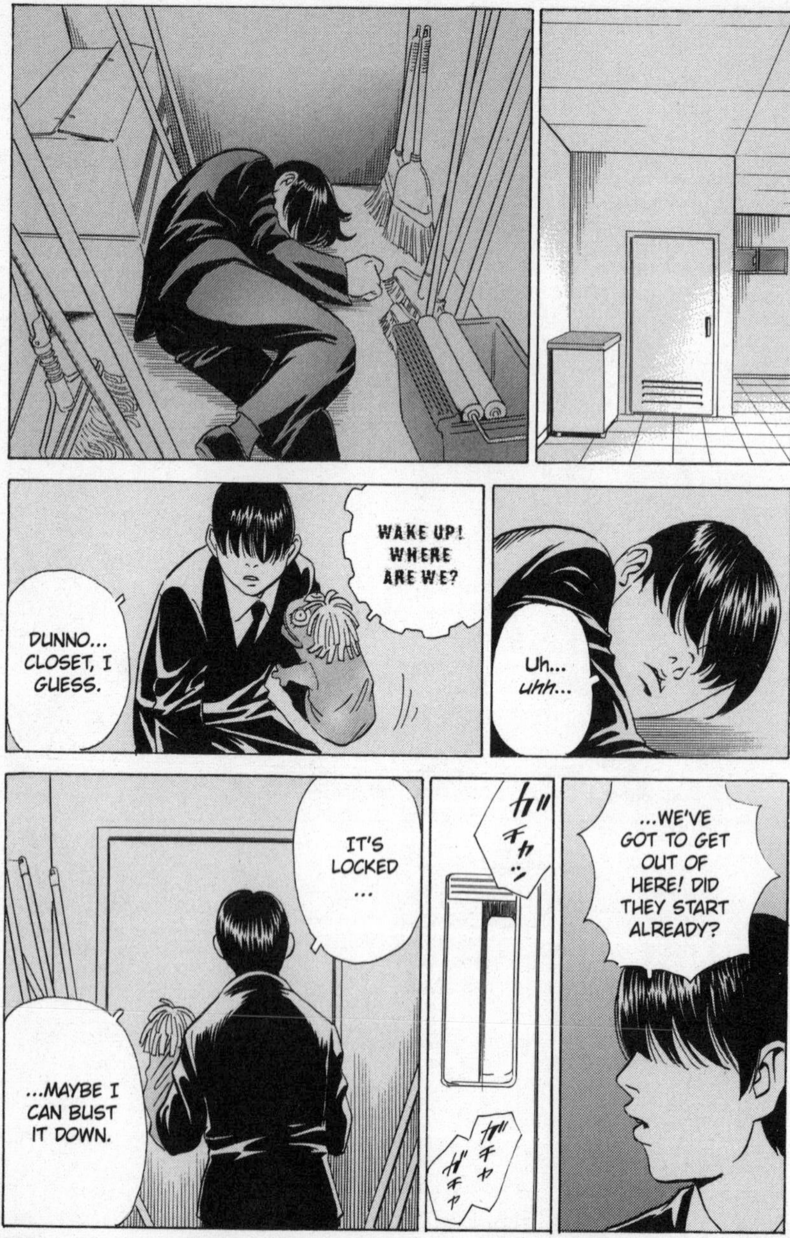
Uh... uhh...
WAKE UP! WHERE ARE WE?
DUNNO... CLOSET, I GUESS.
...WE'VE GOT TO GET OUT OF HERE! DID THEY START ALREADY?
ガチャッ
ガチャガチャ
IT'S LOCKED ...
...MAYBE I CAN BUST IT DOWN.

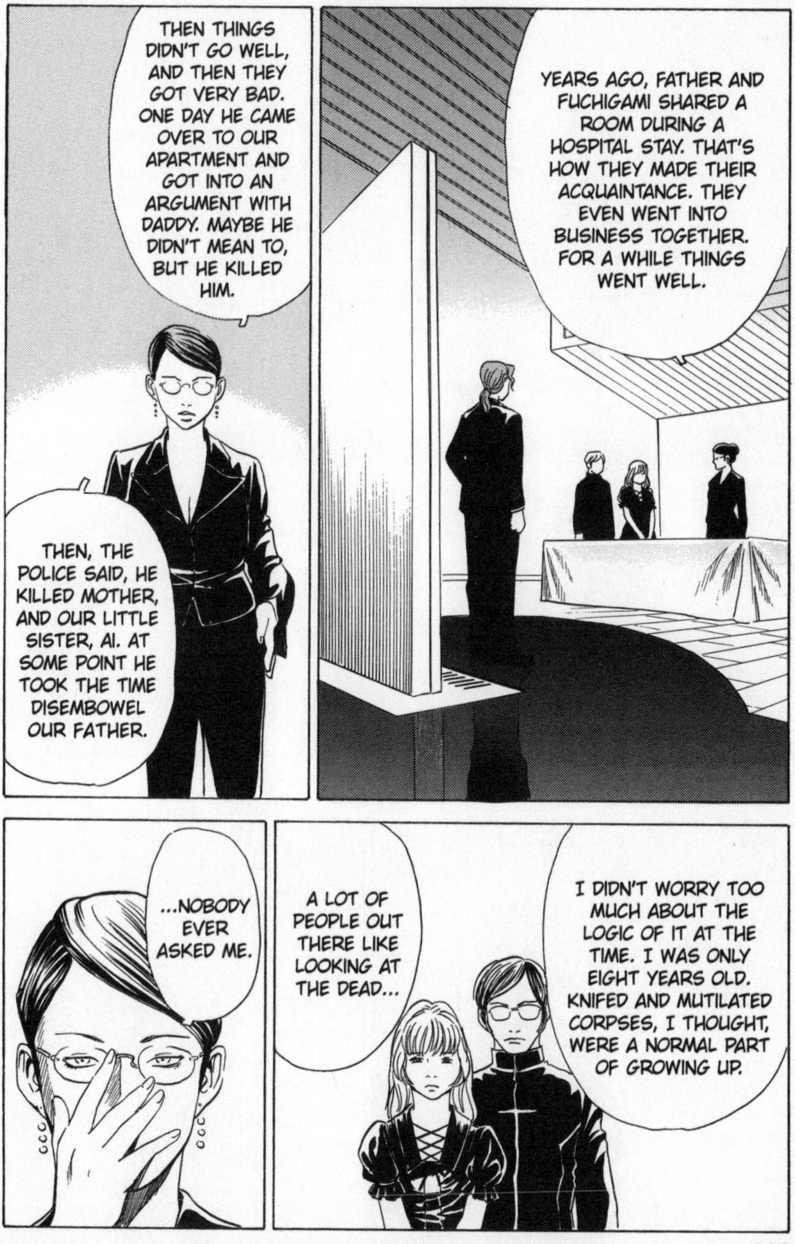
YEARS AGO, FATHER AND FUCHIGAMI SHARED A ROOM DURING A HOSPITAL STAY. THAT'S HOW THEY MADE THEIR ACQUAINTANCE. THEY EVEN WENT INTO BUSINESS TOGETHER. FOR A WHILE THINGS WENT WELL.
THEN THINGS DIDN'T GO WELL, AND THEN THEY GOT VERY BAD. ONE DAY HE CAME OVER TO OUR APARTMENT AND GOT INTO AN ARGUMENT WITH DADDY. MAYBE HE DIDN'T MEAN TO, BUT HE KILLED HIM.
THEN, THE POLICE SAID, HE KILLED MOTHER, AND OUR LITTLE SISTER, AI. AT SOME POINT HE TOOK THE TIME DISEMBOWEL OUR FATHER.
I DIDN'T WORRY TOO MUCH ABOUT THE LOGIC OF IT AT THE TIME. I WAS ONLY EIGHT YEARS OLD. KNIFED AND MUTILATED CORPSES, I THOUGHT, WERE A NORMAL PART OF GROWING UP.
A LOT OF PEOPLE OUT THERE LIKE LOOKING AT THE DEAD...
...NOBODY EVER ASKED ME.

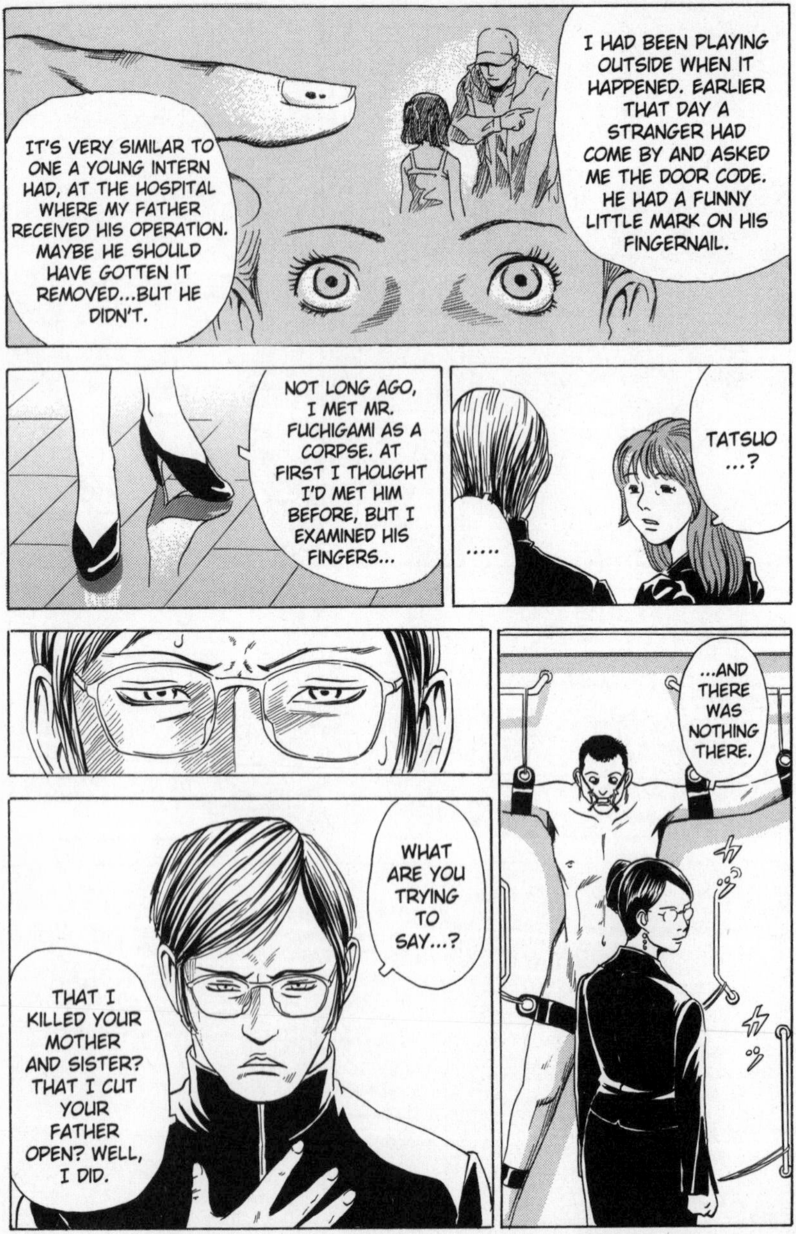

I HAD BEEN PLAYING OUTSIDE WHEN IT HAPPENED. EARLIER THAT DAY A STRANGER HAD COME BY AND ASKED ME THE DOOR CODE. HE HAD A FUNNY LITTLE MARK ON HIS FINGERNAIL.
IT'S VERY SIMILAR TO ONE A YOUNG INTERN HAD, AT THE HOSPITAL WHERE MY FATHER RECEIVED HIS OPERATION. MAYBE HE SHOULD HAVE GOTTEN IT REMOVED...BUT HE DIDN'T.
TATSUO ...?
.....
NOT LONG AGO, I MET MR. FUCHIGAMI AS A CORPSE. AT FIRST I THOUGHT I'D MET HIM BEFORE, BUT I EXAMINED HIS FINGERS...
...AND THERE WAS NOTHING THERE.
WHAT ARE YOU TRYING TO SAY...?
THAT I KILLED YOUR MOTHER AND SISTER? THAT I CUT YOUR FATHER OPEN? WELL, I DID.

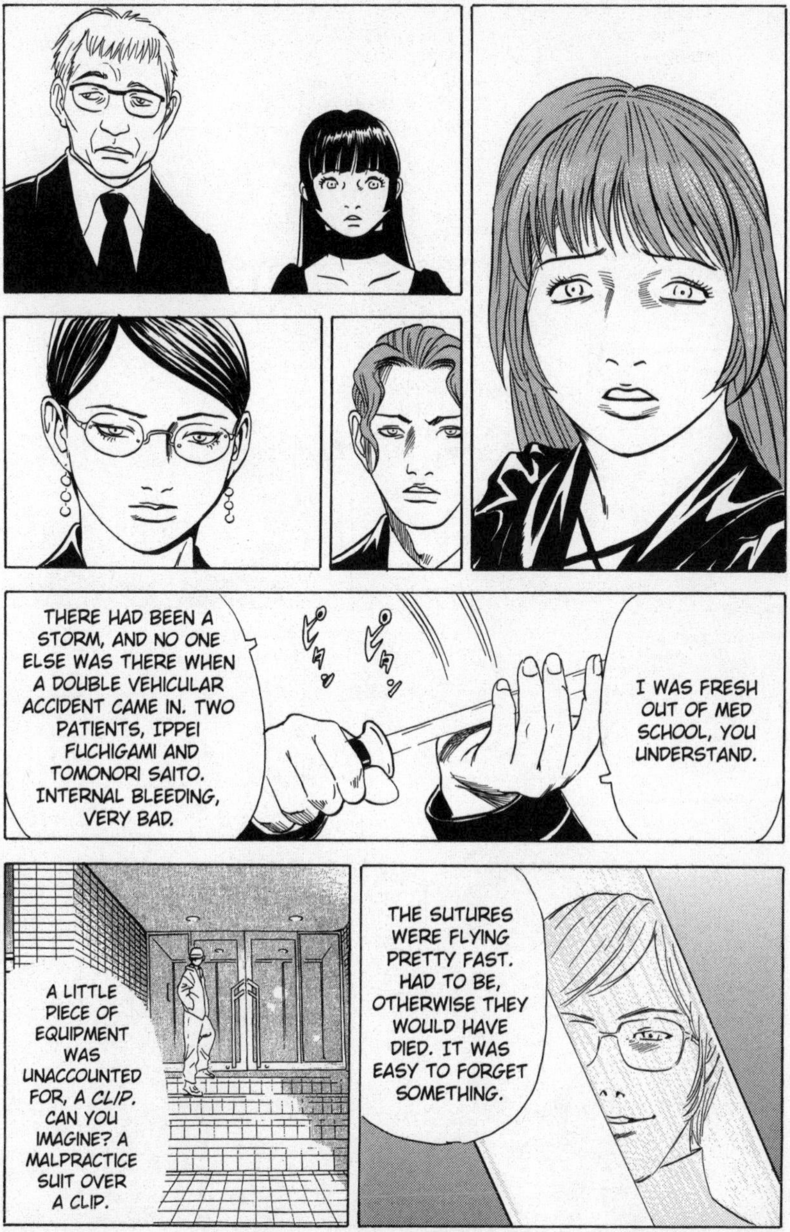
I WAS FRESH OUT OF MED SCHOOL, YOU UNDERSTAND.
THERE HAD BEEN A STORM, AND NO ONE ELSE WAS THERE WHEN A DOUBLE VEHICULAR ACCIDENT CAME IN. TWO PATIENTS, IPPEI FUCHIGAMI AND TOMONORI SAITO. INTERNAL BLEEDING, VERY BAD.
THE SUTURES WERE FLYING PRETTY FAST. HAD TO BE, OTHERWISE THEY WOULD HAVE DIED. IT WAS EASY TO FORGET SOMETHING.
A LITTLE PIECE OF EQUIPMENT WAS UNACCOUNTED FOR, A *CLIP*. CAN YOU IMAGINE? A MALPRACTICE SUIT OVER A CLIP.

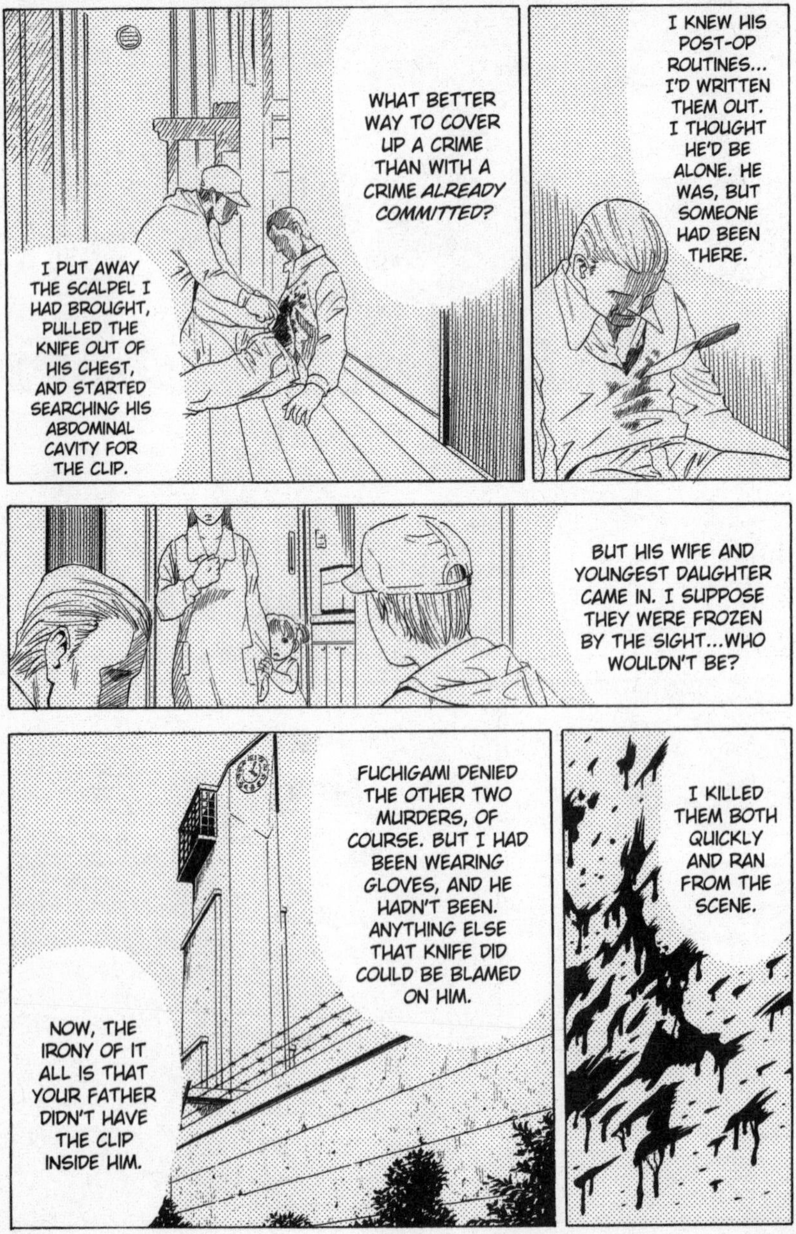
I KNEW HIS POST-OP ROUTINES... I'D WRITTEN THEM OUT. I THOUGHT HE'D BE ALONE. HE WAS, BUT SOMEONE HAD BEEN THERE.
WHAT BETTER WAY TO COVER UP A CRIME THAN WITH A CRIME *ALREADY COMMITTED?*
I PUT AWAY THE SCALPEL I HAD BROUGHT, PULLED THE KNIFE OUT OF HIS CHEST, AND STARTED SEARCHING HIS ABDOMINAL CAVITY FOR THE CLIP.
BUT HIS WIFE AND YOUNGEST DAUGHTER CAME IN. I SUPPOSE THEY WERE FROZEN BY THE SIGHT...WHO WOULDN'T BE?
I KILLED THEM BOTH QUICKLY AND RAN FROM THE SCENE.
FUCHIGAMI DENIED THE OTHER TWO MURDERS, OF COURSE. BUT I HAD BEEN WEARING GLOVES, AND HE HADN'T BEEN. ANYTHING ELSE THAT KNIFE DID COULD BE BLAMED ON HIM.
NOW, THE IRONY OF IT ALL IS THAT YOUR FATHER DIDN'T HAVE THE CLIP INSIDE HIM.

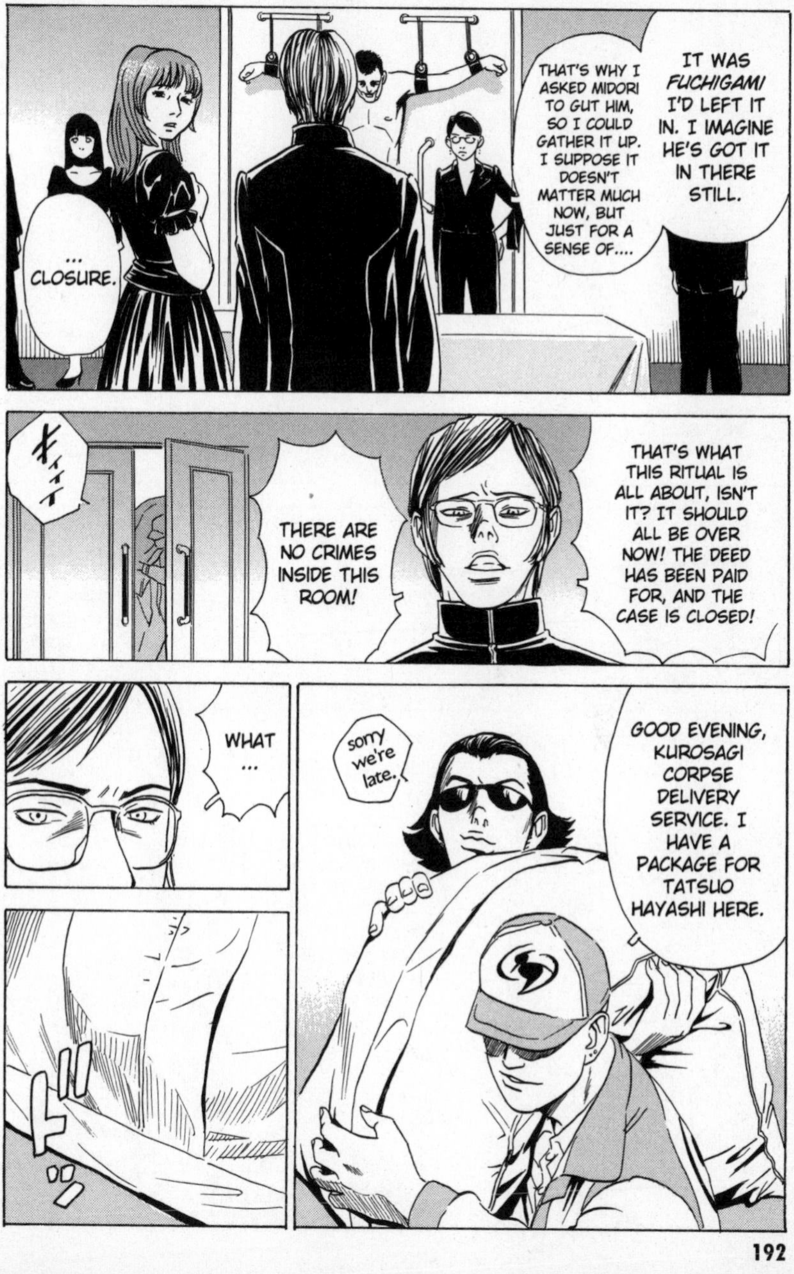
IT WAS *FUCHIGAMI* I'D LEFT IT IN. I IMAGINE HE'S GOT IT IN THERE STILL.
THAT'S WHY I ASKED MIDORI TO GUT HIM, SO I COULD GATHER IT UP. I SUPPOSE IT DOESN'T MATTER MUCH NOW, BUT JUST FOR A SENSE OF....
... CLOSURE.
THAT'S WHAT THIS RITUAL IS ALL ABOUT, ISN'T IT? IT SHOULD ALL BE OVER NOW! THE DEED HAS BEEN PAID FOR, AND THE CASE IS CLOSED!
THERE ARE NO CRIMES INSIDE THIS ROOM!
GOOD EVENING, KUROSAGI CORPSE DELIVERY SERVICE. I HAVE A PACKAGE FOR TATSUO HAYASHI HERE.
sorry we're late.
WHAT ...

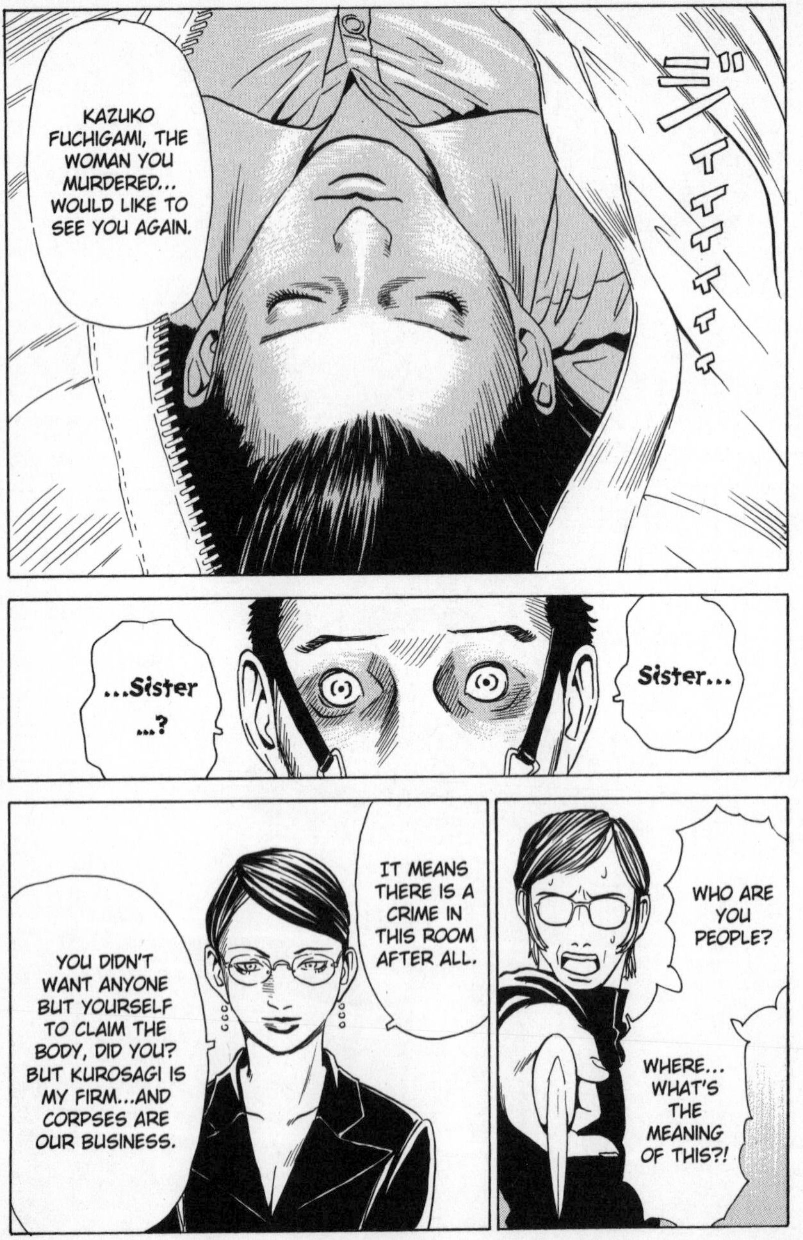
KAZUKO FUCHIGAMI, THE WOMAN YOU MURDERED... WOULD LIKE TO SEE YOU AGAIN.
Sister...
...Sister ...?
WHO ARE YOU PEOPLE?
WHERE... WHAT'S THE MEANING OF THIS?!
IT MEANS THERE IS A CRIME IN THIS ROOM AFTER ALL.
YOU DIDN'T WANT ANYONE BUT YOURSELF TO CLAIM THE BODY, DID YOU? BUT KUROSAGI IS MY FIRM...AND CORPSES ARE OUR BUSINESS.

Fu... fugu... guuuu
ギリリリ
ギイイッ
パキン
ブチ
...Ha... ha... Hayashi...
...I... I... kill... you...

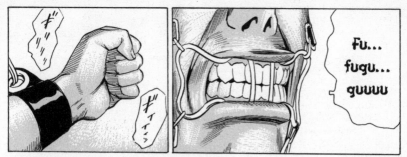

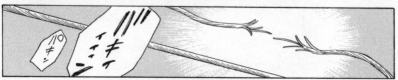

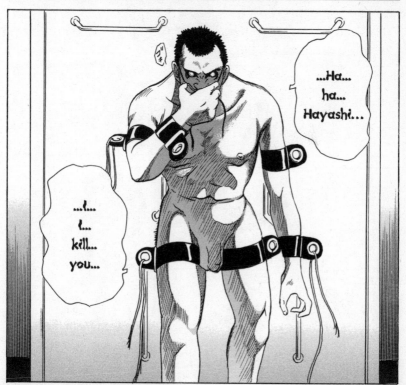

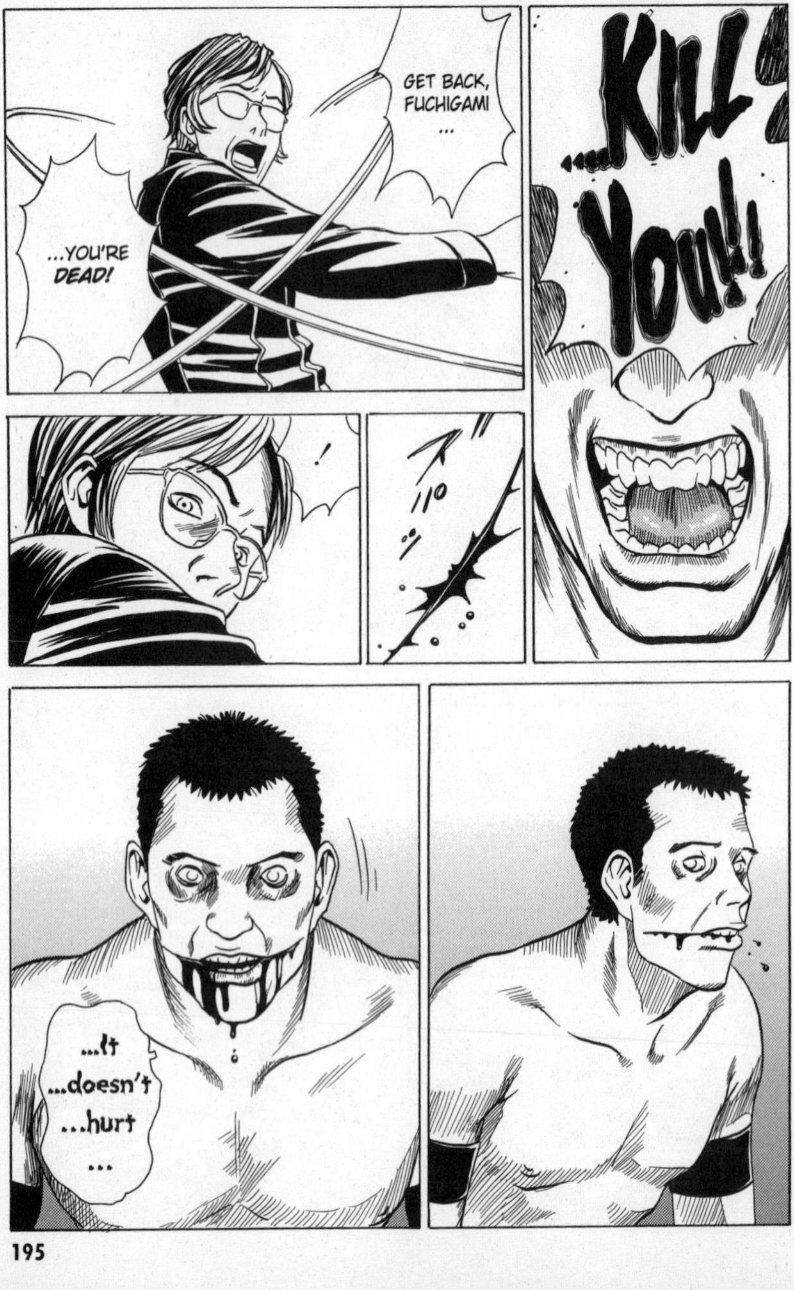

...KILL YOU!!
GET BACK, FUCHIGAMI ...
...YOU'RE DEAD!
!
...It ...doesn't ...hurt ...

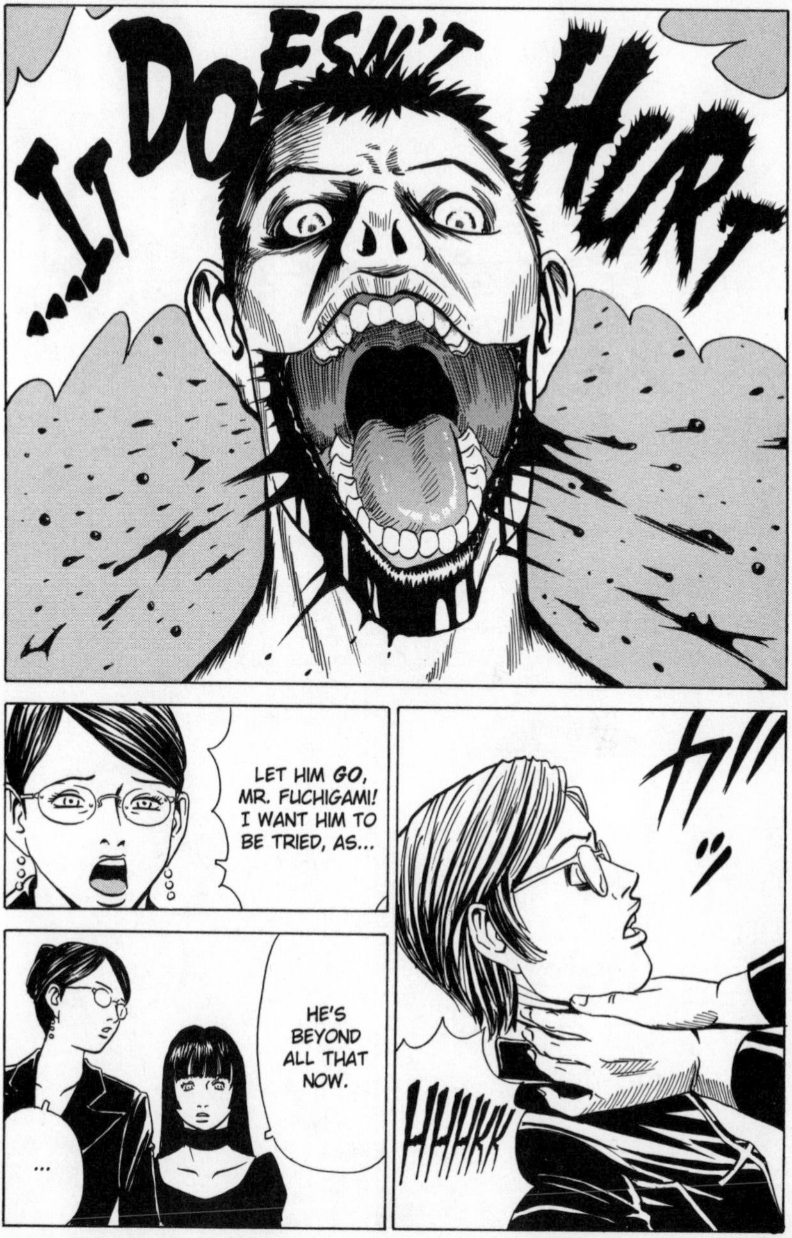
...IT DOESN'T HURT
カッ
HHHKK
LET HIM GO, MR. FUCHIGAMI! I WANT HIM TO BE TRIED, AS...
HE'S BEYOND ALL THAT NOW.
...

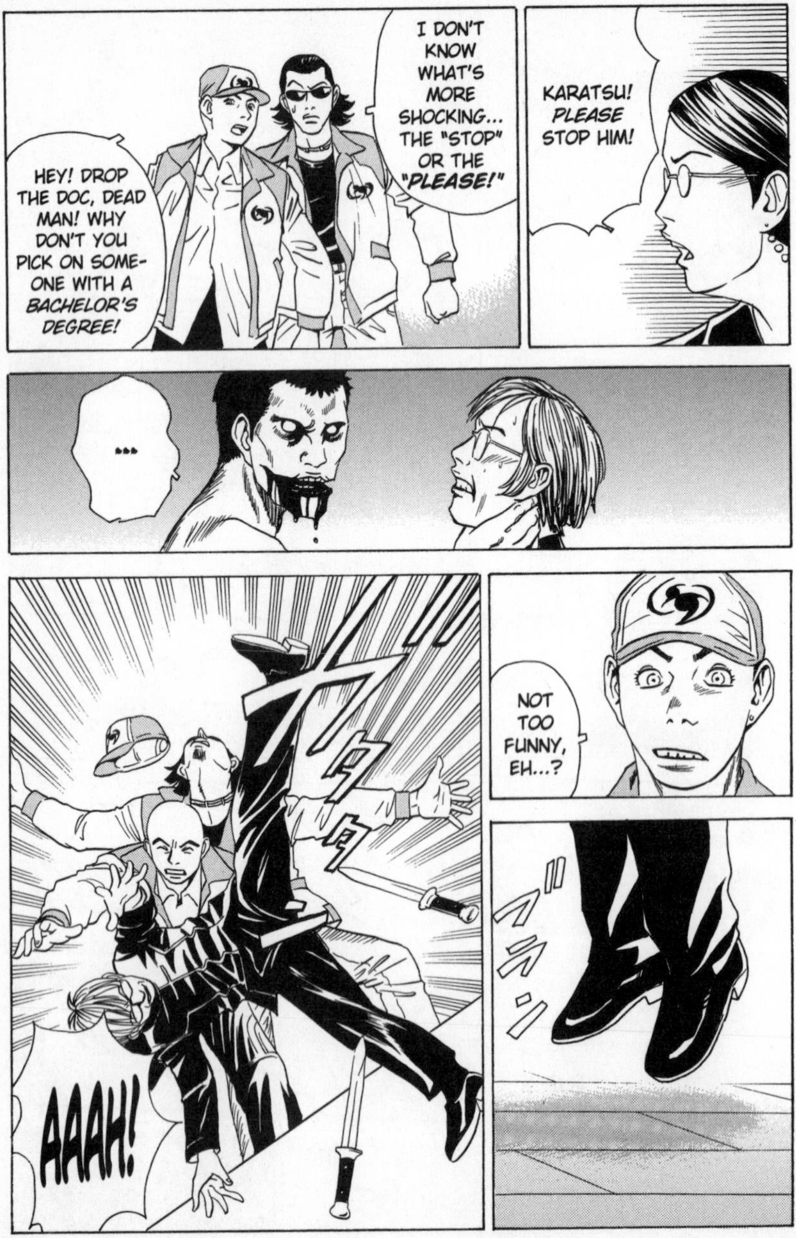
KARATSU! PLEASE STOP HIM!
I DON'T KNOW WHAT'S MORE SHOCKING... THE "STOP" OR THE "PLEASE!"
HEY! DROP THE DOC, DEAD MAN! WHY DON'T YOU PICK ON SOME-ONE WITH A BACHELOR'S DEGREE!
...
NOT TOO FUNNY, EH...?
AAAH!

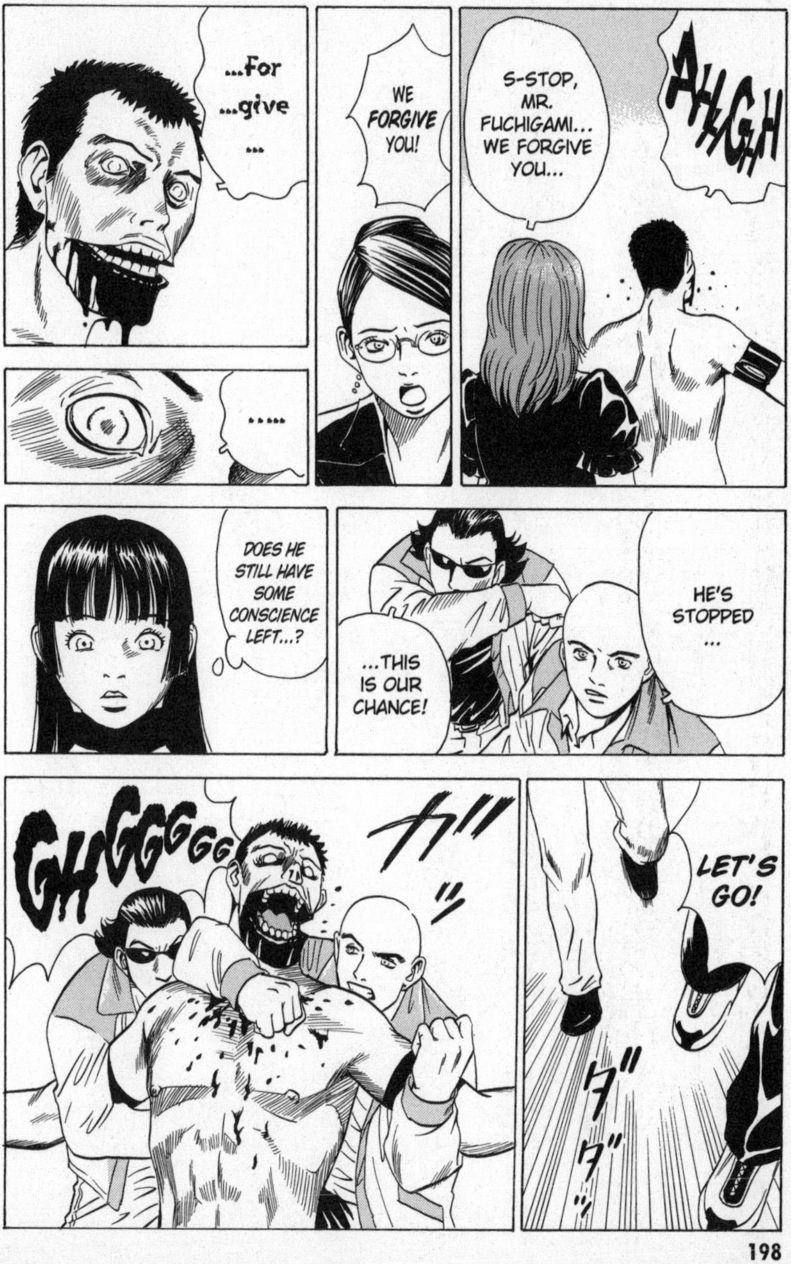
AHGH
S-STOP, MR. FUCHIGAMI... WE FORGIVE YOU...
WE FORGIVE YOU!
...For ...give ...
.....
HE'S STOPPED ...
...THIS IS OUR CHANCE!
DOES HE STILL HAVE SOME CONSCIENCE LEFT...?
LET'S GO!
ダダッ
GHGGGGG

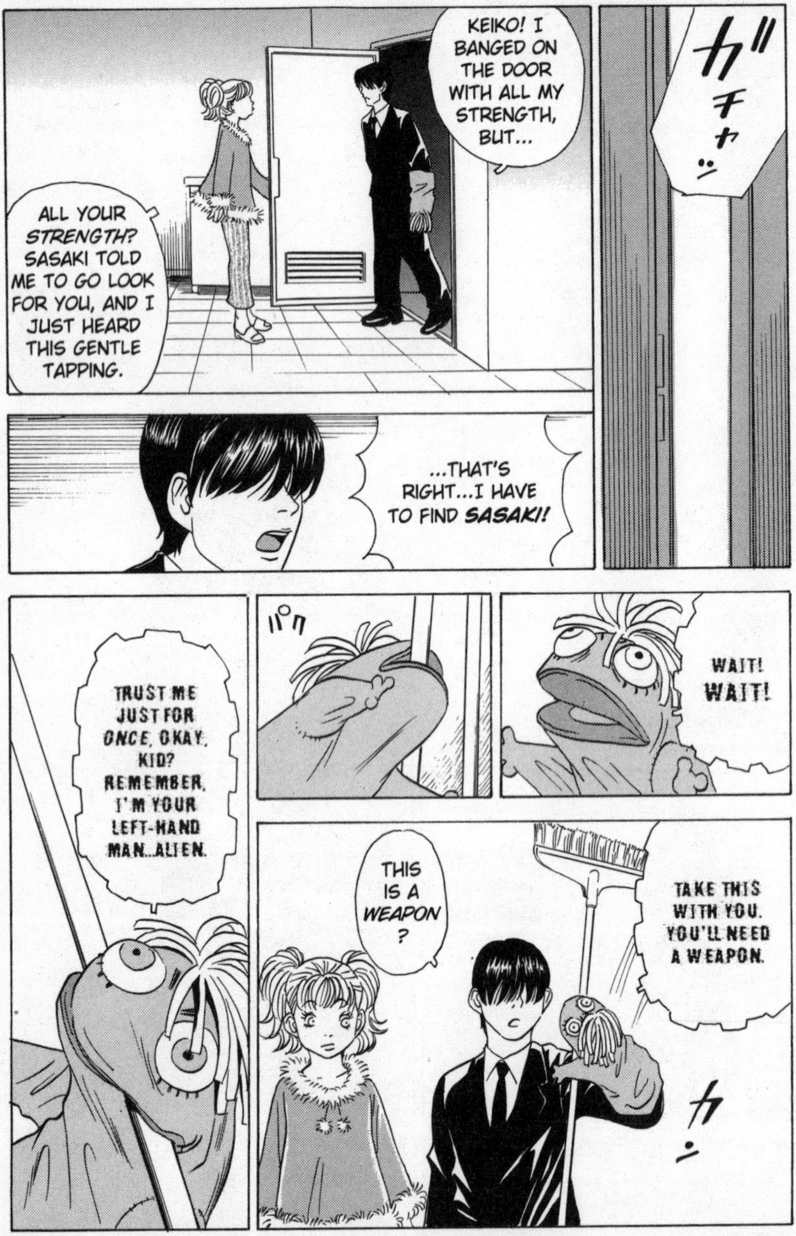
ガチャッ
KEIKO! I BANGED ON THE DOOR WITH ALL MY STRENGTH, BUT...
ALL YOUR *STRENGTH?* SASAKI TOLD ME TO GO LOOK FOR YOU, AND I JUST HEARD THIS GENTLE TAPPING.
...THAT'S RIGHT...I HAVE TO FIND *SASAKI!*
WAIT! WAIT!
パク
TAKE THIS WITH YOU. YOU'LL NEED A WEAPON.
THIS IS A *WEAPON* ?
カッ
TRUST ME JUST FOR *ONCE*, OKAY, KID? REMEMBER, I'M YOUR LEFT-HAND MAN...ALIEN.

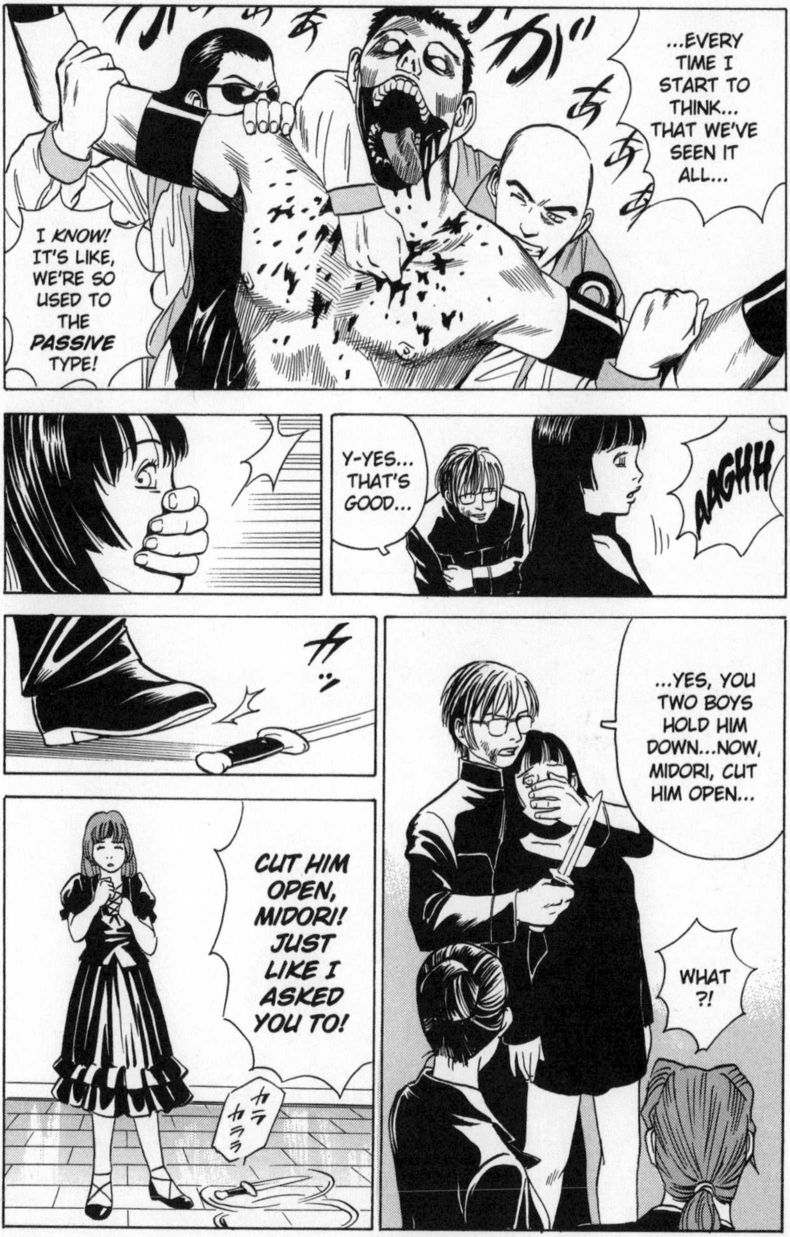
...EVERY TIME I START TO THINK... THAT WE'VE SEEN IT ALL...
I *KNOW!* IT'S LIKE, WE'RE SO USED TO THE ***PASSIVE*** TYPE!
Y-YES... THAT'S GOOD...
AAGHH
...YES, YOU TWO BOYS HOLD HIM DOWN...NOW, MIDORI, CUT HIM OPEN...
WHAT ?!
カッ
CUT HIM OPEN, MIDORI! JUST LIKE I ASKED YOU TO!
カラカラ

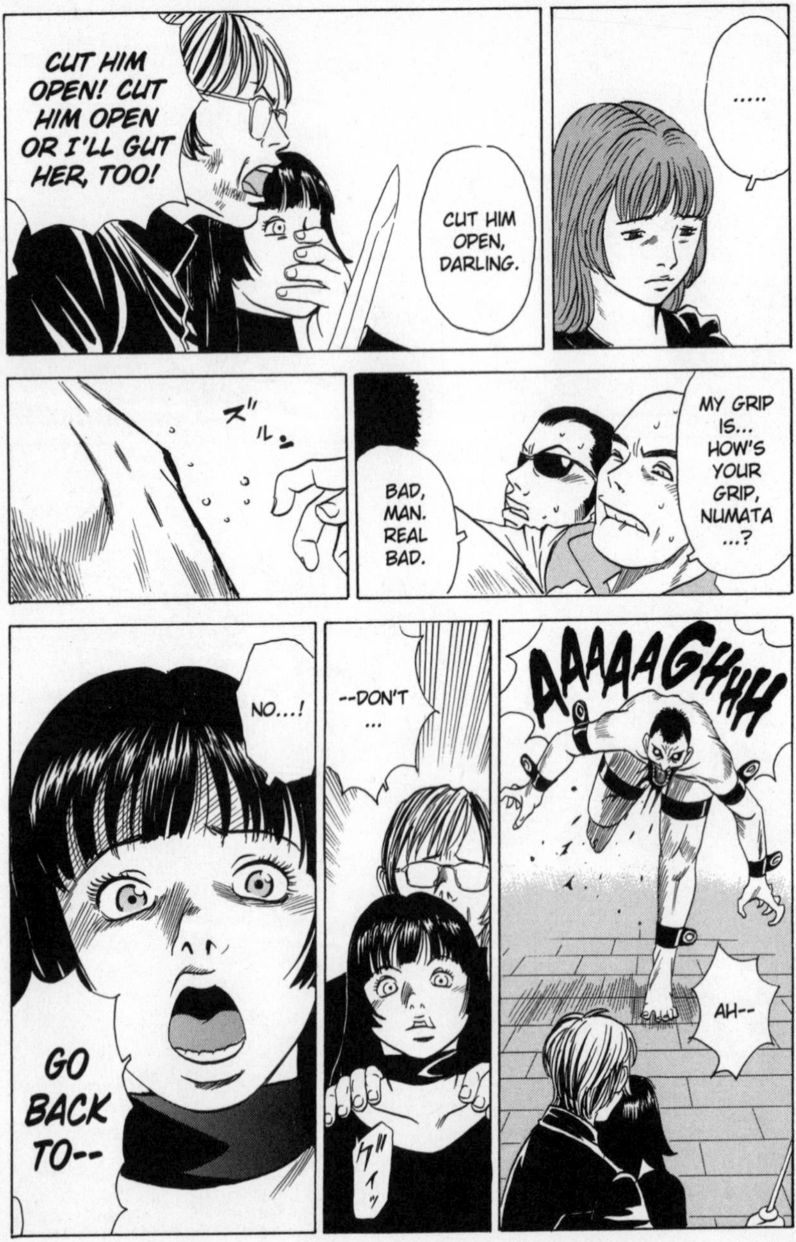
.....
CUT HIM OPEN! CUT HIM OPEN OR I'LL GUT HER, TOO!
CUT HIM OPEN, DARLING.
MY GRIP IS... HOW'S YOUR GRIP, NUMATA ...?
BAD, MAN. REAL BAD.
ズル
AAAAAGHHH
AH--
--DON'T ...
グイッ
NO...!
GO BACK TO--

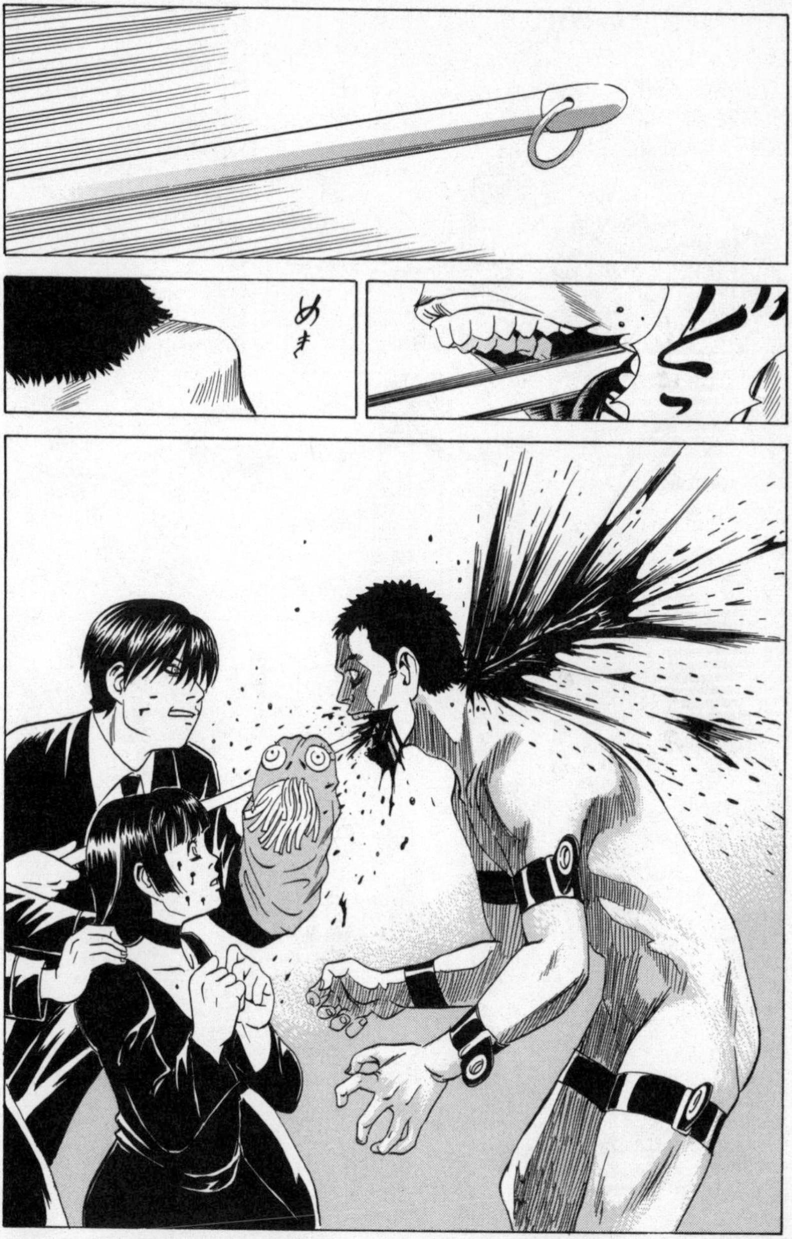

どくっ
めき

OH, YES, YATA.

YOU ALL RIGHT, MUTSUMI?

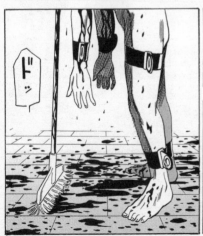

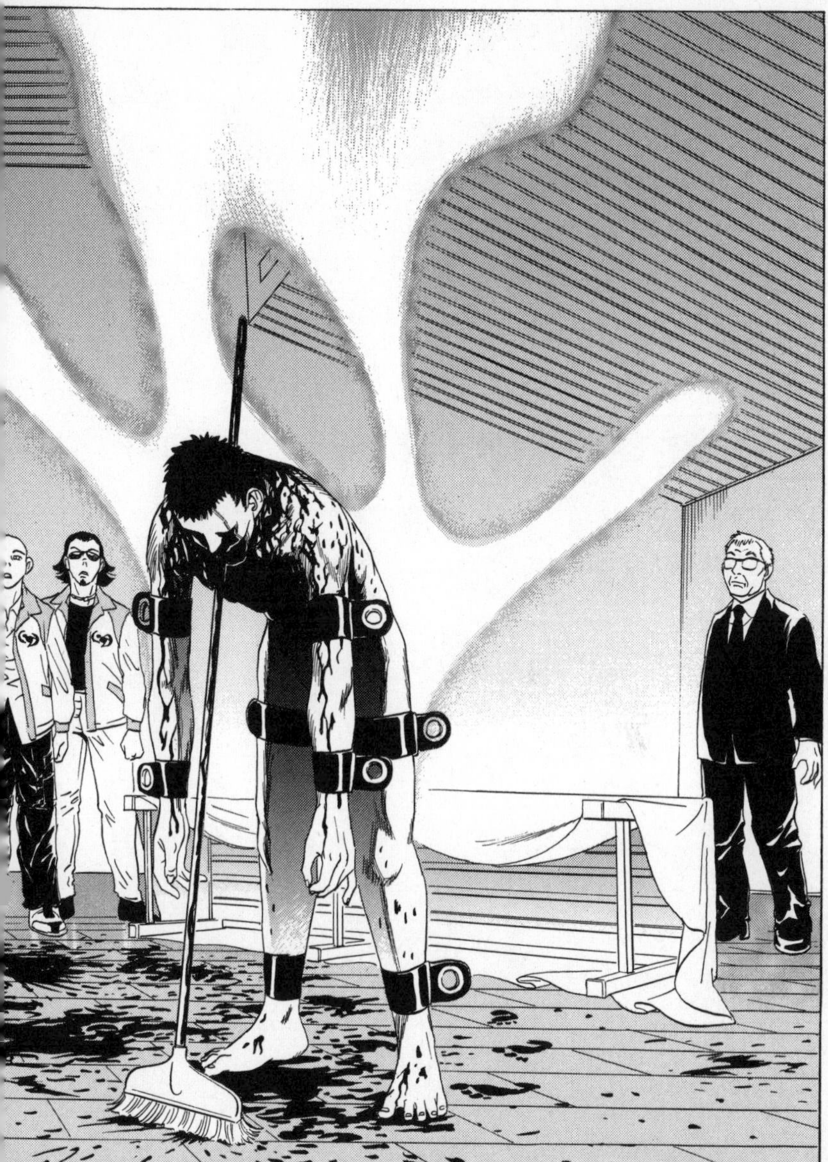

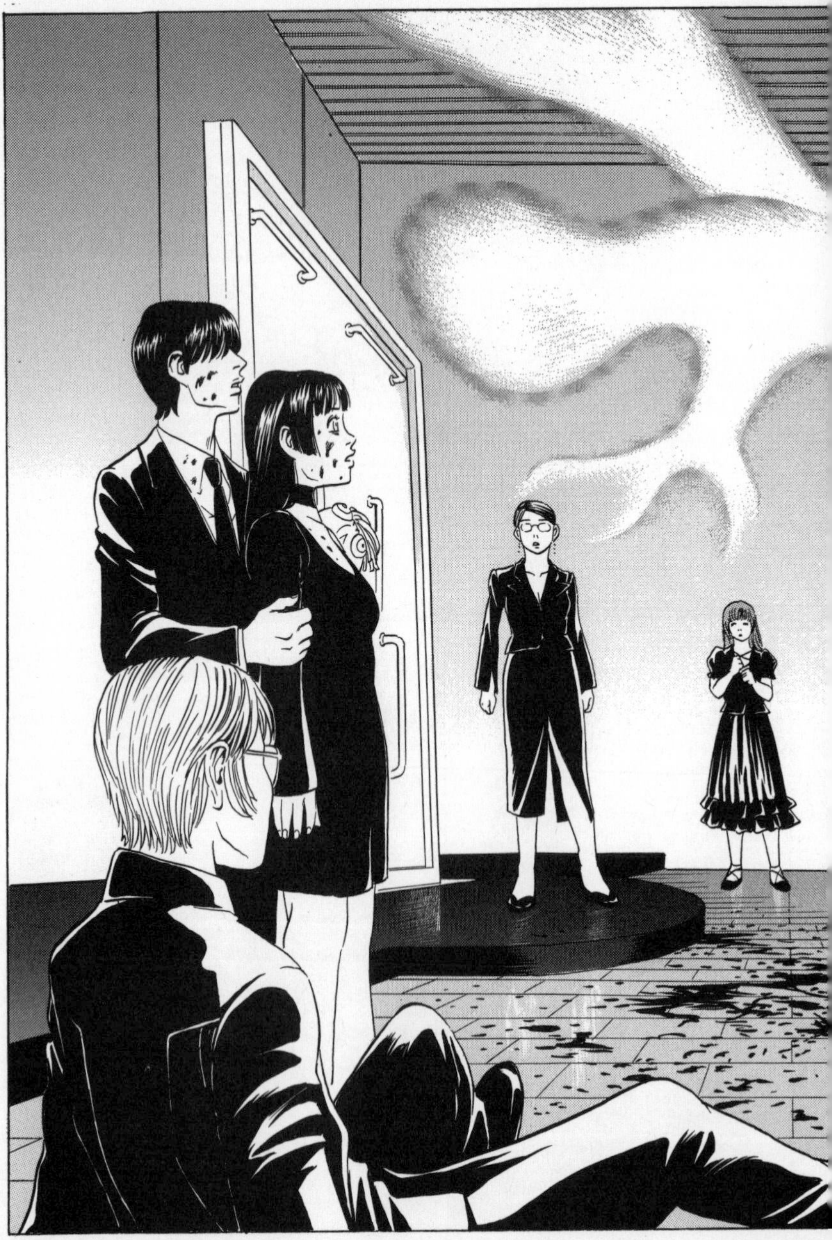

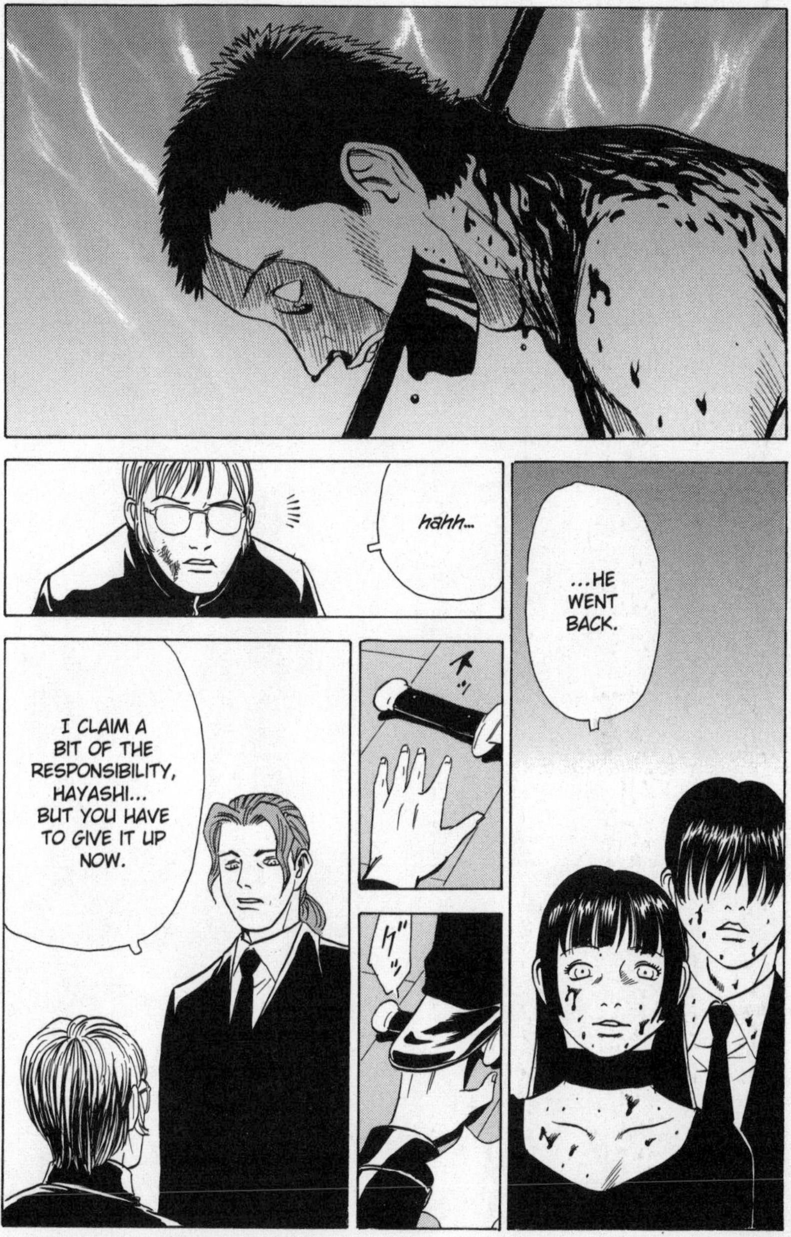
...HE WENT BACK.
hahh...
スッ
グッ
I CLAIM A BIT OF THE RESPONSIBILITY, HAYASHI... BUT YOU HAVE TO GIVE IT UP NOW.

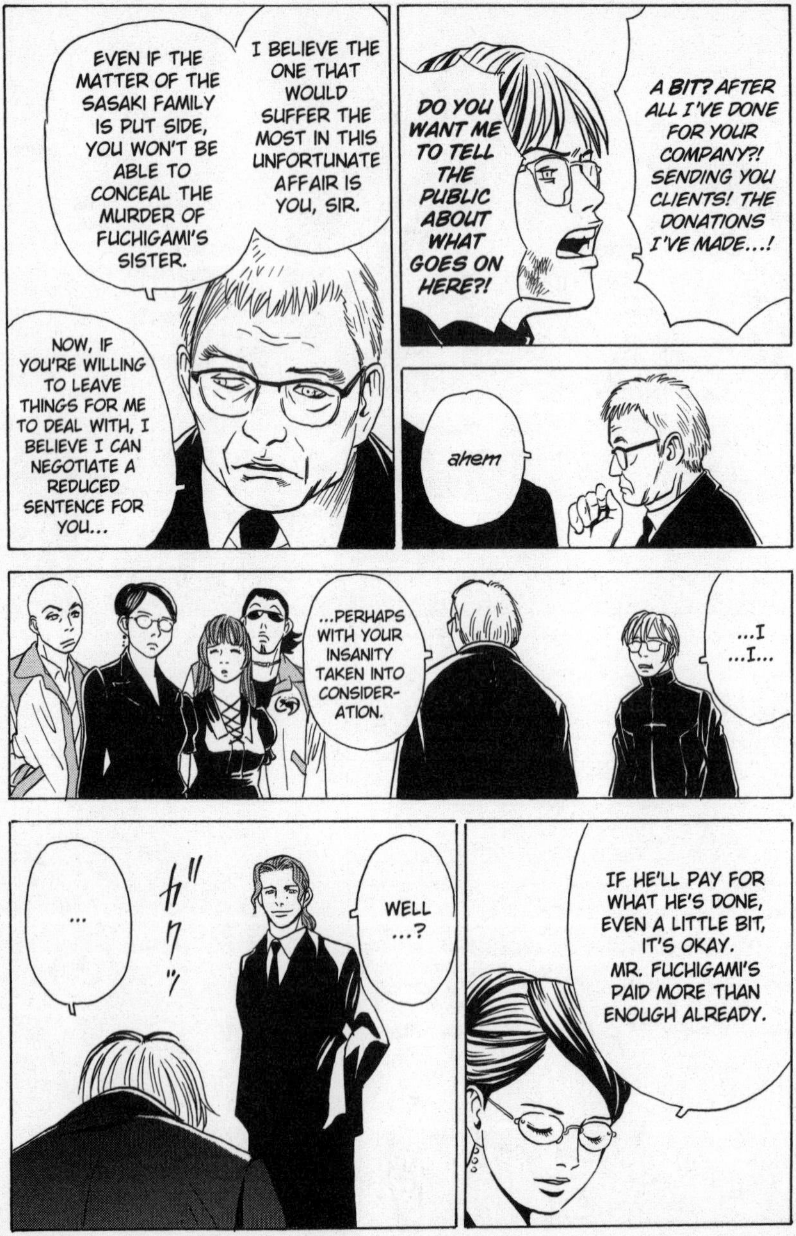
A BIT? AFTER ALL I'VE DONE FOR YOUR COMPANY?! SENDING YOU CLIENTS! THE DONATIONS I'VE MADE...!
DO YOU WANT ME TO TELL THE PUBLIC ABOUT WHAT GOES ON HERE?!
ahem
I BELIEVE THE ONE THAT WOULD SUFFER THE MOST IN THIS UNFORTUNATE AFFAIR IS YOU, SIR.
EVEN IF THE MATTER OF THE SASAKI FAMILY IS PUT SIDE, YOU WON'T BE ABLE TO CONCEAL THE MURDER OF FUCHIGAMI'S SISTER.
NOW, IF YOU'RE WILLING TO LEAVE THINGS FOR ME TO DEAL WITH, I BELIEVE I CAN NEGOTIATE A REDUCED SENTENCE FOR YOU...
...I ...I...
...PERHAPS WITH YOUR INSANITY TAKEN INTO CONSIDER-ATION.
IF HE'LL PAY FOR WHAT HE'S DONE, EVEN A LITTLE BIT, IT'S OKAY. MR. FUCHIGAMI'S PAID MORE THAN ENOUGH ALREADY.
WELL ...?
ガクッ
...

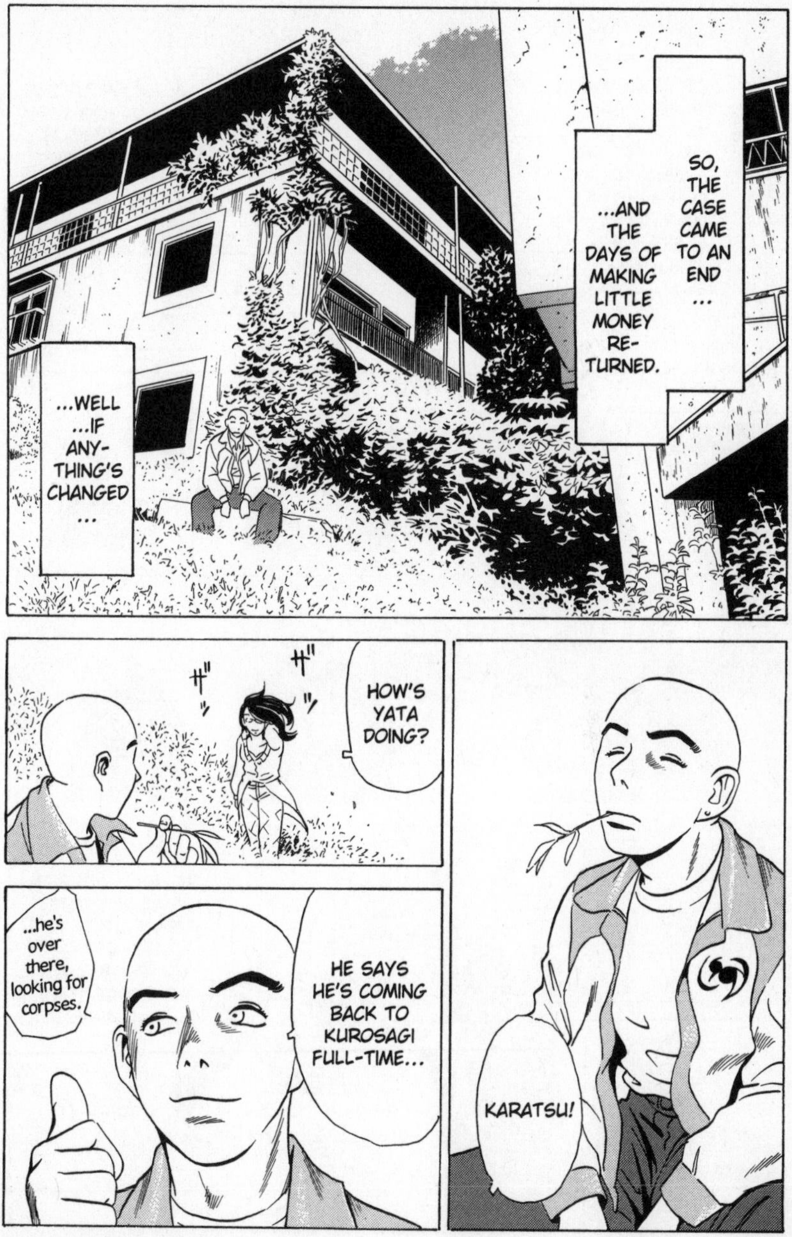
SO, THE CASE CAME TO AN END ...
...AND THE DAYS OF MAKING LITTLE MONEY RE-TURNED.
...WELL ...IF ANY-THING'S CHANGED ...
KARATSU!
ザッ
ザッ
HOW'S YATA DOING?
HE SAYS HE'S COMING BACK TO KUROSAGI FULL-TIME...
...he's over there, looking for corpses.

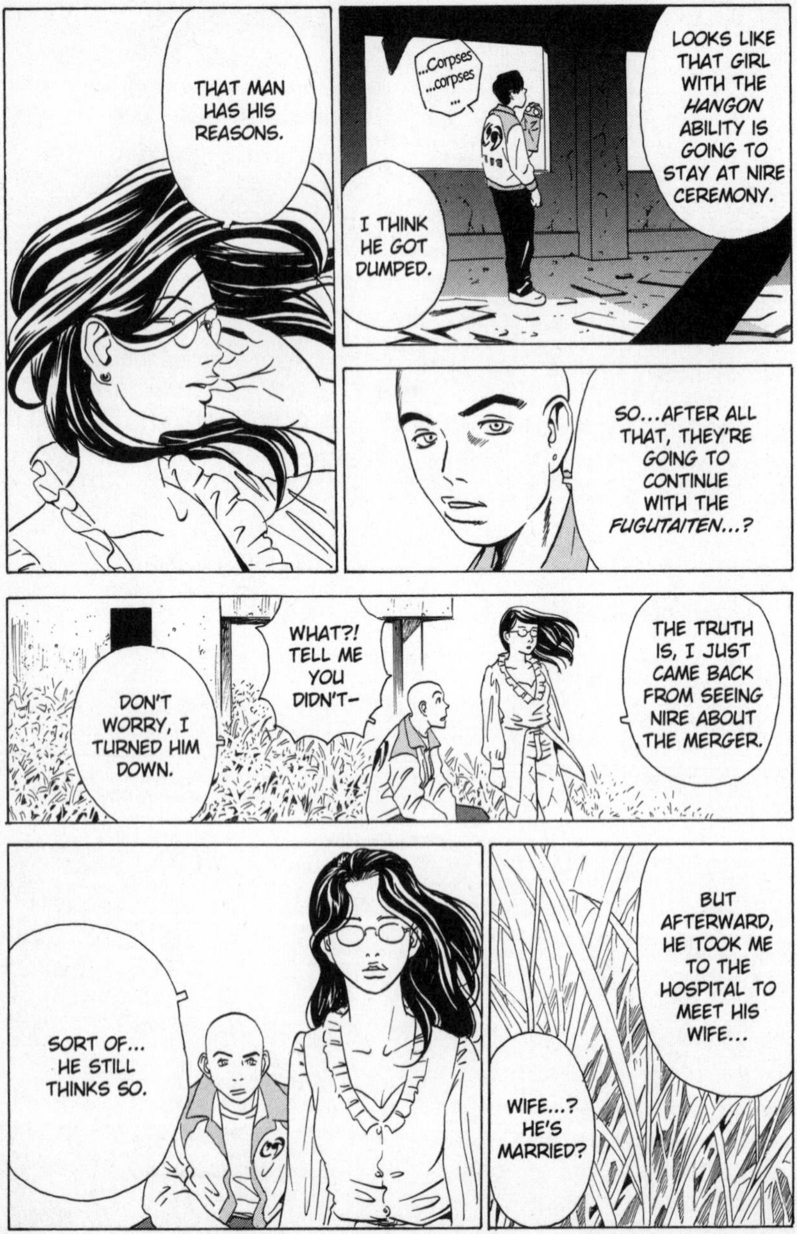
LOOKS LIKE THAT GIRL WITH THE *HANGON* ABILITY IS GOING TO STAY AT NIRE CEREMONY.
...Corpses ...corpses ...
I THINK HE GOT DUMPED.
SO...AFTER ALL THAT, THEY'RE GOING TO CONTINUE WITH THE *FUGUTAITEN*...?
THAT MAN HAS HIS REASONS.
THE TRUTH IS, I JUST CAME BACK FROM SEEING NIRE ABOUT THE MERGER.
WHAT?! TELL ME YOU DIDN'T-
DON'T WORRY, I TURNED HIM DOWN.
BUT AFTERWARD, HE TOOK ME TO THE HOSPITAL TO MEET HIS WIFE...
WIFE...? HE'S MARRIED?
SORT OF... HE STILL THINKS SO.

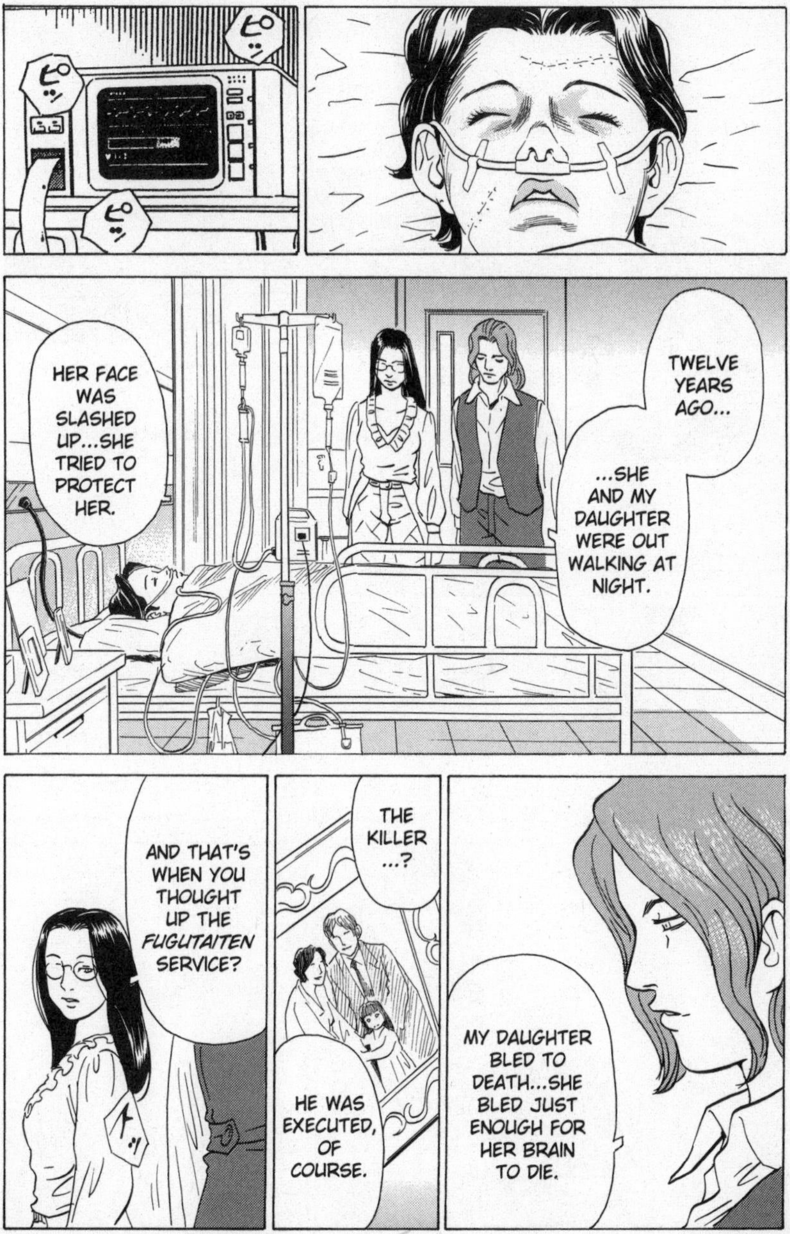
ピッ
ピッ
ピッ
TWELVE YEARS AGO...
...SHE AND MY DAUGHTER WERE OUT WALKING AT NIGHT.
HER FACE WAS SLASHED UP...SHE TRIED TO PROTECT HER.
MY DAUGHTER BLED TO DEATH...SHE BLED JUST ENOUGH FOR HER BRAIN TO DIE.
THE KILLER ...?
HE WAS EXECUTED, OF COURSE.
AND THAT'S WHEN YOU THOUGHT UP THE *FUGUTAITEN* SERVICE?

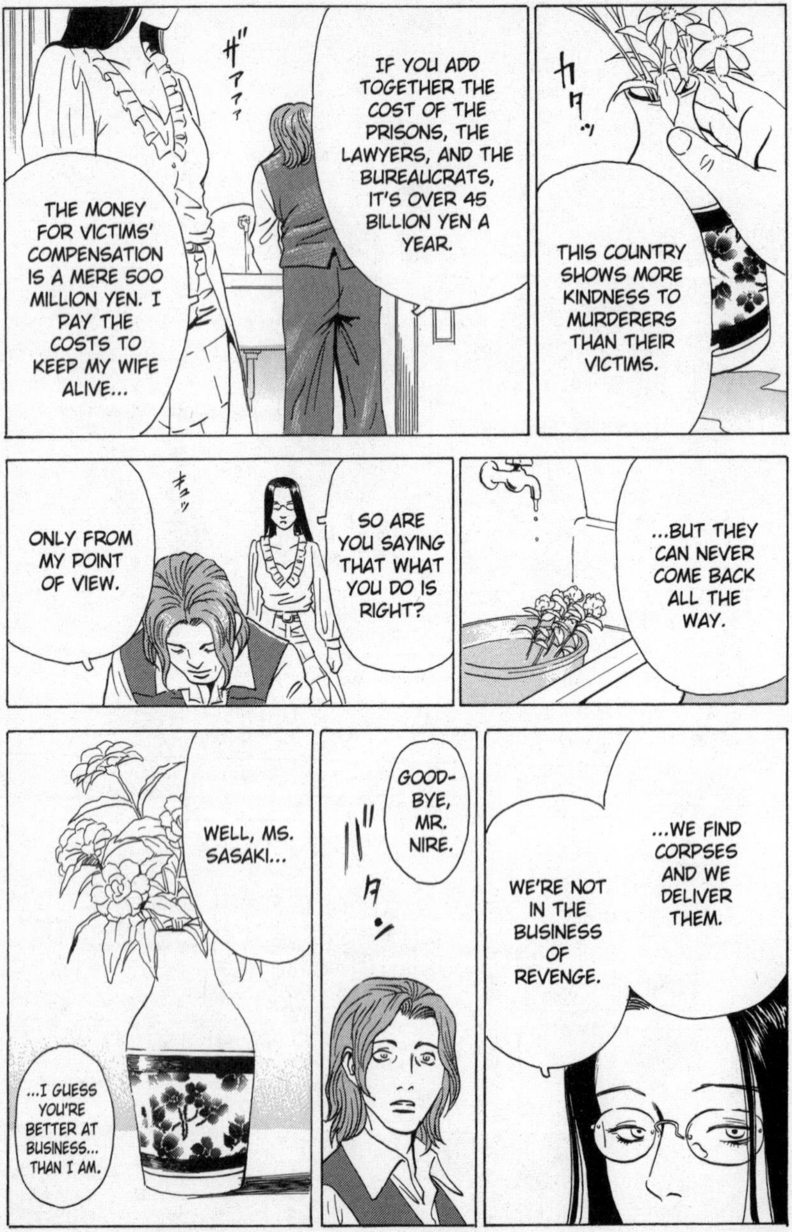
カタッ
THIS COUNTRY SHOWS MORE KINDNESS TO MURDERERS THAN THEIR VICTIMS.
ザァァァ
IF YOU ADD TOGETHER THE COST OF THE PRISONS, THE LAWYERS, AND THE BUREAUCRATS, IT'S OVER 45 BILLION YEN A YEAR.
THE MONEY FOR VICTIMS' COMPENSATION IS A MERE 500 MILLION YEN. I PAY THE COSTS TO KEEP MY WIFE ALIVE...
...BUT THEY CAN NEVER COME BACK ALL THE WAY.
SO ARE YOU SAYING THAT WHAT YOU DO IS RIGHT?
キュッ
ONLY FROM MY POINT OF VIEW.
...WE FIND CORPSES AND WE DELIVER THEM.
WE'RE NOT IN THE BUSINESS OF REVENGE.
GOOD-BYE, MR. NIRE.
WELL, MS. SASAKI...
...I GUESS YOU'RE BETTER AT BUSINESS... THAN I AM.

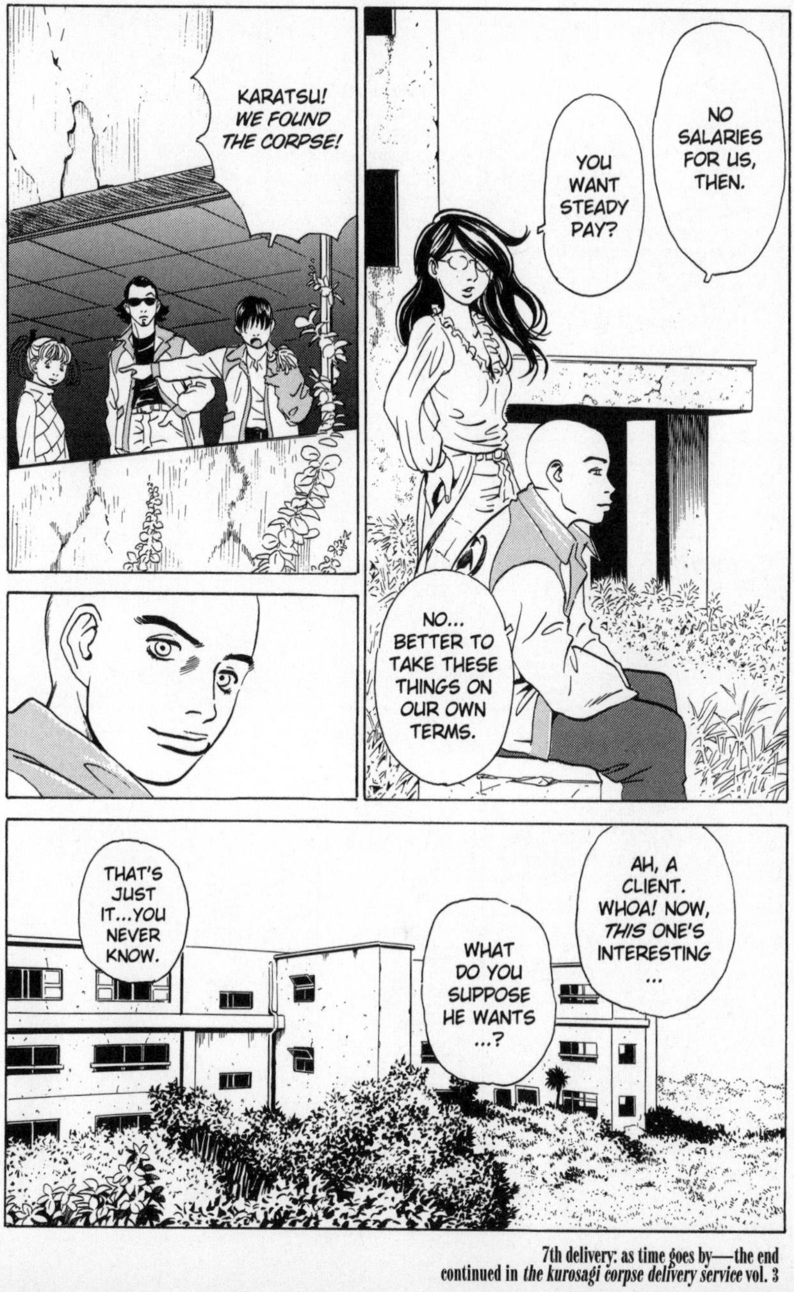
NO SALARIES FOR US, THEN.
YOU WANT STEADY PAY?
NO... BETTER TO TAKE THESE THINGS ON OUR OWN TERMS.
KARATSU! WE FOUND THE CORPSE!
AH, A CLIENT. WHOA! NOW, *THIS* ONE'S INTERESTING ...
WHAT DO YOU SUPPOSE HE WANTS ...?
THAT'S JUST IT...YOU NEVER KNOW.

7th delivery: as time goes by—the end

continued in *the kurosagi corpse delivery service* vol. 3

AFTERWORD FROM THE AUTHOR

AFTERWORD BY THE AUTHOR

My father died of cancer the January just before I graduated college. The doctors said he had very little time to live, and so my family and I went to the hospital to be there in his last days. But his death lasted longer than they had thought, and so, the strain upon those lying by his side, waiting for it.

I awoke one morning just before daybreak on one of the cots the hospital provides. My mother and sister were asleep upon another, and so I was the first to know that my father had passed during the night. I didn't check him or take his pulse; I just knew. I didn't call the nurse nor wake the rest of my weary family; what would have been the point? Let them sleep a little longer; let me sleep again now, too.

My mother died twenty years after—not too long ago. Due to work and other troubles, I couldn't visit her before; I couldn't even make the funeral. Sometimes these things can't be helped as a writer. But the truth is I hadn't seen her in several years, and my sister's family had become worn out from her care, so what I felt was again relief.

Recently things came full circle from my college days, when I went to visit the grave of my old anthropology professor, Tokuji Chiba, with the classmates I hadn't seen in a generation. It was in the professor's will that his old students be notified only after he had been buried. When we came to the site, we saw he'd even left his name off the headstone—and we all agreed that this was just like him. Then we started wondering what the proper procedure was to burn incense at a grave, and how ironic it was that students of anthropology weren't sure. We said, well, we're the kind of students the professor raised.

It hit me later that both my parents and my mentor had now all passed on. I find myself thinking that in few years, the time may come for the first of our generation to be buried.

The Kurosagi Corpse Delivery Service is a story I created out of my desire to write an orthodox horror story. I thought it was odd how the walking dead had become such a normal sight in movies and video games—how much the idea of a zombie had been taken for granted. I wanted to get back to the fear any real person would feel, should death's work appear to be unfinished.

The office I work for comes up with plans for dozens of manga every year, but only a few ever actually get made. In most cases, it's the problem of not being able to find a manga artist that fits the plans, but fortunately for *Kurosagi*, I was paired up with Housui Yamazaki, and together we were able to express this concept as I had hoped.

With most of the readers being desensitized to corpses and zombies from pop culture, I would like to voice how wonderful it is to be able to work with an artist who can depict a sense of fear as Yamazaki can do by simply making the dead move in the way that he does.

Serialized in *Kadowaka Mystery,* a companion title to *Shonen Ace*, this is a series that seems to have a hard time finding a permanent home, but I have an entire story ready to explain why the members have those strange powers, so I hope it can see the light of day in some publication soon. (Editor's note: *Kurosagi* did return, this time to *Shonen Ace* magazine itself, in October of 2006).

See you in Volume Three.

— eiji otsuka

DISJECTA MEMBRA

SOUND FX GLOSSARY AND NOTES ON KUROSAGI VOL. 2 BY TOSHIFUMI YOSHIDA
introduction and additional comments by the editor

TO INCREASE YOUR ENJOYMENT of the distinctive Japanese visual style of this manga, we've included a guide to the sound effects (or "FX") used in this manga adaptation of the anime film. It is suggested the reader not constantly consult this glossary as they read through, but regard it as supplemental information, in the manner of footnotes. If you want to imagine it being read aloud by Osaka, after the manner of her lecture to Sakaki on hemorrhoids in episode five, please go right ahead. In either Yuki Matsuoka or Kira Vincent-Davis's voice—I like them both.

Japanese, like English, did not independently invent its own writing system, but instead borrowed and modified the system used by the then-dominant cultural power in their part of the world. We still call the letters we use to write English today the "Roman" alphabet, for the simple reason that about 1600 years ago the earliest English speakers, living on the frontier of the Roman Empire, began to use the same letters the Romans used to write their Latin language, to write out English.

Around that very same time, on the other side of the planet, Japan, like England, was another example of an island civilization lying across the sea from a great empire, in this case, that of China. Likewise, the Japanese borrowed from the Chinese writing system, which then as now consists of thousands of complex symbols—today in China officially referred

to in the Roman alphabet as *hanzi*, but which the Japanese pronounce as *kanji*. For example, all the Japanese characters you see on the front cover of *The Kurosagi Corpse Delivery Service*—the seven which make up the original title and the four each which make up the creators' names—are examples of kanji. Of course, all of them were hanzi first; although the Japanese did later invent some original kanji of their own, just as new hanzi have been created over the centuries as Chinese evolved.

Note that whereas both kanji and hanzi are methods of writing foreign words in Roman letters, "kanji" gives English speakers a fairly good idea of how the Japanese word is really pronounced—*khan-gee*—whereas "hanzi" does not—in Mandarin Chinese it sounds something like *n-tsuh*. The reason is fairly simple: whereas the most commonly used method of writing Japanese in Roman letters, called the Hepburn system, was developed by a native English speaker, the most commonly used method of writing Chinese in Roman letters, called the Pinyin system, was developed by native Mandarin speakers. In fact Pinyin was developed to help teach Mandarin pronunciation to speakers of other Chinese dialects; unlike Hepburn, it was not intended as a learning tool for English speakers *per se*, and hence has no particular obligation to "make sense" to English speakers or, indeed, users of

other languages spelled with the Roman alphabet).

Whereas the various dialects of Chinese are written entirely in hanzi, it is impractical to render the Japanese language entirely in them. To compare once more, English is a notoriously difficult language in which to spell properly, and this is in part because it uses an alphabet designed for another language, Latin, whose sounds are different. The challenges the Japanese faced in using the Chinese writing system for their own language were even greater, for whereas spoken English and Latin are at least from a common language family, spoken Japanese is unrelated to any of the various dialects of spoken Chinese. The complicated writing system Japanese evolved represents an adjustment to these differences.

When the Japanese borrowed hanzi to become kanji, what they were getting was a way to write out (remember, they already had ways to say) their vocabulary. Nouns, verbs, many adjectives, the names of places and people—that's what kanji are used for, the fundamental data of the written language. The practical use and processing of that "data"—its grammar and pronunciation—is another matter entirely. Because spoken Japanese neither sounds nor functions like Chinese, the first work-around tried was a system called *manyogana*, where individual kanji were picked to represent certain syllables in Japanese (a similar method is still used in Chinese today to spell out foreign names).

The commentary in *Katsuya Terada's The Monkey King* (also available from Dark Horse, and also translated by To-shifumi Yoshida) notes the importance that not only Chinese, but Indian culture had on Japan at this time in history—particularly, Buddhism. It is believed the Northeast Indian *Siddham* script studied by Kukai (died 835 AD), founder of the Shingon sect of Japanese Buddhism, inspired him to create the solution for writing Japanese still used today. Kukai is credited with the idea of taking the manyogana and making the shorthand versions of them now known simply as *kana*. The improvement in efficiency was dramatic—a kanji, used previously to represent a sound, that might have taken a dozen strokes to draw, was now reduced to three or four.

Unlike the original kanji it was based on, the new kana had *only* a sound meaning. And unlike the thousands of kanji, there are only 46 kana, which can be used to spell out any word in the Japanese language, including the many ordinarily written with kanji (Japanese keyboards work on this principle). The same set of 46 kana is written two different ways depending on their intended use; cursive style, *hiragana*, and block style, *katakana*. Naturally, sound FX in manga are almost always written out using kana.

Kana works somewhat differently than the Roman alphabet. For example, while there are separate kana for each of the five vowels (the Japanese order is not A-E-I-O-U as in English, but A-I-U-E-O), there are, except for "n," no separate kana for consonants (the middle "n" in the word ninja illustrates this exception). Instead, kana work by grouping together consonants with vowels: for example, there are five kana for sounds starting

with "k," depending on which vowel follows it—in Japanese vowel order, they go KA, KI, KU, KE, KO. The next set of kana begins with "s" sounds, so SA, SHI, SU, SE, SO, and so on. You will observe this kind of consonant-vowel pattern in the FX listings for *Kurosagi* Vol. 2 below.

Katakana is almost always the kind that gets used for manga sound FX, but on occasion (often when the sound is one made by a person) hiragana are used instead. In *Kurosagi* Vol. 2 you can see one of several examples on page 55, panel 6, when Mutsumi exhales with a "FUU" sound, which in hiragana style is written ふうっ. Note its more cursive appearance compared to the other FX. If it had been written in katakana style, it would look like フウツ.

To see how to use this glossary, take an example from page 4: "4.1 FX: GA-KON—sound of trap door dropping open." 4.1 means the FX is the one on page 4, in panel 1. GAKON is the sound these kana—ガコン—literally stands for. After the dash comes an explanation of what the sound represents (in some cases, such as this one, it will be more obvious than others). Note that in cases where there are two or more different sounds in a single panel, an extra number is used to differentiate them from right to left; or, in cases where right and left are less clear (for example, 4.2.1 and 4.2.2) in clockwise order.

The use of kana in these FX also illustrates another aspect of written Japanese—its flexible reading order. For example, the way you're reading the pages and panels of this book in general: going from right-to-left, and from top to bottom—is the order in which Japanese is also written in most forms of print: books, magazines, and newspapers. However, if you examine those kana examples given above, you'll notice something interesting. They read "Western" style—left-to-right! In fact, many of the FX in *Kurosagi* (and manga in general) read left-to-right. On page 23 you can find the direction switching from right-to-left (23.3) to left-to-right (23.4) in two successive panels. This kind of flexibility is also to be found on Japanese web pages, which usually also read left-to-right. In other words, Japanese doesn't simply read "the other way" from English; the Japanese themselves are used to reading it in several different directions.

As might be expected, some FX "sound" short, and others "sound" long. Manga represent this in different ways. One of many examples of "short sounds" in *Kurosagi* Vol. 2 is to be found in the example 55.6 given above: FUU. Note the small つ mark it has at the end. This is ordinarily reprsents the sound "tsu" (the katakana form, more commonly seen in manga FX, is ツ) but its half-size use at the end of FX like this means the sound is the kind which stops or cuts off suddenly; that's why the sound is written as FUU and not FUUTSU—you don't "pronounce" the TSU in such cases.

Note the small "tsu" has another occasional use *inside*, rather than at the end, of a particular FX, as seen in 23.3's TA TTA TA—running sound—here it's at work between two "TA" タ sounds to indicate a doubling of the consonant sound that follows it.

There are three different ways you may see "long sounds"—where a vowel sound is extended—written out as FX. One is with an ellipsis, as in 21.1's GOTO. Another is with an extended line, as in 50.3's PIN-POON PINPOON. Still another is by simply repeating a vowel several times, as in 17.4's ZUZUUU. You will note this last example also has an ellipsis at its end; the methods may be combined within a single FX. As a visual element in manga, FX are an art rather than a science, and are used in a less rigorous fashion than kana are in standard written Japanese.

The explanation of what the sound represents may sometimes be surprising; but every culture "hears" sounds differently. Note that manga FX do not even necessarily represent literal sounds. Such "mimetic" words, which represent an imagined sound, or even a state of mind, are called *gitaigo* in Japanese. Like the onomatopoeic *giseigo* (the words used to represent literal sounds—i.e., most FX in this glossary are classed as giseigo), they are also used in colloquial speech and writing. A Japanese, for example, might say that something bounced by saying PURIN, or talk about eating by saying MUGU MUGU. It's something like describing chatter in English by saying "yadda yadda yadda" instead.

One important last note: all these spelled-out kana vowels should be pronounced as they are in Japanese: "A" as *ah*, "I" as *eee*, "U" as *ooh*, "E" as *eh*, and "O" as *oh*.

3   People are sometimes surprised to hear that the death penalty still exists in Japan, or that it is carried out by hanging (one might expect something more high-tech, like a laser beam). About two or three people on average are hung every year in Japan—the penalty is given in recent decades only for multiple murders or murder under aggravated circumstances; perhaps the most infamous prisoners on death row in Japan are several members of the cult Aum Shinri Kyo, for their participation in the Japanese nerve-gas terrorist attacks of 1995, and the serial killer Tsutomu Miyazaki, whose arrest in 1989 sparked condemnation of otaku (it was later understood that the media had exaggerated his participation in otaku culture). In Japan, both the defense and the prosecution can appeal a death sentence—that is, the prosecution can argue to a higher court that a person sentenced to life in prison should have their sentence "upgraded" to death!

3.5   **FX: KOKU**—nodding sound

4.1   **FX: GAKON**—sound of trap door dropping open

4.2.1   **FX: BAN**—body convulsing back and forth

4.2.2   **FX: BATAN**—body convulsing

4.3   **FX: GAKU GAKU**—fingers twitching

4.4   **FX: HEKO BEKO**—sound of chest trying to move/convulsing

4.5   **FX: GI GI**—legs twitching

5.1   **FX: PURAN**—legs hanging limp

6 All the chapters in Vol. 2 are titles of songs by Kenji Sawada, known to his fans as "Julie" (it's a little hard to explain). Sawada was the lead singer of The Tigers, one of the most famous of Japan's 1960s GS ("Group Sounds") bands, which, inspired by the Beatles, emphasized guitar and harmonies (Isao Takahata's classic anime film *Only Yesterday* features a brief glimpse of the scene). Today Sawada is a successful actor, appearing in such films as Takashi Miike (who directed the TV adaptation of Eiji Otsuka's *MPD Psycho*)'s *The Happiness of the Katakuris.*

8.2 FX: **DODODODODO**—sound of the bus engine

8.3 FX: **ZA ZA**—footsteps

10.5.1 "Alien hand syndrome" is a genuine neurological disorder where one of a person's hands acts in a way that is apparently not under the person's control, as in the movie *Dr. Strangelove.* The joke, of course, is that the puppet on Yuji's left hand actually *is* supposed to be (channeling) an alien.

10.5.2 FX: **MOZO MOZO GOSO GOSO**—sound of the puppet digging around in Yata's jacket.

11.1 FX: **PASA**—sound of paper being flipped open

12.2 FX: **GACHA**—sound of door opening

13.2 FX: **GOTOTO**—tires coming to a stop

13.3 FX: **GACHA**—door opening

13.4 FX: **HENAA**—sound of the two slumping lifelessly.

14.1 FX: **DOBOBOBO**—pouring hot water

14.3 FX: **PACHIN**—snapping chopsticks apart

14.5 FX: **BARI BORI KARI**—sound of crunching still-hard instant noodles. In other words, Kuro is so hungry he didn't even bother to take the pitcher of boiling water from Numata for his chicken ramen; he just starts crunching them dry. In 15.2 you can see that he's got most of the "brick" between his chopsticks.

14.7 FX/balloons: **KAKO KAKOKO KOKO**—keyboard sounds

16.5 *Nire* (said "nih-reh"—please see note on vowel pronunciation above) is the Japanese word for an elm tree. As with *Kurosagi* ("black heron") it has generally been left untranslated in the script.

17.2 FX: **KAKOKO KOKO KAKOKO KAKOKO**—keyboard sounds

17.4 FX: **ZUZUUU**—sound of photo printer

17.5 FX: **PASARI**—sound of photo hitting floor

18.1 FX/balloon: **KATA**—putting beer can on table

19.1 In case you think the editor learned about the Internet from a CD-ROM he got in the mail, that is what it said in the original; literally, the phrase *yuuga meeru!* written in katakana. The translator, by the way, was the first person the editor ever met who had a Sony VAIO.

21.1 FX: **GOTO**—putting down box

22.6 **FX: GOTO**—putting down heavy coffin

23.3 **FX: TA TTA TA**—running sound

23.4 **FX: ZURI**—dragging sound

23.5 **FX/balloon: BAN**—slamming door shut

24.1 **FX: BATAM**—closing car door

24.2 **FX: BURORO**—car starting up

24.3 **FX: GWOOO**—car speeding along. You may have already noticed this in Vol. 1, but naturally they don't drive around with their *full* company name written on the outside of the van; if you compare it with the front cover, you'll notice it's missing the two critical kanji for "corpse," and hence to the public they're just "The Kurosagi Delivery Service."

24.4 **FX: WOOO**—car speeding along

25.2 As you might observe, the sign on the hearse says "Nire Ceremony."

25.3 **FX: FUBA**—sound of the wind as the two cars pass by each other

27.2 **FX: GWOOO**—car sound

27.3 **FX: YURA YURA**—sound of pendulum swinging

28.1 **FX: GOTO GATA GOTO GATA**—sound of car hitting bumps in road

28.6 **FX/balloon: KEEE**—sound of brakes

28.7 **FX: CHAKA CHAKA CHAKA**—sound of the hazard lights blinking

29.1 **FX: HYUN HYUN HYUN**—sound of pendulum swinging

29.3 **FX/balloon: BA**—sound of the two looking back

33.4 **FX: SU**—reaching out with his hand

35.6 **FX: BOBON**—exhaust backfire as the engine starts

36.1 **FX/balloon: DORURURUN**—car engine sound

37.2 **FX/balloon: KWOOOO**—sound of approaching car

39.2 **FX: GOTO**—putting down coffin

39.4 **FX/Makino:** It's just a corpse right? Boring.

39.6 **FX: PASA**—pulling out a page of the paper

45.4 **FX: KACHA**—opening door

45.5 **FX: BATAN**—door slamming

50.3 **FX: PINPOON PINPOON**—doorbell sounds

50.5 **FX: GACHA**—sound of opening door

51.1 **FX/balloon: KOTO**—sound of cup being put on to plate

51.5 The peculiarities of how capital punishment is administered in Japan make this scenario not as bizarre as it may seem, as indicated by Hayashi's remarks on the system in page 130.

52.2 **FX/balloon: DON GARA GARA DOCHA**—sound of many things falling over

53.6 **FX: POTA POTA POTA**—sound of dripping blood

54.1 **FX/balloons: POTA POTA**—drip drip

FX/balloon: POTA—drip

55.1 **FX/balloon: DOSARI**—sound of cat being tossed down

55.4 **FX: HITA**—hand touching cat

55.5 **FX/balloon: SUUUU**—inhale of air

55.6 **FX: FUU**—soft exhale

56.1 **FX: ZAWA ZAWA ZAWA ZAWA ZAWA**—sound of the leaves moving in the wind

56.2 **FX: ZA ZA ZA ZA ZA**—leaves being blown around by a gust of wind

57.1 **FX/balloon: KASA**—sound of leaves moving under paw

57.2 **FX/balloons: BIKU BIKU**—sound of mouth twitching

57.3 **FX/balloon: PACHI**—sound of eye opening

57.5 **FX: SUKU**—sound of cat getting up

58.2 **FX/balloon: PERO PERO**—sound of cat licking paw

58.3 **FX: GASA**—sound of cat moving off

59.3 Pronounced "keh-reh-ell-is." Bullmark (the logo, appropriately enough, was of a charging bull) made soft vinyl and die-cast toys based on such series as *Godzilla* and *Ultraman* between 1969 and 1977. If this really is his/Yata's/its hobby, it's a relatively expensive one; the originals can sell for several hundred dollars each.

60.2 **FX: KO KO**—footsteps

60.3 **FX: GASA**—something moving in the bushes

61.2 **FX: PURAN PURAN**—wiggling sausage

61.4 **FX: BABA**—sound of cat attacking

62.1 **FX: KUCHA BARI GUCHA**—chomping and bone cracking sounds

62.3 **FX: SHITA SHITA**—quiet cat footsteps

62.4.1 **FX: SHITA SHITA**—more cat footsteps

62.4.2 **FX/balloon: PERON**—licking mouth sound

63.1 **FX: BA**—sound of cat jumping

63.3 **FX: GATSU GATSU**—biting sounds

63.6 **FX: BAKI DOKA**—sound of hitting wall with cat

64.1 **FX: DOKA GA DOKA GA**—repeatedly hitting wall with cat

64.2 **FX: DOTA**—thud

64.4 **FX: MUKO**—sound of cat getting up

64.5 **FX: NU**—sound of spirit leaving cat's body

65.1 **FX: DO**—sound of lifeless cat hitting ground

65.2 **FX: FU**—sound of the spirit fading away

66.4 **FX: KACHA**—opening door

67.1 **FX: BASA BASA**—newspapers being tossed onto the floor

68.6 **FX: PAKU PAKU**—sound of puppet's mouth flapping. Notice Kereellis is now wearing a tie as well, presumably so as to help Yata not look out of place on the job.

70.3 **FX: BATAN**—door closing

71.2 **FX: PIRA**—sound of paper being held up

71.3 It is very common for a Japanese

to use as a form of personal ID when dealing with government records (taxes, registrations, etc.) a *jitsuin*—an ink seal carved with the individual's name. The person makes an impression with it, and registers it on file with a government office, who can then bring it out for comparison when the person brings the seal in on any future occasion. An an acceptable alternative, as Numata alluded to in 69.3, might be a signature (probably in conjunction with a personal identification number), or a thumbprint.

73.5 FX: JAN CHAN JA JACHACHACHA CHAN—ringtone playing

74.3 FX: TSUU TSUU TSUU—dial tone

75.1 In the original "joke," Karatsu misheard it as *nira*, meaning "leek." In the extremely unlikely event you haven't yet seen Orihime from *Bleach* spin a leek to the tune of the nostalgic Finnish song *Eva's Polka*, go directly to leekspin.com for the looped experience.

76.3 FX/balloon: TOPOPO—pouring tea

77.3 FX: HO—sigh of relief

78.3 FX: KYUKYU—sound of a squeaky wheel

78.4 FX: KYU KYU—more squeaks

79.4 FX: GACHA—opening door

80.3 FX: PEKORI—bowing sound

80.5 FX: GATA—getting up

80.6 FX: KACHA—putting cup down on plate

82.1 FX: KON KON—knock knock

82.3 FX: KACHI—door opening

82.7 FX: KACHA—cup being put down

83.6 FX: GA—getting up

85.4 FX: ZA—turning to leave

85.6.1 FX/black: KACHA—door opening

85.6.2 FX/white: BATAN—door slamming

86.2 FX: BATAM—closing car door

87.4 FX: SU—starting to turn to leave

88.1 FX: BUUUN—fluorescent light buzzing

88.2 FX: CHIKA CHIKA CHIKA—fluorescent light flickering

88.3 FX/balloon: PA—light turning on

89.3 FX: KO—footstep

90.3 FX: FUUU—exhale sound

90.8 FX: GO—pulling on door

93.1 FX: RIRII RIRII RII—sound of crickets

93.3 FX: GACHA—door opening

93.4 FX: KO KO GO GO—several footsteps

94.4 FX: KO KO—footsteps walking up

98.1 FX: PAKU PAKU—sound of mouth moving

99.1 FX: PAKU PAKU—flapping mouth sound

101.1 FX: GATAN—pulling chair out

101.3 FX: SU—sliding envelope forward

101.6 Sasaki is commenting on the casual nature of how Hayashi is calling her name without any honorifics such as *-san*, *-chan*, or *-kun*.

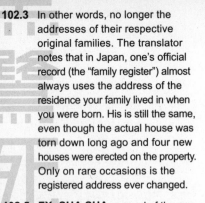

102.3 In other words, no longer the addresses of their respective original families. The translator notes that in Japan, one's official record (the "family register") almost always uses the address of the residence your family lived in when you were born. His is still the same, even though the actual house was torn down long ago and four new houses were erected on the property. Only on rare occasions is the registered address ever changed.

102.5 **FX: SHA SHA**—sound of the pen on paper

103.1 **FX: GATA**—getting up

104.1 **FX/balloon: KOOOO**—car engine sounds

104.4 **FX: KEEE**—sound of brakes

105.1 The ubiquitous roadside or sidewalk vending machines, where you can buy hot or cold food and drinks (as well as alcohol and cigarattes) any time of day or night, are one of the great charms of Japan. As with the remark about gun violence in Vol. 1's "Disjecta Membra," the disturbing scenes portrayed in this volume should perhaps be balanced against the simple remark that such outdoor vending machines can exist in Japan without being vandalized into oblivion; Japan has a much lower crime rate than the U.S.

105.3 **FX/balloon: PI**—pressing button

FX/balloon: GARA GOSHON—sound of bottle dropping

105.4 **FX: SU**—taking bottle out

106.1 **FX: PI**—pressing bottle against cheek

106.3 **FX: GOKYU**—gulp

106.7 **FX: BASA**—sound of map dropping

106.8 **FX: GON**—head slumping onto window

107.2 **FX/balloon: DOTA**—puppet falling onto armrest

107.4 **FX/balloon: SHA**—moving curtain aside. Note the hinged doors on the coffin so that the face of the dead can be viewed.

107.5 **FX: GOTO**—sound of crowbar being put down on coffin

108.2 **FX/balloons: DON DON DADAN DON**—banging on door

108.3.1 **FX/balloons: DON DON**—banging

108.3.2 **FX/balloon: BAN**—banging

109.1 **FX: GACHA**—opening door

109.4.1 **FX/balloon: GABU**—biting sound

109.4.2 **FX/balloon: BAKI**—sound of breaking bones

110.7 **FX/balloon: BURORORO**—car engine sound

112.1 **FX: BASA**—sound of newspaper being tossed onto table

112.5 **FX: BOSO**—mumbling sound effect

113.3 **FX/balloon: BATAN**—door slam

116.1 **FX: GACHA**—opening car door

116.2 **FX: BAN**—car door being shut

116.3 **FX/balloon: KUI**—pointing at driver seat

116.4 **FX/balloon: BAN**—car door shutting

116.6 **FX: KYUTOTOTO**—engine turning over

116.7 **FX/balloon: BUROROROON**—engine starting

117.1 **FX/balloon: PIPAPII PIPAPIPA PIIPAPAAPII**—ringtone

117.2 **FX/balloon: PI**—answering cell phone

118.6 **FX: KO KO**—footsteps

119.1 **FX: PINPOON PINPOON**—doorbell

119.3 **FX/balloon: GACHA**—door opening

119.5 **FX/balloon: KACHI BO**—sound of turning on a gas stove and the fire igniting

120.5 **FX: KACHA**—putting down coffee cups

121.2 **FX: KOTO**—putting video down

121.4 **FX: TATA**—running off

121.5 **FX: BATAN**—door closing

122.2 **FX: TATATATA**—running sound

123.1 **FX: SU**—sound of tape being taken out of sleeve

123.2 **FX: GAKON**—putting tape in

123.4 **FX: WHEEEN**—VCR starting up

125.3 **FX: GAKON**—sound of the trap door opening

126.5 **FX: SU**—picking up remote to stop tape

126.7 *Fugutaiten* means having to take revenge against another even if it means one's own death. The kanji literally mean that one person cannot live under the same

heavens if the other is to stay alive.

127.1 **FX: PA**—sound of the screen changing

130.6 **FX: GATA**—getting up

131.4 **FX: KO KO**—footsteps

132.1 **FX: KYU KYUKYU**—sound of squeaky wheels

132.4 **FX: JYARI**—sound of footsteps in gravel

133.4 **FX: PAKU PAKU**—mouth flapping

137.3 **FX: PINPOON PINPOON**—doorbell

137.4 **FX: GARA**—sliding door opening

138.5 **FX: GAPA**—rice cooker being opened

139.2 **FX/balloon: KU**—putting ring on

139.3 **FX: CHARA**—letting pendulum drop

139.4 **FX: SUUU**—reaching out with his arm

139.5 **FX: HYUN HYUN HYUN**—pendulum beginning to swing

140.2 **FX: GI**—grabbing handle

140.3 **FX: GIIIII**—door being opened

142.4 **FX: GACHA**—opening door

143.4 **FX/balloon: GASHA**—loading videotape

143.5 **FX/balloon: ZAAA**—static

143.6 **FX/balloon: PA**—screen turning on

145.2 **FX: FUU FUU**—heavy breathing

145.3 **FX/box: DOSU BYU**—stabbing then spurting sound

145.5 **FX/box: GACHA GACHA**—rattling against restraints

146.2 **FX/box: ZAKU**—stab

146.4 **FX/box: DOKA**—thud

146.7.1 **FX/box: KOTSU KOTSU**—footsteps

146.7.2 **FX/box: KOTSU**—footstep

147.1 **FX/box: DOSU GUCHU**—stab then wet stabbing sound

147.2 In the original, Yata refers to the myth of the *Hangon* ritual, meaning "half a spirit," supposedly able to reanimate the dead.

148.1 **FX/balloon: GATA**—getting up angrily

148.4 **FX: GA**—grasping shoulder

152.2 **FX/balloons: PI PO PA**—dialing cell phone

153.1 **FX/balloon: PIII**—hanging up cell

153.2 **FX: PATAN**—closing flip phone

153.4 **FX: KUSHA**—crushing business card

153.5 **FX/balloon: KORO**—sound of balled up card rolling

154.2 **FX/balloon: PA**—lights coming on

154.3 **FX/balloon: ZAAAA**—static on TV

155.3 The term as used in Western culture comes from Matthew 27:7, alluding to the practice of soils full of clay (and thus useful to potters) being also used for graveyards—although the Japanese term was *choshinda*, meaning "forsaken ground."

156.1 **FX/balloon: KU**—lifting up chin

157.6 **FX/balloon: BATAN**—door closing

158.1 **FX: GWOOOO**—car sound

159.1 **FX: GATA GOTO GOTON GATAN**—sound of the rattling inside the car

159.2 **FX: GOGO AGO GOGO**—vibrations inside car

159.3 **FX: GOGOGOGOGO**—vibrations

161.1 **FX: SU**—touching sound

162.1 **FX: GOGO GOGO GOGO**—car sound

164.2 **FX: GACHA**—door opening sound

165.5.1 **FX: GATAN**—getting up

165.5.2 **FX/balloon: DOSA**—putting laptop into bag

165.7 **FX: BATAAN**—door slamming

167.1 **FX/balloon: KASHAN**—putting in key

167.3 In the West, a corpse might be laid out in formal dress, but the equivalent Japanese practice is to clothe them in a white kimono.

167.7 **FX/balloon: BATAN**—door closing

168.1.1 **FX/balloon: KOTSU**—footstep

168.1.2 **FX/balloon: KOTSU**—footstep

169.1 **FX: SUU**—inhale

169.2 **FX: FUUU**—exhale

169.3.1 **FX/balloon: PIKU**—eye twitch

169.3.2 **FX/balloons: PIKU PIKU**—more twitching

169.4 **FX/balloon: PACHI**—eyes snapping open

170.2 **FX: PAKU PAKU**—mouth flapping

170.4 **FX: KACHA**—opening door

170.5 **FX/balloon: KACHA**—opening door

171.5 **FX/balloon: BASA**—sound of raincoat falling

172.4 **FX/balloons: TOKU TOKU**—chloroform being poured onto handkerchief

172.5 **FX: BA**—hand jerking up

172.6 **FX: SA**—hand going over mouth and nose

173.2 **FX/balloon: YORO**—stagger

173.3 **FX: DOTA**—sound of Yata falling

174.3 **FX/balloon: PACHIN**—snapping open knife

174.4 **FX: GIRI GIRI**—putting cuts into wire

174.6 **FX: CHIKA**—small LED lighting up

176.1 **FX: TON TON**—straightening papers

176.6 **FX/balloon: GAA**—sound of automatic doors sliding open

177.4 **FX/balloon: BAMUN**—car door closing

177.5 **FX/balloon: VWOON**—engine revving

178.4.1 FX/balloon: PIIPAPI HOPAP-IPAA PIIPAAPI—ringtone

178.4.2 FX/balloon: PIIPAPI HOPAP-IPAA PIIPAA—ringtone

178.5.1 FX/balloon: KYUKO—sound of shower being turned off

178.5.2 FX/balloon: PIIPAPI HOPAP-IPAA PIIPAAPI—ringtone

178.6 **FX/balloon: PI**—answering phone

179.2 **FX: SU**—picking up glasses

179.6 **FX: PASA**—sound of towel falling

181.1 **FX/balloon: KIII**—brake sound

181.2 **FX/balloons: KACHA BAN**—door opening and closing

181.5 **FX/balloon: KUI**—gesturing with head

187.7 **FX/balloons: KO KO KO**—sound of footsteps

183.2 **FX/balloon: PECHI PECHI**—light slapping on face

184.4 **FX: KA KA**—footsteps

184.7 **FX: GAKON GEEE**—doors being unlatched and creaking open

187.6.1 FX/balloon: GACHA—rattling doorknob

187.6.2 FX/balloon: GACHA GACHA—more rattling

189.4 **FX: KATSU KATSU**—walking toward Fuchigami

190.5 **FX: PITAN PITAN**—slapping knife blade against palm

192.2 **FX/balloon: KII**—door creaking open

192.5 **FX: DO**—putting body down

193.1 **FX: JIIII**—sound of zipper being pulled down

194.2.1 FX/balloon: GIIII—sound of straining wire

194.2.2 FX/balloon: GIRIRIRI—more straining

194.3.1 FX/balloon: BAKIIIN—wire breaking

194.3.2 FX/small: PAKI—twang of wire

195.3 **FX: ZUPAA**—sound of slicing flesh

196.2 **FX: GA**—sound of neck being grasped

197.5 **FX: BURAN**—sound of Hayashi's legs hanging off the ground

197.6 **FX: GATATAN**—sound of everyone falling as Hayashi's body is thrown

198.7 **FX: DADA**—running sound

198.8 **FX: GA**—grabbing sound

199.1 **FX: GACHA**—door being opened

199.5 **FX: PAKU**—biting down on broom handle

199.6 **FX: KAN**—sound of the broomstick hitting floor

200.1 **FX: GAAAAAA GAAAAAH**—screaming

200.5 **FX: KA**—kicking knife

200.6 **FX/balloon: KARA KARARA**—sound of knife spinning on floor

201.4 **FX: ZURU**—hand slipping

201.6 **FX/balloon: GUI**—pushing Mutsumi forward

202.2 **FX: DO**—sound of broomstick hitting back of throat

202.3 **FX: MEKI**—sound of the neck/spine starting to break

203.5 **FX/balloon: DON**—tip of broom hitting floor

206.4 **FX: SU**—reaching for knife

206.5 **FX/balloon: GU**—stepping on hand

207.6 **FX: GAKUN**—slumping in defeat

208.3 **FX: ZA ZA**—walking thought field sound

210.2.1 **FX/balloon: PI**—beep

210.2.2 **FX/balloon: PI**—beep

210.2.3 **FX/balloon: PI**—beep

210.6 **FX/balloon: SU**—moving away

211.1 **FX: KATA**—picking up vase

211.2 **FX: ZAA**—sound of running water

211.4 **FX: KYU**—closing tap

211.6 **FX: BATAN**—door closing

STAFF D

Embalming
［エンバーミング］：死体修復

STAFF E

Channeling
［チャネリング］：宇宙人と交信

STAFF E'

Puppet
［マペット］：宇宙人が憑依

お 届 け 物 は 死 体 で す 。

黒鷺死体宅配便

the KUROSAGI corpse delivery service

story
EIJI OTSUKA

art
HOUSUI YAMAZAKI

original cover design
BUNPEI YORIFUJI

translation
TOSHIFUMI YOSHIDA

editor and english adaptation
CARL GUSTAV HORN

lettering and touch-up
IHL

contents

THE KAZUO KOIKE LIBRARY FROM DARK HORSE MANGA

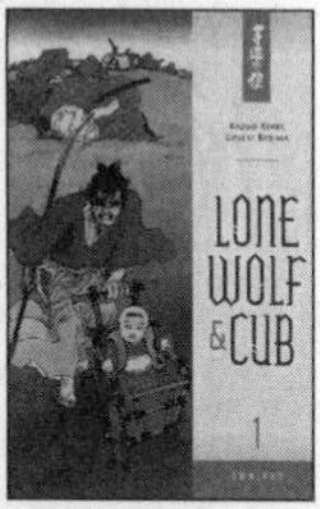

LONE WOLF & CUB
1

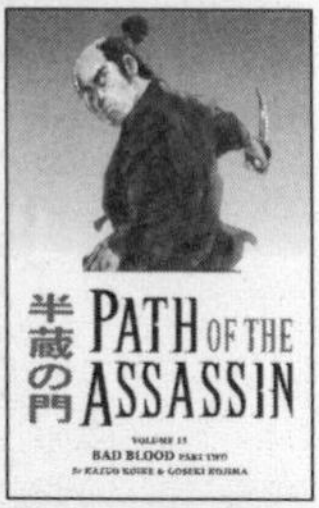

半蔵の門
PATH OF THE ASSASSIN
BAD BLOOD

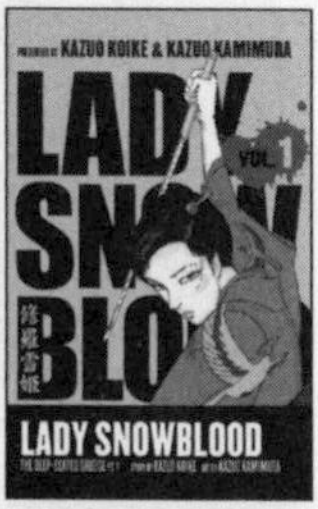

KAZUO KOIKE & KAZUO KAMIMURA
VOL. 1
LADY SNOWBLOOD

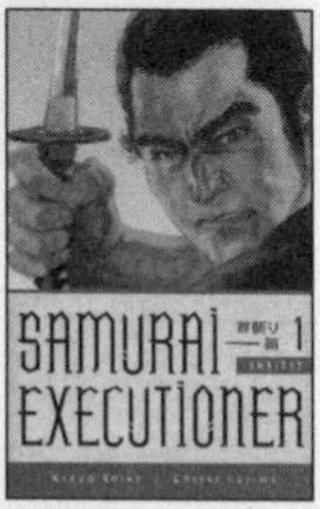

SAMURAI EXECUTIONER
1

LONE WOLF AND CUB OMNIBUS
Volume 1: ISBN 978-1-61655-134-6
Volume 2: ISBN 978-1-61655-135-3
Volume 3: ISBN 978-1-61655-200-8
Volume 4: ISBN 978-1-61655-392-0
Volume 5: ISBN 978-1-61655-393-7
Volume 6: ISBN 978-1-61655-394-4
Volume 7: ISBN 978-1-61655-569-6
Volume 8: ISBN 978-1-61655-584-9
$19.99 each

NEW LONE WOLF AND CUB
Volume 1: ISBN 978-1-59307-649-8
Volume 2: ISBN 978-1-61655-357-9
Volume 3: ISBN 978-1-61655-358-6
Volume 4: ISBN 978-1-61655-359-3
$13.99 each

SAMURAI EXECUTIONER OMNIBUS
Volume 1: ISBN 978-1-61655-319-7
Volume 2: ISBN 978-1-61655-320-3
Volume 3: ISBN 978-1-61655-531-3
Volume 4: ISBN 978-1-61655-567-2
$19.99 each

PATH OF THE ASSASSIN
Volume 1: ISBN 978-1-59307-502-6
Volume 2: ISBN 978-1-59307-503-3
Volume 3: ISBN 978-1-59307-504-0
Volume 4: ISBN 978-1-59307-505-7
Volume 5: ISBN 978-1-59307-506-4
Volume 6: ISBN 978-1-59307-507-1
Volume 7: ISBN 978-1-59307-508-8
Volume 8: ISBN 978-1-59307-509-5
Volume 9: ISBN 978-1-59307-510-1
Volume 10: ISBN 978-1-59307-511-8
Volume 11: ISBN 978-1-59307-512-5
Volume 12: ISBN 978-1-59307-513-2
Volume 13: ISBN 978-1-59307-514-9
Volume 14: ISBN 978-1-59307-515-6
Volume 15: ISBN 978-1-59307-516-3
$9.99 each

COLOR OF RAGE
ISBN 978-1-59307-900-0
$14.99

CRYING FREEMAN
Volume 1: ISBN 978-1-59307-478-4
Volume 2: ISBN 978-1-59307-488-3
Volume 3: ISBN 978-1-59307-489-0
Volume 4: ISBN 978-1-59307-498-2
Volume 5: ISBN 978-1-59307-499-9
$14.99 each

LADY SNOWBLOOD
Volume 1: ISBN 978-1-59307-385-5
Volume 2: ISBN 978-1-59307-443-2
Volume 3: ISBN 978-1-59307-458-6
Volume 4: ISBN 978-1-59307-532-3
$14.99 each

FOR MATURE READERS

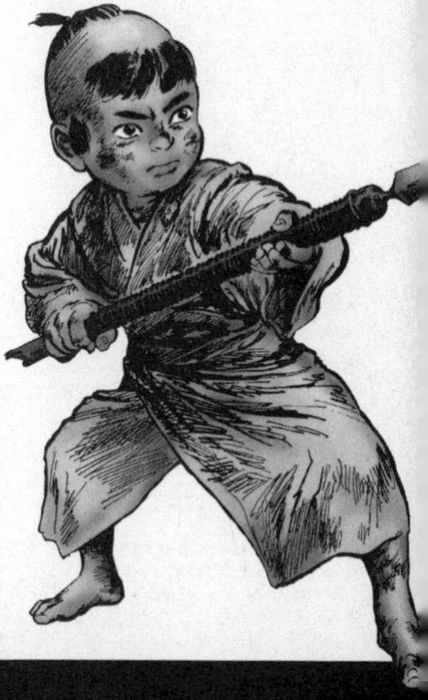

AVAILABLE AT YOUR LOCAL COMICS SHOP OR BOOKSTORE! • To find a comics shop in your area, call 1-888-266-4226.
For more information or to order direct visit DarkHorse.com or call 1-800-862-0052 Mon.–Fri. 9 AM to 5 PM Pacific Time. Prices and availability subject to change without notice.

EDEN

It's an Endless World!

Volume 1
ISBN 978-1-59307-406-7

Volume 2
ISBN 978-1-59307-454-8

Volume 3
ISBN 978-1-59307-529-3

Volume 4
ISBN 978-1-59307-544-6

Volume 5
ISBN 978-1-59307-634-4

Volume 6
ISBN 978-1-59307-702-0

Volume 7
ISBN 978-1-59307-765-5

Volume 8
ISBN 978-1-59307-787-7

Volume 9
ISBN 978-1-59307-851-5

Volume 10
ISBN 978-1-59307-957-4

Volume 11
ISBN 978-1-59582-244-4

Volume 12
ISBN 978-1-59582-296-3

Volume 13
ISBN 978-1-59582-763-0

Volume 14
ISBN 978-1-61655-288-6

$12.99 each

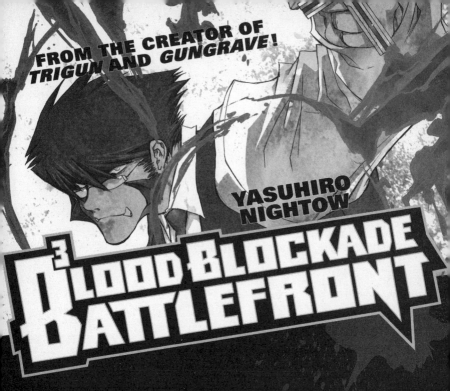

FROM THE CREATOR OF *TRIGUN* AND *GUNGRAVE*!

YASUHIRO NIGHTOW

BLOOD BLOCKADE BATTLEFRONT 3

Three years ago, a gateway between Earth and the Beyond opened over New York City. In one terrible night, New York was destroyed and rebuilt, trapping New Yorkers and extradimensional creatures alike in an impenetrable bubble. New York is now Jerusalem's Lot, a paranormal melting pot where magic and madness dwell alongside the mundane, where human vermin gather to exploit otherworldly assets for earthly profit. Now someone is threatening to breach the bubble and release New Jerusalem's horrors, but the mysterious superagents of Libra fight to prevent the unthinkable.

Trigun creator Yasuhiro Nightow returns with *Blood Blockade Battlefront*, an action-packed supernatural science-fiction steamroller as only Nightow can conjure.

VOLUME ONE
ISBN 978-1-59582-718-0 | $10.99

VOLUME TWO
ISBN 978-1-59582-912-2 | $10.99

VOLUME THREE
ISBN 978-1-59582-913-9 | $10.99

VOLUME FOUR
ISBN 978-1-61655-223-7 | $12.99

VOLUME FIVE
ISBN 978-1-61655-224-4 | $12.99

VOLUME SIX
ISBN 978-1-61655-557-3 | $12.99

VOLUME SEVEN
ISBN 978-1-61655-568-9 | $12.99

DARK HORSE MANGA

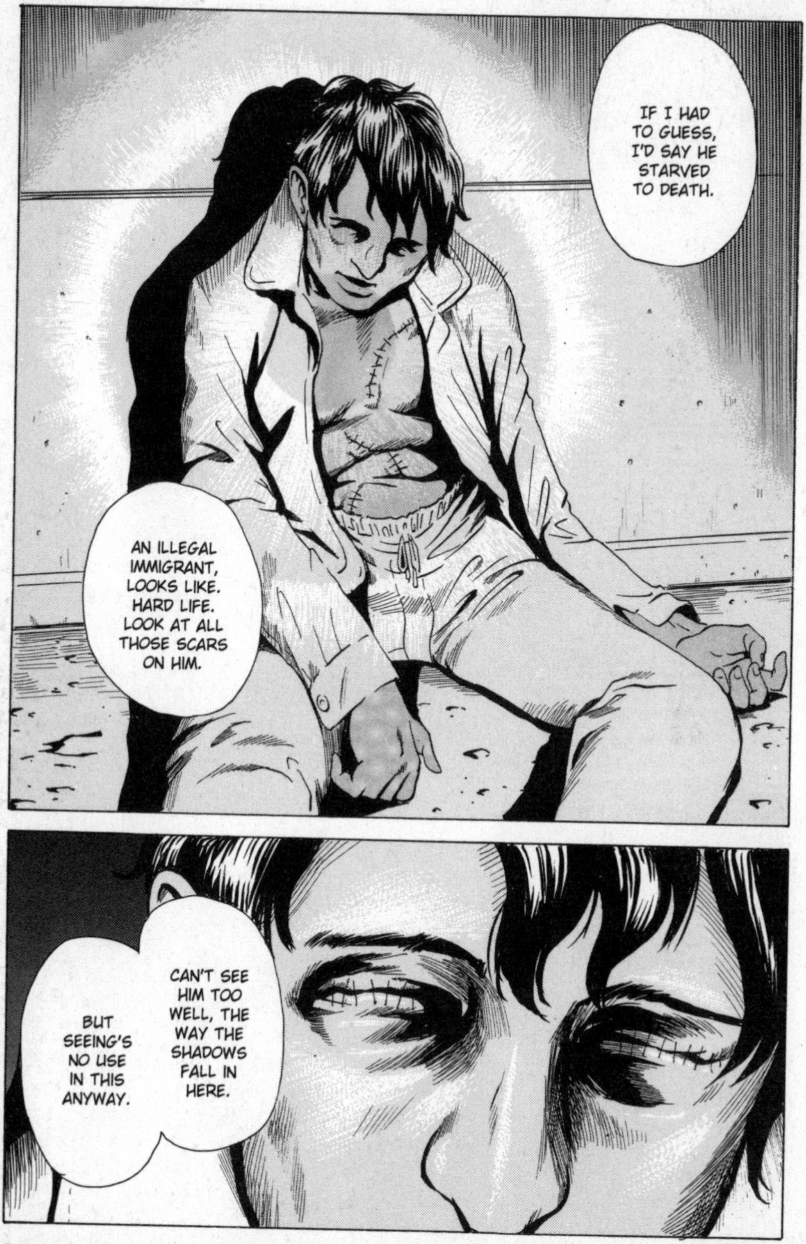
IF I HAD TO GUESS, I'D SAY HE STARVED TO DEATH.
AN ILLEGAL IMMIGRANT, LOOKS LIKE. HARD LIFE. LOOK AT ALL THOSE SCARS ON HIM.
CAN'T SEE HIM TOO WELL, THE WAY THE SHADOWS FALL IN HERE.
BUT SEEING'S NO USE IN THIS ANYWAY.

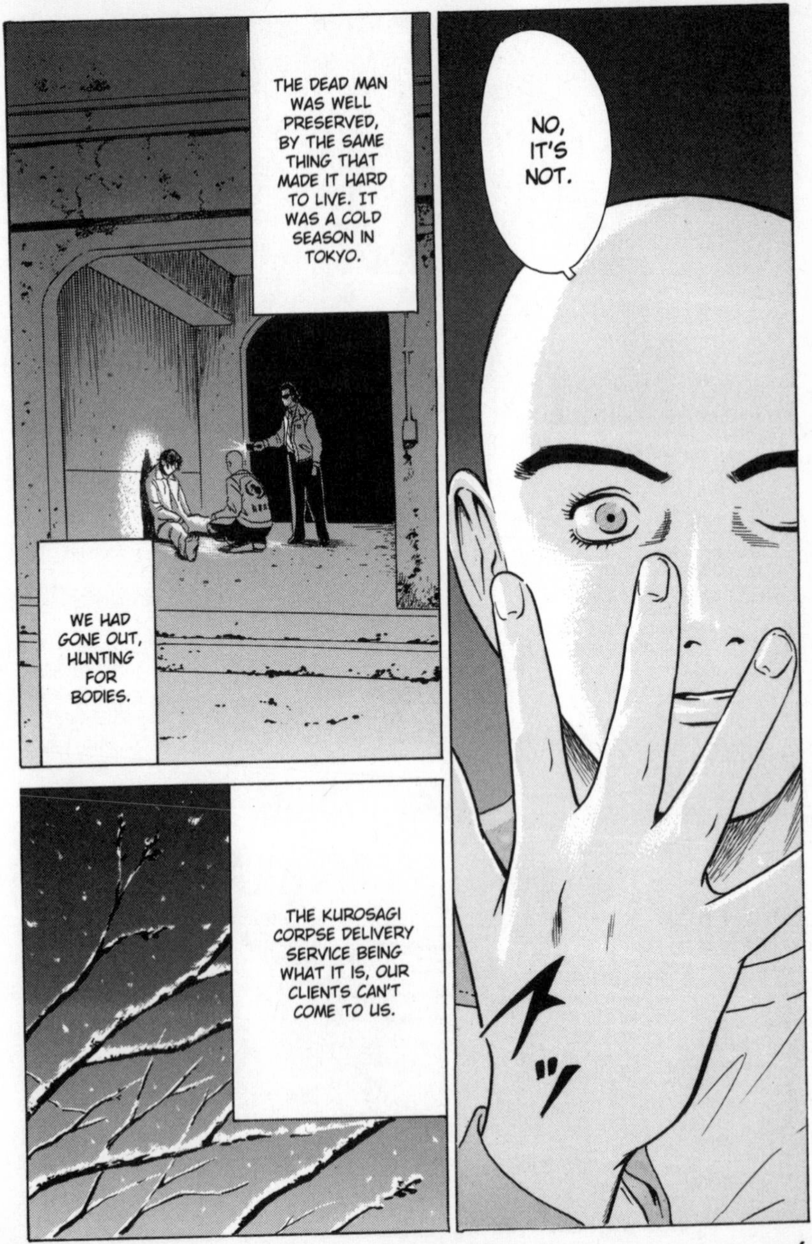

NO, IT'S NOT.
スッ
THE DEAD MAN WAS WELL PRESERVED, BY THE SAME THING THAT MADE IT HARD TO LIVE. IT WAS A COLD SEASON IN TOKYO.
WE HAD GONE OUT, HUNTING FOR BODIES.
THE KUROSAGI CORPSE DELIVERY SERVICE BEING WHAT IT IS, OUR CLIENTS CAN'T COME TO US.

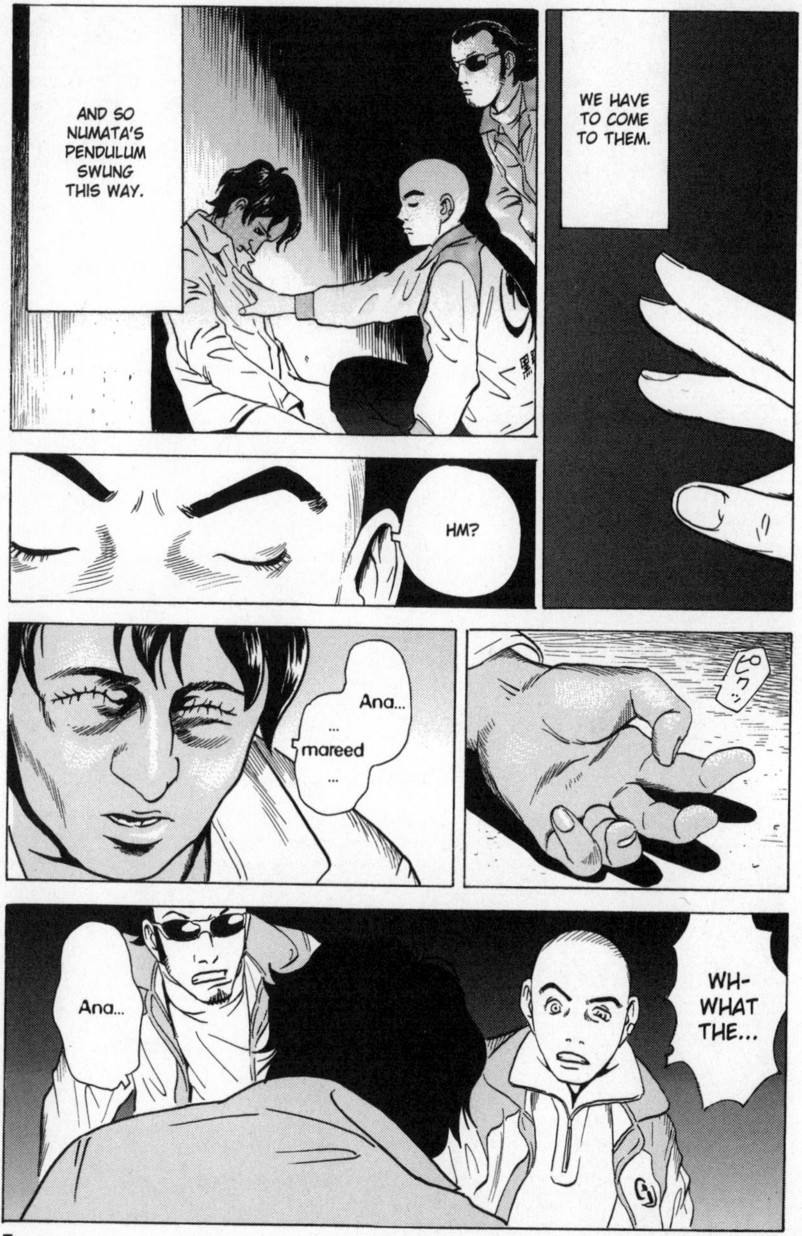
WE HAVE TO COME TO THEM.
AND SO NUMATA'S PENDULUM SWUNG THIS WAY.
HM?
ピクッ
Ana... ... mareed ...
WH- WHAT THE...
Ana...

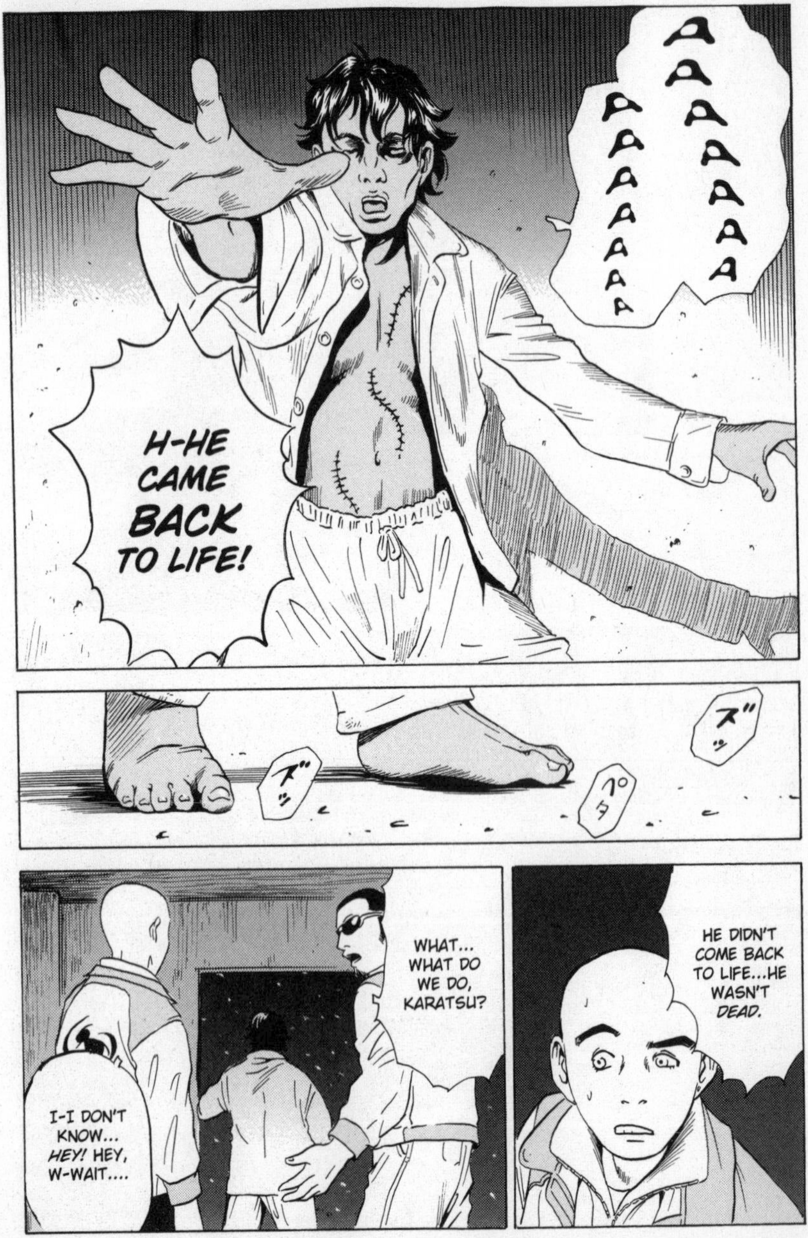
AAAAAAA
AAAAAAA
H-HE CAME BACK TO LIFE!
ズッ
ペタ
ズッ
HE DIDN'T COME BACK TO LIFE...HE WASN'T DEAD.
WHAT... WHAT DO WE DO, KARATSU?
I-I DON'T KNOW... HEY! HEY, W-WAIT....

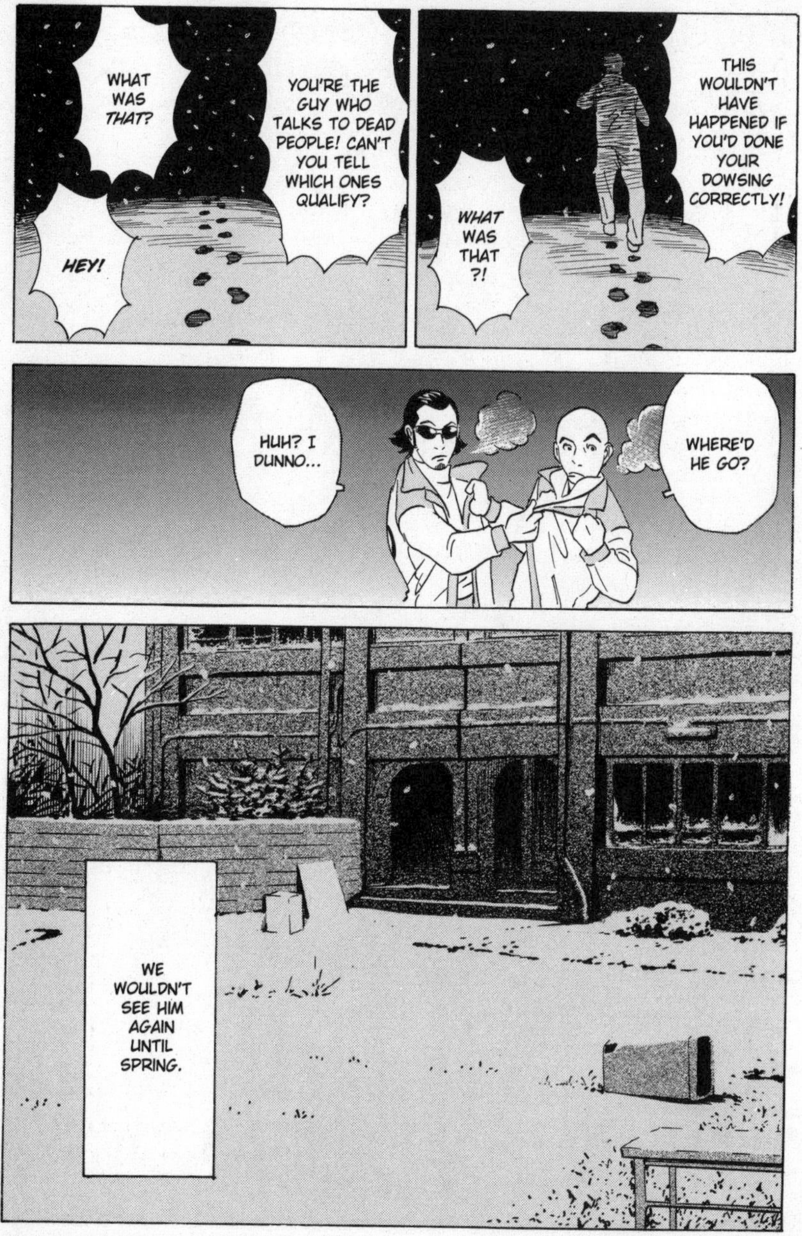
THIS WOULDN'T HAVE HAPPENED IF YOU'D DONE YOUR DOWSING CORRECTLY!
WHAT WAS THAT?!
YOU'RE THE GUY WHO TALKS TO DEAD PEOPLE! CAN'T YOU TELL WHICH ONES QUALIFY?
WHAT WAS THAT?
HEY!
WHERE'D HE GO?
HUH? I DUNNO...
WE WOULDN'T SEE HIM AGAIN UNTIL SPRING.

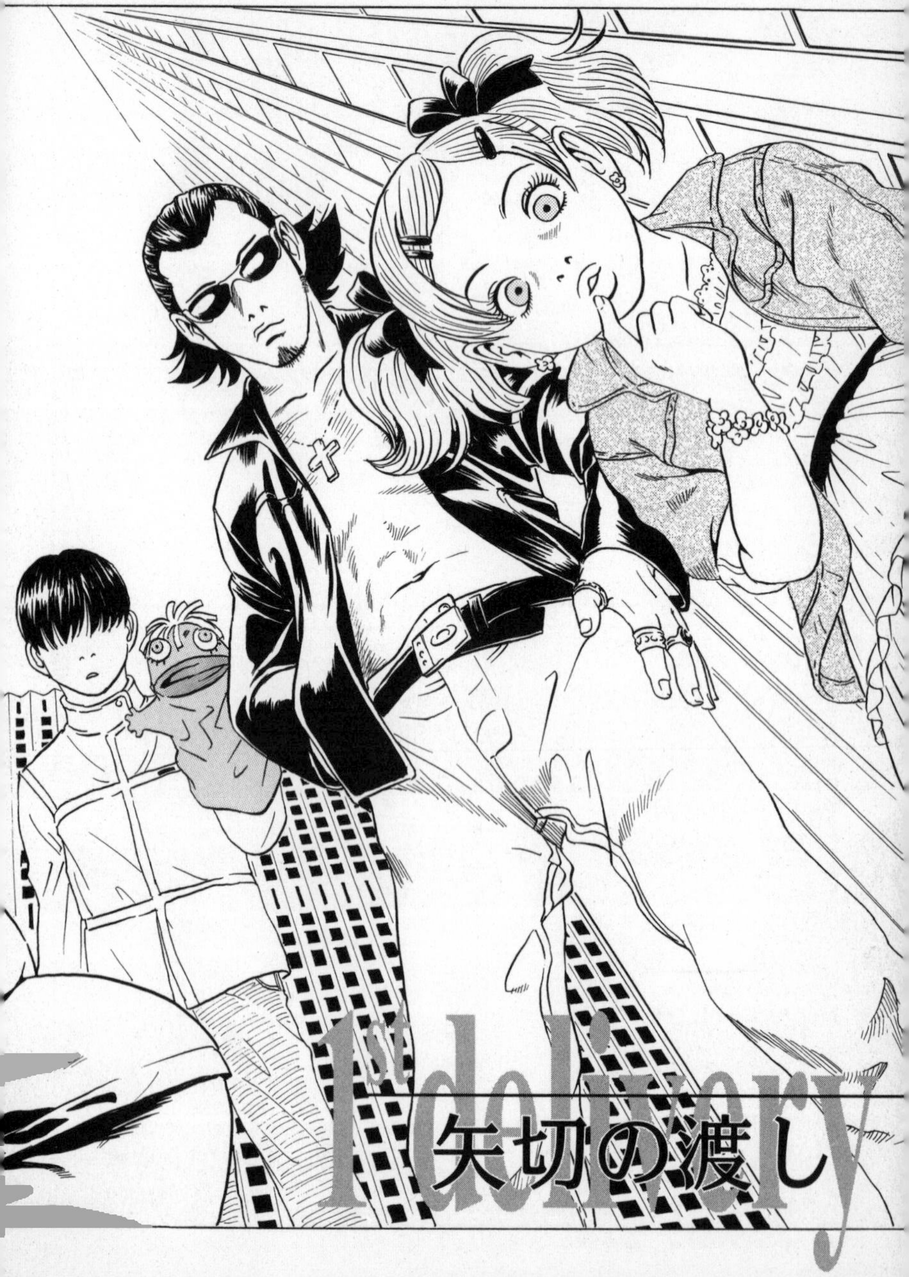
1st delivery
矢切の渡し

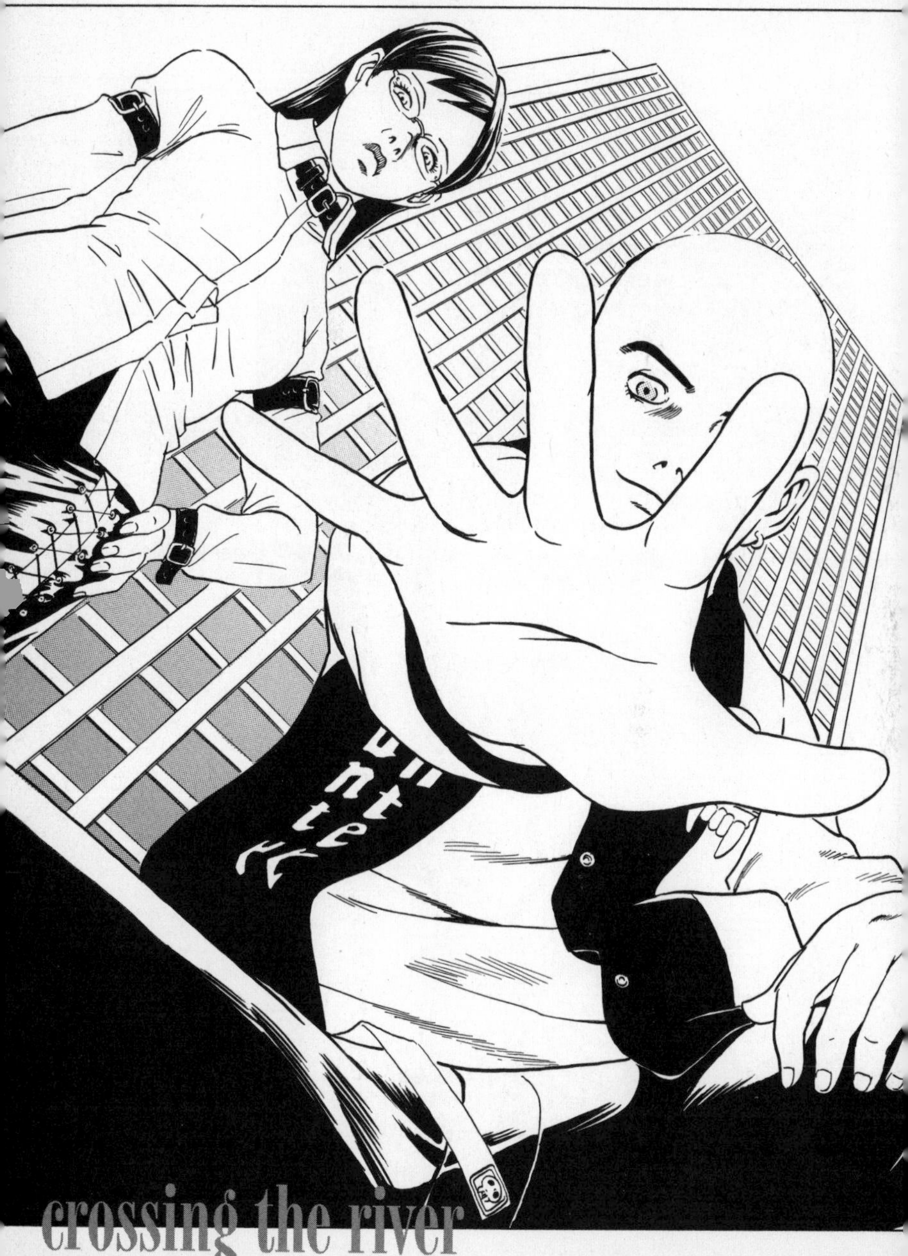

crossing the river

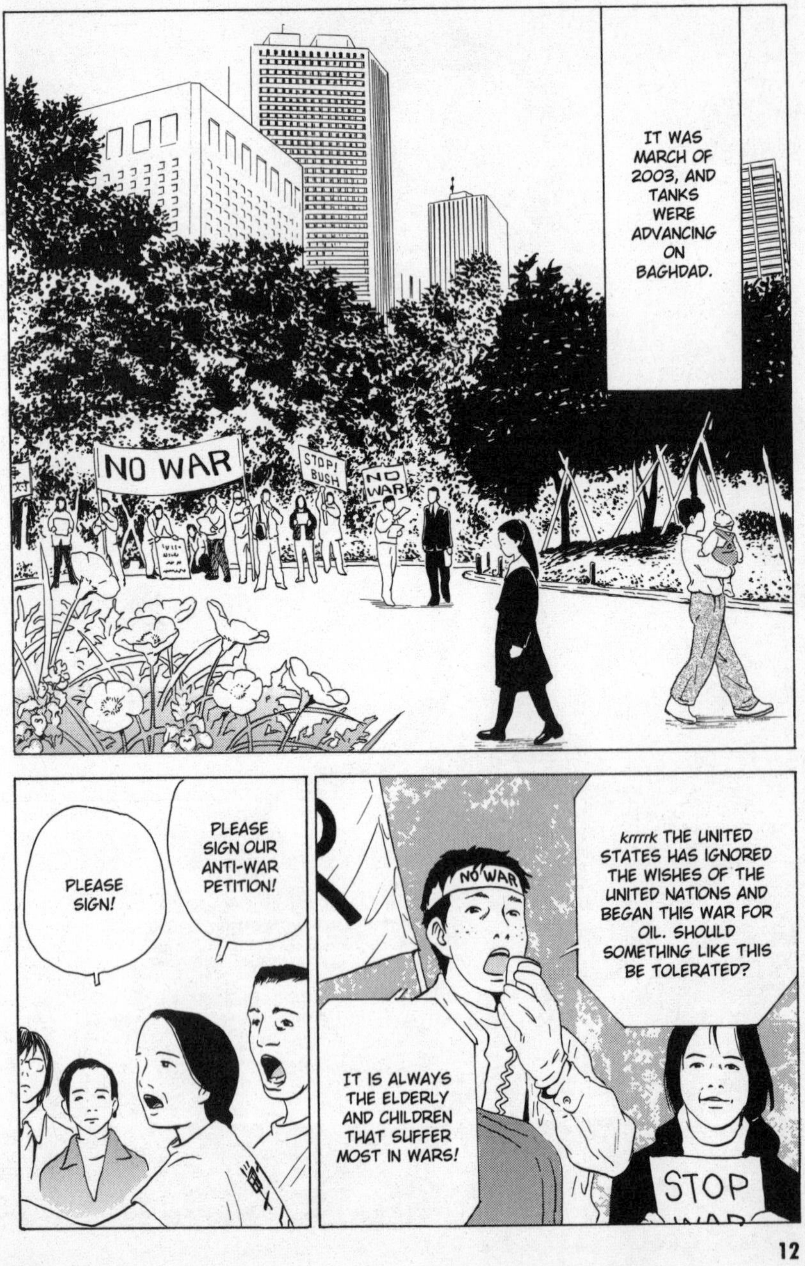
IT WAS MARCH OF 2003, AND TANKS WERE ADVANCING ON BAGHDAD.
NO WAR
STOP! BUSH
NO WAR
krrrk THE UNITED STATES HAS IGNORED THE WISHES OF THE UNITED NATIONS AND BEGAN THIS WAR FOR OIL. SHOULD SOMETHING LIKE THIS BE TOLERATED?
NO WAR
IT IS ALWAYS THE ELDERLY AND CHILDREN THAT SUFFER MOST IN WARS!
STOP
PLEASE SIGN OUR ANTI-WAR PETITION!
PLEASE SIGN!

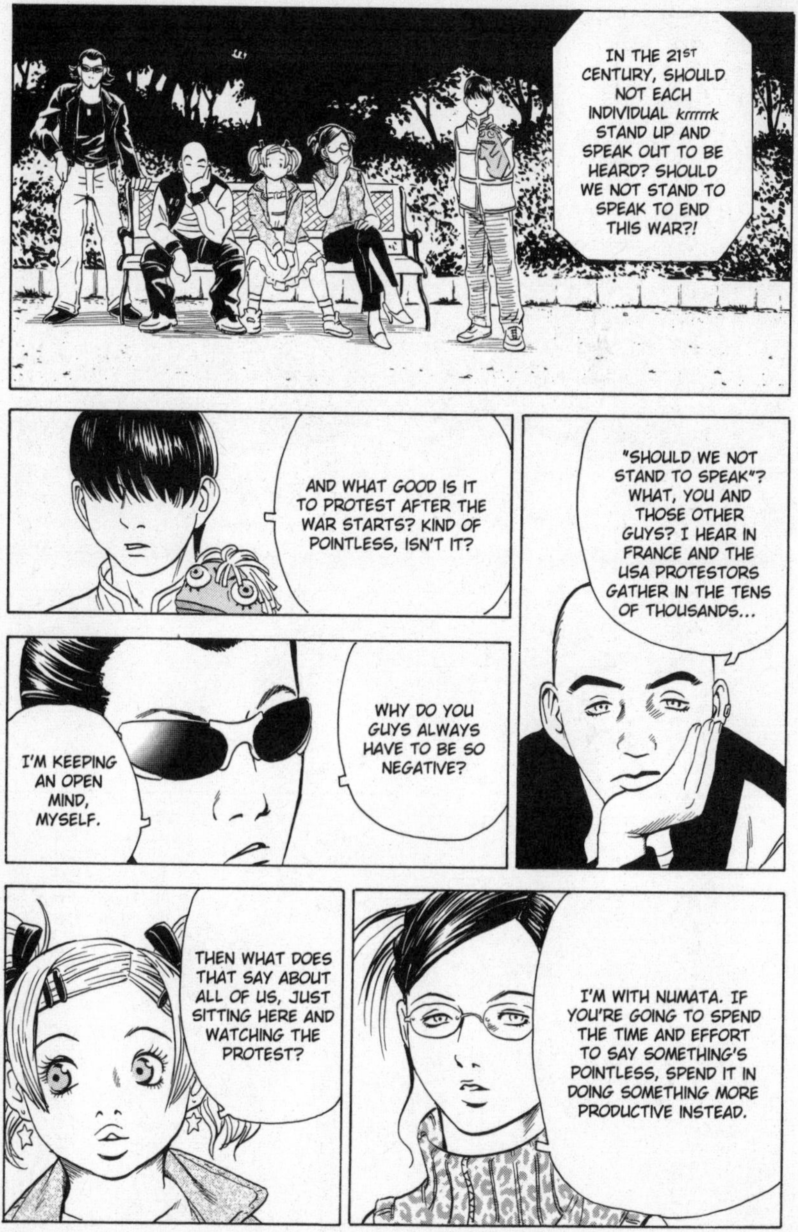
IN THE 21ST CENTURY, SHOULD NOT EACH INDIVIDUAL *krrrrrk* STAND UP AND SPEAK OUT TO BE HEARD? SHOULD WE NOT STAND TO SPEAK TO END THIS WAR?!
"SHOULD WE NOT STAND TO SPEAK"? WHAT, YOU AND THOSE OTHER GUYS? I HEAR IN FRANCE AND THE USA PROTESTORS GATHER IN THE TENS OF THOUSANDS...
AND WHAT GOOD IS IT TO PROTEST AFTER THE WAR STARTS? KIND OF POINTLESS, ISN'T IT?
WHY DO YOU GUYS ALWAYS HAVE TO BE SO NEGATIVE?
I'M KEEPING AN OPEN MIND, MYSELF.
I'M WITH NUMATA. IF YOU'RE GOING TO SPEND THE TIME AND EFFORT TO SAY SOMETHING'S POINTLESS, SPEND IT IN DOING SOMETHING MORE PRODUCTIVE INSTEAD.
THEN WHAT DOES THAT SAY ABOUT ALL OF US, JUST SITTING HERE AND WATCHING THE PROTEST?

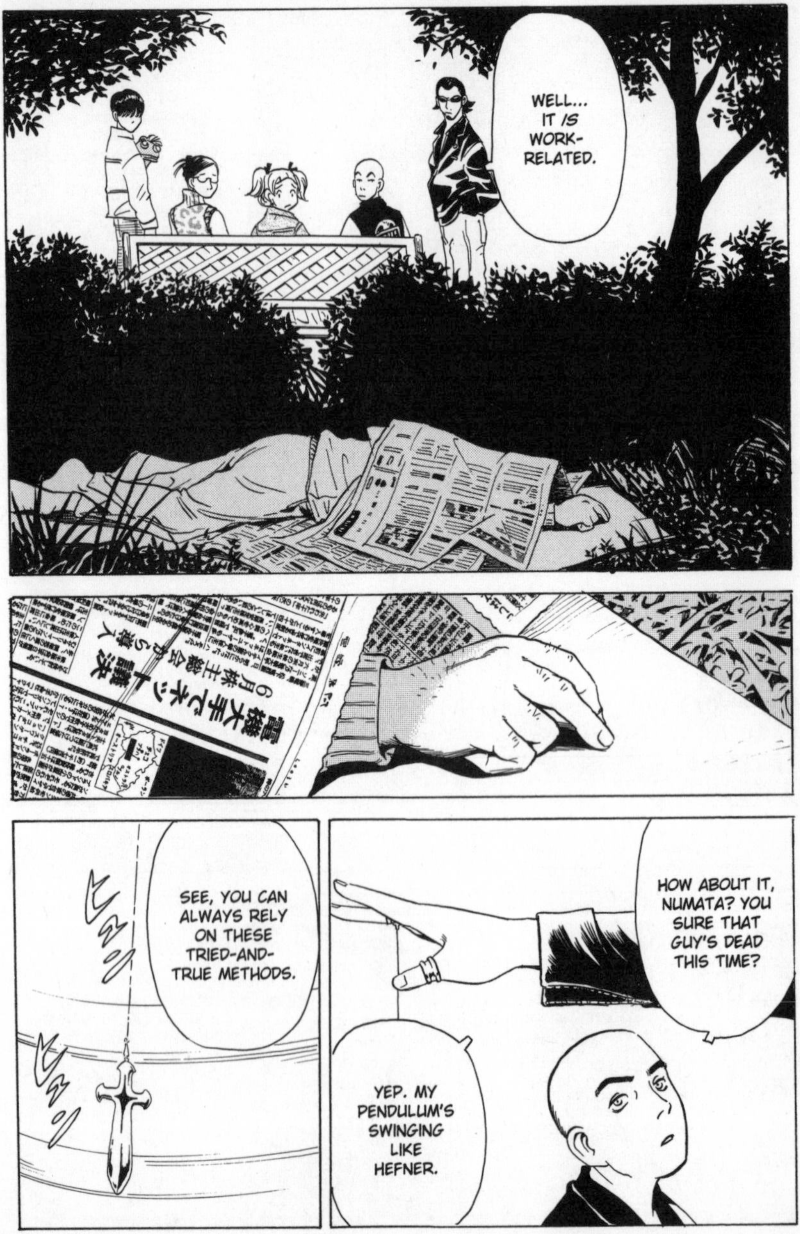
WELL... IT *IS* WORK-RELATED.
HOW ABOUT IT, NUMATA? YOU SURE THAT GUY'S DEAD THIS TIME?
YEP. MY PENDULUM'S SWINGING LIKE HEFNER.
SEE, YOU CAN ALWAYS RELY ON THESE TRIED-AND-TRUE METHODS.

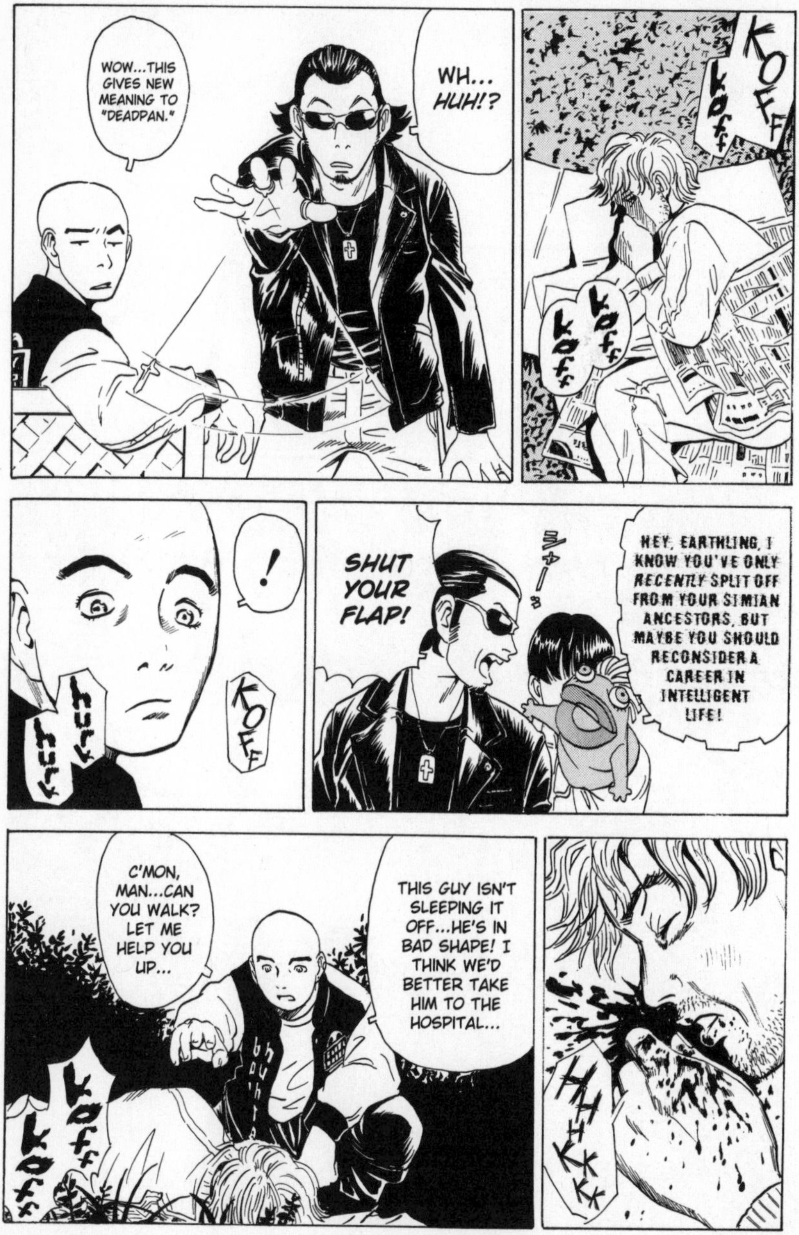
KOFF
koff
koff koff
WH... HUH!?
WOW...THIS GIVES NEW MEANING TO "DEADPAN."
HEY, EARTHLING, I KNOW YOU'VE ONLY RECENTLY SPLIT OFF FROM YOUR SIMIAN ANCESTORS, BUT MAYBE YOU SHOULD RECONSIDER A CAREER IN INTELLIGENT LIFE!
SHUT YOUR FLAP!
!
KOFF
hurk hurk
HHHKKK
THIS GUY ISN'T SLEEPING IT OFF...HE'S IN BAD SHAPE! I THINK WE'D BETTER TAKE HIM TO THE HOSPITAL...
C'MON, MAN...CAN YOU WALK? LET ME HELP YOU UP...
koff koff

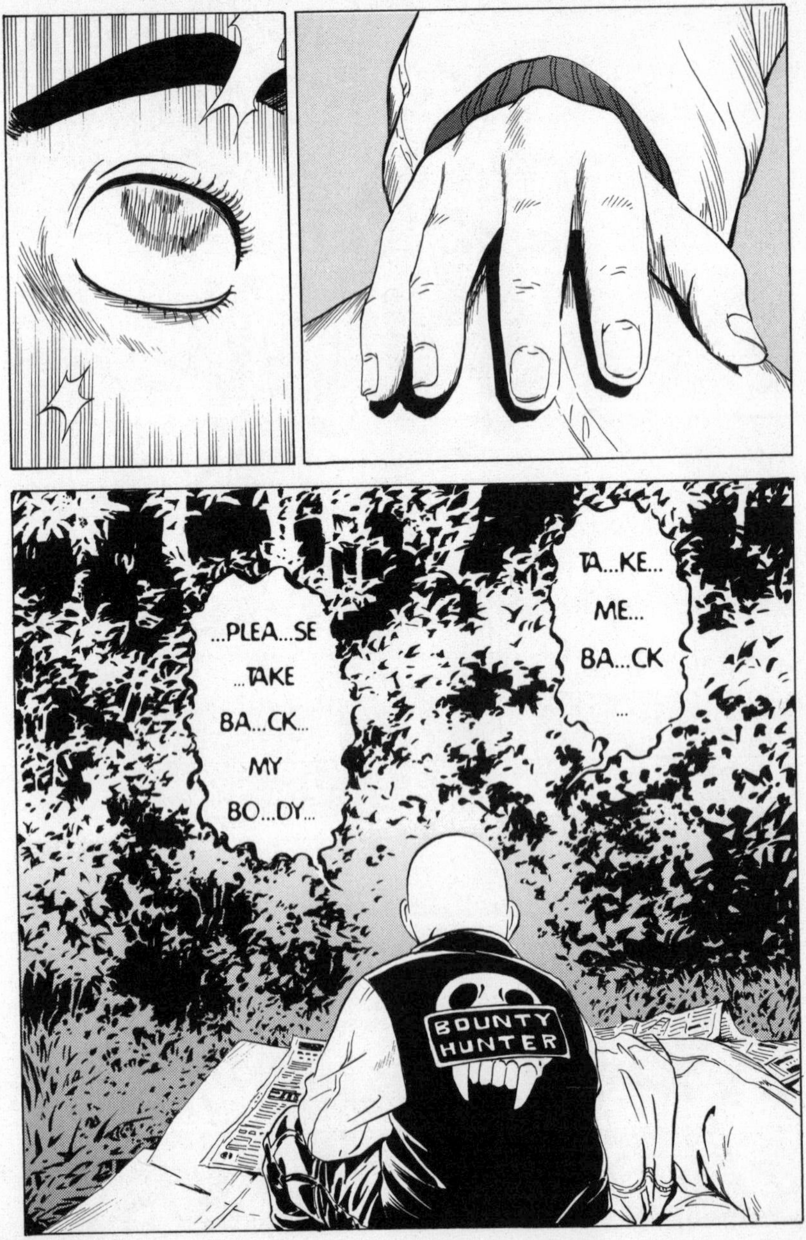
TA...KE... ME... BA...CK ...
...PLEA...SE ...TAKE BA...CK... MY BO...DY...
BOUNTY HUNTER

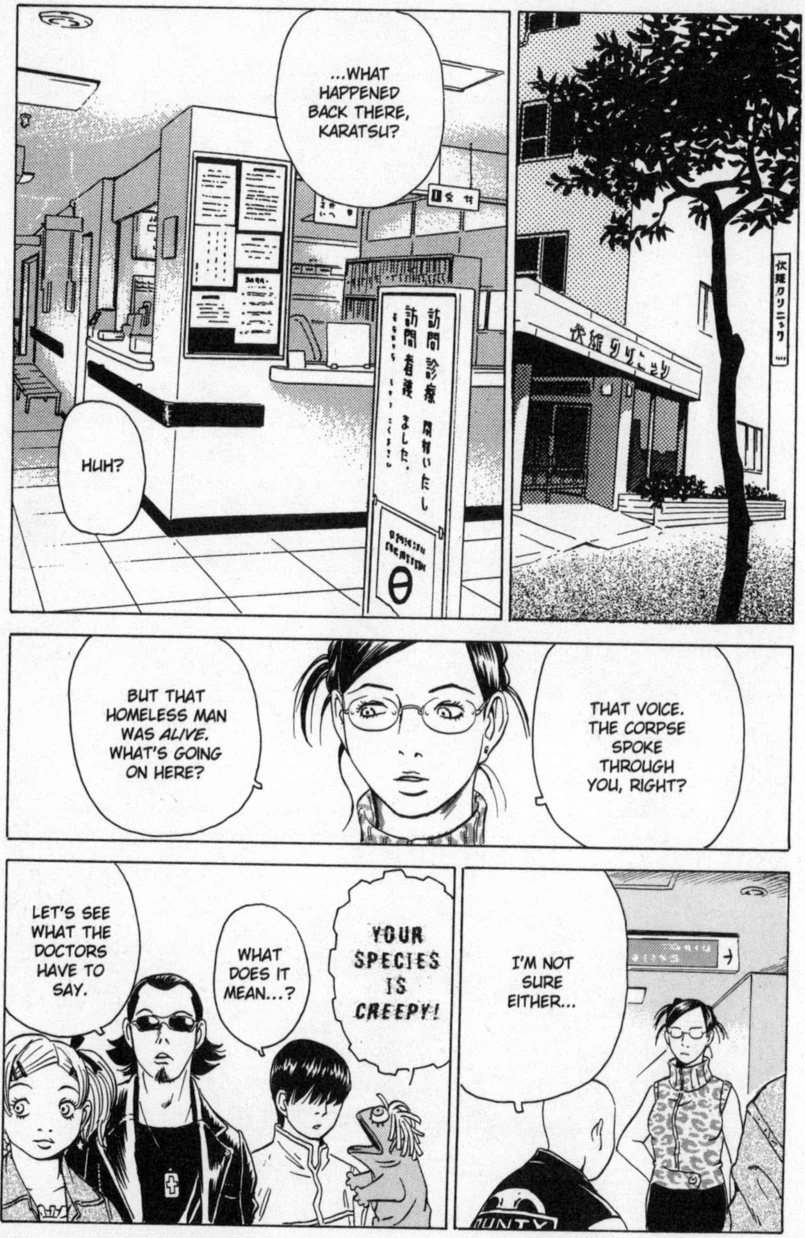
...WHAT HAPPENED BACK THERE, KARATSU?
HUH?
THAT VOICE. THE CORPSE SPOKE THROUGH YOU, RIGHT?
BUT THAT HOMELESS MAN WAS *ALIVE*. WHAT'S GOING ON HERE?
I'M NOT SURE EITHER...
YOUR SPECIES IS *CREEPY!*
WHAT DOES IT MEAN...?
LET'S SEE WHAT THE DOCTORS HAVE TO SAY.

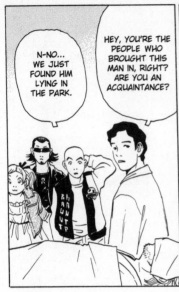

ガコォン
キュッ
キュッ
HEY, YOU'RE THE PEOPLE WHO BROUGHT THIS MAN IN, RIGHT? ARE YOU AN ACQUAINTANCE?
N-NO... WE JUST FOUND HIM LYING IN THE PARK.
DID HE, *uh*, PASS AWAY?
YES, JUST NOW.
HOW... DID HE DIE?
ORGAN FAILURE. HIS BODY SEEMS TO HAVE REJECTED A TRANSPLANT. WE TRIED TO REMOVE IT, BUT WE WERE TOO LATE.

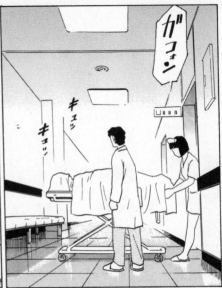

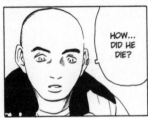

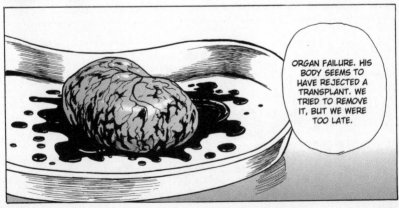

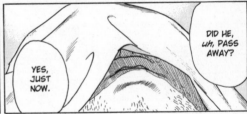

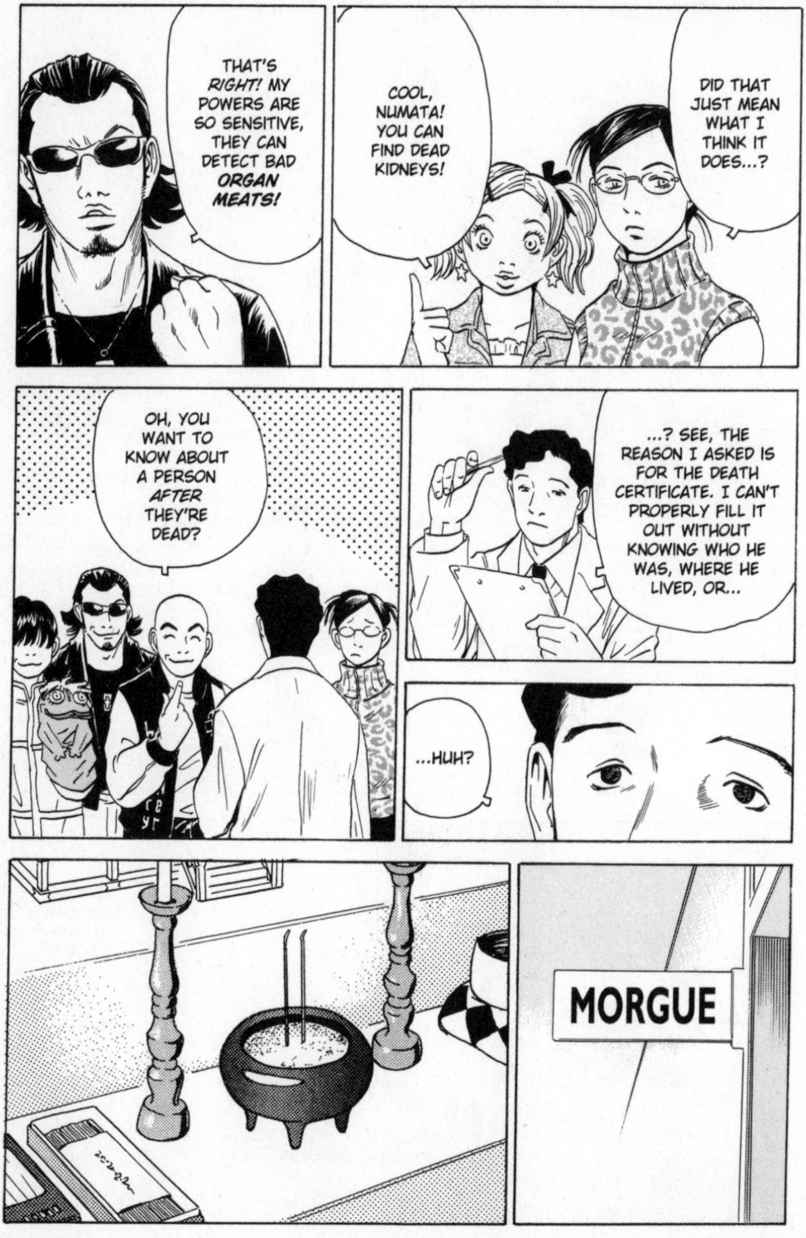
DID THAT JUST MEAN WHAT I THINK IT DOES...?
COOL, NUMATA! YOU CAN FIND DEAD KIDNEYS!
THAT'S *RIGHT!* MY POWERS ARE SO SENSITIVE, THEY CAN DETECT BAD ***ORGAN MEATS!***
...? SEE, THE REASON I ASKED IS FOR THE DEATH CERTIFICATE. I CAN'T PROPERLY FILL IT OUT WITHOUT KNOWING WHO HE WAS, WHERE HE LIVED, OR...
...HUH?
OH, YOU WANT TO KNOW ABOUT A PERSON *AFTER* THEY'RE DEAD?
MORGUE

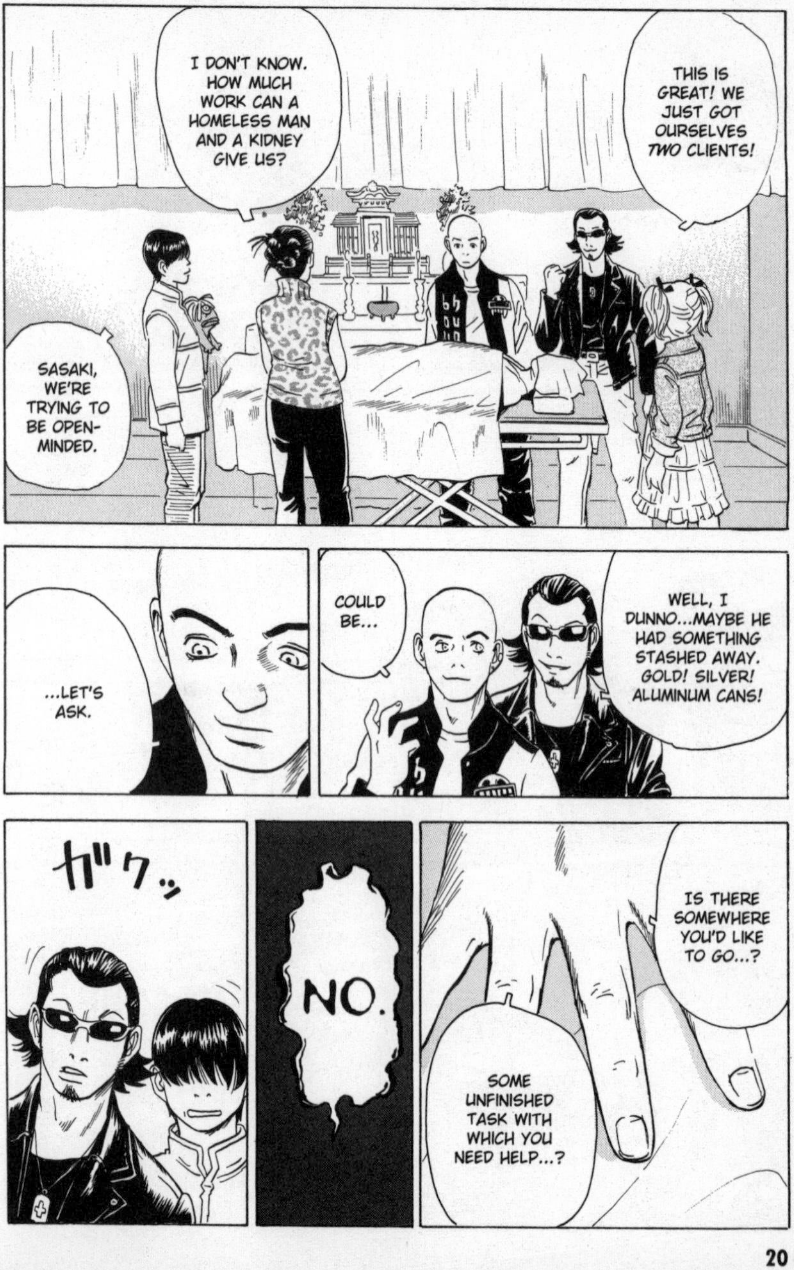
THIS IS GREAT! WE JUST GOT OURSELVES *TWO* CLIENTS!
I DON'T KNOW. HOW MUCH WORK CAN A HOMELESS MAN AND A KIDNEY GIVE US?
SASAKI, WE'RE TRYING TO BE OPEN-MINDED.
WELL, I DUNNO...MAYBE HE HAD SOMETHING STASHED AWAY. GOLD! SILVER! ALUMINUM CANS!
COULD BE...
...LET'S ASK.
IS THERE SOMEWHERE YOU'D LIKE TO GO...?
SOME UNFINISHED TASK WITH WHICH YOU NEED HELP...?
NO.
ガクッ

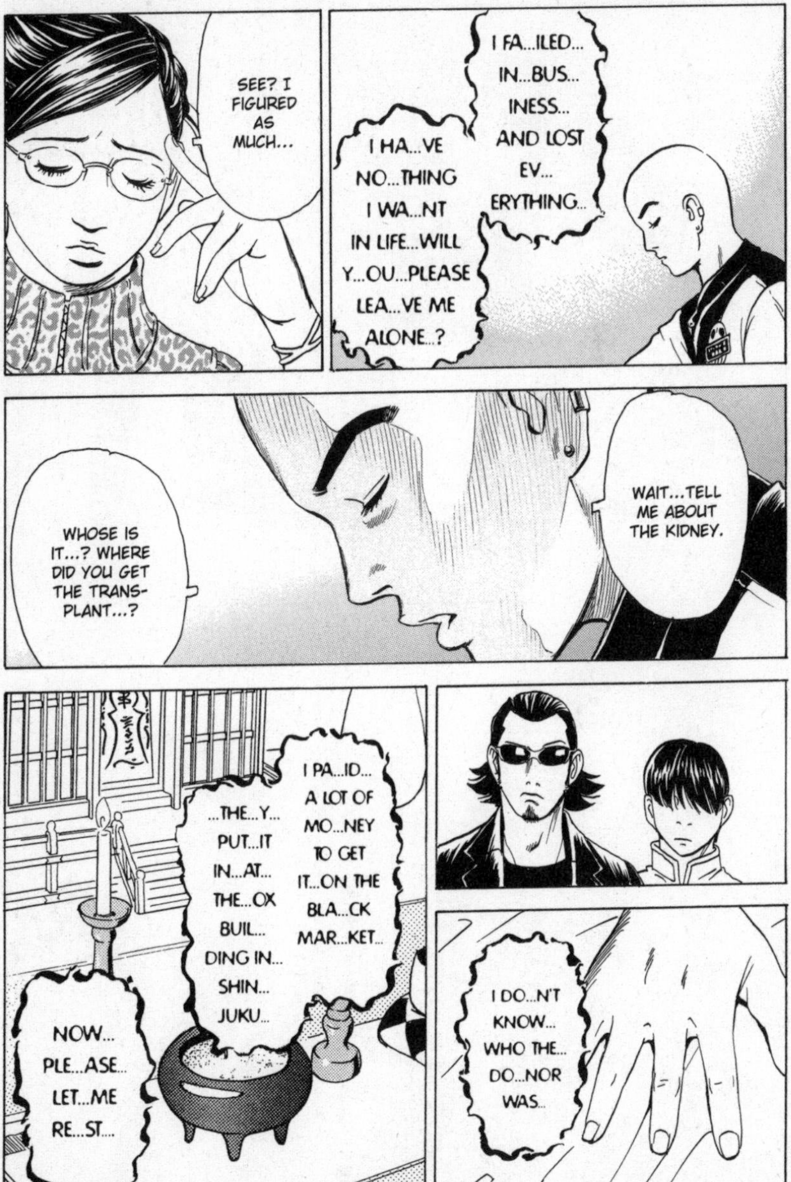
I FA...ILED... IN...BUS... INESS... AND LOST EV... ERYTHING...
I HA...VE NO...THING I WA...NT IN LIFE...WILL Y...OU...PLEASE LEA...VE ME ALONE...?
SEE? I FIGURED AS MUCH...
WAIT...TELL ME ABOUT THE KIDNEY.
WHOSE IS IT...? WHERE DID YOU GET THE TRANS-PLANT...?
I DO...N'T KNOW... WHO THE... DO...NOR WAS...
I PA...ID... A LOT OF MO...NEY TO GET IT...ON THE BLA...CK MAR...KET...
...THE...Y... PUT...IT IN...AT... THE...OX BUIL... DING IN... SHIN... JUKU...
NOW... PLE...ASE... LET...ME RE...ST...

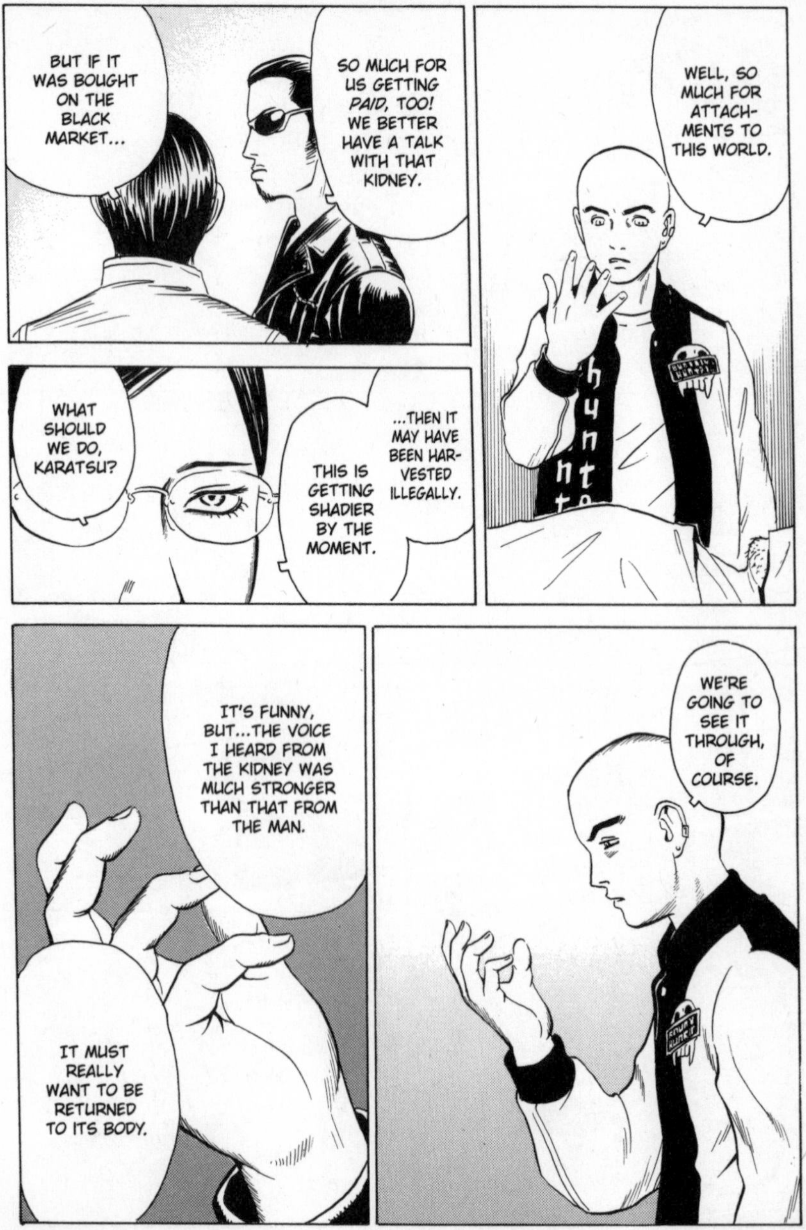
WELL, SO MUCH FOR ATTACH-MENTS TO THIS WORLD.
SO MUCH FOR US GETTING *PAID*, TOO! WE BETTER HAVE A TALK WITH THAT KIDNEY.
BUT IF IT WAS BOUGHT ON THE BLACK MARKET...
...THEN IT MAY HAVE BEEN HAR-VESTED ILLEGALLY.
THIS IS GETTING SHADIER BY THE MOMENT.
WHAT SHOULD WE DO, KARATSU?
WE'RE GOING TO SEE IT THROUGH, OF COURSE.
IT'S FUNNY, BUT...THE VOICE I HEARD FROM THE KIDNEY WAS MUCH STRONGER THAN THAT FROM THE MAN.
IT MUST REALLY WANT TO BE RETURNED TO ITS BODY.

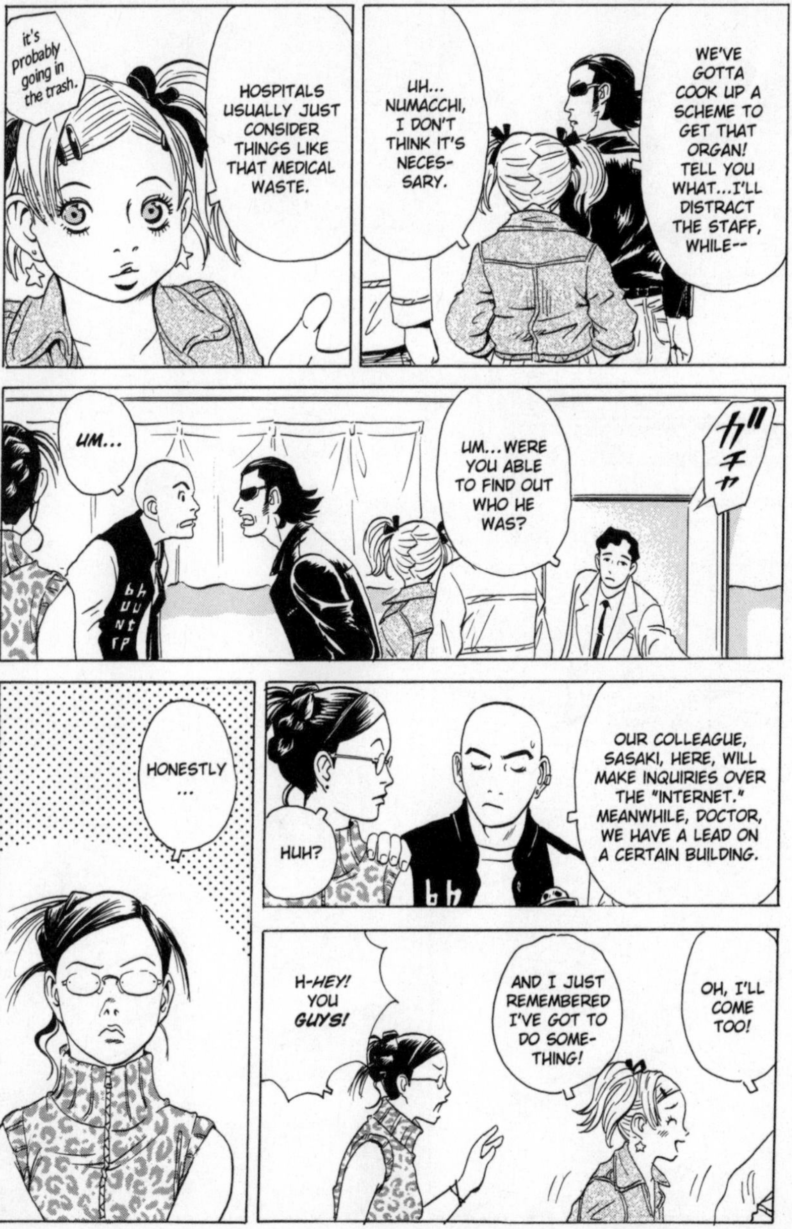
WE'VE GOTTA COOK UP A SCHEME TO GET THAT ORGAN! TELL YOU WHAT...I'LL DISTRACT THE STAFF, WHILE--
UH... NUMACCHI, I DON'T THINK IT'S NECES-SARY.
HOSPITALS USUALLY JUST CONSIDER THINGS LIKE THAT MEDICAL WASTE.
it's probably going in the trash.
ガチャ
UM...WERE YOU ABLE TO FIND OUT WHO HE WAS?
UM...
OUR COLLEAGUE, SASAKI, HERE, WILL MAKE INQUIRIES OVER THE "INTERNET." MEANWHILE, DOCTOR, WE HAVE A LEAD ON A CERTAIN BUILDING.
HUH?
OH, I'LL COME TOO!
AND I JUST REMEMBERED I'VE GOT TO DO SOME-THING!
H-*HEY!* YOU *GUYS!*
HONESTLY ...

THIS CERTAINLY LOOKS LIKE A FLY-BY-NIGHT OPERATION.

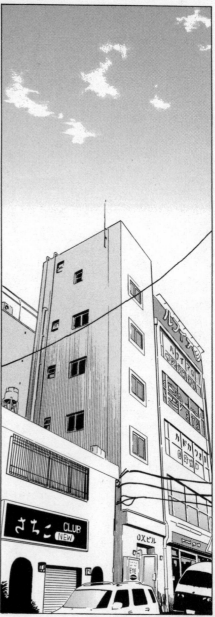

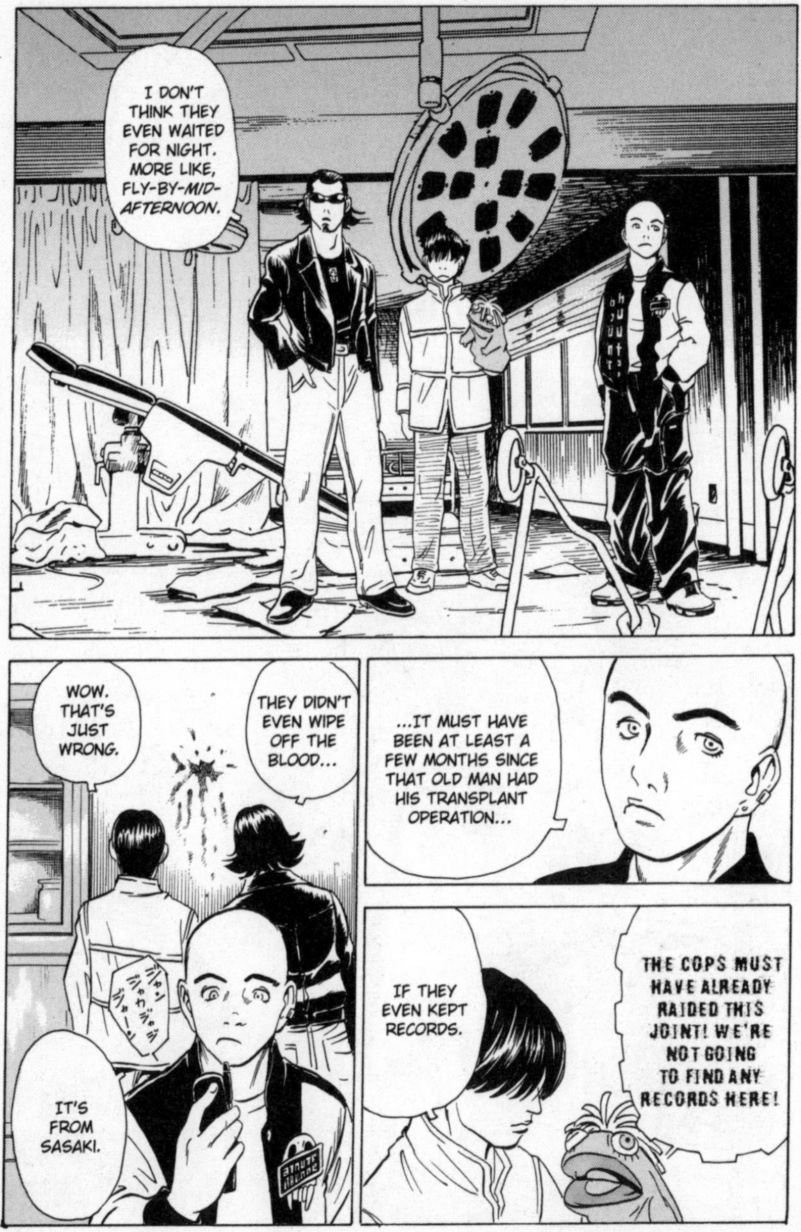
I DON'T THINK THEY EVEN WAITED FOR NIGHT. MORE LIKE, FLY-BY-*MID*-AFTERNOON.
...IT MUST HAVE BEEN AT LEAST A FEW MONTHS SINCE THAT OLD MAN HAD HIS TRANSPLANT OPERATION...
THE COPS MUST HAVE ALREADY RAIDED THIS JOINT! WE'RE NOT GOING TO FIND ANY RECORDS HERE!
IF THEY EVEN KEPT RECORDS.
THEY DIDN'T EVEN WIPE OFF THE BLOOD...
WOW. THAT'S JUST WRONG.
ジャ・ン ジャカジャジャ ジャー・ン
IT'S FROM SASAKI.

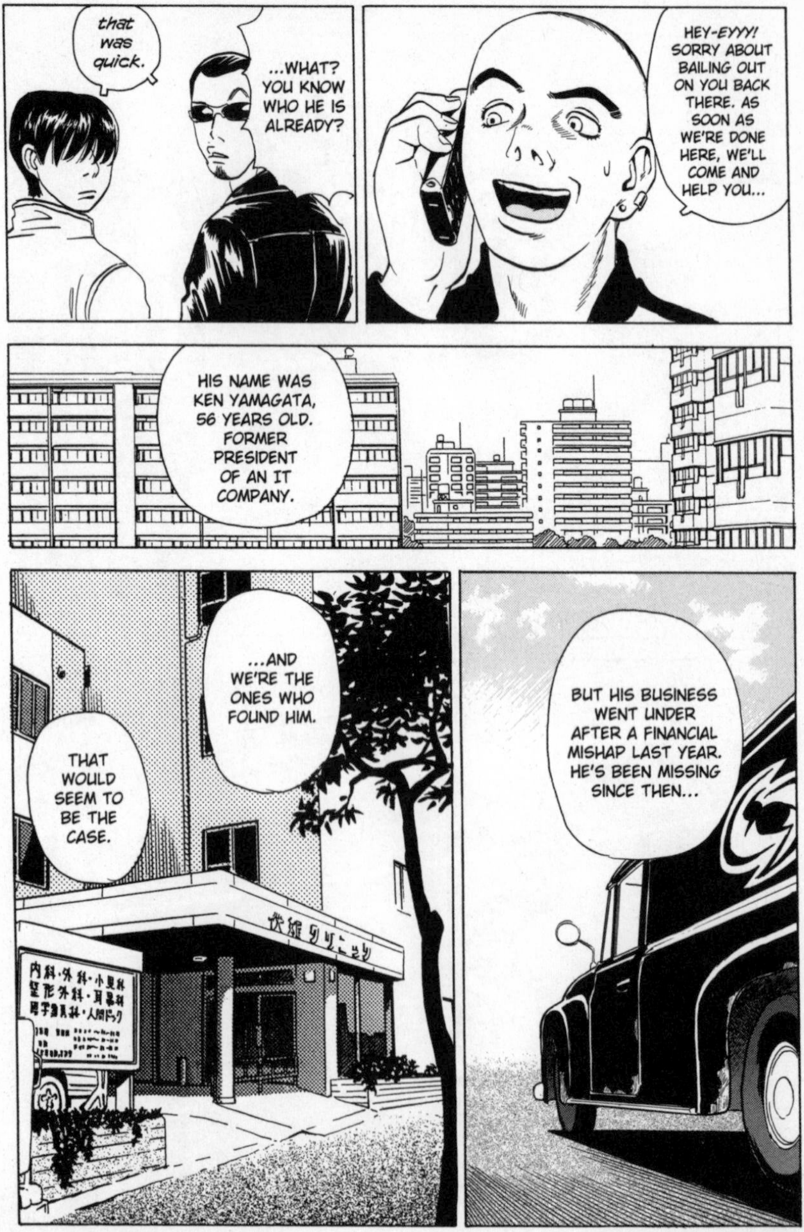
HEY-EYYY! SORRY ABOUT BAILING OUT ON YOU BACK THERE. AS SOON AS WE'RE DONE HERE, WE'LL COME AND HELP YOU...
that was quick.
...WHAT? YOU KNOW WHO HE IS ALREADY?
HIS NAME WAS KEN YAMAGATA, 56 YEARS OLD. FORMER PRESIDENT OF AN IT COMPANY.
BUT HIS BUSINESS WENT UNDER AFTER A FINANCIAL MISHAP LAST YEAR. HE'S BEEN MISSING SINCE THEN...
...AND WE'RE THE ONES WHO FOUND HIM.
THAT WOULD SEEM TO BE THE CASE.

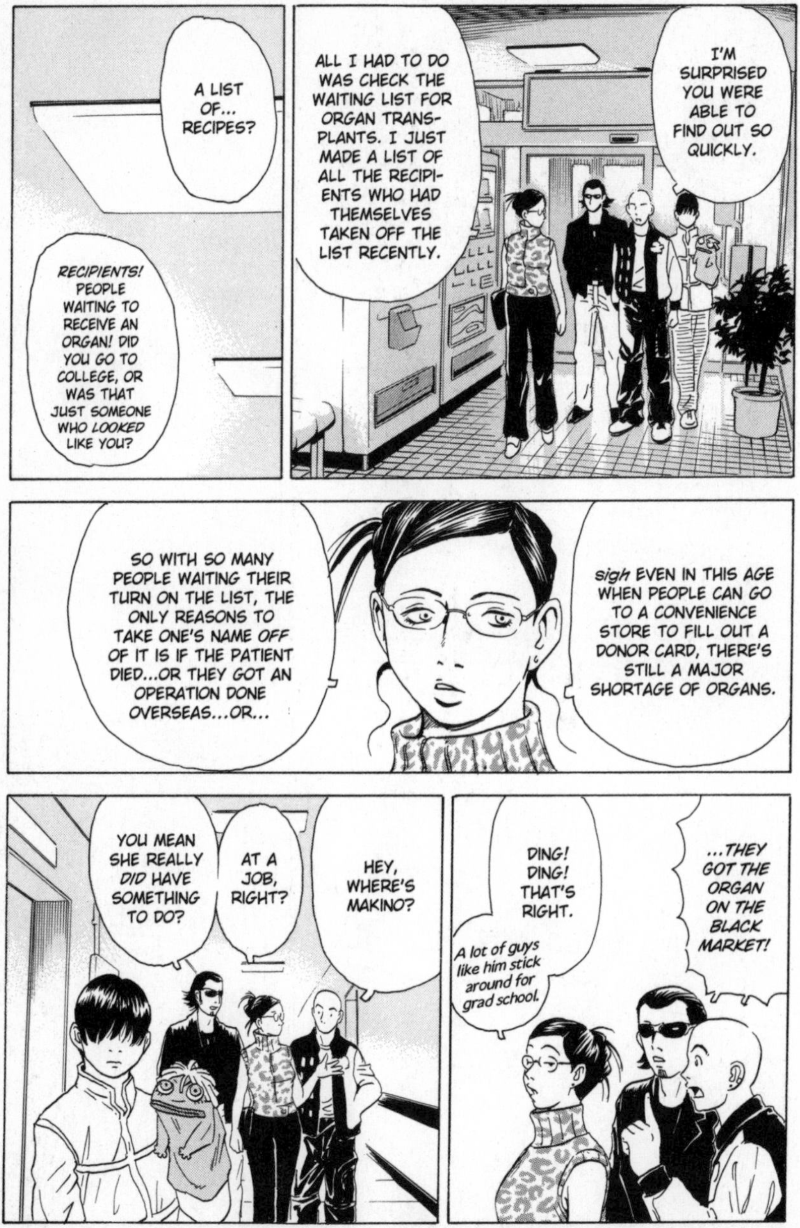
I'M SURPRISED YOU WERE ABLE TO FIND OUT SO QUICKLY.
ALL I HAD TO DO WAS CHECK THE WAITING LIST FOR ORGAN TRANS-PLANTS. I JUST MADE A LIST OF ALL THE RECIPI-ENTS WHO HAD THEMSELVES TAKEN OFF THE LIST RECENTLY.
A LIST OF... RECIPES?
RECIPIENTS! PEOPLE WAITING TO RECEIVE AN ORGAN! DID YOU GO TO COLLEGE, OR WAS THAT JUST SOMEONE WHO *LOOKED* LIKE YOU?
sigh EVEN IN THIS AGE WHEN PEOPLE CAN GO TO A CONVENIENCE STORE TO FILL OUT A DONOR CARD, THERE'S STILL A MAJOR SHORTAGE OF ORGANS.
SO WITH SO MANY PEOPLE WAITING THEIR TURN ON THE LIST, THE ONLY REASONS TO TAKE ONE'S NAME *OFF* OF IT IS IF THE PATIENT DIED...OR THEY GOT AN OPERATION DONE OVERSEAS...OR...
...THEY GOT THE ORGAN ON THE BLACK MARKET!
DING! DING! THAT'S RIGHT.
A lot of guys like him stick around for grad school.
HEY, WHERE'S MAKINO?
AT A JOB, RIGHT?
YOU MEAN SHE REALLY *DID* HAVE SOMETHING TO DO?

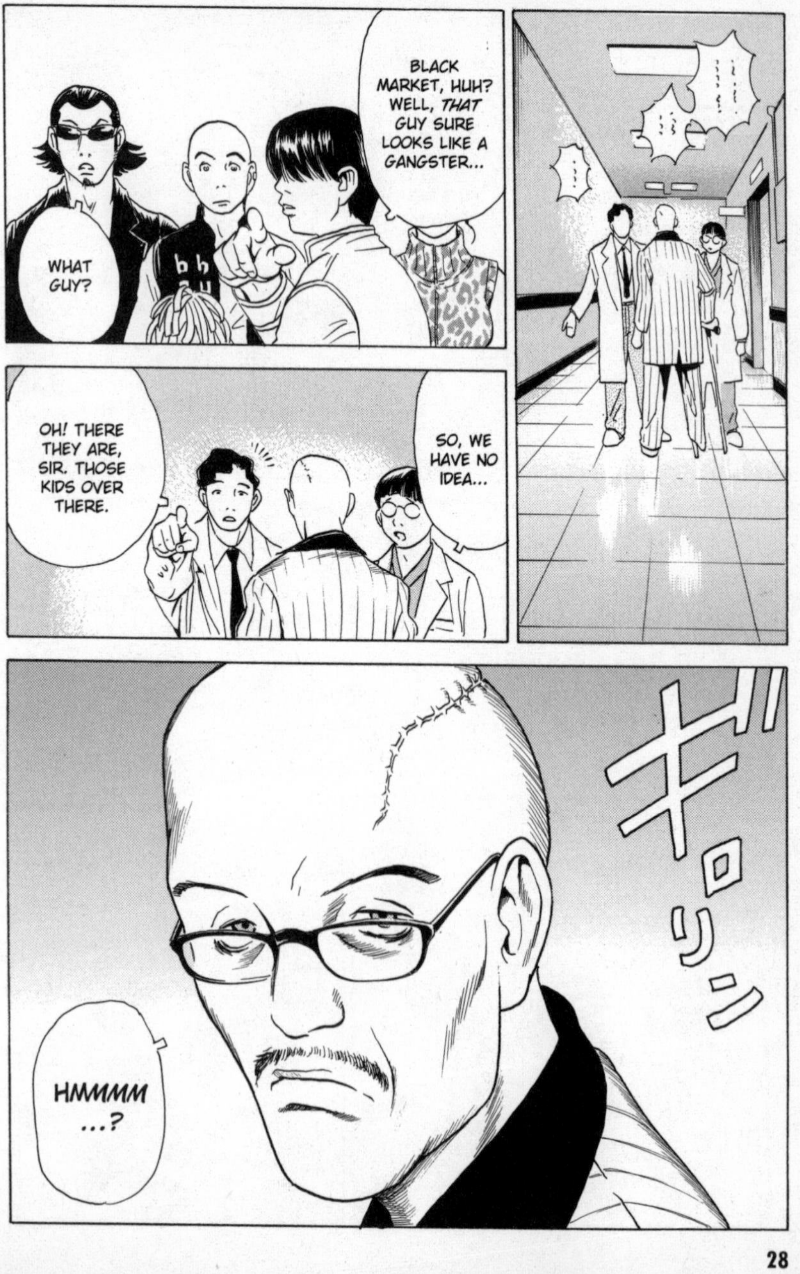
BLACK MARKET, HUH? WELL, *THAT* GUY SURE LOOKS LIKE A GANGSTER...
WHAT GUY?
SO, WE HAVE NO IDEA...
OH! THERE THEY ARE, SIR. THOSE KIDS OVER THERE.
ギロリン
HMMMM ...?

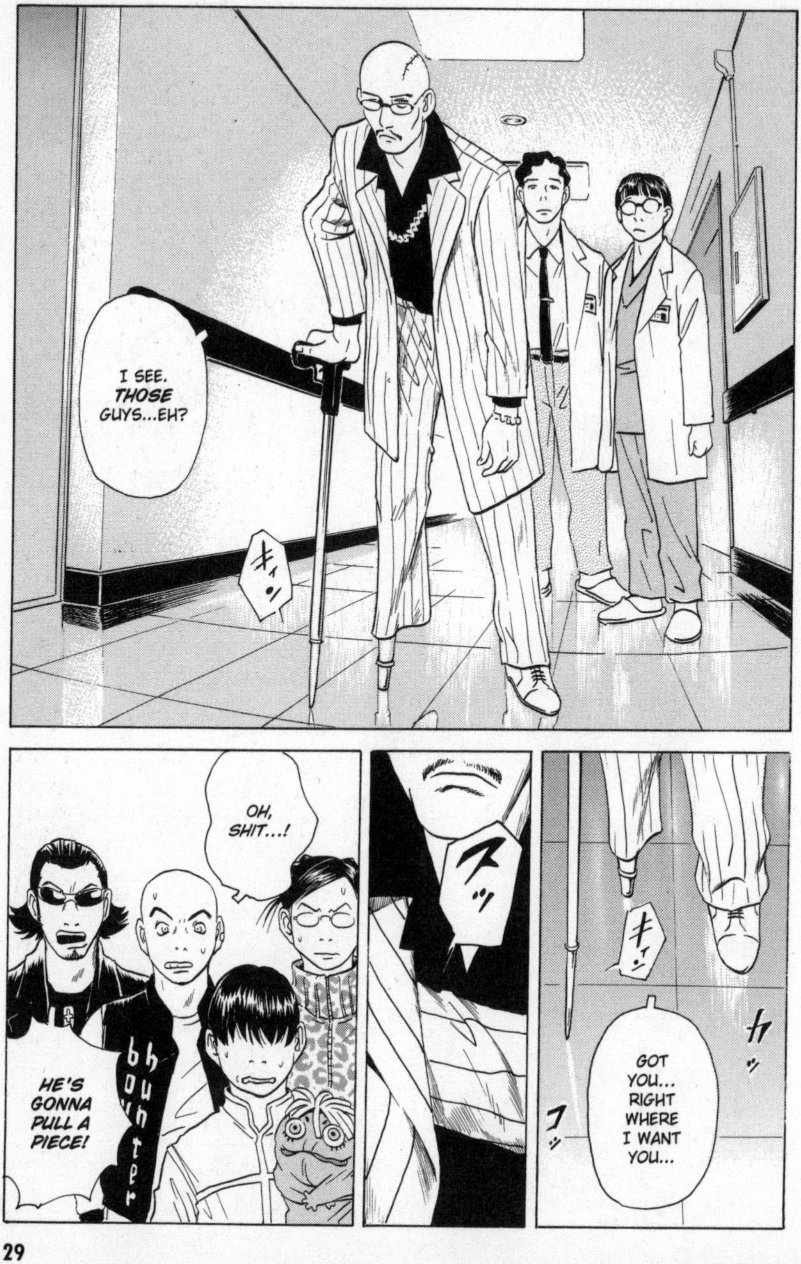

I SEE. THOSE GUYS...EH?
キィン
GOT YOU... RIGHT WHERE I WANT YOU...
キィン
カッ
コッ
スッ
OH, SHIT...!
HE'S GONNA PULL A PIECE!

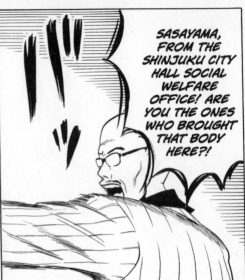

SASAYAMA, FROM THE SHINJUKU CITY HALL SOCIAL WELFARE OFFICE! ARE YOU THE ONES WHO BROUGHT THAT BODY HERE?!

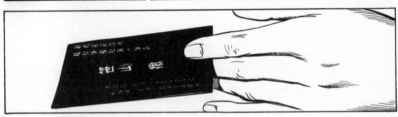

...WHAT'S YOUR PROBLEM?

IS THAT THING LOADED?!?

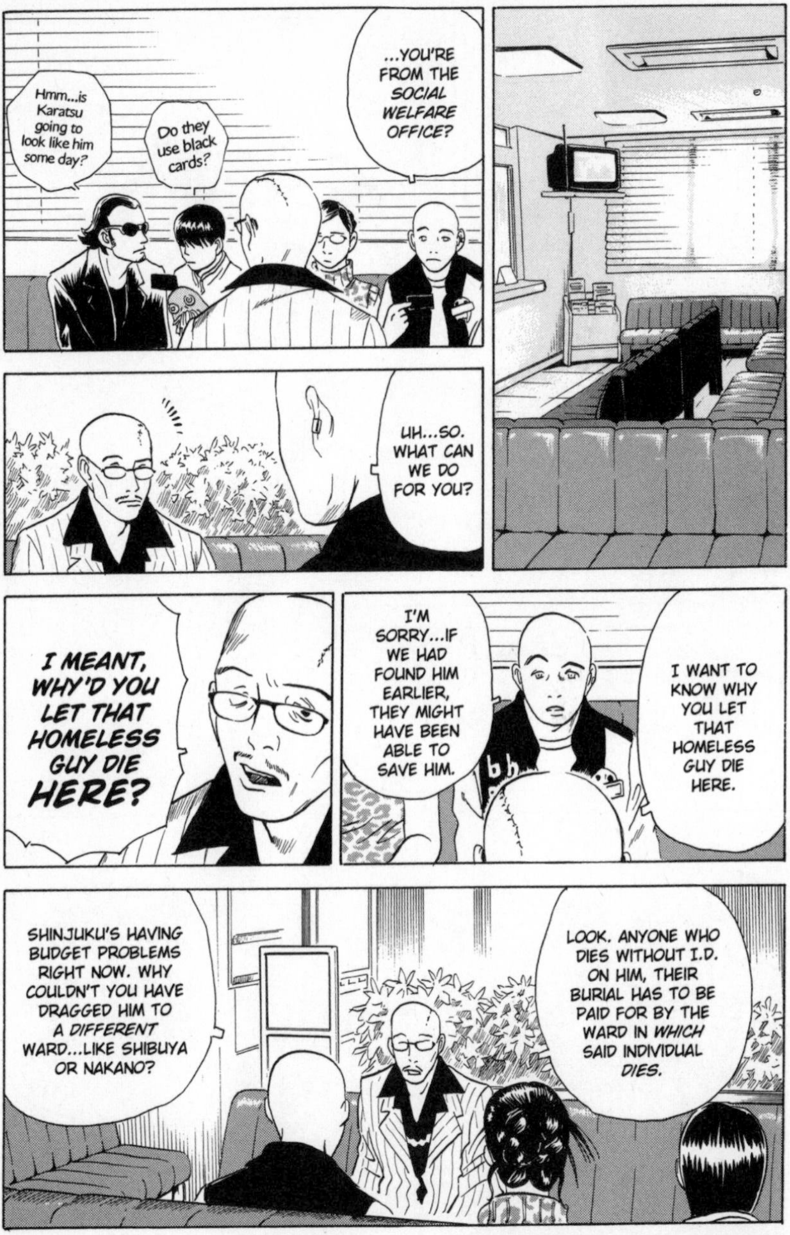
...YOU'RE FROM THE SOCIAL WELFARE OFFICE?
Do they use black cards?
Hmm...is Karatsu going to look like him some day?
UH...SO. WHAT CAN WE DO FOR YOU?
I WANT TO KNOW WHY YOU LET THAT HOMELESS GUY DIE HERE.
I'M SORRY...IF WE HAD FOUND HIM EARLIER, THEY MIGHT HAVE BEEN ABLE TO SAVE HIM.
I MEANT, WHY'D YOU LET THAT HOMELESS GUY DIE HERE?
LOOK. ANYONE WHO DIES WITHOUT I.D. ON HIM, THEIR BURIAL HAS TO BE PAID FOR BY THE WARD IN WHICH SAID INDIVIDUAL DIES.
SHINJUKU'S HAVING BUDGET PROBLEMS RIGHT NOW. WHY COULDN'T YOU HAVE DRAGGED HIM TO A DIFFERENT WARD...LIKE SHIBUYA OR NAKANO?

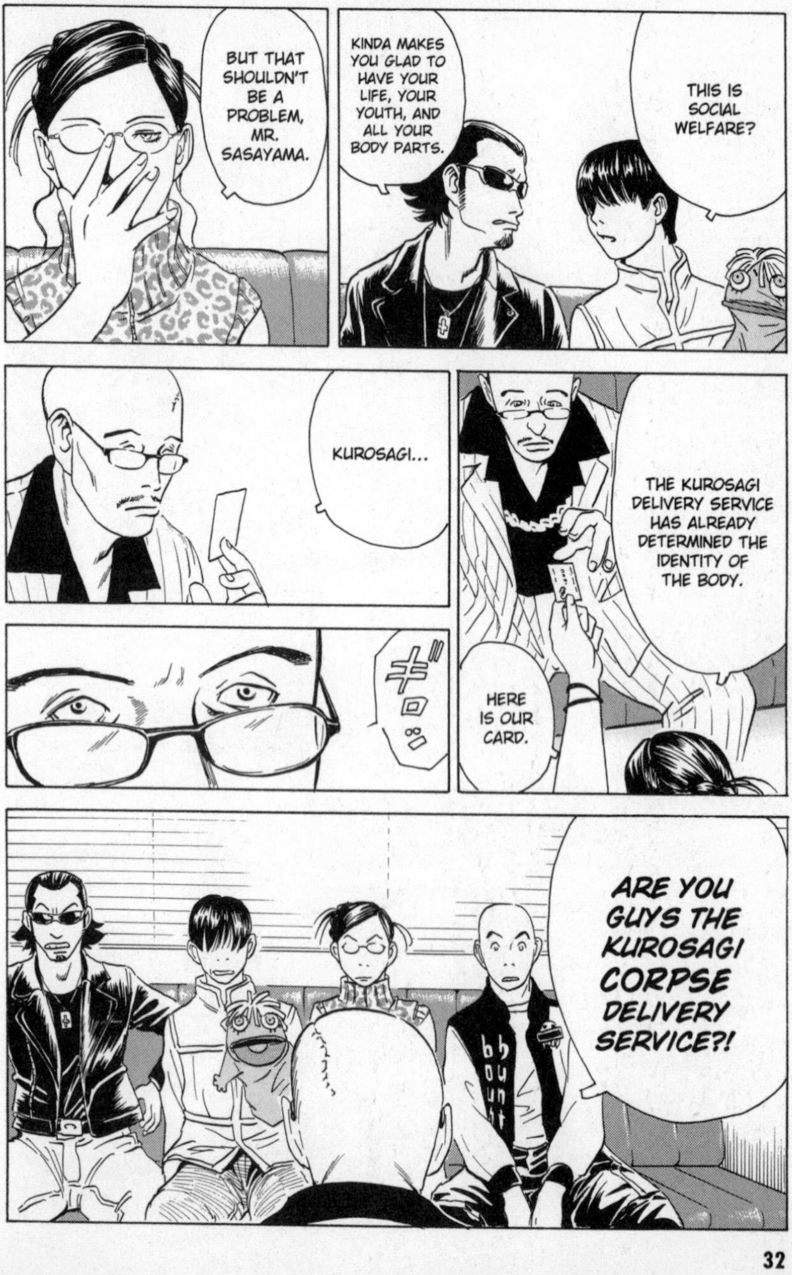
THIS IS SOCIAL WELFARE?
KINDA MAKES YOU GLAD TO HAVE YOUR LIFE, YOUR YOUTH, AND ALL YOUR BODY PARTS.
BUT THAT SHOULDN'T BE A PROBLEM, MR. SASAYAMA.
THE KUROSAGI DELIVERY SERVICE HAS ALREADY DETERMINED THE IDENTITY OF THE BODY.
HERE IS OUR CARD.
KUROSAGI...
ギロッ
ARE YOU GUYS THE KUROSAGI CORPSE DELIVERY SERVICE?!

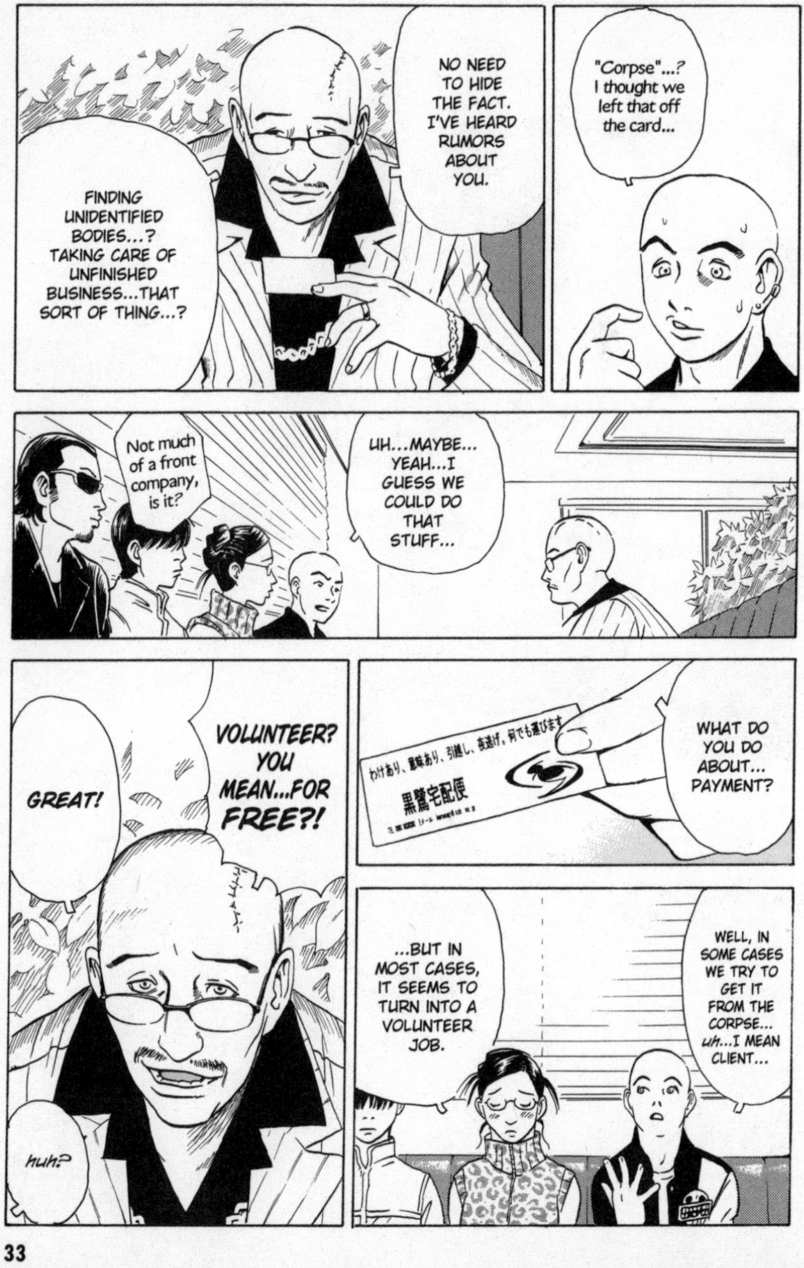
"Corpse"...? I thought we left that off the card...
NO NEED TO HIDE THE FACT. I'VE HEARD RUMORS ABOUT YOU.
FINDING UNIDENTIFIED BODIES...? TAKING CARE OF UNFINISHED BUSINESS...THAT SORT OF THING...?
UH...MAYBE... YEAH...I GUESS WE COULD DO THAT STUFF...
Not much of a front company, is it?
WHAT DO YOU DO ABOUT... PAYMENT?
わけあり、意味あり、引越し、夜逃げ、何でも運びます
黒鷺宅配便
WELL, IN SOME CASES WE TRY TO GET IT FROM THE CORPSE... *uh*...I MEAN CLIENT...
...BUT IN MOST CASES, IT SEEMS TO TURN INTO A VOLUNTEER JOB.
VOLUNTEER? YOU MEAN...FOR FREE?!
GREAT!
huh?

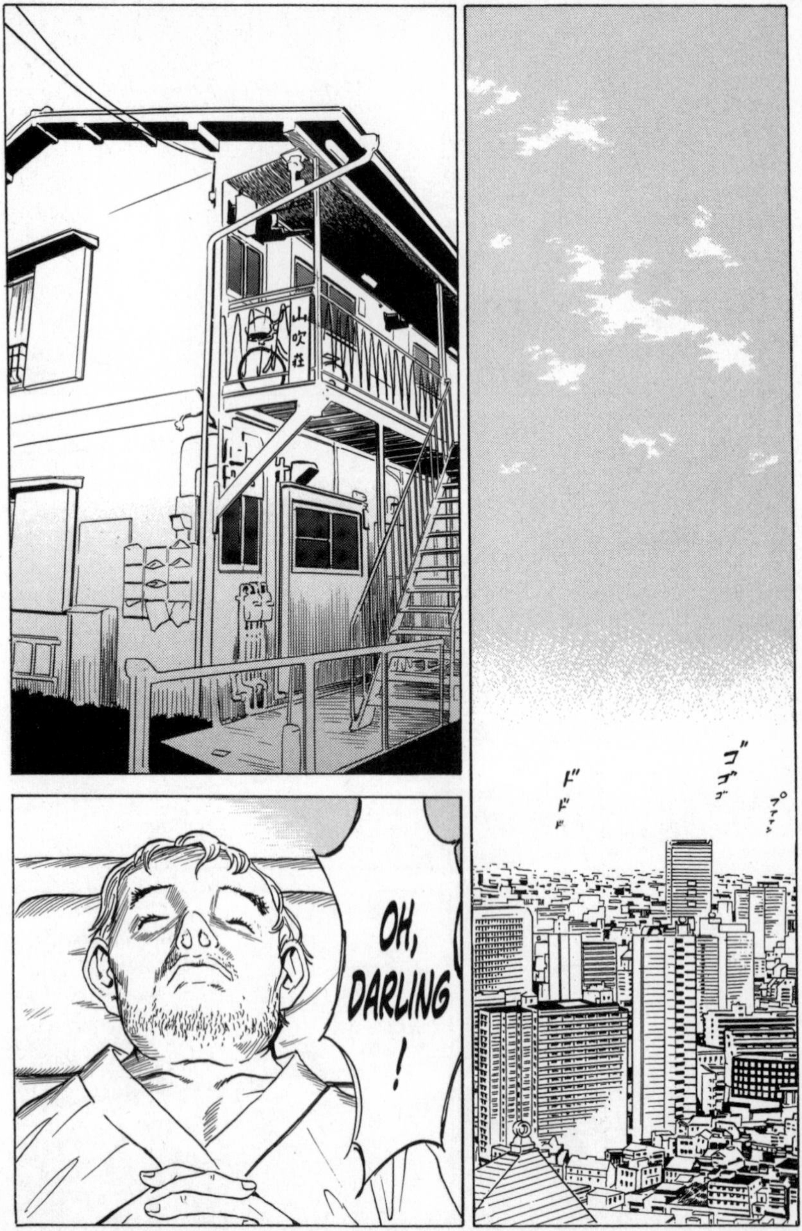
プァァァン
ゴゴゴ
ドドド
山吹荘
OH, DARLING!

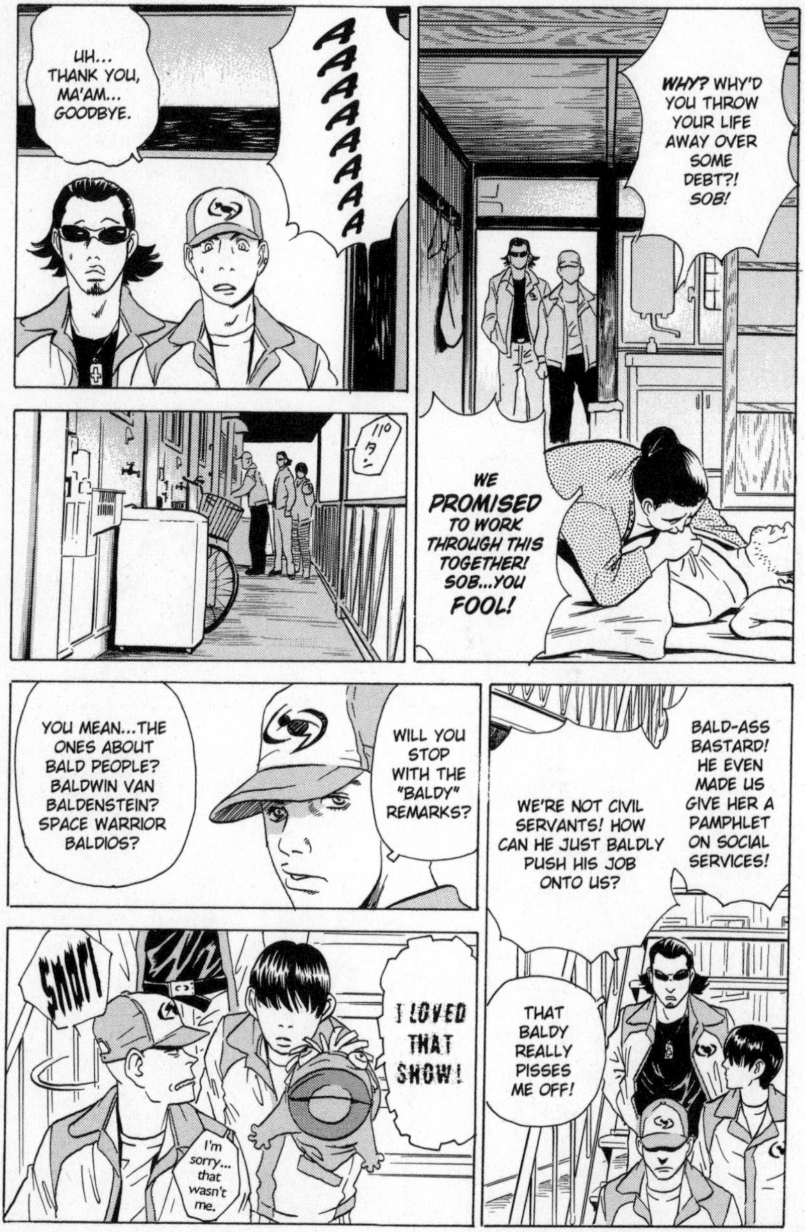
WHY? WHY'D YOU THROW YOUR LIFE AWAY OVER SOME DEBT?! SOB!
WE PROMISED TO WORK THROUGH THIS TOGETHER! SOB...YOU FOOL!
AAAAAAAAAA
UH... THANK YOU, MA'AM... GOODBYE.
BALD-ASS BASTARD! HE EVEN MADE US GIVE HER A PAMPHLET ON SOCIAL SERVICES!
WE'RE NOT CIVIL SERVANTS! HOW CAN HE JUST BALDLY PUSH HIS JOB ONTO US?
THAT BALDY REALLY PISSES ME OFF!
WILL YOU STOP WITH THE "BALDY" REMARKS?
YOU MEAN...THE ONES ABOUT BALD PEOPLE? BALDWIN VAN BALDENSTEIN? SPACE WARRIOR BALDIOS?
I LOVED THAT SHOW!
Snort
I'm sorry... that wasn't me.

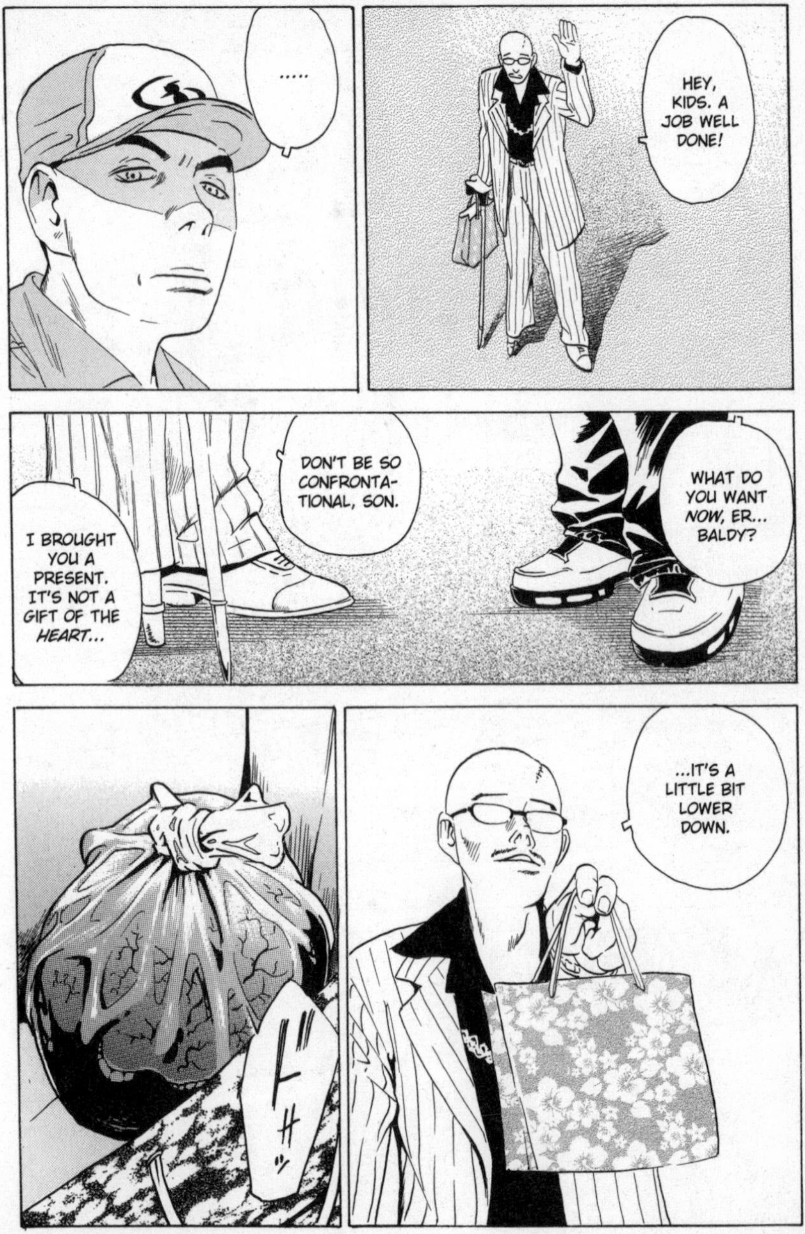
HEY, KIDS. A JOB WELL DONE!
......
WHAT DO YOU WANT *NOW*, ER... BALDY?
DON'T BE SO CONFRONTA-TIONAL, SON.
I BROUGHT YOU A PRESENT. IT'S NOT A GIFT OF THE *HEART*...
...IT'S A LITTLE BIT LOWER DOWN.

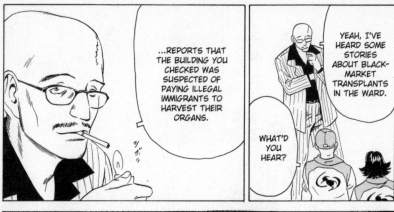

YEAH, I'VE HEARD SOME STORIES ABOUT BLACK-MARKET TRANSPLANTS IN THE WARD.
WHAT'D YOU HEAR?
...REPORTS THAT THE BUILDING YOU CHECKED WAS SUSPECTED OF PAYING ILLEGAL IMMIGRANTS TO HARVEST THEIR ORGANS.
シボッ
SEE, THE MAN YOU BROUGHT IN ISN'T THE FIRST PERSON ASSOCIATED WITH THAT CLINIC TO DIE.
HE WAS THE *FIFTH* TO DIE. THIS WEEK.
HEY, WAIT A SECOND.
WHY ARE *YOU* WORKING ON THIS CASE? SHOULDN'T IT BE SOMETHING FOR THE COPS?
WELL, THEY USED TO CALL ME *DETECTIVE* SASAYAMA... IN HOMICIDE.
キィッ
FOR CERTAIN REASONS I HAD TO LEAVE THE FORCE.

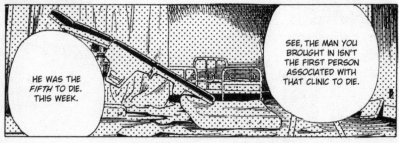

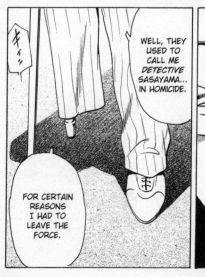

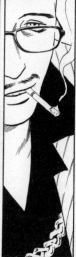

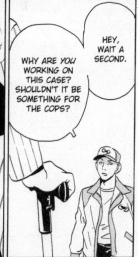

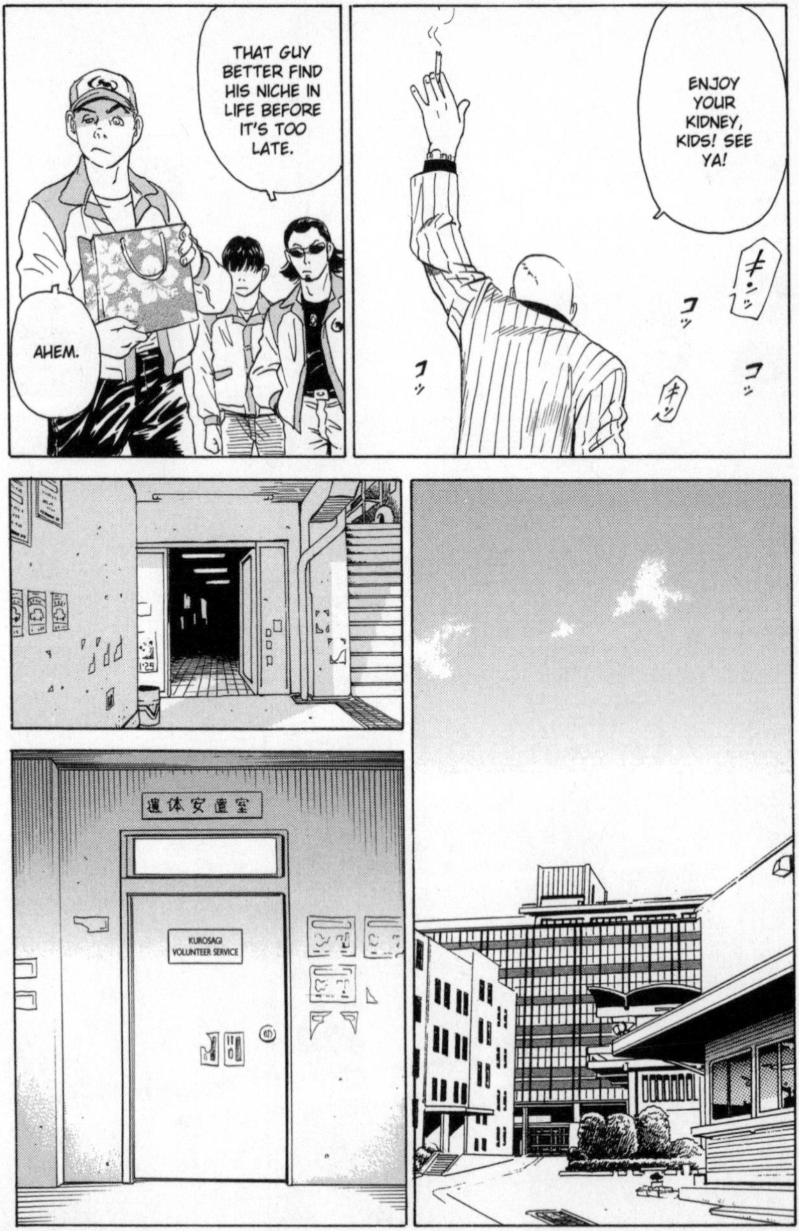
ENJOY YOUR KIDNEY, KIDS! SEE YA!
キンッ
コッ
コッ
キンッ
コッ
THAT GUY BETTER FIND HIS NICHE IN LIFE BEFORE IT'S TOO LATE.
AHEM.
遺体安置室
KUROSAGI VOLUNTEER SERVICE

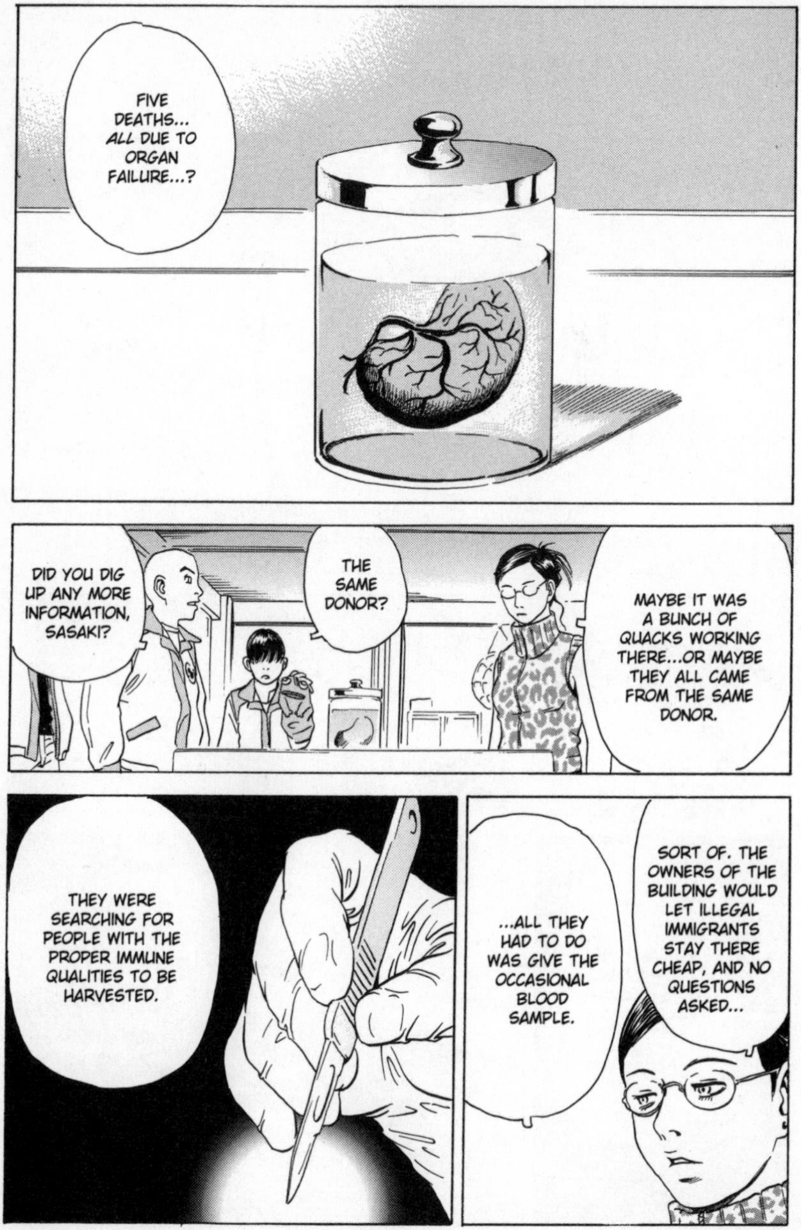
FIVE DEATHS... ALL DUE TO ORGAN FAILURE...?
MAYBE IT WAS A BUNCH OF QUACKS WORKING THERE...OR MAYBE THEY ALL CAME FROM THE SAME DONOR.
THE SAME DONOR?
DID YOU DIG UP ANY MORE INFORMATION, SASAKI?
SORT OF. THE OWNERS OF THE BUILDING WOULD LET ILLEGAL IMMIGRANTS STAY THERE CHEAP, AND NO QUESTIONS ASKED...
...ALL THEY HAD TO DO WAS GIVE THE OCCASIONAL BLOOD SAMPLE.
THEY WERE SEARCHING FOR PEOPLE WITH THE PROPER IMMUNE QUALITIES TO BE HARVESTED.

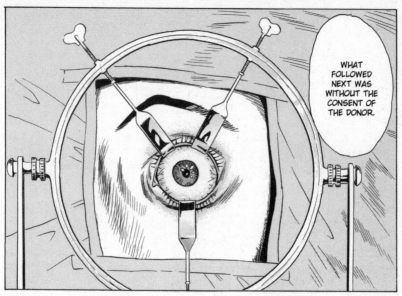

WHAT FOLLOWED NEXT WAS WITHOUT THE CONSENT OF THE DONOR.

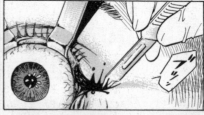

IT'S AMAZING HOW MANY THINGS CAN BE REMOVED FROM A BODY BEFORE IT DIES.

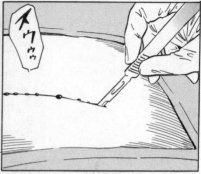

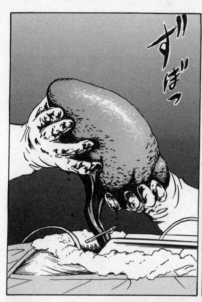

スウゥゥ
ガパッ
ずぼっ
TO KEEP THEM AS FRESH AS POSSIBLE, THEY BEGAN WITH THE ORGANS UNNECESSARY FOR SURVIVAL.
TWO EYES... A LENGTH OF INTESTINE...ONE LUNG...AND ONE KIDNEY.

SOMEHOW HE NOT ONLY MANAGED TO LIVE...

...BUT BLIND AND SUTURED, HE ESCAPED THEM.

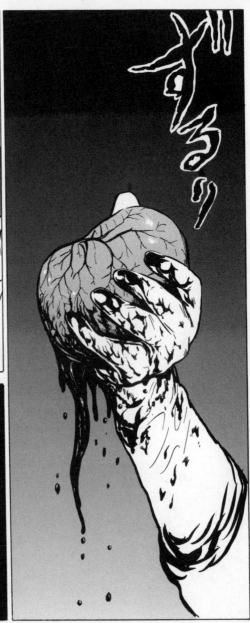

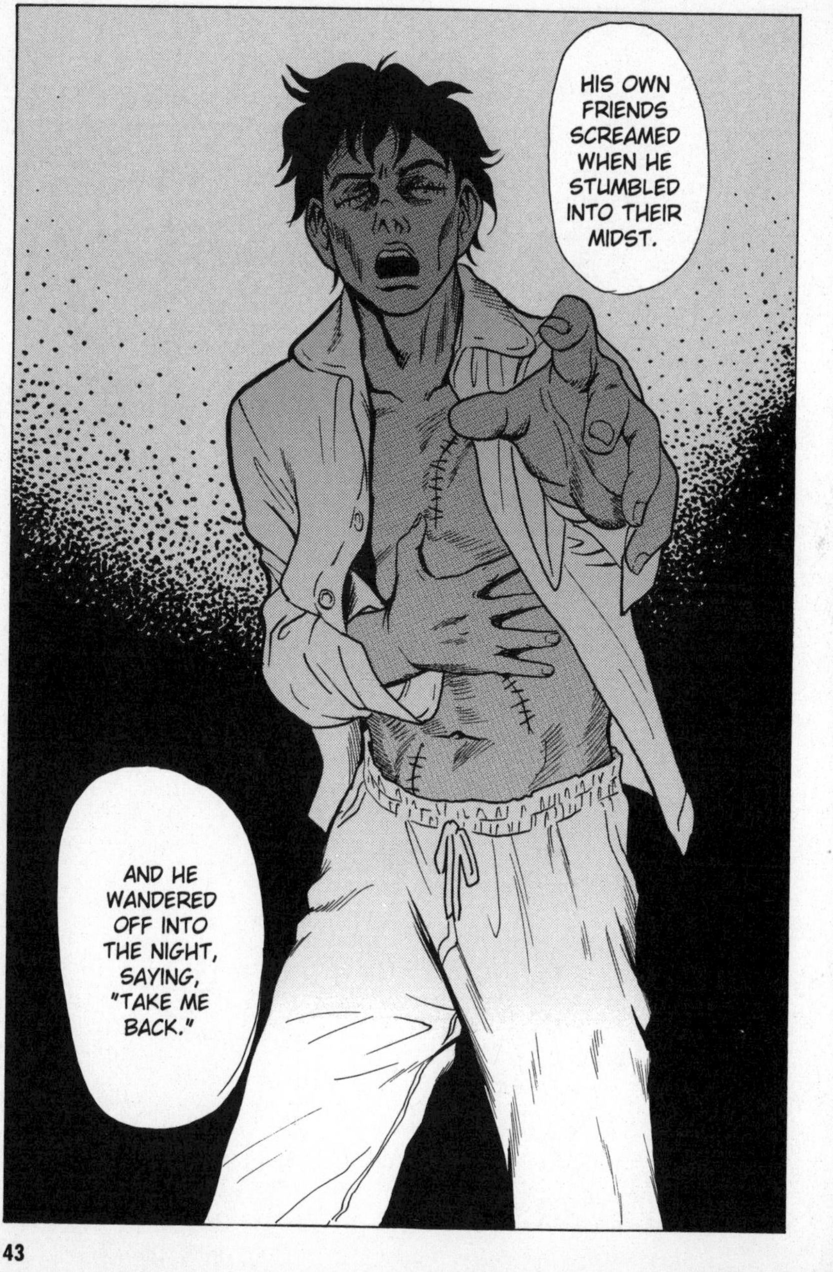
HIS OWN FRIENDS SCREAMED WHEN HE STUMBLED INTO THEIR MIDST.
AND HE WANDERED OFF INTO THE NIGHT, SAYING, "TAKE ME BACK."

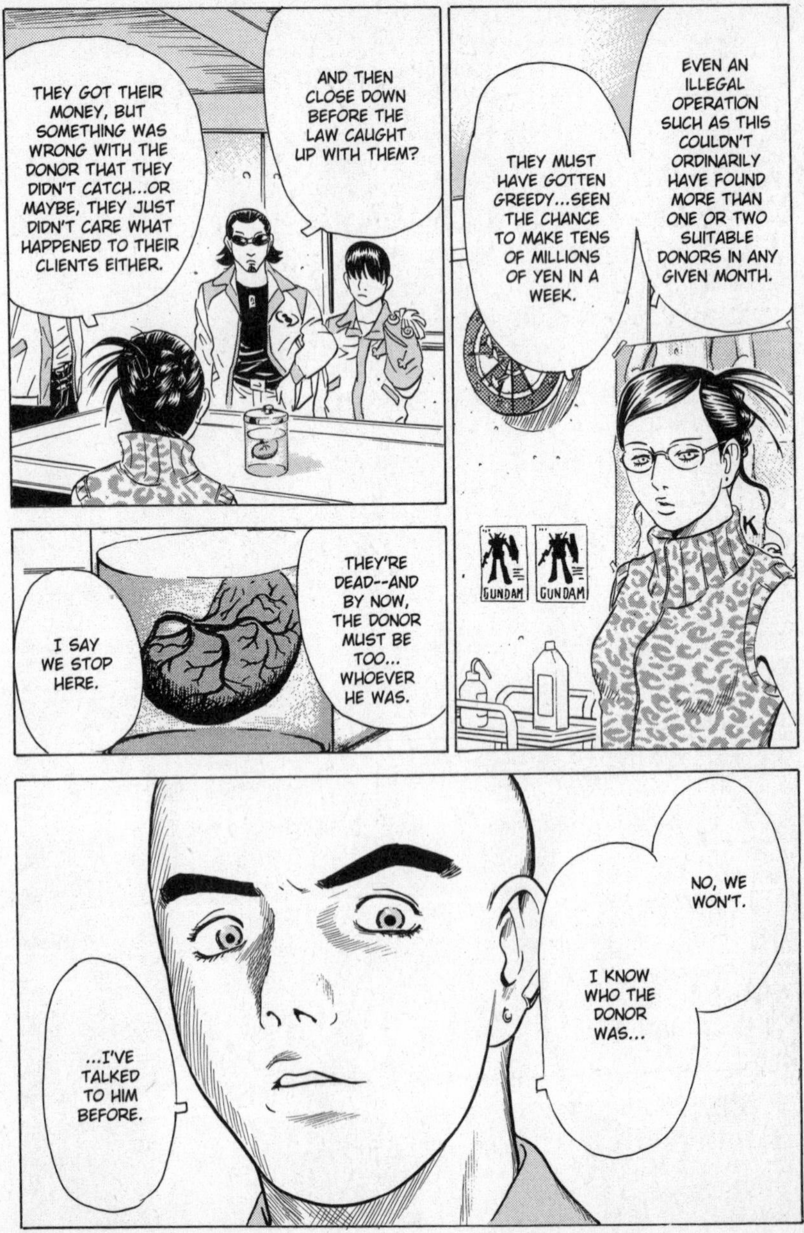
EVEN AN ILLEGAL OPERATION SUCH AS THIS COULDN'T ORDINARILY HAVE FOUND MORE THAN ONE OR TWO SUITABLE DONORS IN ANY GIVEN MONTH.
THEY MUST HAVE GOTTEN GREEDY...SEEN THE CHANCE TO MAKE TENS OF MILLIONS OF YEN IN A WEEK.
GUNDAM
GUNDAM
AND THEN CLOSE DOWN BEFORE THE LAW CAUGHT UP WITH THEM?
THEY GOT THEIR MONEY, BUT SOMETHING WAS WRONG WITH THE DONOR THAT THEY DIDN'T CATCH...OR MAYBE, THEY JUST DIDN'T CARE WHAT HAPPENED TO THEIR CLIENTS EITHER.
THEY'RE DEAD--AND BY NOW, THE DONOR MUST BE TOO... WHOEVER HE WAS.
I SAY WE STOP HERE.
NO, WE WON'T.
I KNOW WHO THE DONOR WAS...
...I'VE TALKED TO HIM BEFORE.

1st delivery: crossing the river—the end

tie
body
a
head
2
1
eyeball

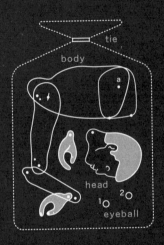

tie
a
b
b
body
bowel

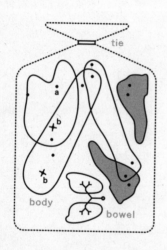

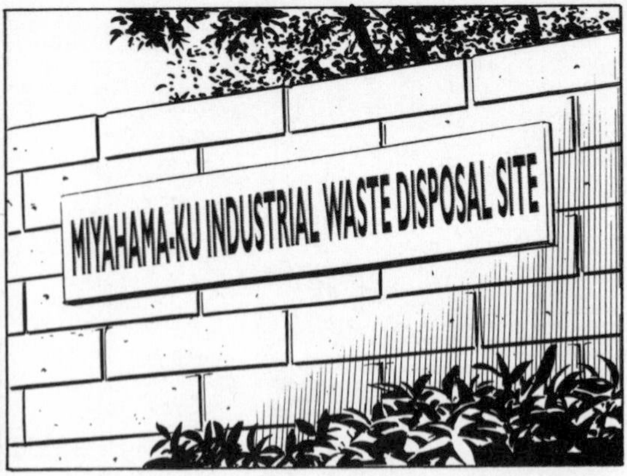
MIYAHAMA-KU INDUSTRIAL WASTE DISPOSAL SITE

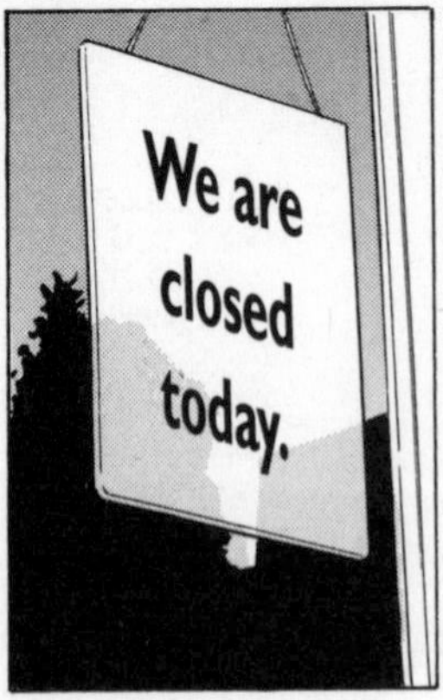
We are closed today.

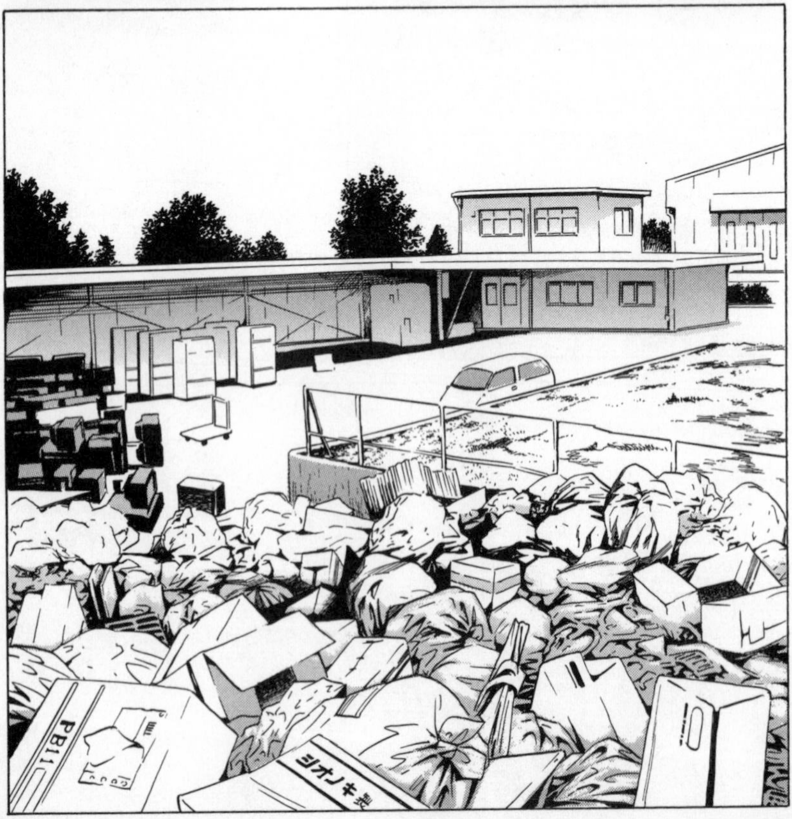
PB11

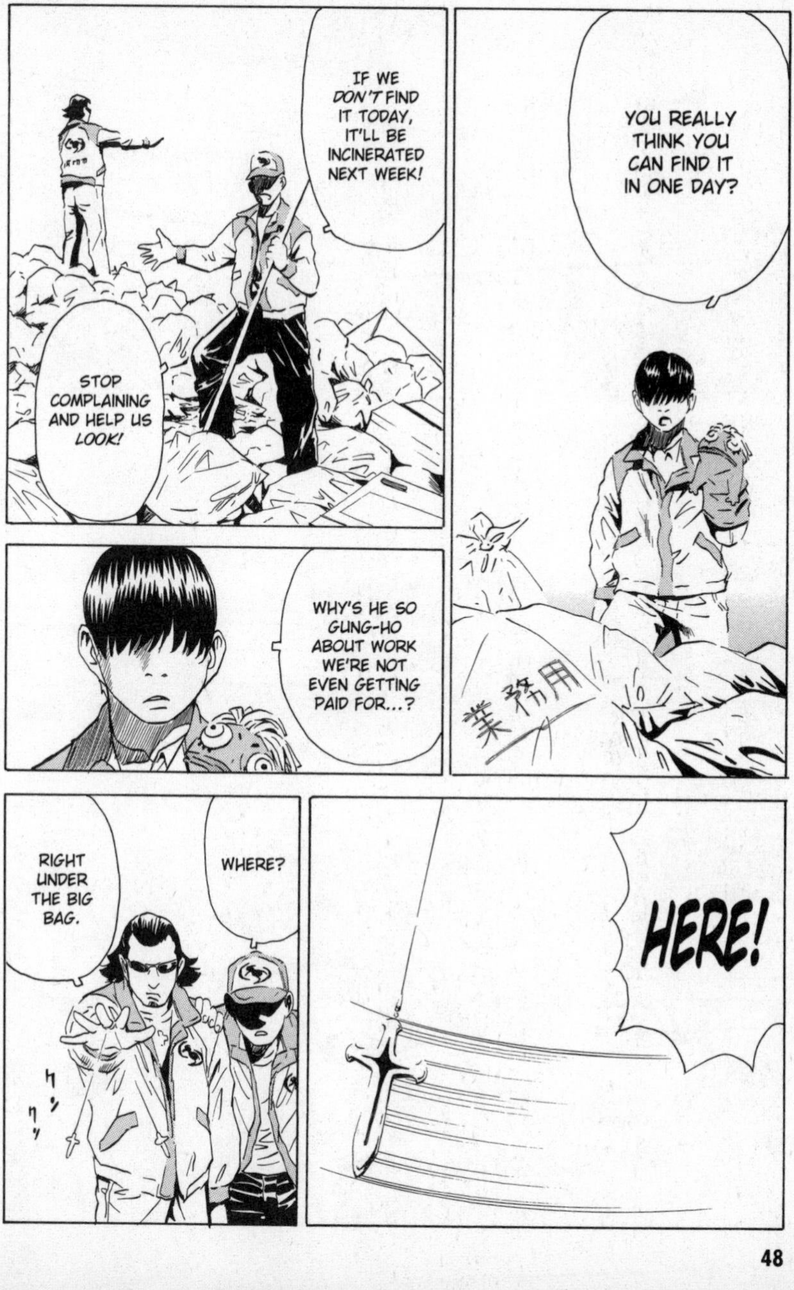

YOU REALLY THINK YOU CAN FIND IT IN ONE DAY?
業務用
IF WE *DON'T* FIND IT TODAY, IT'LL BE INCINERATED NEXT WEEK!
STOP COMPLAINING AND HELP US *LOOK!*
WHY'S HE SO GUNG-HO ABOUT WORK WE'RE NOT EVEN GETTING PAID FOR...?
HERE!
WHERE?
RIGHT UNDER THE BIG BAG.

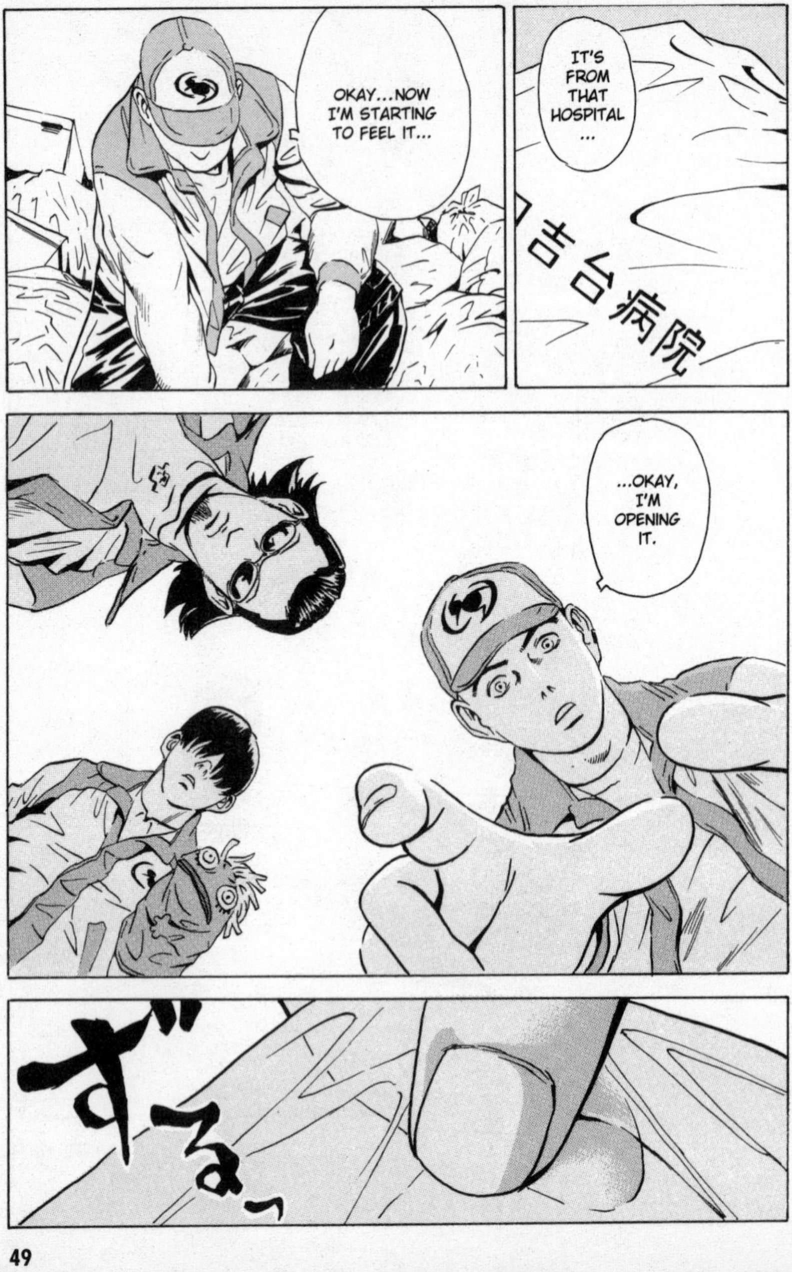
IT'S FROM THAT HOSPITAL ...
吉台病院
OKAY...NOW I'M STARTING TO FEEL IT...
...OKAY, I'M OPENING IT.
ずるっ

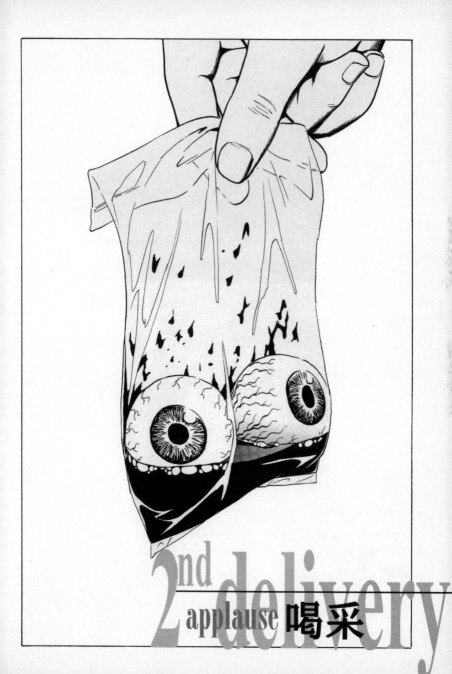

2nd delivery
applause 喝采

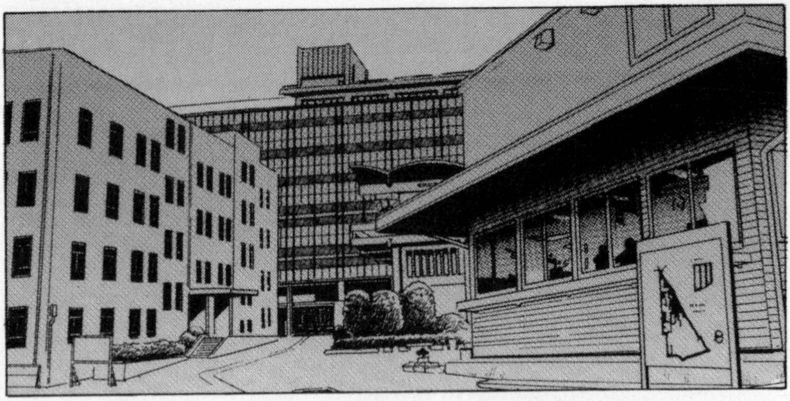

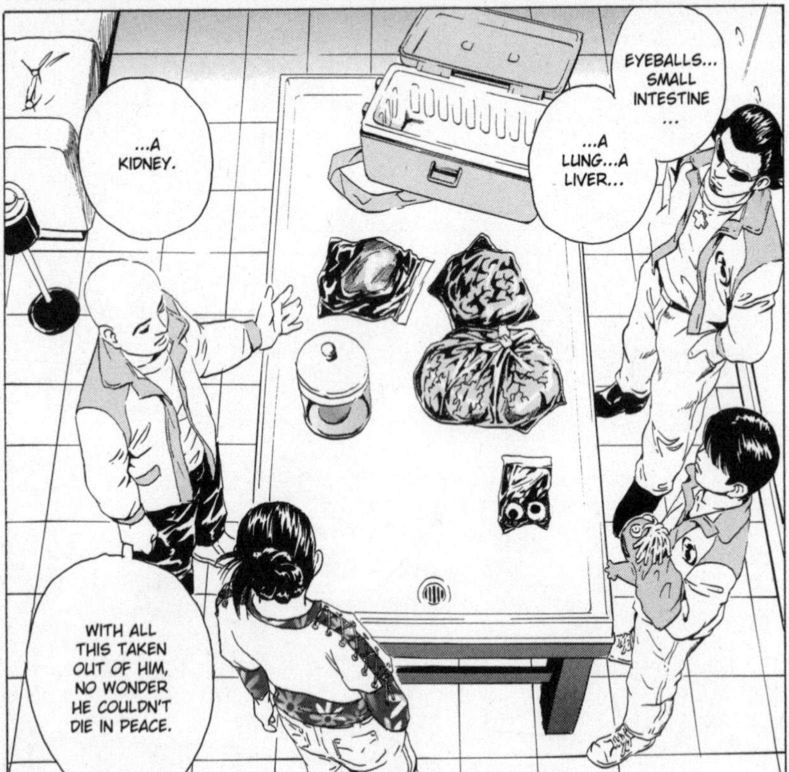

EYEBALLS... SMALL INTESTINE ...
...A LUNG...A LIVER...
...A KIDNEY.
WITH ALL THIS TAKEN OUT OF HIM, NO WONDER HE COULDN'T DIE IN PEACE.

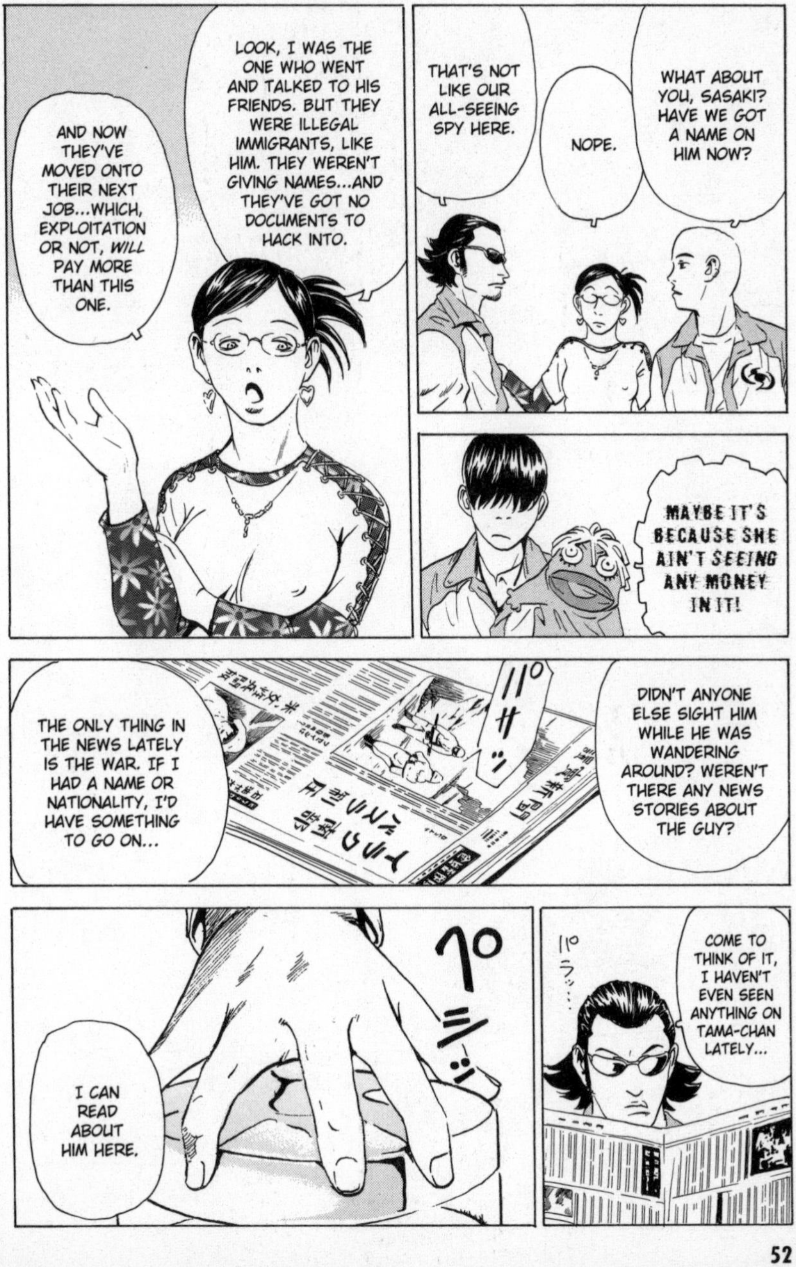
WHAT ABOUT YOU, SASAKI? HAVE WE GOT A NAME ON HIM NOW?
NOPE.
THAT'S NOT LIKE OUR ALL-SEEING SPY HERE.
MAYBE IT'S BECAUSE SHE AIN'T *SEEING* ANY MONEY IN IT!
LOOK, I WAS THE ONE WHO WENT AND TALKED TO HIS FRIENDS. BUT THEY WERE ILLEGAL IMMIGRANTS, LIKE HIM. THEY WEREN'T GIVING NAMES...AND THEY'VE GOT NO DOCUMENTS TO HACK INTO.
AND NOW THEY'VE MOVED ONTO THEIR NEXT JOB...WHICH, EXPLOITATION OR NOT, *WILL* PAY MORE THAN THIS ONE.
DIDN'T ANYONE ELSE SIGHT HIM WHILE HE WAS WANDERING AROUND? WEREN'T THERE ANY NEWS STORIES ABOUT THE GUY?
バサッ
THE ONLY THING IN THE NEWS LATELY IS THE WAR. IF I HAD A NAME OR NATIONALITY, I'D HAVE SOMETHING TO GO ON...
パラッ…
COME TO THINK OF IT, I HAVEN'T EVEN SEEN ANYTHING ON TAMA-CHAN LATELY...
パシッ
I CAN READ ABOUT HIM HERE.

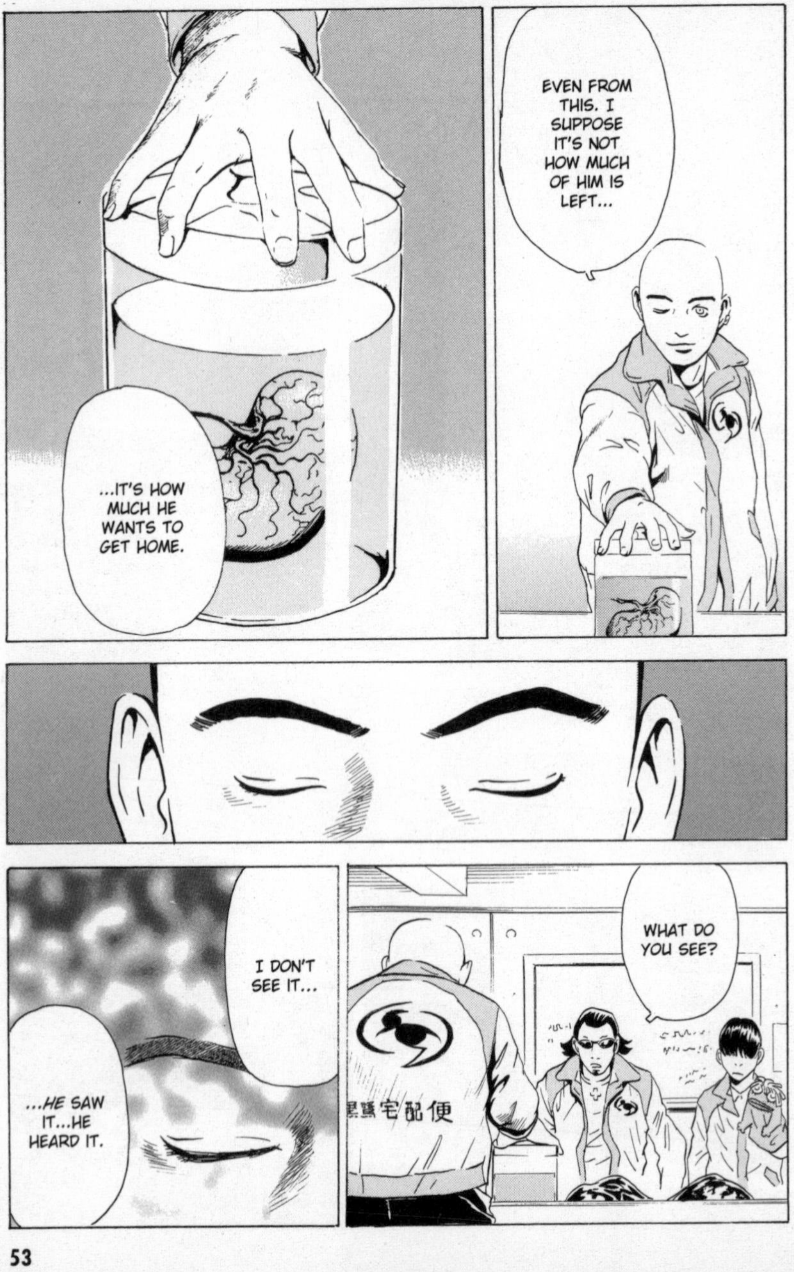
EVEN FROM THIS. I SUPPOSE IT'S NOT HOW MUCH OF HIM IS LEFT...
...IT'S HOW MUCH HE WANTS TO GET HOME.
WHAT DO YOU SEE?
黒鷺宅配便
I DON'T SEE IT...
...*HE* SAW IT...HE HEARD IT.

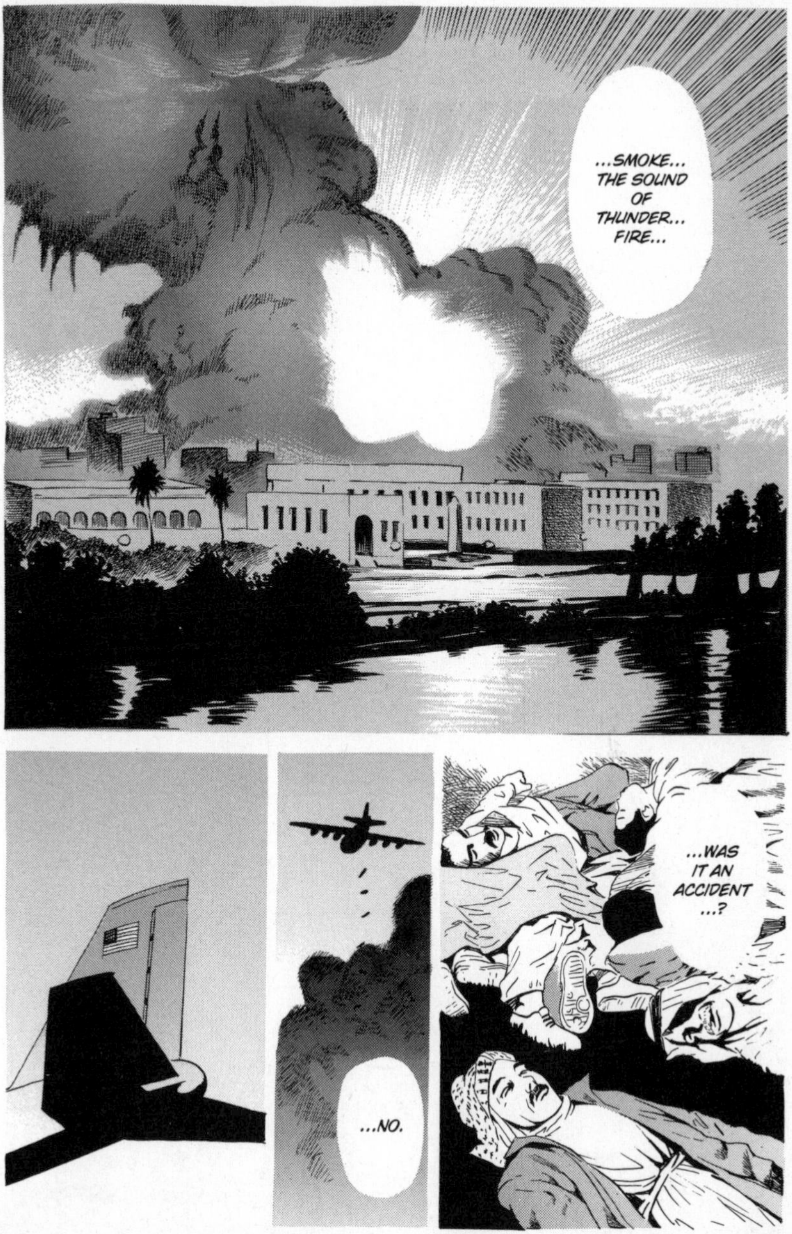
...SMOKE... THE SOUND OF THUNDER... FIRE...
...WAS IT AN ACCIDENT ...?
...NO.

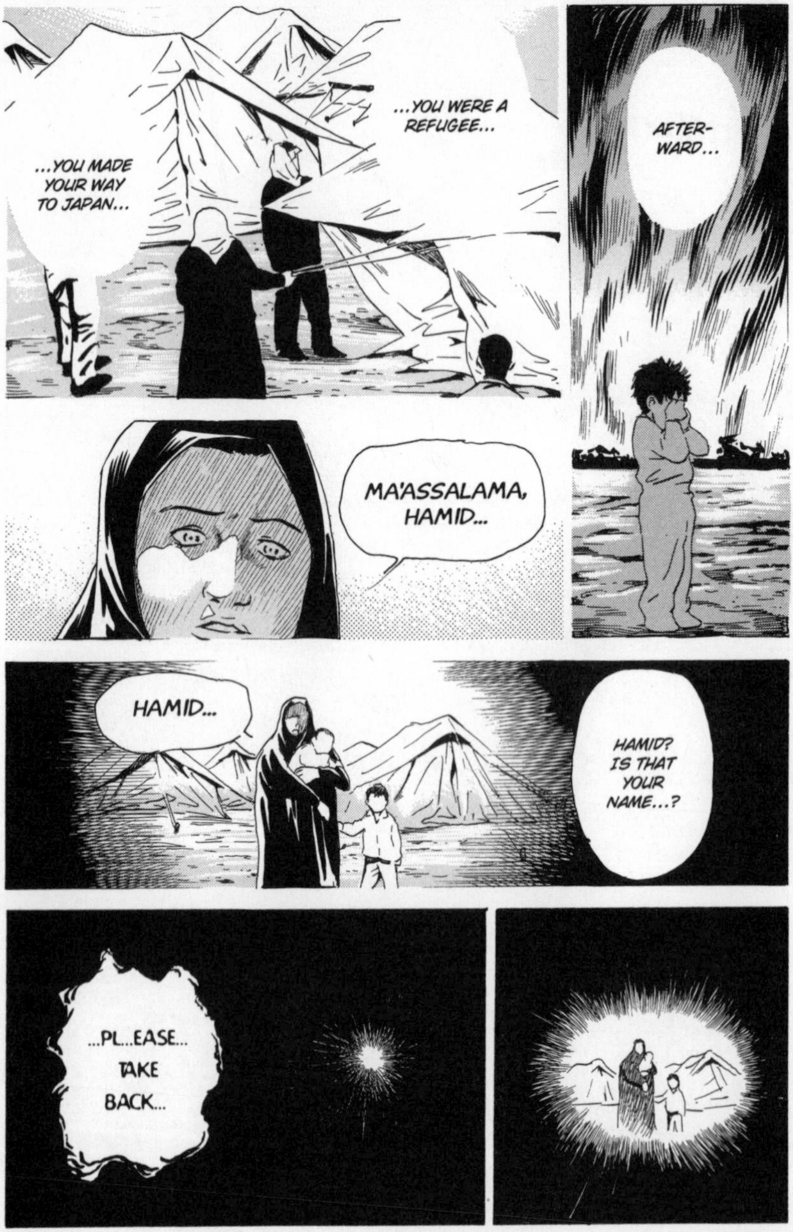
AFTER-WARD...
...YOU WERE A REFUGEE...
...YOU MADE YOUR WAY TO JAPAN...
MA'ASSALAMA, HAMID...
HAMID? IS THAT YOUR NAME...?
HAMID...
...PL...EASE... TAKE BACK...

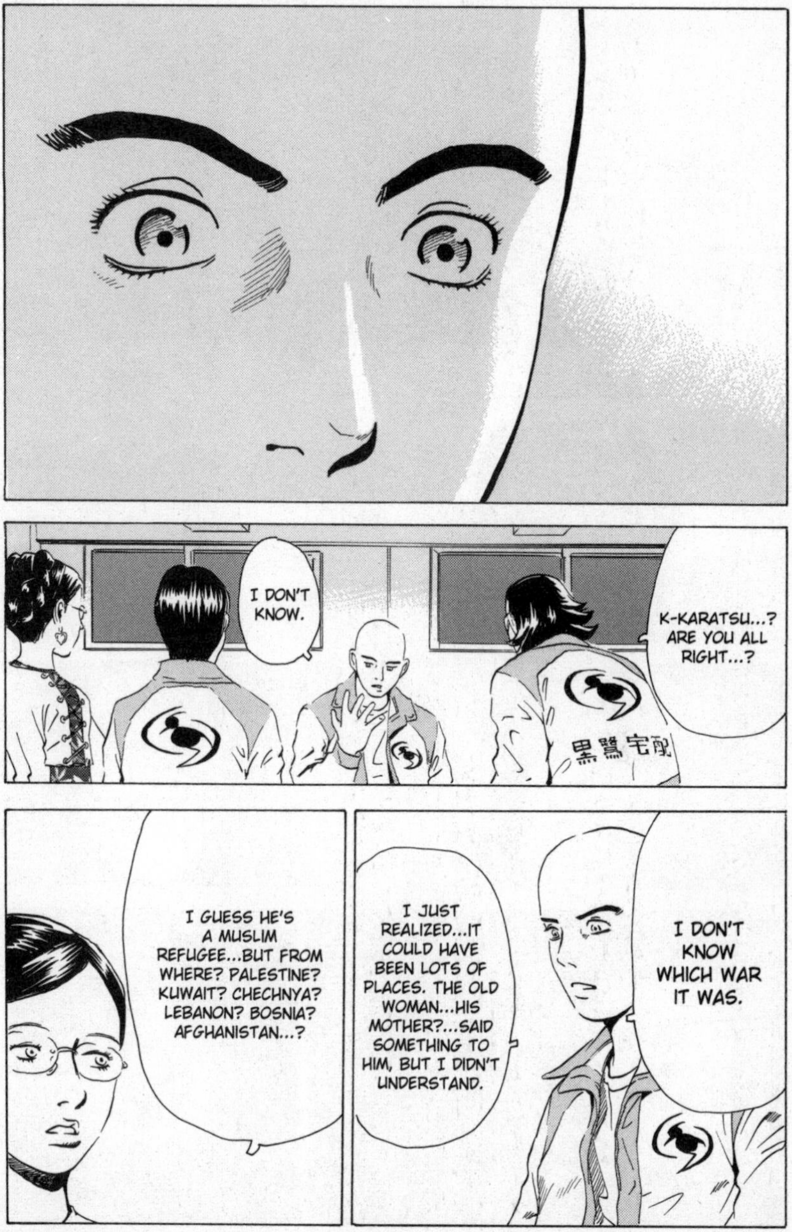
K-KARATSU...? ARE YOU ALL RIGHT...?
I DON'T KNOW.
黒鷺宅配
I DON'T KNOW WHICH WAR IT WAS.
I JUST REALIZED...IT COULD HAVE BEEN LOTS OF PLACES. THE OLD WOMAN...HIS MOTHER?...SAID SOMETHING TO HIM, BUT I DIDN'T UNDERSTAND.
I GUESS HE'S A MUSLIM REFUGEE...BUT FROM WHERE? PALESTINE? KUWAIT? CHECHNYA? LEBANON? BOSNIA? AFGHANISTAN...?

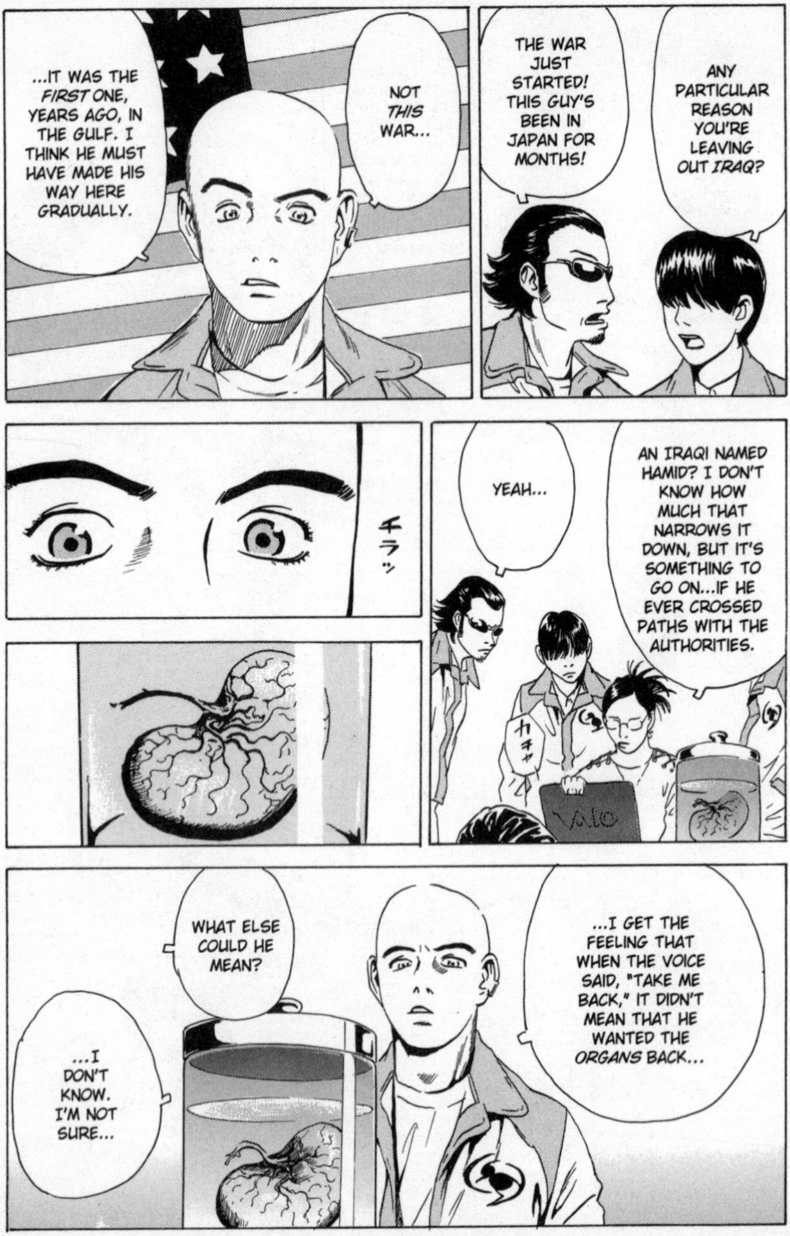
ANY PARTICULAR REASON YOU'RE LEAVING OUT *IRAQ*?
THE WAR JUST STARTED! THIS GUY'S BEEN IN JAPAN FOR MONTHS!
NOT *THIS* WAR...
...IT WAS THE *FIRST* ONE, YEARS AGO, IN THE GULF. I THINK HE MUST HAVE MADE HIS WAY HERE GRADUALLY.
AN IRAQI NAMED HAMID? I DON'T KNOW HOW MUCH THAT NARROWS IT DOWN, BUT IT'S SOMETHING TO GO ON...IF HE EVER CROSSED PATHS WITH THE AUTHORITIES.
YEAH...
カチャ
VAIO
チラッ
...I GET THE FEELING THAT WHEN THE VOICE SAID, "TAKE ME BACK," IT DIDN'T MEAN THAT HE WANTED THE *ORGANS* BACK...
WHAT ELSE COULD HE MEAN?
...I DON'T KNOW. I'M NOT SURE...

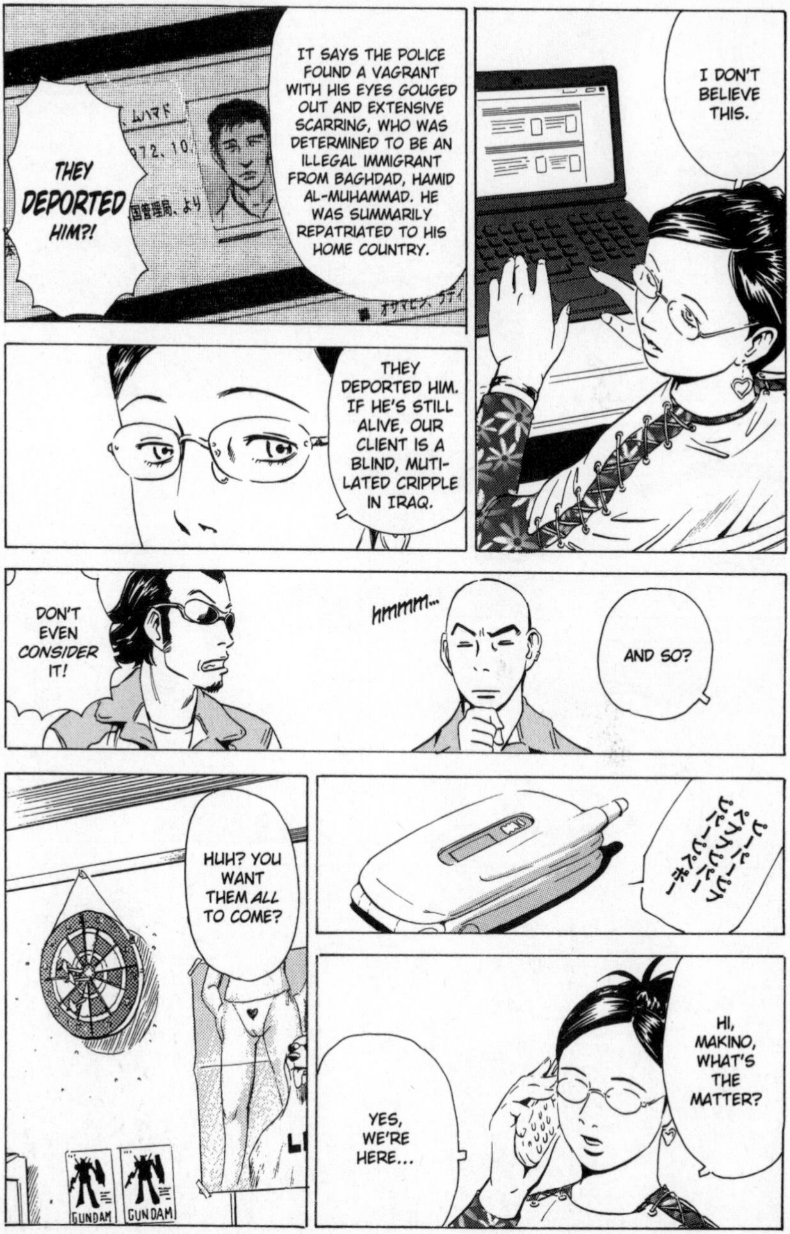

I DON'T BELIEVE THIS.
IT SAYS THE POLICE FOUND A VAGRANT WITH HIS EYES GOUGED OUT AND EXTENSIVE SCARRING, WHO WAS DETERMINED TO BE AN ILLEGAL IMMIGRANT FROM BAGHDAD, HAMID AL-MUHAMMAD. HE WAS SUMMARILY REPATRIATED TO HIS HOME COUNTRY.
THEY DEPORTED HIM?!
THEY DEPORTED HIM. IF HE'S STILL ALIVE, OUR CLIENT IS A BLIND, MUTI-LATED CRIPPLE IN IRAQ.
AND SO?
hmmm...
DON'T EVEN CONSIDER IT!
ピーパーピペ
ペププピパー
ピパーピペポー
HI, MAKINO, WHAT'S THE MATTER?
YES, WE'RE HERE...
HUH? YOU WANT THEM ALL TO COME?
GUNDAM
GUNDAM

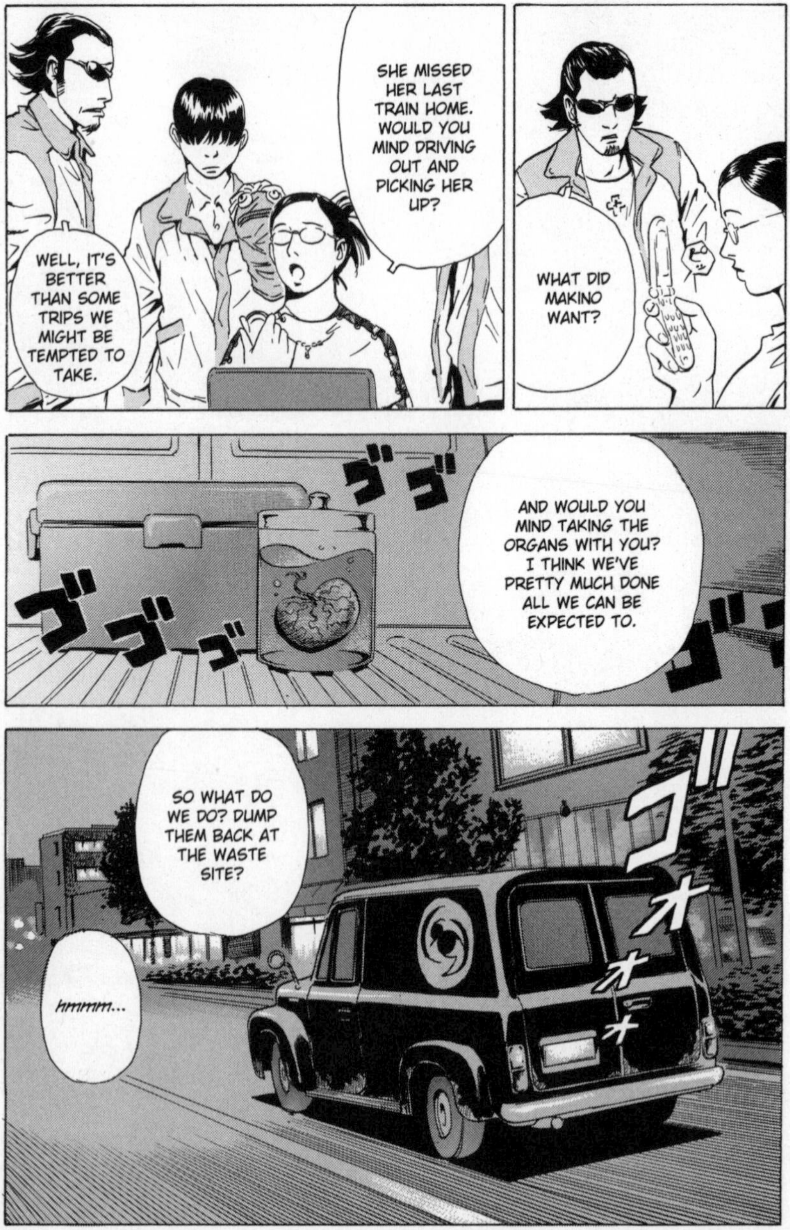
WHAT DID MAKINO WANT?
SHE MISSED HER LAST TRAIN HOME. WOULD YOU MIND DRIVING OUT AND PICKING HER UP?
WELL, IT'S BETTER THAN SOME TRIPS WE MIGHT BE TEMPTED TO TAKE.
AND WOULD YOU MIND TAKING THE ORGANS WITH YOU? I THINK WE'VE PRETTY MUCH DONE ALL WE CAN BE EXPECTED TO.
ゴゴ
ゴゴゴ
SO WHAT DO WE DO? DUMP THEM BACK AT THE WASTE SITE?
hmmm...
ゴオオオ

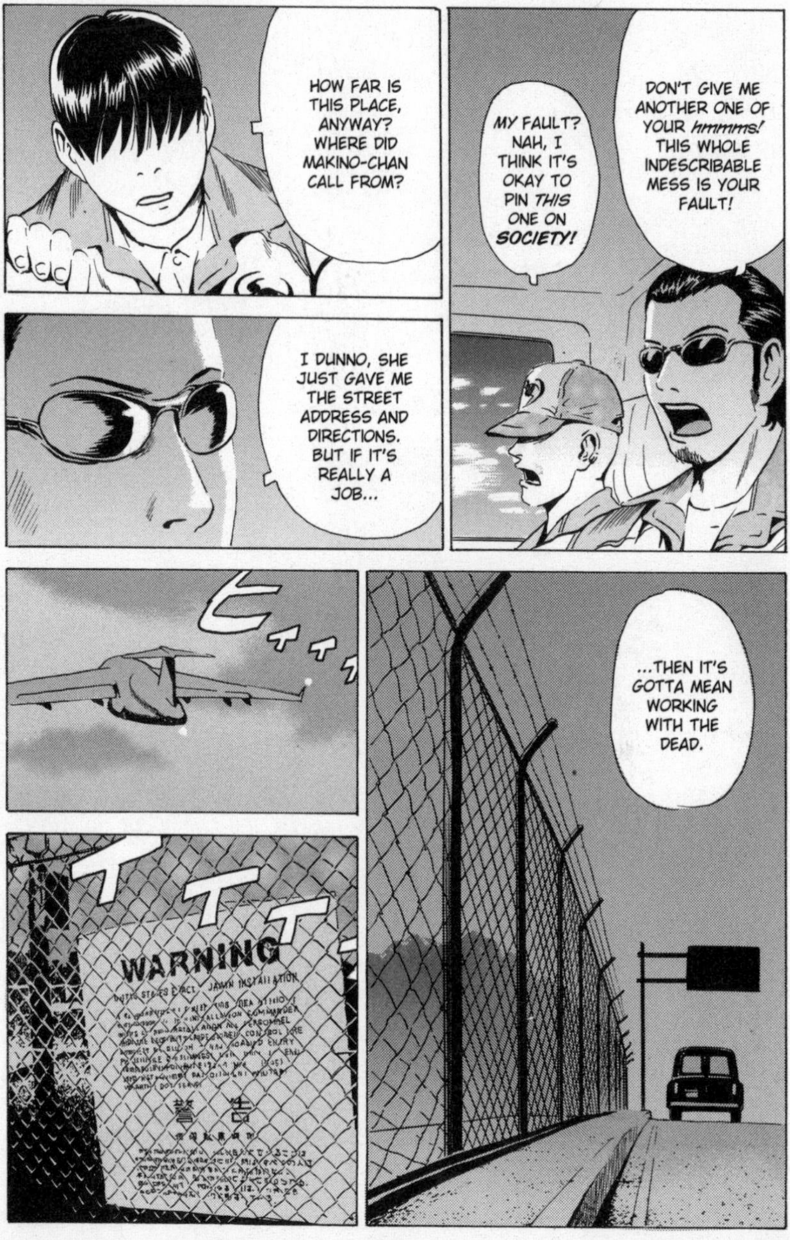

DON'T GIVE ME ANOTHER ONE OF YOUR *hmmms!* THIS WHOLE INDESCRIBABLE MESS IS YOUR FAULT!
MY FAULT? NAH, I THINK IT'S OKAY TO PIN *THIS* ONE ON ***SOCIETY!***
HOW FAR IS THIS PLACE, ANYWAY? WHERE DID MAKINO-CHAN CALL FROM?
I DUNNO, SHE JUST GAVE ME THE STREET ADDRESS AND DIRECTIONS. BUT IF IT'S REALLY A JOB...
...THEN IT'S GOTTA MEAN WORKING WITH THE DEAD.
WARNING

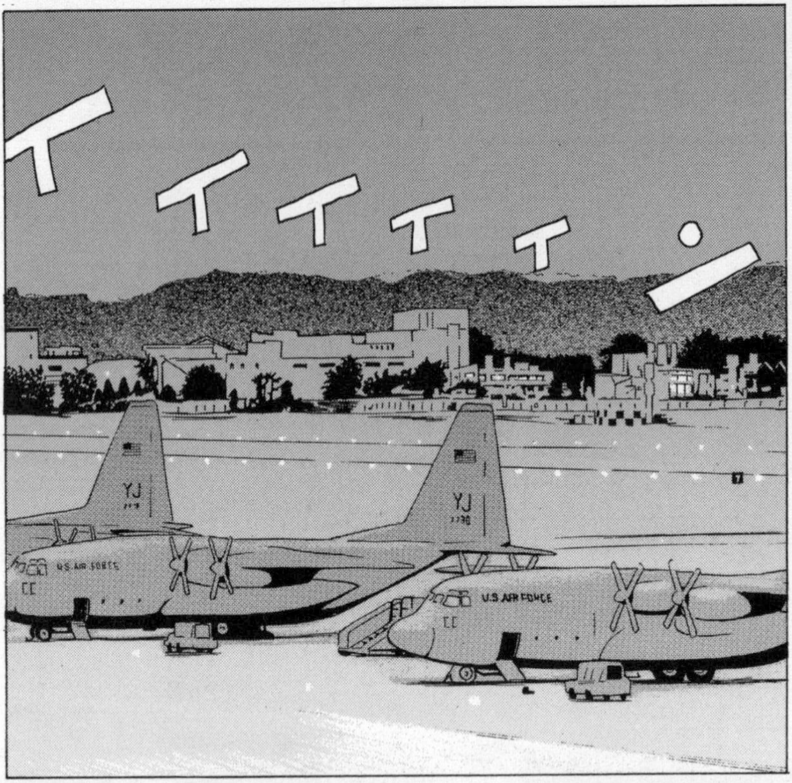
イイイイイン
YJ
U.S. AIR FORCE
YJ
U.S. AIR FORCE
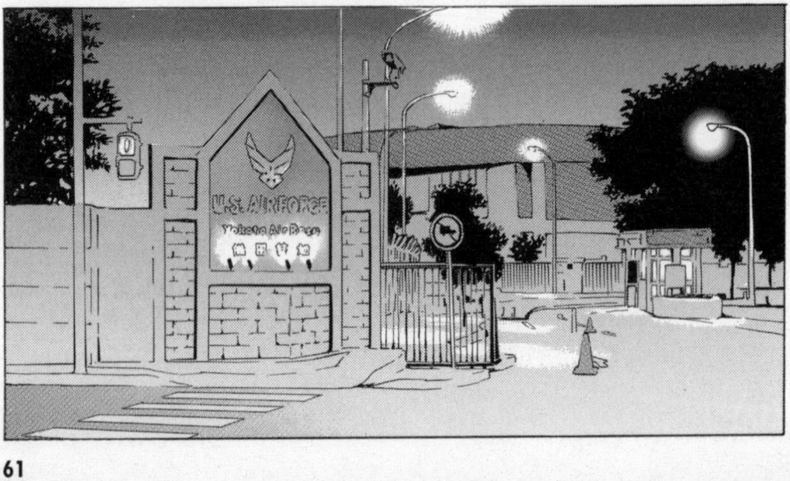
U.S. AIR FORCE
Yokota Air Base
横田基地

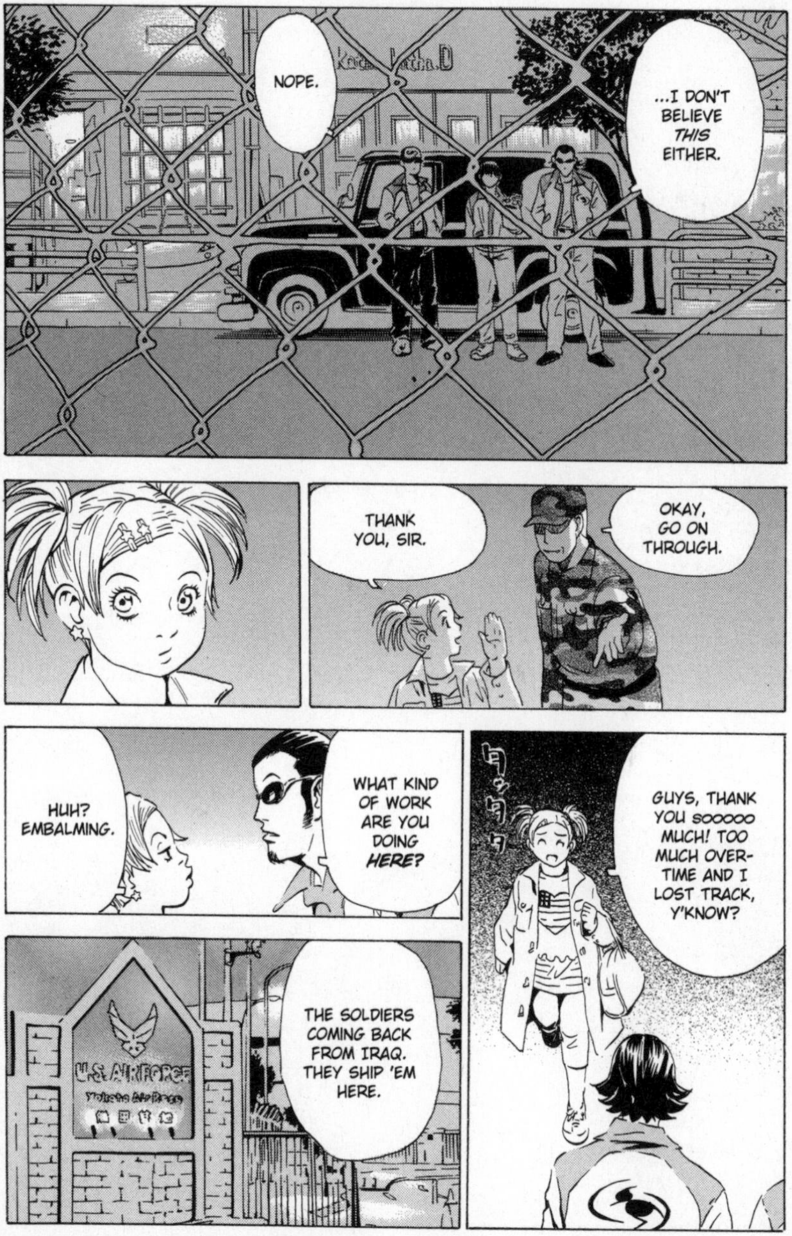
...I DON'T BELIEVE *THIS* EITHER.
NOPE.
OKAY, GO ON THROUGH.
THANK YOU, SIR.
GUYS, THANK YOU SOOOOO MUCH! TOO MUCH OVER-TIME AND I LOST TRACK, Y'KNOW?
WHAT KIND OF WORK ARE YOU DOING *HERE*?
HUH? EMBALMING.
THE SOLDIERS COMING BACK FROM IRAQ. THEY SHIP 'EM HERE.
U.S. AIR FORCE

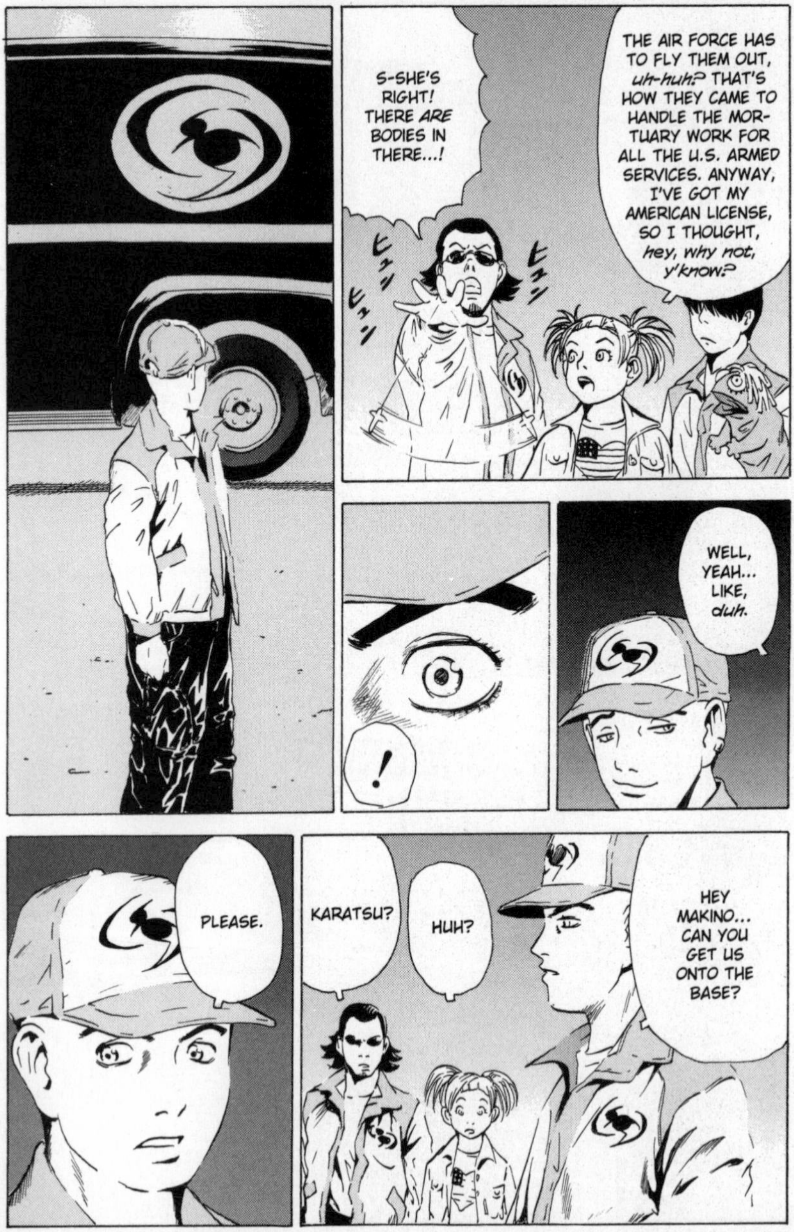

THE AIR FORCE HAS TO FLY THEM OUT, *uh-huh?* THAT'S HOW THEY CAME TO HANDLE THE MORTUARY WORK FOR ALL THE U.S. ARMED SERVICES. ANYWAY, I'VE GOT MY AMERICAN LICENSE, SO I THOUGHT, *hey, why not, y'know?*
S-SHE'S RIGHT! THERE *ARE* BODIES IN THERE...!
ヒュン
ヒュン
ヒュン
WELL, YEAH... LIKE, *duh.*
!
HEY MAKINO... CAN YOU GET US ONTO THE BASE?
HUH?
KARATSU?
PLEASE.

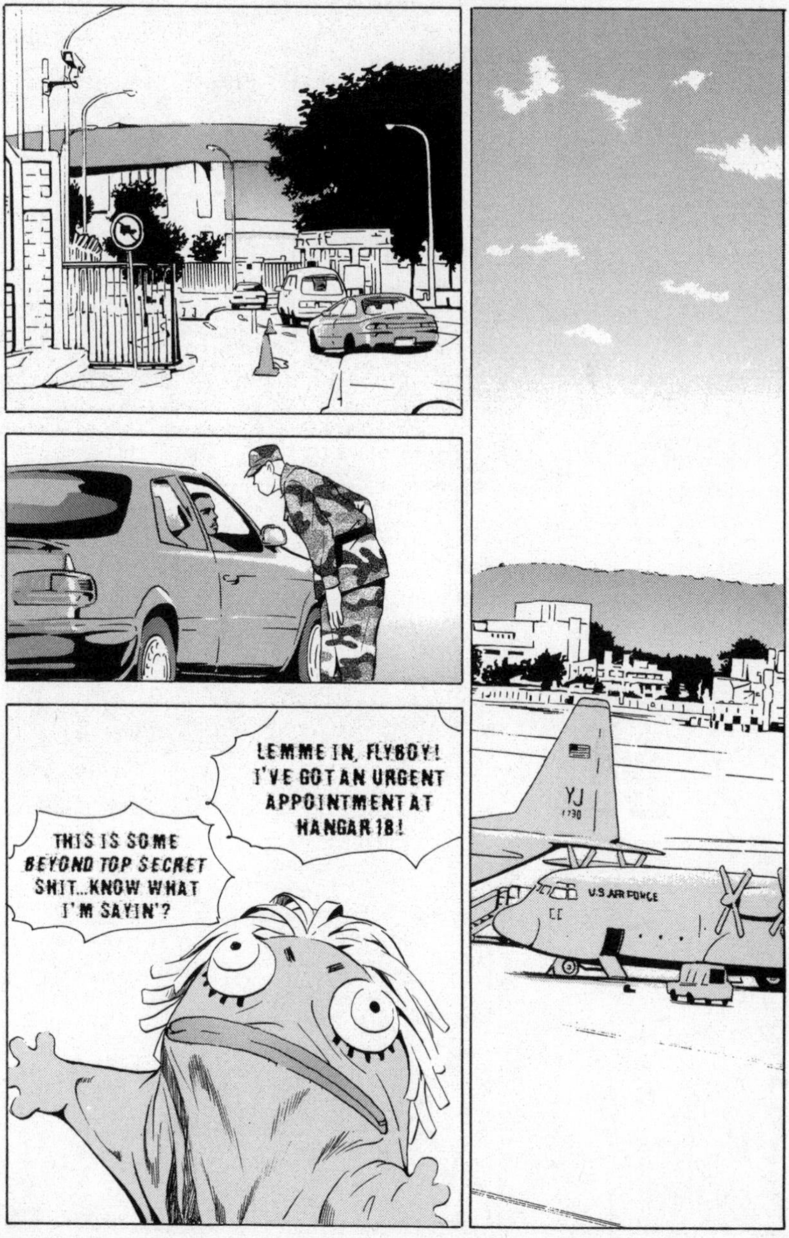
YJ
U.S AIR FORCE
LEMME IN, FLYBOY! I'VE GOT AN URGENT APPOINTMENT AT HANGAR 18!
THIS IS SOME *BEYOND TOP SECRET* SHIT...KNOW WHAT I'M SAYIN'?

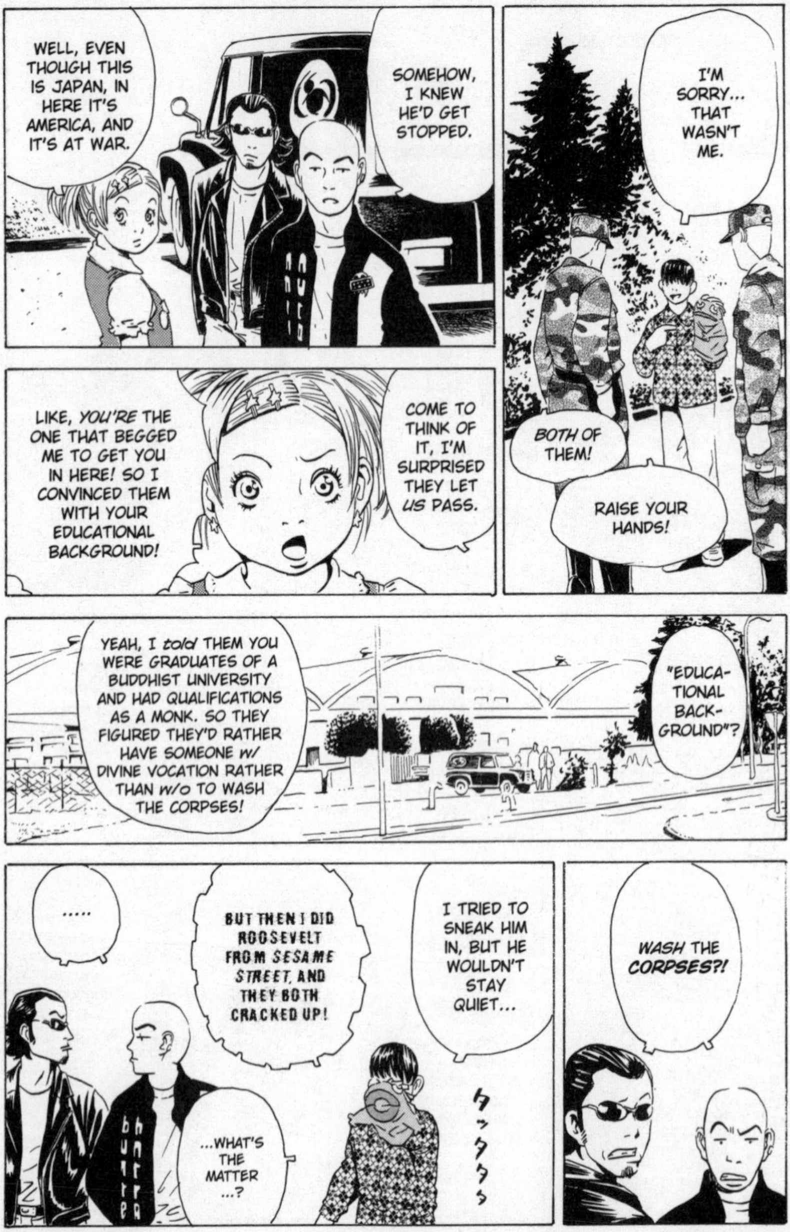
I'M SORRY... THAT WASN'T ME.
BOTH OF THEM!
RAISE YOUR HANDS!
SOMEHOW, I KNEW HE'D GET STOPPED.
WELL, EVEN THOUGH THIS IS JAPAN, IN HERE IT'S AMERICA, AND IT'S AT WAR.
COME TO THINK OF IT, I'M SURPRISED THEY LET *US* PASS.
LIKE, *YOU'RE* THE ONE THAT BEGGED ME TO GET YOU IN HERE! SO I CONVINCED THEM WITH YOUR EDUCATIONAL BACKGROUND!
"EDUCATIONAL BACKGROUND"?
YEAH, I *told* THEM YOU WERE GRADUATES OF A BUDDHIST UNIVERSITY AND HAD QUALIFICATIONS AS A MONK. SO THEY FIGURED THEY'D RATHER HAVE SOMEONE *w/* DIVINE VOCATION RATHER THAN *w/o* TO WASH THE CORPSES!
WASH THE *CORPSES?!*
I TRIED TO SNEAK HIM IN, BUT HE WOULDN'T STAY QUIET...
タッタタタ
BUT THEN I DID ROOSEVELT FROM *SESAME STREET*, AND THEY BOTH CRACKED UP!
.....
...WHAT'S THE MATTER ...?

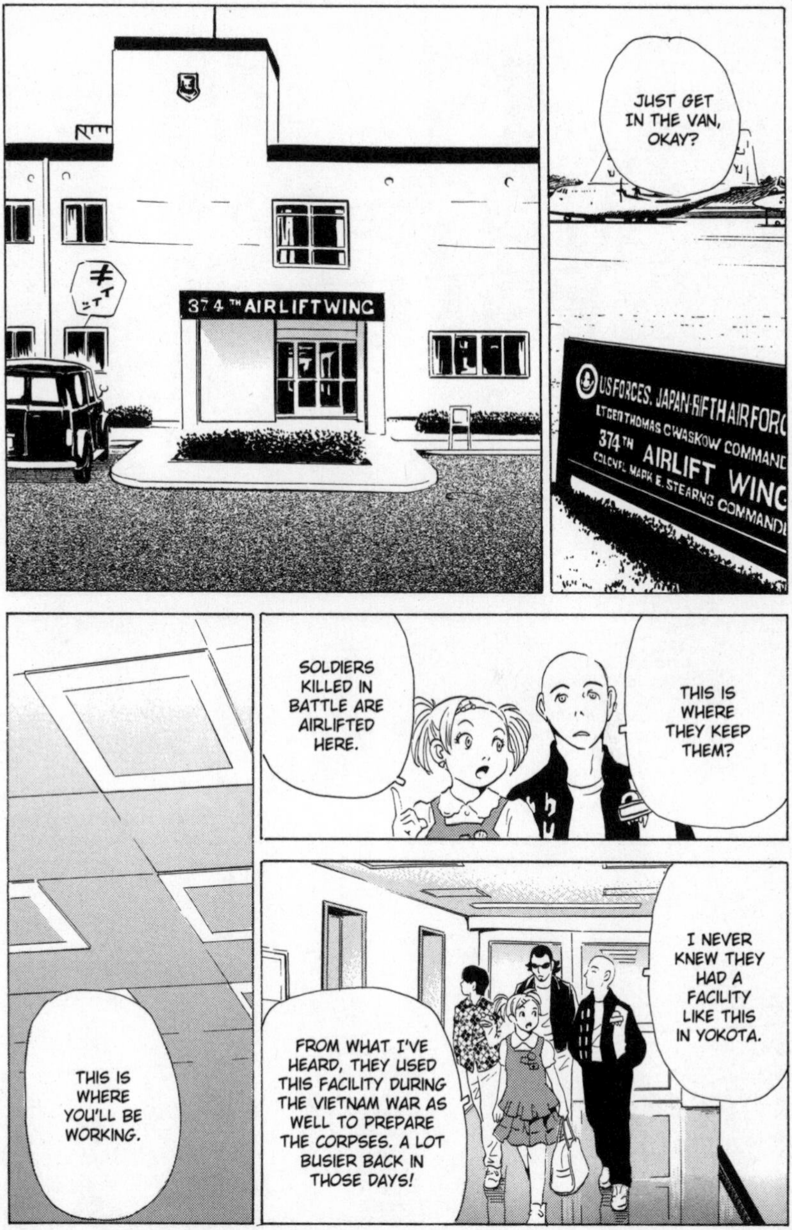
JUST GET IN THE VAN, OKAY?
US FORCES, JAPAN-FIFTH AIR FORC
LT GEN THOMAS C WASKOW COMMAND
374TH AIRLIFT WING
COLONEL MARK E. STEARNS COMMAND
374TH AIRLIFT WING
THIS IS WHERE THEY KEEP THEM?
SOLDIERS KILLED IN BATTLE ARE AIRLIFTED HERE.
I NEVER KNEW THEY HAD A FACILITY LIKE THIS IN YOKOTA.
FROM WHAT I'VE HEARD, THEY USED THIS FACILITY DURING THE VIETNAM WAR AS WELL TO PREPARE THE CORPSES. A LOT BUSIER BACK IN THOSE DAYS!
THIS IS WHERE YOU'LL BE WORKING.

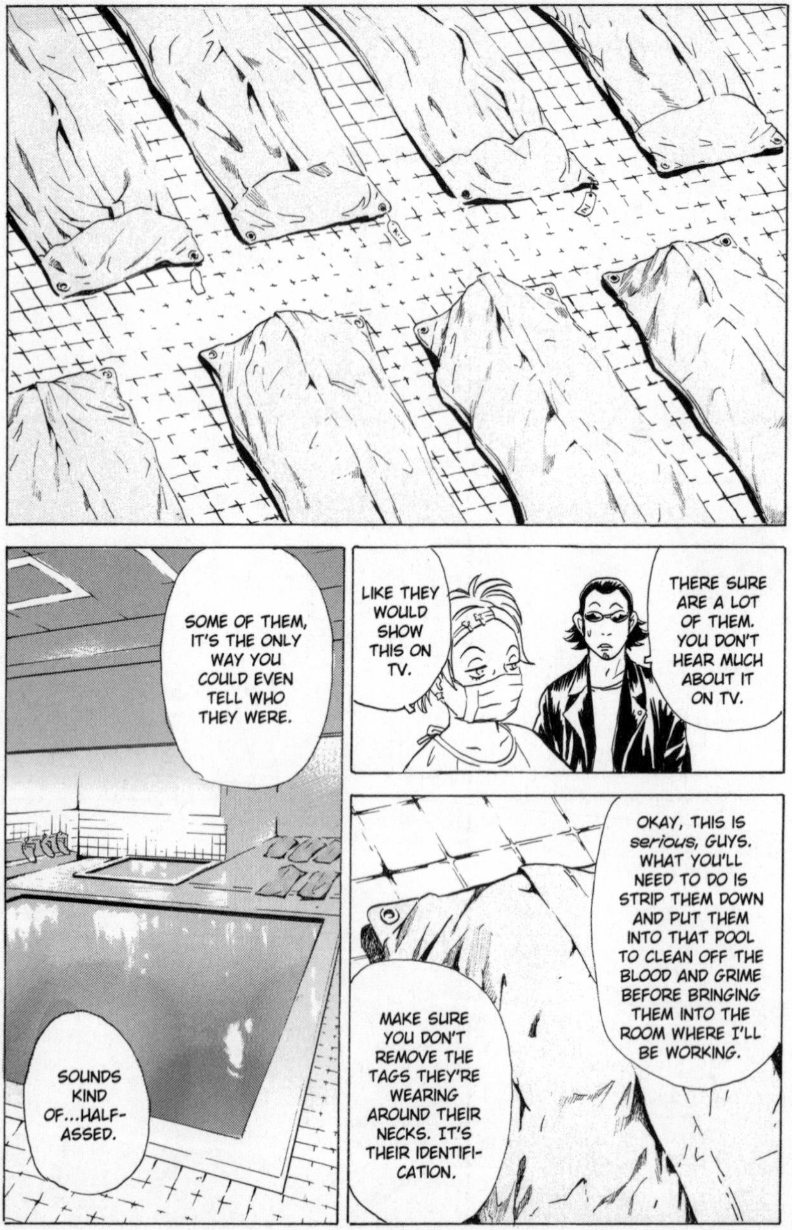
THERE SURE ARE A LOT OF THEM. YOU DON'T HEAR MUCH ABOUT IT ON TV.
LIKE THEY WOULD SHOW THIS ON TV.
OKAY, THIS IS *serious*, GUYS. WHAT YOU'LL NEED TO DO IS STRIP THEM DOWN AND PUT THEM INTO THAT POOL TO CLEAN OFF THE BLOOD AND GRIME BEFORE BRINGING THEM INTO THE ROOM WHERE I'LL BE WORKING.
MAKE SURE YOU DON'T REMOVE THE TAGS THEY'RE WEARING AROUND THEIR NECKS. IT'S THEIR IDENTIFI-CATION.
SOME OF THEM, IT'S THE ONLY WAY YOU COULD EVEN TELL WHO THEY WERE.
SOUNDS KIND OF...HALF-ASSED.

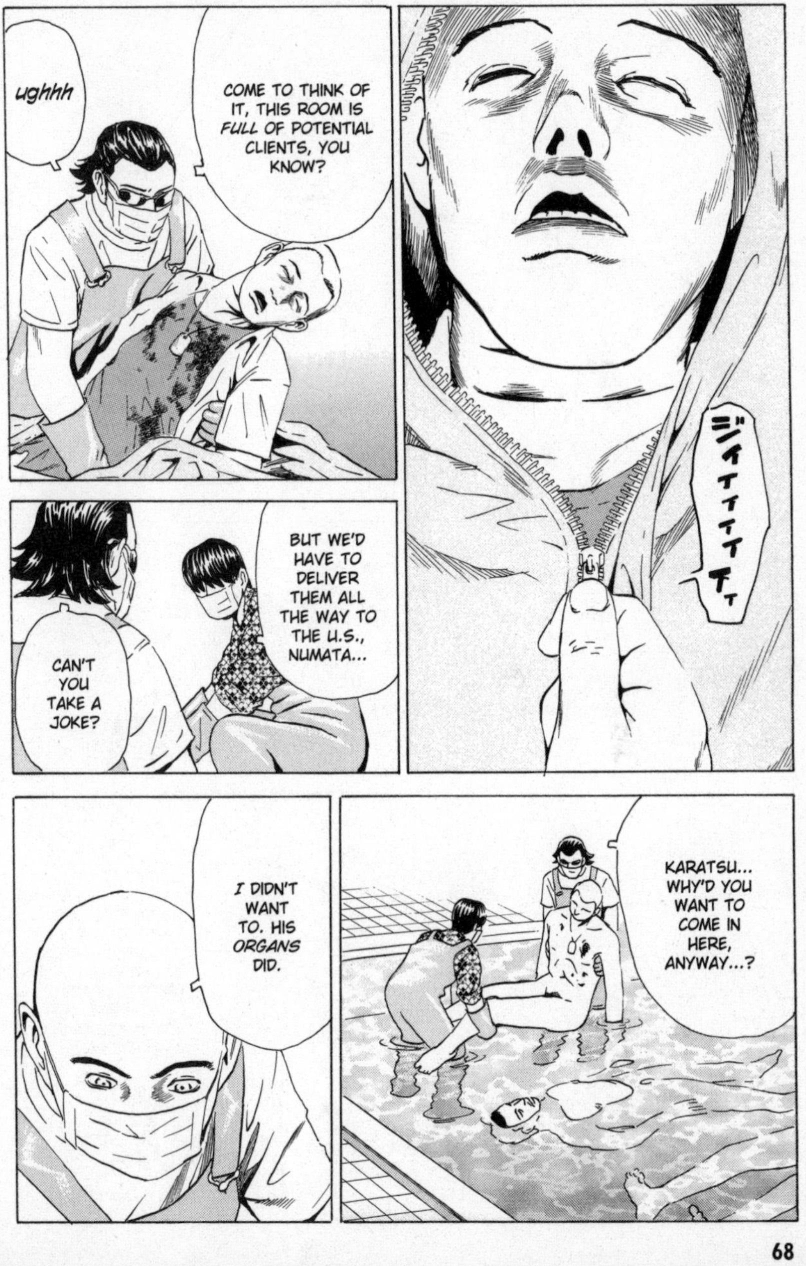
ジイイイイイイイィ
COME TO THINK OF IT, THIS ROOM IS *FULL OF POTENTIAL* CLIENTS, YOU KNOW?
ughhh
BUT WE'D HAVE TO DELIVER THEM ALL THE WAY TO THE U.S., NUMATA...
CAN'T YOU TAKE A JOKE?
KARATSU... WHY'D YOU WANT TO COME IN HERE, ANYWAY...?
I DIDN'T WANT TO. HIS *ORGANS* DID.

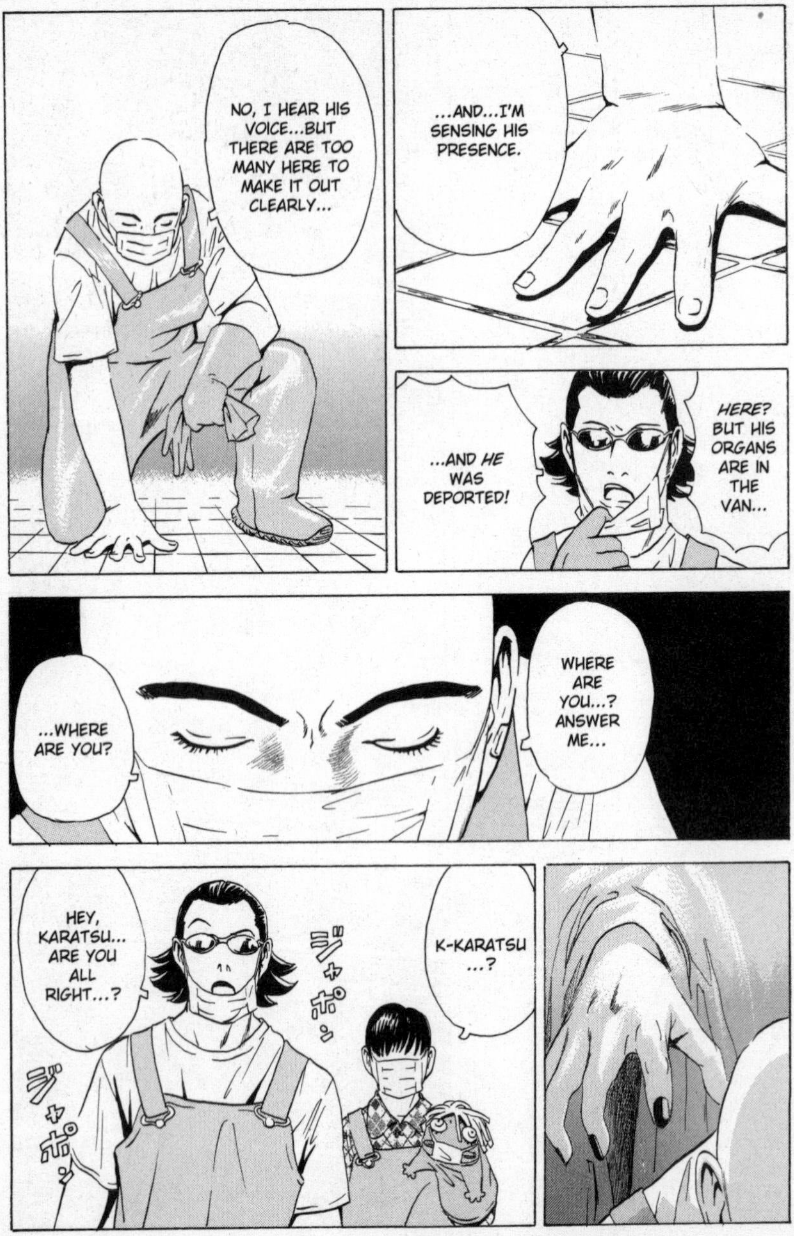
...AND...I'M SENSING HIS PRESENCE.
HERE? BUT HIS ORGANS ARE IN THE VAN...
...AND HE WAS DEPORTED!
NO, I HEAR HIS VOICE...BUT THERE ARE TOO MANY HERE TO MAKE IT OUT CLEARLY...
WHERE ARE YOU...? ANSWER ME...
...WHERE ARE YOU?
K-KARATSU ...?
ジャポン
HEY, KARATSU... ARE YOU ALL RIGHT...?
ジャポン

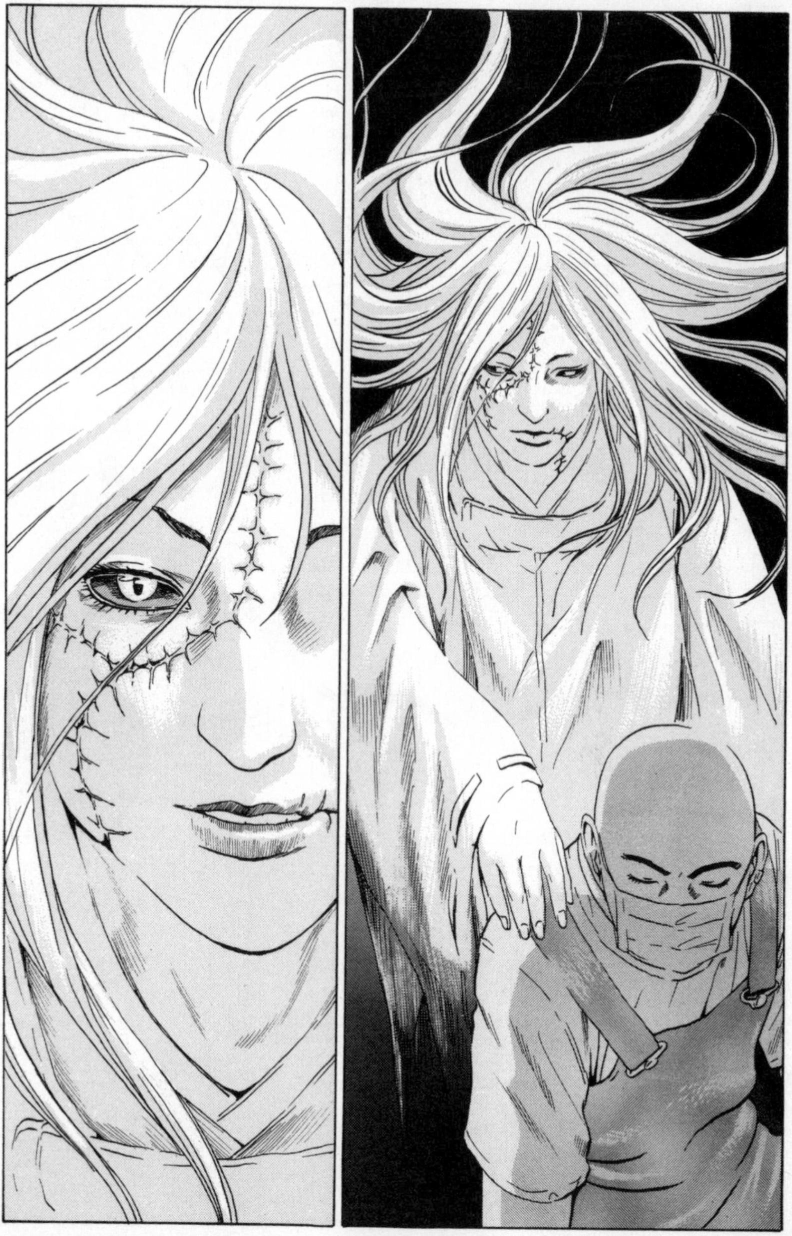

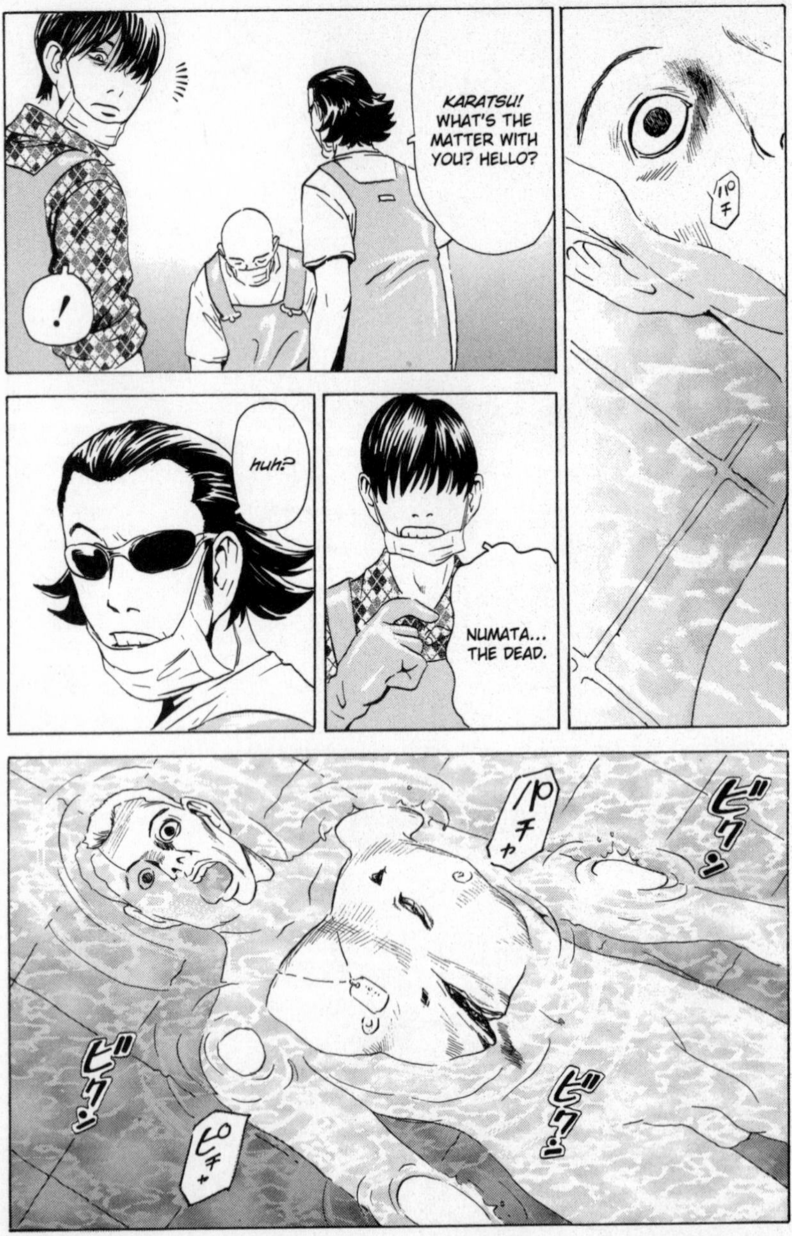
パチ
KARATSU! WHAT'S THE MATTER WITH YOU? HELLO?
!
NUMATA... THE DEAD.
huh?
ビクッ
パチャ
ビクッ
ビクッ
ピチャ

ババシャ
バシャ
ババシャ
ババシャ
パチャ
バシャ
パチャ
ババシャ
バタッ
ドサッ!!
バタ
ヴッ
ウイッ

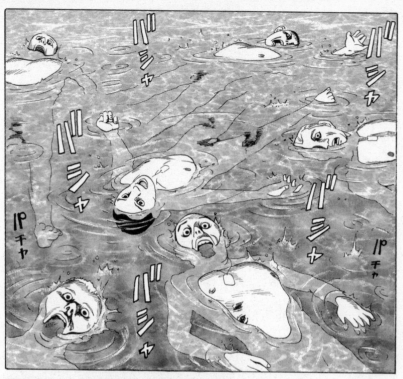

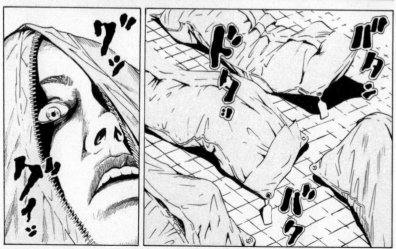

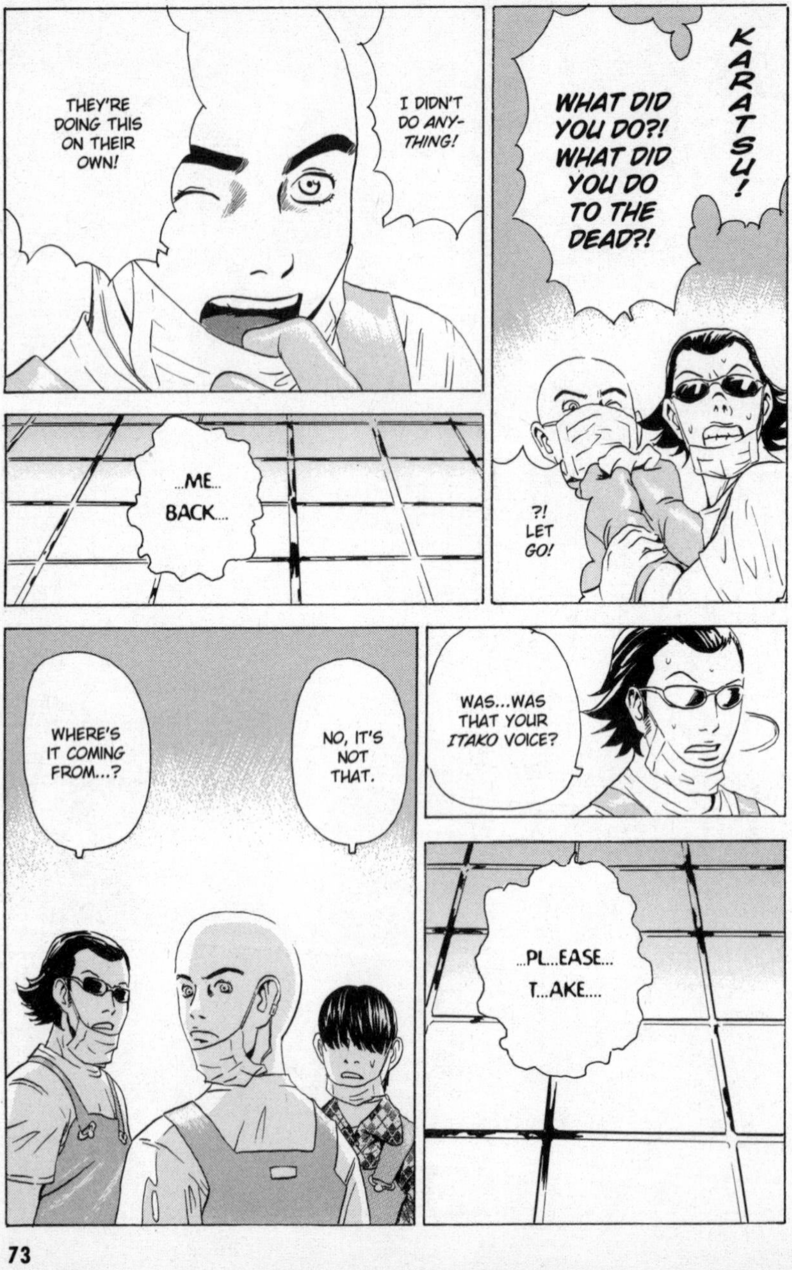
KARATSU!
WHAT DID YOU DO?! WHAT DID YOU DO TO THE DEAD?!
?! LET GO!
I DIDN'T DO ANY-THING!
THEY'RE DOING THIS ON THEIR OWN!
...ME... BACK....
WAS...WAS THAT YOUR ITAKO VOICE?
...PL...EASE... T...AKE....
NO, IT'S NOT THAT.
WHERE'S IT COMING FROM...?

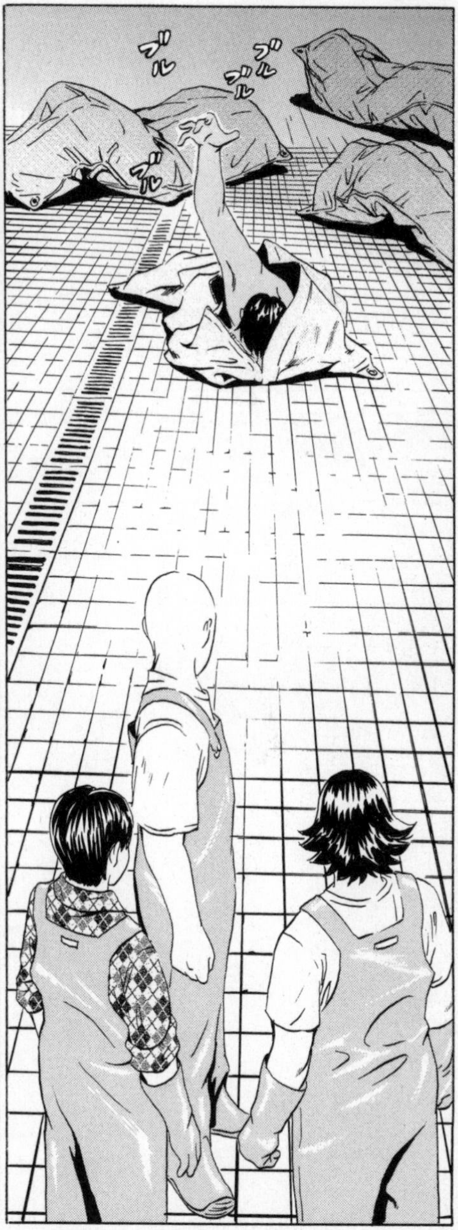
ブル
ブル
ブル
ブル

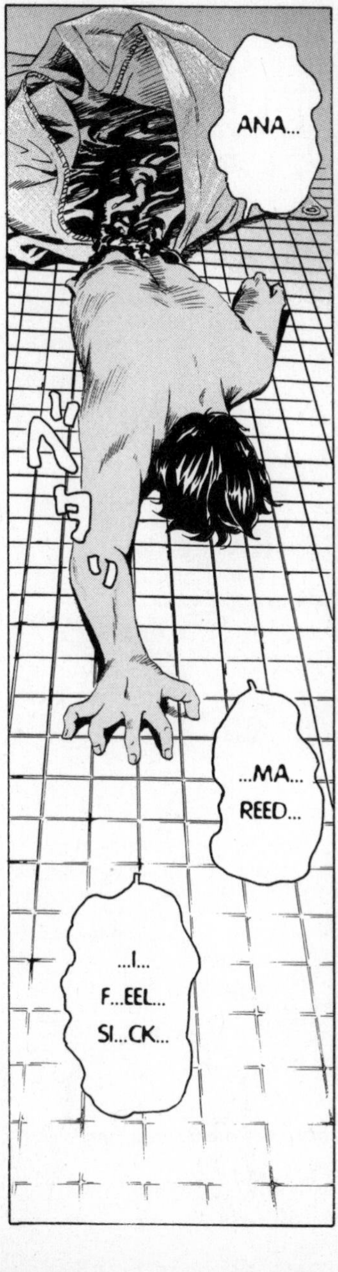
ANA...
ズヨリ
...MA... REED...
...I... F...EEL... SI...CK...

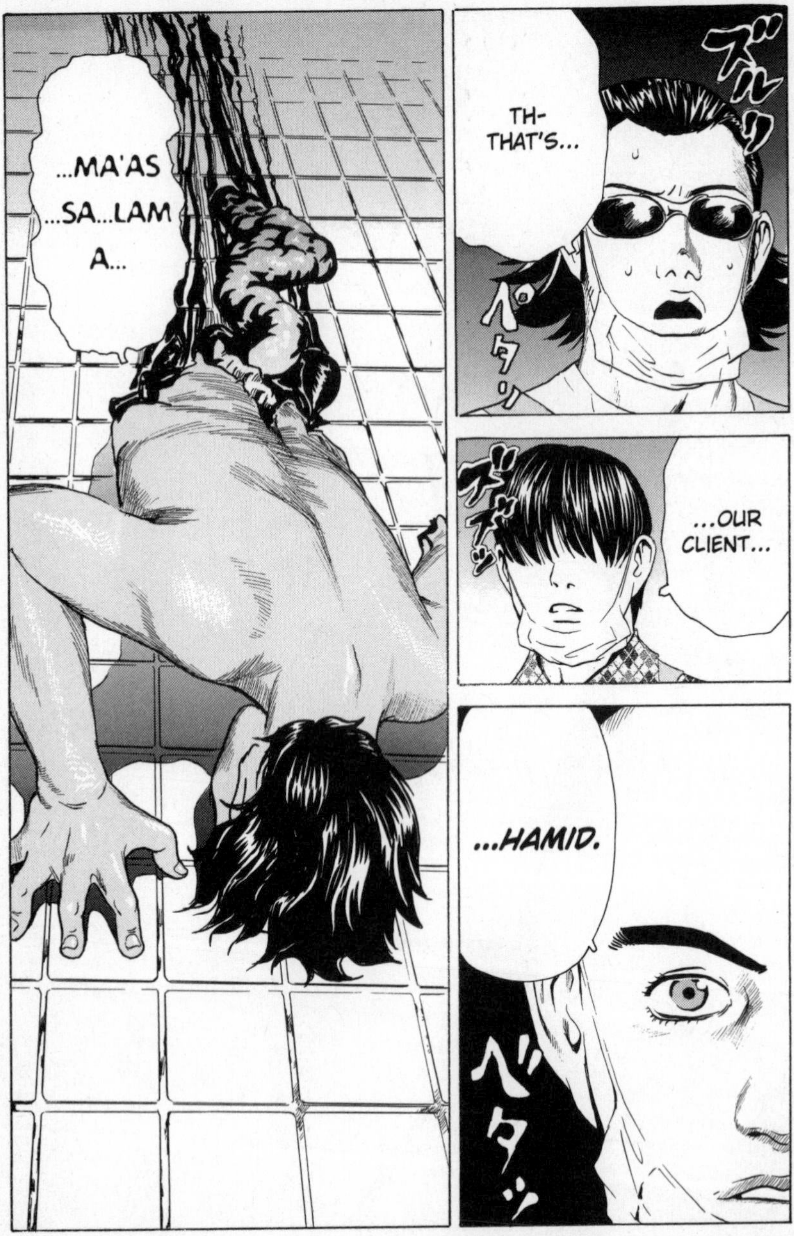
TH-
THAT'S...
...OUR
CLIENT...
...HAMID.
...MA'AS
...SA...LAM
A...

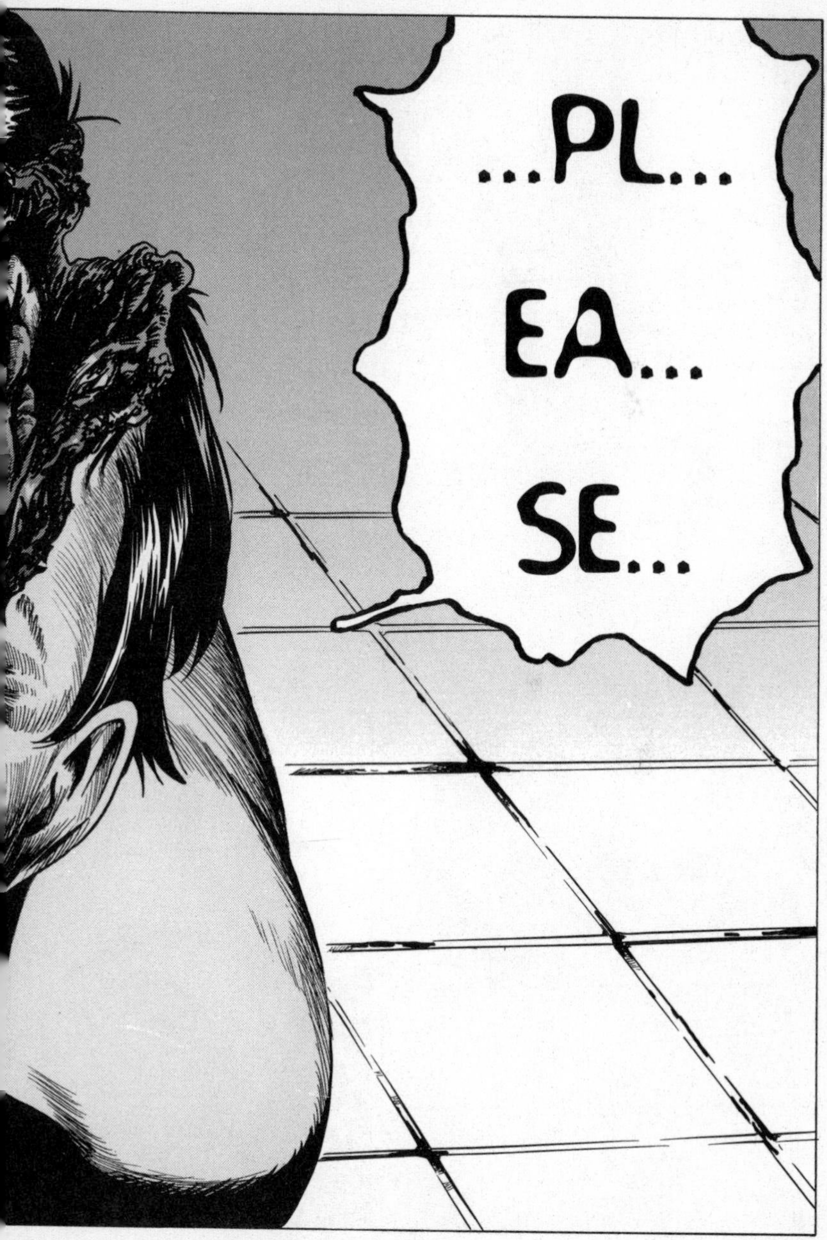
...PL... EA... SE...

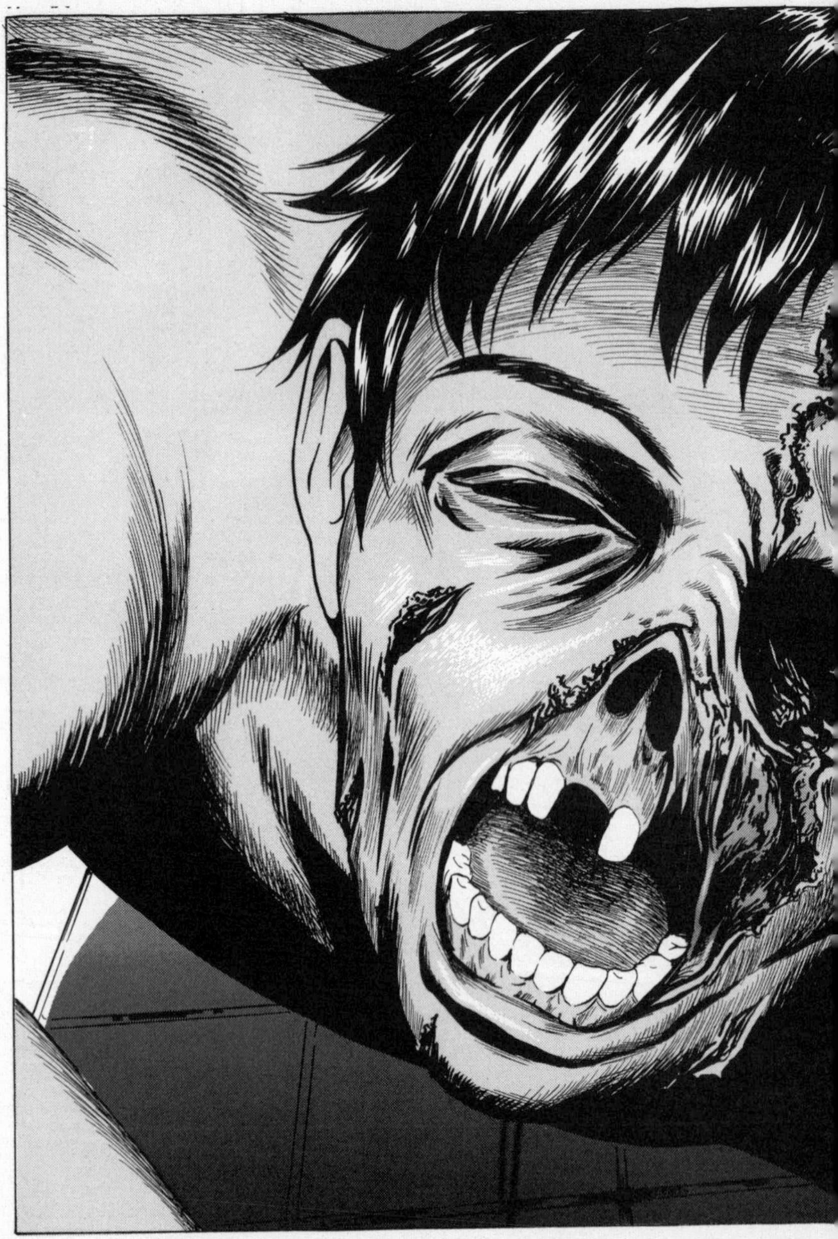

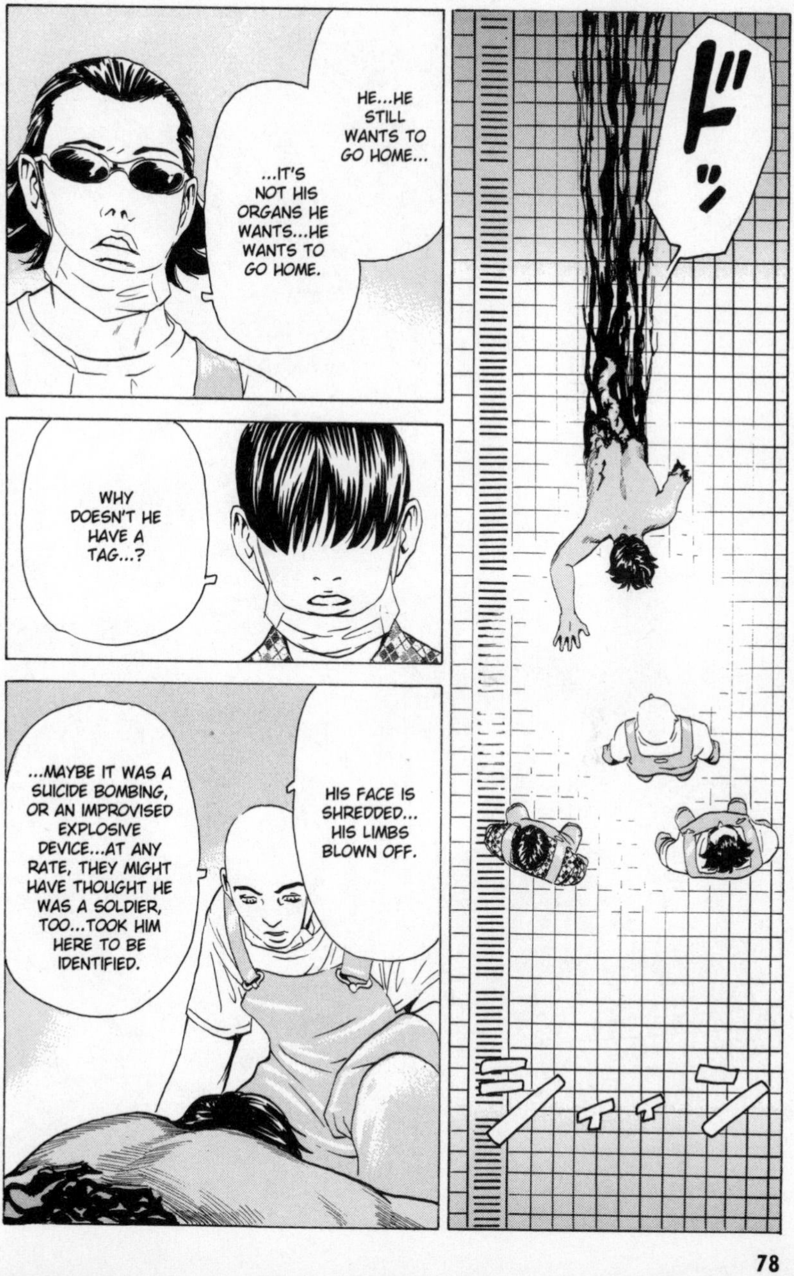
ドッ
HE...HE STILL WANTS TO GO HOME...
...IT'S NOT HIS ORGANS HE WANTS...HE WANTS TO GO HOME.
WHY DOESN'T HE HAVE A TAG...?
HIS FACE IS SHREDDED... HIS LIMBS BLOWN OFF.
...MAYBE IT WAS A SUICIDE BOMBING, OR AN IMPROVISED EXPLOSIVE DEVICE...AT ANY RATE, THEY MIGHT HAVE THOUGHT HE WAS A SOLDIER, TOO...TOOK HIM HERE TO BE IDENTIFIED.

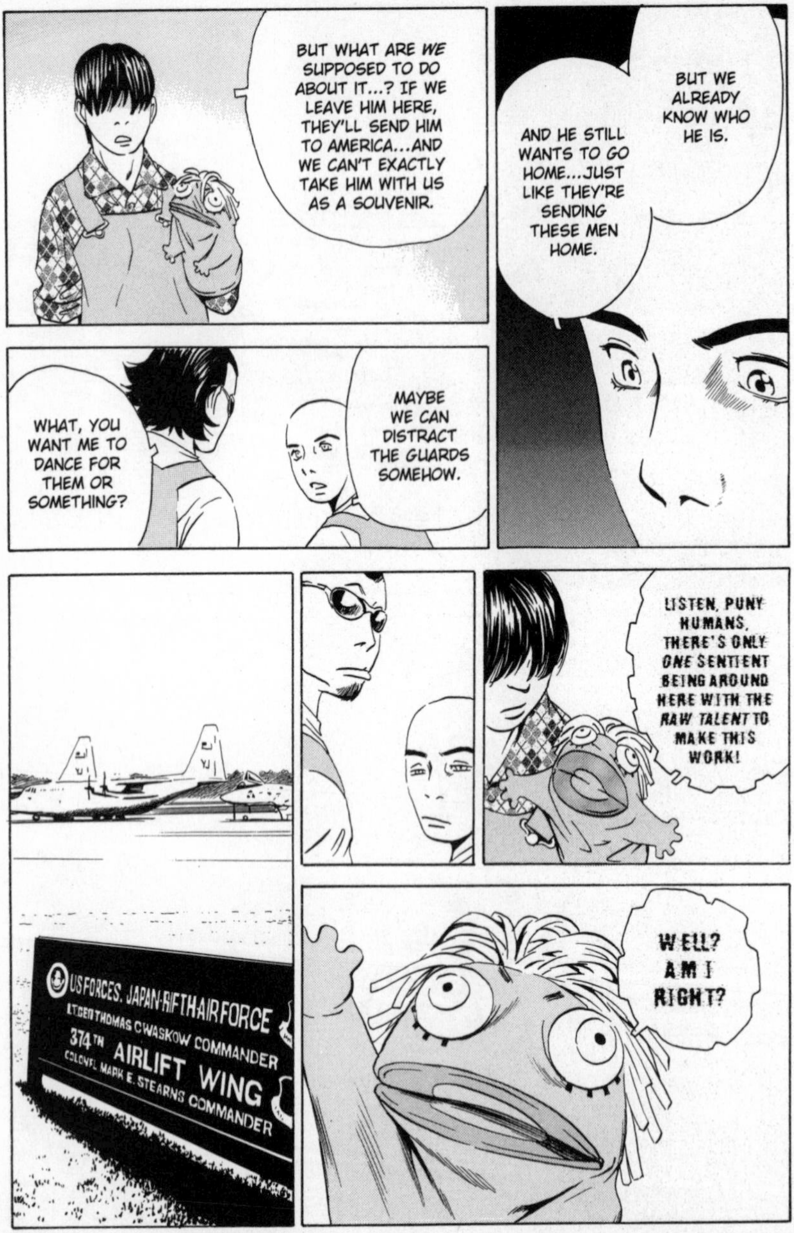
BUT WE ALREADY KNOW WHO HE IS.
AND HE STILL WANTS TO GO HOME...JUST LIKE THEY'RE SENDING THESE MEN HOME.
BUT WHAT ARE *WE* SUPPOSED TO DO ABOUT IT...? IF WE LEAVE HIM HERE, THEY'LL SEND HIM TO AMERICA...AND WE CAN'T EXACTLY TAKE HIM WITH US AS A SOUVENIR.
MAYBE WE CAN DISTRACT THE GUARDS SOMEHOW.
WHAT, YOU WANT ME TO DANCE FOR THEM OR SOMETHING?
LISTEN, PUNY HUMANS, THERE'S ONLY *ONE* SENTIENT BEING AROUND HERE WITH THE *RAW TALENT* TO MAKE THIS WORK!
WELL? AM I RIGHT?
US FORCES, JAPAN·FIFTH·AIR FORCE
LT.GEN THOMAS C.WASKOW COMMANDER
374TH AIRLIFT WING
COLONEL MARK E. STEARNS COMMANDER

RIGHT.

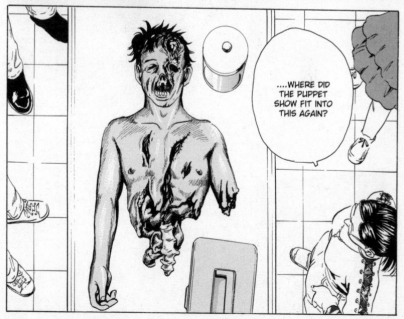

....WHERE DID THE PUPPET SHOW FIT INTO THIS AGAIN?

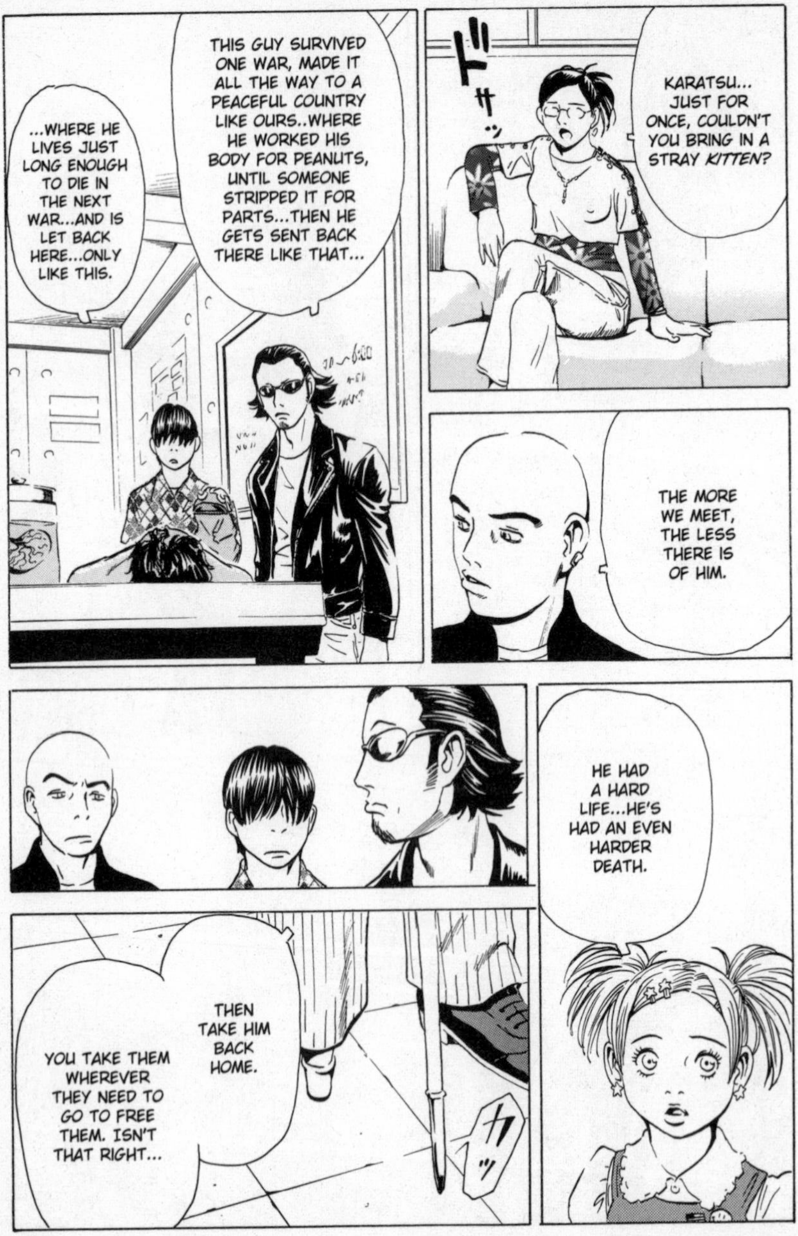
ドサッ
KARATSU... JUST FOR ONCE, COULDN'T YOU BRING IN A STRAY *KITTEN?*
THE MORE WE MEET, THE LESS THERE IS OF HIM.
THIS GUY SURVIVED ONE WAR, MADE IT ALL THE WAY TO A PEACEFUL COUNTRY LIKE OURS..WHERE HE WORKED HIS BODY FOR PEANUTS, UNTIL SOMEONE STRIPPED IT FOR PARTS...THEN HE GETS SENT BACK THERE LIKE THAT...
...WHERE HE LIVES JUST LONG ENOUGH TO DIE IN THE NEXT WAR...AND IS LET BACK HERE...ONLY LIKE THIS.
HE HAD A HARD LIFE...HE'S HAD AN EVEN HARDER DEATH.
THEN TAKE HIM BACK HOME.
YOU TAKE THEM WHEREVER THEY NEED TO GO TO FREE THEM. ISN'T THAT RIGHT...
カッ

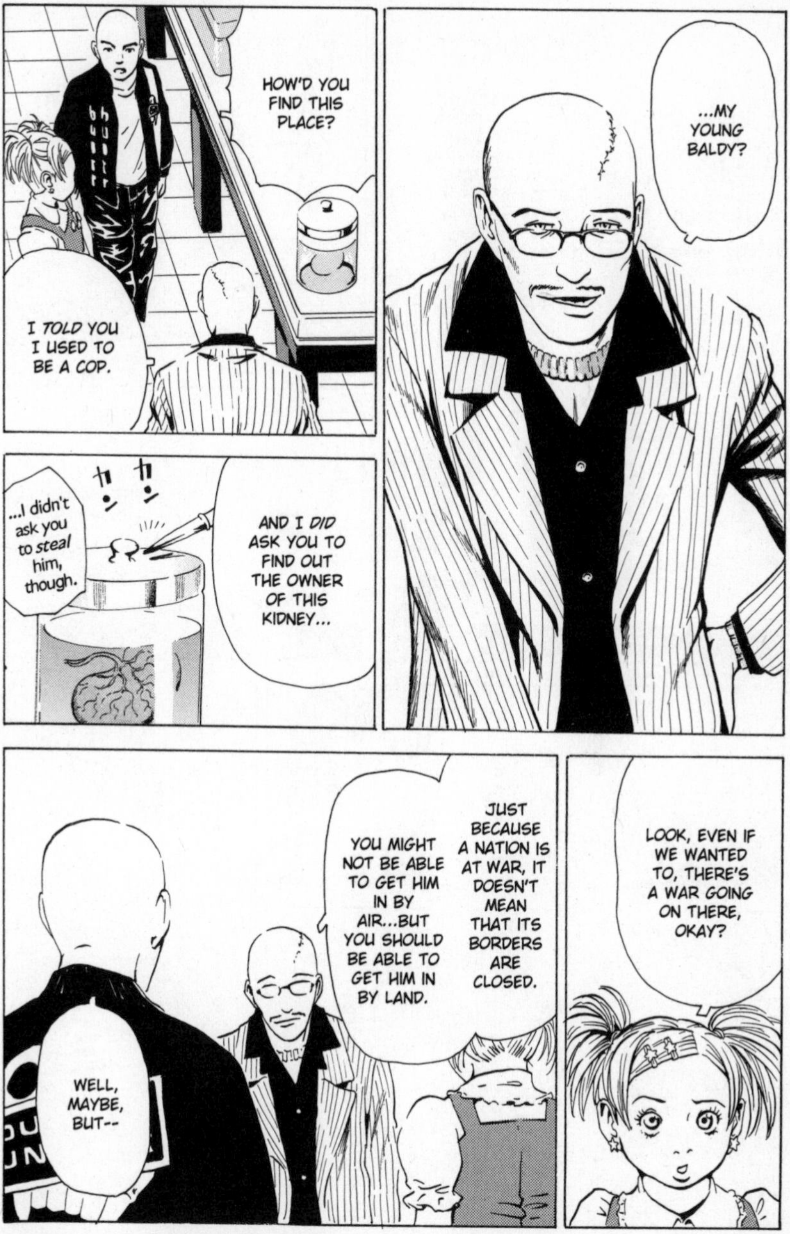

...MY YOUNG BALDY?
HOW'D YOU FIND THIS PLACE?
I *TOLD* YOU I USED TO BE A COP.
AND I *DID* ASK YOU TO FIND OUT THE OWNER OF THIS KIDNEY...
カン カン
...I didn't ask you to *steal* him, though.
LOOK, EVEN IF WE WANTED TO, THERE'S A WAR GOING ON THERE, OKAY?
JUST BECAUSE A NATION IS AT WAR, IT DOESN'T MEAN THAT ITS BORDERS ARE CLOSED.
YOU MIGHT NOT BE ABLE TO GET HIM IN BY AIR...BUT YOU SHOULD BE ABLE TO GET HIM IN BY LAND.
WELL, MAYBE, BUT--

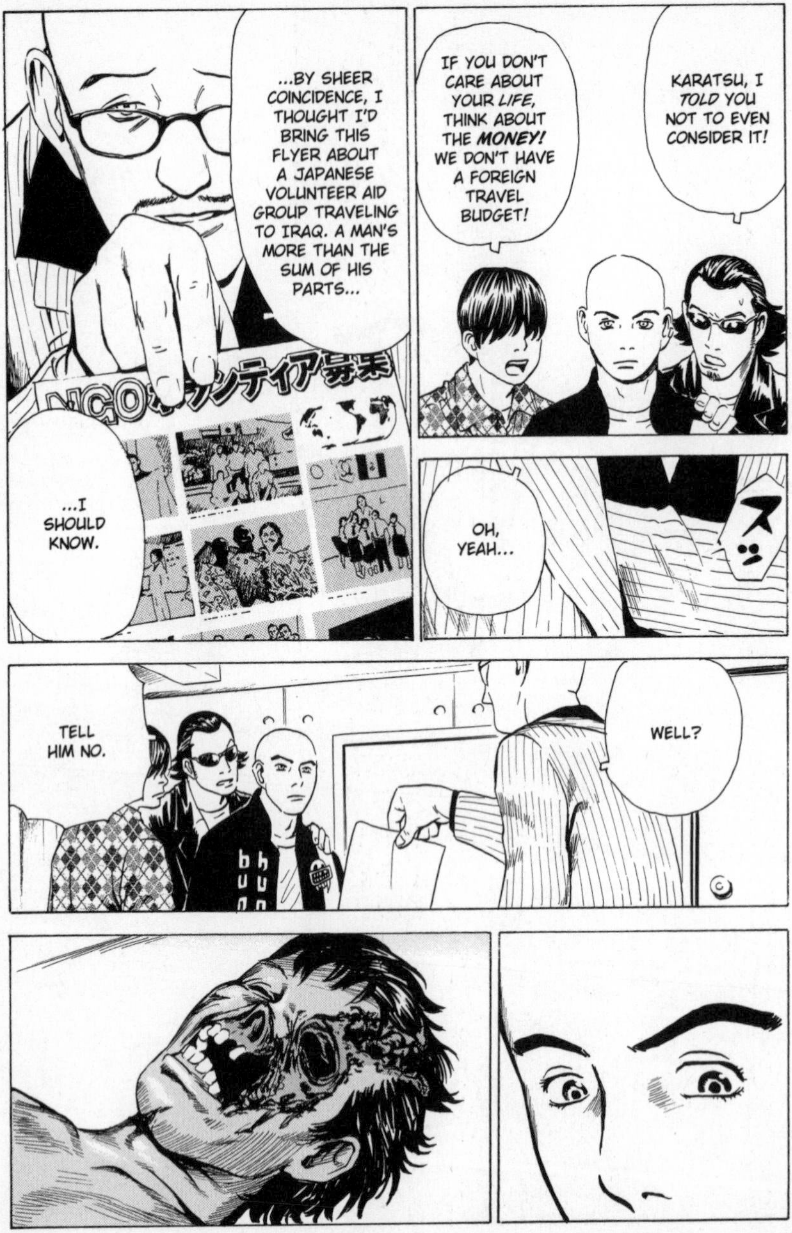
KARATSU, I *TOLD* YOU NOT TO EVEN CONSIDER IT!
IF YOU DON'T CARE ABOUT YOUR *LIFE*, THINK ABOUT THE ***MONEY!*** WE DON'T HAVE A FOREIGN TRAVEL BUDGET!
OH, YEAH...
スッ
...BY SHEER COINCIDENCE, I THOUGHT I'D BRING THIS FLYER ABOUT A JAPANESE VOLUNTEER AID GROUP TRAVELING TO IRAQ. A MAN'S MORE THAN THE SUM OF HIS PARTS...
...I SHOULD KNOW.
WELL?
TELL HIM NO.

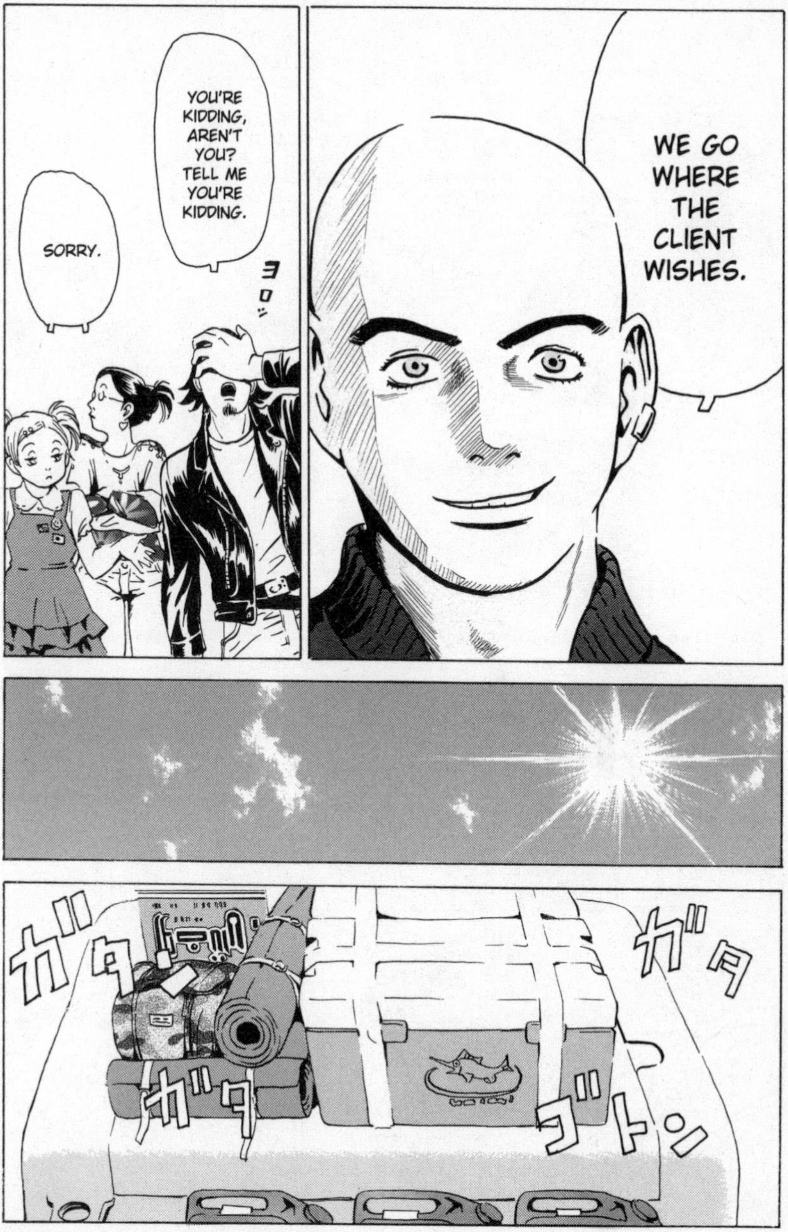
WE GO WHERE THE CLIENT WISHES.
YOU'RE KIDDING, AREN'T YOU? TELL ME YOU'RE KIDDING.
ヨロッ
SORRY.
ガタ
ゴトン
ガタ
ガタ

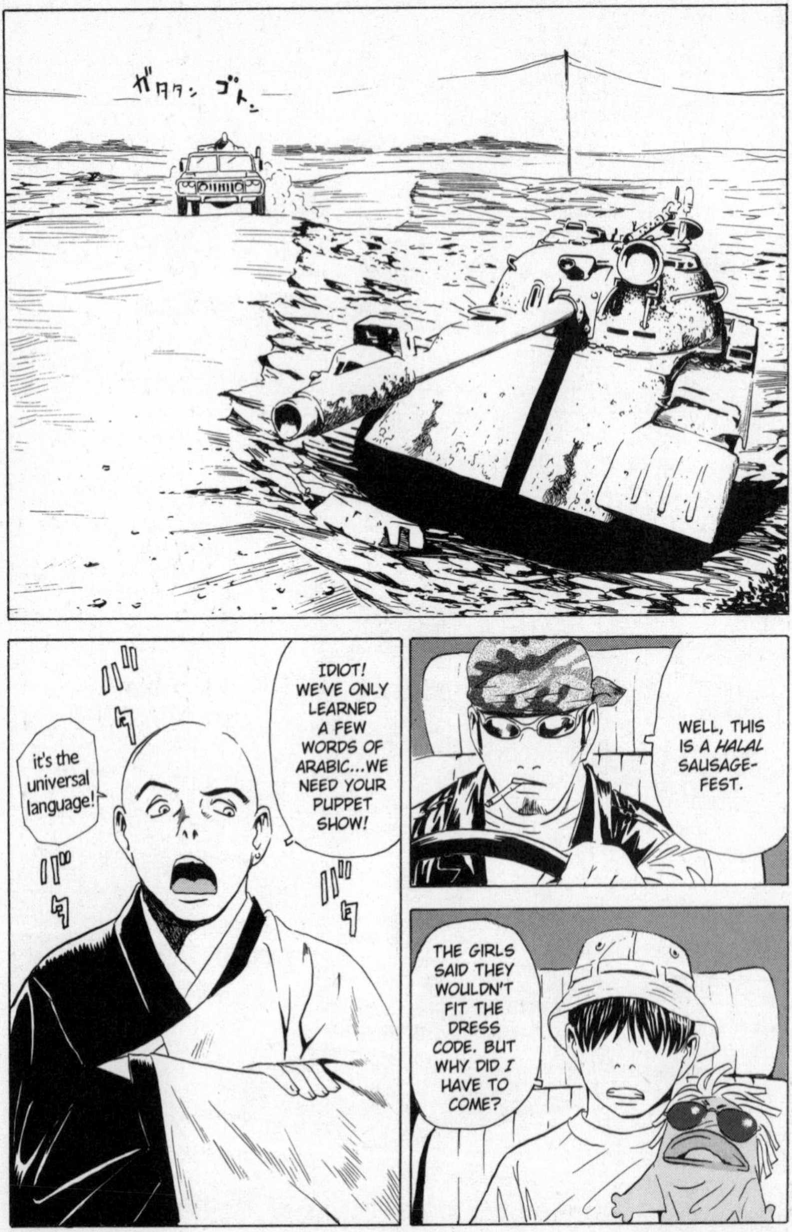
ガタタン ゴトン
WELL, THIS IS A *HALAL* SAUSAGE-FEST.
THE GIRLS SAID THEY WOULDN'T FIT THE DRESS CODE. BUT WHY DID *I* HAVE TO COME?
バタ
IDIOT! WE'VE ONLY LEARNED A FEW WORDS OF ARABIC...WE NEED YOUR PUPPET SHOW!
it's the universal language!
バタ
バタ

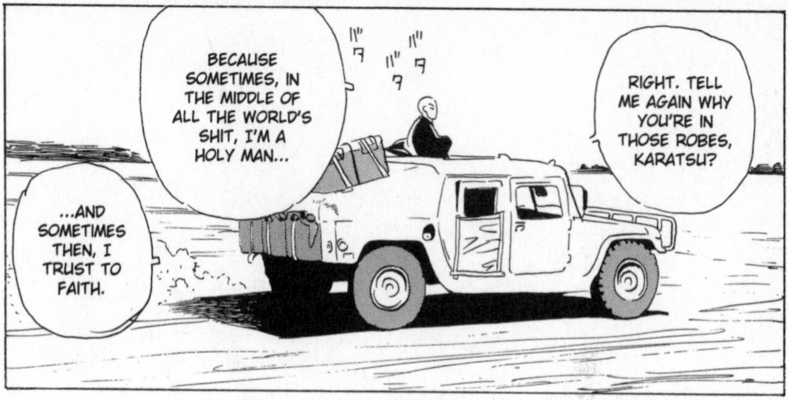
RIGHT. TELL ME AGAIN WHY YOU'RE IN THOSE ROBES, KARATSU?
バッ バッ バッ
BECAUSE SOMETIMES, IN THE MIDDLE OF ALL THE WORLD'S SHIT, I'M A HOLY MAN...
...AND SOMETIMES THEN, I TRUST TO FAITH.

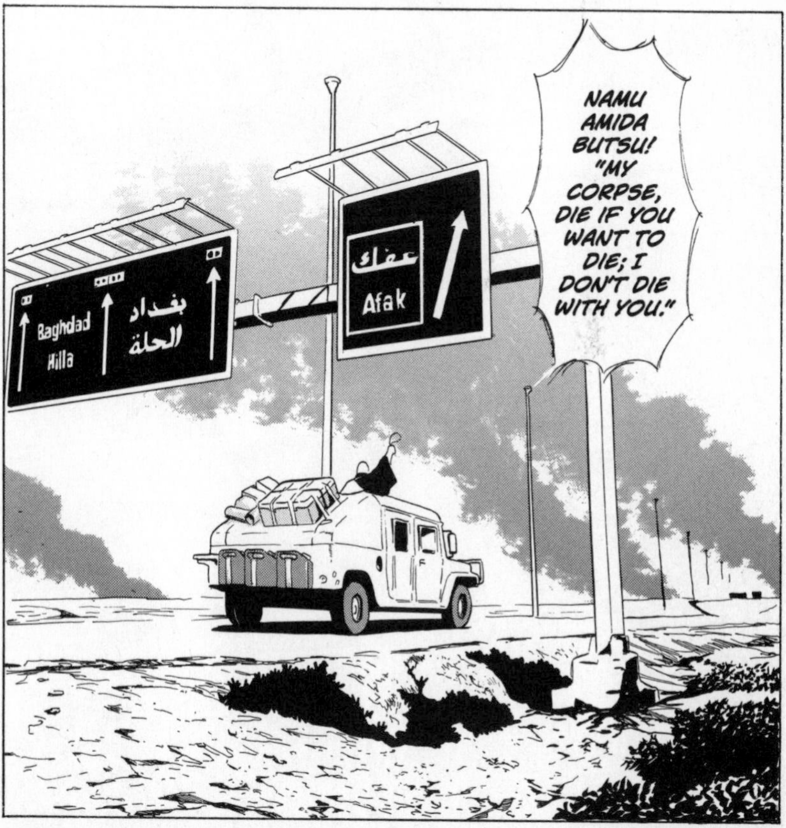
NAMU AMIDA BUTSU! "MY CORPSE, DIE IF YOU WANT TO DIE; I DON'T DIE WITH YOU."
عفك
Afak
بغداد
الحلة
Baghdad
Hilla

2nd delivery: applause—the end

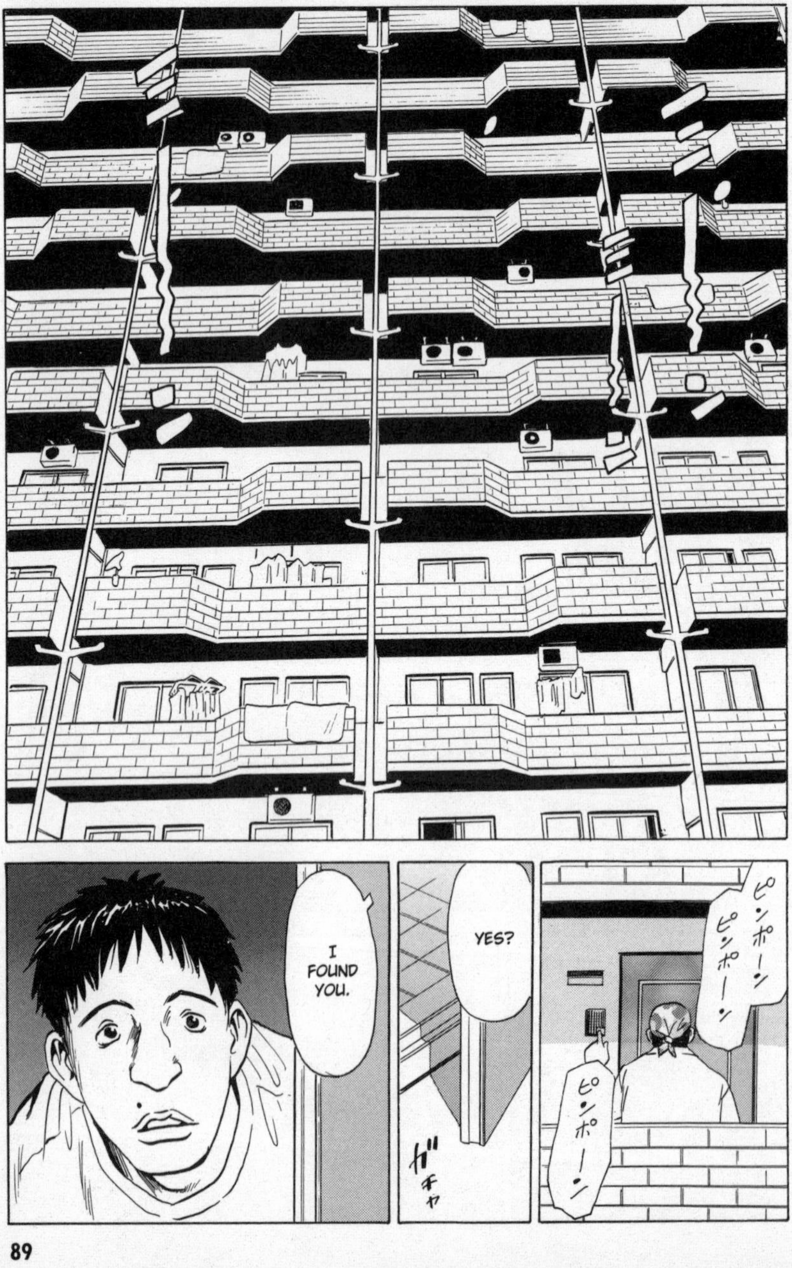
ピンポーン
ピンポーン
ピンポーン
YES?
ガチャ
I FOUND YOU.

ドドカッッ
ビチャ
ズズッ
hahhh
hahhh
hahhh
チキ
チキ
チキ

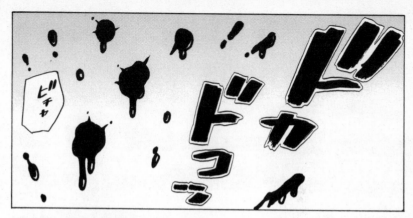

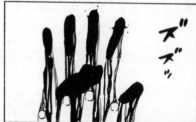

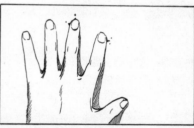

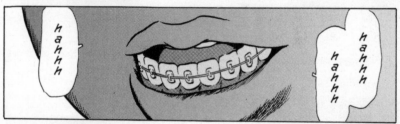

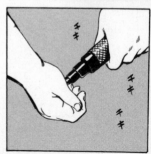

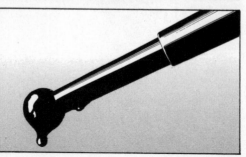

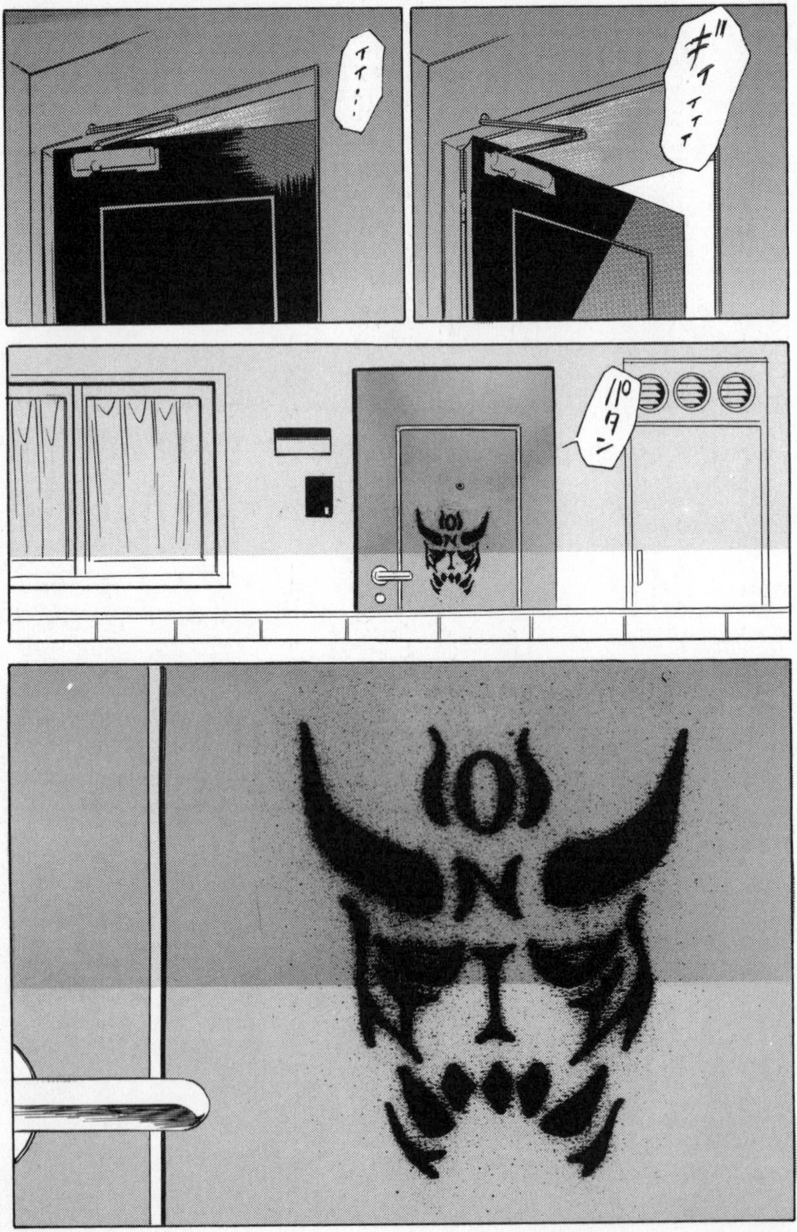
ギイイイイ
イイ…
パタン

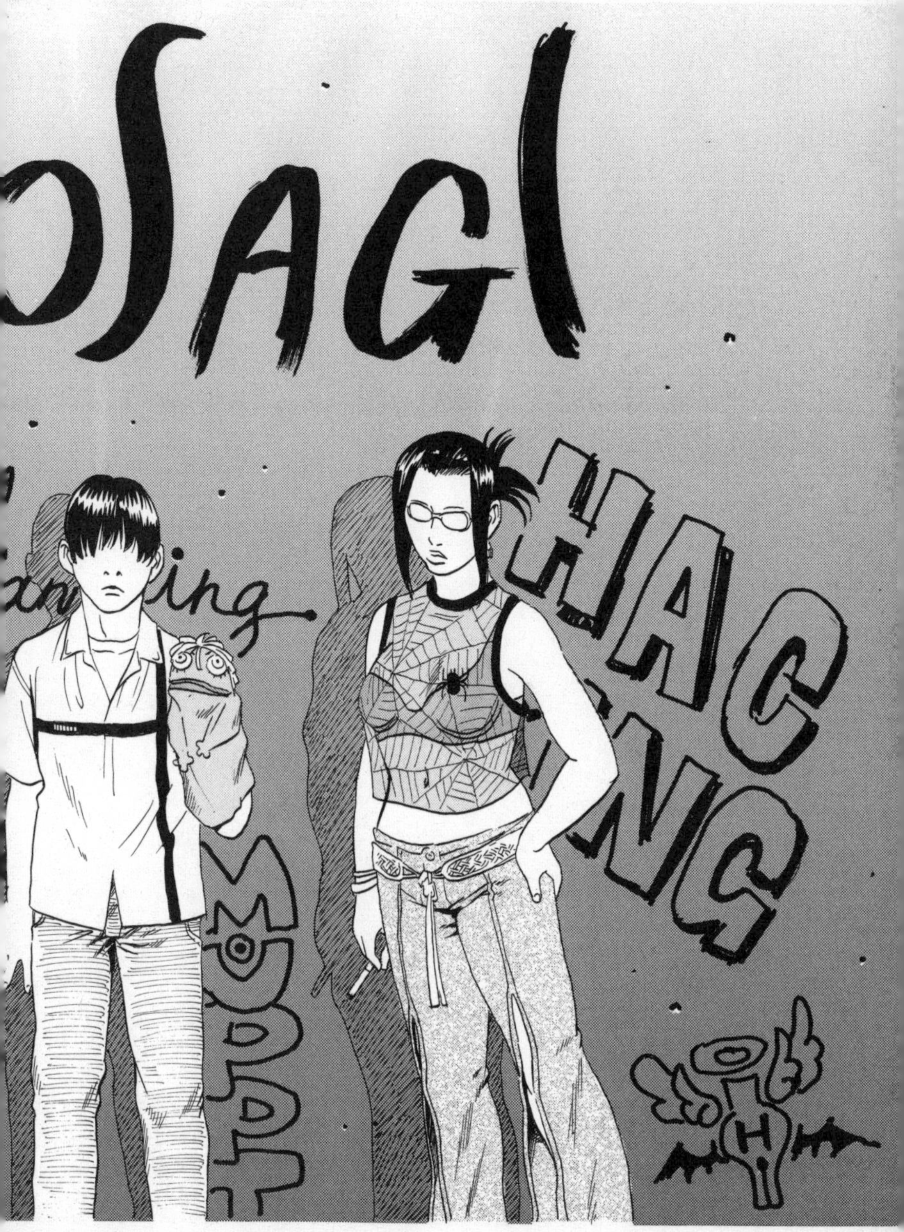

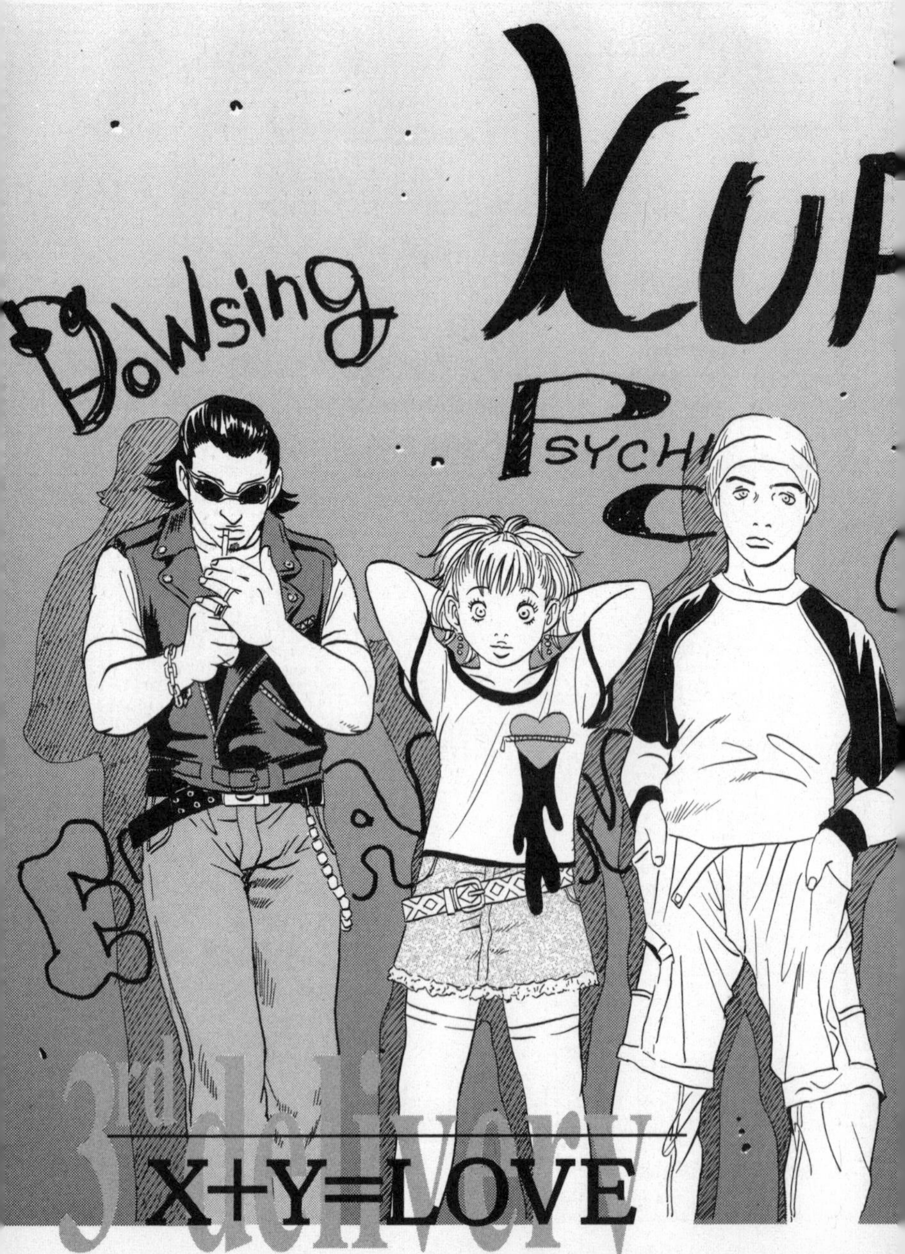

3rd delivery
X+Y=LOVE

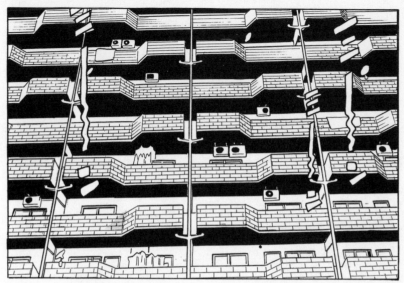

THIS STUFF IS *HEAVY*...

5 0 3

DON'T ANY OF THESE PEOPLE PUT THEIR NAMES ON THE DOOR?

SHHH! GOTTA BE BUSINESS-LIKE AND PROFES-SIONAL.

...AND IT'S *HOT*.

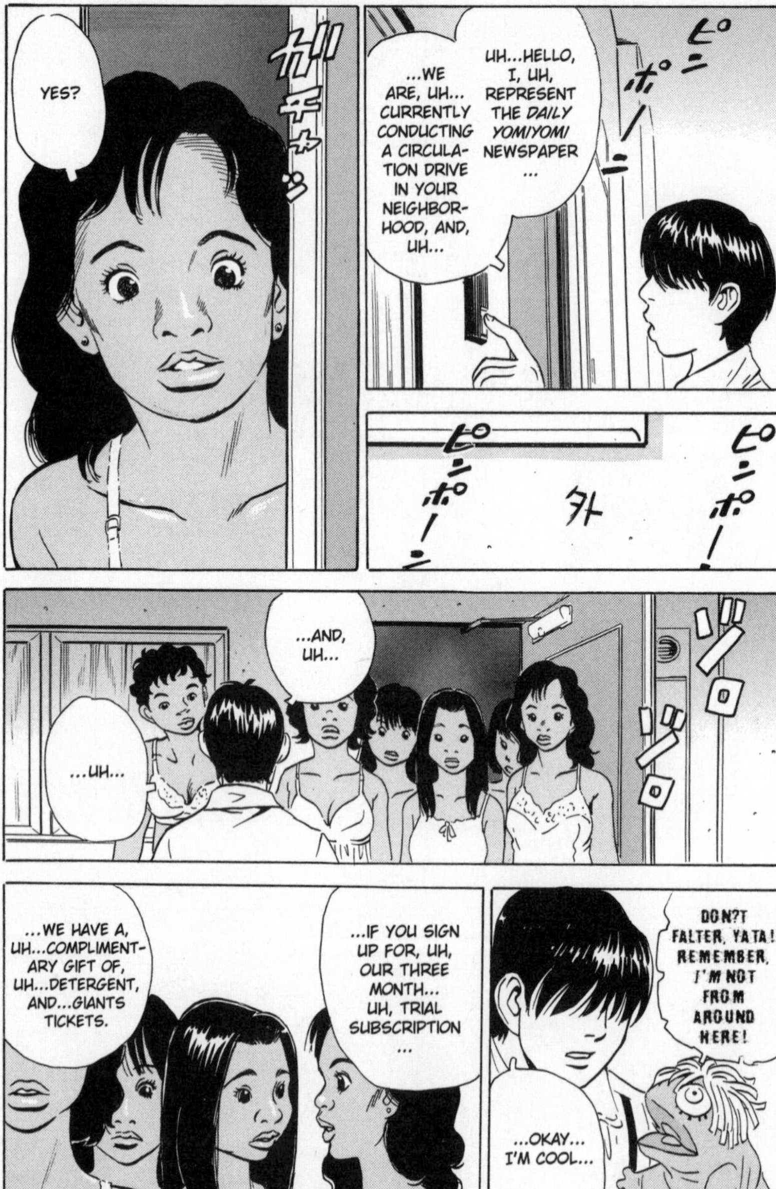
ピンポーン
UH...HELLO, I, UH, REPRESENT THE *DAILY YOMIYOMI* NEWSPAPER...
...WE ARE, UH... CURRENTLY CONDUCTING A CIRCULATION DRIVE IN YOUR NEIGHBORHOOD, AND, UH...
ピンポーン
外
ピンポーン
ガチャ
YES?
ゾロ
ゾロ
...AND, UH...
...UH...
DON?T FALTER, YATA! REMEMBER, *I'M* NOT FROM AROUND HERE!
...OKAY... I'M COOL...
...IF YOU SIGN UP FOR, UH, OUR THREE MONTH... UH, TRIAL SUBSCRIPTION...
...WE HAVE A, UH...COMPLIMENTARY GIFT OF, UH...DETERGENT, AND...GIANTS TICKETS.

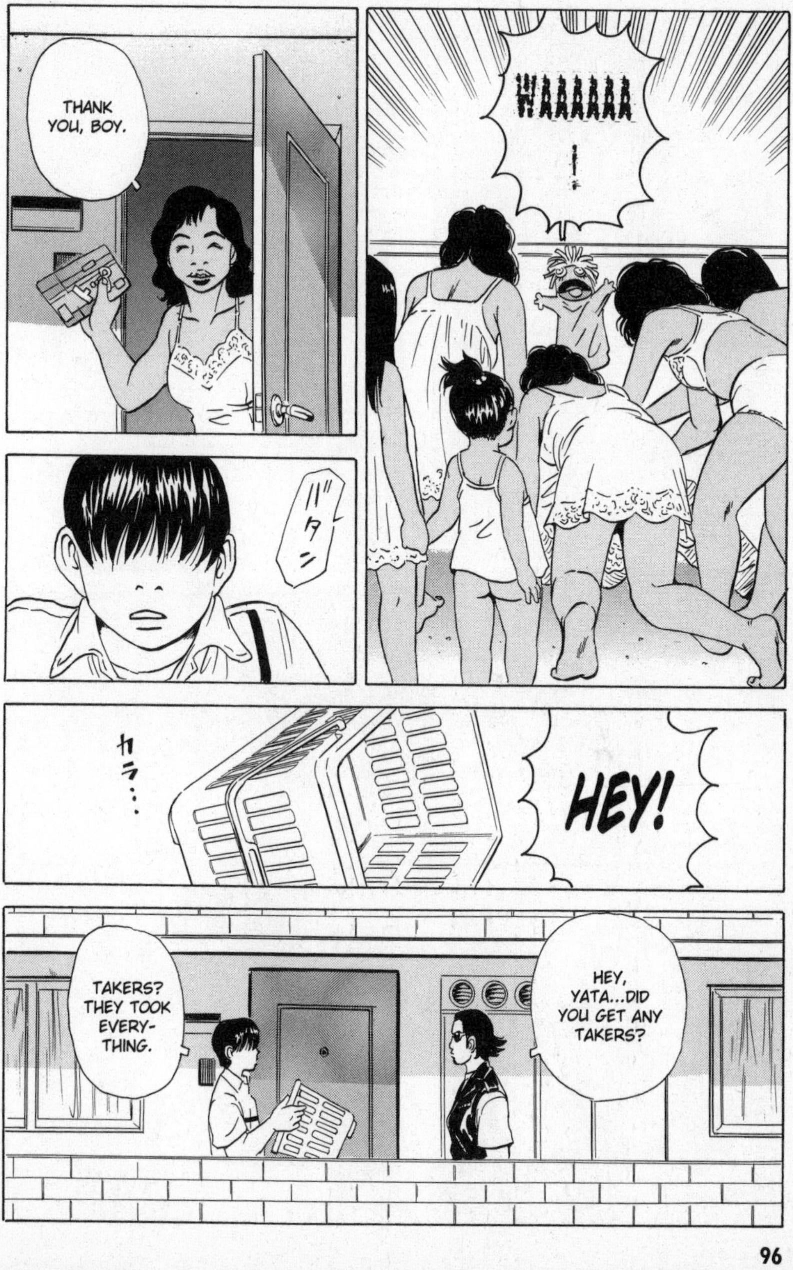
WAAAAAA!!
THANK YOU, BOY.
バタン
HEY!
カラ…
HEY, YATA...DID YOU GET ANY TAKERS?
TAKERS? THEY TOOK EVERY-THING.

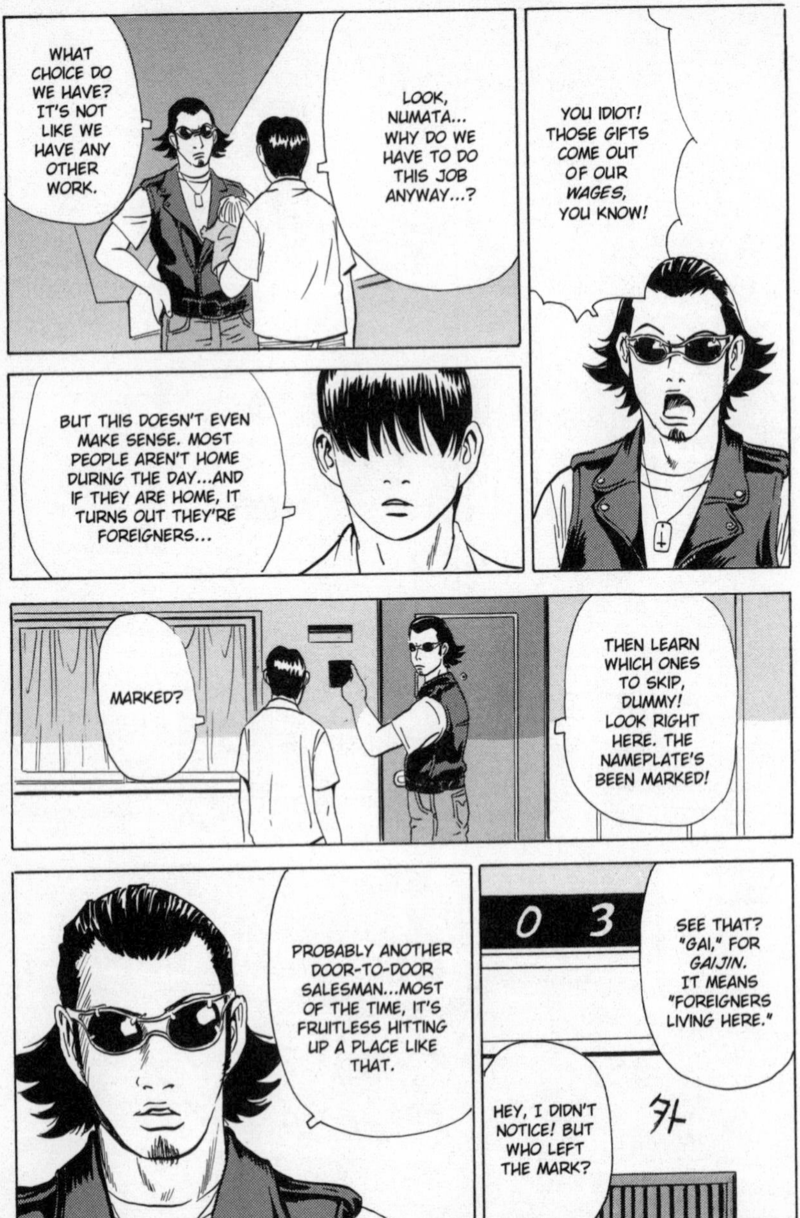
YOU IDIOT! THOSE GIFTS COME OUT OF OUR *WAGES*, YOU KNOW!
LOOK, NUMATA... WHY DO WE HAVE TO DO THIS JOB ANYWAY...?
WHAT CHOICE DO WE HAVE? IT'S NOT LIKE WE HAVE ANY OTHER WORK.
BUT THIS DOESN'T EVEN MAKE SENSE. MOST PEOPLE AREN'T HOME DURING THE DAY...AND IF THEY ARE HOME, IT TURNS OUT THEY'RE FOREIGNERS...
THEN LEARN WHICH ONES TO SKIP, DUMMY! LOOK RIGHT HERE. THE NAMEPLATE'S BEEN MARKED!
MARKED?
0 3
SEE THAT? "GAI," FOR *GAIJIN*. IT MEANS "FOREIGNERS LIVING HERE."
外
HEY, I DIDN'T NOTICE! BUT WHO LEFT THE MARK?
PROBABLY ANOTHER DOOR-TO-DOOR SALESMAN...MOST OF THE TIME, IT'S FRUITLESS HITTING UP A PLACE LIKE THAT.

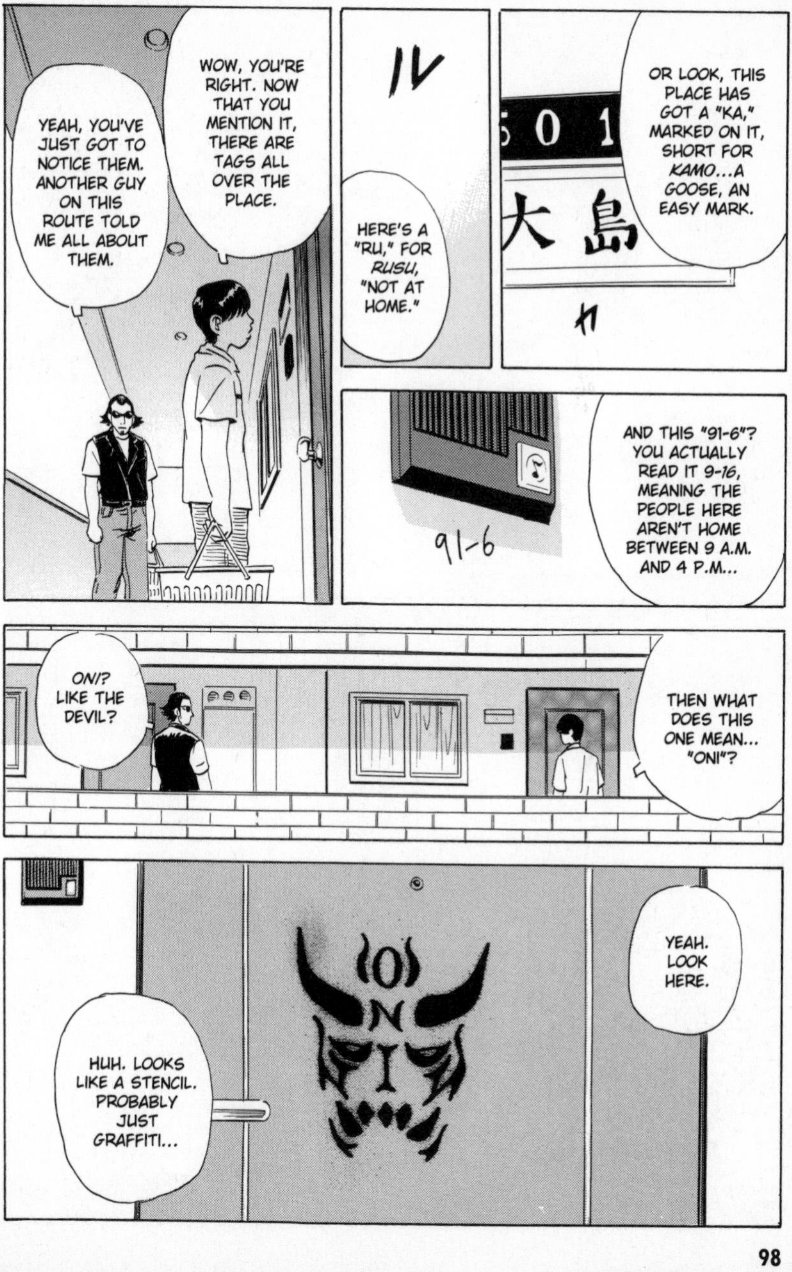

501
大島
カ
OR LOOK, THIS PLACE HAS GOT A "KA," MARKED ON IT, SHORT FOR *KAMO*...A GOOSE, AN EASY MARK.
ル
HERE'S A "RU," FOR *RUSU*, "NOT AT HOME."
91-6
AND THIS "91-6"? YOU ACTUALLY READ IT 9-16, MEANING THE PEOPLE HERE AREN'T HOME BETWEEN 9 A.M. AND 4 P.M...
WOW, YOU'RE RIGHT. NOW THAT YOU MENTION IT, THERE ARE TAGS ALL OVER THE PLACE.
YEAH, YOU'VE JUST GOT TO NOTICE THEM. ANOTHER GUY ON THIS ROUTE TOLD ME ALL ABOUT THEM.
THEN WHAT DOES THIS ONE MEAN... "ONI"?
ONI? LIKE THE DEVIL?
YEAH. LOOK HERE.
ONI
HUH. LOOKS LIKE A STENCIL. PROBABLY JUST GRAFFITI...

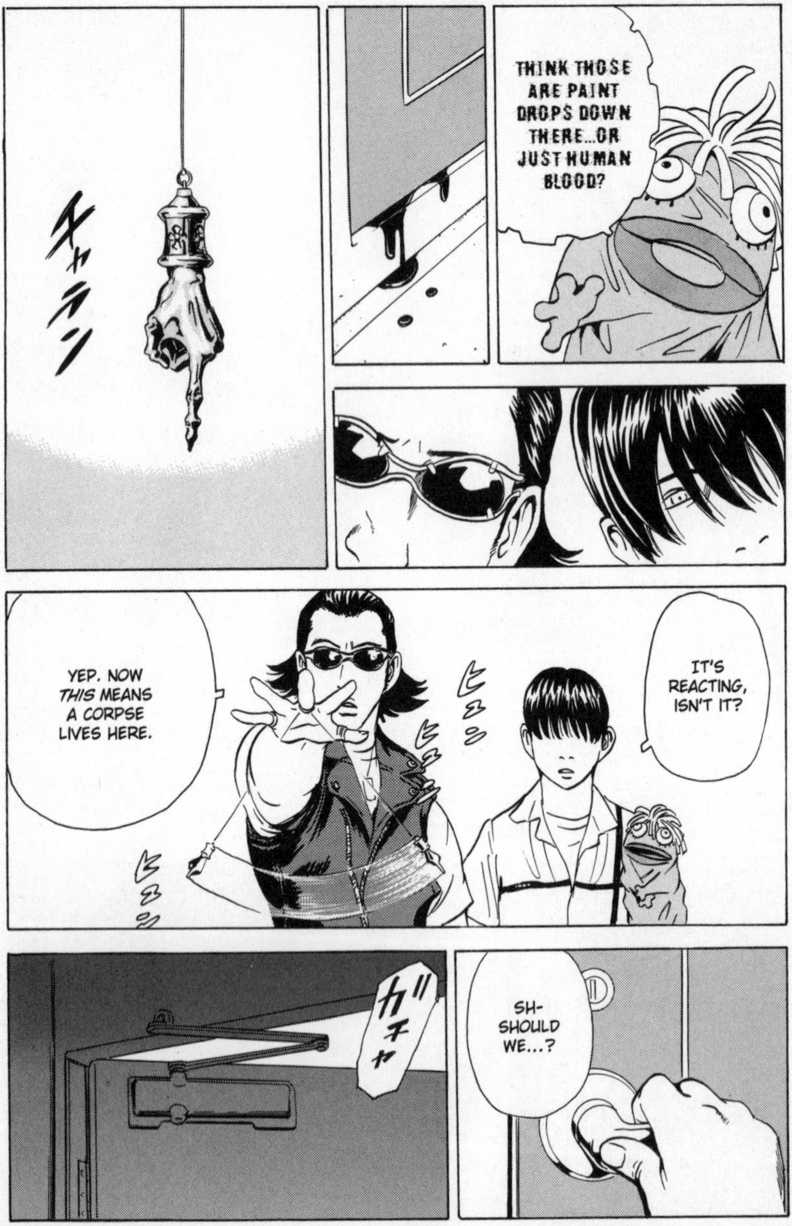
THINK THOSE ARE PAINT DROPS DOWN THERE...OR JUST HUMAN BLOOD?
チャラン
IT'S REACTING, ISN'T IT?
YEP. NOW *THIS* MEANS A CORPSE LIVES HERE.
SH- SHOULD WE...?
ガチャ

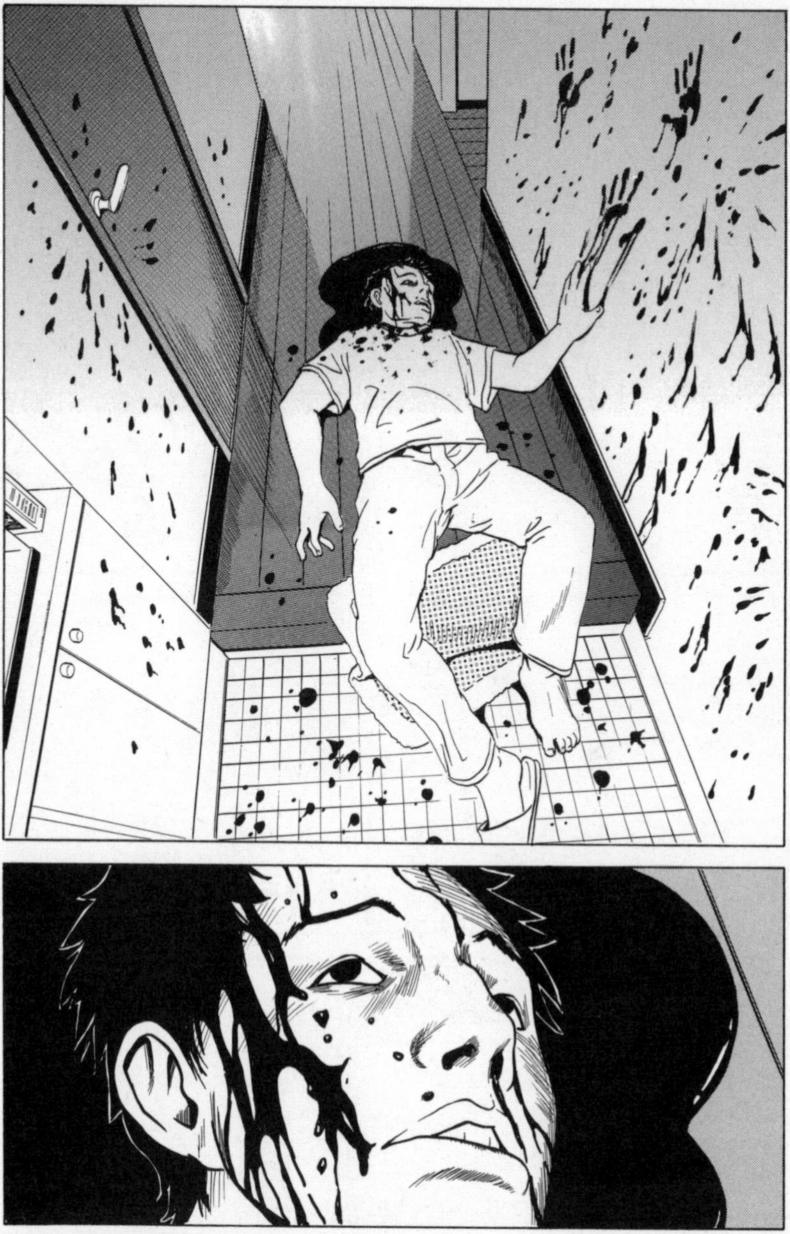

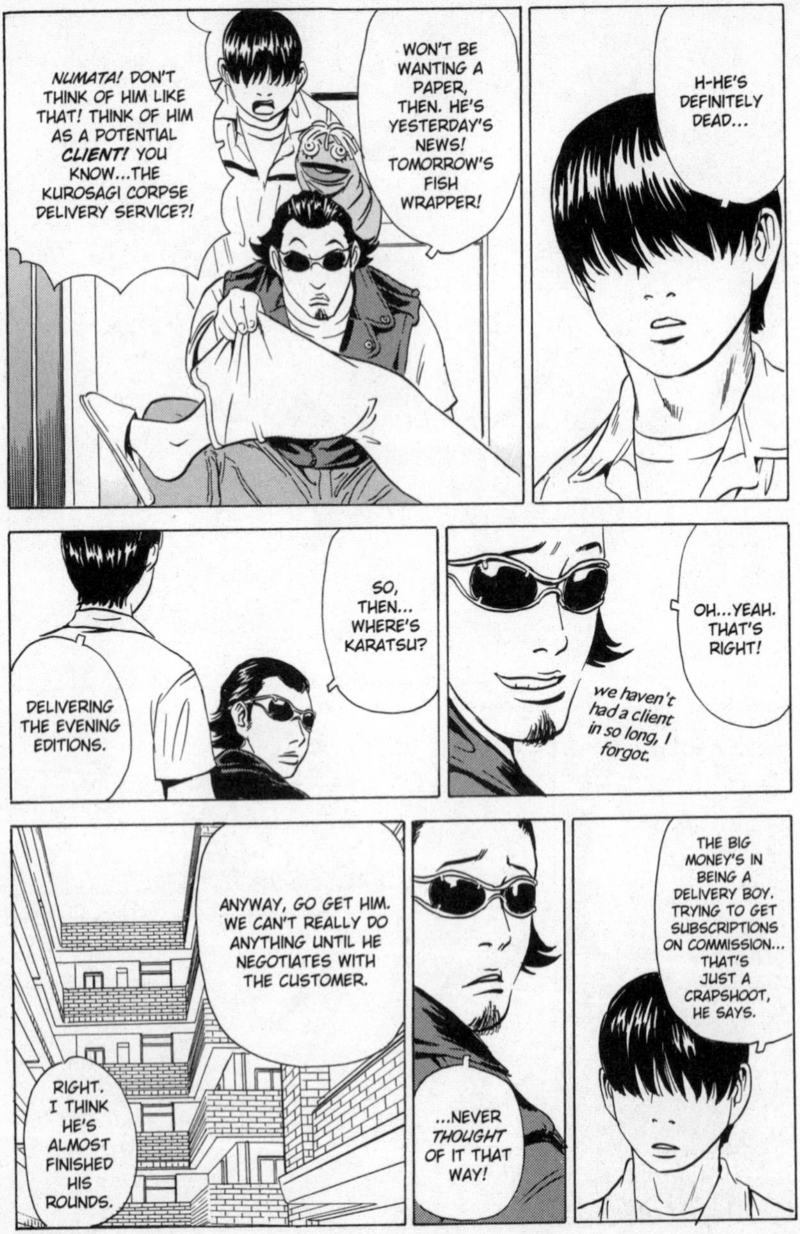

H-HE'S DEFINITELY DEAD...
WON'T BE WANTING A PAPER, THEN. HE'S YESTERDAY'S NEWS! TOMORROW'S FISH WRAPPER!
NUMATA! DON'T THINK OF HIM LIKE THAT! THINK OF HIM AS A POTENTIAL ***CLIENT!*** YOU KNOW...THE KUROSAGI CORPSE DELIVERY SERVICE?!
OH...YEAH. THAT'S RIGHT!
we haven't had a client in so long, I forgot.
SO, THEN... WHERE'S KARATSU?
DELIVERING THE EVENING EDITIONS.
THE BIG MONEY'S IN BEING A DELIVERY BOY. TRYING TO GET SUBSCRIPTIONS ON COMMISSION... THAT'S JUST A CRAPSHOOT, HE SAYS.
...NEVER *THOUGHT* OF IT THAT WAY!
ANYWAY, GO GET HIM. WE CAN'T REALLY DO ANYTHING UNTIL HE NEGOTIATES WITH THE CUSTOMER.
RIGHT. I THINK HE'S ALMOST FINISHED HIS ROUNDS.

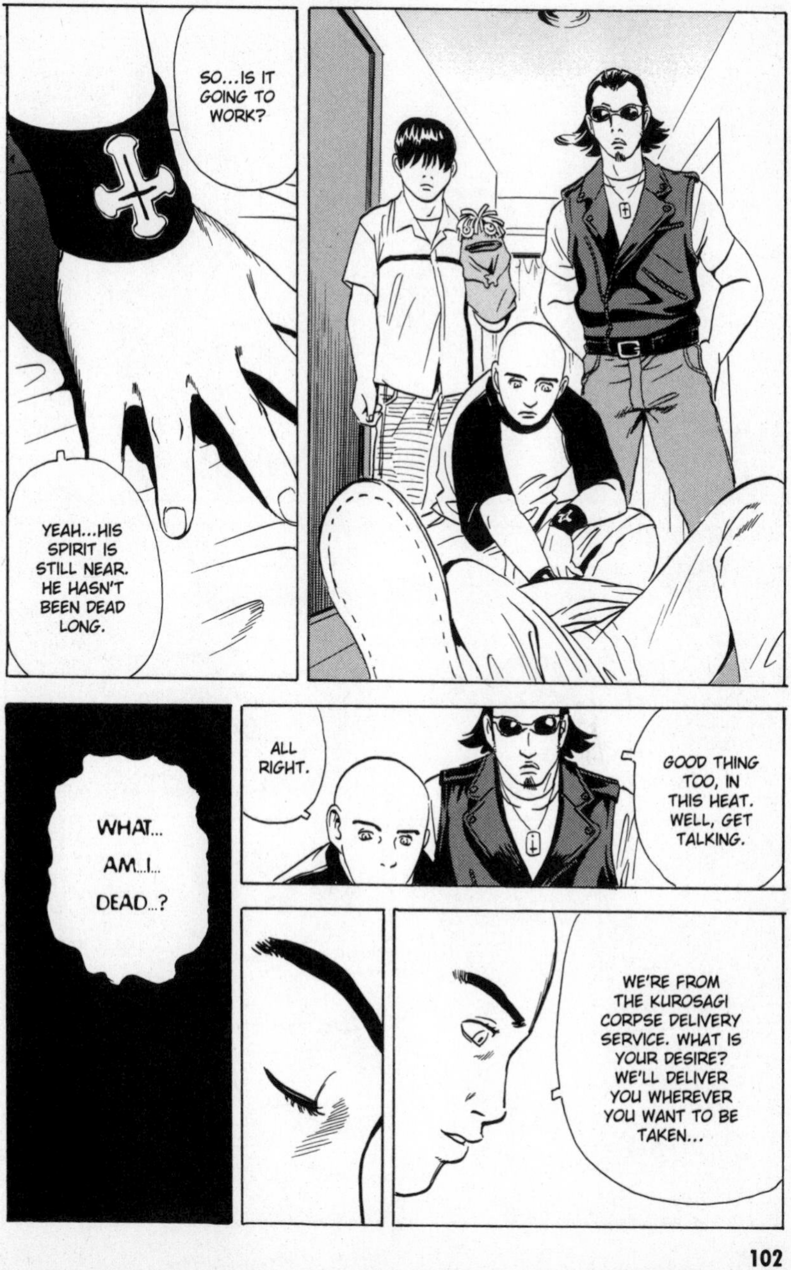
SO...IS IT GOING TO WORK?
YEAH...HIS SPIRIT IS STILL NEAR. HE HASN'T BEEN DEAD LONG.
GOOD THING TOO, IN THIS HEAT. WELL, GET TALKING.
ALL RIGHT.
WE'RE FROM THE KUROSAGI CORPSE DELIVERY SERVICE. WHAT IS YOUR DESIRE? WE'LL DELIVER YOU WHEREVER YOU WANT TO BE TAKEN...
WHAT... AM...I... DEAD...?

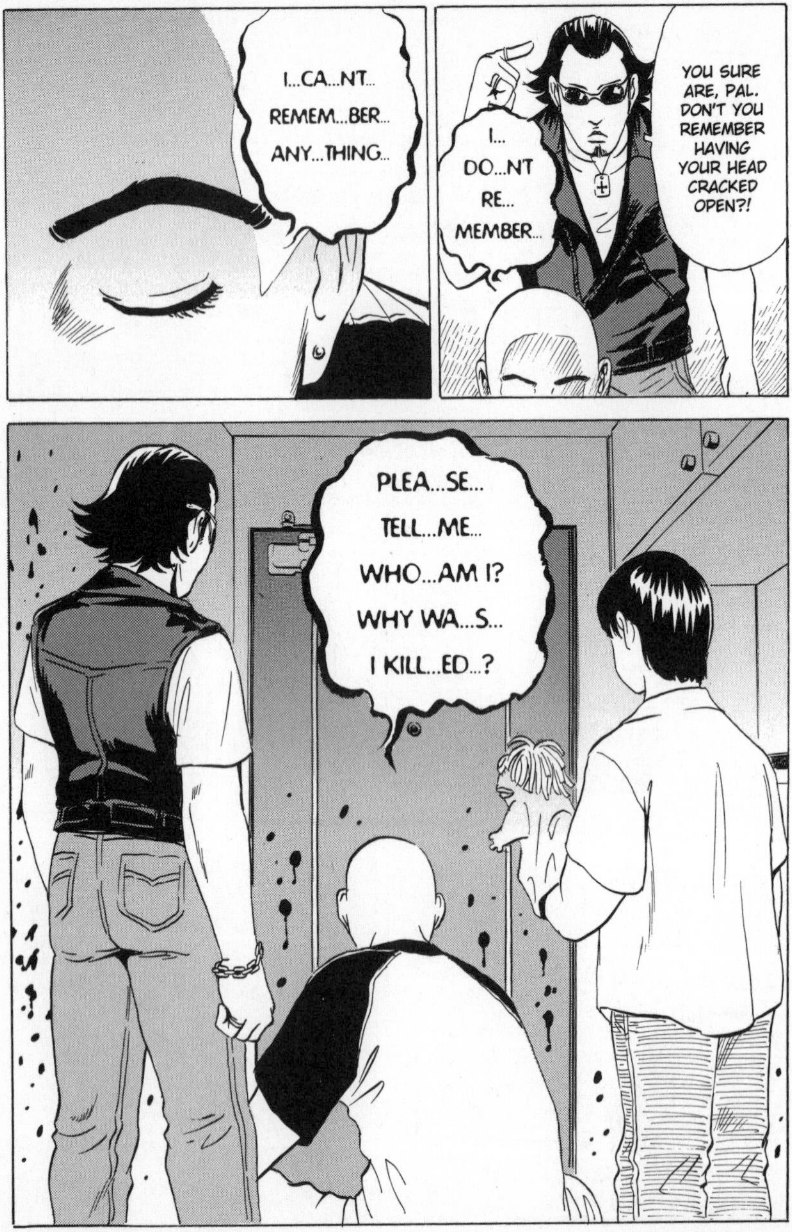
YOU SURE ARE, PAL. DON'T YOU REMEMBER HAVING YOUR HEAD CRACKED OPEN?!
I... DO...N'T RE... MEMBER...
I...CA...N'T... REMEM...BER... ANY...THING...
PLEA...SE... TELL...ME... WHO...AM I? WHY WA...S... I KILL...ED...?

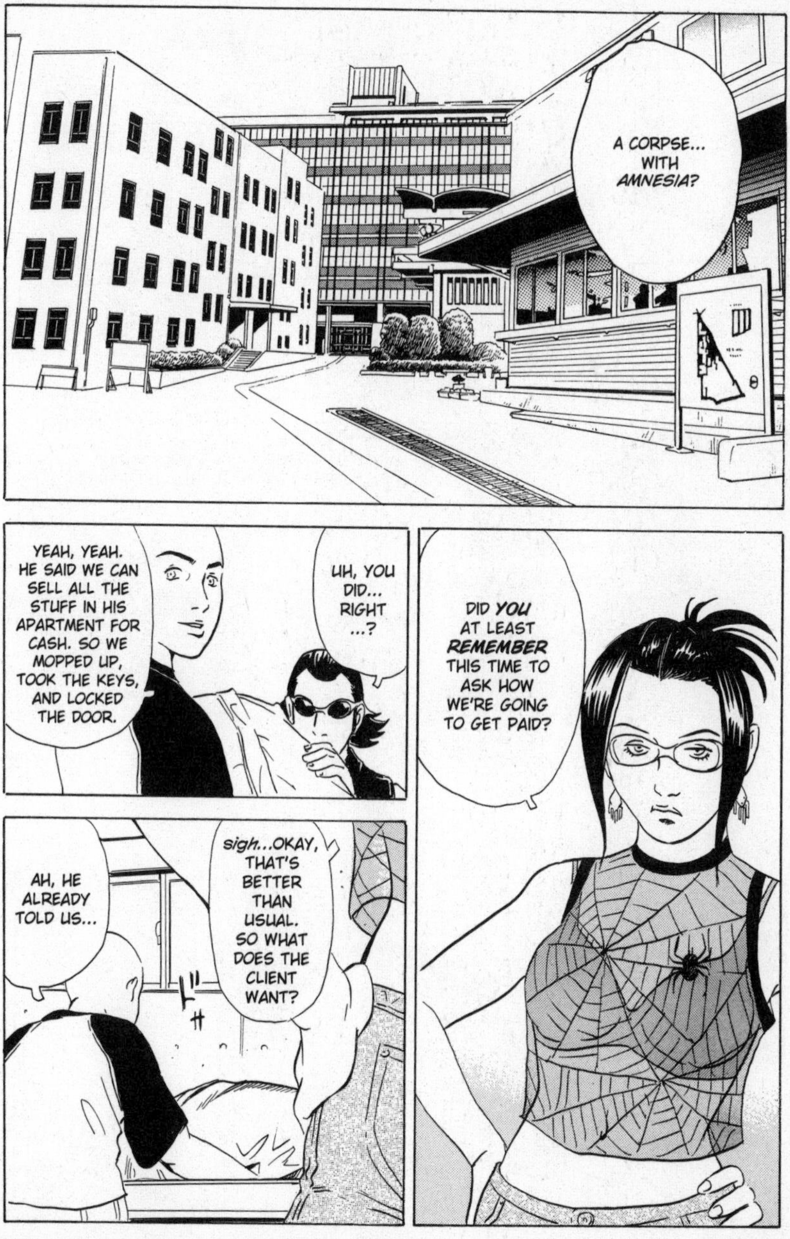
A CORPSE... WITH *AMNESIA?*
DID *YOU* AT LEAST ***REMEMBER*** THIS TIME TO ASK HOW WE'RE GOING TO GET PAID?
UH, YOU DID... RIGHT ...?
YEAH, YEAH. HE SAID WE CAN SELL ALL THE STUFF IN HIS APARTMENT FOR CASH. SO WE MOPPED UP, TOOK THE KEYS, AND LOCKED THE DOOR.
sigh...OKAY, THAT'S BETTER THAN USUAL. SO WHAT DOES THE CLIENT WANT?
AH, HE ALREADY TOLD US...

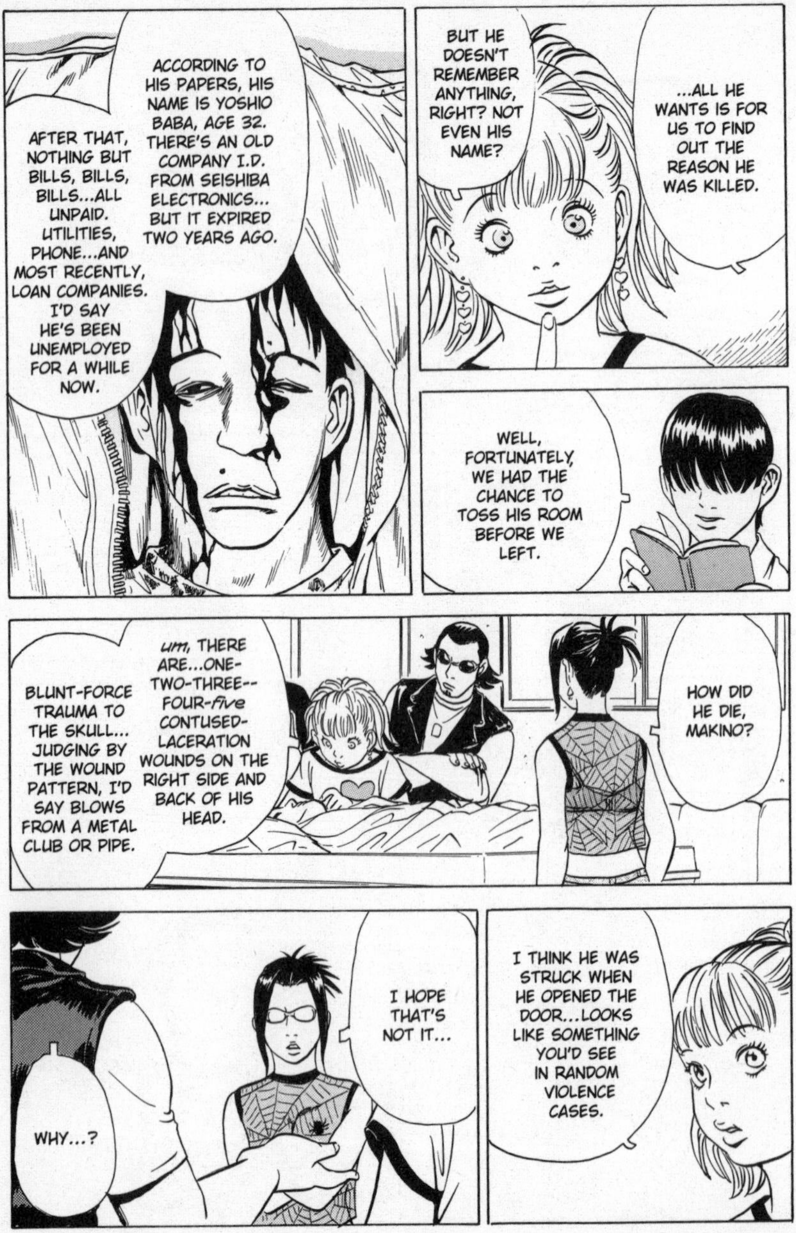
...ALL HE WANTS IS FOR US TO FIND OUT THE REASON HE WAS KILLED.
BUT HE DOESN'T REMEMBER ANYTHING, RIGHT? NOT EVEN HIS NAME?
WELL, FORTUNATELY, WE HAD THE CHANCE TO TOSS HIS ROOM BEFORE WE LEFT.
ACCORDING TO HIS PAPERS, HIS NAME IS YOSHIO BABA, AGE 32. THERE'S AN OLD COMPANY I.D. FROM SEISHIBA ELECTRONICS... BUT IT EXPIRED TWO YEARS AGO.
AFTER THAT, NOTHING BUT BILLS, BILLS, BILLS...ALL UNPAID. UTILITIES, PHONE...AND MOST RECENTLY, LOAN COMPANIES. I'D SAY HE'S BEEN UNEMPLOYED FOR A WHILE NOW.
HOW DID HE DIE, MAKINO?
um, THERE ARE...ONE-TWO-THREE--FOUR-*five* CONTUSED-LACERATION WOUNDS ON THE RIGHT SIDE AND BACK OF HIS HEAD.
BLUNT-FORCE TRAUMA TO THE SKULL... JUDGING BY THE WOUND PATTERN, I'D SAY BLOWS FROM A METAL CLUB OR PIPE.
I THINK HE WAS STRUCK WHEN HE OPENED THE DOOR...LOOKS LIKE SOMETHING YOU'D SEE IN RANDOM VIOLENCE CASES.
I HOPE THAT'S NOT IT...
WHY...?

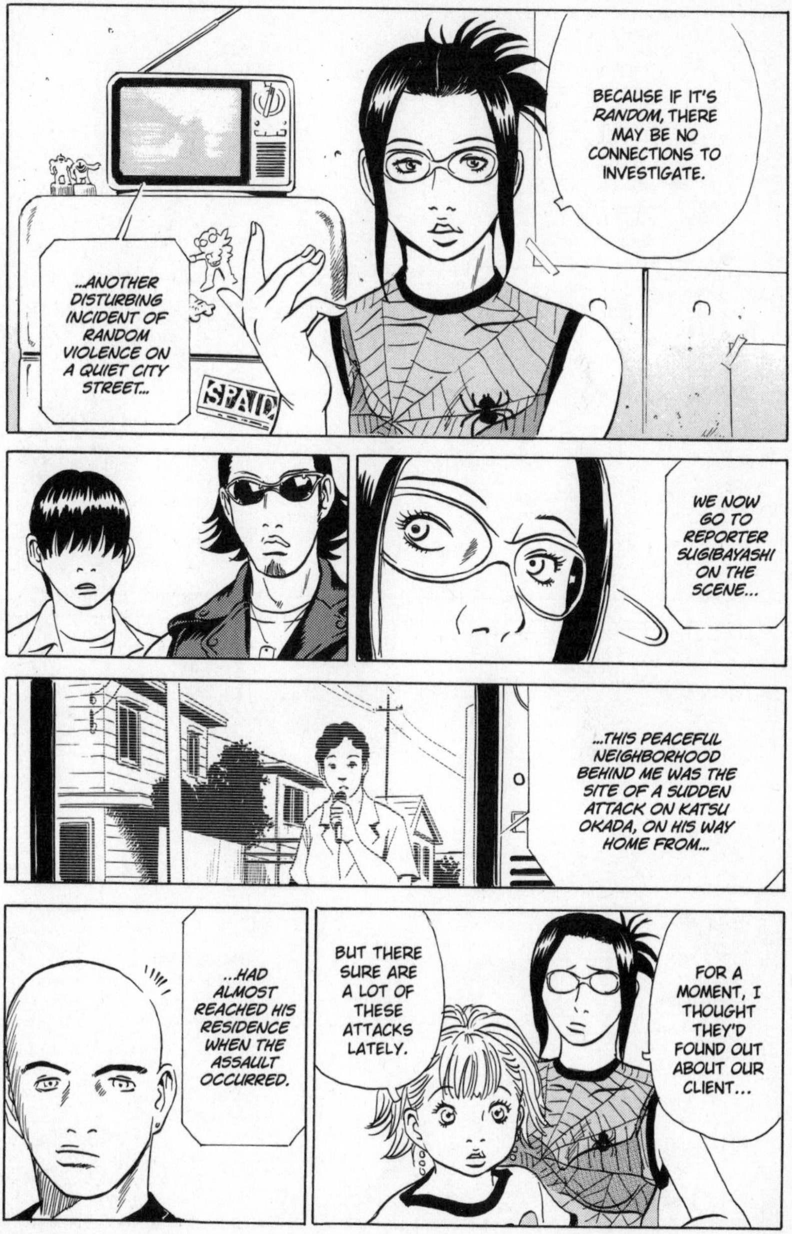
BECAUSE IF IT'S *RANDOM*, THERE MAY BE NO CONNECTIONS TO INVESTIGATE.
...ANOTHER DISTURBING INCIDENT OF RANDOM VIOLENCE ON A QUIET CITY STREET...
WE NOW GO TO REPORTER SUGIBAYASHI ON THE SCENE...
...THIS PEACEFUL NEIGHBORHOOD BEHIND ME WAS THE SITE OF A SUDDEN ATTACK ON KATSU OKADA, ON HIS WAY HOME FROM...
FOR A MOMENT, I THOUGHT THEY'D FOUND OUT ABOUT OUR CLIENT...
BUT THERE SURE ARE A LOT OF THESE ATTACKS LATELY.
...HAD ALMOST REACHED HIS RESIDENCE WHEN THE ASSAULT OCCURRED.

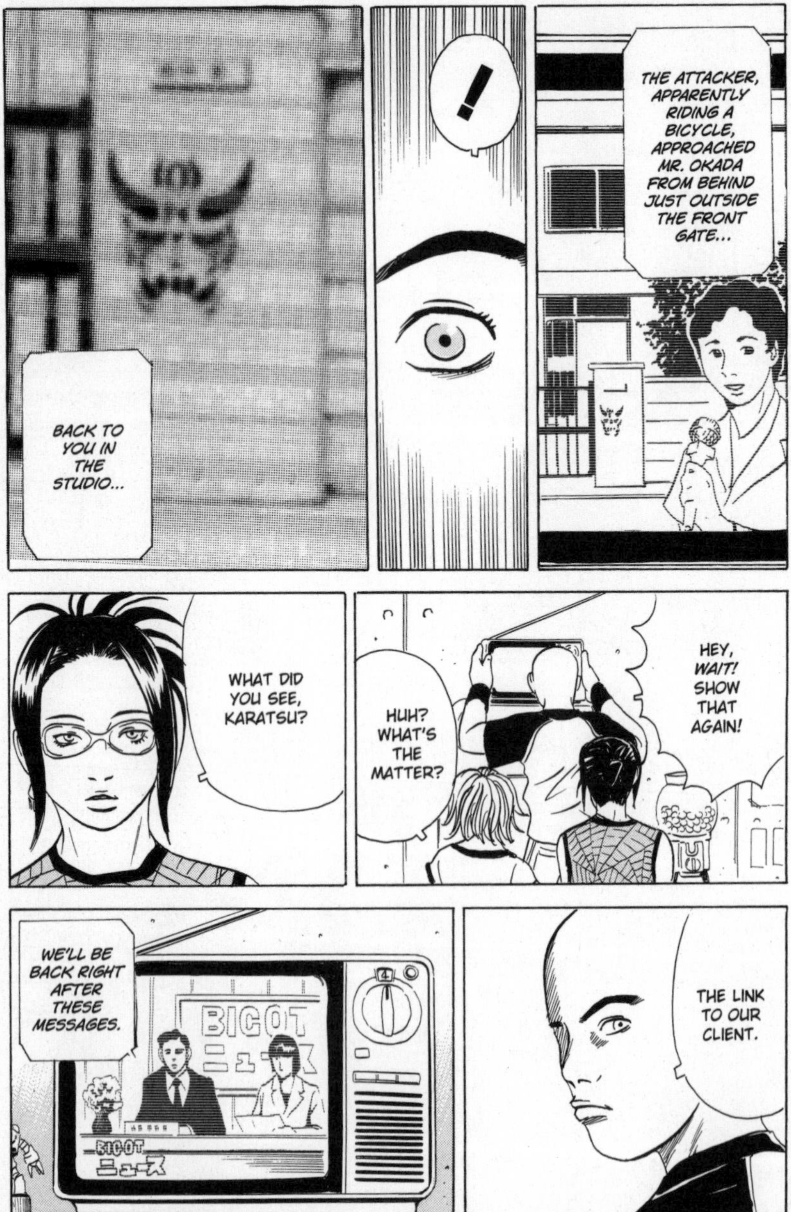
THE ATTACKER, APPARENTLY RIDING A BICYCLE, APPROACHED MR. OKADA FROM BEHIND JUST OUTSIDE THE FRONT GATE...
!
BACK TO YOU IN THE STUDIO...
HEY, WAIT! SHOW THAT AGAIN!
HUH? WHAT'S THE MATTER?
WHAT DID YOU SEE, KARATSU?
THE LINK TO OUR CLIENT.
WE'LL BE BACK RIGHT AFTER THESE MESSAGES.
BIGOT
ニュース

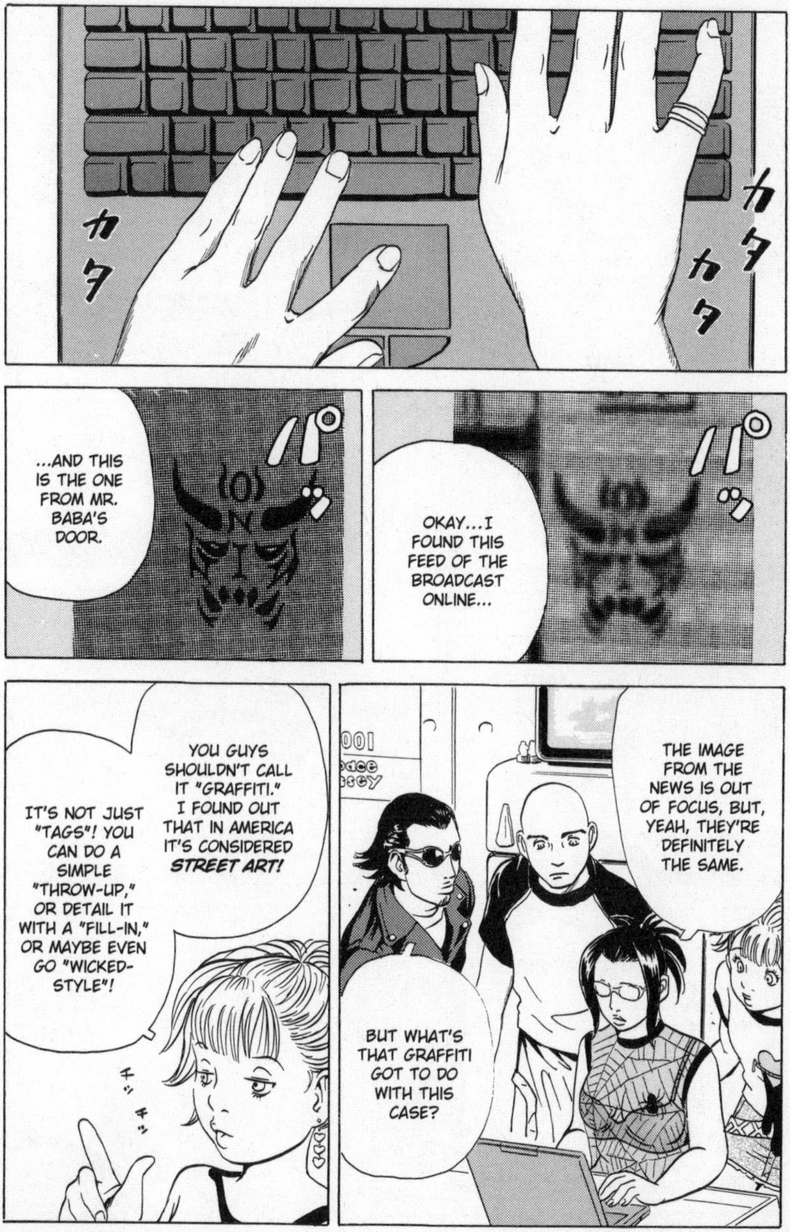
カタカタ
カタ
パッ
OKAY...I FOUND THIS FEED OF THE BROADCAST ONLINE...
パ
...AND THIS IS THE ONE FROM MR. BABA'S DOOR.
THE IMAGE FROM THE NEWS IS OUT OF FOCUS, BUT, YEAH, THEY'RE DEFINITELY THE SAME.
BUT WHAT'S THAT GRAFFITI GOT TO DO WITH THIS CASE?
YOU GUYS SHOULDN'T CALL IT "GRAFFITI." I FOUND OUT THAT IN AMERICA IT'S CONSIDERED ***STREET ART!***
IT'S NOT JUST "TAGS"! YOU CAN DO A SIMPLE "THROW-UP," OR DETAIL IT WITH A "FILL-IN," OR MAYBE EVEN GO "WICKED-STYLE"!
チッ チッ

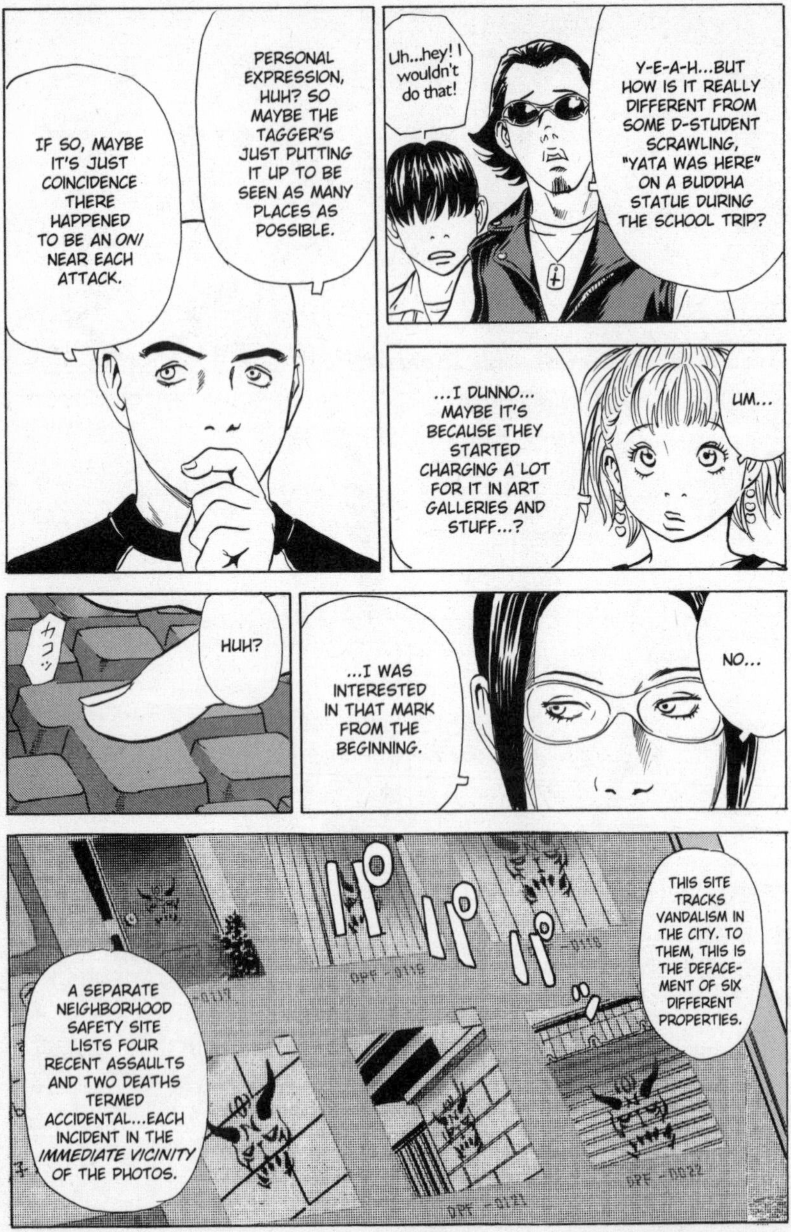
Y-E-A-H...BUT HOW IS IT REALLY DIFFERENT FROM SOME D-STUDENT SCRAWLING, "YATA WAS HERE" ON A BUDDHA STATUE DURING THE SCHOOL TRIP?
Uh...hey! I wouldn't do that!
UM...
...I DUNNO... MAYBE IT'S BECAUSE THEY STARTED CHARGING A LOT FOR IT IN ART GALLERIES AND STUFF...?
PERSONAL EXPRESSION, HUH? SO MAYBE THE TAGGER'S JUST PUTTING IT UP TO BE SEEN AS MANY PLACES AS POSSIBLE.
IF SO, MAYBE IT'S JUST COINCIDENCE THERE HAPPENED TO BE AN *ONI* NEAR EACH ATTACK.
NO...
...I WAS INTERESTED IN THAT MARK FROM THE BEGINNING.
HUH?
カコッ
THIS SITE TRACKS VANDALISM IN THE CITY. TO THEM, THIS IS THE DEFACEMENT OF SIX DIFFERENT PROPERTIES.
A SEPARATE NEIGHBORHOOD SAFETY SITE LISTS FOUR RECENT ASSAULTS AND TWO DEATHS TERMED ACCIDENTAL...EACH INCIDENT IN THE *IMMEDIATE VICINITY* OF THE PHOTOS.

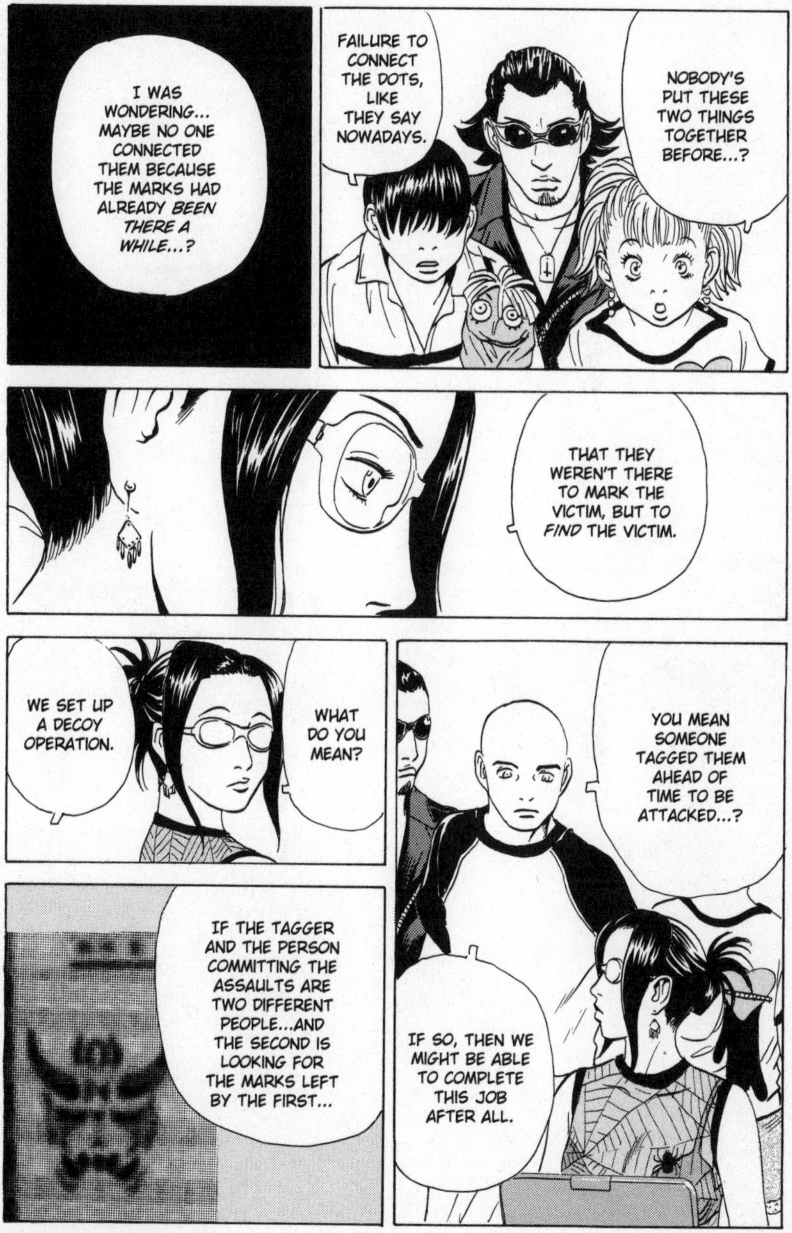
NOBODY'S PUT THESE TWO THINGS TOGETHER BEFORE...?
FAILURE TO CONNECT THE DOTS, LIKE THEY SAY NOWADAYS.
I WAS WONDERING... MAYBE NO ONE CONNECTED THEM BECAUSE THE MARKS HAD ALREADY *BEEN THERE A WHILE*...?
THAT THEY WEREN'T THERE TO MARK THE VICTIM, BUT TO *FIND* THE VICTIM.
YOU MEAN SOMEONE TAGGED THEM AHEAD OF TIME TO BE ATTACKED...?
IF SO, THEN WE MIGHT BE ABLE TO COMPLETE THIS JOB AFTER ALL.
WHAT DO YOU MEAN?
WE SET UP A DECOY OPERATION.
IF THE TAGGER AND THE PERSON COMMITTING THE ASSAULTS ARE TWO DIFFERENT PEOPLE...AND THE SECOND IS LOOKING FOR THE MARKS LEFT BY THE FIRST...

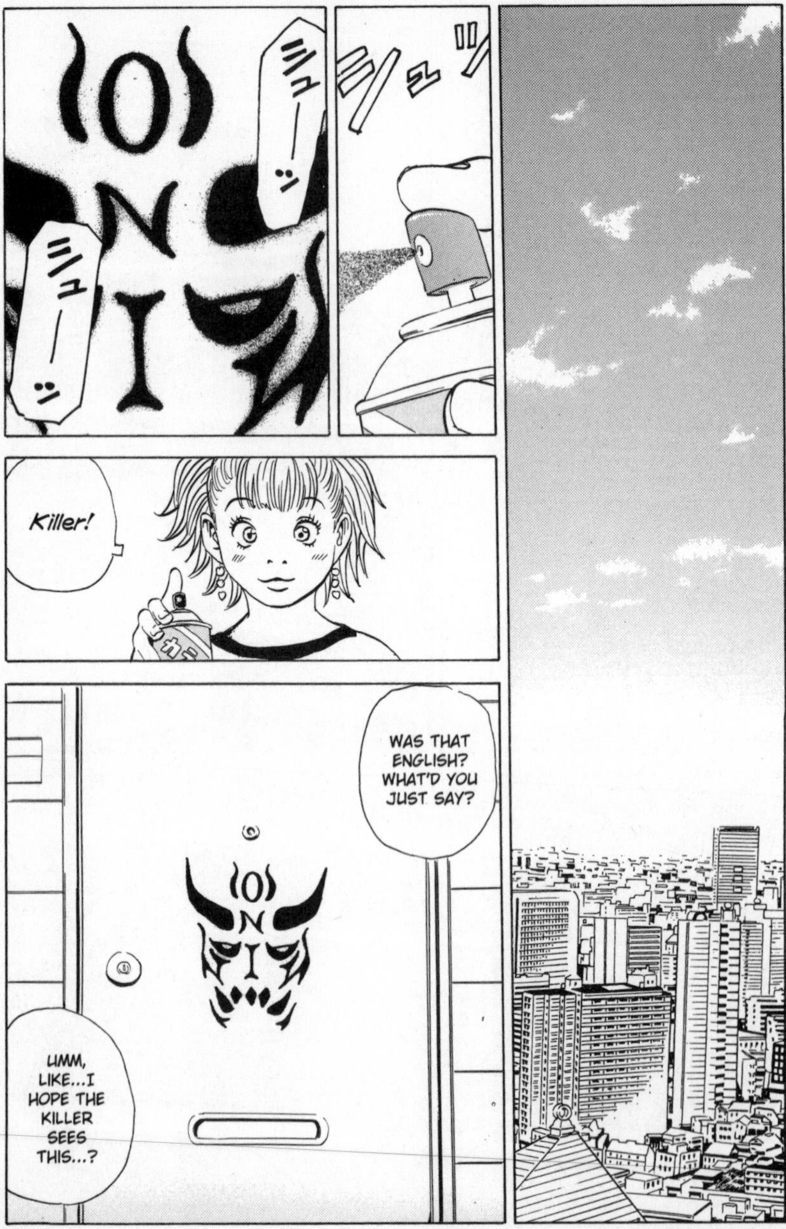

シュッ
シュ――ッ
シュ――ッ
Killer!
WAS THAT ENGLISH? WHAT'D YOU JUST SAY?
UMM, LIKE...I HOPE THE KILLER SEES THIS...?

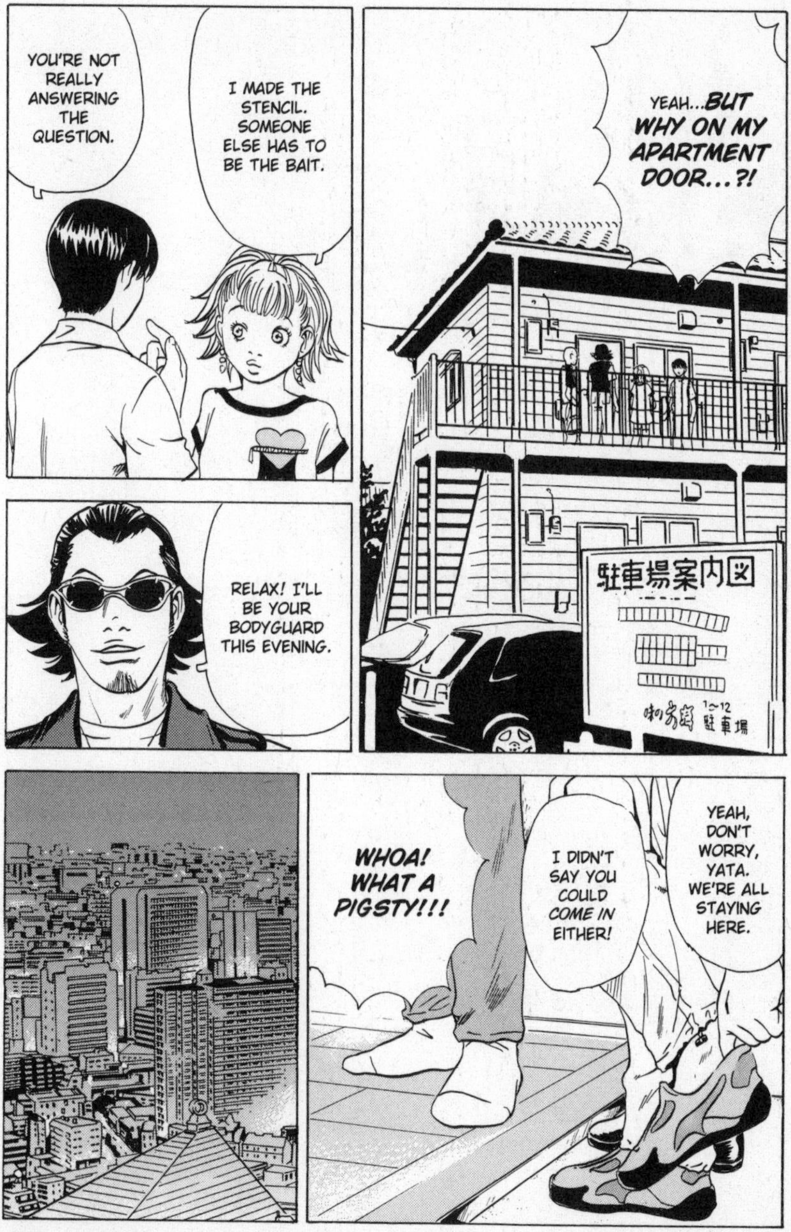
YEAH...BUT WHY ON MY APARTMENT DOOR...?!
駐車場案内図
1~12 駐車場
I MADE THE STENCIL. SOMEONE ELSE HAS TO BE THE BAIT.
YOU'RE NOT REALLY ANSWERING THE QUESTION.
RELAX! I'LL BE YOUR BODYGUARD THIS EVENING.
YEAH, DON'T WORRY, YATA. WE'RE ALL STAYING HERE.
I DIDN'T SAY YOU COULD COME IN EITHER!
WHOA! WHAT A PIGSTY!!!

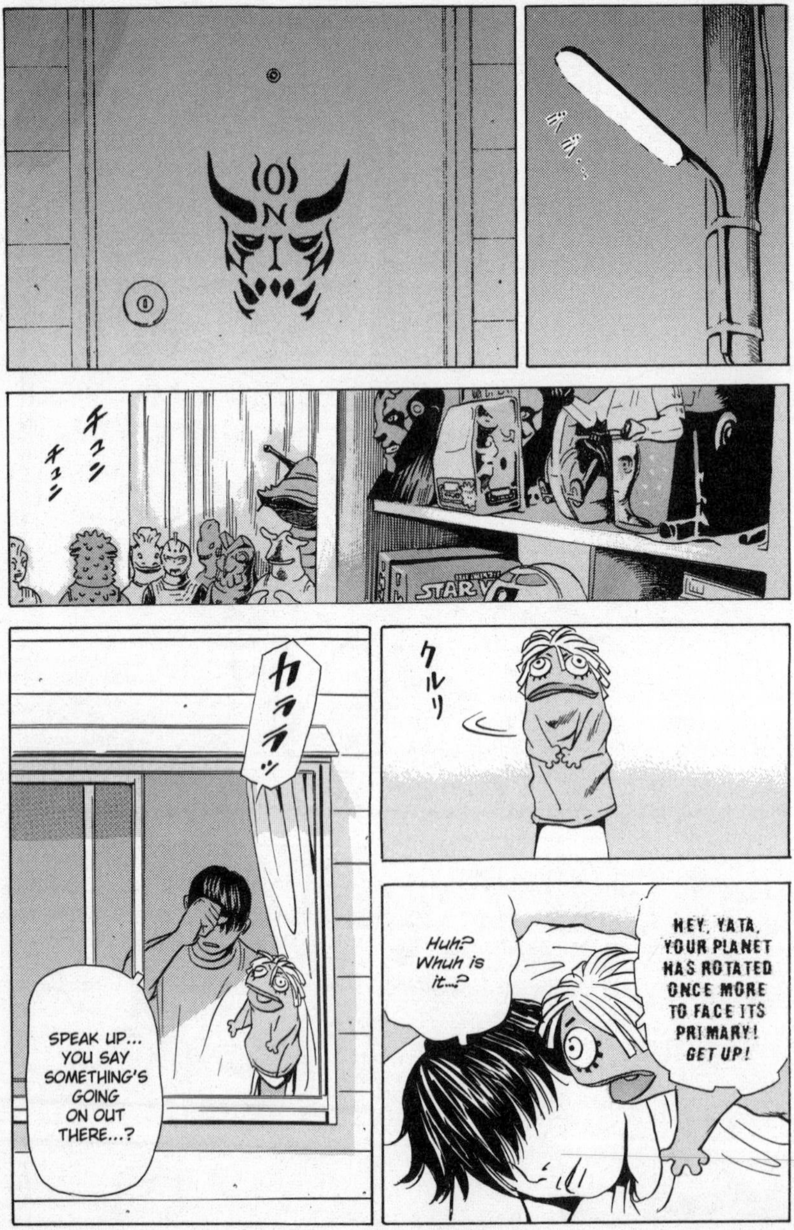

チュン
チュン
クルリ
HEY, YATA, YOUR PLANET HAS ROTATED ONCE MORE TO FACE ITS PRIMARY! GET UP!
Huh? Whuh is it...?
カララッ
SPEAK UP... YOU SAY SOMETHING'S GOING ON OUT THERE...?

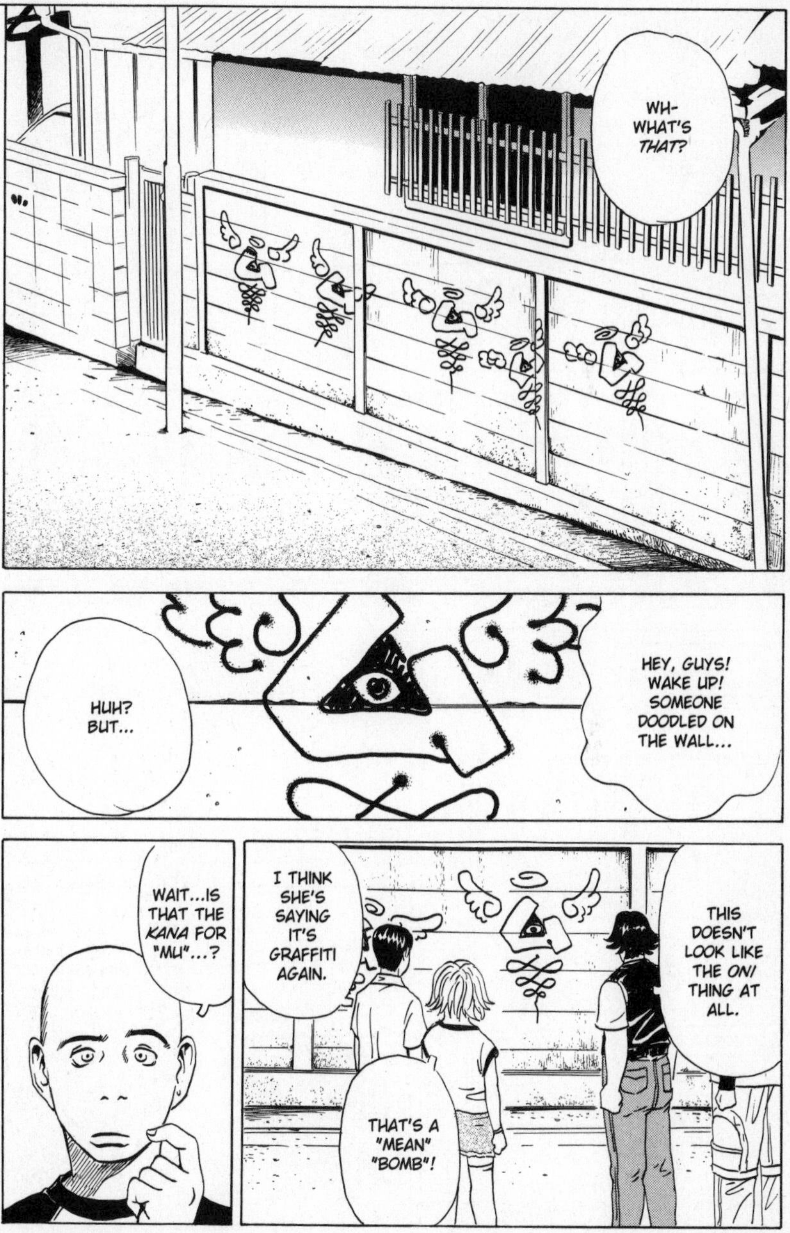
WH- WHAT'S *THAT?*
HEY, GUYS! WAKE UP! SOMEONE DOODLED ON THE WALL...
HUH? BUT...
THIS DOESN'T LOOK LIKE THE *ONI* THING AT ALL.
I THINK SHE'S SAYING IT'S GRAFFITI AGAIN.
THAT'S A "MEAN" "BOMB"!
WAIT...IS THAT THE *KANA* FOR "MU"...?

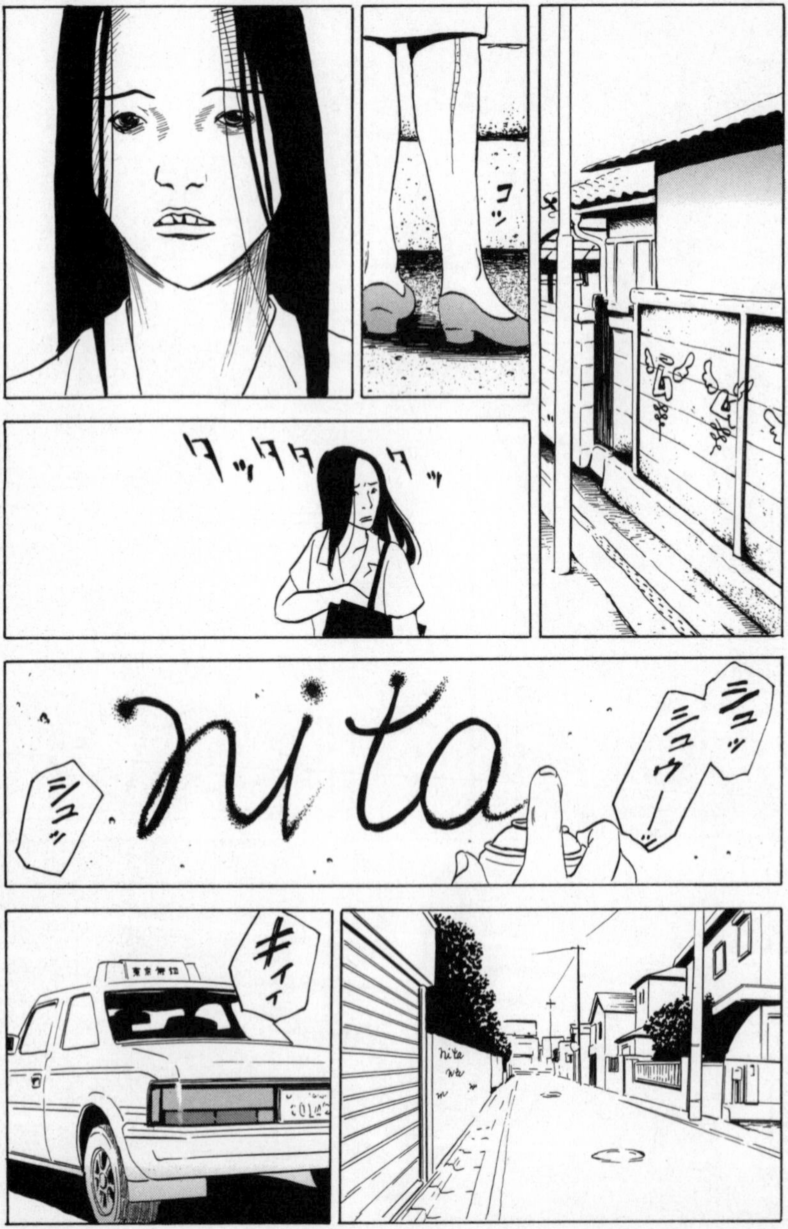
コッ
タッタタ タッ
シュッ シュウー…
nita
シュッ
nita
キイイ

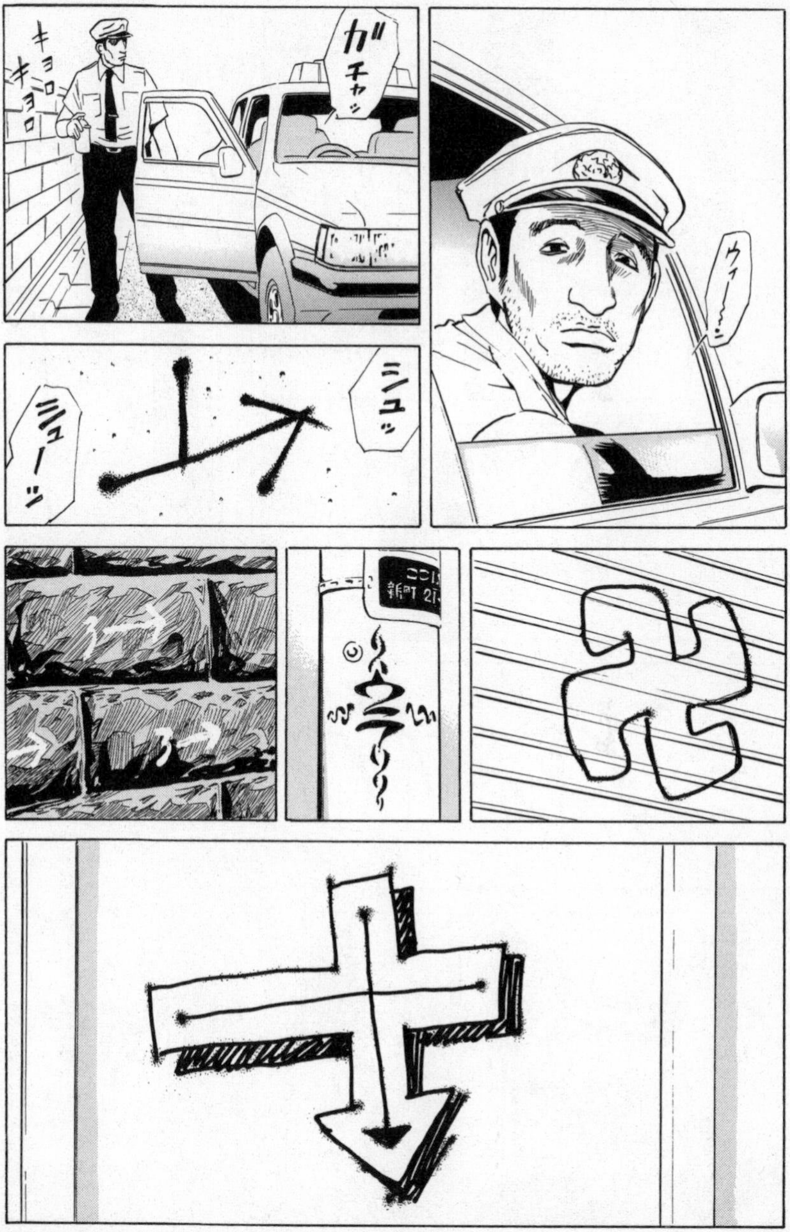
ヴィ～…
ガチャッ
キョロ キョロ
シュッ
シューッ
ココ

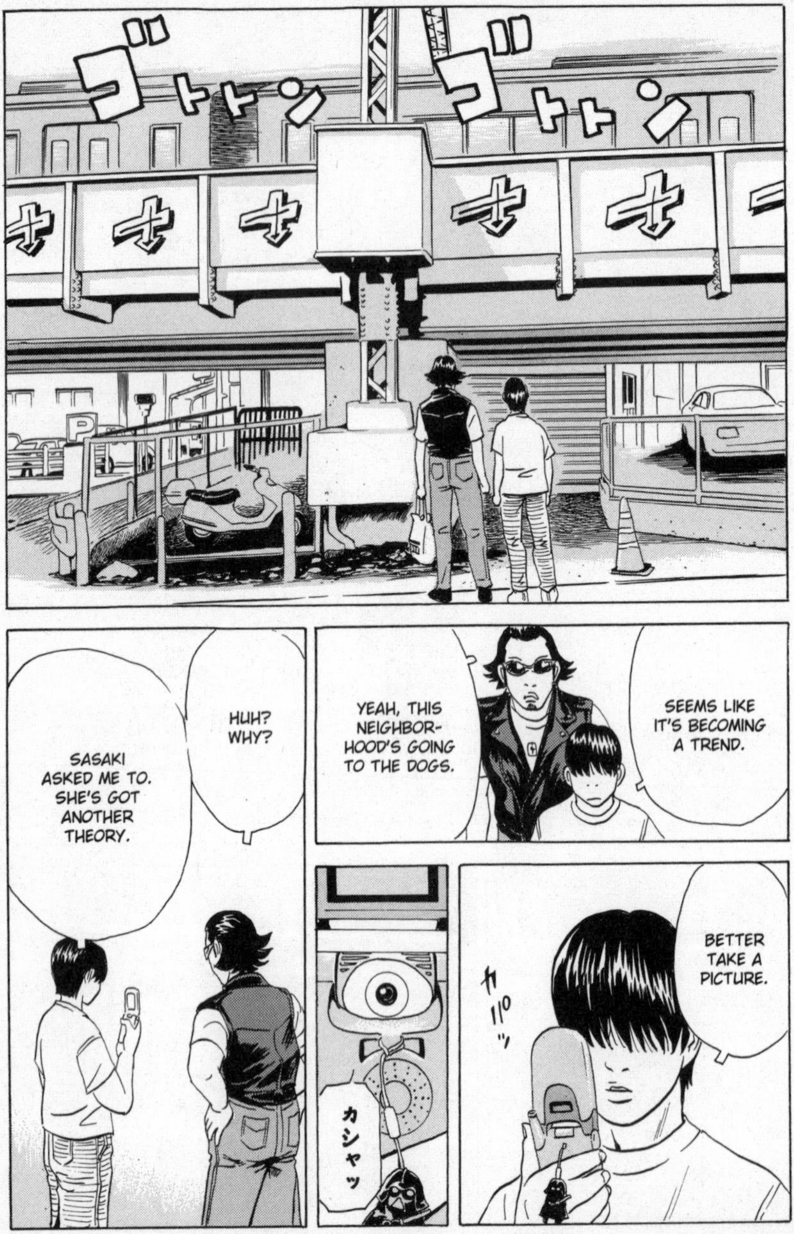
ゴトトン
ゴトトン
SEEMS LIKE IT'S BECOMING A TREND.
YEAH, THIS NEIGHBOR-HOOD'S GOING TO THE DOGS.
BETTER TAKE A PICTURE.
カパッ
カシャッ
HUH? WHY?
SASAKI ASKED ME TO. SHE'S GOT ANOTHER THEORY.

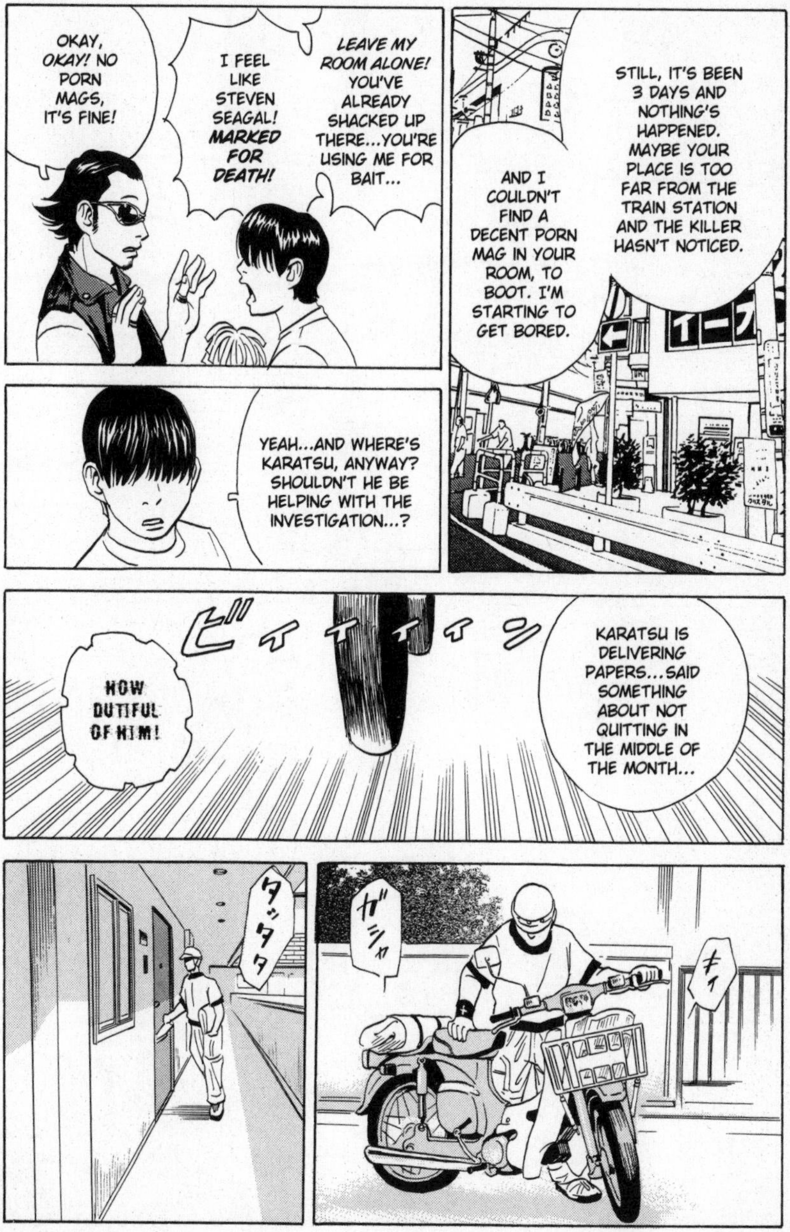
STILL, IT'S BEEN 3 DAYS AND NOTHING'S HAPPENED. MAYBE YOUR PLACE IS TOO FAR FROM THE TRAIN STATION AND THE KILLER HASN'T NOTICED.
AND I COULDN'T FIND A DECENT PORN MAG IN YOUR ROOM, TO BOOT. I'M STARTING TO GET BORED.
LEAVE MY ROOM ALONE! YOU'VE ALREADY SHACKED UP THERE...YOU'RE USING ME FOR BAIT...
I FEEL LIKE STEVEN SEAGAL! MARKED FOR DEATH!
OKAY, OKAY! NO PORN MAGS, IT'S FINE!
YEAH...AND WHERE'S KARATSU, ANYWAY? SHOULDN'T HE BE HELPING WITH THE INVESTIGATION...?
KARATSU IS DELIVERING PAPERS...SAID SOMETHING ABOUT NOT QUITTING IN THE MIDDLE OF THE MONTH...
ビィイイイン
HOW DUTIFUL OF HIM!
キィ
ガシャ
タッタタ

IT'S HERE, TOO...?

HUH?

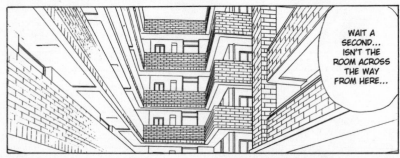

WAIT A SECOND... ISN'T THE ROOM ACROSS THE WAY FROM HERE...

MU... "MUKAI"...

...ACROSS.

YEAH. IT'S WHERE OUR CLIENT LIVED.

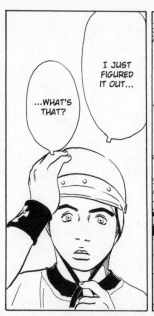

HEY! WHERE'S YATA?!
IT'S JUST US HERE. WHAT'S GOING ON?
I JUST FIGURED IT OUT...
...WHAT'S THAT?
HUH? THIS? THESE ARE ALL THE TAGS THAT HAVE SHOWN UP AROUND YATA'S NEIGHBORHOOD.
SO MANY ALREADY? THIS IS BAD.
BAD? HOW DO YOU MEAN, BAD...?
THEY AREN'T TAGS.
THEY'RE ROUTE CODES. WITH JUST THE *ONI* MARK, THERE'S NO WAY THE KILLER COULD HAVE SEARCHED EVERY DOOR IN THE AREA.
APER ROUTE CODE
Straight at Intersection
Bend
Switchback
Forward
T-Intersection
LOOK. THESE ARE THE CODES DELIVERY PEOPLE ARE GIVEN FOR PAPER ROUTES.

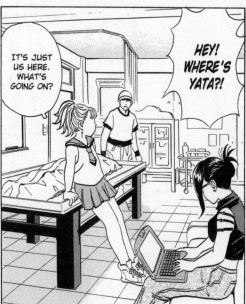

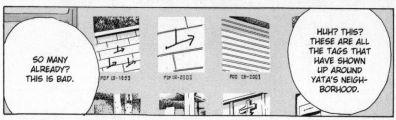

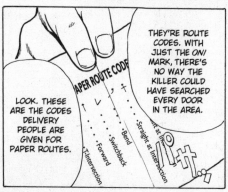

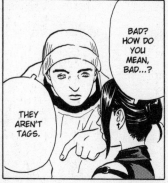

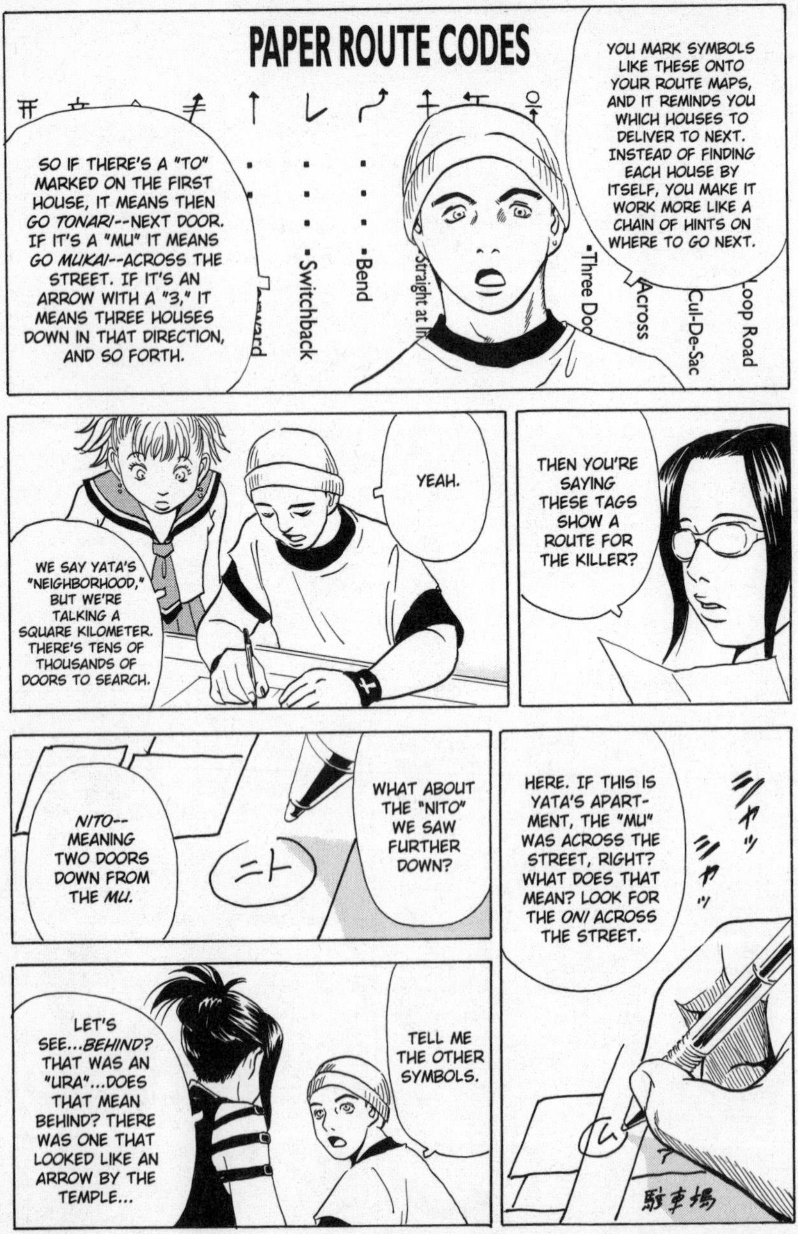
PAPER ROUTE CODES
YOU MARK SYMBOLS LIKE THESE ONTO YOUR ROUTE MAPS, AND IT REMINDS YOU WHICH HOUSES TO DELIVER TO NEXT. INSTEAD OF FINDING EACH HOUSE BY ITSELF, YOU MAKE IT WORK MORE LIKE A CHAIN OF HINTS ON WHERE TO GO NEXT.
Loop Road
Cul-De-Sac
Across
Bend
Switchback
SO IF THERE'S A "TO" MARKED ON THE FIRST HOUSE, IT MEANS THEN GO *TONARI*--NEXT DOOR. IF IT'S A "MU" IT MEANS GO *MUKAI*--ACROSS THE STREET. IF IT'S AN ARROW WITH A "3," IT MEANS THREE HOUSES DOWN IN THAT DIRECTION, AND SO FORTH.
THEN YOU'RE SAYING THESE TAGS SHOW A ROUTE FOR THE KILLER?
YEAH.
WE SAY YATA'S "NEIGHBORHOOD," BUT WE'RE TALKING A SQUARE KILOMETER. THERE'S TENS OF THOUSANDS OF DOORS TO SEARCH.
シャッ
シャッ
HERE. IF THIS IS YATA'S APARTMENT, THE "MU" WAS ACROSS THE STREET, RIGHT? WHAT DOES THAT MEAN? LOOK FOR THE *ONI* ACROSS THE STREET.
ム
駐車場
WHAT ABOUT THE "NITO" WE SAW FURTHER DOWN?
ニト
NITO--MEANING TWO DOORS DOWN FROM THE *MU*.
TELL ME THE OTHER SYMBOLS.
LET'S SEE...*BEHIND?* THAT WAS AN "URA"...DOES THAT MEAN BEHIND? THERE WAS ONE THAT LOOKED LIKE AN ARROW BY THE TEMPLE...

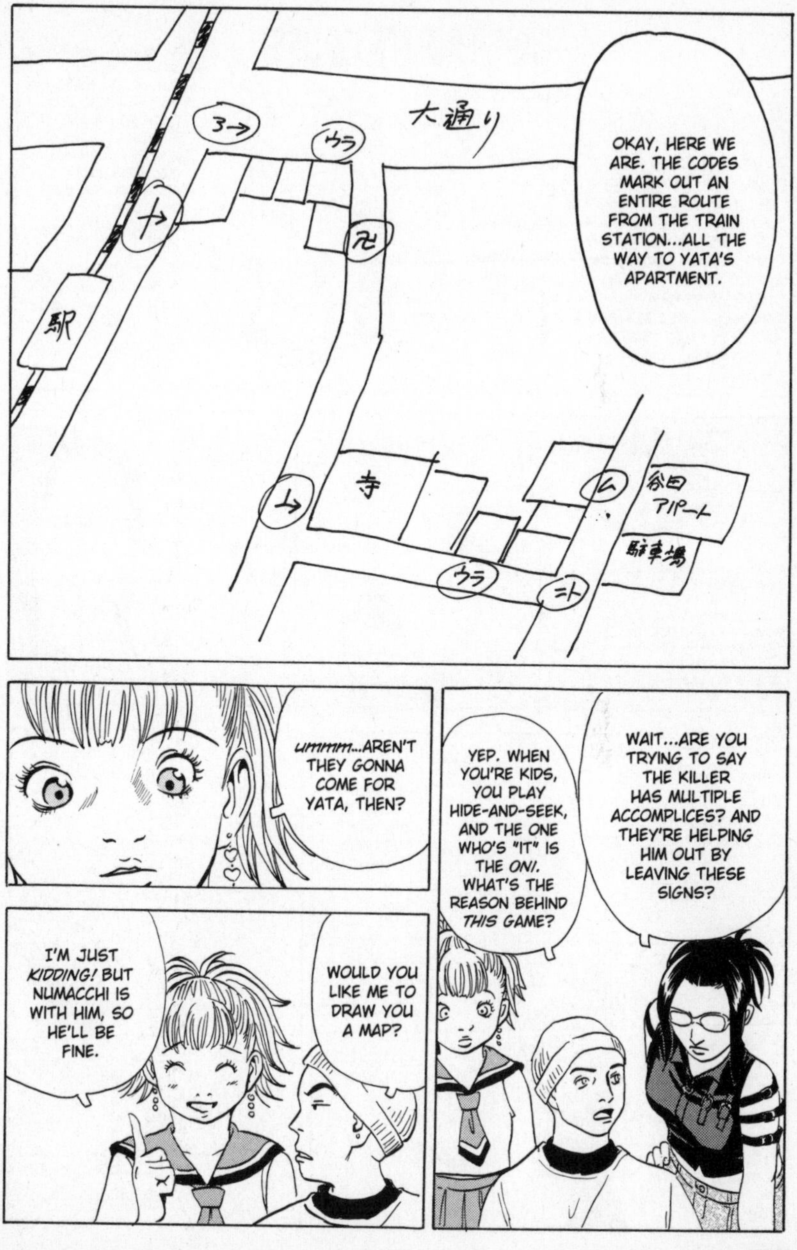
大通り
駅
寺
谷田
アパート
駐車場
ウラ
OKAY, HERE WE ARE. THE CODES MARK OUT AN ENTIRE ROUTE FROM THE TRAIN STATION...ALL THE WAY TO YATA'S APARTMENT.
WAIT...ARE YOU TRYING TO SAY THE KILLER HAS MULTIPLE ACCOMPLICES? AND THEY'RE HELPING HIM OUT BY LEAVING THESE SIGNS?
YEP. WHEN YOU'RE KIDS, YOU PLAY HIDE-AND-SEEK, AND THE ONE WHO'S "IT" IS THE *ONI*. WHAT'S THE REASON BEHIND *THIS* GAME?
ummm...AREN'T THEY GONNA COME FOR YATA, THEN?
WOULD YOU LIKE ME TO DRAW YOU A MAP?
I'M JUST *KIDDING!* BUT NUMACCHI IS WITH HIM, SO HE'LL BE FINE.

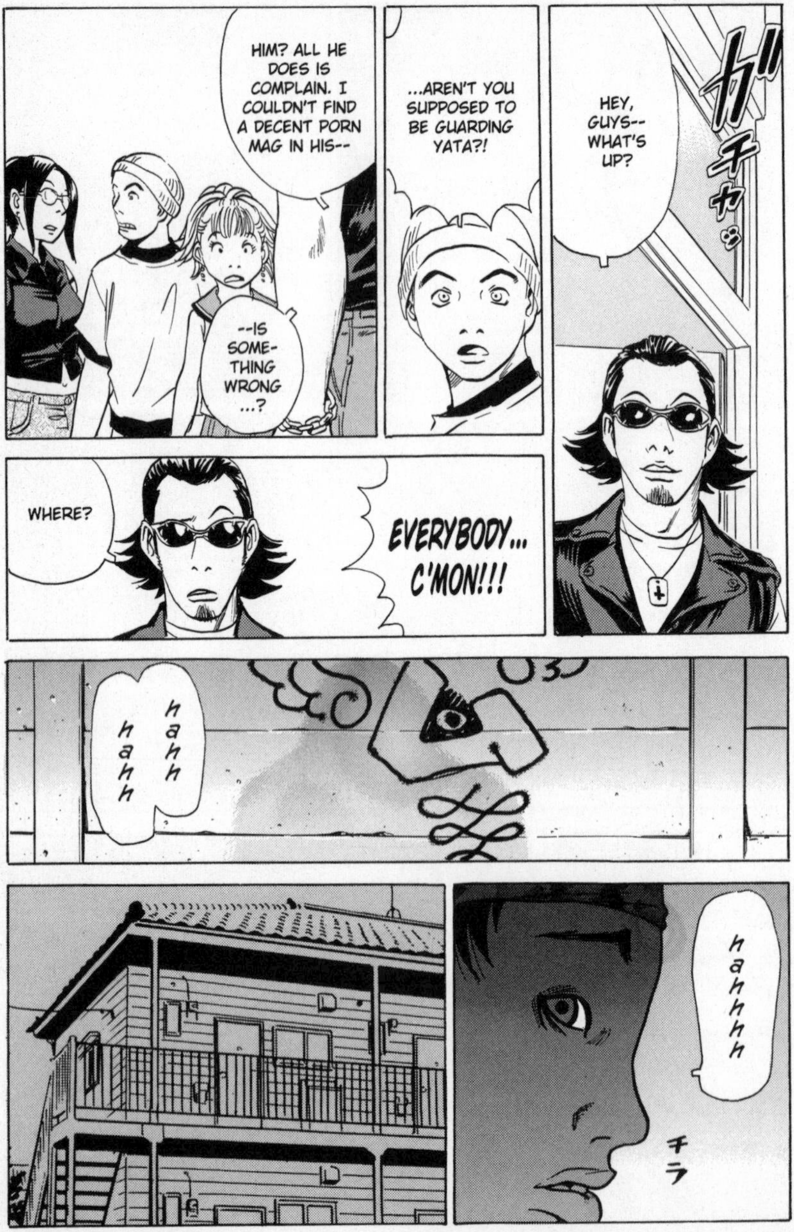
ガチャッ
HEY, GUYS-- WHAT'S UP?
...AREN'T YOU SUPPOSED TO BE GUARDING YATA?!
HIM? ALL HE DOES IS COMPLAIN. I COULDN'T FIND A DECENT PORN MAG IN HIS--
--IS SOMETHING WRONG ...?
EVERYBODY... C'MON!!!
WHERE?
hahh hahh
hahhhh
チラ

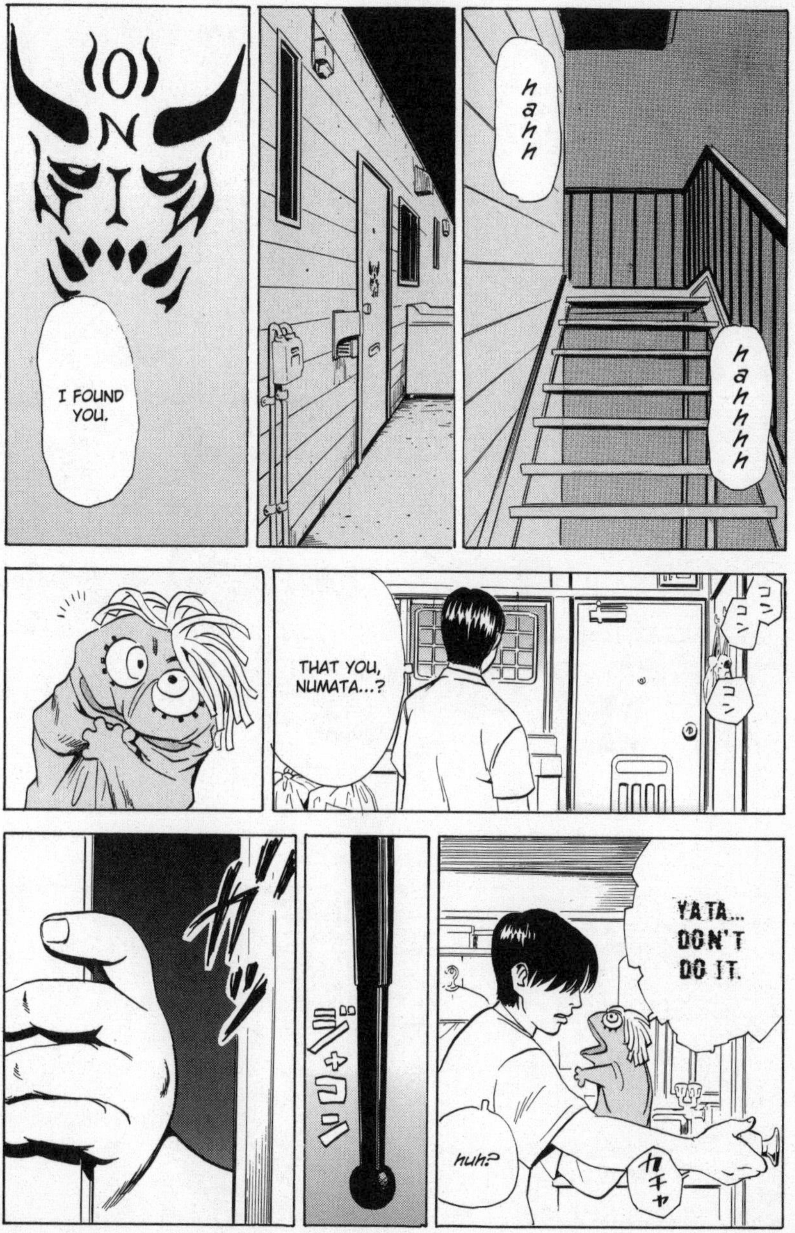
hahh
hahhhh
ONI
I FOUND YOU.
コン
コン
コン
THAT YOU, NUMATA...?
YATA... DON'T DO IT.
huh?
カチャ
ジャコン
ガッ

ドカッ
UM...
..HEY!!
hahhhhhh
hahhhhhh
WHAT...DO YOU THINK YOU'RE DOING... HUH?
I FOUND YOU...FAIR AND SQUARE...

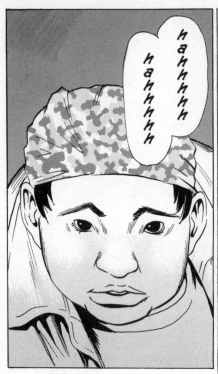

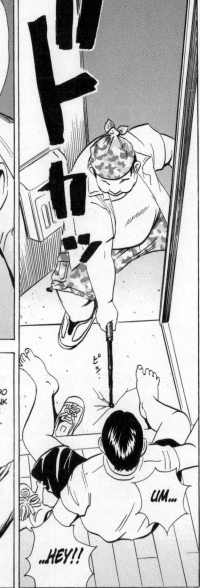

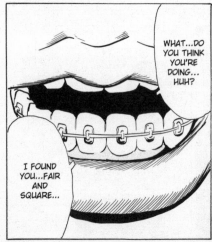

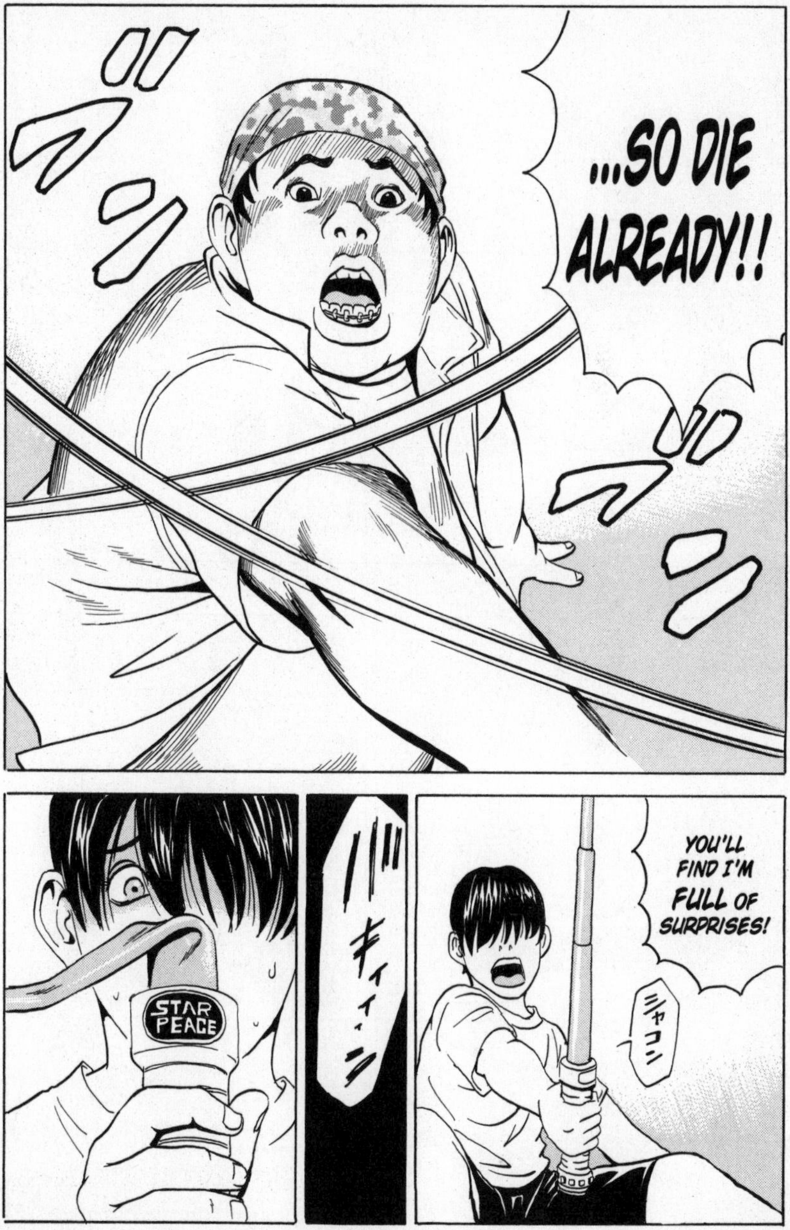
...SO DIE ALREADY!!
YOU'LL FIND I'M FULL OF SURPRISES!
シャコン
バキィィン
STAR PEACE

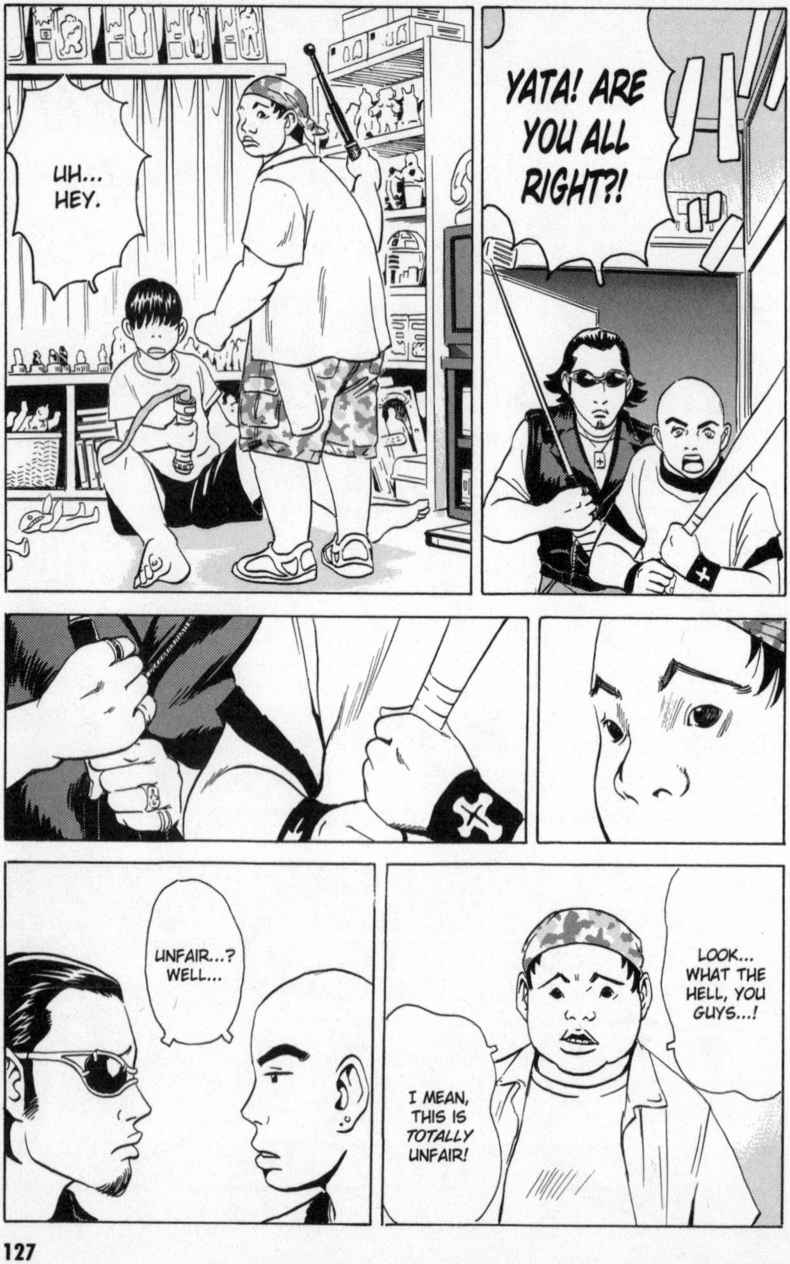
YATA! ARE YOU ALL RIGHT?!
UH... HEY.
LOOK... WHAT THE HELL, YOU GUYS...!
I MEAN, THIS IS *TOTALLY* UNFAIR!
UNFAIR...? WELL...

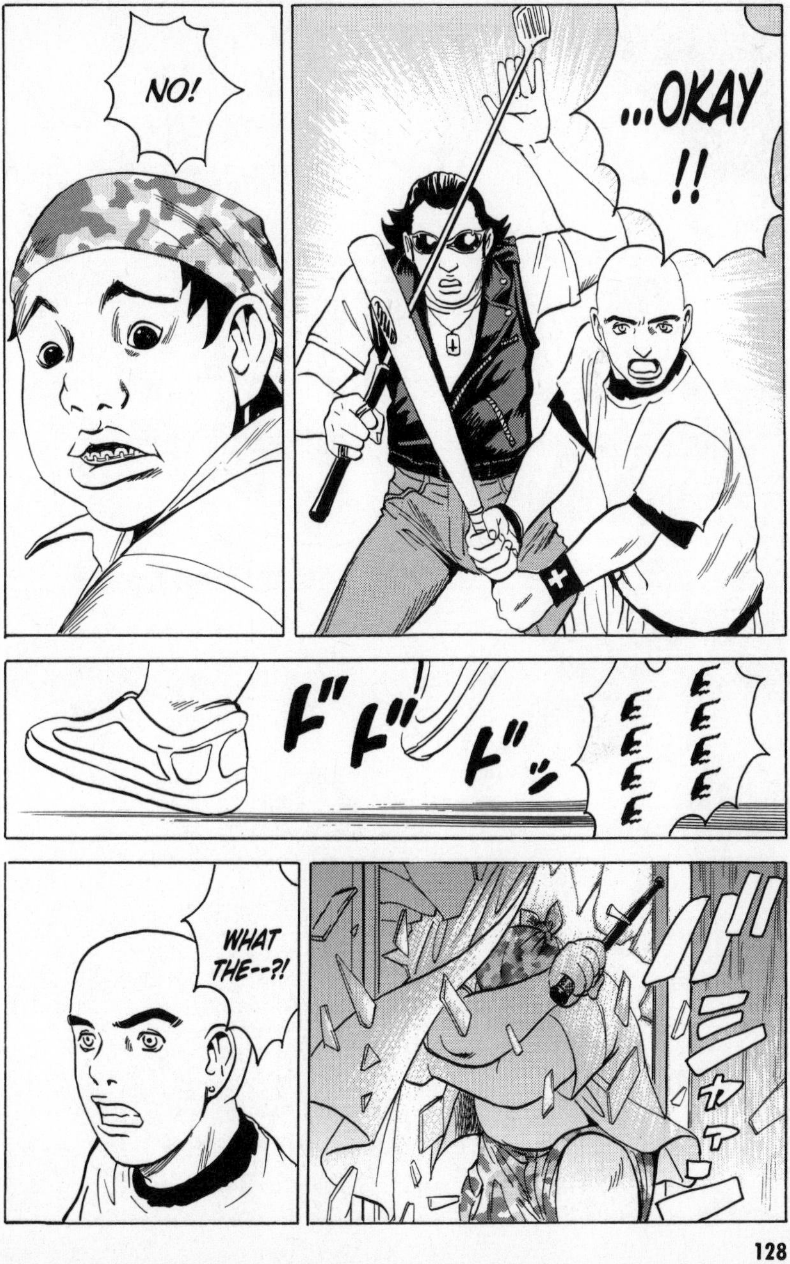
...OKAY !!
NO!
ドドドッ
EEEEEEEEE
WHAT THE--?!

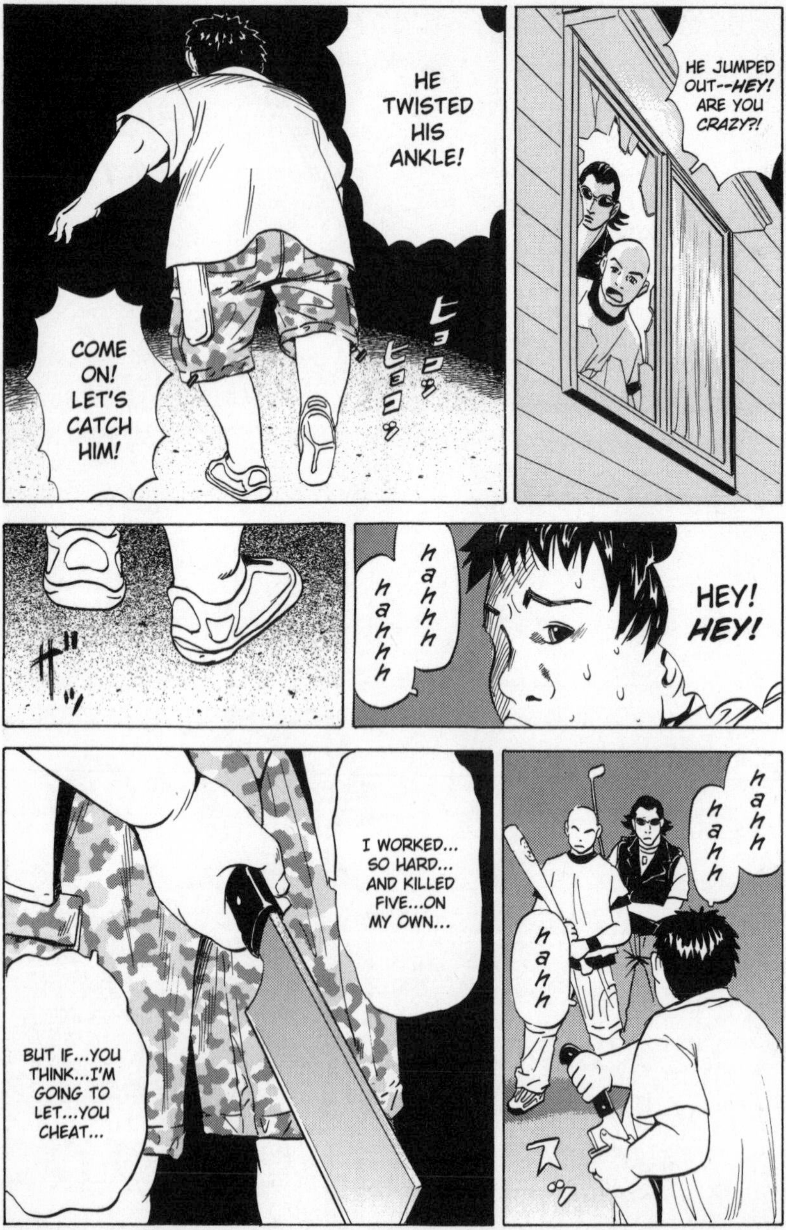
HE JUMPED OUT--*HEY!* ARE YOU *CRAZY?!*
HE TWISTED HIS ANKLE!
COME ON! LET'S CATCH HIM!
HEY! *HEY!*
hahhh
hahhh
hahh
hahh
hahh
I WORKED... SO HARD... AND KILLED FIVE...ON MY OWN...
BUT IF...YOU THINK...I'M GOING TO LET...YOU CHEAT...

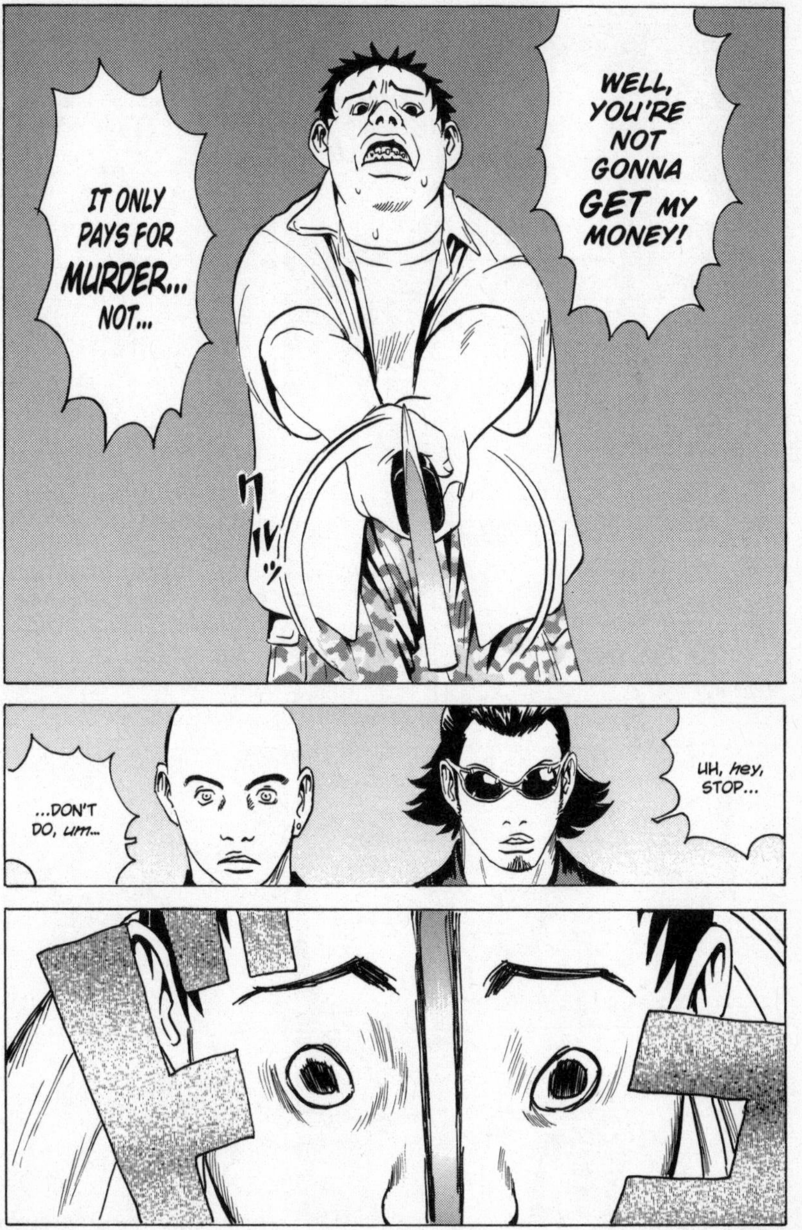
WELL, YOU'RE NOT GONNA GET MY MONEY!
IT ONLY PAYS FOR MURDER... NOT...
UH, hey, STOP...
...DON'T DO, um...

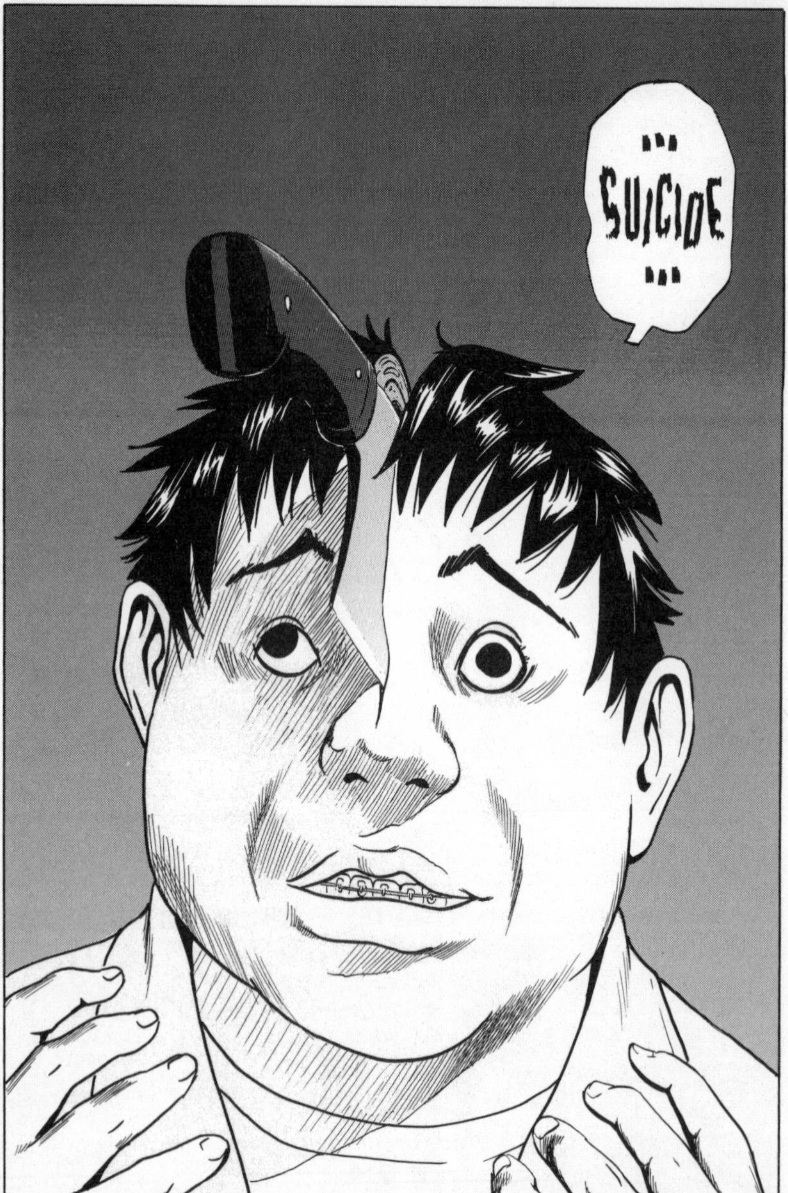
...SUICIDE...

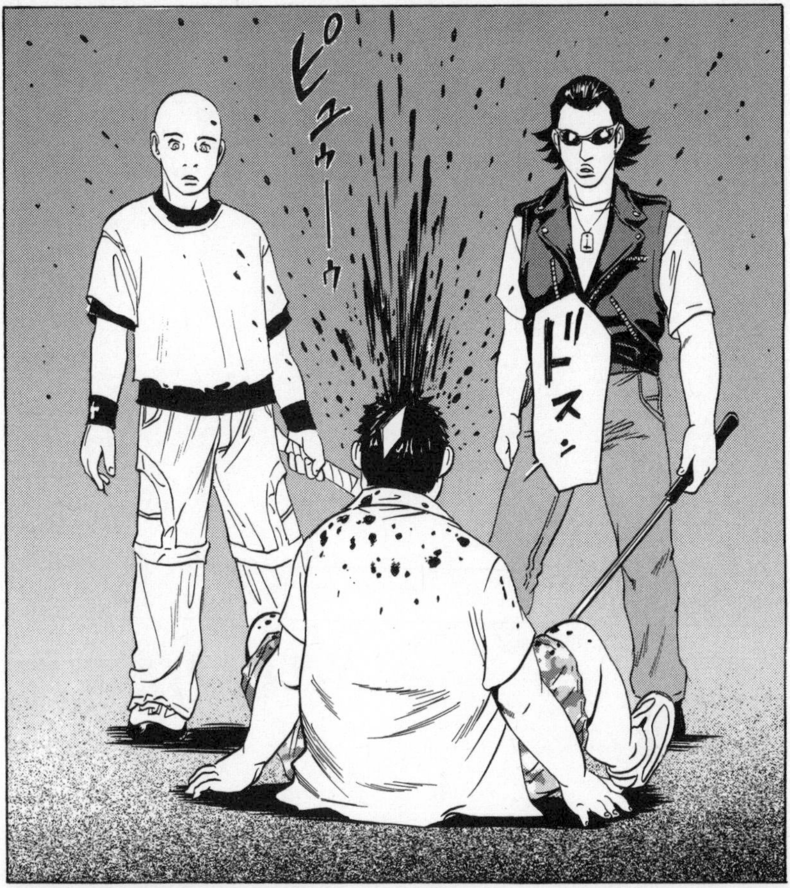
ピュゥーーゥ
ドスッ

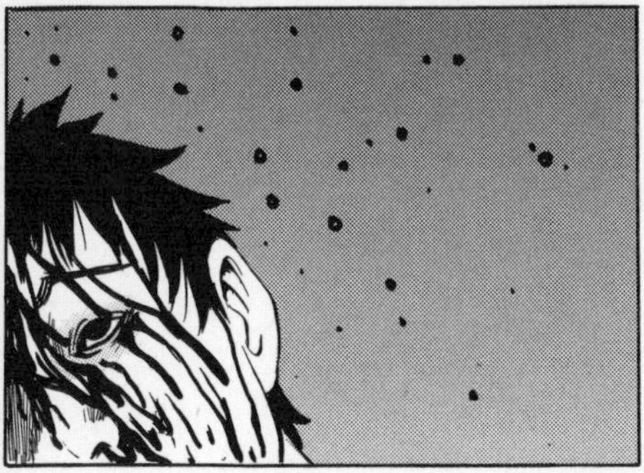

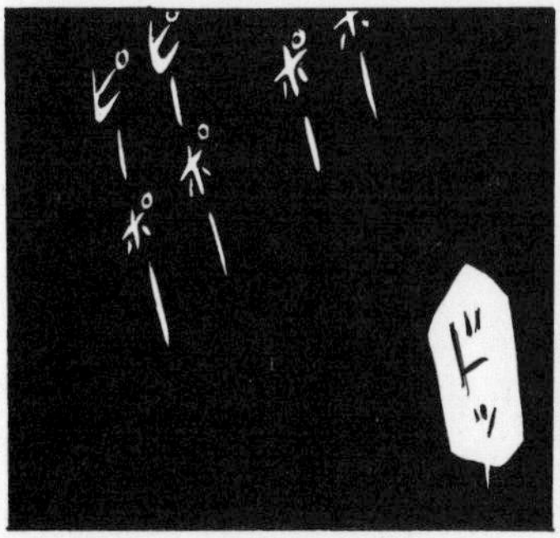
ポー
ポー
ピーポー
ピーポー
ドッ

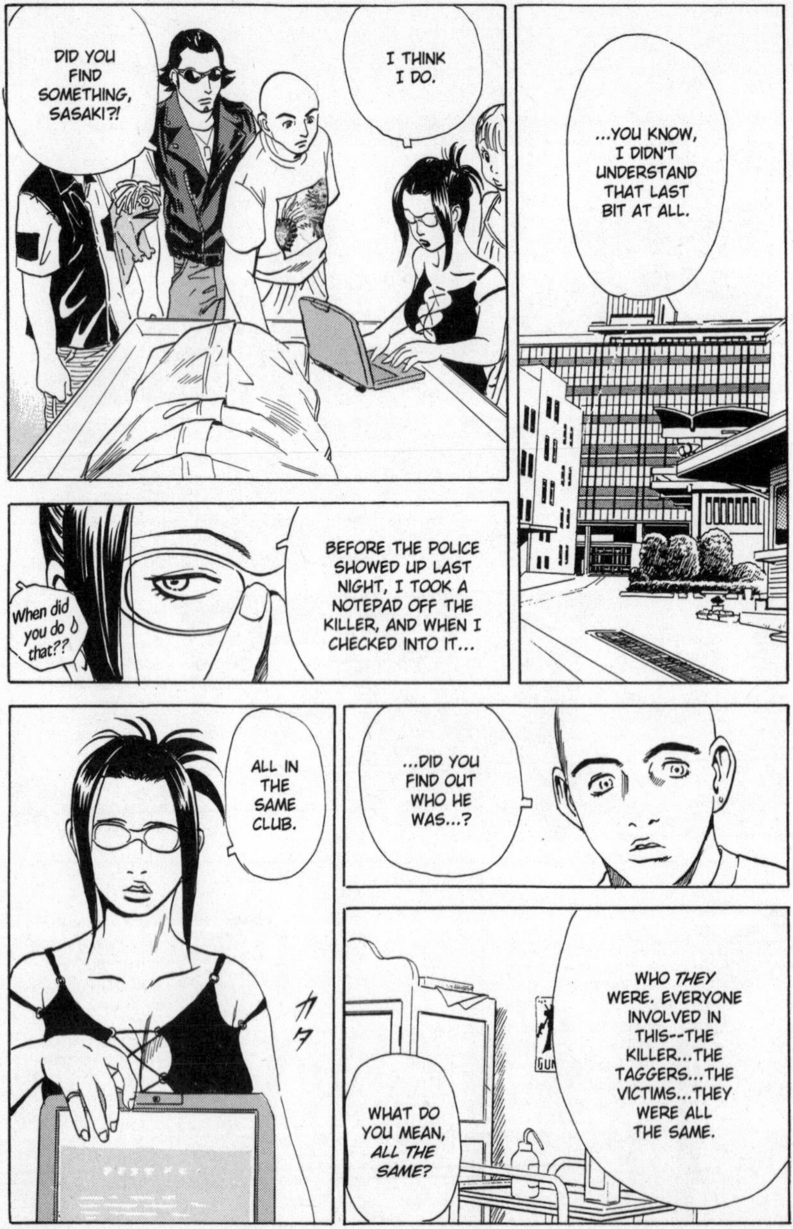
...YOU KNOW, I DIDN'T UNDERSTAND THAT LAST BIT AT ALL.
I THINK I DO.
DID YOU FIND SOMETHING, SASAKI?!
BEFORE THE POLICE SHOWED UP LAST NIGHT, I TOOK A NOTEPAD OFF THE KILLER, AND WHEN I CHECKED INTO IT...
When did you do that??
...DID YOU FIND OUT WHO HE WAS...?
WHO *THEY* WERE. EVERYONE INVOLVED IN THIS--THE KILLER...THE TAGGERS...THE VICTIMS...THEY WERE ALL THE SAME.
WHAT DO YOU MEAN, *ALL THE SAME?*
ALL IN THE SAME CLUB.
カタ

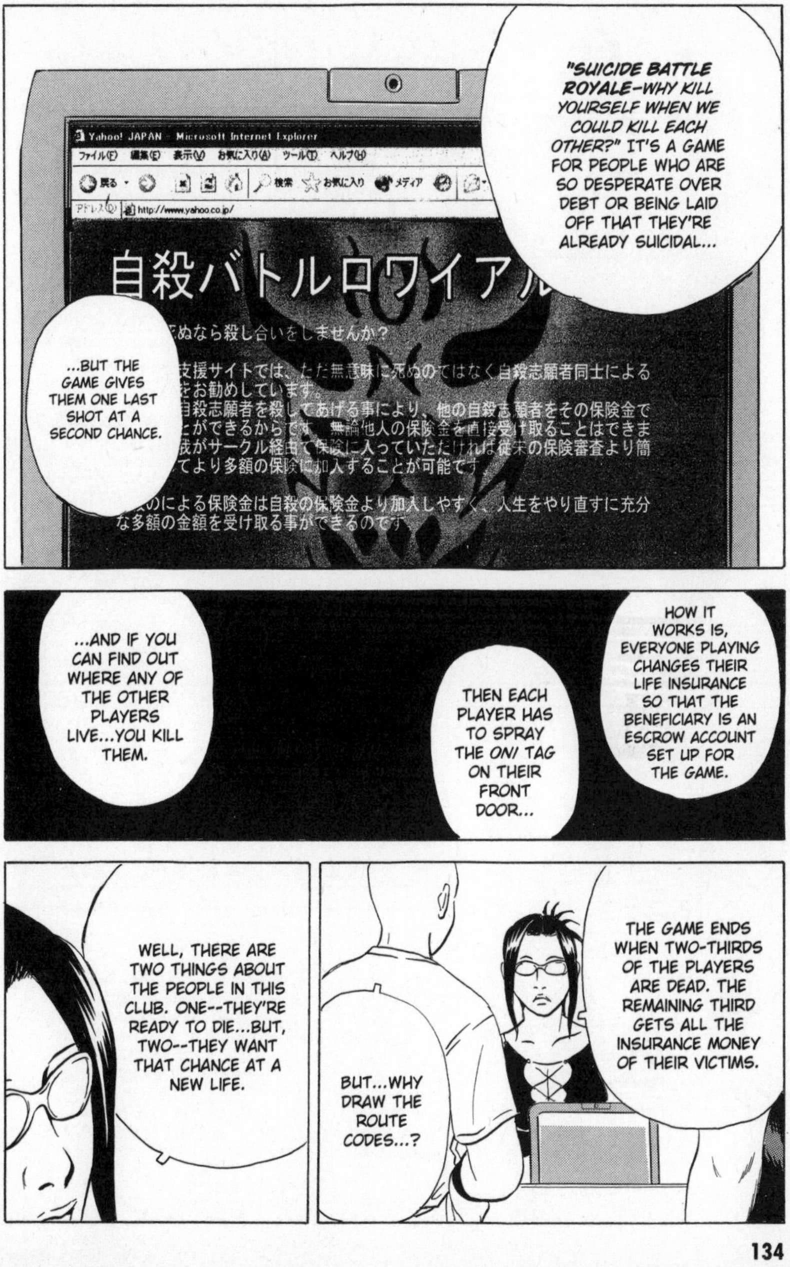
"SUICIDE BATTLE ROYALE–WHY KILL YOURSELF WHEN WE COULD KILL EACH OTHER?" IT'S A GAME FOR PEOPLE WHO ARE SO DESPERATE OVER DEBT OR BEING LAID OFF THAT THEY'RE ALREADY SUICIDAL...
自殺バトルロワイアル
...BUT THE GAME GIVES THEM ONE LAST SHOT AT A SECOND CHANCE.
HOW IT WORKS IS, EVERYONE PLAYING CHANGES THEIR LIFE INSURANCE SO THAT THE BENEFICIARY IS AN ESCROW ACCOUNT SET UP FOR THE GAME.
THEN EACH PLAYER HAS TO SPRAY THE *ONI* TAG ON THEIR FRONT DOOR...
...AND IF YOU CAN FIND OUT WHERE ANY OF THE OTHER PLAYERS LIVE...YOU KILL THEM.
THE GAME ENDS WHEN TWO-THIRDS OF THE PLAYERS ARE DEAD. THE REMAINING THIRD GETS ALL THE INSURANCE MONEY OF THEIR VICTIMS.
BUT...WHY DRAW THE ROUTE CODES...?
WELL, THERE ARE TWO THINGS ABOUT THE PEOPLE IN THIS CLUB. ONE--THEY'RE READY TO DIE...BUT, TWO--THEY WANT THAT CHANCE AT A NEW LIFE.

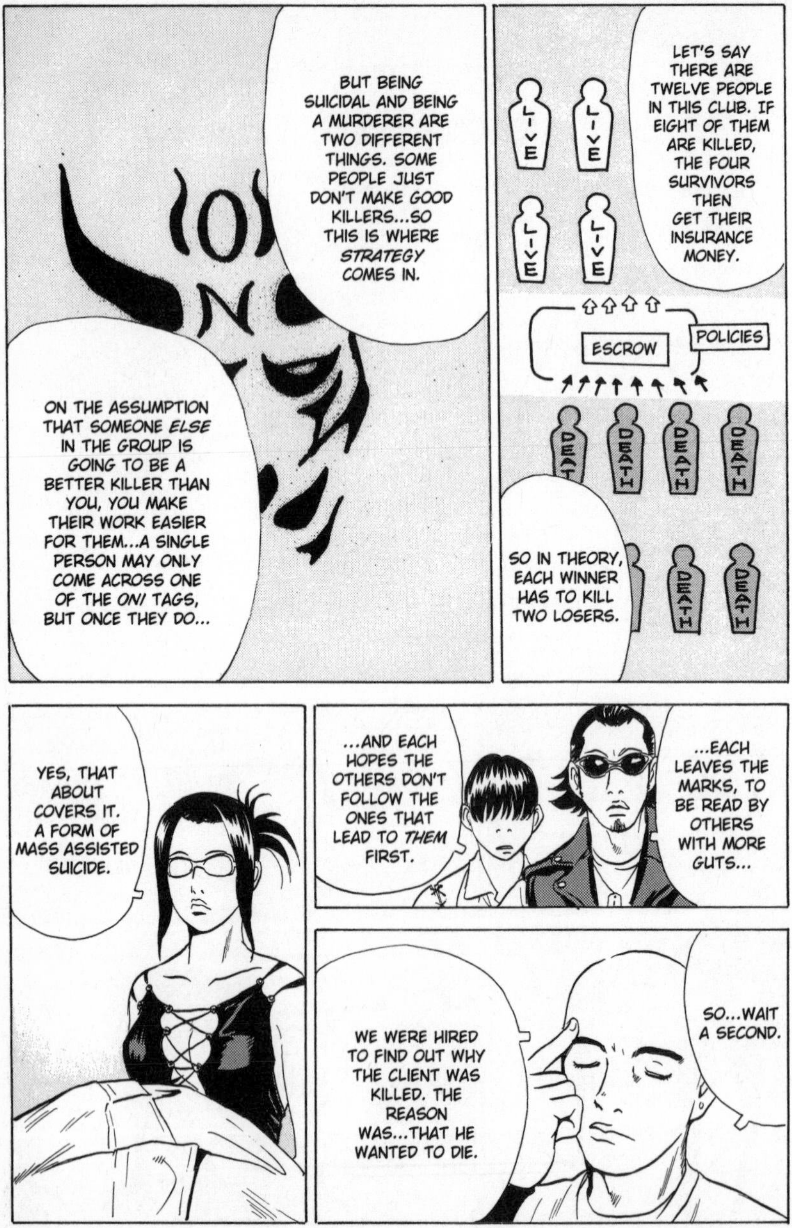
LET'S SAY THERE ARE TWELVE PEOPLE IN THIS CLUB. IF EIGHT OF THEM ARE KILLED, THE FOUR SURVIVORS THEN GET THEIR INSURANCE MONEY.
LIVE
LIVE
LIVE
LIVE
POLICIES
ESCROW
DEATH
DEATH
DEATH
DEATH
DEATH
DEATH
SO IN THEORY, EACH WINNER HAS TO KILL TWO LOSERS.
BUT BEING SUICIDAL AND BEING A MURDERER ARE TWO DIFFERENT THINGS. SOME PEOPLE JUST DON'T MAKE GOOD KILLERS...SO THIS IS WHERE *STRATEGY* COMES IN.
ON THE ASSUMPTION THAT SOMEONE *ELSE* IN THE GROUP IS GOING TO BE A BETTER KILLER THAN YOU, YOU MAKE THEIR WORK EASIER FOR THEM...A SINGLE PERSON MAY ONLY COME ACROSS ONE OF THE *ONI* TAGS, BUT ONCE THEY DO...
...EACH LEAVES THE MARKS, TO BE READ BY OTHERS WITH MORE GUTS...
...AND EACH HOPES THE OTHERS DON'T FOLLOW THE ONES THAT LEAD TO *THEM* FIRST.
SO...WAIT A SECOND.
WE WERE HIRED TO FIND OUT WHY THE CLIENT WAS KILLED. THE REASON WAS...THAT HE WANTED TO DIE.
YES, THAT ABOUT COVERS IT. A FORM OF MASS ASSISTED SUICIDE.

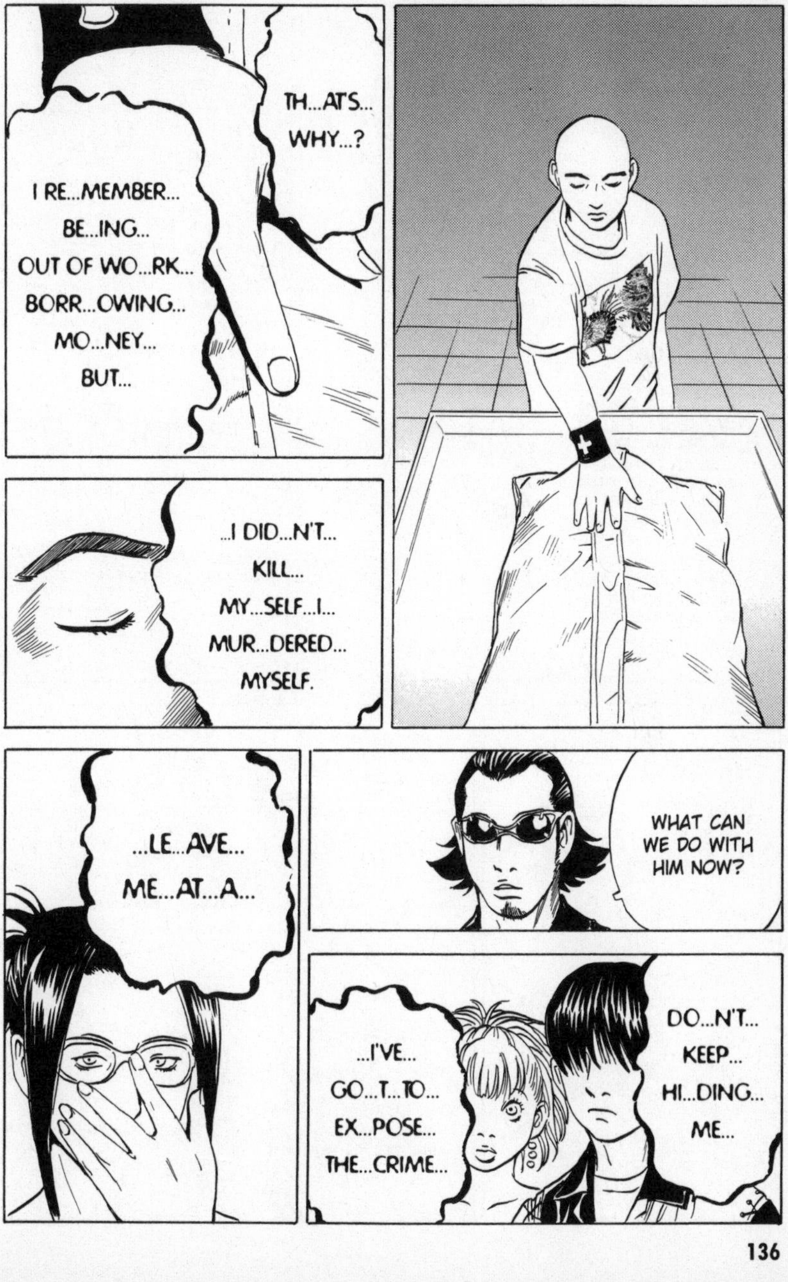
TH...AT'S... WHY...?
I RE...MEMBER... BE...ING... OUT OF WO...RK... BORR...OWING... MO...NEY... BUT...
...I DID...N'T... KILL... MY...SELF...I... MUR...DERED... MYSELF.
WHAT CAN WE DO WITH HIM NOW?
DO...N'T... KEEP... HI...DING... ME...
...I'VE... GO...T...TO... EX...POSE... THE...CRIME...
...LE...AVE... ME...AT...A...

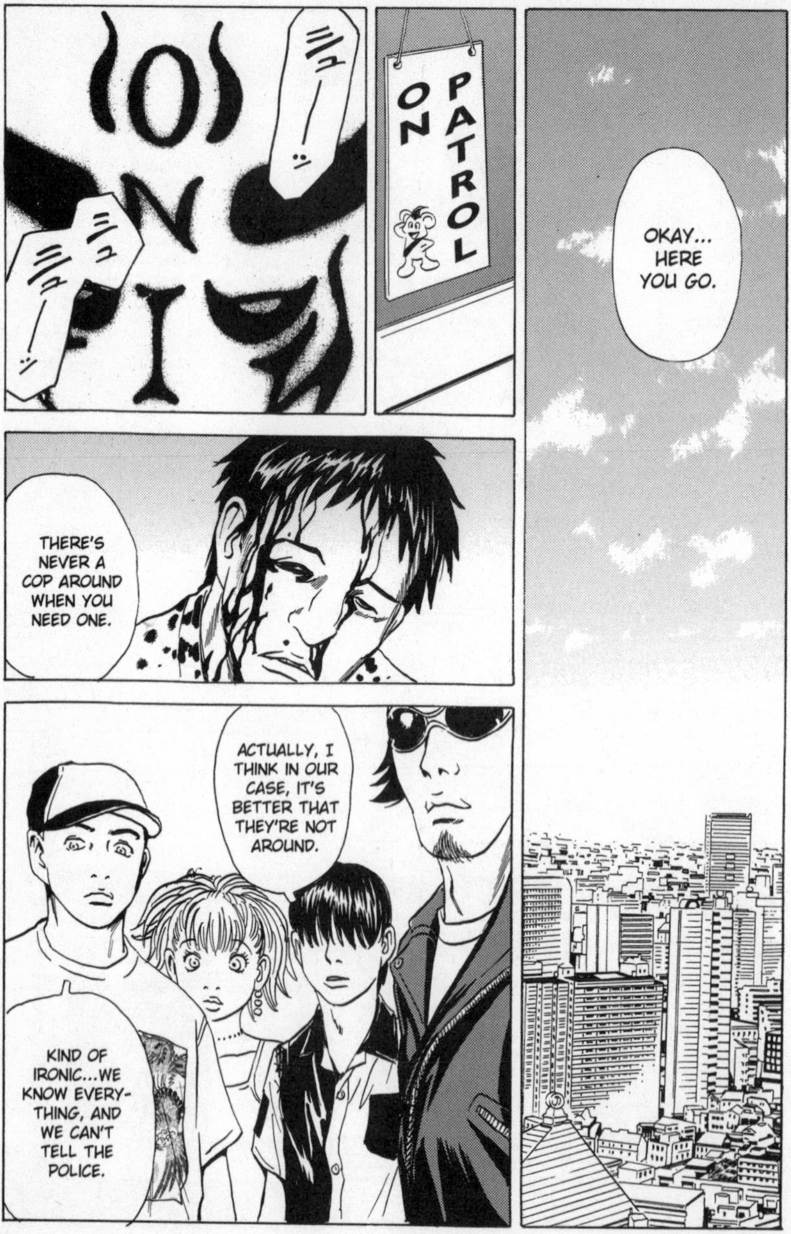
OKAY... HERE YOU GO.
ON PATROL
ミュー
ミュー
ミュー
THERE'S NEVER A COP AROUND WHEN YOU NEED ONE.
ACTUALLY, I THINK IN OUR CASE, IT'S BETTER THAT THEY'RE NOT AROUND.
KIND OF IRONIC...WE KNOW EVERY-THING, AND WE CAN'T TELL THE POLICE.

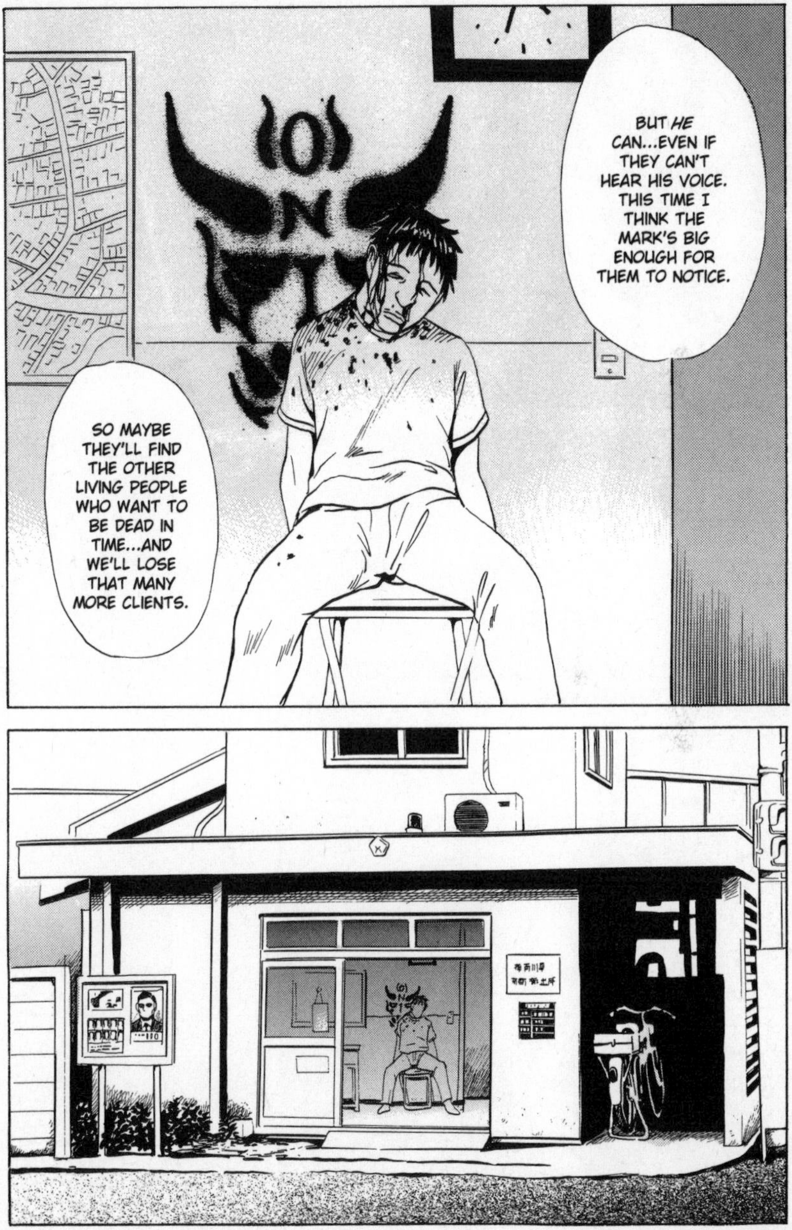
BUT HE CAN...EVEN IF THEY CAN'T HEAR HIS VOICE. THIS TIME I THINK THE MARK'S BIG ENOUGH FOR THEM TO NOTICE.
SO MAYBE THEY'LL FIND THE OTHER LIVING PEOPLE WHO WANT TO BE DEAD IN TIME...AND WE'LL LOSE THAT MANY MORE CLIENTS.

3rd delivery: x+y=love—the end

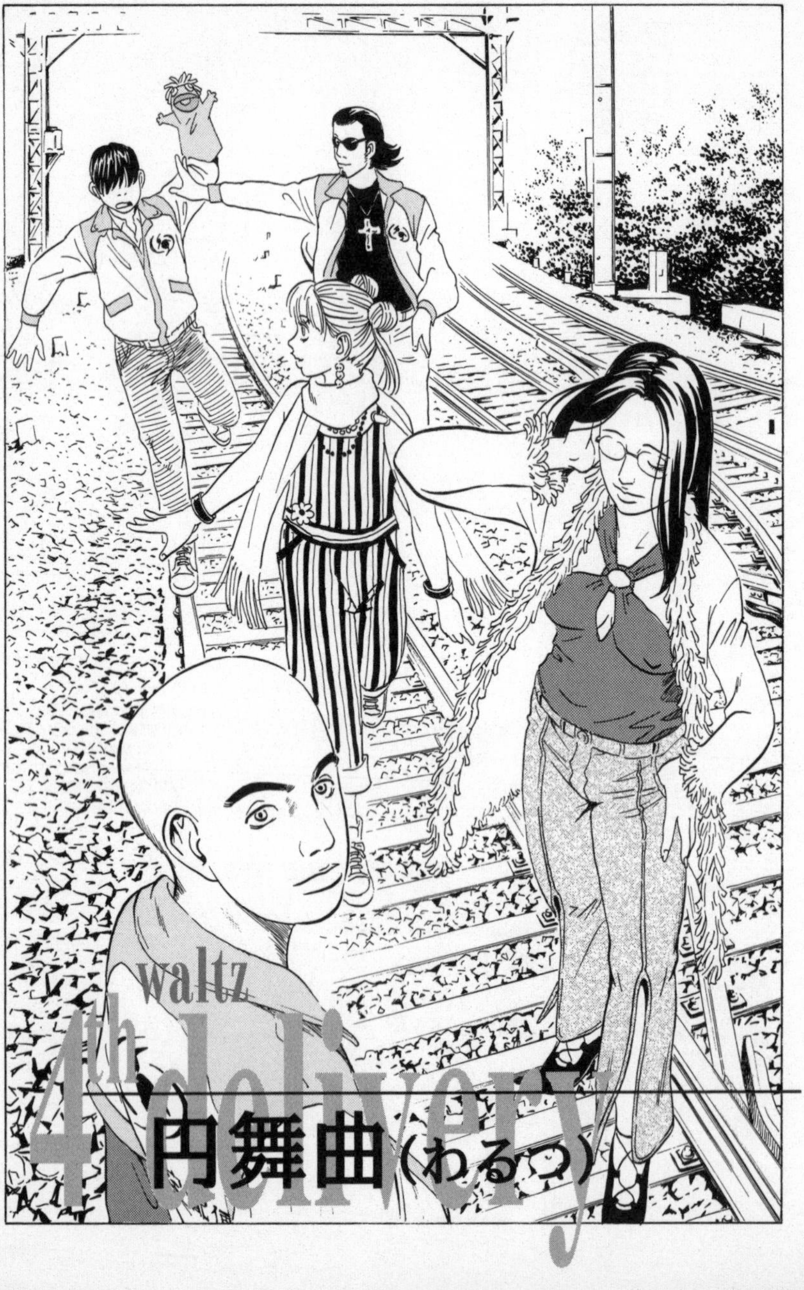

waltz
4th delivery
円舞曲（わるつ）

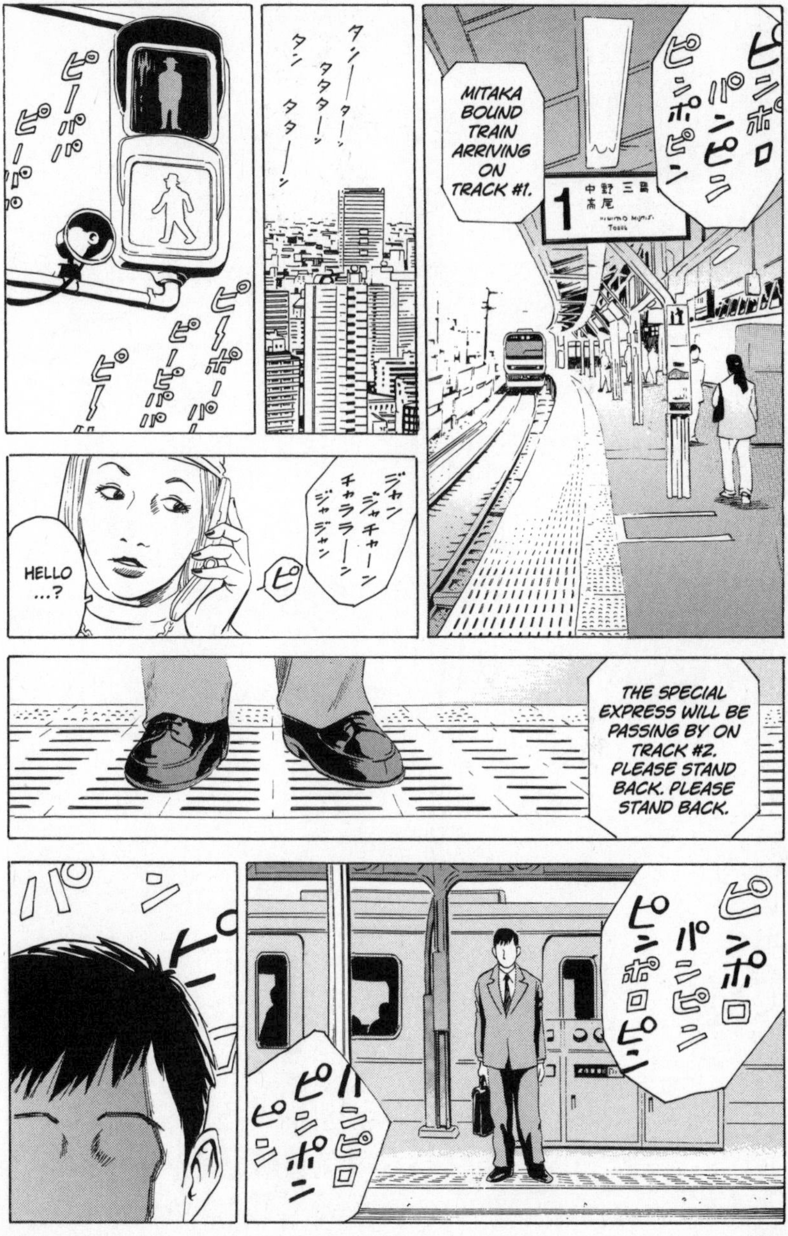

MITAKA BOUND TRAIN ARRIVING ON TRACK #1.
HELLO ...?
THE SPECIAL EXPRESS WILL BE PASSING BY ON TRACK #2. PLEASE STAND BACK. PLEASE STAND BACK.

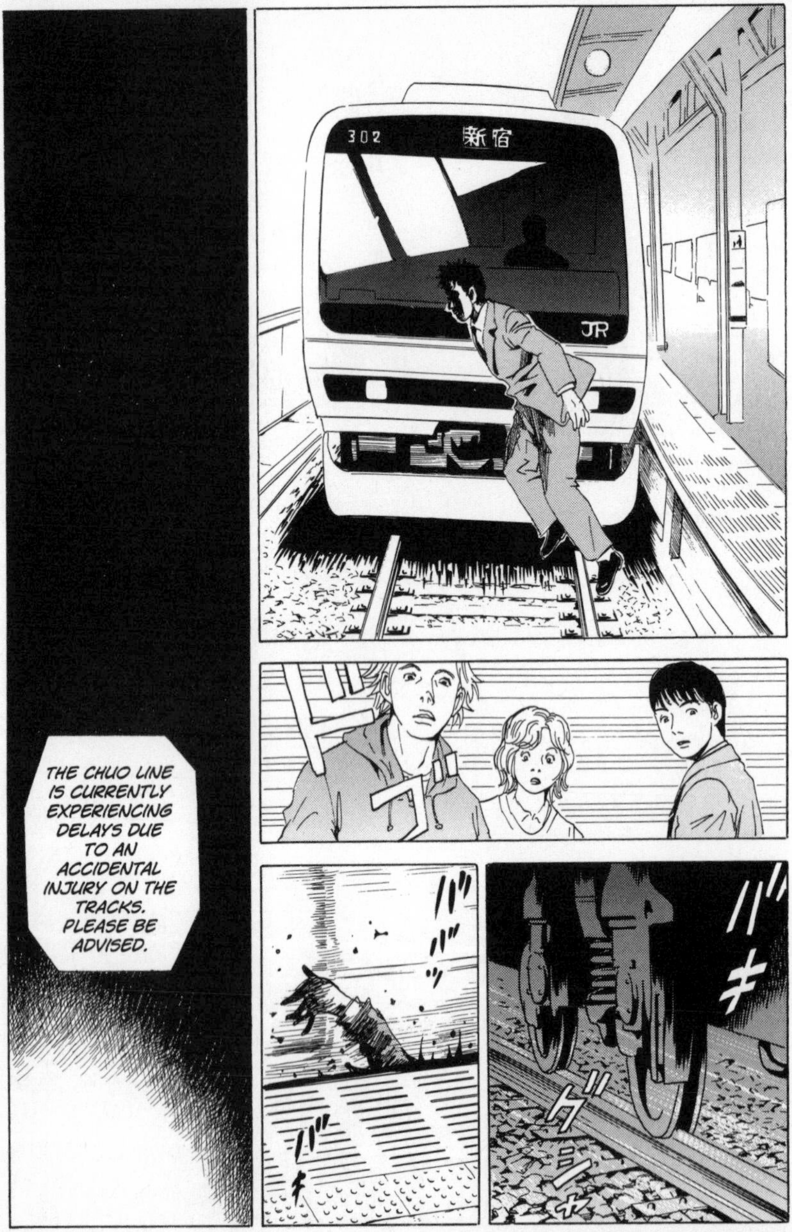
302
新宿
JR
THE CHUO LINE IS CURRENTLY EXPERIENCING DELAYS DUE TO AN ACCIDENTAL INJURY ON THE TRACKS. PLEASE BE ADVISED.

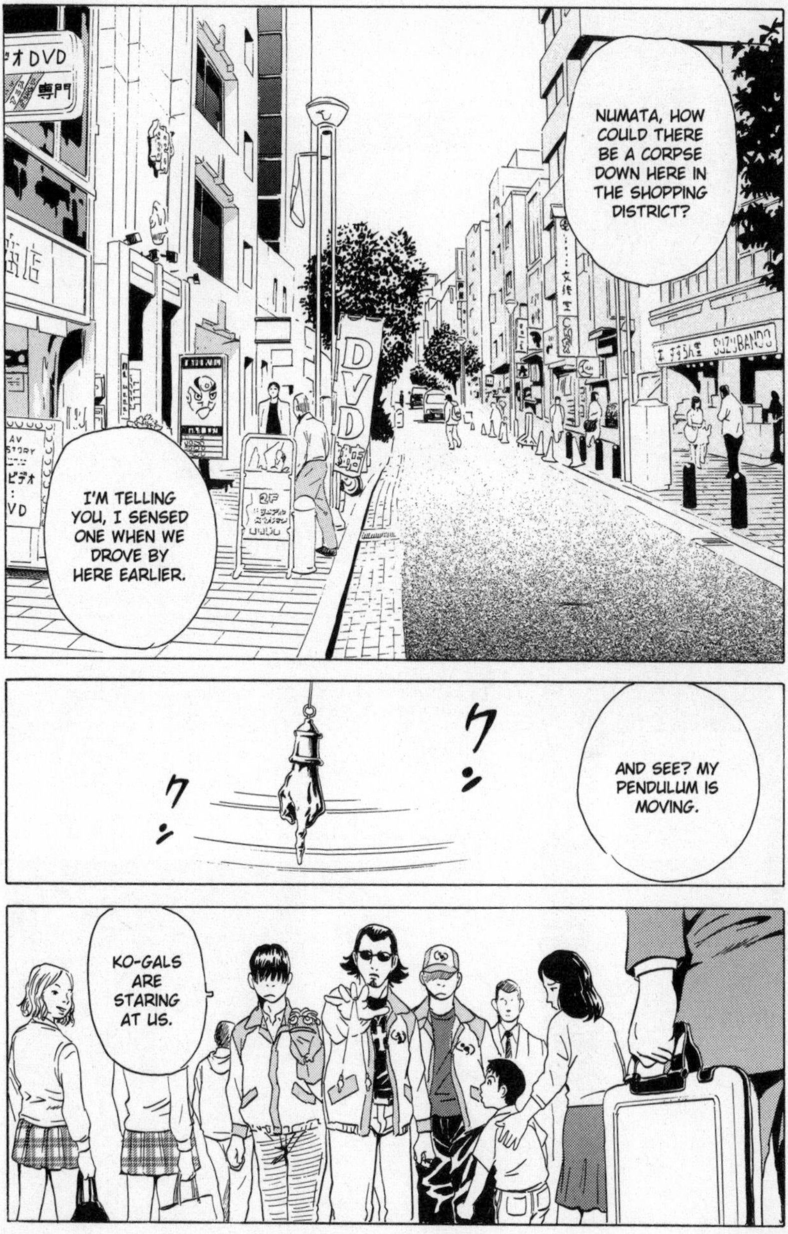
NUMATA, HOW COULD THERE BE A CORPSE DOWN HERE IN THE SHOPPING DISTRICT?
I'M TELLING YOU, I SENSED ONE WHEN WE DROVE BY HERE EARLIER.
AND SEE? MY PENDULUM IS MOVING.
クン
クン
KO-GALS ARE STARING AT US.

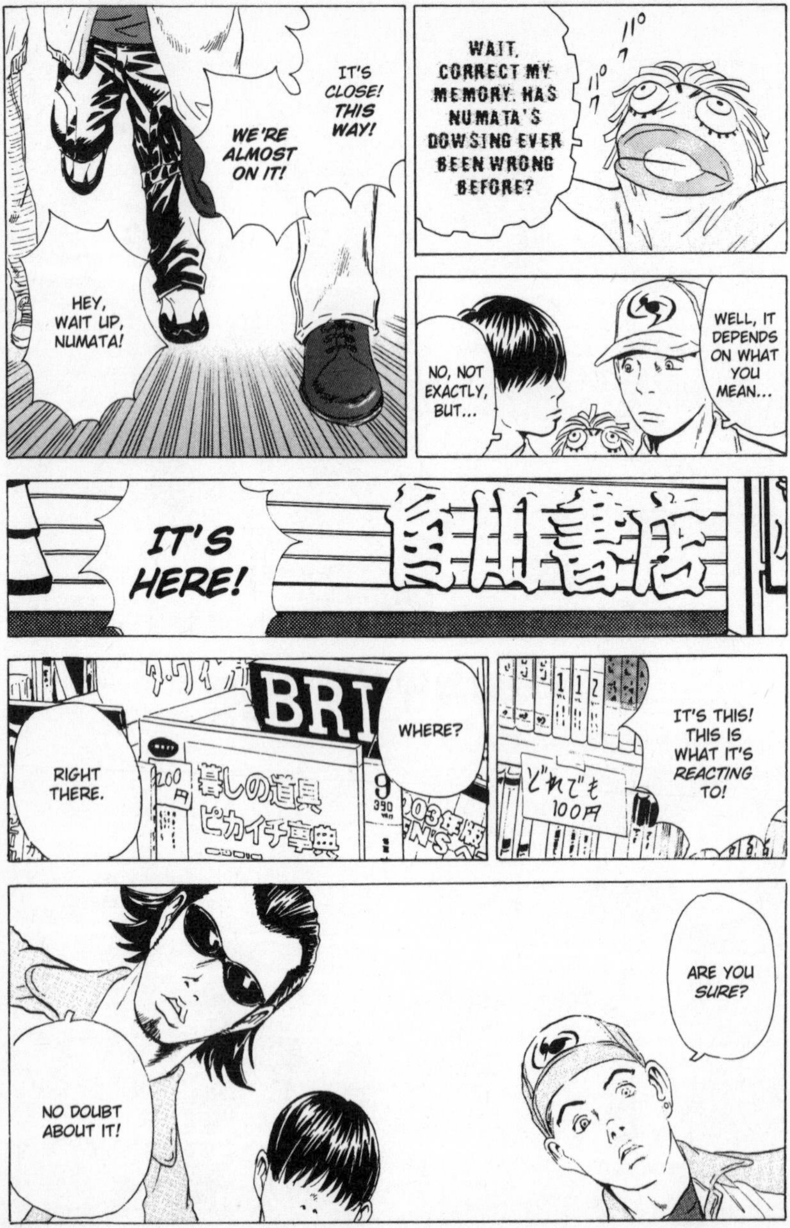
WAIT, CORRECT MY MEMORY. HAS NUMATA'S DOWSING EVER BEEN WRONG BEFORE?
WELL, IT DEPENDS ON WHAT YOU MEAN...
NO, NOT EXACTLY, BUT...
IT'S CLOSE! THIS WAY!
WE'RE ALMOST ON IT!
HEY, WAIT UP, NUMATA!
IT'S HERE!
IT'S THIS! THIS IS WHAT IT'S REACTING TO!
どれでも
100円
WHERE?
BRI
暮しの道具
ピカイチ事典
RIGHT THERE.
ARE YOU SURE?
NO DOUBT ABOUT IT!

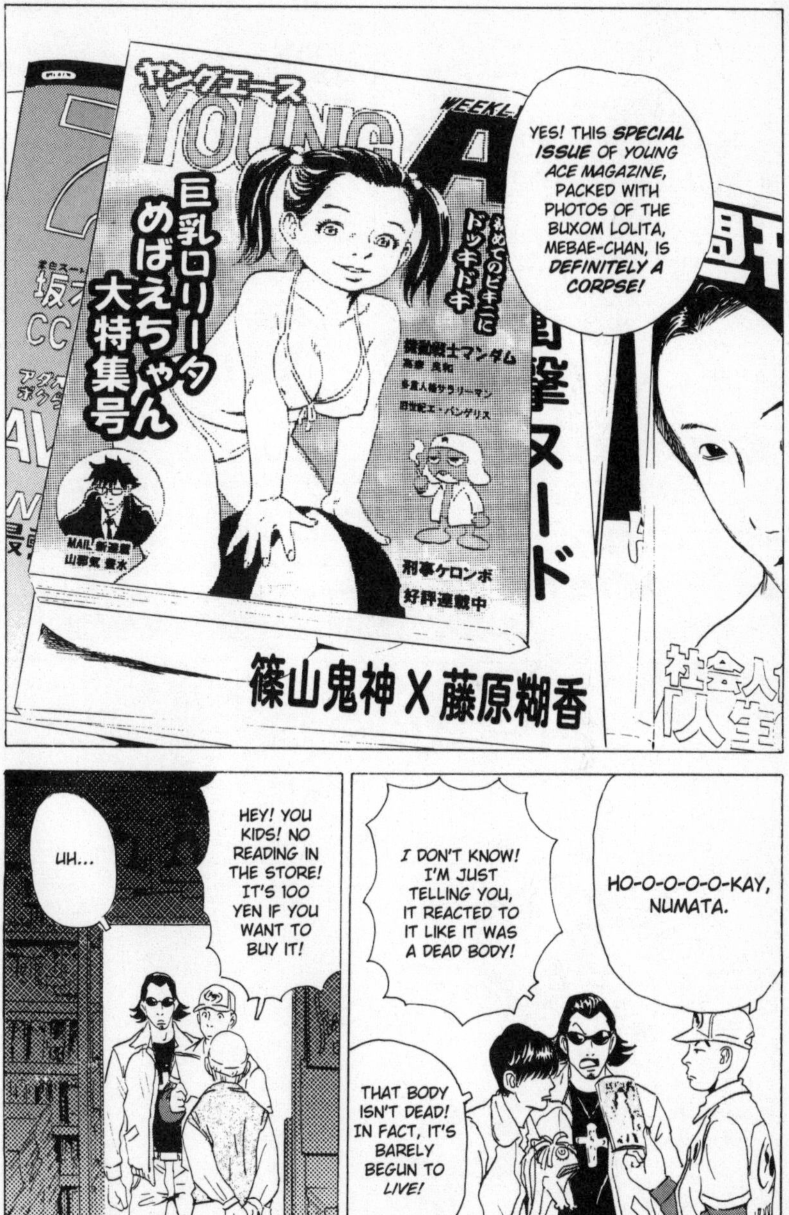
YES! THIS SPECIAL ISSUE OF YOUNG ACE MAGAZINE, PACKED WITH PHOTOS OF THE BUXOM LOLITA, MEBAE-CHAN, IS DEFINITELY A CORPSE!
ヤングエース
YOUNG A
巨乳ロリータめばえちゃん大特集号
ドッキドキ
刑事ケロンボ
好評連載中
篠山鬼神X藤原糊香
HO-O-O-O-O-KAY, NUMATA.
I DON'T KNOW! I'M JUST TELLING YOU, IT REACTED TO IT LIKE IT WAS A DEAD BODY!
THAT BODY ISN'T DEAD! IN FACT, IT'S BARELY BEGUN TO LIVE!
HEY! YOU KIDS! NO READING IN THE STORE! IT'S 100 YEN IF YOU WANT TO BUY IT!
UH...

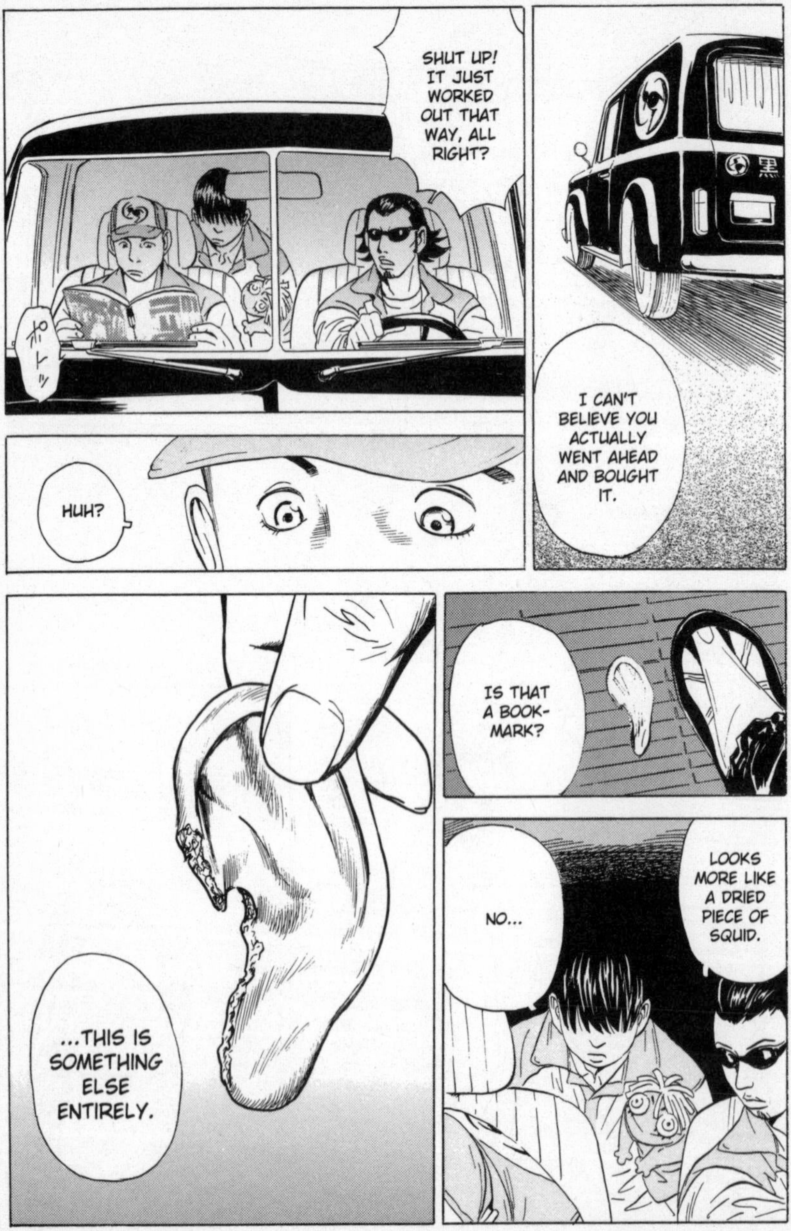

I CAN'T BELIEVE YOU ACTUALLY WENT AHEAD AND BOUGHT IT.
SHUT UP! IT JUST WORKED OUT THAT WAY, ALL RIGHT?
ポトッ
HUH?
IS THAT A BOOK-MARK?
LOOKS MORE LIKE A DRIED PIECE OF SQUID.
NO...
...THIS IS SOMETHING ELSE ENTIRELY.

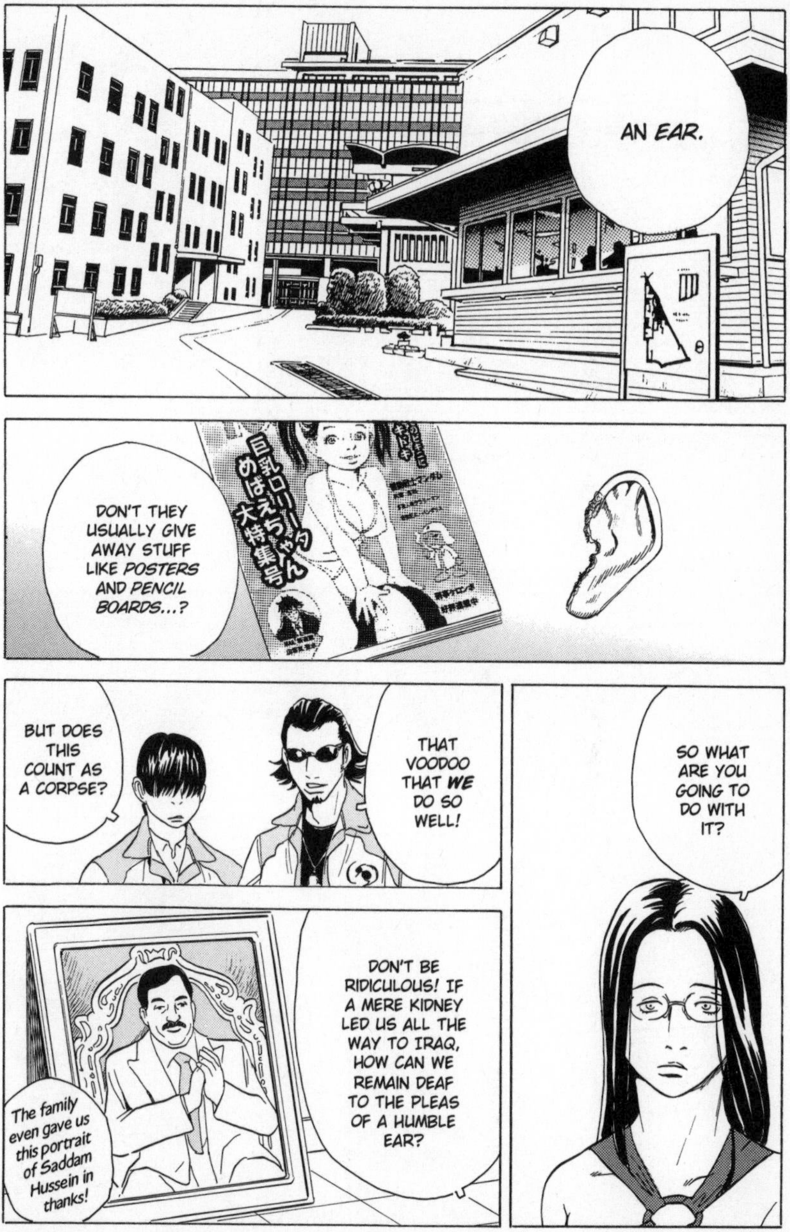
AN EAR.
巨乳ロリータ めばえちゃん 大特集号
DON'T THEY USUALLY GIVE AWAY STUFF LIKE POSTERS AND PENCIL BOARDS...?
SO WHAT ARE YOU GOING TO DO WITH IT?
THAT VOODOO THAT WE DO SO WELL!
BUT DOES THIS COUNT AS A CORPSE?
DON'T BE RIDICULOUS! IF A MERE KIDNEY LED US ALL THE WAY TO IRAQ, HOW CAN WE REMAIN DEAF TO THE PLEAS OF A HUMBLE EAR?
The family even gave us this portrait of Saddam Hussein in thanks!

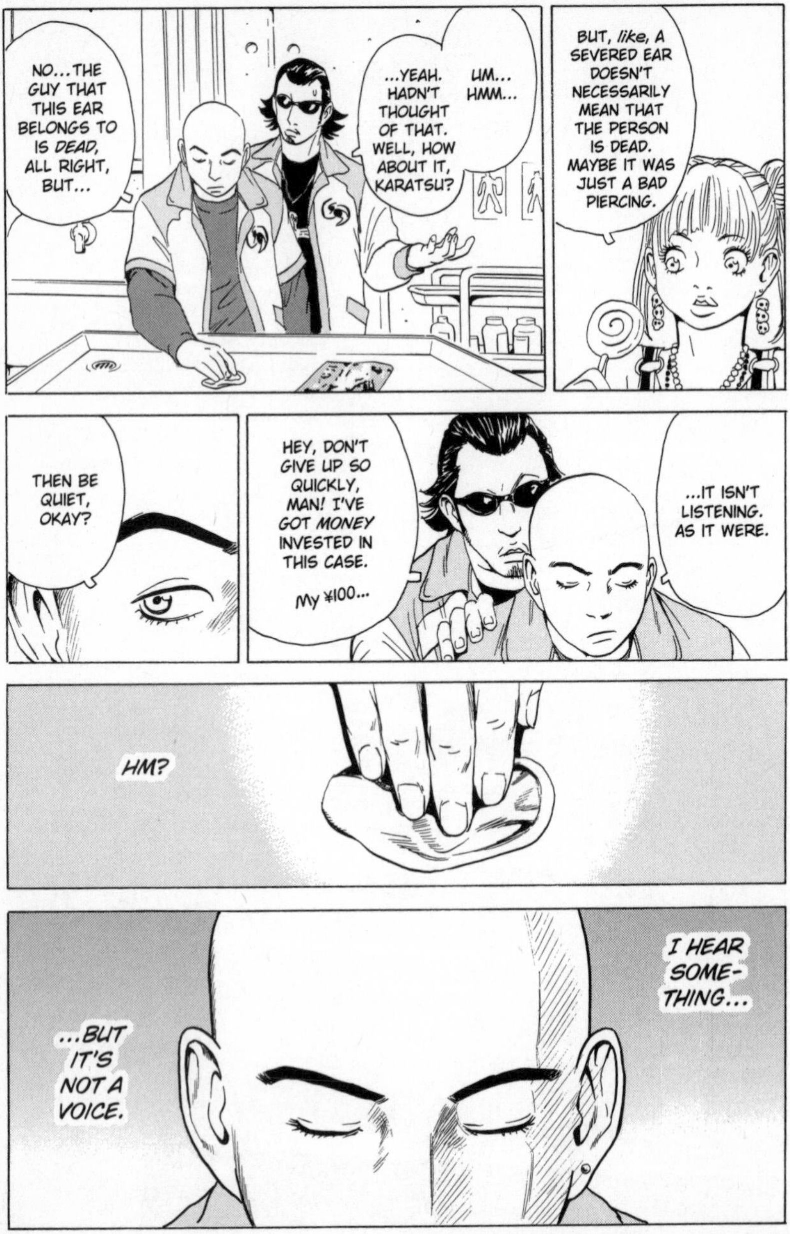
BUT, *like*, A SEVERED EAR DOESN'T NECESSARILY MEAN THAT THE PERSON IS DEAD. MAYBE IT WAS JUST A BAD PIERCING.
UM... HMM...
...YEAH. HADN'T THOUGHT OF THAT. WELL, HOW ABOUT IT, KARATSU?
NO... THE GUY THAT THIS EAR BELONGS TO IS *DEAD*, ALL RIGHT, BUT...
...IT ISN'T LISTENING. AS IT WERE.
HEY, DON'T GIVE UP SO QUICKLY, MAN! I'VE GOT *MONEY* INVESTED IN THIS CASE.
My ¥100...
THEN BE QUIET, OKAY?
HM?
I HEAR SOME-THING...
...BUT IT'S NOT A VOICE.

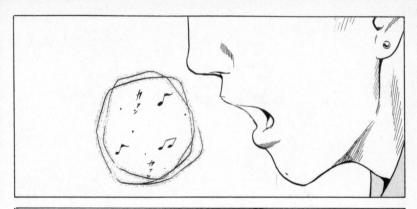

HE'S... SINGING.

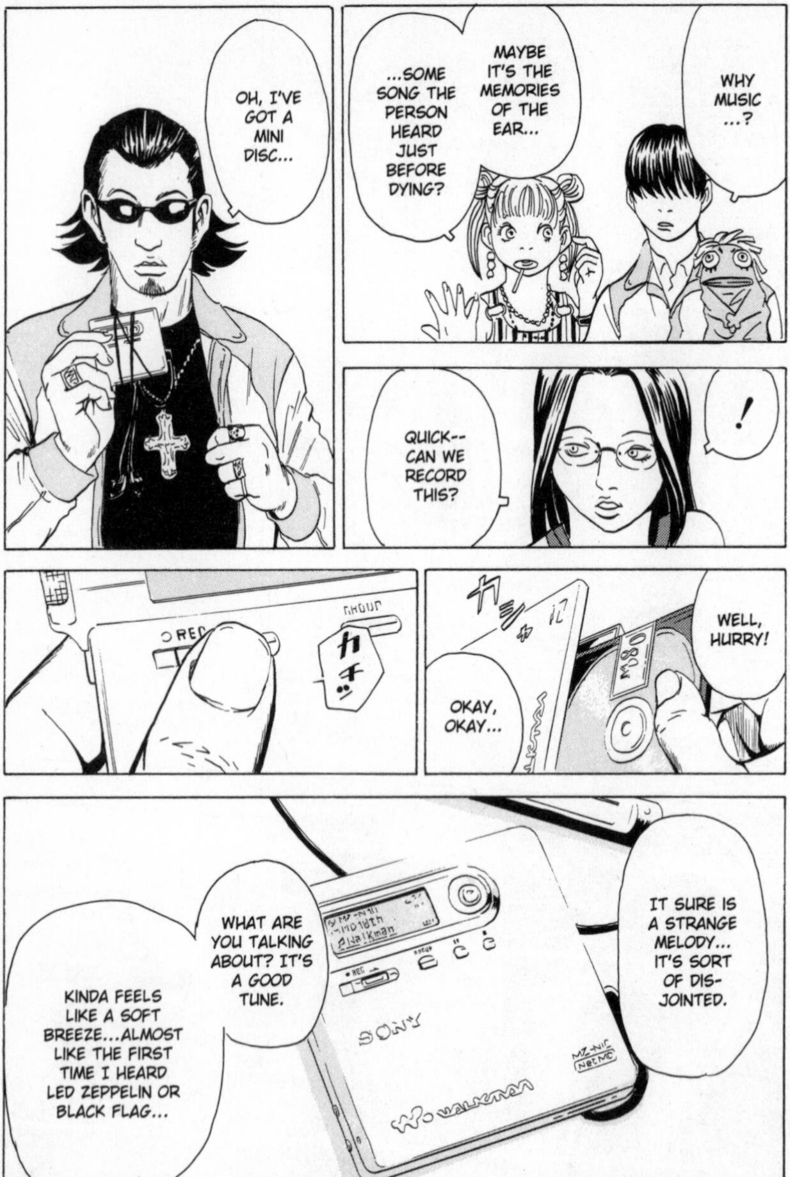
WHY MUSIC ...?
MAYBE IT'S THE MEMORIES OF THE EAR...
...SOME SONG THE PERSON HEARD JUST BEFORE DYING?
!
QUICK-- CAN WE RECORD THIS?
OH, I'VE GOT A MINI DISC...
WELL, HURRY!
OKAY, OKAY...
カチッ
IT SURE IS A STRANGE MELODY... IT'S SORT OF DIS-JOINTED.
WHAT ARE YOU TALKING ABOUT? IT'S A GOOD TUNE.
SONY
KINDA FEELS LIKE A SOFT BREEZE...ALMOST LIKE THE FIRST TIME I HEARD LED ZEPPELIN OR BLACK FLAG...

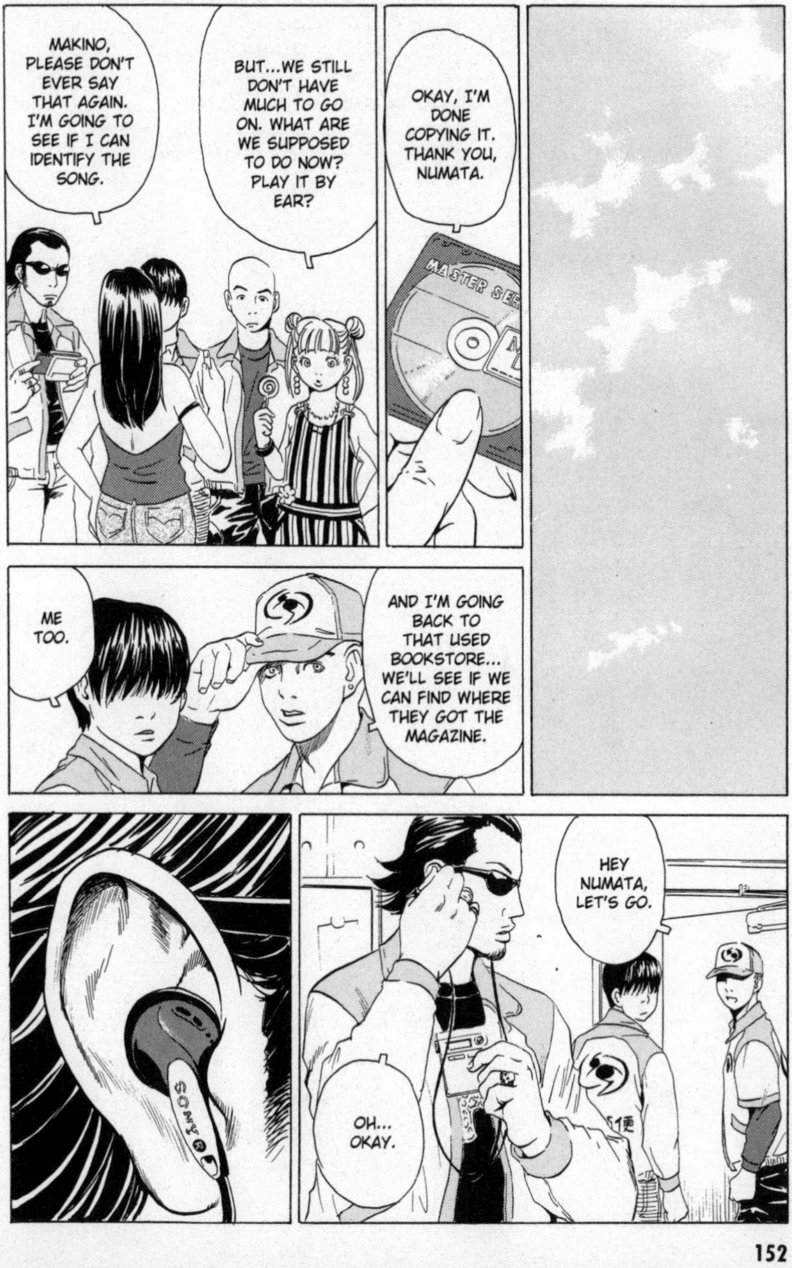
OKAY, I'M DONE COPYING IT. THANK YOU, NUMATA.
MASTER SER
BUT...WE STILL DON'T HAVE MUCH TO GO ON. WHAT ARE WE SUPPOSED TO DO NOW? PLAY IT BY EAR?
MAKINO, PLEASE DON'T EVER SAY THAT AGAIN. I'M GOING TO SEE IF I CAN IDENTIFY THE SONG.
AND I'M GOING BACK TO THAT USED BOOKSTORE... WE'LL SEE IF WE CAN FIND WHERE THEY GOT THE MAGAZINE.
ME TOO.
HEY NUMATA, LET'S GO.
OH... OKAY.
SONY

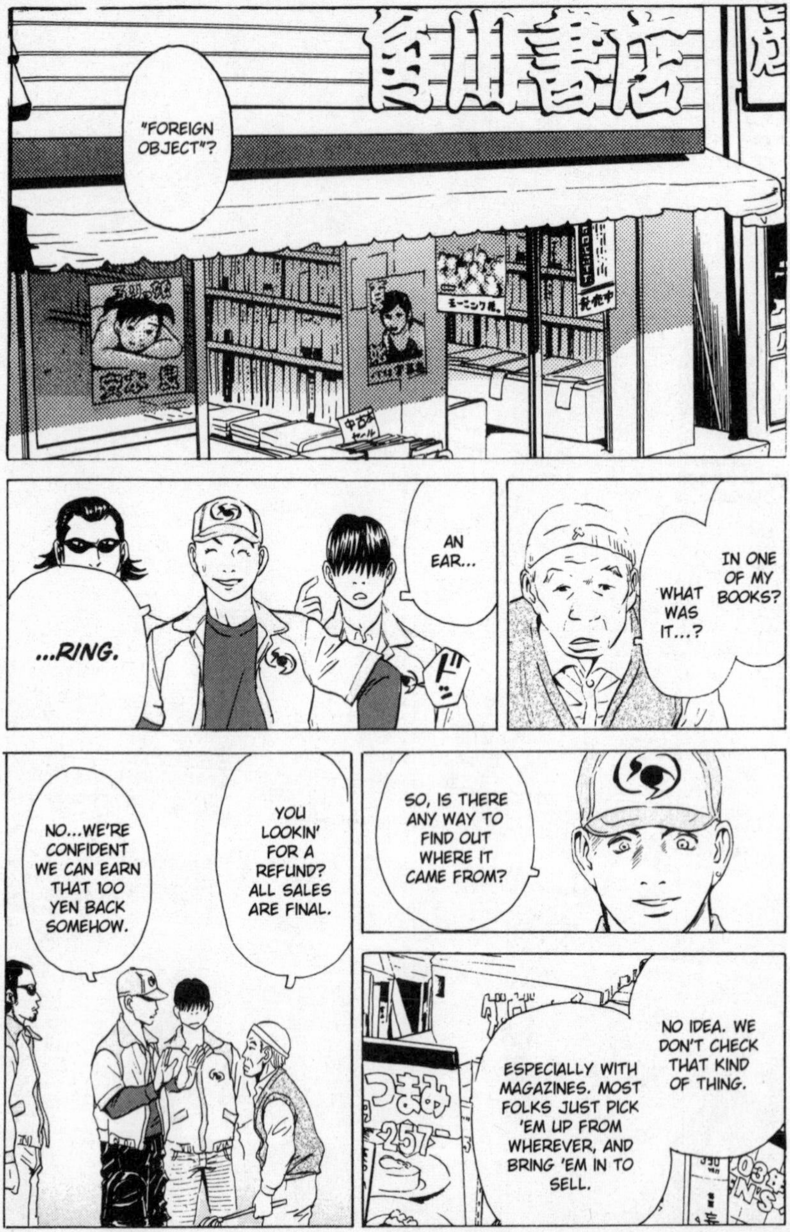
"FOREIGN OBJECT"?
IN ONE OF MY BOOKS?
WHAT WAS IT...?
AN EAR...
...RING.
SO, IS THERE ANY WAY TO FIND OUT WHERE IT CAME FROM?
NO IDEA. WE DON'T CHECK THAT KIND OF THING.
ESPECIALLY WITH MAGAZINES. MOST FOLKS JUST PICK 'EM UP FROM WHEREVER, AND BRING 'EM IN TO SELL.
YOU LOOKIN' FOR A REFUND? ALL SALES ARE FINAL.
NO...WE'RE CONFIDENT WE CAN EARN THAT 100 YEN BACK SOMEHOW.

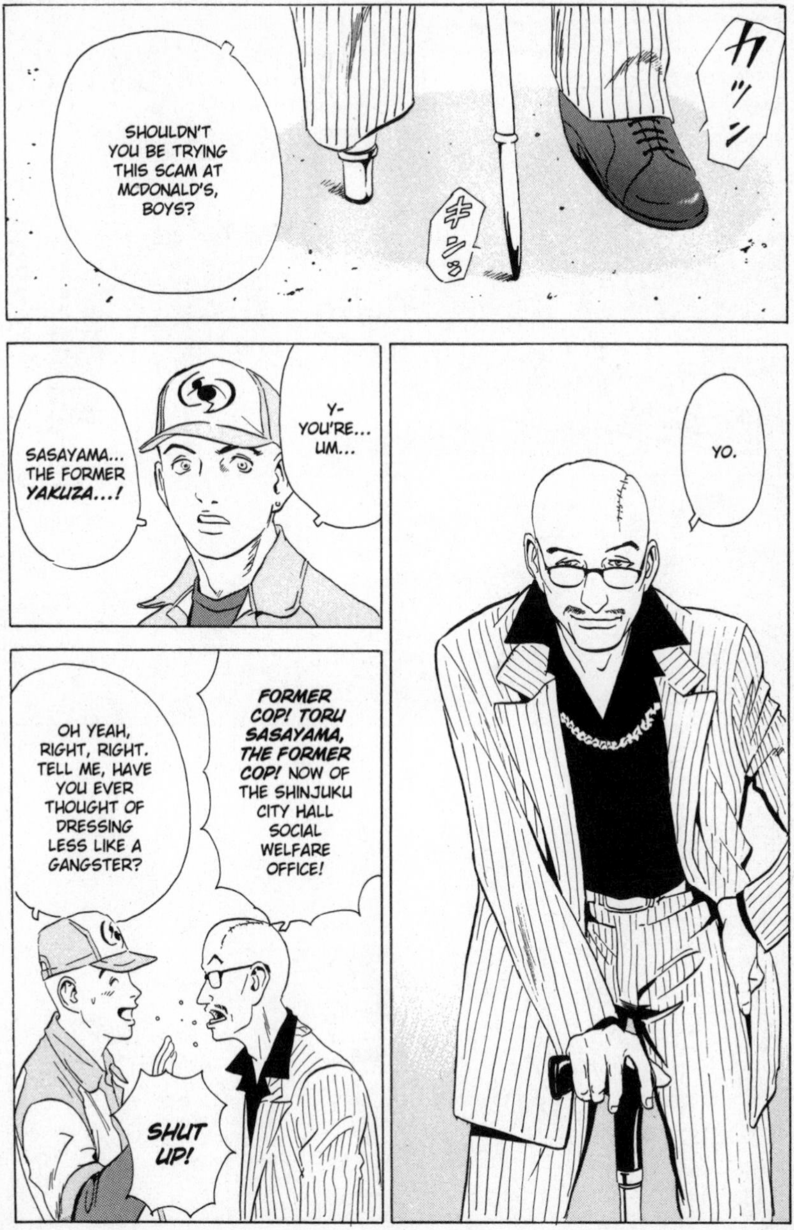

カッン
SHOULDN'T YOU BE TRYING THIS SCAM AT MCDONALD'S, BOYS?
YO.
Y- YOU'RE... UM...
SASAYAMA... THE FORMER YAKUZA...!
FORMER COP! TORU SASAYAMA, THE FORMER COP! NOW OF THE SHINJUKU CITY HALL SOCIAL WELFARE OFFICE!
OH YEAH, RIGHT, RIGHT. TELL ME, HAVE YOU EVER THOUGHT OF DRESSING LESS LIKE A GANGSTER?
SHUT UP!

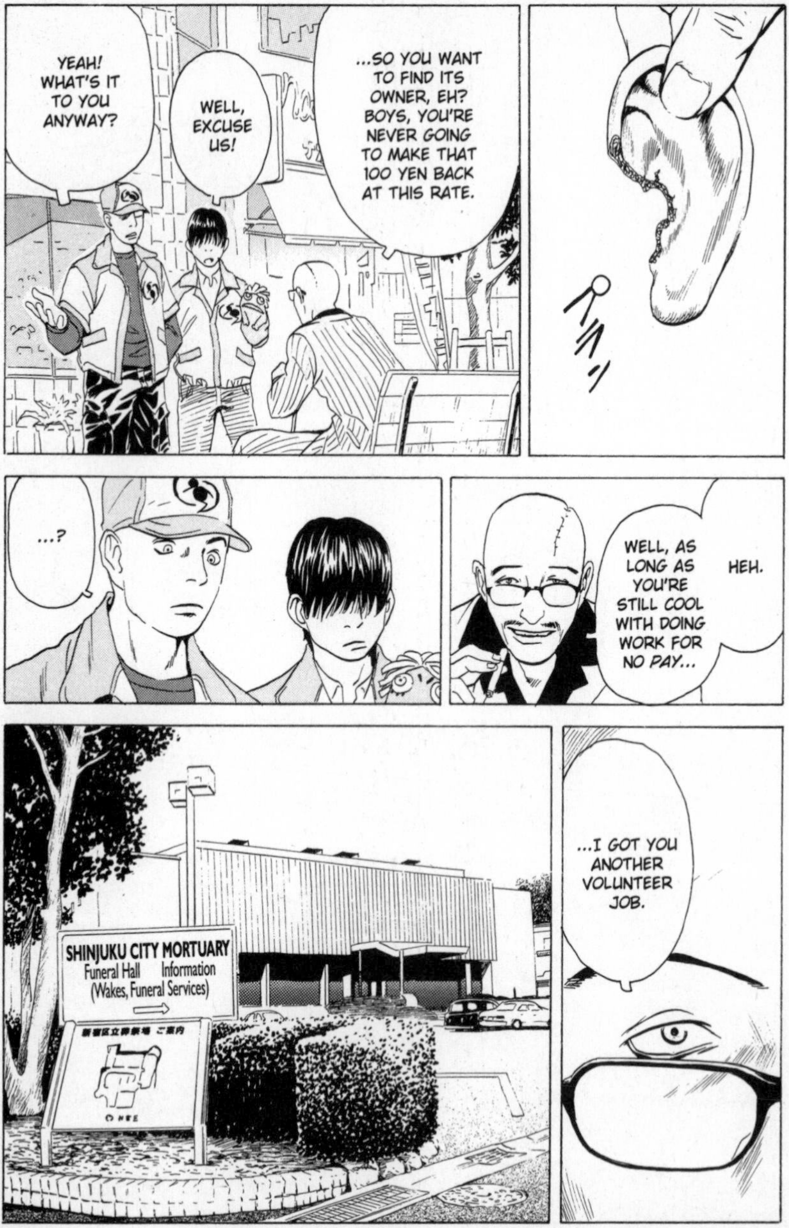
...SO YOU WANT TO FIND ITS OWNER, EH? BOYS, YOU'RE NEVER GOING TO MAKE THAT 100 YEN BACK AT THIS RATE.
WELL, EXCUSE US!
YEAH! WHAT'S IT TO YOU ANYWAY?
HEH.
WELL, AS LONG AS YOU'RE STILL COOL WITH DOING WORK FOR NO *PAY*...
...?
...I GOT YOU ANOTHER VOLUNTEER JOB.
SHINJUKU CITY MORTUARY
Funeral Hall Information
(Wakes, Funeral Services)

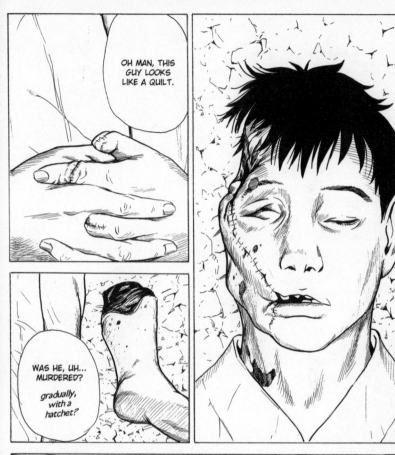

OH MAN, THIS GUY LOOKS LIKE A QUILT.
WAS HE, UH... MURDERED?
gradually, with a hatchet?
IF HE WAS, I WOULDN'T BE ASKING FOR YOUR HELP.
HE JUMPED INTO THE FRONT OF A SPEEDING EXPRESS AT OKUBO STATION.
SUICIDE, HUH...?

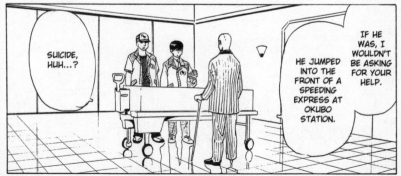

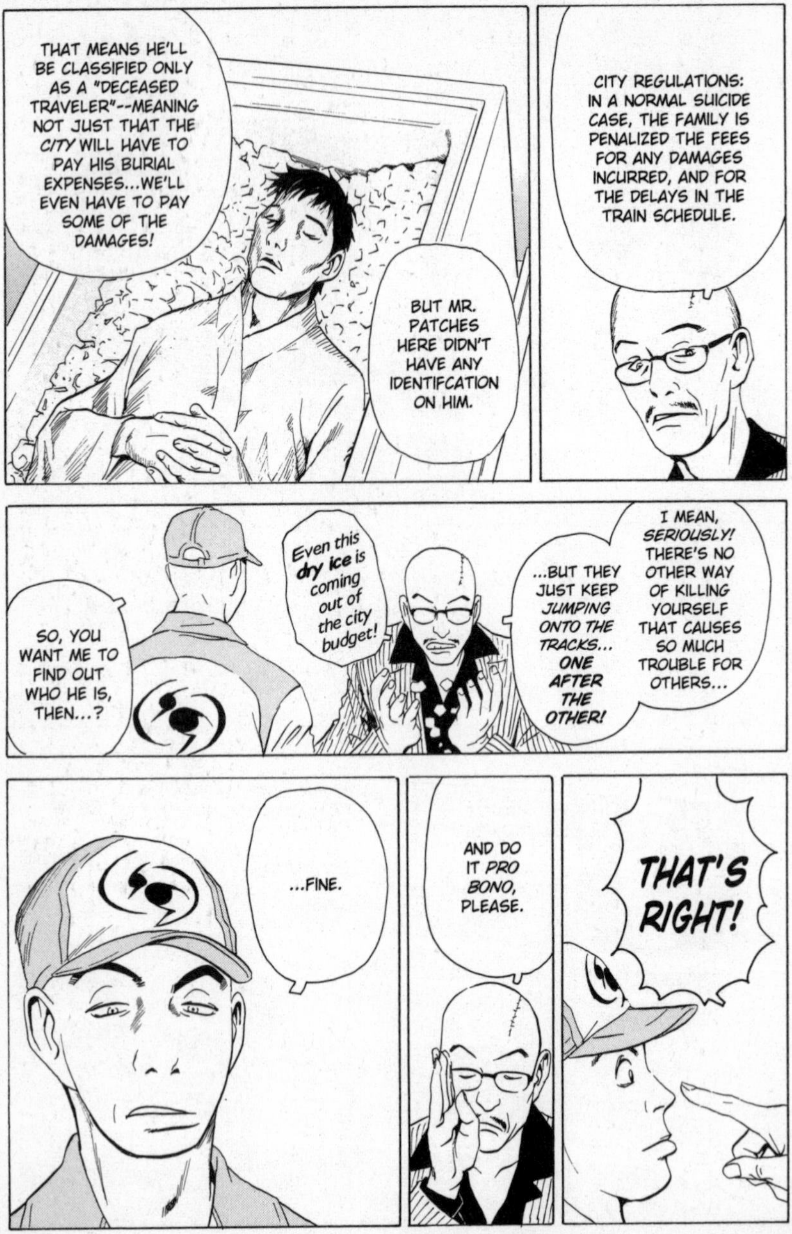
CITY REGULATIONS: IN A NORMAL SUICIDE CASE, THE FAMILY IS PENALIZED THE FEES FOR ANY DAMAGES INCURRED, AND FOR THE DELAYS IN THE TRAIN SCHEDULE.
BUT MR. PATCHES HERE DIDN'T HAVE ANY IDENTIFCATION ON HIM.
THAT MEANS HE'LL BE CLASSIFIED ONLY AS A "DECEASED TRAVELER"--MEANING NOT JUST THAT THE *CITY* WILL HAVE TO PAY HIS BURIAL EXPENSES...WE'LL EVEN HAVE TO PAY SOME OF THE DAMAGES!
I MEAN, *SERIOUSLY!* THERE'S NO OTHER WAY OF KILLING YOURSELF THAT CAUSES SO MUCH TROUBLE FOR OTHERS...
...BUT THEY JUST KEEP *JUMPING ONTO THE TRACKS...* ***ONE AFTER THE OTHER!***
Even this **dry ice** is coming out of the city budget!
SO, YOU WANT ME TO FIND OUT WHO HE IS, THEN...?
THAT'S RIGHT!
AND DO IT *PRO BONO*, PLEASE.
...FINE.

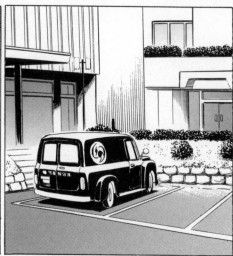

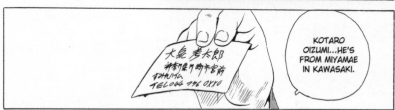

フン フン フン フフーン
KOTARO OIZUMI...HE'S FROM MIYAMAE IN KAWASAKI.
THANKS. YOU SAVED ME A LOT OF TROUBLE.
HE SAID YOU WERE BEING A LITTLE HARD ON HIM...ANYWAY, HE WAS CARRYING HIS COMPANY I.D. ...
HMM? IT PROBABLY BLEW AWAY AND GOT LOST SOMEWHERE.
...?

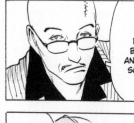

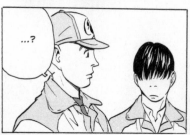

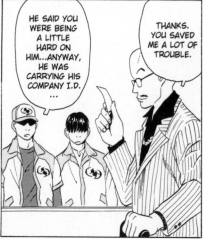

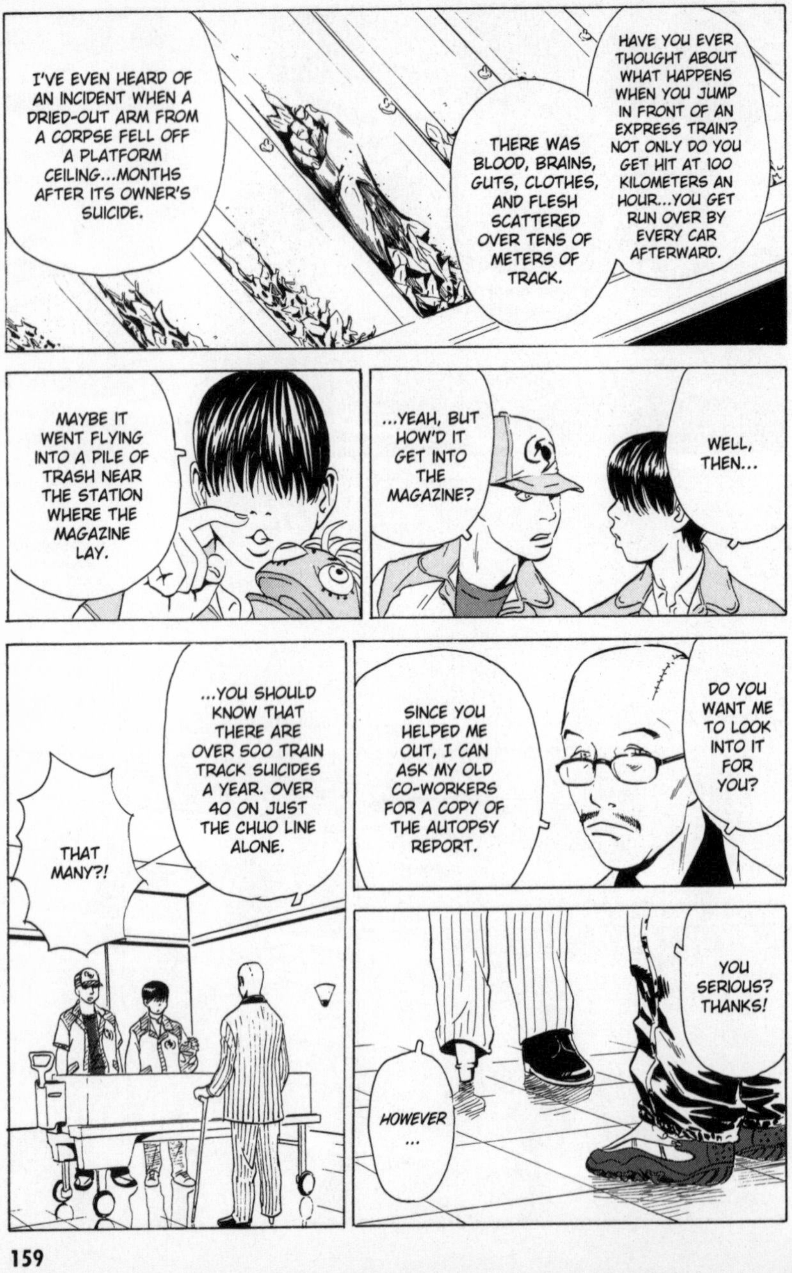
HAVE YOU EVER THOUGHT ABOUT WHAT HAPPENS WHEN YOU JUMP IN FRONT OF AN EXPRESS TRAIN? NOT ONLY DO YOU GET HIT AT 100 KILOMETERS AN HOUR...YOU GET RUN OVER BY EVERY CAR AFTERWARD.
THERE WAS BLOOD, BRAINS, GUTS, CLOTHES, AND FLESH SCATTERED OVER TENS OF METERS OF TRACK.
I'VE EVEN HEARD OF AN INCIDENT WHEN A DRIED-OUT ARM FROM A CORPSE FELL OFF A PLATFORM CEILING...MONTHS AFTER ITS OWNER'S SUICIDE.
WELL, THEN...
...YEAH, BUT HOW'D IT GET INTO THE MAGAZINE?
MAYBE IT WENT FLYING INTO A PILE OF TRASH NEAR THE STATION WHERE THE MAGAZINE LAY.
DO YOU WANT ME TO LOOK INTO IT FOR YOU?
SINCE YOU HELPED ME OUT, I CAN ASK MY OLD CO-WORKERS FOR A COPY OF THE AUTOPSY REPORT.
YOU SERIOUS? THANKS!
HOWEVER ...
...YOU SHOULD KNOW THAT THERE ARE OVER 500 TRAIN TRACK SUICIDES A YEAR. OVER 40 ON JUST THE CHUO LINE ALONE.
THAT MANY?!

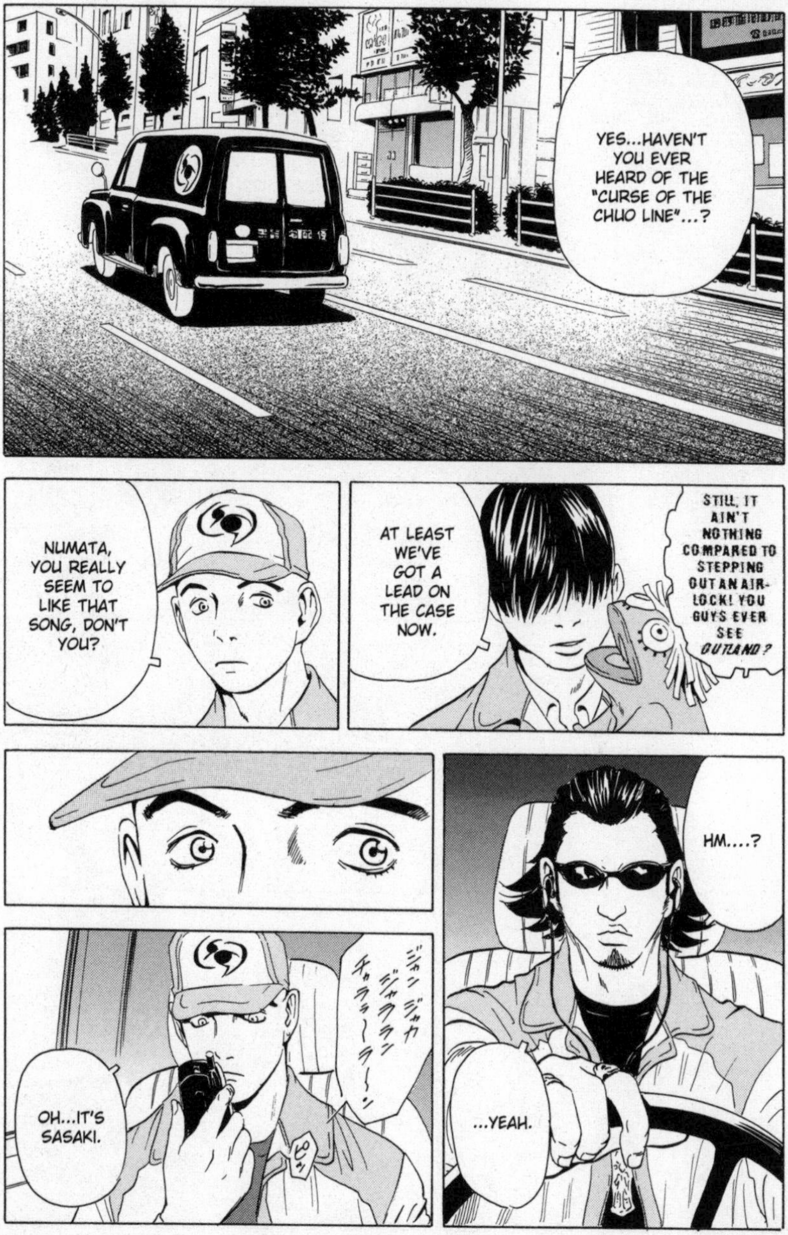
YES...HAVEN'T YOU EVER HEARD OF THE "CURSE OF THE CHUO LINE"...?
STILL, IT AIN'T NOTHING COMPARED TO STEPPING OUT AN AIR-LOCK! YOU GUYS EVER SEE *OUTLAND*?
AT LEAST WE'VE GOT A LEAD ON THE CASE NOW.
NUMATA, YOU REALLY SEEM TO LIKE THAT SONG, DON'T YOU?
HM....?
...YEAH.
ジャン ジャカ ジャララン チャララ〜ラ〜ン
OH...IT'S SASAKI.
ピッ

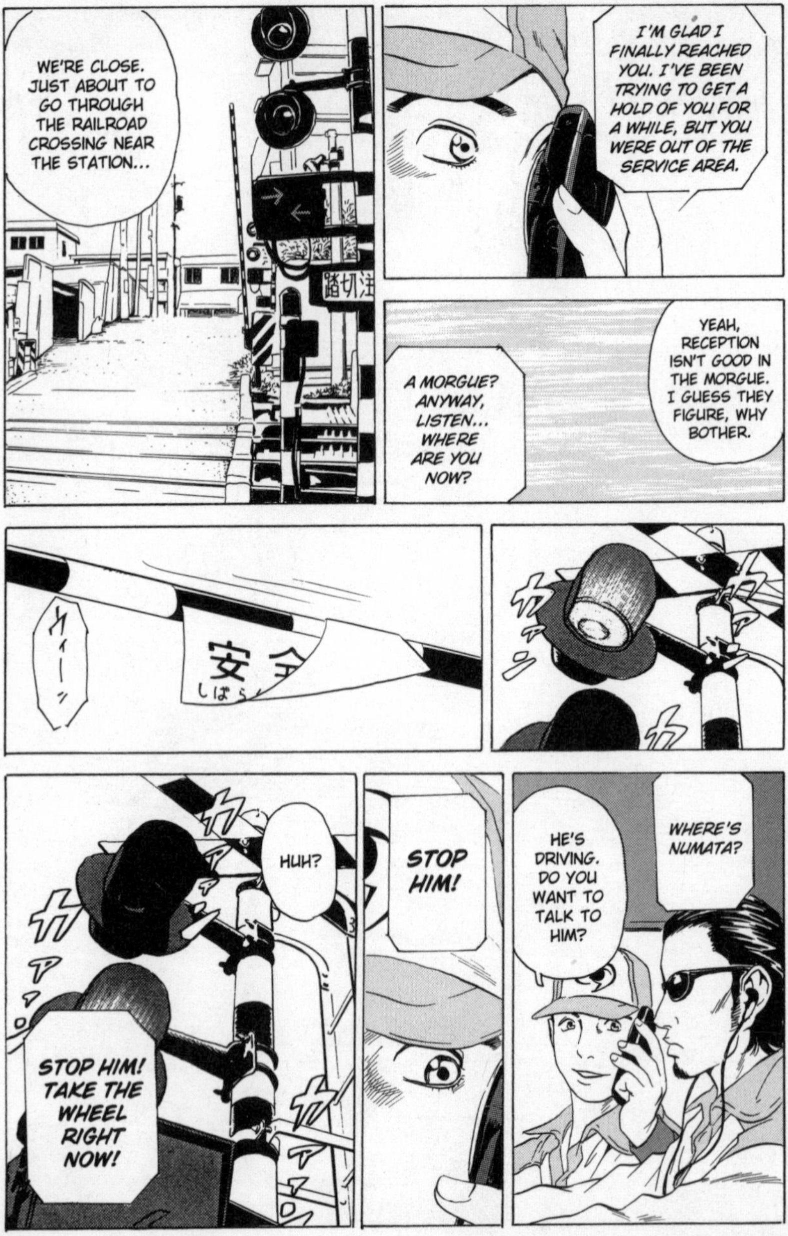
I'M GLAD I FINALLY REACHED YOU. I'VE BEEN TRYING TO GET A HOLD OF YOU FOR A WHILE, BUT YOU WERE OUT OF THE SERVICE AREA.
YEAH, RECEPTION ISN'T GOOD IN THE MORGUE. I GUESS THEY FIGURE, WHY BOTHER.
A MORGUE? ANYWAY, LISTEN... WHERE ARE YOU NOW?
WE'RE CLOSE. JUST ABOUT TO GO THROUGH THE RAILROAD CROSSING NEAR THE STATION...
ウィーン
WHERE'S NUMATA?
HE'S DRIVING. DO YOU WANT TO TALK TO HIM?
STOP HIM!
HUH?
STOP HIM! TAKE THE WHEEL RIGHT NOW!

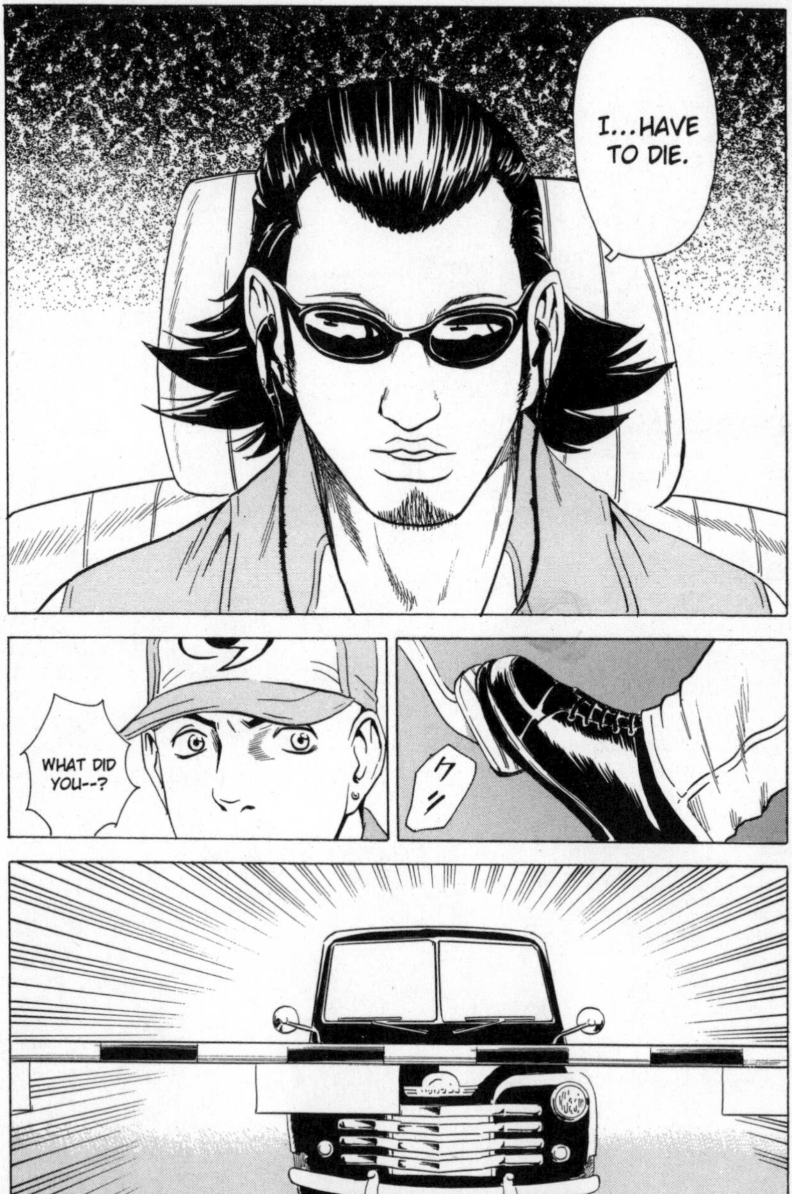
I...HAVE TO DIE.
クン
WHAT DID YOU--?

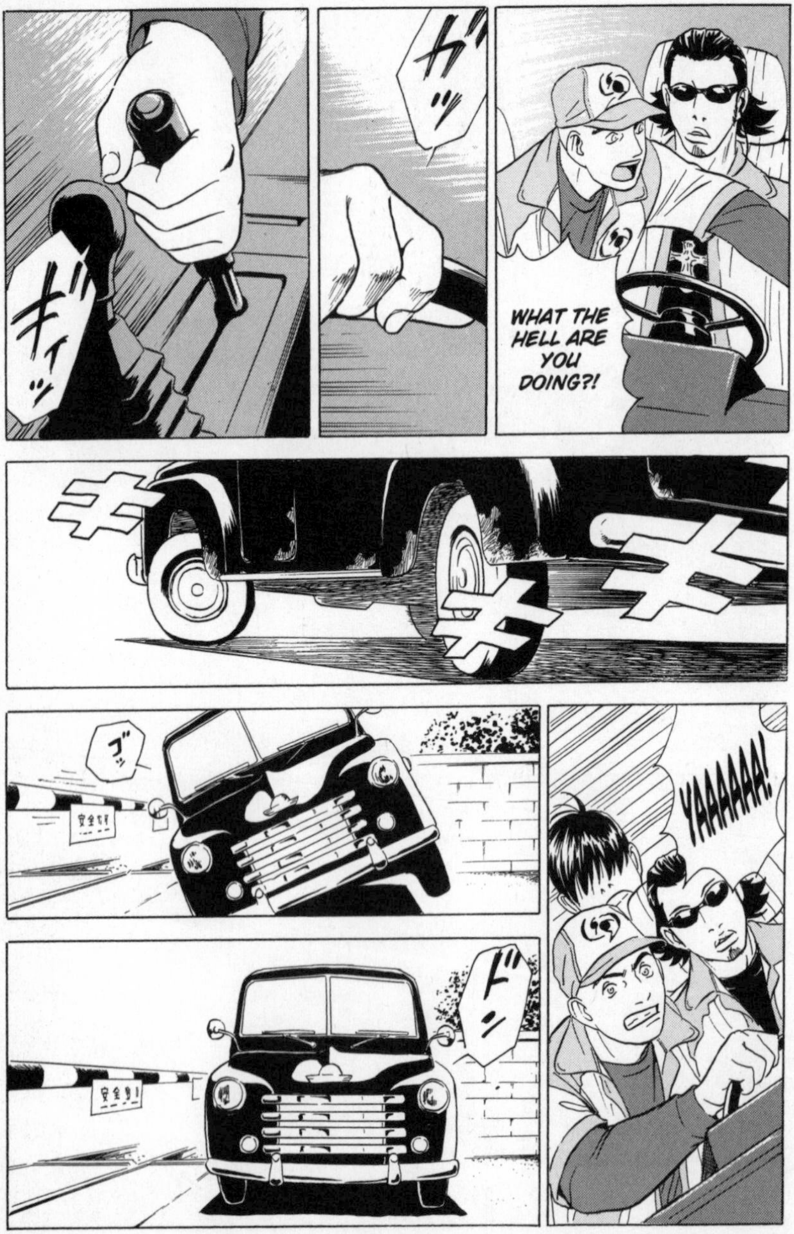
WHAT THE HELL ARE YOU DOING?!
ガッ
ギィッ
キ
キ
キ
キ
YAAAAAA!
ゴッ
ドン

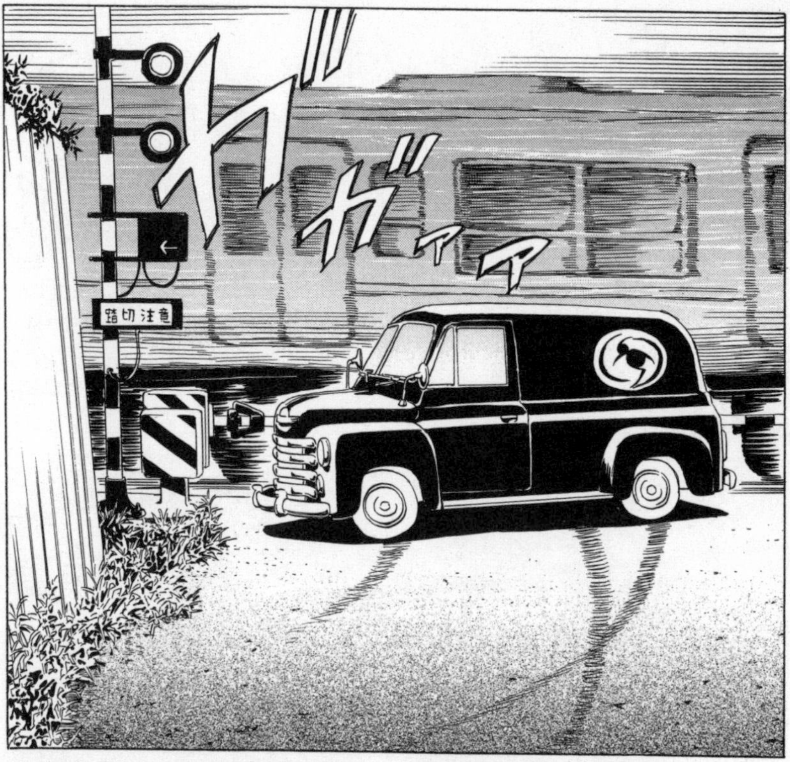
踏切注意

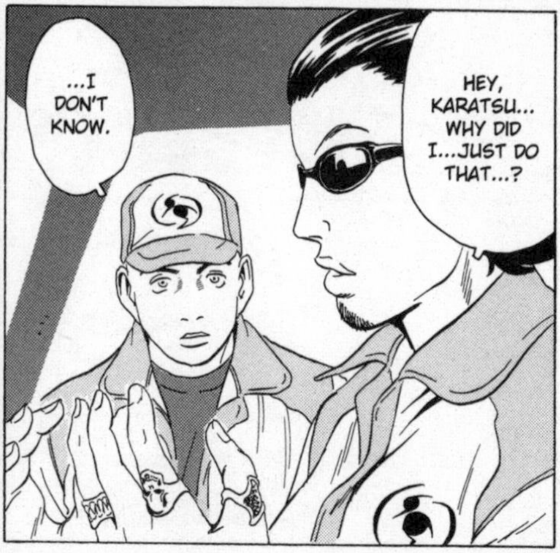
HEY, KARATSU... WHY DID I...JUST DO THAT...?
...I DON'T KNOW.

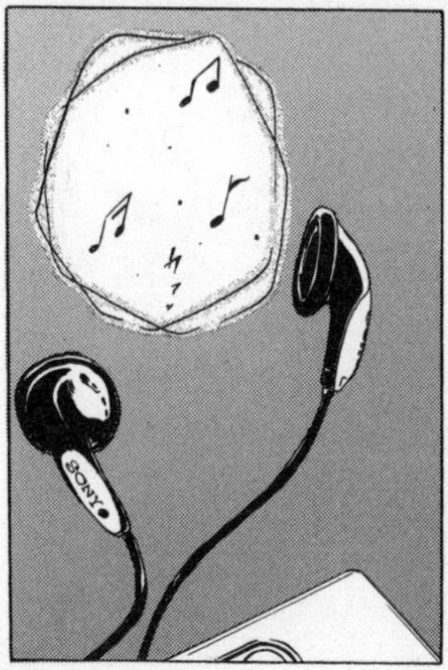
SONY

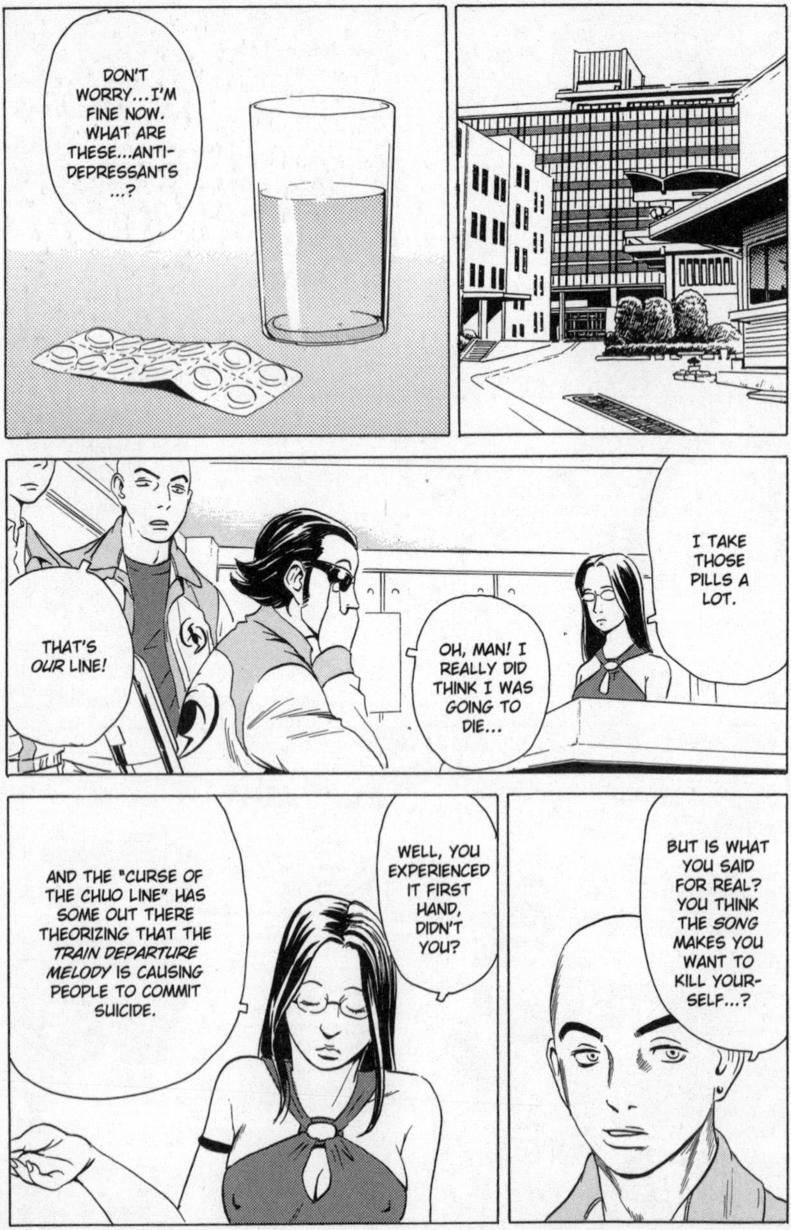
DON'T WORRY...I'M FINE NOW. WHAT ARE THESE...ANTI-DEPRESSANTS ...?
I TAKE THOSE PILLS A LOT.
OH, MAN! I REALLY DID THINK I WAS GOING TO DIE...
THAT'S *OUR* LINE!
BUT IS WHAT YOU SAID FOR REAL? YOU THINK THE *SONG* MAKES YOU WANT TO KILL YOURSELF...?
WELL, YOU EXPERIENCED IT FIRST HAND, DIDN'T YOU?
AND THE "CURSE OF THE CHUO LINE" HAS SOME OUT THERE THEORIZING THAT THE *TRAIN DEPARTURE MELODY* IS CAUSING PEOPLE TO COMMIT SUICIDE.

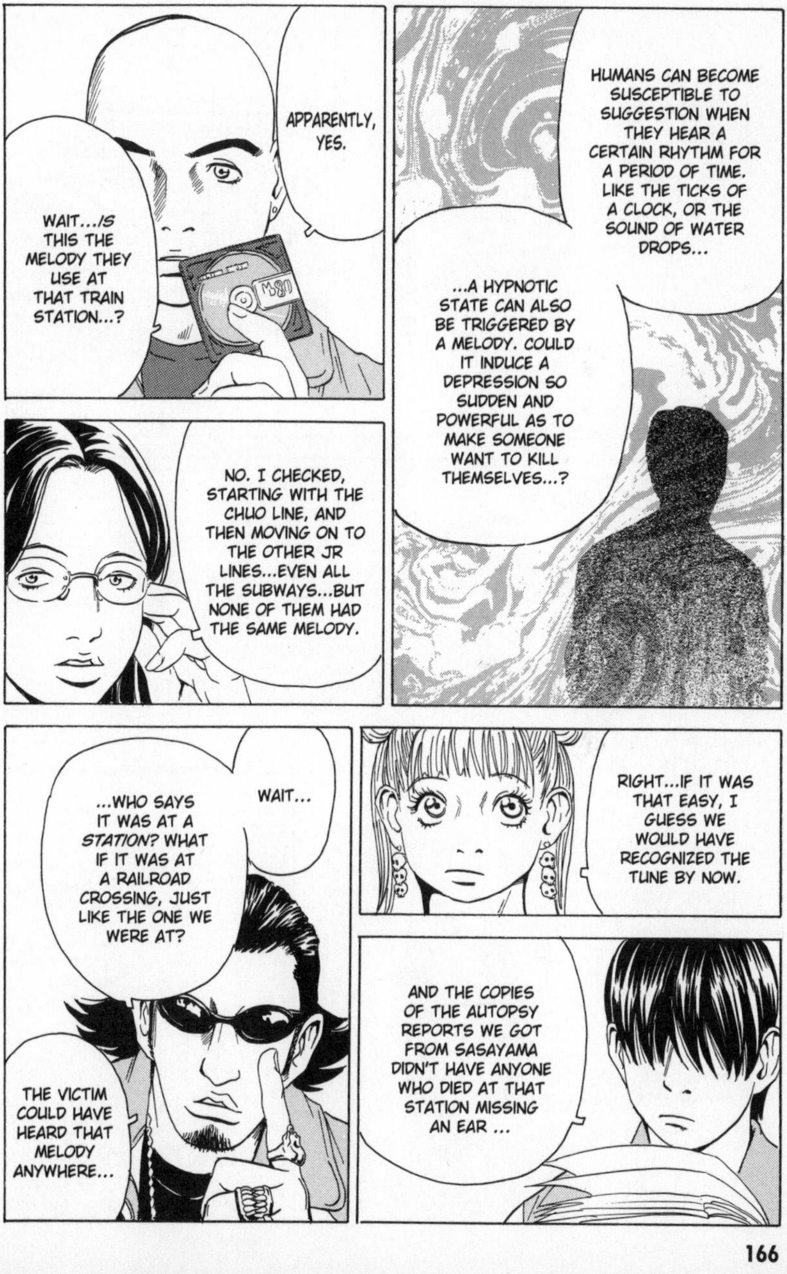
HUMANS CAN BECOME SUSCEPTIBLE TO SUGGESTION WHEN THEY HEAR A CERTAIN RHYTHM FOR A PERIOD OF TIME. LIKE THE TICKS OF A CLOCK, OR THE SOUND OF WATER DROPS...
...A HYPNOTIC STATE CAN ALSO BE TRIGGERED BY A MELODY. COULD IT INDUCE A DEPRESSION SO SUDDEN AND POWERFUL AS TO MAKE SOMEONE WANT TO KILL THEMSELVES...?
APPARENTLY, YES.
WAIT...*IS* THIS THE MELODY THEY USE AT THAT TRAIN STATION...?
M80
NO. I CHECKED, STARTING WITH THE CHUO LINE, AND THEN MOVING ON TO THE OTHER JR LINES...EVEN ALL THE SUBWAYS...BUT NONE OF THEM HAD THE SAME MELODY.
RIGHT...IF IT WAS THAT EASY, I GUESS WE WOULD HAVE RECOGNIZED THE TUNE BY NOW.
AND THE COPIES OF THE AUTOPSY REPORTS WE GOT FROM SASAYAMA DIDN'T HAVE ANYONE WHO DIED AT THAT STATION MISSING AN EAR ...
WAIT...
...WHO SAYS IT WAS AT A *STATION*? WHAT IF IT WAS AT A RAILROAD CROSSING, JUST LIKE THE ONE WE WERE AT?
THE VICTIM COULD HAVE HEARD THAT MELODY ANYWHERE...

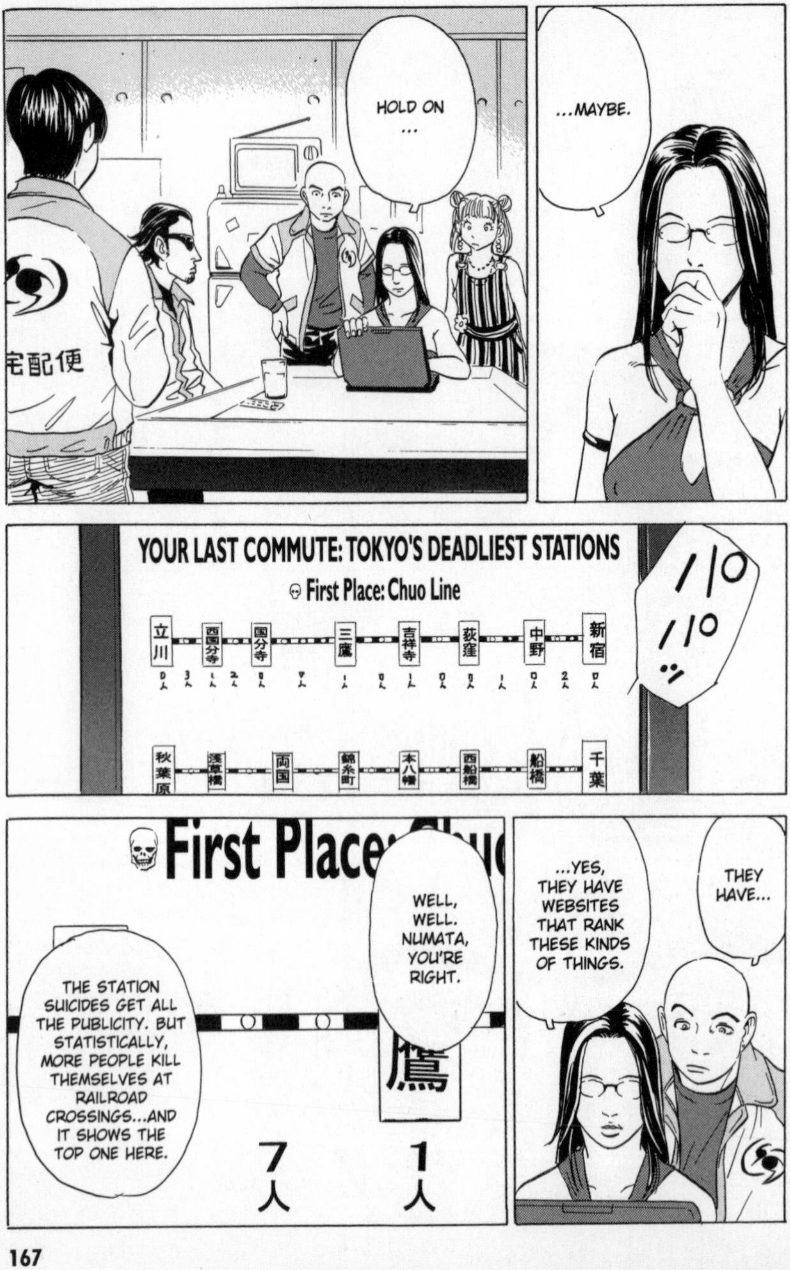
...MAYBE.
HOLD ON ...
宅配便
パパッ
YOUR LAST COMMUTE: TOKYO'S DEADLIEST STATIONS
First Place: Chuo Line
新宿 中野 荻窪 吉祥寺 三鷹 国分寺 西国分寺 立川
千葉 船橋 西船橋 本八幡 錦糸町 両国 浅草橋 秋葉原
THEY HAVE...
...YES, THEY HAVE WEBSITES THAT RANK THESE KINDS OF THINGS.
First Place
WELL, WELL. NUMATA, YOU'RE RIGHT.
THE STATION SUICIDES GET ALL THE PUBLICITY. BUT STATISTICALLY, MORE PEOPLE KILL THEMSELVES AT RAILROAD CROSSINGS...AND IT SHOWS THE TOP ONE HERE.
鷹
1人
7人

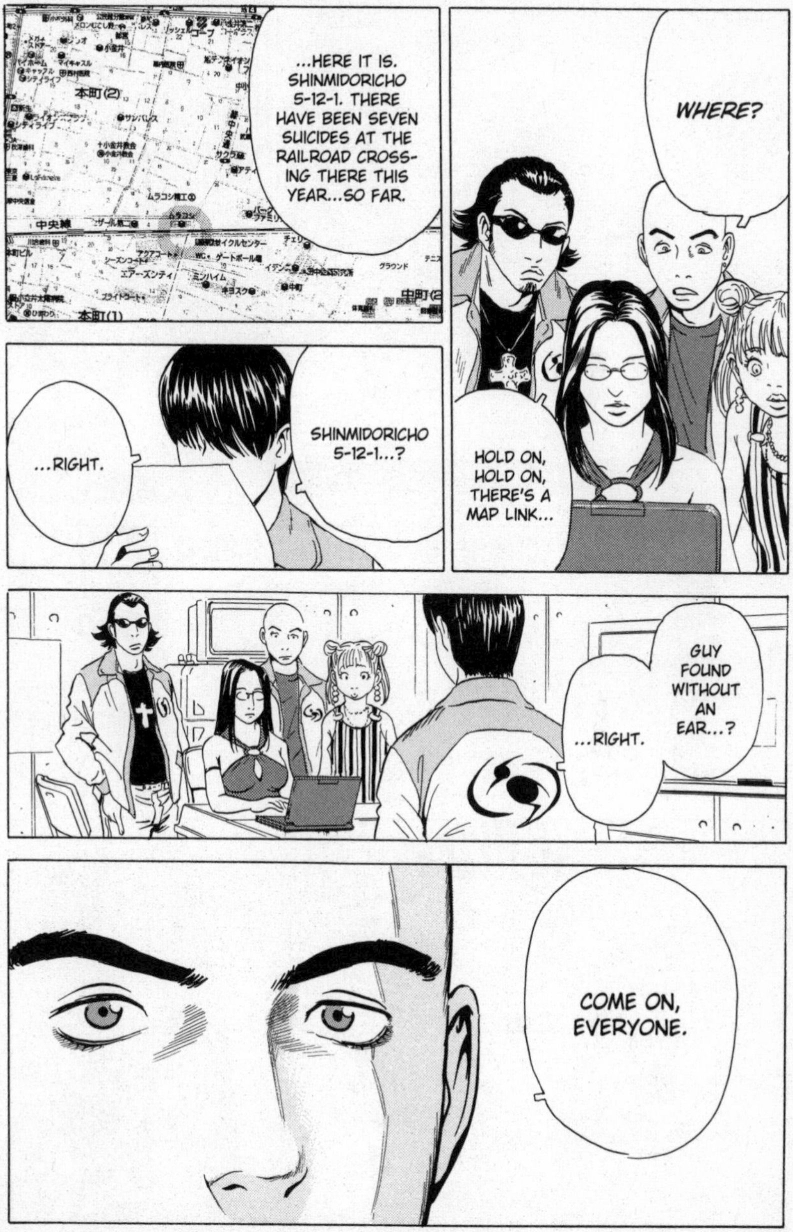
WHERE?
HOLD ON, HOLD ON, THERE'S A MAP LINK...
...HERE IT IS. SHINMIDORICHO 5-12-1. THERE HAVE BEEN SEVEN SUICIDES AT THE RAILROAD CROSSING THERE THIS YEAR...SO FAR.
本町(2)
中央線
本町(1)
SHINMIDORICHO 5-12-1...?
...RIGHT.
GUY FOUND WITHOUT AN EAR...?
...RIGHT.
COME ON, EVERYONE.

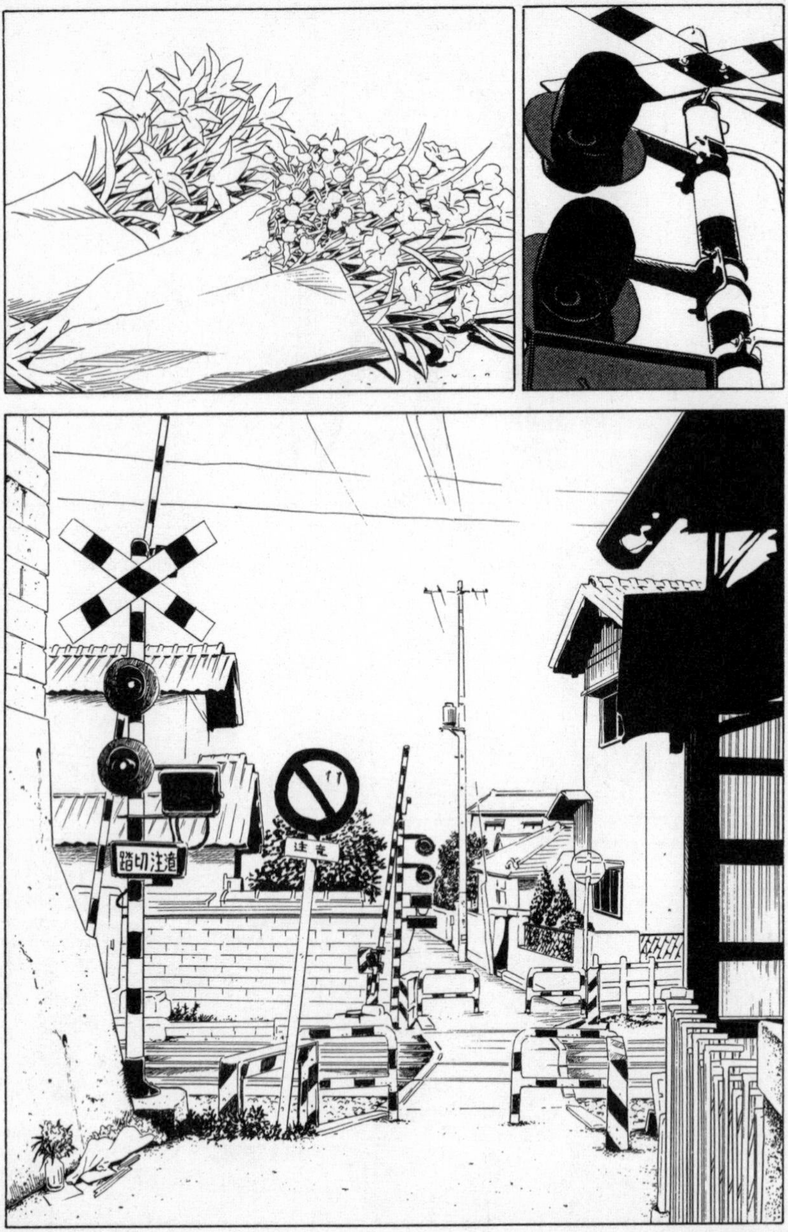
踏切注意
注意

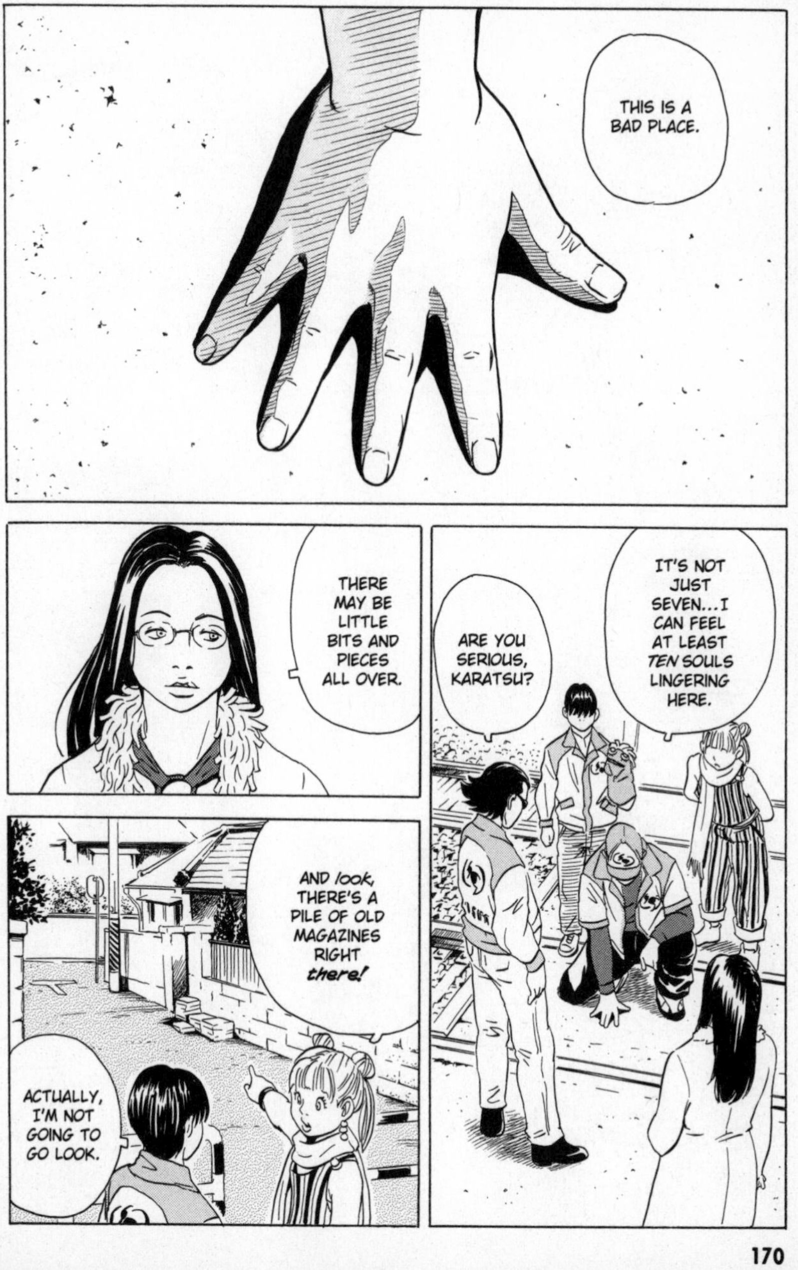

THIS IS A BAD PLACE.
IT'S NOT JUST SEVEN...I CAN FEEL AT LEAST *TEN* SOULS LINGERING HERE.
ARE YOU SERIOUS, KARATSU?
THERE MAY BE LITTLE BITS AND PIECES ALL OVER.
AND *look*, THERE'S A PILE OF OLD MAGAZINES RIGHT *there!*
ACTUALLY, I'M NOT GOING TO GO LOOK.

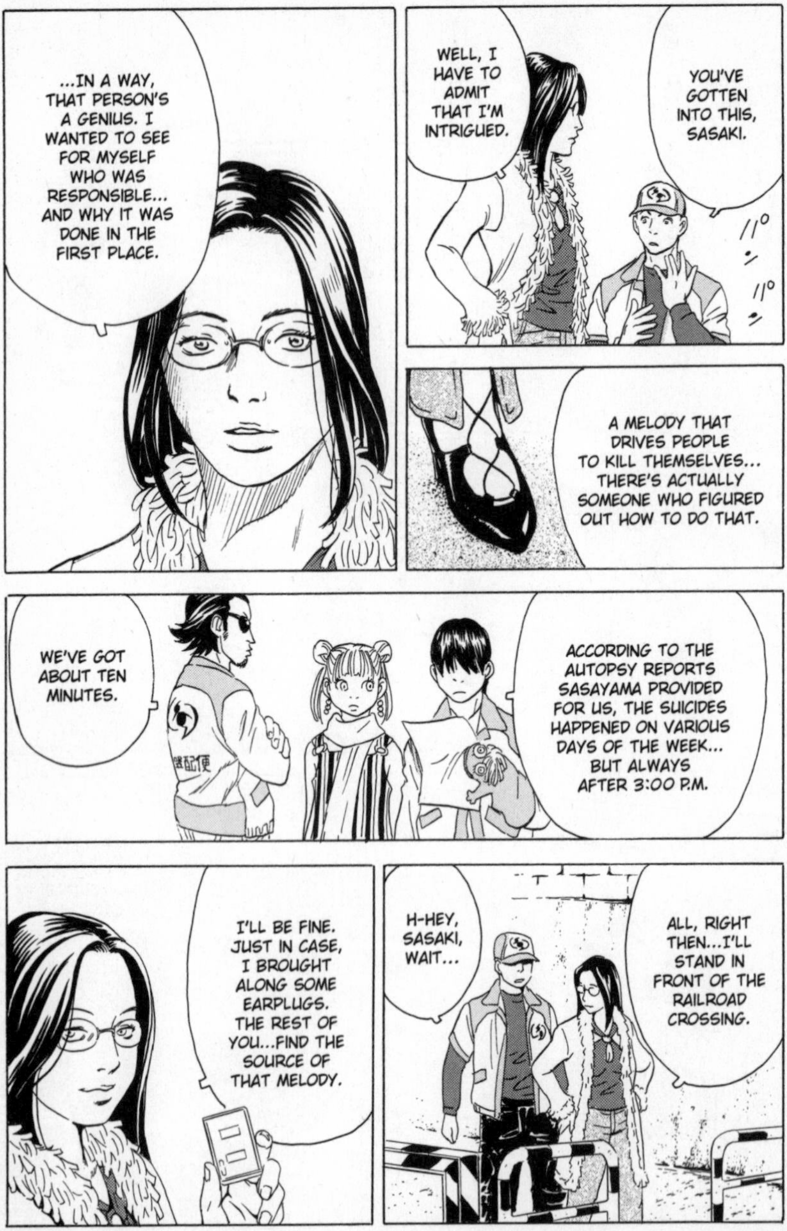
YOU'VE GOTTEN INTO THIS, SASAKI.
WELL, I HAVE TO ADMIT THAT I'M INTRIGUED.
A MELODY THAT DRIVES PEOPLE TO KILL THEMSELVES... THERE'S ACTUALLY SOMEONE WHO FIGURED OUT HOW TO DO THAT.
...IN A WAY, THAT PERSON'S A GENIUS. I WANTED TO SEE FOR MYSELF WHO WAS RESPONSIBLE... AND WHY IT WAS DONE IN THE FIRST PLACE.
ACCORDING TO THE AUTOPSY REPORTS SASAYAMA PROVIDED FOR US, THE SUICIDES HAPPENED ON VARIOUS DAYS OF THE WEEK... BUT ALWAYS AFTER 3:00 P.M.
WE'VE GOT ABOUT TEN MINUTES.
ALL, RIGHT THEN...I'LL STAND IN FRONT OF THE RAILROAD CROSSING.
H-HEY, SASAKI, WAIT...
I'LL BE FINE. JUST IN CASE, I BROUGHT ALONG SOME EARPLUGS. THE REST OF YOU...FIND THE SOURCE OF THAT MELODY.

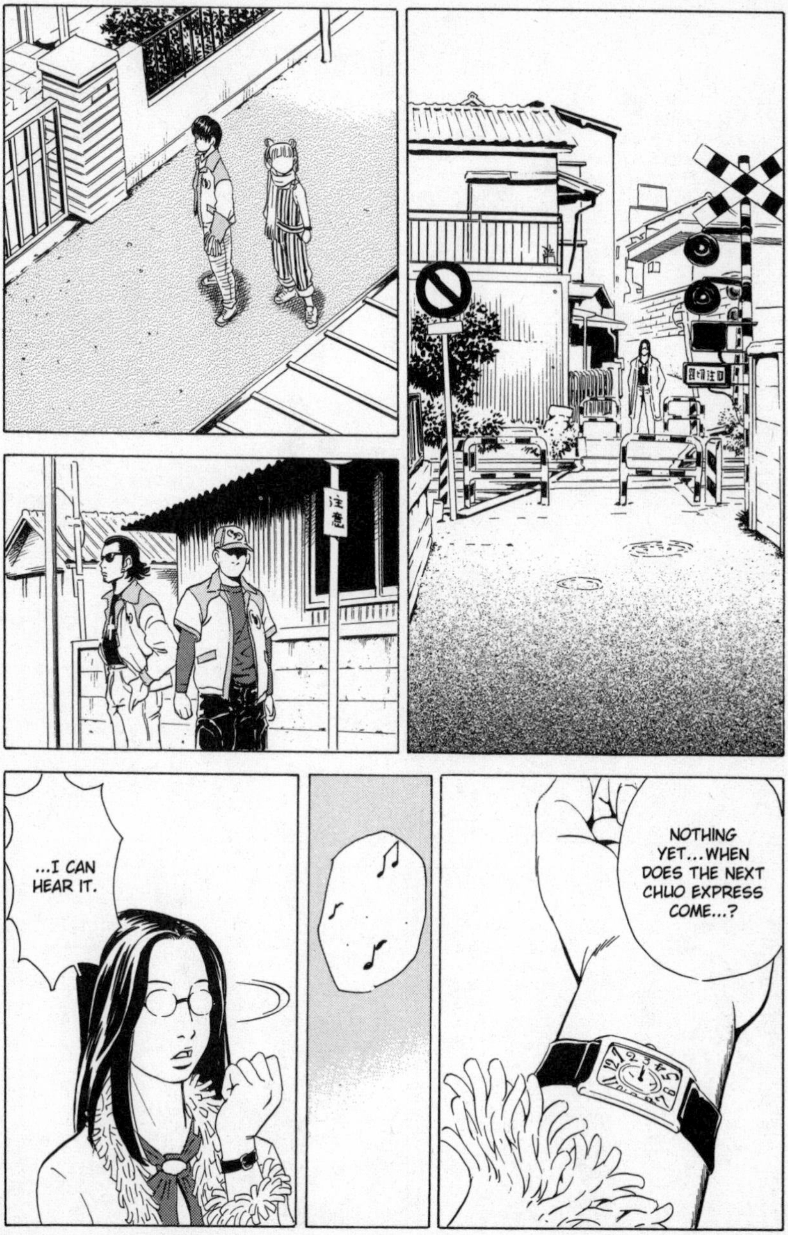
注意
NOTHING YET...WHEN DOES THE NEXT CHUO EXPRESS COME...?
...I CAN HEAR IT.

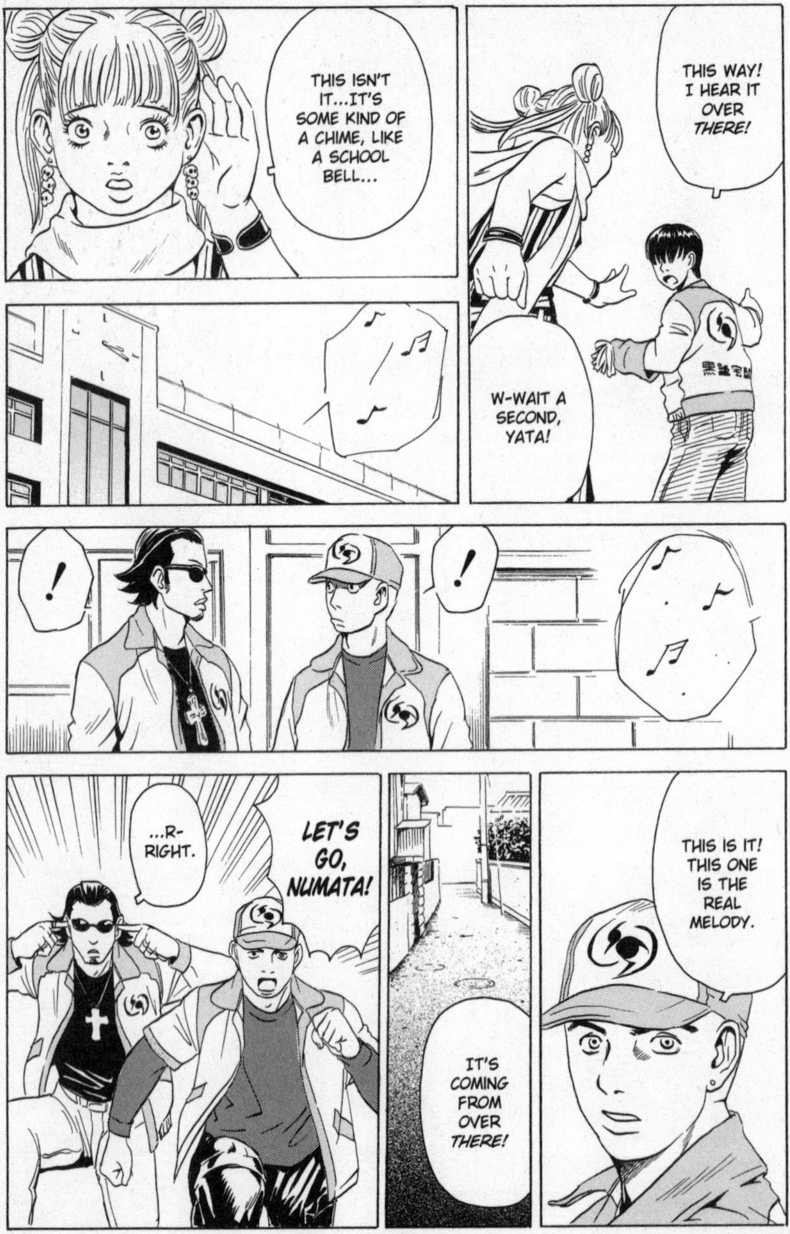
THIS WAY! I HEAR IT OVER *THERE!*
W-WAIT A SECOND, YATA!
THIS ISN'T IT...IT'S SOME KIND OF A CHIME, LIKE A SCHOOL BELL...
!
!
THIS IS IT! THIS ONE IS THE REAL MELODY.
IT'S COMING FROM OVER *THERE!*
LET'S GO, NUMATA!
...R-RIGHT.

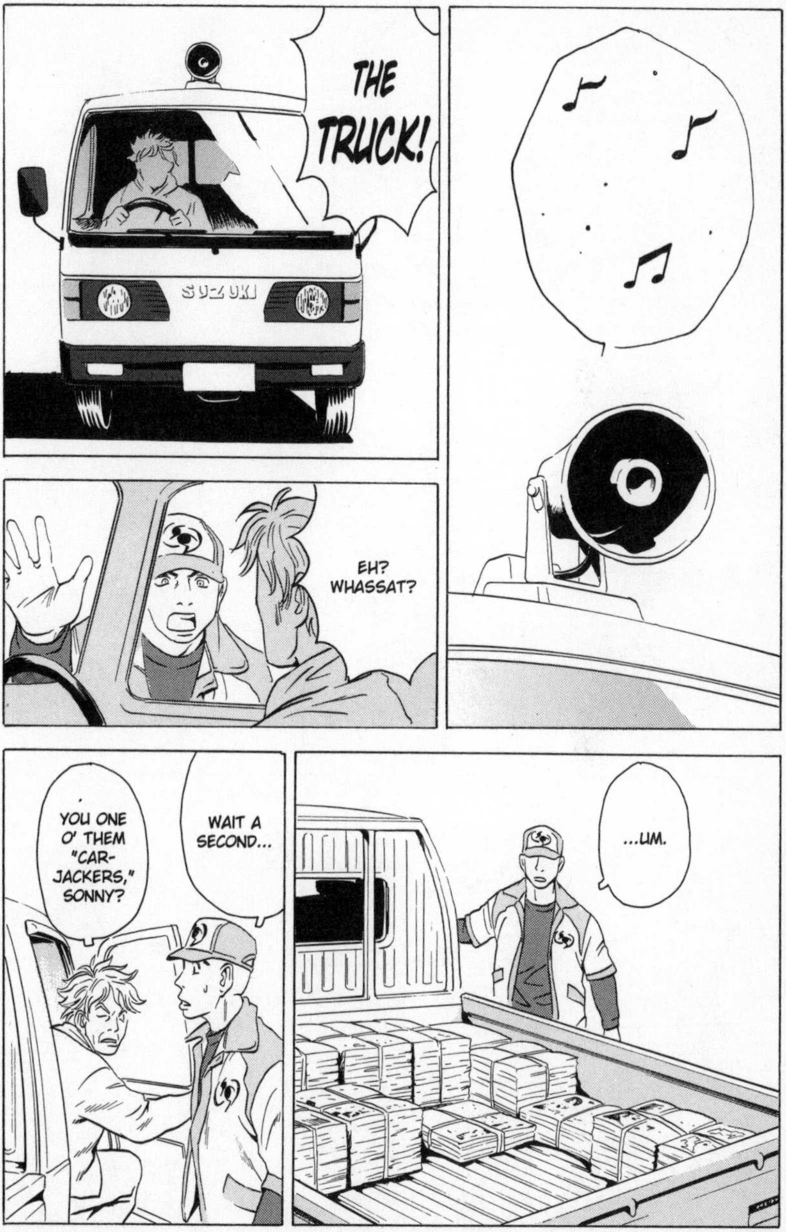
THE TRUCK!
EH? WHASSAT?
...UM.
WAIT A SECOND...
YOU ONE O' THEM "CAR-JACKERS," SONNY?

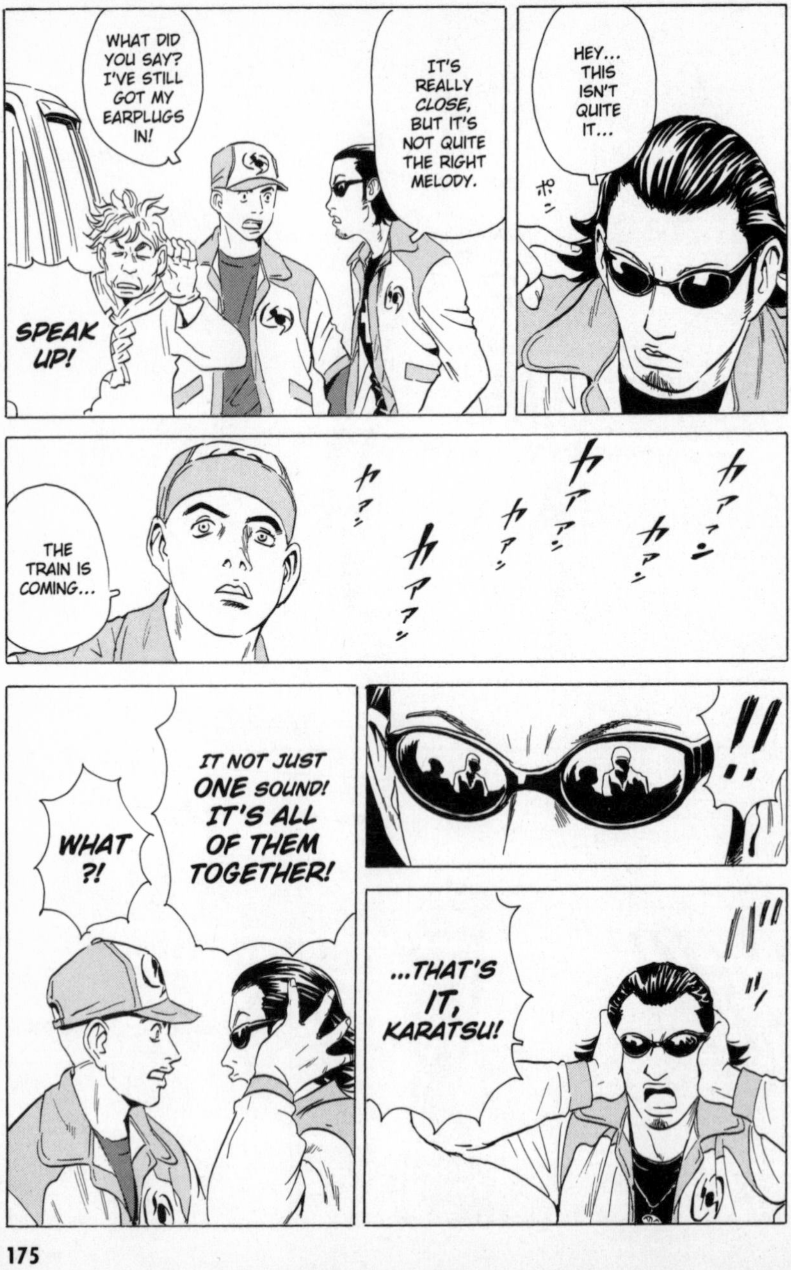
HEY... THIS ISN'T QUITE IT...
ポン
IT'S REALLY CLOSE, BUT IT'S NOT QUITE THE RIGHT MELODY.
WHAT DID YOU SAY? I'VE STILL GOT MY EARPLUGS IN!
SPEAK UP!
THE TRAIN IS COMING...
!!
...THAT'S IT, KARATSU!
IT NOT JUST ONE SOUND! IT'S ALL OF THEM TOGETHER!
WHAT?!

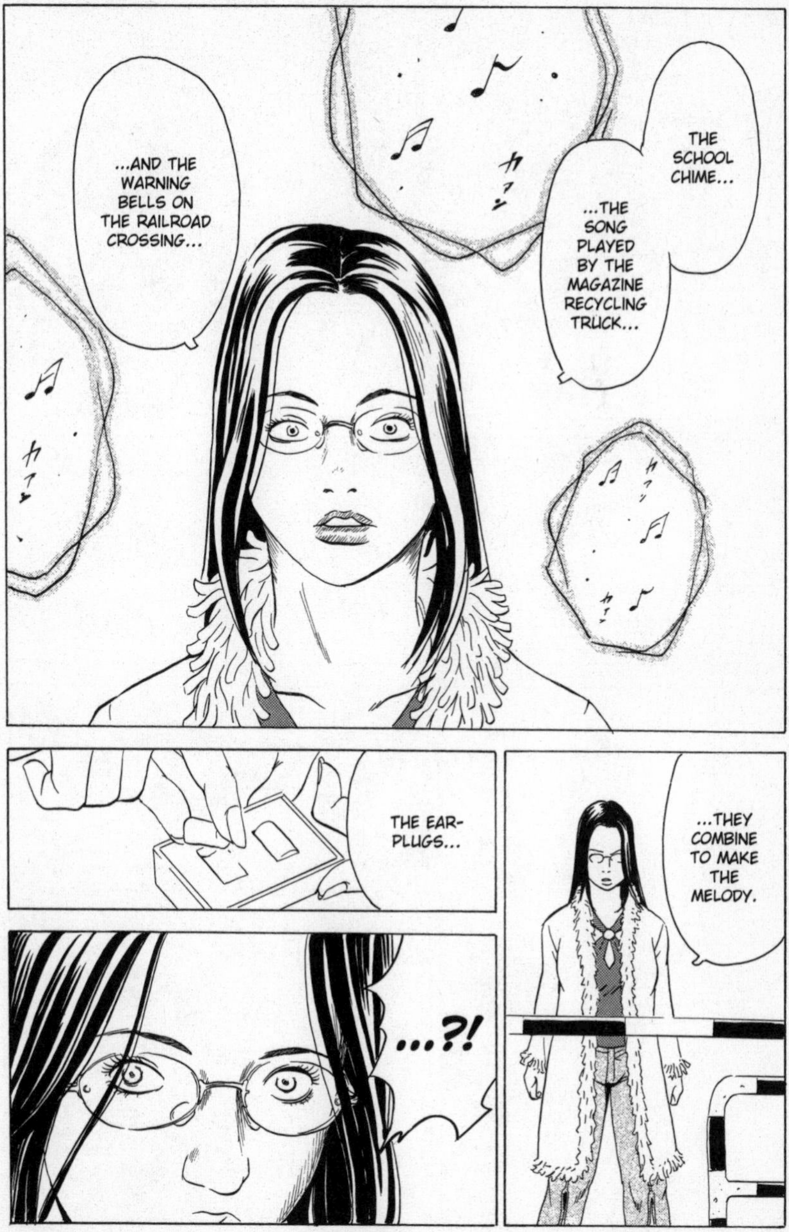
THE SCHOOL CHIME...
...THE SONG PLAYED BY THE MAGAZINE RECYCLING TRUCK...
...AND THE WARNING BELLS ON THE RAILROAD CROSSING...
...THEY COMBINE TO MAKE THE MELODY.
THE EAR-PLUGS...
...?!

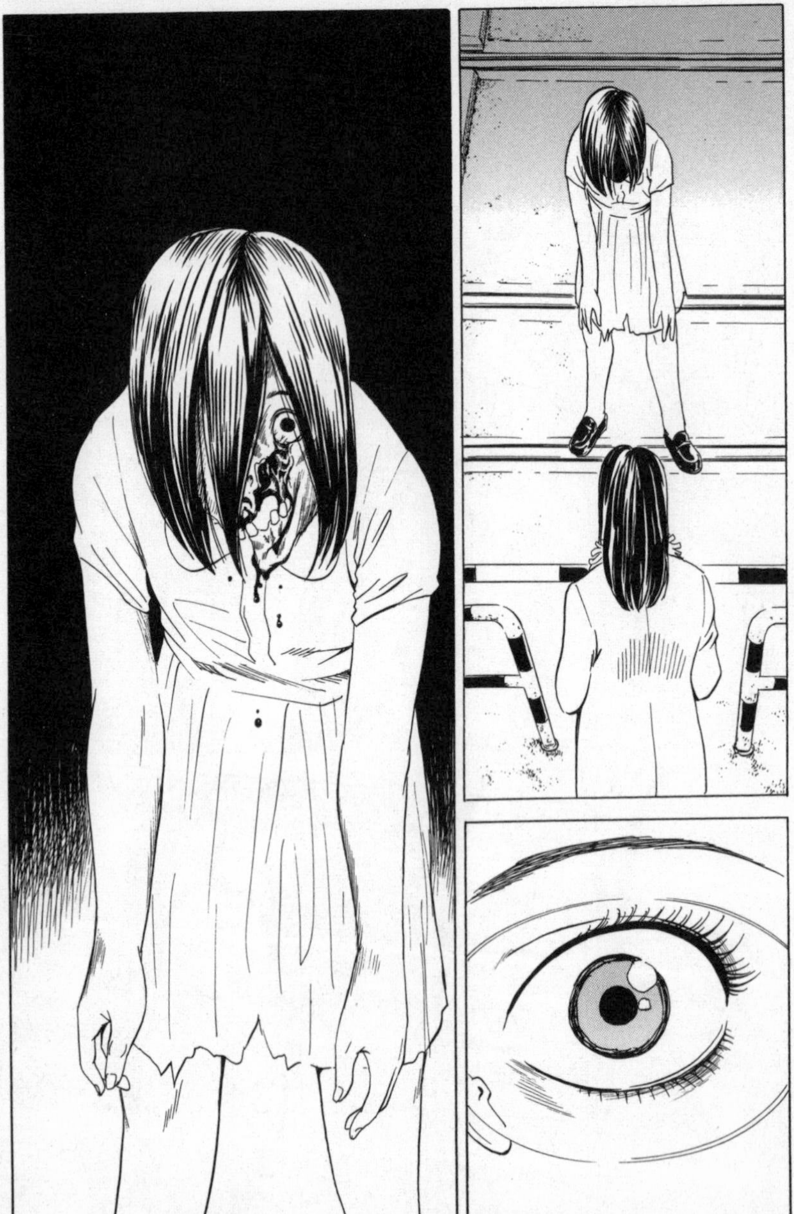

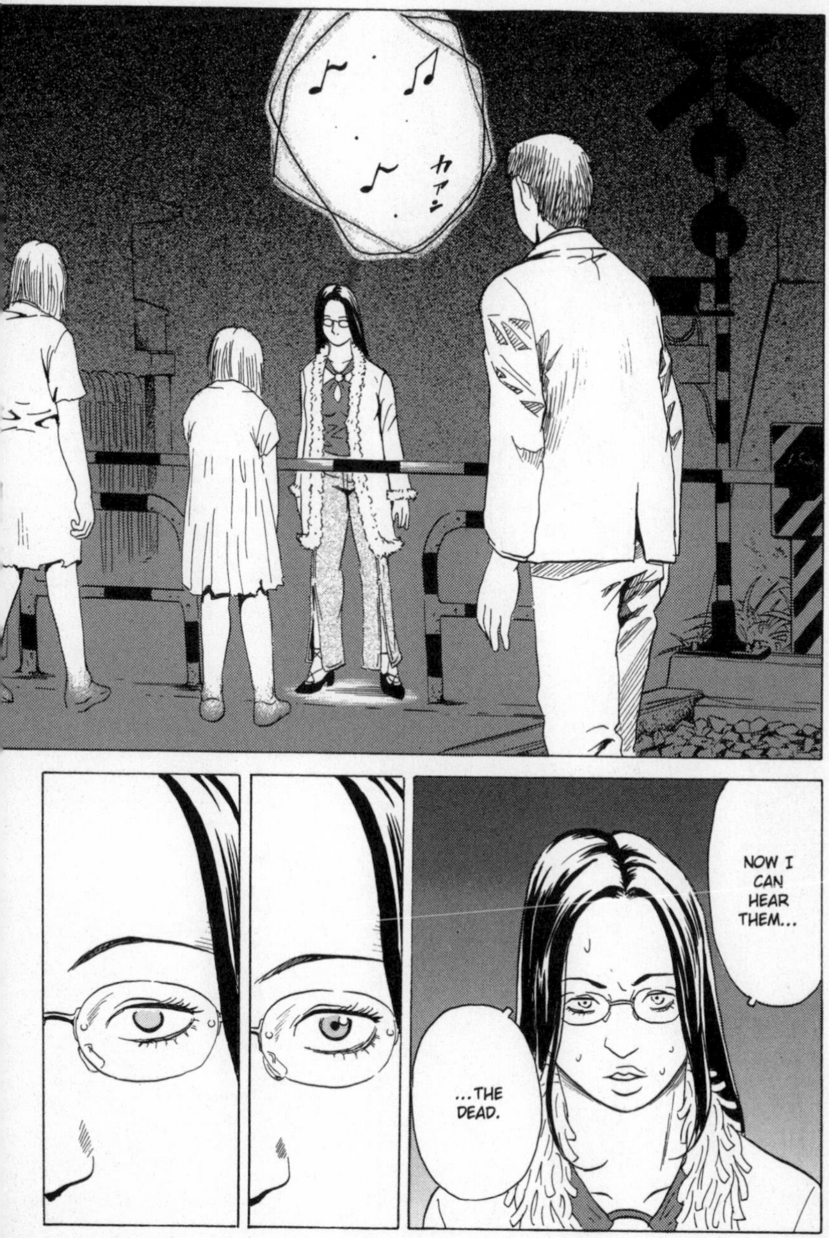
カァン
NOW I CAN HEAR THEM...
...THE DEAD.

I HAVE TO DIE TOO...

...SO I CAN SEE...MY MOTHER AND MY FATHER.

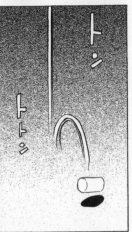

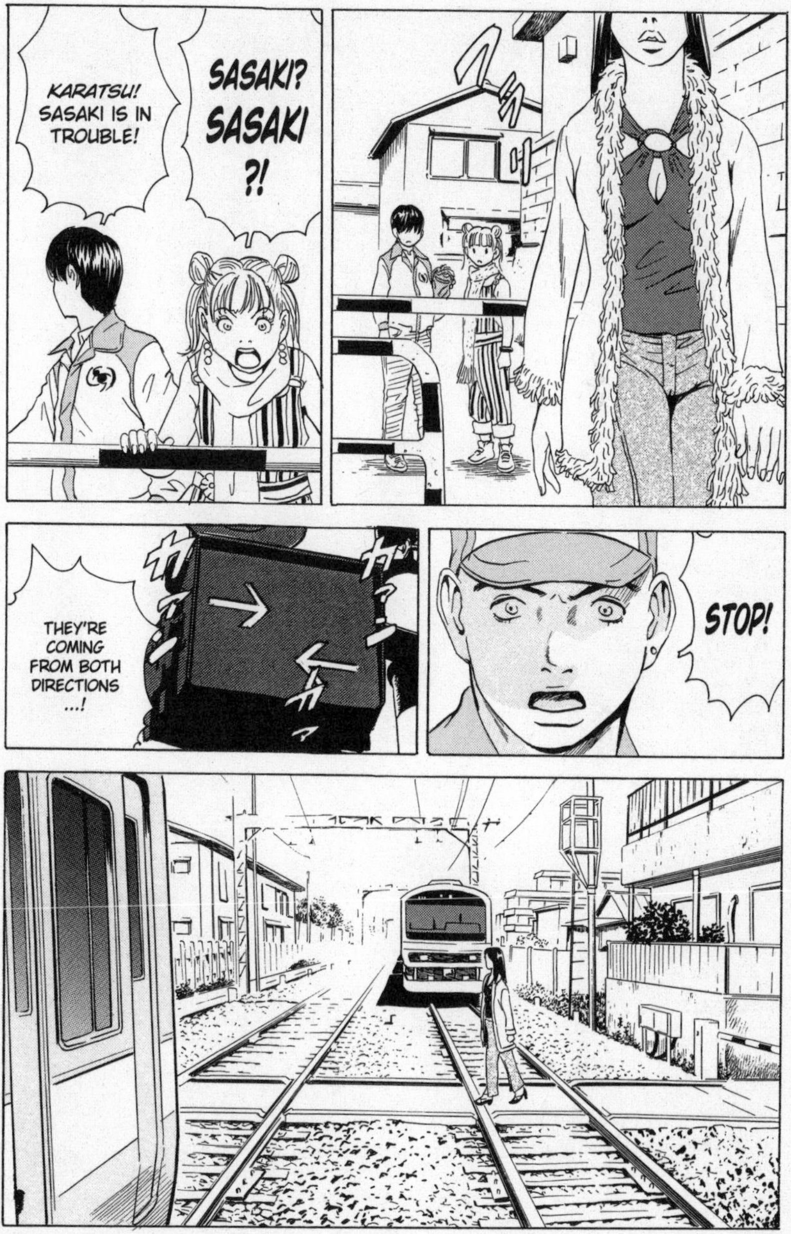
SASAKI? SASAKI ?!
KARATSU! SASAKI IS IN TROUBLE!
STOP!
THEY'RE COMING FROM BOTH DIRECTIONS ...!

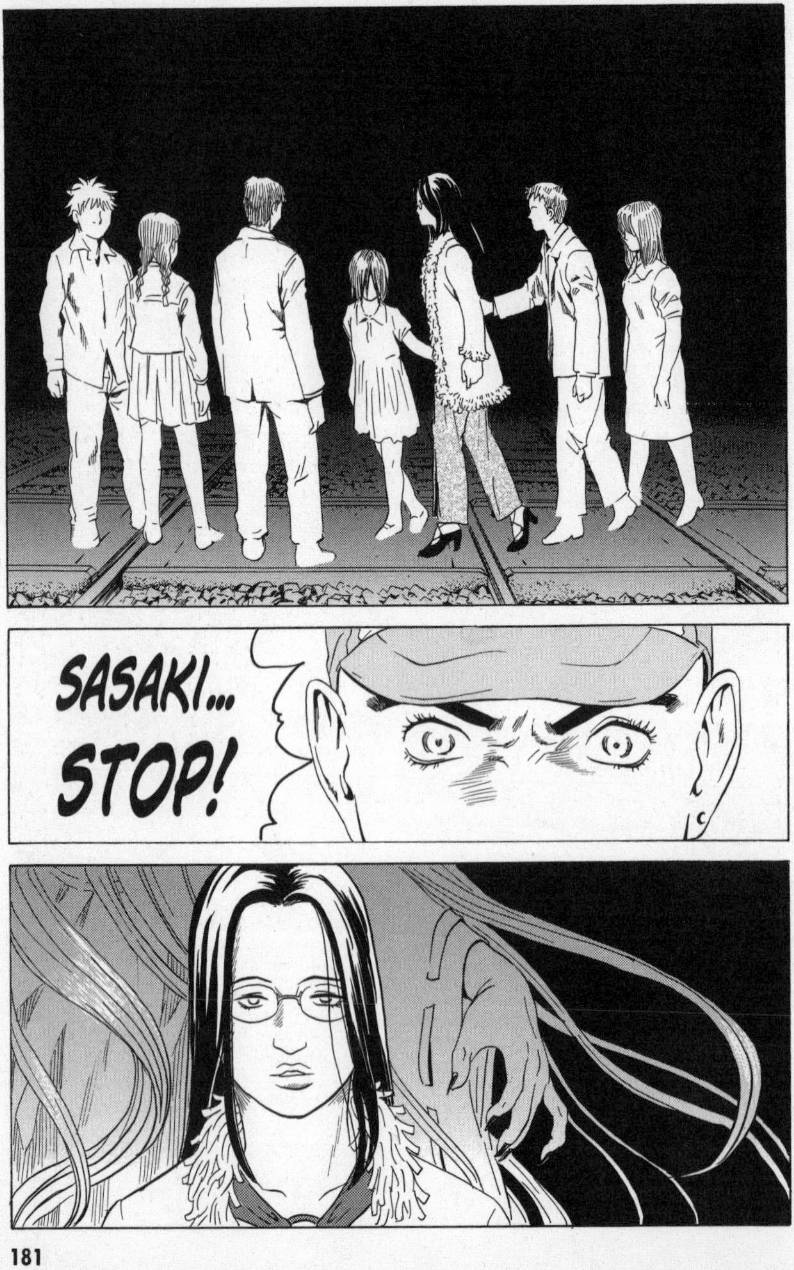
SASAKI... STOP!

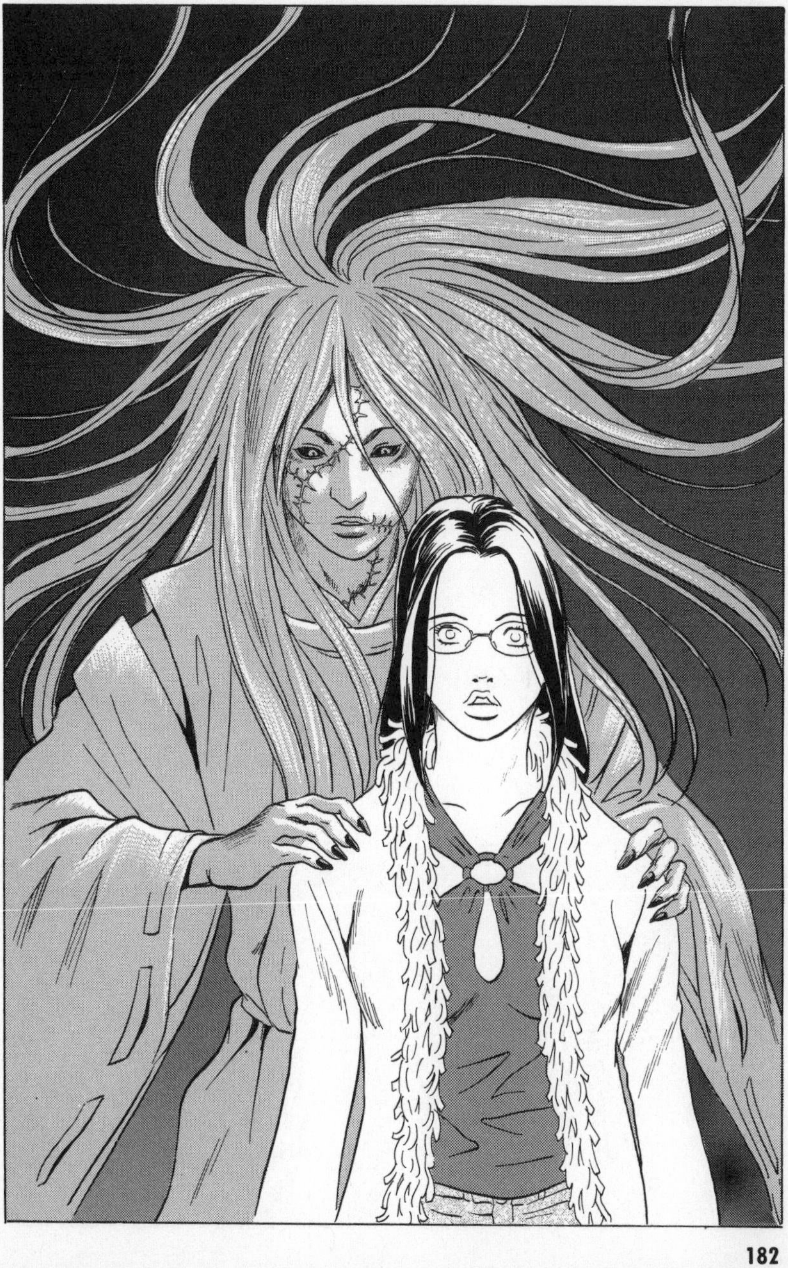

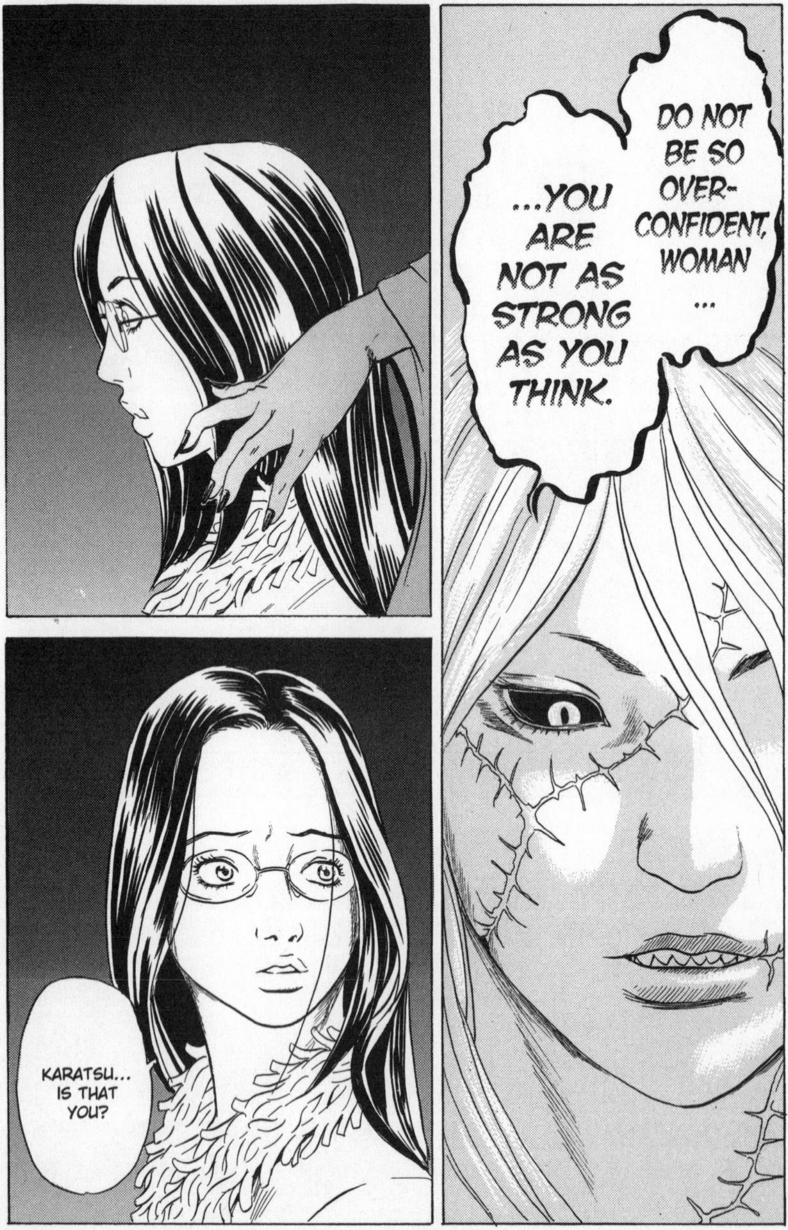
DO NOT BE SO OVER-CONFIDENT, WOMAN ...
...YOU ARE NOT AS STRONG AS YOU THINK.
KARATSU... IS THAT YOU?

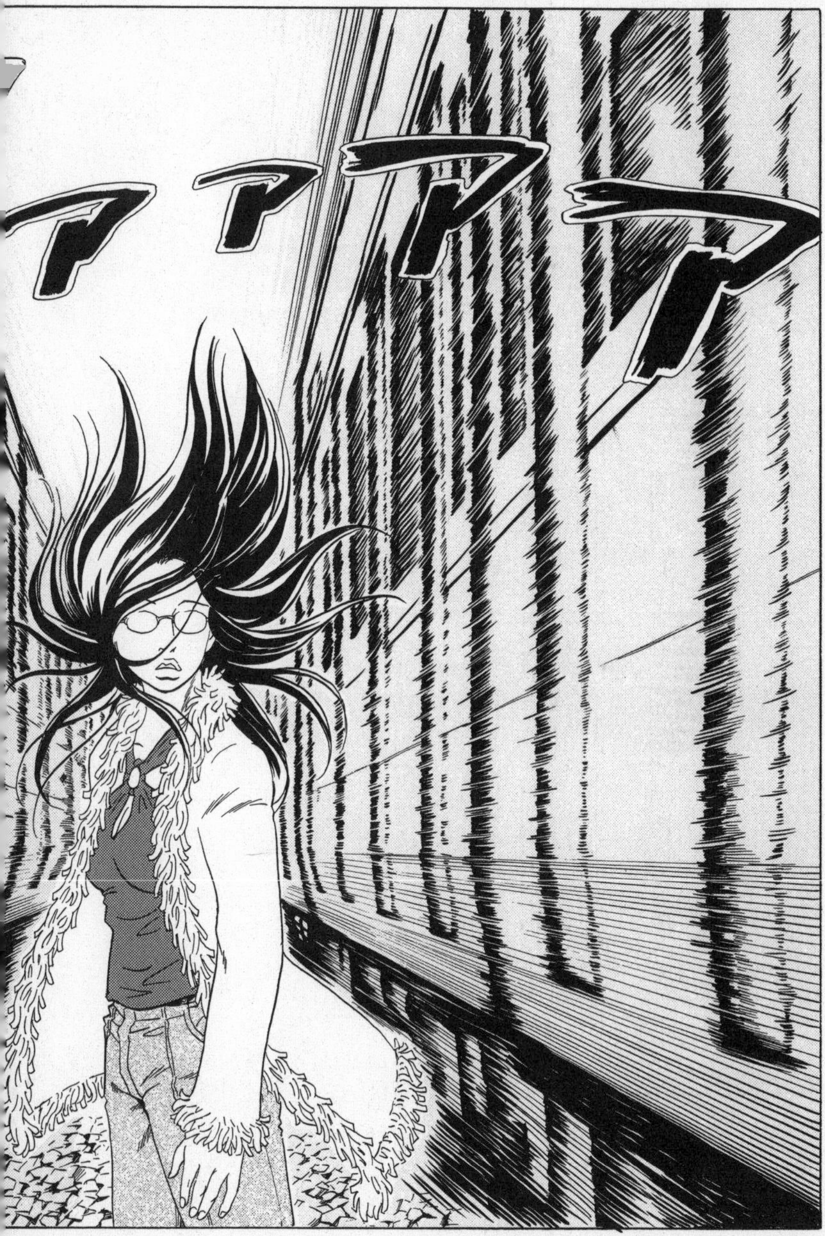
アアアア

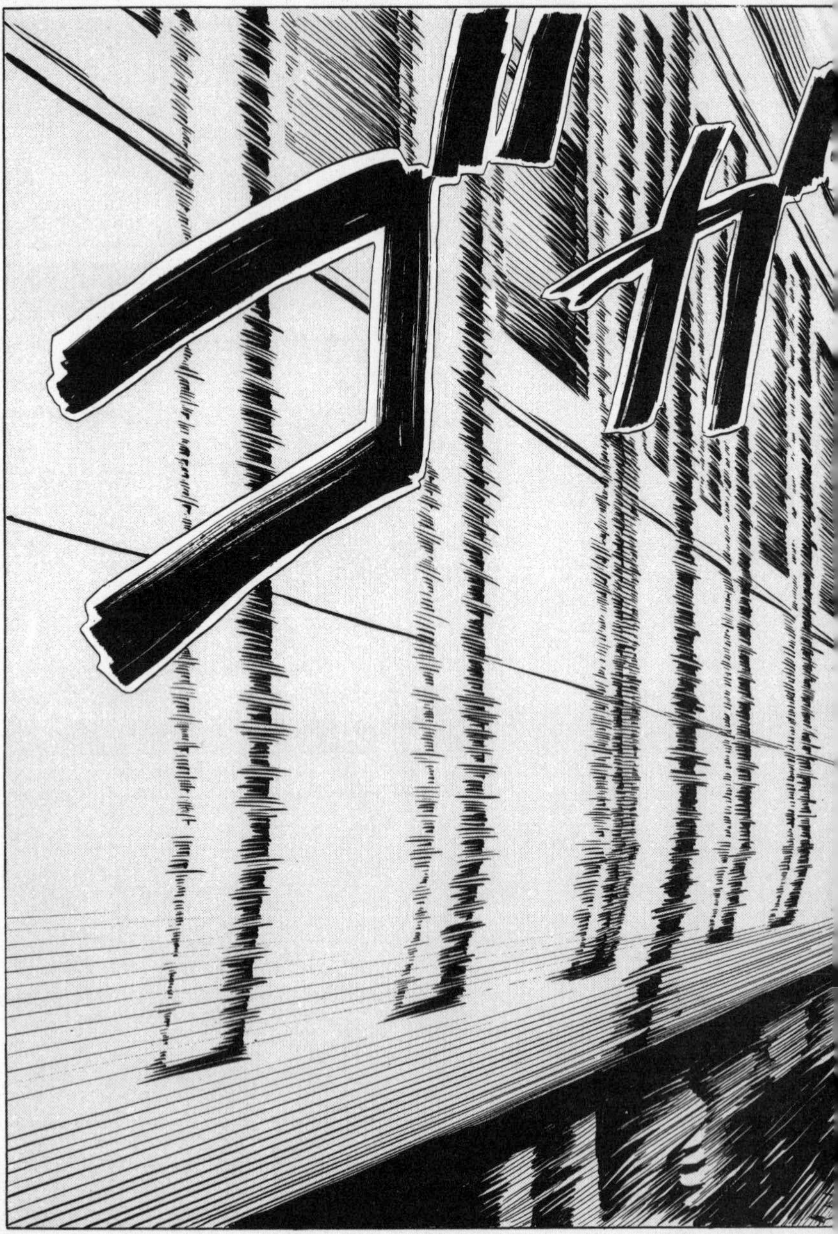
ゴオ

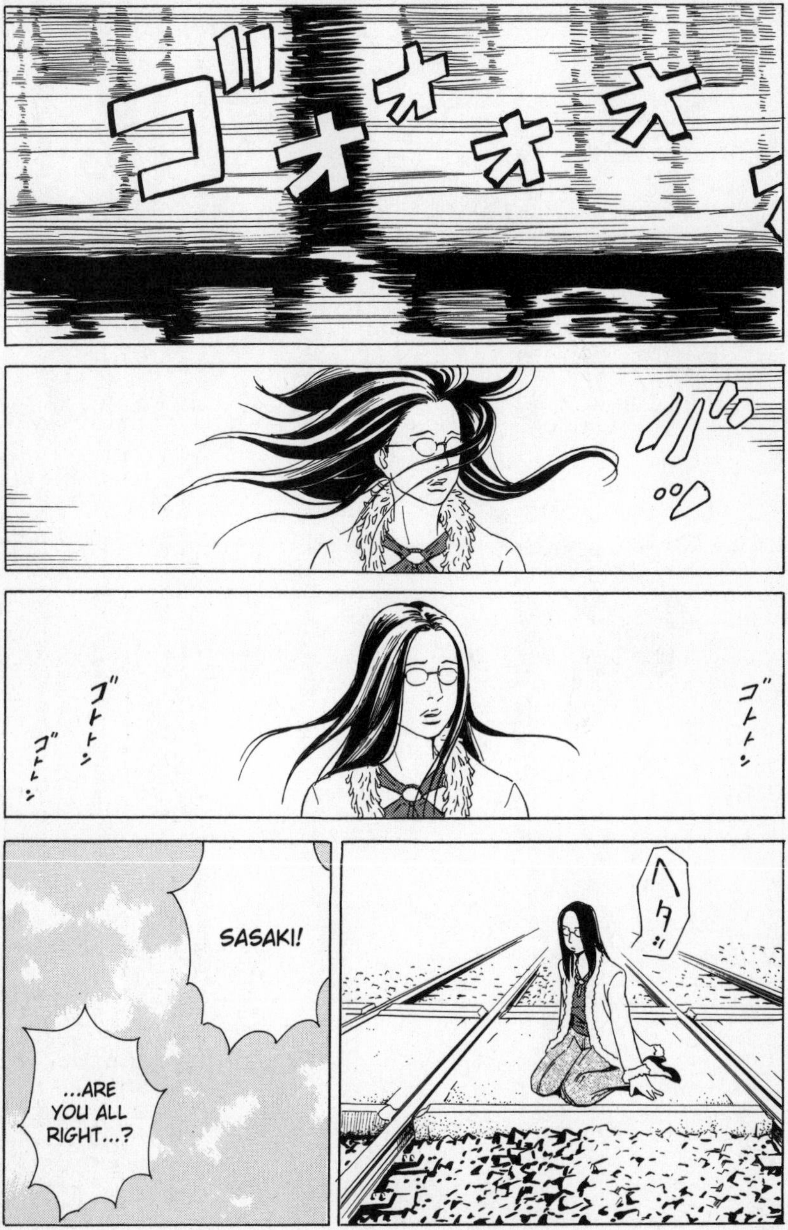
SASAKI!
...ARE YOU ALL RIGHT...?

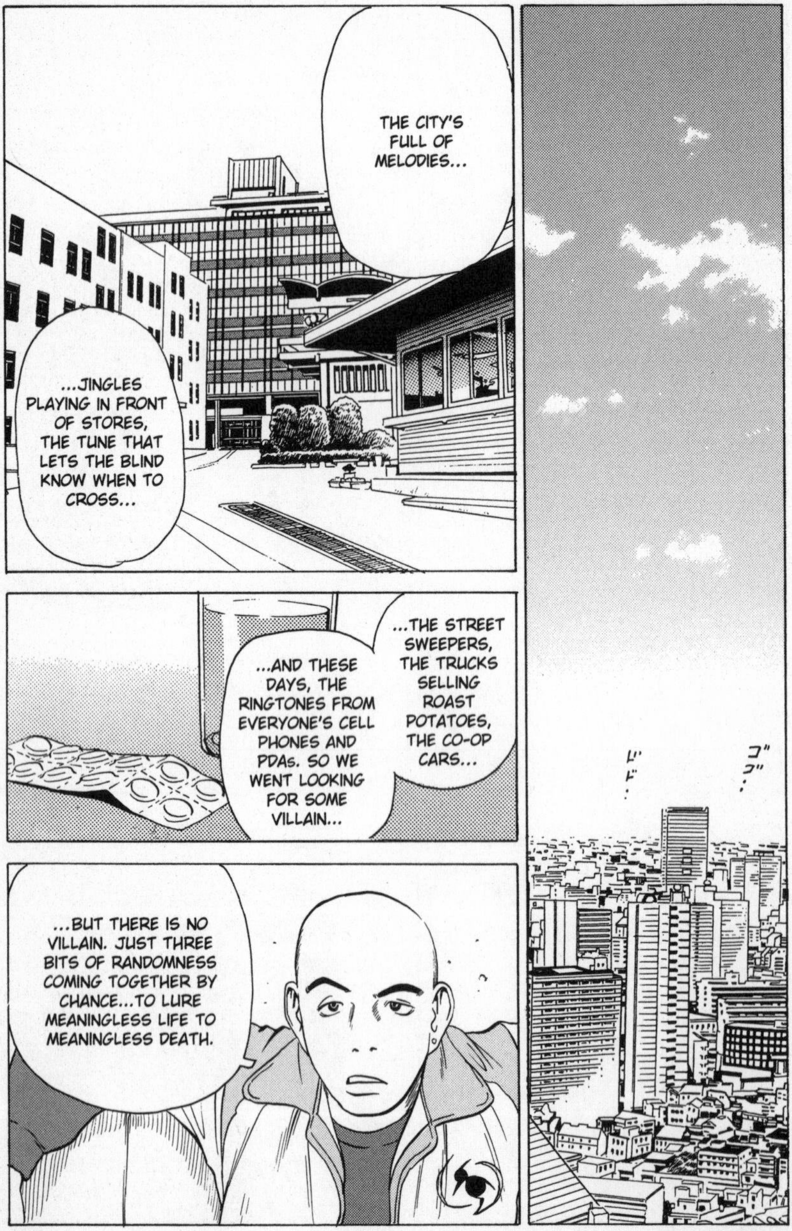
ゴゴ
ドド
THE CITY'S FULL OF MELODIES...
...JINGLES PLAYING IN FRONT OF STORES, THE TUNE THAT LETS THE BLIND KNOW WHEN TO CROSS...
...THE STREET SWEEPERS, THE TRUCKS SELLING ROAST POTATOES, THE CO-OP CARS...
...AND THESE DAYS, THE RINGTONES FROM EVERYONE'S CELL PHONES AND PDAs. SO WE WENT LOOKING FOR SOME VILLAIN...
...BUT THERE IS NO VILLAIN. JUST THREE BITS OF RANDOMNESS COMING TOGETHER BY CHANCE...TO LURE MEANINGLESS LIFE TO MEANINGLESS DEATH.

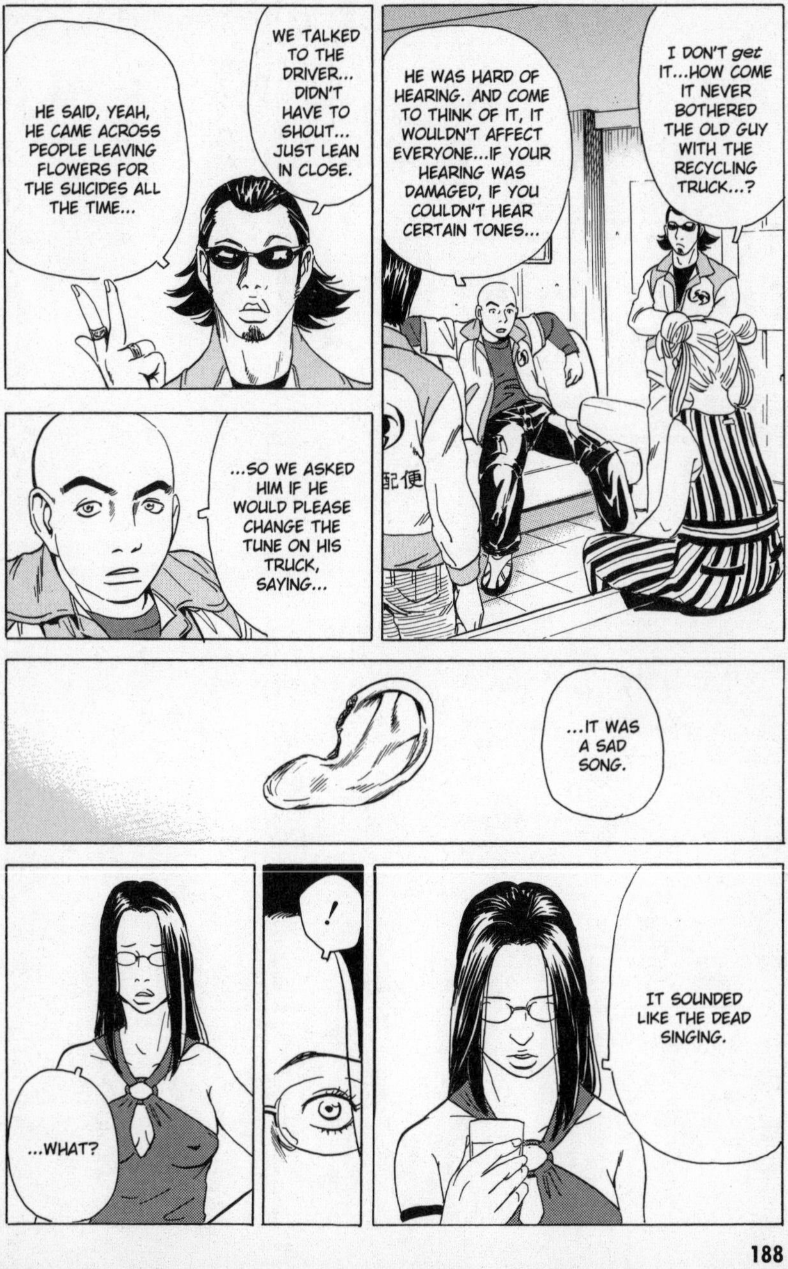
I DON'T get IT...HOW COME IT NEVER BOTHERED THE OLD GUY WITH THE RECYCLING TRUCK...?
HE WAS HARD OF HEARING. AND COME TO THINK OF IT, IT WOULDN'T AFFECT EVERYONE...IF YOUR HEARING WAS DAMAGED, IF YOU COULDN'T HEAR CERTAIN TONES...
配便
WE TALKED TO THE DRIVER... DIDN'T HAVE TO SHOUT... JUST LEAN IN CLOSE.
HE SAID, YEAH, HE CAME ACROSS PEOPLE LEAVING FLOWERS FOR THE SUICIDES ALL THE TIME...
...SO WE ASKED HIM IF HE WOULD PLEASE CHANGE THE TUNE ON HIS TRUCK, SAYING...
...IT WAS A SAD SONG.
IT SOUNDED LIKE THE DEAD SINGING.
!
...WHAT?

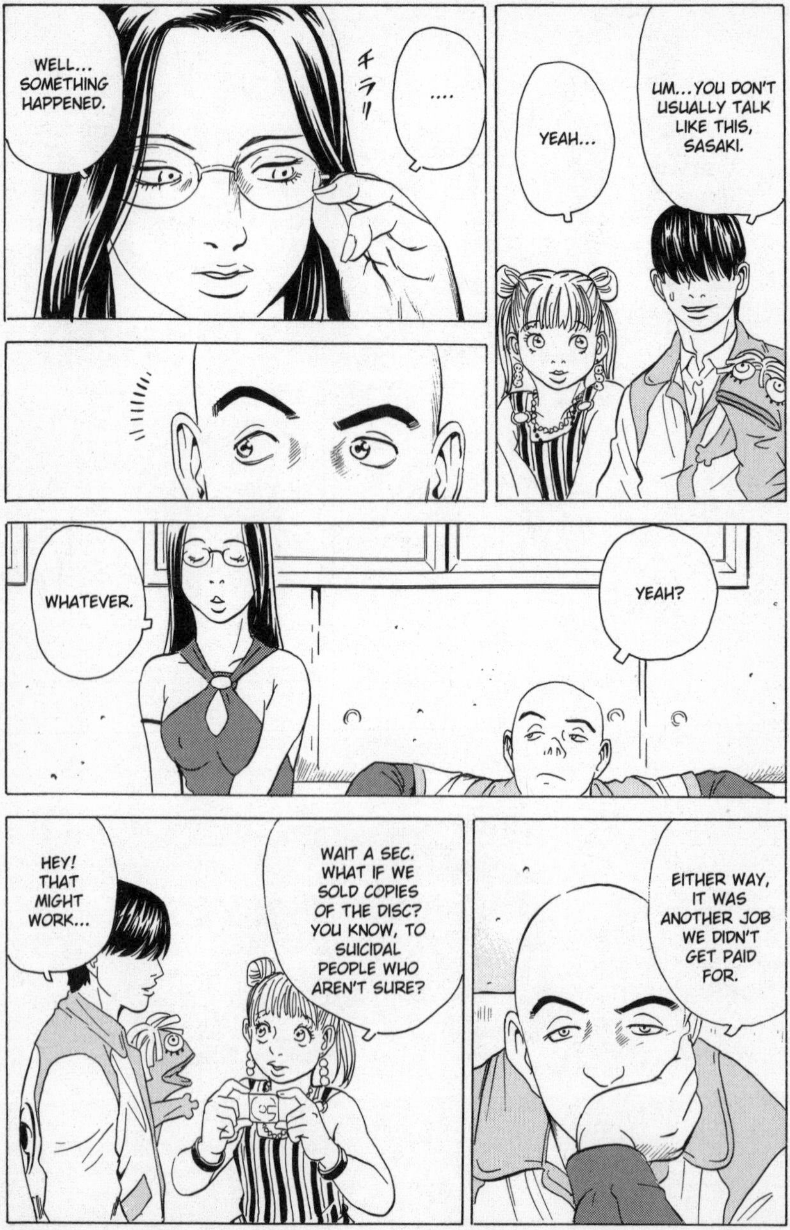
UM...YOU DON'T USUALLY TALK LIKE THIS, SASAKI.
YEAH...
....
チラリ
WELL... SOMETHING HAPPENED.
YEAH?
WHATEVER.
EITHER WAY, IT WAS ANOTHER JOB WE DIDN'T GET PAID FOR.
WAIT A SEC. WHAT IF WE SOLD COPIES OF THE DISC? YOU KNOW, TO SUICIDAL PEOPLE WHO AREN'T SURE?
HEY! THAT MIGHT WORK...

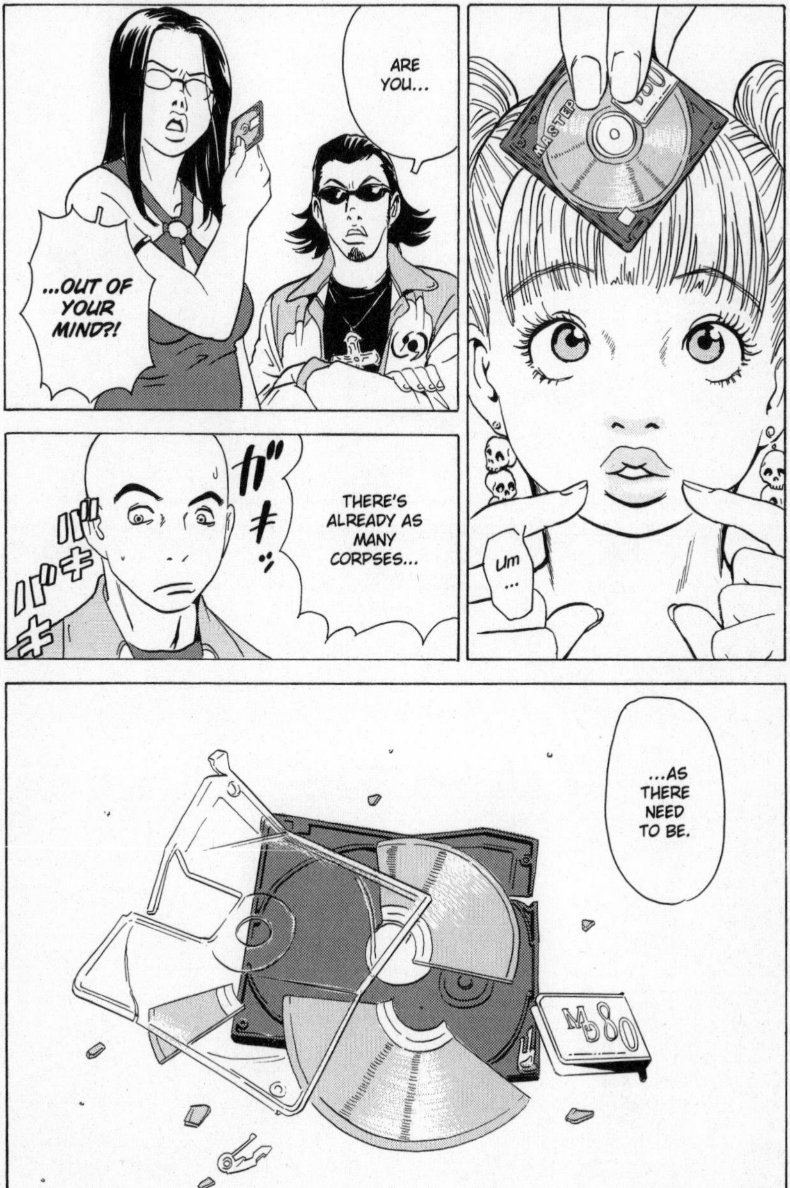

MASTER
Um ...
ARE YOU...
...OUT OF YOUR MIND?!
ガチッ
THERE'S ALREADY AS MANY CORPSES...
バキバキ
...AS THERE NEED TO BE.
MD80

4th delivery: waltz—the end

DISJECTA MEMBRA

SOUND FX GLOSSARY AND NOTES ON *KUROSAGI* VOL. 3 BY TOSHIFUMI YOSHIDA
introduction and additional comments by the editor

To increase your enjoyment of the distinctive Japanese visual style of this manga, we've included a guide to the sound effects (or "FX") used in this manga-style adaptation of the anime film. It is suggested the reader *not* constantly consult this glossary as they read through, but regard it as supplemental information, in the manner of footnotes. If you want to imagine it being read aloud by Osaka, after the manner of her lecture to Sakaki on hemorrhoids in episode five, please go right ahead. In either Yuki Matsuoka or Kira Vincent-Davis's voice—I like them both.

Japanese, like English, did not independently invent its own writing system, but instead borrowed and modified the system used by the then-dominant cultural power in their part of the world. We still call the letters we use to write English today the "Roman" alphabet, for the simple reason that about 1600 years ago the earliest English speakers, living on the frontier of the Roman Empire, began to use the same letters the Romans used to write their Latin language to write out English.

Around that very same time, on the other side of the planet, Japan, like England, was another example of an island civilization lying across the sea from a great empire, in this case, that of China. Likewise the Japanese borrowed from the Chinese writing system, which then as now consists of thousands of complex symbols—today in China officially referred to in the Roman alphabet as *hanzi*, but which the Japanese pronounce as *kanji*. For example, all the Japanese characters you see on the front cover of *The Kurosagi Corpse Delivery Service*—the seven which make up the original title and the four which make up the creators' names—are examples of kanji. Of course, all of them were hanzi first; although the Japanese did invent some original kanji of their own, just as new hanzi have been created over the centuries as Chinese evolved.

(Note that whereas both *kanji* and *hanzi* are methods of writing foreign words in Roman letters, "kanji" gives English-speakers a fairly good idea of how the Japanese word is really pronounced—*khan-gee*—whereas "hanzi" does not—in Mandarin Chinese it sounds something like *n-tsuh*). The reason is fairly simple: whereas the most commonly used method of writing Japanese in Roman letters, called the Hepburn system, was developed by a native English speaker, the most commonly used method of writing Chinese in Roman letters, called the *Pinyin* system, was developed by native Mandarin speakers. In fact Pinyin was developed to help teach Mandarin pronunciation to speakers of other Chinese dialects; unlike Hepburn, it was not intended as a learning tool for English-speakers *per se*, and hence has no particular obligation to "make sense" to English speakers or, indeed, users of other languages spelled with the Roman alphabet).

Whereas the various dialects of Chinese are written entirely in hanzi, it is practical to render the Japanese language entirely in them. To compare once more, English is a notoriously difficult language in which to spell properly, and this is in part because it uses an alphabet designed for another language, Latin, whose sounds are different. The challenges the Japanese faced in using the Chinese writing system for their own language were even greater, for whereas spoken English and Latin are at least from a common language family, spoken Japanese is unrelated to any of the various dialects of spoken Chinese. The complicated writing system Japanese evolved represents an adjustment to these differences.

When the Japanese borrowed hanzi to become kanji, what they were getting was a way to write out (remember, they already had ways to *say*) their vocabulary. Nouns, verbs, many adjectives, the names of places and people—that's what kanji are used for, the fundamental data of the written language. The practical use and processing of that "data"—its grammar and pronunciation—is another matter entirely. Because spoken Japanese neither sounds nor functions like Chinese, the first work-around tried was a system called *manyogana*, where individual kanji were picked to represent certain syllables in Japanese (a similar method is still used in Chinese today to spell out foreign names).

The commentary in *Katsuya Terada's The Monkey King* (also available from Dark Horse, and also translated by Toshifumi Yoshida) notes the importance that not only Chinese, but Indian culture had on Japan at this time in history—particularly, Buddhism. It is believed the Northeast In-

dian *Siddham* script studied by Kukai (died 835 AD), founder of the Shingon sect of Japanese Buddhism inspired him to create the solution for writing Japanese still used today. Kukai is credited with the idea of taking the manyogana and making shorthand versions of them now known simply as *kana*. The improvement in efficiency was dramatic—a kanji, used previously to represent a sound, that might have taken a dozen strokes to draw, was now reduced to three or four.

Unlike the original kanji it was based on, the new kana had *only* a sound meaning. And unlike the thousands of kanji, there are only 46 kana, which can be used to spell out any word in the Japanese language, including the many ordinarily written with kanji (Japanese keyboards work on this principle). The same set of 46 kana is written two different ways depending on their intended use: cursive style, *hiragana*, and block style, *katakana*. Naturally, sound FX in manga are almost always written out using kana.

Kana works somewhat differently than the Roman alphabet. For example, while there are separate kana for each of the five vowels (the Japanese order is not A-E-I-O-U as in English, but A-I-U-E-O), except for "n," there are no separate kana for consonants (the middle "n" in the word *ninja* illustrates this exception). Instead, kana work by grouping together consonants with vowels: for example, there are five kana for sounds starting with "k," depending on which vowel follows it—in Japanese vowel order, they go KA, KI, KU, KE, KO. The next set of kana begins with "s" sounds, so SA, SHI, SU, SE, SO, and so on. You will observe this kind of

consonant-vowel pattern in the FX listings for *Kurosagi* Vol. 3 below.

Katakana is almost always the kind that gets used for manga sound FX, but on occasion (often when the sound is one associated with a person's body) hiragana are used instead. In *Kurosagi* Vol. 3 you can see one of several examples on page 41, panel 3, when the liver is extracted with a "ZUBO" sound, which in hiragana style is written ずぼっ. Note its more cursive appearance compared to the other FX. If it had been written in katakana style, it would look like ズボッ.

To see how to use this glossary, take an example from page 7: "7.4 FX/balloon: PIKU – twitch." 7.4 means the FX is the one on page 7, in panel 4 (the "balloon" note, of course, means the FX is inside a balloon, although just as many FX in *Kurosagi* are free on the page). PIKU is the sound these kana—ピクツ—literally stand for. After the dash comes an explanation of what the sound represents (in some cases, such as this one, it will be less obvious than others). Note that in cases where there are two or more different sounds in a single panel, an extra number is used to differentiate them from right to left; or, in cases where right and left are less clear, in clockwise order.

The use of kana in these FX also illustrates another aspect of written Japanese—its flexible reading order. For example, the way you're reading the pages and panels of this book in general: going from right-to-left, and from top to bottom—is the order in which Japanese is also written in most forms of print: books, magazines, and newspapers. However, if you examine those kana examples given above, you'll notice something interesting. They read "Western" style—left-

to-right! In fact, many of the FX in *Kurosagi* (and manga in general) read left-to-right. This kind of flexibility is also to be found on Japanese web pages, which usually also read left-to-right. In other words, Japanese doesn't simply read "the other way" from English; the Japanese themselves are used to reading it in several different directions.

As might be expected, some FX "sound" short, and others "sound" long. Manga represent this in different ways. One of many examples of "short sounds" in *Kurosagi* Vol. 3 is to be found in the example from 41.3 given above: ZUBO. Note the small つ mark it has at the end. This ordinarily represents the sound "tsu" (the katakana form, more commonly seen in manga FX, is ツ) but its half-size use at the end of FX like this means the sound is the kind which stops or cuts off suddenly; that's why the sound is written as ZUBO and not ZUBOTSU—you don't "pronounce" the TSU in such cases.

Note the small "tsu" has another occasional use *inside*, rather than at the end, of a particular FX, as seen in 65.6's TATTATATA—the sound of Yata running up—here it's at work between two "TA" タ sounds to indicate a doubling of the consonant sound that follows it.

There are three different ways you may see "long sounds"—where a vowel sound is extended—written out as FX. One is with an ellipsis, as in 52.5's PARA. Another is with an extended line, as in 15.3's SHAAA. Still another is by simply repeating a vowel several times, as in 61.1's IIIIIN. You will note that 52.5 has *both* the "tsu" and an ellipsis at its end, even though they would seem to be working at cross purposes; the methods may be combined within a single

FX. As a visual element in manga, FX are an art rather than a science, and are used in a less rigorous fashion than kana are in standard written Japanese.

The explanation of what the sound represents may sometimes be surprising; but every culture "hears" sounds differently. Note that manga FX do not even necessarily represent literal sounds; for example 78.1.2 FX: SHIIIN—in manga this is the figurative "sound" of silence. 28.4 FX: GI-RORIN, representing a glare, is another one of this type. Such "mimetic" words, which represent an imagined sound, or even a state of mind, are called *gitaigo* in Japanese. Like the onomatopoeic *giseigo* (the words used to represent literal sounds—i.e., most FX in this glossary are classed as giseigo), they are also used in colloquial speech and writing. A Japanese, for example, might say that something bounced by saying PURIN, or talk about eating by saying MUGU MUGU. It's something like describing chatter in English by saying "yadda yadda yadda" instead.

One important last note: all these spelled-out kana vowels should be pronounced as they are in Japanese: "A" as *ah*, "I" as *eee*, "U" as *ooh*, "E" as *eh*, and "O" as *oh*.

2.1 As has been Eiji Otsuka's style throughout *Kurosagi*, all of these titles are again song names. For this volume, the songs are that of Naomi Chiaki. The title of the first story refers to the river ferry that connects Shibamata in Katsushika-ku, Tokyo, with Shimoyagiri, across the Edogawa River (that marks the eastern border of Tokyo proper) in Matsudo, Chiba. The ferry started long ago in the early Edo Period (that is, in the seventeenth century)

and today remains the only such service where the boat is still rowed manually by the guides. The original title is *Yagiri no watashi*, "Crossing the Yagiri" or "River Crossing"—note this is not the *watashi* meaning "I" in Japanese, but a homophone spelled with a different kanji. The title of the second story literally means "Applause" but it's also the Japanese title of the US movie *Country Girl* (1954) starring Bing Crosby and Grace Kelly. It's *probably* not pertinent, but an interesting bit of trivia nevertheless. ^_^

7.4 **FX/balloon:** PIKU—twitch

8.2.1 **FX/balloon:** ZU—sound of dragging feet

8.2.2 **FX/balloon:** PETA—sound of feet slapping on floor

8.2.3 **FX/balloon:** ZU—sound of dragging feet

12.2 Japanese anti-Iraq War protest signs in real life often *are* in English as you see here, perhaps for the benefit of the international media (although just as the English expression "Oh my God!" is sometimes portrayed in manga with the stress placed oddly—"Oh! MY God"—you will also often see signs that read "No!! War"). The editor saw a few more stylish protests in Japan back in 2003 (this story appeared in July of that year), with skaters in hoodies chalking their slogans on their decks. But all in all, Karatsu has a point on page 13 about the size of the protests—very different from the radical Japanese marches of the 1960s and early '70s that

director Mamoru Oshii describes in the semi-autobiographical portions of the novel *Blood: Night of the Beasts*, available, naturally, from Dark Horse.

14.4 **FX:** HYUN—sound of the pendulum swinging.

15.3 **FX:** SHAAA—hissing sound (like a cat)

15.4.1 **FX/balloon:** KOHO—cough

15.4.2 **FX/balloons:** GOHO GEHO—cough getting worse

15.5 **FX/balloon:** BUHA—coughing up blood

15.6.1 **FX/balloon:** GEHO GOHO—coughing

17.3 Sasaki uses, as is common in Japan, the English word for "homeless," which is pronounced as *hoomuresu*. Of course, there have been homeless people in Japan for decades (millions of people had at least some experience with it due to WWII), but the editor was shocked in the late 1990s to see tent encampments *inside* the Tokyo subway stations—not only because it seemed such a change from 1980s' confidence and prosperity (during which time there were, of course, also homeless people in Japan), but in that the municipal authorities would allow people to set up shelters there, which would seem unlikely in America.

18.1.1 **FX/balloon:** GAKON—sound of door being pushed open

18.1.2 **FX:** KYU KYU—sound of a squeaky wheel

19.5 I love how Kereellis has the same smile as Yata, Numata, and Karatsu.

19.7 Note the traditional offering to the dead of a bowl or rice, with chopsticks straight up. Foreigners are often warned not to put their chopsticks straight up in a bowl of rice when eating with Japanese (that's what the chopstick rest is for).

20.6 **FX:** GAKU—pratfall/depressed sound

23.3 **FX/balloon:** GACHA—door opening

25.4 **FX/balloon:** JAN JYAKA JIJI JYAAN—ringtone

28.4 **FX:** GIRORIN—glare

29.1 **FX/balloon:** KIN—sound of metal end of cane ringing on floor

29.2.1 **FX:** KA KO—footsteps

29.2.2 **FX/balloon:** KIN—sound of metal end of cane ringing on floor

29.3 **FX/balloon:** SU—reaching into jacket

30.1 **FX:** BA—quickly extending arm

31.6 Tokyo, which is usually thought of as a city, is legally a prefecture unto itself, and is divided into twenty-three wards with a high degree of self-government. Probably the best known of Tokyo's wards outside of Japan (and the editor's favorite) is Shinjuku; the Beastie Boys shot their video for "Intergalactic" in Shinjuku Station, the world's busiest commuter train junction (Michael Gombos is somewhat amazed that they were granted permission to do this, though the effect is classic, as Mike D., MCA, and Adrock dance and throw B-boy gestures into the camera as hordes of confused salarymen walk around them). Although "wards" is the official translation of the Japanese original

ku, many of the wards themselves use "city" to refer to themselves in English, and, with individual populations reaching into the hundreds of thousands (Shinjuku alone has 300,000 permanent residents, to say nothing of temporary commuters and shoppers) they indeed qualify.

32.5 **FX/balloon:** GIRO—glare

33.4 Their "Kurosagi Delivery Service" card (like the sign on their van, they leave the "Corpse" out of it) has the slogan "Any reason, any purpose—moving, fleeing by night, we'll deliver it, no questions asked." The telephone number and e-mail are, regrettably, obscured.

34.1 **FX:** PUAAN GOGOGO DODO-DO—car and construction sounds

35.3 **FX/balloon:** PATAN—door closing

35.6 **FX/balloon:** KI—angry reaction sound

36.5 **FX/balloon:** DOSA—thud

37.2 **FX:** SHIBO—lighter igniting

37.6 **FX/balloon:** KIN—sound of metal tip of cane hitting ground

38.1.1 **FX/balloon:** KIN—sound of metal tip of cane hitting ground

38.1.2 **FX:** KO KO KO—footsteps

38.1.3 **FX/balloon:** KI—sound of metal tip of cane hitting ground.

40.2 **FX/balloon:** BU—scalpel cutting into skin

40.3 **FX/balloon:** GU GU—tugging sound

40.4 **FX:** BOTO—plop

41.1 **FX/balloon:** SUUU—sound of skin being sliced

41.2 **FX:** GAPA—sound of chest being opened

41.3 **FX:** ZUBO—sound of an organ being pulled out

41.5 **FX/balloon:** SUUU—sound of skin being sliced

41.6 **FX/balloon:** ZUBU GUCHU—fingers digging into body followed by a wet digging sound

42.1 **FX:** ZURURI—sound of a kidney being pulled out

48.5 **FX:** KUN KUN—sound of pendulum swinging

49.4 **FX:** ZURU—sound of a plastic bag being slid out

52.4 **FX:** PASA—dropping newspaper

52.5 **FX:** PARA—flipping newspaper page. Note that Tama-chan is the name of a baby seal that first turned up in Tamagawa River in the summer of 2002. The seal continued to appear in various rivers in the Tokyo area for two years, spawned a fandom of its own and had a swarm of media coverage. There were several songs written about it, and some "Tama-chan" character goods even appeared on the market.

52.6 **FX:** PESHI—putting hand on jar

57.3 **FX/balloon:** KACHA—keyboard sound

57.4 **FX:** CHIRA—glancing down at jar

58.5 **FX/balloon:** PIIPAAPIPU PEPU-PUPIPAA PIPAAPIIPEPO—ringtone

59.3 **FX:** GOGOGOGO—sound of the car rumbling

59.4 **FX:** GWOOOO—sound of the car being driven

60.5 **FX:** HIIII—sound of a transport plane flying away

60.6 **FX:** IIII—sound of jet engines

61.1 **FX:** IIIIIN—more sound of jets

62.1 Many Americans have voiced concerns about our building bases in Iraq, wondering just how longterm our military presence there will prove to be—but a good *sixty years* after the end of WWII, the U.S. still has literally dozens of bases in Japan, containing 47,000 soldiers, sailors, and airmen. The HQ of all military forces in Japan is located at Yokota Air Base, the site of this scene in the story. It's located in the suburb of Fussa in Saitama Prefecture, about 19 miles west of downtown Tokyo. The controversial presence of the U.S. bases has itself made them the focus of occasional demonstrations, and a ready locale for intrigue and conspiracy stories; perhaps most notably in anime, the film *Blood: The Last Vampire* was set at Yokota.

62.4 **FX:** TA TA TA—jogging sound

63.1 The USAF in fact does adminster the largest mortuary in the American armed forces, but it is located at Dover Air Base in Delaware, under the 436th Services Squadron. Mortuary affairs at Yokota are handled under the auspices of the Honor Guard of the 374th Airlift Wing Services Division.

FX: HYUN HYUN HYUN—pendulum swinging wildly

65.6 **FX:** TATTATATA—Yata running up

65.6.1 This isn't a change—he said *Sesame Street* in the original. A dubbed version of the U.S. show was aired on NHK in Japan for many years, but shortly after this story appeared, a new locally made version (many countries have created such versions to better reflect their own cultures) began showing on TV Tokyo, the network that aired *Neon Genesis Evangelion*!

66.4 Although interrupted by the recent detoriation of relations with North Korea, in the late 1990s and early years of this decade, there was an ongoing effort where the North Korean government cooperated in U.S. efforts to locate the remains of servicemen killed in the Korean War (over 8,000 American soldiers became missing in action in Korea, far more than in Vietnam). From this effort, nearly 200 bodies were found and returned to the United States, passing through Yokota on their way home. This recent example of Yokota being used to handle U.S. war dead possibly inspired Eiji Otsuka to portray it happening today with the Iraq War. It is also true that the mortuary at Yokota was a transshipment point for many of the American casualties during the Vietnam War; an Army surgeon stationed there in the 1960s, Ronald Glasser, gives an account of the period in his acclaimed book *365 Days*. The use of Yokota for dead servicemen from the Iraq War appears to be a literary conceit (or perhaps, an echo of past history) on Otsuka's part; in reality

such casualties are often sent first to Sather Air Base at Baghdad International Airport, then to Kuwait, and onward to Dover Air Base, where the actual embalming takes place.

67.3-4 The notion of bodies that are so badly damaged that their dog tags provide the only identification is again something of a throwback to the Vietnam era, as today DNA samples are taken of all military recruits, permitting eventual identification of remains no matter their condition. However, it is true, for example, that looking for ID tags remains part of the mortuary procedure at Sather Air Base in an attempt to establish a tentative identification; final, positive identification is again the responsibility of the 436th Services Squadron at Dover Air Base.

68.1 **FX/balloon:** JIIII—zipper sound

68.4 The idea of placing dead bodies in a pool is probably a reference to the Japanese urban legend (mentioned also in Dark Horse's *Reiko the Zombie Shop* Vol. 2) that some hospitals have a morgue where the bodies are stored in a pool filled with formaldehyde, where attendants stand around with long sticks to keep poking them under again as they bob up.

69.6 **FX:** JAPPO JAPPO—sound of rubber boots sloshing in the pool

71.5.1 **FX:** BIKUN BIKUN BIKUN—corpse twitching

71.5.2 **FX/balloon:** PACHA PISHA—splashing sounds

72.1.1 **FX/white:** BASHA BASHA BASHA BASHA BASHA—loud splashes

72.1.2 **FX/black:** PACHA PACHA—smaller splashes

72.2 **FX:** BATAN DOTAN BATA—Corpses in body bags moving around

72.3 **FX:** GU GUI—face trying to push out of the bag

74.1 **FX:** BURU BURU BURU BURU—hand shaking/waving

75.1 **FX:** PETAN—sound of hand slapping the tile floor as it moves along

75.2 **FX:** ZU ZU—dragging sound

75.3 **FX:** BETA—sound of flesh slapping against tile floor.

78.1.1 **FX:** DO—thud

78.1.2 **FX/white:** SHIIIN—sound of silence

81.1 **FX:** DOSA—slumping into sofa

81.6 **FX/balloon:** KA—metal end of cane hitting floor

82.3 **FX:** KAN KAN—tapping metal lid of jar with tip of cane

83.2 **FX/balloon:** SU—reaching into jacket

83.3 In 2004, Japan deployed a force of 550 Self-Defense Force soldiers to aid in reconstruction efforts in Iraq—strictly non-combatants, they were themselves guarded by Australian and Dutch members of the "coalition of the willing." While the SDF troops remained unharmed, a number of civilian Japanese did in fact face danger in Iraq, many as NGO (Non-Governmental Organization) volunteers. Seven were kidnapped and two killed—one, in a notorious incident in October 2004, beheaded by masked terrorists upon an American flag, his corpse

then wrapped in it for people to find. Such gruesome and symbolically charged incidents in real life make the editor reflect upon how much of *Kurosagi* might be called shock value, and how much just stylized truth.

84.2 **FX:** YORO—stagger

84.4 **FX:** GATA GOTON GATAN GATA—sound of Hummer bouncing on the road

85.1 **FX:** GATAKON GOTON—Hummer riding on uneven ground

85.4 **FX:** BATA BATA BATA—sound of his monk robes billowing in the wind

86.1 **FX:** BATA BATA BATA—sound of his monk robes billowing in the wind

89.1 **FX:** MIIIN MIIIN MIIIN—sound of cicadas

89.2 **FX/balloon:** PINPOON PINPOON PINPOON—sound of doorbell

89.3 **FX:** GACHA—sound of door latch

90.1.1 **FX:** DOKA DOKO—sound of club striking bone

90.1.2 **FX/balloon:** BICHA—blood spatter

90.3 **FX:** ZU ZU—hand sliding down wall

90.6 **FX:** CHIKI CHIKI CHIKI—retracting baton

91.1 **FX/balloon:** KIIIIII—door creaking closed

91.2 **FX/balloon:** IIII—continuing to close

91.3 **FX/balloon:** PATAN—door shutting

92.1 Is the winged pen nib with the "H" Housui Yamazaki's personal tag?

94.1 **FX:** MEEN MEEN MEEN—sound of cicadas

94.3 **FX:** GASHA—dropping heavy basket

95.1 **FX:** PINPOON—doorbell. *Yomiyomi* is a satire on the name of the Japanese newspaper *Yomiuri Shimbun*, which has claimed to have a circulation of as much as 14 million daily.

95.3 **FX:** GACHA—door opening

95.4 **FX:** ZORO ZORO—women pouring out of room

96.2 She actually says it this way in the original: *sankyuu booi*—how a Japanese would pronounce the English phrase; most Japanese know enough English to understand it.

96.3 **FX/balloon:** PATAN—door closing

96.4 **FX:** KARA—rattle of empty basket falling over

98.3 Japan uses a twenty-four-hour clock, so whereas Americans would say "4 P.M.," they'd say "16." As is the case here, the fact that the number refers to a time of day is made clear by context, or by the use of an English lower-case "h" (as in "16h") or the kanji 時, *ji* (as in 16時).

99.4 **FX:** CHARAN—dangling pendulum

99.5 **FX:** HYUN HYUN HYUN—pendulum swinging

99.7 **FX/balloon:** GACHA—opening door

104.4 **FX:** DOSA—thud

108.1 **FX:** KATA KATA KATA—keyboard sound

108.2 **FX:** PA—picture coming up

108.3 **FX:** PA—another picture coming up

108.5 **FX:** CHI CHI—giving a tut-tut expression

109.5 **FX/button:** KAKON—pressing key

109.6 **FX:** PA PA PA—multiple images popping up

111.2 **FX:** SHU—spray paint sound

111.3.1 FX/balloon: SHUUU—spraying sound

111.3.2 FX/balloon: SHUUU—spraying sound

113.1 **FX:** JI JI—streetlight buzzing

113.3 **FX:** CHUN CHUN—chirping birds. Note Yata's *Star Wars* gear. You may or may not be aware that Dark Horse has published dozens of original comics set in the *Star Wars* galaxy since 1991—almost, but not quite as long as we've been publishing manga. In fact, Dark Horse has even published *Star Wars* manga—translations of the licensed adaptations of *A New Hope* (by Hisao Tamaki), *The Empire Strikes Back* (by Toshiki Kudo), *Return of the Jedi* (by Shin-ichi Hiromoto), and *The Phantom Menace* (by Kia Asamiya).

113.4 **FX:** KURURI—Puppet turning around

113.6 **FX/balloon:** KARARA—sliding window open

115.2 **FX:** KOTSU—footstep

115.4 **FX:** TA TA TA TA—running sound

115.5.1 FX/balloons: SHU SHUUU—spraying sound

115.5.2 FX/balloon: SHU—spraying sound

115.7 **FX/balloon:** KII—sound of brakes

116.1 **FX/balloon:** WIIIN—power window rolling down

116.2.1 FX/balloon: GACHA—car door opening

116.2.2 FX: KYORO KYORO—looking around

116.3.1 FX/balloon: SHU—spraying sound

116.3.2 FX/balloons: SHU SHUUU—spraying sound

117.1 **FX:** GOTOTON GOTOTON—train moving on tracks

117.3 **FX:** KAPA—opening mobile phone

117.4 **FX/balloon:** KASHA—click

118.2 Although he shouldn't worry too much, because, remember, Steven Seagal is also *Hard to Kill* (and also a Buddhist, for that matter). As you may know, Seagal has two children by his first Japanese wife, model Kentaro Seagal and actress Ayako Fujitani, whom *Evangelion*'s Hideaki Anno directed in his second live-action film, *Shiki-Jitsu*.

118.4 **FX:** BIIIIIN—sound of a moped

118.5.1 FX/balloon: KII—brake sound

118.5.2 FX/balloon: GASHA—putting kick-stand down

118.6 **FX/balloon:** TA TA TA—running sound

120.5 **FX:** PASA—flipping open piece of paper

121.4 **FX:** SHU SHU—quick scribbling

122.2 *Oni* is also sometimes translated as "ogre," but, depending on how the reference is used, the connotations of "devil" can seem more appropri-

ate in English. Sometimes, one might use both at once, as in *Urusei Yatsura*, where Lum is devilish, but her dad is definitely an ogre.

123.1 FX: GACHA—door opening

123.6 FX: CHIRA—peering to the side

124.4 FX/balloons: KON KON KON—knocking

124.6 FX: KACHA—doorknob being turned

124.7 FX: JAKON—telescoping club being extended

124.8 FX: GA—grabbing door

125.1.1 FX: DOKA—impact sound

125.1.2 FX/small: PISHI—floor cracking

126.1 FX: BUN BUN—swinging truncheon

126.2 FX/balloon: SHAKON—toy lightsaber being extended

126.3 FX/balloon: BAKEEN—breaking sound

126.4 Just to note that "Star Peace" wasn't a change by Dark Horse, but a gag in the original.

127.1 FX: BA—jumping into room

128.3 FX: DO DO DO—running sound

128.4 FX: BASHAN—breaking glass

129.2 FX: HYOKO HYOKO—hobbled walking sound

129.4 FX: ZA—coming to a stop

129.5 FX: SU—drawing out cleaver

130.1 FX: KURU—twisting over

130.3 FX: DOKO—impact sound

132.1.1 FX: PYUU—spurting blood

132.1.2 FX/balloon: DOSUN—thudding onto ground

132.3.1 FX/balloon: DO—sound of body hitting ground

132.3.2 FX: PEE POO PEE POO PEE POO PEE POO—sirens

133.6 FX: KATA—turning laptop around

137.3.1 FX/balloon: SHUUU—spraying sound

137.3.2 FX/balloon: SHU SHUUU—spraying sound

138.2 The body has been left in a *koban*, a kiosk typical of the neighborhood police in Japan—hence the sign saying they're out on patrol. Perhaps oddly, you can often find anime- and manga-themed public service announcement posters inside such koban (for example, in the summer of 1996, there was a *Neon Genesis Evangelion* one printed urging people not to waste water—was the idea to use LCL instead?). Hiroyuki Yamaga, co-producer of *Evangelion*, said he never met a cop who wasn't an otaku.

142.1 FX: PINPORO PANPIN PIN-POIN—train attention tones

142.2 FX: TANNNN TAAA TATATAAAA TAN TAAA—car horns

142.3 FX: PIIPAPA PIPAPA PPPPOOPAA PIIPIPAPA PIIHA —crossing signal

142.4.1 FX: JAN JACHAAN CHARARAAN JAJAN —phone chatter

142.4.2 FX: PI —phone beep

142.6.1 FX: PINPORO PANPIN PINPORO-PIN—train attention tones

142.6.2 FX: PANPIRO PINPON PIN—train attention tones

142.7 **FX:** PANPIRO—train attention tones

143.2 **FX:** DOGO—impact sound

143.3 **FX:** BAKI GUSHA—breaking and crushing sounds

143.4.1 FX/top: BABA—train speeding by

143.4.2 FX/bottom: BAKI—breaking bone sound

144.2 **FX:** KUN KUN—pendulum swinging

145.1 **FX:** PAKU PAKU—puppet's mouth flapping

146.1 The magazine title, *Young A* (for "Ace") *Weekly*, is a play on two magazines: Kodansha's *Weekly Young* (the original home of *Akira*, and in more recent years hits like *Chobits* and *Initial D*), which actually is famous for its nubile swimsuit covers, and Kadokawa's *Shonen Ace* (in real life a monthly), the current home of *The Kurosagi Corpse Delivery Service* as well as several other manga published in English (including Dark Horse's forthcoming *MPD Psycho*, as well as such titles as *Neon Genesis Evangelion*, *Eureka Seven*, and *Sgt. Frog*). The cover parodies several actual *Shonen Ace* titles, claiming to contain manga such as *Neon Genesis Vangelis* and *Multiple Personality Salaryman*. Note the cameo by Akiba from Housui Yamazaki's other manga *Mail*—Akiba will be making an actual cameo in the next volume of *Kurosagi*.

147.2 **FX/balloon:** POTO—something falling out from between the pages

151.4 **FX:** KASHA—MD recorder being opened

151.5 **FX:** KACHI—hitting record switch

151.6 The Sony MiniDisc, introduced in 1991, was the thing you were supposed to buy to replace your Sony Walkman, but it never really caught on in North America. Unlike portable CD players, MiniDisc players can record as well as play, and provide good audio editing functions. The editor notes that the translator of *Kurosagi*, Toshi Yoshida, was also the producer of the English-dubbed versions of *Inu-Yasha*, *Ranma 1/2*, *Maison Ikkoku*, and *Jin-Roh* among many others, and made extensive use of the MiniDisc in his work.

153.3 **FX/balloon:** DON—elbow hitting chest. Note that rather than "earring," Karatsu originally said "an ear of bread," which is how Japanese often refer to a piece of bread crust.

154.1.1 FX/black: KATSUN—footstep

154.1.2 FX/white: KIN—metal tip of cane hitting ground

155.1 **FX:** PURAN—dangling sound

158.2 **FX/Numata:** FU FU FU FU-FUU—humming along to music

160.6 **FX/balloon:** JYAKA JYAKA JYARA-RAN CHARARARAAN—ringtone

161.4 **FX:** KAAN KAAN KAAN—bells ringing as a train approaches

161.5 **FX/balloon:** WIII—crossbar coming down

161.8 **FX:** KAAN KAAN KAAN—bells ringing as a train approaches

162.2 **FX/balloon:** KUN—pressing on accelerator

163.2 **FX/balloon:** GA—grabbing wheel

163.3 **FX/balloon:** GII—pulling on emergency brakes

163.4 **FX:** KI KI KI—brakes squealing

163.6 **FX/balloon:** GO—mirror touching crossbar

163.7 **FX/balloon:** DON—wheels landing on ground

164.1 **FX:** GAGAAAAA—train speeding by

166.3 A charming aspect of Japan is the use of individual melodies, like theme songs, that are played over the loudspeaker to mark arrivals at train and subway stations. Andy Raskin did a story about them that aired on National Public Radio in September of 2003, and you can find an archive of them at the site http://melody.pos.to/.

167.3 **FX/balloon:** PA PA—screen coming up. Note that the screen lists stations on the Chuo line in Tokyo, whose reputation as a method of suicide is in fact quite real (as is the practice of billing the deceased's family). Many Tokyo subway stations have installed transparent anti-suicide walls along the track edges (the trains stop so that their own doors are lined up with doors in the wall, which only then open), but of course this does nothing to prevent suicides at ground-level crossings, such as you see in this story.

171.1 **FX:** PAN PAN—hitting dirt off of hands

175.1 **FX:** PON—taking out earplug

175.3 **FX:** KAAN KAAN KAAN KAAN KAAN KAAN KAAN—sound of the warning bell for an approaching train

175.5 **FX:** BA—covering ears

178-179.1 FX/balloon: KAAN—warning bell amongst other musical notes

178-179.2 FX/balloon: KAAN KAAN—warning bells amongst other musical notes

178-179.5 FX: TON TOTON—earplug bouncing on the ground

180.1 **FX:** FURARI—a staggering walk sound

180.4 **FX:** KAAN KAAN KAAN—warning bell

184-185.1 FX: GOKAAAAAAA—train speeding by on both sides

186.1 **FX:** GWOOOO—sound of speeding train

186.2 **FX:** BA—sound of last train passing by

186.3 **FX:** GOTOTO GOTOTON GOTOTON—sound of train moving on tracks on both sides

186.4 **FX/balloon:** HETA—sound of Sasaki crumpling to her knees

187.1 **FX:** GOGO DODO—construction noise in the distance

187.3 Such cooperatively run vehicles range from ones shared by farmers to market produce to city dwellers, to colleges providing a shuttle service between dorms and train stations.

189.2 **FX:** CHIRA—peering at Kuro

190.3 **FX:** GAKI BAKI BAKI— stomping and breaking sounds

STAFF D

Embalming
［エンバーミング］：死体修復

STAFF E

Channeling
［チャネリング］：宇宙人と交信

STAFF E'

Puppet
［マペット］：宇宙人が憑依

お届け物は死体です。

the KUROSAGI corpse delivery service

黒鷺死体宅配便

eiji otsuka 大塚英志 housui yamazaki 山崎峰水

publisher **MIKE RICHARDSON**
editor **CARL GUSTAV HORN**
editorial assistant **RACHEL MILLER**
omnibus edition designer **BRENNAN THOME**
original series designer **HEIDI FAINZA**
digital art technician **CHRISTINA McKENZIE**

English-language version
produced by Dark Horse Comics

Published by
Dark Horse Manga
A division of Dark Horse Comics, Inc.
10956 SE Main Street
Milwaukie, OR 97222
DarkHorse.com

To find a comics shop in your area,
call the Comic Shop Locator Service
toll-free at 1-888-266-4226

First edition: August 2015
ISBN 978-1-61655-754-6

1 3 5 7 9 10 8 6 4 2

Printed in the United States of America

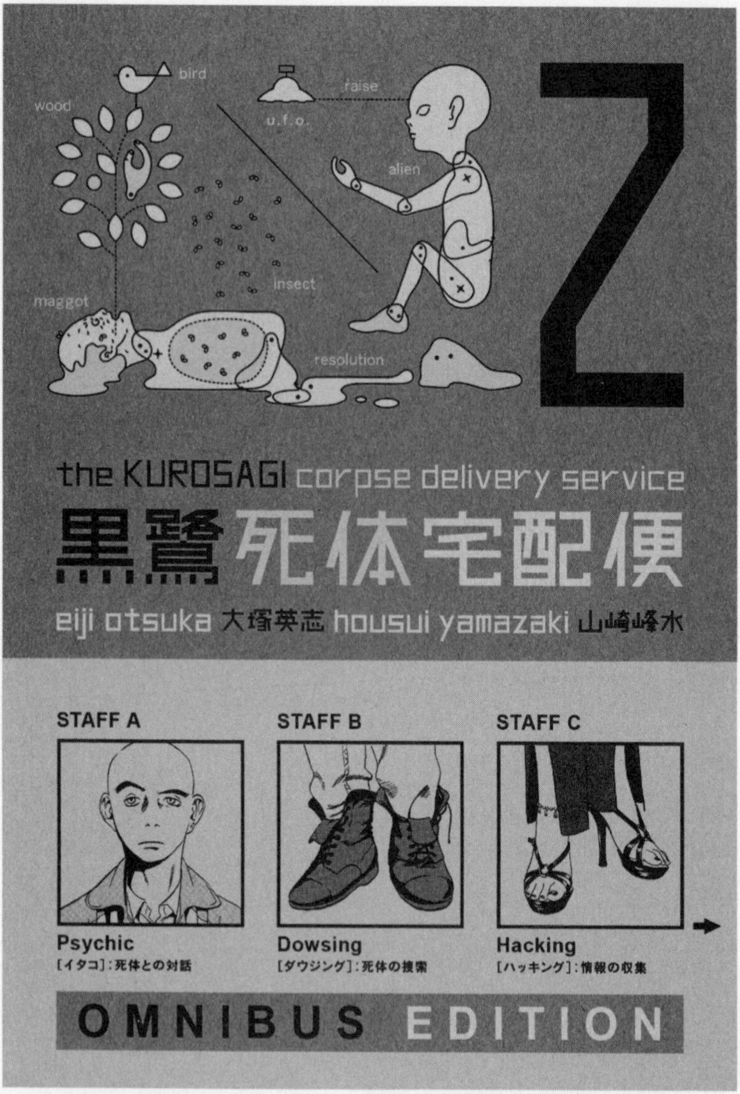
bird
wood
raise
u.f.o.
alien
insect
maggot
resolution
2
the KUROSAGI corpse delivery service
黒鷺死体宅配便
eiji otsuka 大塚英志 housui yamazaki 山崎峰水
STAFF A
STAFF B
STAFF C
Psychic
[イタコ]：死体との対話
Dowsing
[ダウジング]：死体の捜索
Hacking
[ハッキング]：情報の収集
OMNIBUS EDITION

DEAD UFO PILOTS . . . MODERN MUMMIES . . .

or just the everyday body rotting away in your attic! Book Two contains eleven more stories of strange happenings for the Kurosagi Corpse Delivery Service . . . as we begin to learn the ancestral secrets of Karatsu's familiar spirit, Yaichi!

M P D - P S Y C H O

多　重　人　格　探　偵

田島昭宇 ✕ 大塚英志
SHO-U TAJIMA   EIJI OTSUKA

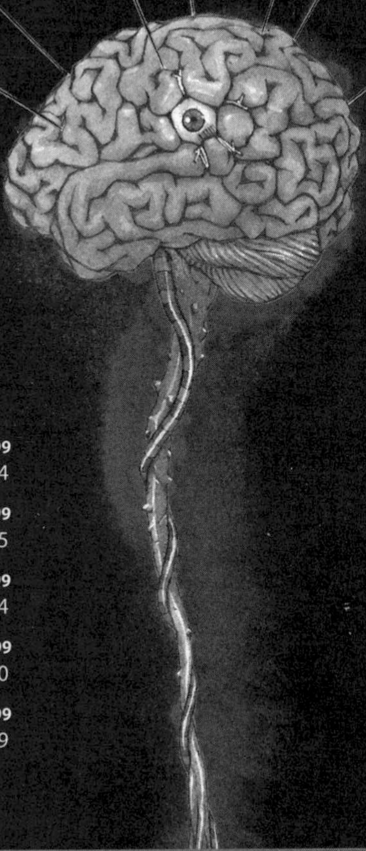

Police detective Yosuke Kobayashi's life is changed forever after a serial killer notices something "special" about him. That same killer mutilates Kobayashi's girlfriend and kick-starts a "multiple personality battle" within Kobayashi that pushes him into a complex tempest of interconnected deviants and evil forces.

Originally licensed by another U.S. publisher, *MPD-Psycho* was deemed too shocking for them to release, but Dark Horse is always prepared to give manga readers what they want and is proud to present *MPD-Psycho* uncensored, in all of its controversial and unflinchingly grotesque glory!

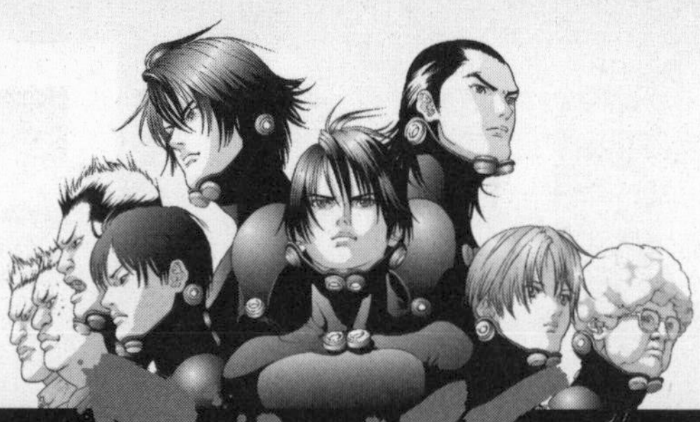

GANTZ

HIROYA OKU Works.

The last thing Kei and Masaru remember was being struck dead by a subway train while saving the life of a drunken bum. What a waste! And yet somehow they're still alive. Or semi-alive? Maybe reanimated . . . by some kind of mysterious orb! And this orb called "Gantz" intends to make them play games of death, hunting all kinds of odd aliens, along with a bunch of other ordinary citizens who've recently met a tragic semi-end. The missions they embark upon are often dangerous. Many die—and die again. This dark and action-packed manga deals with the moral conflicts of violence, teenage sexual confusion and angst, and our fascination with death.

Dark Horse is proud to deliver one of the most requested manga ever to be released. Hang on to your gear and keep playing the game, whatever you do; *Gantz* is unrelenting!

VOLUME ONE
ISBN 978-1-59307-949-9

VOLUME TWO
ISBN 978-1-59582-188-1

VOLUME THREE
ISBN 978-1-59582-232-1

VOLUME FOUR
ISBN 978-1-59582-250-5

VOLUME FIVE
ISBN 978-1-59582-301-4

VOLUME SIX
ISBN 978-1-59582-320-5

VOLUME SEVEN
ISBN 978-1-59582-373-1

VOLUME EIGHT
ISBN 978-1-59582-383-0

VOLUME NINE
ISBN 978-1-59582-452-3

VOLUME TEN
ISBN 978-1-59582-459-2

VOLUME ELEVEN
ISBN 978-1-59582-518-6

VOLUME TWELVE
ISBN 978-1-59582-526-1

VOLUME THIRTEEN
ISBN 978-1-59582-587-2

VOLUME FOURTEEN
ISBN 978-1-59582-598-8

VOLUME FIFTEEN
ISBN 978-1-59582-662-6

VOLUME SIXTEEN
ISBN 978-1-59582-663-3

VOLUME SEVENTEEN
ISBN 978-1-59582-664-0

VOLUME EIGHTEEN
ISBN 978-1-59582-776-0

VOLUME NINETEEN
ISBN 978-1-59582-813-2

VOLUME TWENTY
ISBN 978-1-59582-846-0

VOLUME TWENTY-ONE
ISBN 978-1-59582-847-7

VOLUME TWENTY-TWO
ISBN 978-1-59582-848-4

VOLUME TWENTY-THREE
ISBN 978-1-59582-849-1

VOLUME TWENTY-FOUR
ISBN 978-1-59582-907-8

VOLUME TWENTY-FIVE
ISBN 978-1-59582-908-5

$12.99 EACH

VOLUME TWENTY-SIX
ISBN 978-1-61655-048-6

VOLUME TWENTY-SEVEN
ISBN 978-1-61655-049-3

VOLUME TWENTY-EIGHT
ISBN 978-1-61655-050-9

VOLUME TWENTY-NINE
ISBN 978-1-61655-150-6

VOLUME THIRTY
ISBN 978-1-61655-151-3

VOLUME THIRTY-ONE
ISBN 978-1-61655-152-0

VOLUME THIRTY-TWO
ISBN 978-1-61655-428-6

VOLUME THIRTY-THREE
ISBN 978-1-61655-429-3

VOLUME THIRTY-FOUR
ISBN 978-1-61655-573-3

VOLUME THIRTY-FIVE
ISBN 978-1-61655-586-3

$13.99 EACH

AVAILABLE AT YOUR LOCAL COMICS SHOP OR BOOKSTORE
TO FIND A COMICS SHOP IN YOUR AREA, CALL 1-888-266-4226

For more information or to order direct: On the web: darkhorse.com · E-mail: mailorder@darkhorse.com
Phone: 1-800-862-0052 Mon.–Fri. 9 A.M. to 5 P.M Pacific Time.

DARK HORSE MANGA

STOP!

THIS IS THE BACK OF THE BOOK!

This manga collection is translated into English, but arranged in right-to-left reading format to maintain the artwork's visual orientation as originally drawn and published in Japan. If you've never read comics this way before, take a look at the diagram below to give yourself an idea of how to go about it. Basically, you'll be starting in the upper right-hand corner, and will read each word balloon and panel moving right-to-left. It may take a little getting used to, but you should get the hang of it very quickly. Have fun! If this is the millionth manga you've read this way, never mind. ^_^

1
...
2
THEY TALK TO YOU BECAUSE YOU'RE THE KIND OF GUY WHO CAN'T SAY NO.
3
...YES.
4
RIGHT. SO LET'S TAKE THIS HORRIBLE, STINKING, ROTTING THING BACK TO CAMPUS. QUICK, BEFORE THE COPS NOTICE.
5
BACK TO CAMPUS?!
6
KARATSU, THERE'S NOTHING IN THE HANDBOOK THAT SAYS STUDENTS CAN'T POSSESS CORPSES--OR, IN YOUR CASE, VICE-VERSA.

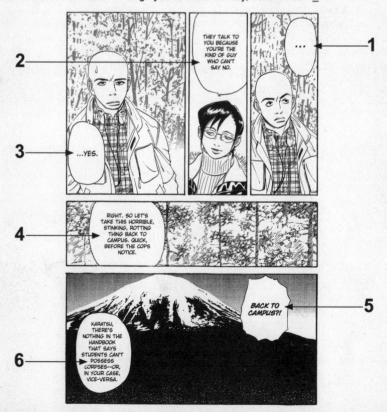